THE THEORY OF PUBLIC FINANCE

A study in public economy

THE THEORY

OF PUBLIC FINANCE

A STUDY IN PUBLIC ECONOMY

by Richard A. Musgrave

PROFESSOR OF ECONOMICS AND PUBLIC AFFAIRS
PRINCETON UNIVERSITY

McGRAW-HILL BOOK COMPANY, INC.

New York   Toronto   London   1959

THE THEORY OF PUBLIC FINANCE
A STUDY IN PUBLIC ECONOMY

IV

44115

THE MAPLE PRESS COMPANY, YORK, PA.

Preface

Public finance, as a branch of economics, has a mixed past. Some of the great economists—notably Ricardo, Wicksell, Edgeworth, and Pigou—ventured forth into the theory of taxation and, less frequently, of public expenditures. Yet these were more or less lonely forays. The mainstream of literature in public finance proper proceeded in a historical and institutional context. Primary concern remained with the more practical aspects of fiscal legislation and administration.

These, to be sure, are important matters. The effects of a tax depend upon what it is, not what it is meant to be; and an understanding of the social and historical setting is needed to interpret the determination of fiscal politics. At the same time, the problems of public finance must be dealt with by economic analysis as well. The general body of economic theory, which has been applied so successfully to such special fields as international trade, must be applied with equal rigor to public finance.

In recent years there has been a growing tendency among writers in public finance to do just this. The present volume is designed to contribute to this approach. The book dates back to my doctoral dissertation, where I first attempted to come to grips with what may be called an economic theory of budget determination. Later, and like most economists of my generation, I had the benefit of direct association with policy making and policy makers, thus observing the link—or the gap, as it may be—between pure theory and affairs of state. Rather than weakening my interest in theoretical questions, this proved invaluable in finding worthwhile questions to ask.

Unlike some economic purists of today, I admit to more than only a scientific motivation; intelligent and civilized conduct of government and the delineation of its responsibilities are at the heart of democracy. Indeed, the conduct of government is the testing ground of social ethics and civilized living. Intelligent conduct of government requires an understanding of the economic relations involved; and the economist, by aiding in this understanding, may hope to contribute to a better society. This is why the field of public finance has seemed of particular interest to me; and this is why my interest in the field has been motivated by a search for the good society, no less than by scientific curiosity. The form of this good society involves value judgment, and value judgment may enter into the issues that the economist chooses to examine. From there on, however, the economist's function is to aim at a scientific and thus objective answer.

At the close of the last century, Continental writers engaged in a lively discussion of the normative theory of budget determination, and the normative approach was continued in the twenties when Pigou applied his theory of welfare economics to public finance. However, there was little interest, between Ricardo and Keynes, in the repercussion of budget policy upon the working of the economy. This line of investigation received a great stimulus during the thirties, when the new concepts of fiscal policy and compensatory finance moved budget policy to the very heart of the economic mechanism. While the new infant hardly lived up to the hopes of its parents (which infant ever will?) it revolutionized the approach to public finance and, most important, directed the interest of theoretical economists to the fiscal problem. As a result, a literature developed on the role of budget policy in macroeconomic theory, comparable in significance to that available in any of the other applied areas in economics.

Yet, this breakthrough of public finance into economics has been one-sided—limited, as it were, to the type of macroeconomic theory which began with Keynes's *The General Theory* and which was continued with the subsequent developments of the post-Keynesian discussion. While the macrotheory of public finance was explored in depth, effects of budget policy upon the distribution of income and the allocation of resources in the private sector received little attention. In preparing this volume, it became evident very quickly that most work remains to be done in precisely these traditional areas of tax and expenditure theory. What I had expected to be a volume in compensatory finance turned out to be one in which stabilization policy occupies but a third of the total space.

Indeed, I have been hesitant to refer to this book as a study in the theory of public *finance*. The problems, to a large degree, are not those of finance. They are problems in resource use and income distribution, rather than liquidity or investment earnings. Thus, it might have been better to describe this as an examination of the theory of public *economy*, following the useful German concept of Staatswirtschaft. If the more conventional title was used, it is only to avoid what the consumer might find an unfamiliar label.

This study is divided into four major parts.   In Part 1, I attempt to provide a general framework for an economic theory of the public household, combining the functional finance of the stabilization type with other equally important objectives of budget policy, including provision for the satisfaction of social wants and adjustments in the distribution of income. I beg the reader not to discard this somewhat utopian scheme with the sterile objection of "utterly impracticable."   Let its practicability be tested not by prospects for speedy enactment but by the contribution it has to make to orderly thinking about the basic issues of budget policy.

In Part 2, I deal with the application of welfare economics to the issues of budget determination.   Assuming a full-employment economy, the task of budget policy is to contribute to an efficient allocation of resources and a "proper" distribution of income.   This involves the problem, central to any theory of public economy, of determining what social wants are to be satisfied and who is to pay for them.   I review the development of doctrine along the lines of the benefit and ability-to-pay theories, and attempt to apply the findings of the newer theories of welfare economics.   Beyond this there is the task of designing efficient tax and expenditure policies that avoid excess burdens, and of devising a tax structure that complies with the basic requirements of horizontal equity. The latter undertaking is engaged in but briefly, since it is here that the available literature, grouped around the basic work of Henry Simons, is at its best.   Finally, I examine some questions of measurement and treatment of budget items in the social accounts.

In Part 3, I consider the general range of problems usually connected with incidence and effects of budget policy.   I begin with an attempt at defining concepts—in particular, the concept of incidence.   Assuming that all empirical difficulties can be overcome, just what is it that we would like to measure?   To answer this, a choice had to be made between examining the consequences of particular taxes and expenditures and dealing with the effects of budget policies (including different taxes and expenditures) on the various decision-making units of the economy. For analytical reasons the latter approach was chosen.   Thus, there follows a set of chapters dealing with the reaction of consumers, workers, business firms, and investors to various tax and expenditure policies, all dealt with in a strictly partial-equilibrium setting.

Thereafter, I reexamine the problem in a general-equilibrium setting, beginning with the simplest possible model of an economy that produces consumer goods only, and proceeding to a classical model where capital formation is allowed for, but where Say's law still holds.   I attempt to cut through the immense complexity of Walrasian analysis by using a workable concept of incidence and certain empirical relationships of key importance.   In this way I hope to obtain results of general interest, even though it remains impossible to determine just what has happened to millions of individual product and factor prices. Undoubtedly this approach needs improvement; but some way must be found to penetrate the solar system of n-1 sets of relative prices, if some progress is to be made.

In Part 4, I turn to the problems of fiscal policy as a means of economic stabilization. By way of introduction, a brief review of the theory of income determination is presented. Thereafter, the mechanics of compensatory finance are examined—first in terms of the traditional approach, where primary attention is paid to effects upon consumption, and then in a system where effects upon investment are taken into account. Having discussed these matters in terms of comparative statics, I examine the budding problems of fiscal dynamics and the bearing of fiscal policy on economic growth. A further consideration of flexibility and efficiency in compensatory finance follows. Thereafter, I turn to the effects of compensatory finance that result from changes in the liquidity structure of the economy, implicit in deficit and surplus budgets. Thereby the problem of debt and monetary policy are joined with those of fiscal policy. A chapter on the classical theory of public debt is inserted, but it may be read also in connection with efficiency problems of Part 2.

In dealing with the issues of compensatory finance, my concern is to show how the effects of fiscal policy depend upon the particular structure of income determination that applies. As our understanding of macrotheory has grown, the theory of compensatory finance has become more complex than it appeared on the basis of the simplest Keynesian system from which it first derived. In particular, I endeavor to allow for the inflation as well as the depression aspects of the problem, and to integrate the effects of fiscal operations upon the structure of claims with the traditional emphasis upon income effects. Most important, an effort is made to view the stabilization function in the broader context of efficient budget policy. This policy must account for the provision of social services and distributional adjustments as well as stabilization, and the stabilization goals must be met so as not to interfere with these other objectives. Indeed, the basic theme of this volume is to integrate the classical with the Keynesian aspects of the problem.

In the course of the study, many aspects of economic theory, solved and unsolved, are encountered. Not all these are handled to satisfaction, and important gaps remain. The reader may wish to touch up or paint over many a spot on the canvas; this will be all to the good. Nevertheless, I hope that the "beginning-advanced" student will find this volume useful in obtaining a systematic introduction to the field. While I have tried to limit the use of mathematics, I have not been successful in doing so in all cases. Not being a mathematical economist by predilection, I have tried to state the argument as simply as possible and at times include what to my sterner friends seems an excessively detailed exposition. In certain connections, the mathematical argument is given in both linear and general form, so as to permit the reader to follow with the use of simple algebra only.

Many people have helped in bringing this volume to fruition. Among them, let me note the late H. H. Burbank, who encouraged my interest in the field of public finance when I first came to the United States in 1933; Alvin Hansen, to whom, for his teaching and his friendship, I owe the greatest debt of all; John H. Williams, whose fiscal policy seminar at Harvard in the late thirties, offered jointly with Hansen, was a mainspring of creative thinking; and the late E. R. Goldenweiser, whose conception of the economist's function in public service ("think straight, but partake in policy making") enriched my years with the Board of Governors in Washington. Evsey D. Domar, during joint years at the Board, shared in the development of many of the ideas here presented. Daniel B. Suits helped to straighten out theoretical points over innumerable cups of coffee. Paul A. Samuelson aided in the discussion of efficient budget determination. Seymour E. Harris and E. Cary Brown read the manuscript in its later stages and made many valuable suggestions. Louis Lefeber gave the entire volume a thorough and productive going-over. Herbert Geyer contributed much to the discussion of dynamics and growth, and helpful suggestions were made by Arthur Goldberger, Assar Lindbäck, and Warren Smith.

Thanks are due, moreover, to the Guggenheim Foundation, whose fellowship enabled me to get started on this volume, to the Faculty Research Fund of the University of Michigan, and to the Ford Foundation, whose grants provided the finance for clerical and research assistance.

I am also indebted to my graduate students at the University of Michigan over the last ten years who, as a captive audience, had to suffer through the manuscript at various stages, and whose response and criticism furnished the push required to carry it to completion. Thanks are due, finally, to my wife, who has shared patiently in the opportunity cost of this effort. Needless to say, I would not have been able to do the job without the help of all these people. They deserve credit for much that is good in this volume and—to vary a familiar theme—may even be responsible for some of the mistakes.

Richard A. Musgrave

University of Michigan
Ann Arbor
Spring, 1959

Contents

PART ONE

Statement of issues

"For any real understanding of public finances, it is necessary to examine very carefully the divergences of substance that underlie similarities in money form." [A. C. PIGOU, A STUDY IN PUBLIC FINANCE, MACMILLAN & CO., LTD., LONDON, 1928, P. 4]

CHAPTER 1

A multiple theory of the public household

Modern capitalism is a mixed economic system. The larger part of the national output is purchased by private consumers and investors, and the larger part of the product is produced and supplied by private firms. The distribution of income is determined largely by the ownership of factors of production and by their earnings in the market. At the same time, a substantial share of the nation's product goes to satisfy public wants, a substantial part of private income originates in the public budget, and public tax and transfer payments significantly influence the state of private distribution. Moreover, budget policy affects the level of employment and prices in the private sector. Thus ours is a mixed system, including a sizable and vitally important sphere of public economy along with the market sector.

A. INTRODUCTION

The complex of problems that center around the revenue-expenditure process of government is referred to traditionally as *public finance*. Following this convention, the same term is used in the title of this volume, but with much hesitation. While operations of the public household involve money flows of receipts and expenditure, the basic problems are not issues of finance. They are not concerned with money, liquidity, or capital markets. Rather, they are problems of resource allocation, the distribution of income, full employment, and price-level stability and growth. Therefore, we must think of our task as an investigation into the principles of public economy; or more precisely, into those aspects of economic policy that arise in the operations of the public budget.

Theories of Public Economy

Economists have paid much attention to the formulation of theories that examine the problems of consumer households, business firms, cooperatives, trade unions, and other decision-making units in the economy. While much remains to be done, we can boast of a fairly adequate framework in which to explore these matters. No such success can be claimed for occasional attempts to develop a corresponding theory of the public sector.

Such a theory can be approached in two ways. First, we attempt to state the rules and principles that make for an efficient conduct of the public economy. In other words, we determine the optimal budget plan on the basis of initially defined conditions and see how it can be achieved. This we refer to as a normative or optimal theory of the public household. In the second approach, we attempt to develop a theory that permits us to explain why existing policies are pursued and to predict which policies will be pursued in the future. Such a theory of budget policy may be thought of as a sociology of fiscal politics. For purposes of either approach, the economic consequences of legislative action must be determined. For the first approach, we must know how the market reacts to various tax or expenditure policies so that we can choose that policy which gives optimal results. For the second approach, we must know how the market reacts so that we can predict further changes in policy that will be generated by these reactions.

For purposes of this study, our concern is primarily with the first or normative view. A theory of fiscal politics is interesting and important but will be referred to only in occasional connections.[1] Our normative model of public economy is not designed to be realistic in the sense of describing what goes on in the capitals of the world. Rather, it is designed to show what would go on if an optimal result were achieved. Nevertheless, our model is not without close relation to social and economic institutions. The framework of a normative theory of public economy itself depends upon the political and social values of the society that it serves; and the implementation of the optimal budget plan depends upon the functional relationships that prevail in the market sector of the economy.

[1] On fiscal politics see Joseph Schumpeter, "Die Krise des Steuerstaates," *Zeitfragen aus dem Gebiete der Soziologie*, Graz, Austria, 1918. (English translation: "The Crisis of the Tax State," *International Economic Papers*, no. 4, pp. 5–38, London, 1954.)

For a Marxist interpretation see Rudolf Goldscheid, "Wesen und Aufgabe der Finanzwissenschaft vom Standpunkte der Soziologie," *Handbuch der Finanzwissenschaft*, Tübingen, Germany, 1926, vol. 1. (English translation: R. A. Musgrave and Alan T. Peacock (eds.), *Classics in the Theory of Public Finance*, International Economic Association, Macmillan & Co., Ltd., London, 1958.)

Our task will be to examine how the objectives of the budget plan can be determined in an optimal fashion, and how they can be implemented accordingly. The introductory chapters of Part I are designed to give a general framework of analysis, covering the entire range of problems to be considered later on. Many difficulties dealt with at a later point are overlooked for the time being. In Part II, we examine how the optimal objectives of budget policy can be determined. In Part III, we deal with the implementation of budget policy in a classical system, where there is no problem of stabilization policy. In Part IV, we consider the implementation of budget policy in a compensatory system.

Three Objectives of Budget Policy

There is no simple set of principles, no uniform rule of normative behavior that may be applied to the conduct of public economy. Rather, we are confronted with a number of separate, though interrelated, functions that require distinct solutions. Our first task is to sort out these objectives, to state the issues, and to see how objectives and issues are related.

In order to obtain a comprehensive, if highly simplified, view of the problem, let us observe the determination of budget policies in an imaginary state, where efficient standards of fiscal planning prevail. The responsibilities of the Fiscal Department in our imaginary state are derived from a multiplicity of objectives. For present purposes these are grouped under three headings: The use of fiscal instruments to (1) secure adjustments in the allocation of resources; (2) secure adjustments in the distribution of income and wealth; and (3) secure economic stabilization.

Let us now think of each of these functions as being performed by a particular branch of our imaginary Fiscal Department. These branches may be referred to respectively as the Allocation, Distribution, and Stabilization Branches. The manager of the Allocation Branch must determine what adjustments in allocation are needed, who is to bear the cost, and what revenue and expenditure policies are required to achieve the desired objectives. The manager of the Distribution Branch must determine what steps are needed to establish the desired or "proper" state of distribution, and the manager of the Stabilization Branch must decide what must be done to secure price-level stability and full employment.

For reasons to be explained later, each manager is to plan his job on the assumption that the other two branches will perform their respective functions properly. In other words, the diversion of resources to satisfy public wants is to be planned in the Allocation Branch on the assumption that resources are fully employed and that the proper distribution of income has been secured. The proper or desired distribution is to be planned in the Distribution Branch on the assumption that a full-employment income is available for distribution and that the satisfaction of public wants is taken care of. Finally, the manager of the Stabilization Branch is to determine what fiscal actions are needed to maintain the required level of aggregate demand, given the proper state of distribution and diversion of resources to the satisfaction of public wants.

In this way, budget policy is determined as the result of three inter-dependent plans, each of which involves different objectives and prin-ciples of action. These subplans may then be cleared and consolidated into a net budget involving but a single set of tax and expenditure measures. This, however, is a matter of convenience only. The basic task is to arrive at efficient budget planning for each of the three levels.

B. THE ALLOCATION BRANCH

One is tempted to describe the function of the Allocation Branch as providing for the satisfaction of public wants, but this does not tell us much. It merely poses the problem of how to define public wants. This cannot be done readily in general terms, since different situations give rise to different types of public wants. We shall get further, there-fore, if we view the function of this branch as that of securing necessary adjustments in the allocation of resources by the market. We may then examine the various situations in which such adjustments are required and thus secure a more specific view of the nature of the public wants to be met in each case.

Situations Calling for Adjustments in Allocation

The pricing mechanism of the market secures an optimal allocation of resources, provided that certain conditions are met.[1] These conditions are met reasonably well over wide areas of economic activity, so that the bulk of the allocating function may be left to the forces of the market. In these areas, public policy need not concern itself with matters of allocation. Yet conditions arise in many connections where the forces of the market cannot secure optimal results. Here we are faced with the problem of how public policy can intervene to secure a more efficient resource allocation. In some cases, the required adjustment is made best through budget policy, while in others, different techniques are more suitable. Let us note briefly the major situations where problems of allocation policy must be faced.

[1] See, for instance, A. P. Lerner, *The Economics of Control*, The Macmillan Company, New York, 1944, chap. 2.

To begin with, an occasion for adjustment arises where, for institutional reasons, the organization of industry precludes free entry, so that allocation diverges from that obtained under purely competitive conditions. This is the general case of monopoly control. The existence of market imperfections must be allowed for in the determination of efficient budget policy, and budget policies may be used to remove them. However, the regulation of competition is not primarily a problem of budget policy. More commonly, it is dealt with by legislation to control industrial organization or to regulate the price and output policies of firms. Since our study is concerned with budget policy, this aspect of allocation control enters our discussion only in a collateral way.

A second and more difficult problem of adjustment arises in the case of lumpiness of productive factors and of production processes that involve decreasing cost. These conditions may not only lead to monopoly, but they make it futile to demand that the monopolist behave like a competitor. Optimal determination of output requires an equating of average revenue with marginal cost. Under conditions of decreasing cost, the firm cannot be expected to follow such a policy, since it involves a loss. A tax-subsidy process—and, hence, budget policy—is required to secure an optimal output.

Next, we have situations where external economies or diseconomies are generated by the operation of particular individuals or firms. Establishment of an expensive store may increase real estate values in the neighborhood, even though the store cannot collect for the services thus rendered. A railroad into new territory may lead to gains in economic development that greatly exceed the profits to the particular railroad. Since the market permits a price to be charged for only a part of the services rendered, the development may be unprofitable from the private, but profitable from the public, point of view. Similarly, private operations may involve social costs that are not reflected in private cost calculations and, hence, are not accounted for by the market. A factory may pollute the air and damage an adjoining resort. The smoke nuisance is a cost to the particular community, yet it is not a private cost to the firm. The resort owners cannot collect from the firm since they cannot prevent its use of the common air. Thus, what is profitable to the private firm may be unprofitable from a social point of view.

Other discrepancies may arise from differences between public and private risk, and again others from differences between public and private time preferences. Indeed, if we assume that any one person's welfare depends on that of all others—a case of keeping up with the Joneses—we must conclude that the satisfaction of all private wants involves gains and losses that are not accounted for in the market.

We thus find a wide array of situations where the market mechanism involves varying degrees of inefficiency in resource allocation—inefficiencies that arise collateral to the satisfaction of private wants. Nevertheless, the satisfaction of such wants in most cases is best left to the market. Depending upon the nature and severity of the inefficiencies, corrective action may be desirable and feasible; but such action as is taken remains more or less marginal.

Let us now turn to situations where the market mechanism fails altogether and where the divergence between the social and private product becomes all-inclusive. This is the case of *social wants* proper, the first type of public wants to be considered. Social wants are those wants satisfied by services that must be consumed in equal amounts by all. People who do not pay for the services cannot be excluded from the benefits that result; and since they cannot be excluded from the benefits, they will not engage in voluntary payments. Hence, the market cannot satisfy such wants. Budgetary provision is needed if they are to be satisfied at all. Determination of the required budget plan is complicated by two factors, both of which arise because the same amount of services must be consumed by all.

A primary difficulty arises because true preferences are unknown. Since, as we have noted, no one can be excluded from the benefits that result, consumers will not readily reveal their true preferences. Yet the government must determine these preferences before it can decide how to satisfy them efficiently. A way must therefore be found by which to induce people to reveal their preferences.

A second difficulty arises even if we assume that the true preferences of all individuals are known. The difficulty arises because there is no single most efficient solution to the satisfaction of social wants or to the problem of supplying services that are consumed in equal amounts by all. This difficulty exists, at least, if we apply the criterion of efficiency as understood in the determination of market price. Therefore, a more specific welfare function is needed to secure an optimal solution. These are the two issues which comprise the crux of the problem to be solved by the Allocation Branch.

The suggested distinction between private and social wants is not of an absolute sort. Inefficiencies arise in the satisfaction of private wants through the market process, and wherever such is the case, one could say that an element of social want is involved. The difference is essentially one of degree, but the same may be said for most categories in economics, e.g., consumption and capital formation. The distinction remains of fundamental importance. In the case of private wants, the divergence between private and social product is a more or less marginal matter; in the case of social wants, the divergence becomes of the essence. Private wants are provided for adequately by the market. Social wants must be satisfied through the budget if they are to be satisfied at all. For purposes of public policy, the difference in degree thus becomes an important difference in substance.

So far, we have considered situations where corrective policy is required in order to secure an allocation of resources that is in line with consumer preferences. A different type of intervention occurs where public policy aims at an allocation of resources which deviates from that reflected by consumer sovereignty. In other words, wants are satisfied that could be serviced through the market but are not, since consumers choose to spend their money on other things. The reason for budgetary action in this case is *not* to be found in the technical difficulties that arise because certain services are consumed in equal amounts by all. Separate amounts of individual consumption are possible. The reason, then, for budgetary action is to correct individual choice. Wants satisfied under these conditions constitute a second type of public wants, and will be referred to as *merit wants*. The problem they pose must be distinguished clearly from that posed by social wants.

Social Wants

Let us now take a closer look at the nature of social wants. Such wants cannot be satisfied through the mechanism of the market because their enjoyment cannot be made subject to price payments.

Exchange in the market depends on the existence of property titles to the things that are to be exchanged. If a consumer wishes to satisfy his desire for any particular commodity, he must meet the terms of exchange set by those who happen to possess this particular commodity, and vice versa. That is to say, he is excluded from the enjoyment of any particular commodity or service unless he is willing to pay the stipulated price to the owner. This may be referred to as the *exclusion principle*. Where it applies, the consumer must bid for the commodities he wants. His offer reveals the value he assigns to them and tells the entrepreneur what to produce under given cost conditions.

This mechanism breaks down with social wants, where the satisfaction derived by any individual consumer is independent of his own contribution. Such, at least, is the case where the individual consumer is but one among many, and any contribution he may render covers only a small part of the total cost. Consider, for instance, such items as a flood-control project, the more general benefits of which accrue to an entire region; a sanitary campaign that raises the general level of health throughout an area; expenditures for the judiciary system that secure internal safety and enforce contractual obligations; or protection against foreign aggression. All these contribute to the welfare of the whole community. The benefits resulting from such services will accrue to all who live in the particular place or society where the services are rendered.[1] Some may benefit more than others, but everyone knows that his benefit will be independent of his particular contribution. Hence, as we have said, he cannot be relied upon to make a voluntary contribution. The government must step in, and compulsion is called for.

The difficulty thus created would be slight if the problem were merely one of collecting tax bills. Unfortunately, this is not the case. The tax collector, while important, does not solve the problem of the economist. The latter must determine what expenditures should be made and what taxes should be collected. To do this, a way must be found to determine people's true preferences in social wants, i.e., the preference pattern by which they rate the satisfaction of their total wants, private and social. The difficulty arises because the market mechanism fails as a device for registering consumer preferences. Since the services that satisfy social wants can be had without payment, the individual consumer need not reveal his evaluation thereof (and invite corresponding tax assessments!) through market bids. Because of this, signals are lacking and true preference scales for social wants are unknown. Such, at least, is the case with central finance. In the case of local finance, some registration of preferences may occur by moving from less to more congenial fiscal communities, a factor that will be disregarded for the time being.

Since the market mechanism fails to reveal consumer preferences in social wants, it may be asked what mechanism there is by which the government can determine the extent to which resources should be released for the satisfaction of such wants; the extent to which particular social wants should be satisfied; and the way in which the cost should be spread among the group. In a democratic society, the decision to satisfy one or another social want cannot be imposed in dictatorial form. It must be derived, somehow, from the effective preferences of the individual member of the group, as determined by his tastes and his "proper" share in full-employment income.[2] A political process must

---

[1] It is evident that the case of social wants must involve joint consumption; but joint consumption, as usually defined, does not necessarily involve social wants. A circus performance involves joint consumption on the part of those who attend. Yet entrance fees can be charged, different amounts can be consumed by various people, and the service can be provided through the market. Demand schedules can be added horizontally. (See p. 76.) For a social want to arise, the condition of equal consumption must apply to all, whether they pay or not. In other words, we must combine the condition of joint consumption with that of inapplicability of the exclusion principle. Only then will demand schedules be added vertically.

[2] As noted before, the budget of the Allocation Branch is planned on the assumption that the Distribution Branch has provided for the proper distribution of income and that the Stabilization Branch has provided for a full-employment level of income.

be substituted for the market mechanism, and individuals must be made to adhere to the group decision. As shown later on, the problem is to determine the kind of voting process or group decision that offers the best approximation to the solution (or one of the solutions) that would be chosen if true preferences were known.

The preceding argument is based on the premise that individuals *can* evaluate social wants, that is, that such wants form part of individual preference scales along with private wants. Without this, no determination of public preferences can be made that meets the requirements of a democratic society as we understand it. This approach differs from an alternative view, according to which social wants are collective in nature and are experienced by the group as a whole or its leaders, as distinct from its members. It is futile to debate which of these is the correct interpretation. Let us look upon our preference for the individualistic over the organic view as a matter of value judgment and be content to show that our formulation makes empirical sense. I see no reason why individuals should not be able to evaluate the benefits they derive from the satisfaction of social wants, along with the benefits they derive from the satisfaction of private wants. To be sure, it may be simpler to assess the advantages of installing a lock in one's own house than to appraise the precise benefits one derives from military protection against foreign invasion; or one may find it simpler to measure the advantages of improving one's own yard than to evaluate one's gain from the installation of public parks. Such differences in degree may exist, but they are not inherently a matter of public versus private wants. Similar distinctions arise between various types of private wants, some of which are more immediate (such as medical consultation in the case of illness) and some of which are more remote (such as preventive medical care). Considerations of this sort, therefore, do not contradict our basic proposition that social wants are an integral part of the individual's preference pattern.

Individuals, at the same time, are social beings, dependent in their preferences and actions on their social environments, and their relations to others. While all wants are evaluated in terms of individual preference patterns, these patterns are not determined in a Robinson Crusoe setting. All sorts of social motivations enter, be it with regard to private or to public wants. While social preference must be anchored in individual valuation, it does not follow that people are selfish monsters. Altruistic or social motivation may be imbedded in the structure of individual-preference patterns. A person may favor expenditures for courts or for education, not only because they will improve his safety, increase his learning, give the pleasure of dealing with more educated neighbors, or because he expects them to think well of him if he appears socially minded; he may favor them simply because he feels that he should contribute to the good life of others.[1]

Such considerations will be present in varying degrees; but they will not be so strong or universal as to justify the assumption that people will reveal their true preferences in social wants on a voluntary basis, independent of any assurance that the same will be done by others. With all due allowance for social interdependence and altruistic motivation, such an assumption would be unrealistic and inconsistent with the premises of all other phases of economic analysis. The first difficulty of the Allocation Branch, therefore, is how to induce people to reveal their individual preferences in social wants.

Suppose, now, that this part of the task has been accomplished in some fashion. We may expect to find that individual preferences differ with regard to social as well as to private wants. In the case of private wants, such differences are reflected in the purchase of varying amounts of goods and services at a common price. This solution is inapplicable to social wants, since the same amount of goods and services must be consumed by all. If costs are to be allocated in response to individual preferences, different prices must be charged to various consumers, or different tax assessments must be placed on various voters. This suggests that a solution may be obtained which is analogous to that of efficient pricing in the market. Unfortunately, this is not the case. The condition of equal consumption by all does not permit a single most efficient solution; or, to put it more precisely, it permits such a solution only on the basis of a social preference function that goes much beyond the conditions of efficiency required to evaluate the allocation of resources in the satisfaction of private wants. This is the second basic difficulty in the provision for social wants, a problem that remains even if individual preferences can be determined.

Taxes imposed by the Allocation Branch are designed to cover the cost of public services. Will the distribution of these tax payments be regressive, proportional or progressive? Since they are to express the individual's valuation of social wants as based on the proper distribution of income, the answer depends on the income elasticity of social wants. If this elasticity in the typical case tends to be unity, tax contributions will be proportional; if it is above unity, they will be progressive; and if it is below unity, they will be regressive. In any case, note that the considerations behind the question of progression are quite different in this context from considerations arising in connection with distributional adjustments.

[1] See p. 88.

Merit Wants

The type of public wants dealt with under social wants are wants whose satisfaction should be subject to the principle of consumer sovereignty. The basic rule is that resources should be allocated in response to the effective demand of consumers, determined by individual preferences and the prevailing state of distribution. Indeed, social wants are quite similar in this fundamental respect to private wants.

We now turn to our second category of public wants. Such wants are met by services subject to the exclusion principle and are satisfied by the market within the limits of effective demand. They become public wants if considered so meritorious that their satisfaction is provided for through the public budget, over and above what is provided for through the market and paid for by private buyers. This second type of public wants will be referred to as *merit wants*. Public services aimed at the satisfaction of merit wants include such items as publicly furnished school luncheons, subsidized low-cost housing, and free education. Alternatively, certain wants may be stamped as undesirable, and their satisfaction may be discouraged through penalty taxation, as in the case of liquor.

The satisfaction of merit wants cannot be explained in the same terms as the satisfaction of social wants. While both are public wants in that they are provided for through the public budget, different principles apply. Social wants constitute a special problem because the same amount must be consumed by all, with all the difficulties to which this gives rise. Otherwise, the satisfaction of social wants falls within the realm of consumer sovereignty, as does the satisfaction of private wants. The satisfaction of merit wants, by its very nature, involves interference with consumer preferences.

In view of this, does the satisfaction of merit wants have a place in a normative theory of public economy, based upon the premise of individual preference in a democratic society? A position of extreme individualism could demand that all merit wants be disallowed, but this is not a sensible view. To begin with, situations arise that seem to involve merit wants but on closer inspection involve social wants. Certain public wants may fall on the border line between private and social wants, where the exclusion principle can be applied to part of the benefits gained but not to all. Budgetary provision for free educational services or for free health measures are cases in point. Such measures are of immediate benefit to the particular pupil or patient, but apart from this, everyone stands to gain from living in a more educated or healthier community. Wants that appear to be merit wants may involve substantial elements of social wants.

Moreover, a case for the satisfaction of merit wants and for inter-ference with consumer sovereignty, narrowly defined, may derive from the role of leadership in a democratic society. While consumer sover-eignty is the general rule, situations may arise, within the context of a democratic community, where an informed group is justified in imposing its decision upon others. Few will deny that there is a case for regulating the sale of drugs or for providing certain health facilities. The advan-tages of education are more evident to the informed than the unin-formed, thus justifying compulsion in the allocation of resources to education; interference in the preference patterns of families may be directed at protecting the interest of minors; the freedom to belong may override the freedom to exclude, and so forth. These are matters of learning and leadership which are an essential part of democracy reason-ably defined and which justify the satisfaction of certain merit wants within a normative model.

The basic doctrine of consumer sovereignty, finally, rests on the assumption of complete market knowledge and rational appraisal. In the modern economy, the consumer is subject to advertising, screaming at him through the media of mass communication and designed to sway his choice rather than to give complete information. Thus, there may arise a distortion in the preference structure that needs to be counteracted. The ideal of consumer sovereignty and the reality of consumer choice in high-pressure markets may be quite different things. At the same time, the satisfaction of merit wants remains a precarious task. Interferences with consumer choice may occur simply because a ruling group considers its particular set of mores superior and wishes to impose it on others. Such determination of wants rests on an authoritarian basis, not per-missible in our normative model based upon a democratic society.

To the extent that merit wants are admitted, the provision for such wants differs basically from the provision for social wants.[1] In the case of the latter, the problem is one of giving effect to individual evaluations. Even though policy will not be determined by unanimous vote, the task remains one of fitting the result as closely as possible to individual tastes and effective demands. Majority rule is a necessary evil to approximate the desired result, not a principle desired as such. In the case of merit wants, however, the very purpose may be one of interference by some, presumably the majority, into the want pattern of others. The solution to the determination of social wants, based on the true preferences of all individuals alike, does not apply in this case.

Providing for the Satisfaction of Public Wants

Suppose, now, that it has been decided which public wants, social or merit, shall be provided for through the public budget. What, precisely,

[1] For further discussion of various types of wants, see pp. 88–89.

do we mean by saying that the government must "provide" for the satisfaction of such wants?

We mean, simply, that the goods and services needed to satisfy public wants must be paid for out of general revenue. The goods and services must be supplied free of direct charge to the user; at the same time, they need *not* be produced under the direct management or supervision of the government. This is an important distinction to be made in order to avoid confusion.

Consider, for instance, the case of military protection. Provision for protection means that resources must be diverted to the construction of guns or of naval vessels. It does *not* mean, necessarily, that the guns or ships should be constructed by a public enterprise—or, necessarily, by private firms. One may consider also the matter of public playgrounds. The problem here is to determine the amount and type of playground facilities to be provided; but the decision to *provide* for such facilities does not tell us whether they should be supplied by public enterprises or through contract by private construction companies.

To bring out this distinction, we may visualize two economies, one in which all goods are produced by the government and sold on the market, and another in which all goods are produced privately but purchased by the government and distributed free of direct charge. In the former case, there is no provision for public wants, while all production is under public management. In the latter case, there is no public production, but all resources are devoted to provision for public wants. Provision for public wants, therefore, does not require public production management, just as public production management does not require provision for public wants. Quite different criteria apply in determining the proper scope of each.

The Function of Expenditures and Taxes in the Allocation Branch

Suppose that the satisfaction of certain public wants is decided upon and that the cost of the necessary resource withdrawals is to be placed upon certain people. It remains to be seen how this plan can be carried out.

The desired transfer of resources may be accomplished by commandeering such resources or products directly. This is done customarily in the case of military service, where the soldier's wage falls short of the value determined in a free market; a somewhat similar situation exists where use is made of the right of eminent domain. The same procedure could be followed in other cases as well. If, for instance, the government wishes to obtain a battleship, and steel is needed, steel may be commandeered and transferred from the production of passenger cars, and labor may be conscripted and transferred from other uses to produce more steel. This would accomplish the purpose of securing the battleship for government use, but it would place the entire cost on the producers of steel. It would be an absurd cost allocation, avoidable by tax finance. By levying taxes, private demand is reduced and resources are released. By spending the proceeds, these resources are transferred from private to public use. The desired result in resource transfer is obtained in both cases, but the distribution of cost is now independent of the particular resources that are transferred. It can be spread in any way that may appear desirable.

The tax-purchase mechanism as a means of resource transfer thus permits a cost allocation quite independent of the ownership distribution of the resources that are to be transferred. The entire process may be thought of as a combination of direct resource transfer by commandeering with a tax-compensation scheme so as to obtain the proper allocation of costs. For the Allocation Branch, the need for securing a cost distribution independent of the particular resource transfer is *the* function and raison d'etre of taxation. This must be kept in mind, lest overemphasis on the function of the Stabilization Branch lead to the misleading conclusion that the only function of taxation is to prevent inflation.

Requirement of Balance in the Budget

The basic task of the Allocation Branch is to choose among alternative uses of resources. Thus, the problem is essentially one of opportunity cost. If resources are to be used for the satisfaction of certain public wants, they will not be available for the satisfaction of other public or private wants. In this basic sense of opportunity cost, the budget of the Allocation Branch must always be balanced. The amount of resources withdrawn from private use must equal the amount of resources added to public use. This much follows from our initial rule that the budget of the Allocation Branch must be planned in a full-employment context.

At the same time, it does not follow that the budget of the Allocation Branch must always be balanced in the sense that expenditures are matched by tax receipts. Such will be the case if the satisfaction of all public wants is in the nature of current consumption, but not if capital outlays are made. In the case of capital outlays, the release of resources from private use and their transfer to the satisfaction of public wants may be accomplished properly through a borrowing-purchase mechanism rather than a tax-purchase mechanism. The charge to be covered currently by tax receipts equals the cost of current services and depreciation in value of public capital assets. Nevertheless, the cost of capital outlays must be imputed to the beneficiaries and be covered in taxes over the lifetime of the capital asset.

With this qualification, we may conclude that the budget of the Allocation Branch must be balanced, even in the financial sense of equality between expenditures and tax receipts. The financial balance merely expresses the underlying real balance between the benefits derived from the satisfaction of public wants and the opportunity cost of withdrawing resources from the satisfaction of private wants. At the same time, we shall find that there is no conflict whatsoever between this principle of balance in the budget of the Allocation Branch and the quite different principle of imbalance in the budget of the Stabilization Branch.

C. THE DISTRIBUTION BRANCH

The function of the Allocation Branch may be considered the classical function of budget policy. Indeed, there was a time when the provision of public services was considered its only legitimate function, and it was argued that "the fiscal problem pure and simple" should not be confused with "alien considerations of social and economic policy." Subsequently, however, most people came to recognize that the revenue-expenditure process of government is bound to have social and economic effects, and that these may be aimed usefully at purposes not directly connected with the immediate objective of satisfying public wants. Adjustments in the state of distribution are one such purpose.

In formulating the budget of the Allocation Branch, we assume that there exists a desired or proper state of distribution to begin with. This is necessary for two reasons. Unless the state of distribution is given, individuals cannot translate their preferences, whether for private or public wants, into a pattern of effective demand. And unless the given state of distribution can be accepted as the proper one, the resulting pattern of effective demand cannot be accepted in furnishing a guide to the efficient use of resources. It is the task of the Distribution Branch to determine and secure this proper state of distribution. In so doing, the Distribution Branch may assume that the satisfaction of public wants is determined correctly by the Allocation Branch and that full employment and price-level stability are maintained by the Stabilization Branch.

The Tax-Transfer Process of the Distribution Branch

The distribution of income and wealth in a market economy depends on a number of factors including the laws of inheritance, the distribution of innate talents, the availability of educational opportunities, social mobility, and the structure of markets. As a result of these factors, a state of distribution, with a given degree of equality or inequality, comes about. This state will seem appropriate to some, while others will prefer a greater, and still others a lesser, degree of equality.

Social philosophies or personal predilection with regard to equality or inequality differ. Yet within certain limits there is likely to exist at any time and place more or less widely accepted mores with regard to certain basic aspects of the problem. In our society it is agreed that babies should not go short of milk, that old people should be cared for, that cases of extreme poverty should be taken care of, and so forth. Beyond this, opinions differ, but few will deny that some situations arise in a democratic society where an interference in the state of distribution is called for. This being the case, a mechanism must be provided by which corrections in the state of distribution can be made in an orderly fashion and in a way that does the least damage to an efficient functioning of the economy.

Such a mechanism is given by the tax and transfer system of the Distribution Branch. This, to be sure, is not the only way in which adjustments in the state of distribution can be made. Minimum-wage legislation, price support for certain farm crops, tariff protection, fair-trade legislation, and so forth are all policies with important distributional results and, to a large degree, distributional objectives. From the economist's point of view there is, however, an a priori preference for the budgetary approach. This approach to income transfer, if implemented properly, involves a minimum of interference in the allocation of resources as determined by the pricing system. Unless such interference is warranted as an objective in itself, this quality of neutrality renders the budgetary approach a superior technique. Budgetary action is also more efficient in that it permits us to reach all members of any desired group and not only those who engage in particular occupations or sets of market transactions, such as farmers, importers, or unionized workers.

Suppose now that the proper state of distribution has been determined. The corrections to be applied are found by comparing this norm with the prevailing state. The easiest and most direct way of implementing the desired adjustment is through a system of taxes and transfer payments. In fact, the latter may be thought of simply as negative taxes.

Contrary to the expenditures and taxes of the Allocation Branch, which are designed to move resources from the satisfaction of private to the satisfaction of public wants, the taxes and transfers of the Distribution Branch are designed to shift resources from the disposal of one individual to that of another. As in the case of the Allocation Branch, the budget of the Distribution Branch is planned on the assumption that full employment is provided for by the Stabilization Branch. The budget must again be balanced in real terms. Since the problem is viewed against the backdrop of a full-employment income, the same amount of real resources that is withdrawn from X will be placed at the disposal of Y.

As with the Allocation Branch, this balance in real terms need not exclude the use of loan finance as a means of accomplishing distributional objectives.   For instance, low incomes may be taxed heavily during a war, but refundable taxes may be used to arrange for a subsequent readjustment.   As in the preceding case, this is a temporary matter only.   Over a longer period, the transfer budget will have to be balanced in both the financial and the real sense.

The "Proper" State of Distribution

It is easy to conclude that distributional adjustments may be needed at times and that such adjustments should be implemented through the budget of the Distribution Branch.   The difficulty is to decide what the proper state of distribution should be.   This decision evidently cannot be made by a market process, since the nature of exchange presupposes title to the things that are to be exchanged.   A political process of decision making is needed, and before this can function, there must be some distribution of weights in the political process.   There must be a distribution of rights to vote.

Leaving for later consideration how this political process can be determined, let us note some of the issues inherent in the matter of distribution.   Democratic thinking, based on the postulate of man's individual worth, seems to establish a presumption in favor of equality, both political and economic.   But equality applied to economic matters can be interpreted in different ways, and the choice among different interpretations is a matter of value judgment.   To some, equality may imply actual equality in economic welfare at any given time; to others, it may imply the quite different concept of equality of opportunity; and still others may interpret equality in terms of maximum welfare to all members of society.

If the criterion of welfare is accepted, this does not necessarily require actual equality in the distribution of income, which would follow only if all people are similar in their propensity to enjoy income.   More likely than not, they will differ in this as in other respects.   The conclusion, therefore, may well be one of uneven distribution, a result that hardly corresponds to the commonly understood meaning of equality.   Moreover, there is doubt whether interpersonal comparisons of welfare can be made at all in meaningful sense.   Indeed, economists now widely hold to the view that such comparisons must be ruled out.   For these reasons, it is tempting to interpret the concept of equality (or degree thereof) as outright equality of objectively measurable income or wealth rather than as subjective equality of welfare.   In other words, social policy could be based on the assumption of equal capacity to enjoy income even though capacities are, in fact, unequal.

If the criterion of equality of opportunity is accepted, we are still faced with a number of different interpretations.   Equality of opportunity can be taken to mean equal educational facilities, allocation of jobs on the basis of competitive performance rather than connections, and so forth. Above all, the idea of equal opportunity involves mobility between various positions in the income scale. Fiscal policies aimed at greater equality in the one sense of the term may interfere with other aspects of equality, thus requiring a careful weighing of the various objectives.

Finally, we must allow for the fact that the total income (defined to include goods and leisure) available for distribution may itself be a function of the state of distribution. Desired changes in the state of distribution may increase the total cake to be divided, or they may decrease it. If there is a conflict, the case is not necessarily in favor of the greater income and against the preferred state of distribution. This is a matter of taste, but it is clear that the cost of lesser output must be weighed in such a case against the advantages of distributional change. Similarly, account must be taken of such changes in social or political environment as may be induced by various distribution policies.

It is evident from all this that the concept of a proper state of distribution, necessary though it is to the formulation of a complete budget theory, leads into a most difficult set of ethical, social, and economic problems. In addition, the implementation of distributional objectives raises difficulties of a technical sort. It is by no means obvious how to measure the relative economic positions that are to be adjusted. While the most widely accepted criterion is income, this is not the only possible one; and granted that income is to be taken as the criterion, it is by no means obvious how income is to be defined.

A proper definition of income is important, not only to establish equity in a vertical sense—that is, to plan taxes and transfers so as to adjust relative positions; it is important also to establish equity in a horizontal sense—that is, to give equal treatment to people in equal positions. The complexity of modern economic organization is such that income may accrue in a variety of forms and through many different channels. Thus, there arises the problem of designing the tax and transfer structure so as to give equal treatment to people who are in basically equal positions but who differ regarding the form in which their income accrues.

Relation to Taxation in the Allocation Branch

In discussing the function of the Allocation Branch, our premise has been that the satisfaction of social wants must be related to individual evaluations of the benefits received. If we assume that this can be done effectively, a clear distinction may be drawn between taxation by the Allocation Branch and taxation by the Distribution Branch. Tax payments to the Allocation Branch may be progressive, proportional, or regressive, depending on the income elasticity of social wants. The tax-transfer mechanism of the Distribution Branch, in turn, may be progressive or regressive, depending on the desired type of distributional adjustment.

The proper state of distribution, as determined by the Distribution Branch, will be defined in terms of income earned, minus such taxes or plus such transfers as the Distribution Branch chooses to impose. Taxes and transfers of the Stabilization Branch, as noted presently, will be distributionally neutral, and the Distribution Branch will disregard taxes collected by the Allocation Branch. Such taxes, like other personal uses of income, may be looked upon as expenditures, whether for consumption or capital formation, that are made in relation to the taxpayer's own evaluation of the social wants being satisfied.

At the same time, there remains an interdependence of the two budgets. The program of the Allocation Branch depends upon the pattern of effective demand as set by the adjustments of the Distribution Branch. The program of the Distribution Branch depends upon the distribution of factor incomes in the market, as affected by the policies of the Allocation Branch.

Unfortunately, such a clear-cut distinction between taxation at the two levels is not quite permissible. For one thing, we have noted that there is no single optimal solution to the satisfaction of social wants even if preferences are known; and the choice between the various possible solutions involves distributional considerations. For another, the satisfaction of merit wants is associated frequently with distributional considerations. Subsidies in kind, for instance, may be given for the satisfaction of certain private wants. Free charity clinics may be furnished, or subsidies may be given to low-cost housing, the benefits of which will accrue to low-income families. Such programs have a dual nature. They may be looked upon both as operations of the Allocation Branch in the satisfaction of merit wants and as operations of the Distribution Branch in the redistribution of income. Alternatively, the same objectives may be achieved through cash subsidies to individuals based on the condition that the payments must be spent in a prescribed way. Thus, subsidies in kind may be looked upon as redistributional arrangements made conditional upon certain uses of the grants received. The Distribution Branch, accordingly, must allow for the distributional implications of provision for merit wants in the Allocation Branch; and the Allocation Branch, in considering the satisfaction of merit wants, must allow for distributional adjustments in kind made by the Distribution Branch.

Notwithstanding these difficulties and overlaps, I think it useful to maintain a distinction between the problems of the Allocation Branch and those of the Distribution Branch. This, at least, is preferable to the other extreme, inherent in the ability-to-pay approach, of discarding the

assignment of benefits from public services and of considering the place-
ment of the entire tax bill as a distributional problem. If this is done,
nothing is gained by maintaining a distinction between taxation by the
Allocation Branch and taxation by the Distribution Branch. To be sure,
we may still think of the taxes of the Allocation Branch as allocated on a
proportional basis, and of the tax-transfer process of the Distribution
Branch as providing for a proper state of distribution, defined now with
reference to income left after payment of taxes to the Allocation Branch.
Or we may assume that the Allocation Branch initially sets aside such
resources as are needed to satisfy public wants, and that the Distribution
Branch concerns itself with the distribution of the remaining resources
only. The result is the same either way. Unless the Allocation Branch
succeeds to a significant degree in imputing benefits to individual taxpayers, there is no point in distinguishing between tax distributions by
the two Branches.

D. THE STABILIZATION BRANCH

The function of the Stabilization Branch differs sharply from that of
the other two. Its concern is not with the allocation of resources between
public and private, or between alternative private, wants. Rather, it is
with maintaining a high level of resource utilization and a stable value of
money. Though the newest of our three branches of budget policy, the
Stabilization Branch has been in the limelight during the last 20 years.
The problem of compensatory finance was posed first by the depression
of the thirties and recast subsequently by the inflation pressure of the war
and the years that followed. There is little reason to expect that future
decades will provide a more stable setting unless appropriate policies are
undertaken. Even if the shadows of war should pass, the problem of
instability will remain. A free economy, if uncontrolled, tends towards
more or less drastic fluctuations in prices and employment; and apart
from relatively short-term swings, maladjustments of a secular sort may
arise towards unemployment or inflation. Public policy must assume a
stabilizing function in order to hold within tolerable limits departures
from high employment and price stability.

No one can predict whether the bias in the years ahead will be towards
inflation or deflation. Much depends on the outlook for peace and war
and on the resulting level of military expenditures in the budget. In
any case, there is little reason to expect that stabilizing policy will become
unnecessary. While much has been said in recent years about the growing strength of built-in stabilizers, these remain to be tested; and contrary
to current belief, the inherent tendency toward instability may increase
rather than decline as the economy develops and gains in complexity.

At the same time, the social climate grows less tolerant toward the hardships of unemployment, and similar attitudes may develop with regard to inflation. It is thus of paramount importance for the success of free economic systems to develop compensatory measures which can maintain high employment when private economic activity threatens to slacken and which can maintain price-level stability when demand threatens to exceed available supplies.

Underlying Principles

The basic logic of compensatory finance is simple enough, and may be summarized in a few rules:

1. If involuntary unemployment prevails, increase the level of demand so as to adjust aggregate expenditures upward to the value of output produced at full employment.

2. If inflation prevails, reduce the level of demand so as to adjust aggregate expenditures downward to the value of output measured in current, rather than rising, prices.

3. If full employment and price-level stability prevail, maintain the aggregate level of money expenditures to prevent unemployment and inflation.

The first rule is based on the propositions that fiscal policy may be used to increase the aggregate level of expenditures and that this will raise the level of employment.   The level of demand may be raised in a number of ways.   The government may undertake to increase its own expenditures on goods and services; it may take steps leading to an increase in the level of private expenditures; or it may combine both measures.   If an increase in private expenditures is desired, this may be secured by raising transfer payments or reducing taxes, thus increasing the amount of income available for private use.   If both public and private expenditures are to be increased, an increase in public goods and service expenditures will be combined with a lesser increase in transfers or a reduction in taxes.   The required magnitude of adjustment under the various approaches will differ in order to obtain the same result. Some measures may serve to induce an independent increase in private expenditures, or have pump-priming effects; others may lower private investment.   However this may be, total expenditures on currently produced goods and services can be increased through continued fiscal action, and such an increase can be obtained either by increasing government expenditures on goods and services and/or by increasing disposable income available for private expenditures.

Under conditions of depression, an increase in expenditures ordinarily leads to an increase in real output and employment.   Unemployment will be substantial, business will have excess capacity, and the supply of additional output will be highly elastic. If there is an increase in demand, supply will increase initially along a more or less horizontal schedule. In the process of approaching full employment, total supply will become less elastic, and increasing expenditures will be dissipated more, largely in rising prices. The level of prices may well begin to rise before reasonably full employment is restored; but this may happen whether the increase in employment is due to public policy or an autonomous recovery of private spending.

The second rule of compensatory finance relates to a situation where total expenditures exceed feasible output valued at current prices. Let us assume a situation of more or less full employment, so that the supply of total output is quite inelastic. An increase in the level of aggregate demand now produces inflation. Fiscal adjustments must be made that prevent a potential increase in the level of expenditures from coming about. The required adjustments are the inverse of those used in the depression case. Government expenditures on goods and services may be reduced, tax rates may be increased, and transfer payments may be cut.

Again, there is no doubt that fiscal adjustments *can* be made that will hold expenditures down. However, a number of difficulties may arise that render control of the inflation more troublesome than control of depression. The rates of taxation needed to reduce expenditures sufficiently to check inflation may be so high as to deter work incentives. More important, market structures and the behavior of power groups may be such that a basic conflict arises between the objectives of price-level stability and full employment. This difficulty again is not peculiar to fiscal measures but has become one of the major problems of stabilization at large.

Turning now to the third rule of compensatory finance, we note that maintenance of a high level of employment with price-level stability does not imply a constant level of aggregate demand. Stabilization policy in a growing economy does not mean that the level of income is to be stabilized. On the contrary, the policy must provide for an expansion of demand commensurate with the growing capacity to produce. It must be designed to result in a rate of growth that moves along an equilibrium path, so that high employment and price-level stability are maintained in the process of expansion. Whether it will always be possible to satisfy all three objectives remains for later consideration; it also remains to be seen how a choice can be made between alternative rates of equilibrium growth. We shall find that the problem of growth enters at the level of the Allocation and Distribution Branches as well as in connection with stabilization. For this reason, growth has not been assigned a separate branch; but the system may be readily adjusted to include it.

Nature of the Budget Plan

In its simplest terms, the budget planning of the Stabilization Branch may be described as follows: First, the manager of the Stabilization Branch must appraise the level of aggregate expenditures that will be forthcoming in the absence of such a budget. This includes expenditures on goods and services by the Allocation Branch as well as private expenditures on investment, consumption, and net exports. Since private expenditures depend on the distribution of income, the plans of both the Allocation and the Distribution Branches must be taken as given. Next, he must estimate the level of aggregate demand needed to maintain full utilization of resources at the present level of prices. Finally, he must compare this hypothetical level of demand with the level of expenditure forthcoming in the absence of a stabilization budget, and provide for taxes or transfer payments to compensate for the difference.

If expansion is needed, the Stabilization Branch will provide for the required level of transfer payments. It will operate with transfer payments because these do not involve decision over the allocation of resources. The Stabilization Branch will not raise the level of public expenditures on goods and services because this would interfere with the satisfaction of public wants as planned by the Allocation Branch. If contraction is needed, the Stabilization Branch will impose the required level of taxation. It will refrain from reducing goods and service expenditures, so as to avoid interfering with the satisfaction of public wants. In other words, countercyclical variations in the level of goods and service expenditures of government will be undertaken only to the extent that the Allocation Branch finds itself confronted with such fluctuations in the demand for the satisfaction of social wants.

Since the Stabilization Branch does not pursue distributional objectives, its transfer payments or taxes will be proportional to the proper distribution of income as determined by the Distribution Branch. Provided that the budget of the Allocation Branch is determined on the basis of individual preferences, taxes paid to, and benefits derived from, the budget of the Allocation Branch will not be deducted in defining the proper state of distribution.

By the very nature of the stabilization function, the budget of the Stabilization Branch will include at any one time either taxes (if the level of expenditure is otherwise excessive) or transfers (if demand is otherwise deficient). It will never include *both* taxes and transfers. The budget of the Stabilization Branch, if it exists at all, will be a surplus or a deficit budget. It will be in balance only in a situation that requires both taxes and transfers to stay at the zero level; that is, a situation where private expenditures plus expenditures by the Allocation Branch are at just the right level in the absence of a stabilizing budget policy.

The function of taxation in the context of the stabilization budget is only to prevent inflation, just as the function of transfers is only to prevent deflation. Thus, we have a third function of the revenue-expenditure process, quite distinct from those observed in the Allocation and the Distribution Branches.

Monetary and Debt Policy

Fiscal adjustments are not the only means by which economic stabilization may be secured. Other approaches such as monetary and debt policies, or possibly wage and price controls, must be considered as well. Just as the budgetary function of the Allocation Branch must be seen in the broader context of all public policies aimed at adjustments in allocation, so the budgetary function of stabilization must be seen in the broader context of other stabilization policies. The budgetary action required by the Stabilization Branch thus depends upon the restrictive or expansionary nature of other measures that are taken. The more that is done by other techniques such as monetary and debt policy, the less need be done through budgetary action. In this way, other techniques of stabilization policy may be readily built into our framework.

For purposes of this study, the array of other approaches to stabilization enters primarily in the form of monetary and debt policy. These policies offer the major alternative to stabilization by budget policy, and they are linked directly to budget measures that involve a deficit or surplus. Since the budget of the Stabilization Branch is necessarily a deficit or a surplus budget, it must be decided how to finance the deficit or how to dispose of the surplus. In either case, there results a change in the structure of claims, which in turn may affect the level of private spending. The most effective solution is through the creation or the destruction of money. This follows from the hypothesis that investment is related inversely to interest and that private consumption is related positively to the value of total claims held.

If tax rates are raised and the additional proceeds are withheld, the resulting effect upon the level of private expenditures will be restrictive in various respects. Not only will consumption expenditures decline because disposable income has been reduced (the income effect on consumption) but they may decline even further because consumer holdings of money claims are reduced (the asset effect on consumption). Moreover, investment may contract because the ratio of money supply to debt supply has been reduced, thus increasing the rate of interest (the claim effect on investment). If the surplus funds are not retained but used to pay off debt, the income effect on consumption will be the same; the asset effect on consumption will prove more questionable, as it now operates through a reduction in holding of debt; and the claim effect on investment will be reversed, since the withdrawal of public debt depresses the rate of interest, thus inducing investment. The net result, therefore, will tend to be less restrictive.

For similar reasons, expansionary action is more effective if the additional expenditures are financed out of new money than if they are financed out of borrowed funds. If new money is used, all effects are expansionary. More income is received, more claims are held, and the mix of outstanding claims has become more liquid. If the transfers are financed by borrowing, the asset effect on consumers is again positive, since total holdings of money and public debt are increased; but the claim effect on investment becomes restrictive, since the asset mix has become less liquid. Thus, the net expansionary effect is weakened.

Similar considerations hold with regard to policies of debt management. The choice in meeting deficit or surplus is not only between money and debt finance but also between various forms of debt finance, involving different types of obligations. Moreover, the problem of debt management is not limited to decisions that relate to changes in the total volume of claims but includes the much broader problem of possible changes between types of claims within a given total. It follows from all this that no sharp line of distinction can be drawn between fiscal and monetary policies for stabilization. In dealing with the former, considerable attention must also be paid to the latter.

Since stabilization may be approached by alternative routes involving different fiscal measures or combinations of fiscal and debt or monetary measures, there remains the question of which policy or which policy mix should be chosen. This decision must be made partly in terms of administrative feasibilities, but they do not decide the whole issue. Consideration must be given as well to important collateral effects— effects that may differ under various approaches. They may bear upon the efficiency of resource use, the state of distribution, or the rate of growth, thus rendering the choice of optimal policy a difficult matter.

CHAPTER 2

Interdependence and consolidation of subbudgets

Thus far we have considered the general problems encountered in preparing the budget plans for each of the three branches. We now turn to a more specific statement of the subbudgets—their interdependence and consolidation into a single net budget plan.

A. ILLUSTRATION OF A HYPOTHETICAL BUDGET

While the subplans of the three branches pursue distinct objectives, they nevertheless comprise an interdependent system. This we have emphasized already by instructing the manager of each branch to assume that the managers of the other branches will do their respective jobs. The formulation of the three budgets in an interdependent system may be shown best by a simple model of equations, but we shall begin with a numerical illustration.

To simplify matters, the illustration of Table 2-1 involves a community consisting of two individuals, X and Z. We begin with the situation shown in case 1. Total expenditures or sales receipts in the economy equal $1,000, including $800 of sales to private buyers and $200 of sales to government. To simplify matters, we assume that earnings from all sales are divided so as to give 30 per cent to X and 70 per cent to Z. We thus obtain the distribution of total earnings shown in lines 1 to 3, where X receives 30 per cent and Z receives 70 per cent. Total earnings equal $1,000, which is the full-employment income at prevailing prices.

In dealing with the subbudget, let us begin with the Allocation Branch. Since we are confronted with an interdependent system, any other

TABLE 2-1. BUDGET DETERMINATION AND CONSOLIDATION*

(In dollars)

	Case 1				Case 2				Case 3			
	Individuals			Budget	Individuals			Budget	Individuals			Budget
	X	Z	X + Z		X	Z	X + Z		X	Z	X + Z	
Private sector:												
1. Earnings from sales to private buyers (6 + 7)	240	560	800		211	493	704		228	533	761	
2. Earnings from sales to government (9)	60	140	200		89	207	296		72	167	239	
3. Total earnings (1 + 2)	300	700	1,000		300	700	1,000		300	700	1,000	
4. Available income after distributional adjustment (3 + 13)	400	600	1,000		400	600	1,000		300	700	1,000	
5. Available income, final amount (3 + 13 + 16)	500	750	1,250		369	554	923		420	981	1,401	
6. Private expenditures on investment			150				225				75	
7. Private expenditures on consumption	350	300	650		258	221	479		294	392	686	
Budget of the Allocation Branch:												
8. Taxes	−50	−150	−200	+200	−74	−222	−296	+296	−42	−197	−239	+239
9. Purchases				−200				−296				−239
10. Balance (8 + 9)	−50	−150	−200	0	−74	−222	−296	0	−42	−197	−239	0
Budget of the Distribution Branch:												
11. Taxes		−100	−100	+100		−100	−100	+100				
12. Transfers	+100		+100	−100	+100		+100	−100				
13. Balance (11 + 12)	+100	−100	0	0	+100	−100	0	0				
Budget of the Stabilization Branch:												
14. Taxes					−31	−46	−77	+77				
15. Transfers	+100	+150	+250	−250					+120	+281	+401	−401
16. Balance (14 + 15)	+100	+150	+250	−250	−31	−46	−77	+77	+120	+281	+401	−401
Net budget:												
17. Taxes, total	−50	−250	−300	+300	−105	−368	−473	+473	−42	−197	−239	+239
18. Transfers, total	+200	+150	+350	−350	+100		+100	−100	+120	+281	+401	−401
19. Purchases (9)				−200				−296				−239
20. Balance (17 + 18 + 19)	+150	−100	+50	−250	−5	−368	−373	+77	+78	+84	+162	−401

* The figures shown in this table are derived from the system of equations given in section B of this chapter; certain simplifications have been made, however. For case 1, we assume that $Y = 1000$, $j = 0.4$, $m = 0.3$, $v = 0.3$, and $I = 150$. To simplify matters, eqs. (2-2) to (2-5) are replaced by the simple assumption that $T_a^x = 0.1(E^x - T_d^x - T_s^x)$ and that $T_a^z = 0.2(E^z - T_d^z - T_s^z)$. Also, eqs. (2-12) and (2-13) have now been replaced by the simple assumption that $C^x = 0.7(E^x - T_d^x - T_s^x)$ and that $C^z = 0.4(E^z - T_d^z - T_s^z)$.
For case 2, we assume $I = 225$, that $X_a^z = 0.4(E^z - T_d^z - T_s^z)$, and that $T_a^z = 0.2(E^z - T_d^z - T_s^z)$. Otherwise, the assumptions are the same as for case 1.
For case 3, we assume $I = 75$ and $j = 0.3$. Otherwise, the assumptions are as in case 1. Where items do not apply, the respective portions of the table are blank.

sequence will do as well.   If social wants are to be satisfied in accordance
with individual preferences, outlays will depend on how much X and Z
wish to spend for this purpose.   This depends on their preferences and
on the amounts of income available to them.   These amounts are shown
in line 5.   They include earnings (line 3), taxes or transfers of the Distribution Branch (line 13), and taxes or transfers of the Stabilization
Branch (line 16).   Both lines 13 and 16 are given for purposes of planning
the budget of the Allocation Branch, so that line 5 may be computed
readily.

Let us now overlook all the difficulties noted in the preceding chapter
and proceed on the heroic assumption that X wishes to spend 10 per cent
of his income for the satisfaction of public wants, while Z wishes to spend
20 per cent.   They are billed the corresponding amounts of tax, as shown
in line 8.   The proceeds are used to purchase goods and services for the
satisfaction of social wants (line 9).   These expenditures are not reflected
as private receipts in line 9 because they are recorded already as earnings
in line 2.   We assume that the outlays of the Allocation Branch do not
involve capital formation, so that the question of loan finance does not
arise.   As shown in line 10, the budget of the Allocation Branch is
balanced.

We now turn to the budget of the Distribution Branch.   The receipt
of earnings in the market, as shown in lines 1 to 3, is given for purposes of
planning by the Distribution Branch.   Of total earnings of $1,000,
30 per cent goes to X and 70 per cent goes to Z.   Let us suppose, now,
that it has been decided to raise X's share to 40 per cent, putting aside
again the difficulties that arise in reaching such a decision.   The tax and
transfer measures required to accomplish this redistribution are shown in
lines 11 to 13.   If line 13 is added to line 3, we obtain the available
income shown in line 4.   This adjusted position conforms to what we
have assumed to be the proper state of distribution.   As seen in line 13,
the budget of the Distribution Branch is in balance.   Payments and
receipts cancel out for X and Z as a group.

There remains the budget of the Stabilization Branch.   From an
analysis of available resources, the full-employment output or income at
prevailing prices is found to equal $1,000.   To obtain full employment,
$1,000 must be spent on current output, including private outlays on
consumption and investment as well as goods and service expenditures of
the Allocation Branch.   Suppose, now, that private investment is independent of income and budget policy and is fixed at $150, as shown in
line 6.   There is no need to specify how this total is divided between
X and Z.   Since goods and service expenditures by the Allocation Branch
have been determined at $200, private outlays on consumption must
equal $1,000 − $200 − $150 = $650.

The manager of the Stabilization Branch now determines the amount of disposable income needed to call forth this level of private consumption and imposes taxes or pay transfers to provide for it. To simplify matters, let us assume that past experience shows that X will consume 70 per cent and that Z will consume 40 per cent of his disposable income. We may then determine what consumption would be in the absence of any action by the Stabilization Branch. By applying these ratios to the adjusted available incomes, as shown in line 4, we find that total consumption would amount to $520. This falls $130 short of the required level of $650. The Stabilization Branch, therefore, must make transfer payments so as to raise consumption by $130.

We know that 40 per cent of these payments must go to X and 60 per cent to Z, so as to leave the "proper" state of distribution undisturbed. We also know that X will spend 70 per cent of his transfers, while Z will spend 40 per cent. From this we can conclude that total transfers of $250 are required. The resulting payments to X and Z are shown in line 16. The resulting total available income is recorded in line 5. The corresponding level of consumption expenditures is shown in line 7, and total expenditures are at the desired level of full employment.

As shown in line 16, the budget of the Stabilization Branch records a deficit equal to its transfers. X and Z together show a net receipt of this amount.

The reader should keep in mind that this model is based on highly simplifying assumptions. The difficulties involved in determining social wants and the proper state of distribution have been assumed away. The relationships by which the level of income is determined have been oversimplified, and functional relationships that are not easily determined have been taken as given. These simplifications will be dropped as our study proceeds. Now we are interested only in the basic principle of simultaneous planning of subbudgets, and this principle continues to apply even if more complex systems are introduced. Thus, investment may be made a dependent variable, asset effects on consumption may be allowed for, and liquidity preference may be introduced. All this complicates the picture, but the general nature of our problem remains the same.

The planning of the subbudgets has thus been completed, and the objectives of all three branches have been met. The manager of the Allocation Branch is satisfied that social wants have been provided for and that the cost has been allocated in accordance with individual preferences; the manager of the Distribution Branch is satisfied that the proper distribution of income has been established; and the manager of the Stabilization Branch is satisfied that aggregate demand has been set so as to maintain full employment and price-level stability.

Turning now to the implementation of the subbudgets, it appears that the goods and service expenditures of the Allocation Branch must be carried out as provided for in its budget. All other items may be submitted to a clearing procedure. Consider, for instance, the case of X, who is to pay $50 in taxes to the Allocation Branch, to receive $100 in transfers from the Distribution Branch, and to obtain another $100 in transfers from the Stabilization Branch. Matters will be simplified by paying him a net transfer of $100 + $100 − $50 = $150. In the case of Z, by a similar procedure we arrive at a net tax obligation of $100.

This consolidation is shown in lines 17 to 20 of Table 2-1. We find that X receives net transfers of $150, while Z pays net taxes of $100. The excess of transfer over taxes is $50. The net budget, as shown in line 20, runs a deficit of $250, obtained by adding the excess of transfers over taxes to the goods and service expenditures of the Allocation Branch. The deficit in the net budget, moreover, equals the deficit of the Stabilization Branch, since the budgets of the other two branches are in balance. Finally, the deficit equals the excess of available income (line 5) over the sum of private expenditures (lines 6 and 7) and public expenditures on goods and services (line 9).

These numerical results follow from our particular assumptions, and a different picture could readily be obtained by varying them. In case 2, we double the fraction of income spent on the satisfaction of public wants and raise private investment by 50 per cent. In case 3, we reduce private investment by 50 per cent and omit distributional adjustments. Otherwise the assumptions of case 1 are held unchanged. The result in case 2 is a situation where both X and Z are subject to tax payments in the net budget, which now incurs a surplus. In case 3, we obtain a situation where both X and Z receive transfers in the net budget, and a large deficit is needed. Case 2 could be taken to reflect a war or a high-level defense economy or a boom situation; and case 3 could be taken to reflect a state of potentially deep depression. Other illustrations may be added to show how various objectives in the subbudgets can combine to different patterns of net budget, but the table should suffice to illustrate the principle involved.

B. A SIMPLE MODEL

We now turn to a more precise statement of the problem in terms of a simple system of interdependent equations. We retain our assumption that there are two taxpayers and only one type of public service, and make use of the following symbols:

Parameters

Y = income at full employment
I = expenditures on private investment

U_a = cost of goods provided for by the Allocation Branch
U_p = cost of goods supplied to satisfy private wants
m = fraction of earnings from sales to private buyers, going to X
v = fraction of earnings from sales to government, going to X
j = fraction of available income under proper distribution going to X

Variables

E = factor earnings
C = private consumption
G = goods and service expenditures of Allocation Branch
T = tax payments (+) or transfer receipts (−)
B = budget balance, surplus (+) and deficit (−)
p_p = price of goods purchased privately
$p_a{}^x$ = price payable by X for goods provided by the Allocation Branch
$p_a{}^z$ = price payable by Z for goods provided by the Allocation Branch

Throughout, we shall use superscripts x and z to indicate individuals X and Z respectively, and subscripts a, d, and s to indicate transactions by the Allocation, Distribution, and Stabilization Branches, respectively. Subscript n will be used to refer to transactions in the net budget.

We may now state the conditions that must be met by the budget plans of the three branches, holding constant in each case the variables determined in the budgets of the other two branches. Thereafter, the three subbudgets will be consolidated into a net budget.

The Subbudgets

The budget of the Allocation Branch must meet the following conditions:

$$G = T_a{}^x + T_a{}^z \tag{2-1}$$

$$T_a{}^x = T_a{}^x \left[(E^x - T_d{}^x - T_s{}^x), \frac{p_a{}^x}{p_p} \right] \tag{2-2}$$

$$T_a{}^z = T_a{}^z \left[(E^z - T_d{}^z - T_s{}^z), \frac{p_a{}^z}{p_p} \right] \tag{2-3}$$

$$\frac{p_a{}^x}{p_p} = \frac{p_a{}^x}{p_p} \left(U_a,\ U_p,\ \frac{T_a{}^x}{T_a{}^z} \right) \tag{2-4}$$

$$\frac{p_a{}^z}{p_p} = \frac{p_a{}^z}{p_p} \left(U_a,\ U_p,\ \frac{T_a{}^z}{T_a{}^x} \right) \tag{2-5}$$

Holding constant the values of $T_d{}^x$, $T_d{}^z$, E^x, and E^z as determined by the budget of the Distribution Branch, and the values of $T_s{}^x$ and $T_s{}^z$ as determined by the budget of the Stabilization Branch, the above five equations permit us to determine the values of G, $T_a{}^x$, $T_a{}^z$, $p_a{}^x/p_p$, and $p_a{}^z/p_p$.

According to equation (2-1), total expenditures for the satisfaction of public wants are determined as the sum of the contributions of X and Z. The budget of the Allocation Branch is in balance, assuming that the social wants provided for are in the nature of current consumption. The contributions of X and Z are determined, according to equations (2-2) and (2-3), as functions of available income, of the relative prices of goods provided for by the Allocation Branch, and of goods purchased privately.[1] Available income is defined as earnings minus taxes (or plus transfers) of the Distribution and the Stabilization Branches. Taxes imposed by the Allocation Branch are not deducted, since they are the very item that is to be determined.

Note that the prices of public services are not the same for X and Z. While both share in the same amount of public services, the allocation of the unit cost of such services between them depends upon their respective valuations of social wants. The nature of these wants is such that differences in effective demand by different consumers must be reflected in different prices. At the same time, both X and Z pay the same price in their private purchases. Thus they are confronted with different sets of relative prices when choosing between goods purchased privately and goods provided for by the Allocation Branch. The respective price ratios are determined in equations (2-4) and (2-5). They are functions of costs as well as of the shares in which X and Z respectively contribute to the outlays of the Allocation Branch.[2]

The budget of the Distribution Branch must meet the following conditions:

$$E^x = m(C + I) + vG \qquad (2\text{-}6)$$
$$E^z = Y - E^x \qquad (2\text{-}7)$$
$$E^x - T_d{}^x = j(E^x + E^z) \qquad (2\text{-}8)$$
$$T_d{}^x = -T_d{}^z \qquad (2\text{-}9)$$

---

[1] If public wants cannot be determined on the basis of individual evaluations, the taxes of the Allocation Branch must be allocated by some pattern determined on an authoritarian basis. Suppose this is proportionate to the "proper" state of distribution. At the Allocation Branch level, eqs. (2-2) and (2-4) are replaced by

$$T_a{}^x = j(T_a{}^x + T_a{}^z)$$

The three equations for the Distribution Branch remain unchanged. Those for the Stabilization Branch remain unchanged as well, with the exception of (2-12) and (2-13). Equation (2-12) now becomes

$$C^x = C^x(E^x - T_a{}^x - T_d{}^x - T_s{}^x)$$

with corresponding adjustments for (2-13). We thus have three equations less. The two price ratios previously counted as unknown drop out, as does G, which is now given by authoritarian decision.

[2] To simplify matters, we assume that goods produced to satisfy social and private wants are both produced under conditions of constant unit cost. Introduction of variable unit costs requires the addition of cost functions and substitution of absolute values for tax ratios in eqs. (2-4) and (2-5).

Holding constant the value of G as determined by the Allocation Branch, and of C as determined by the Stabilization Branch, the above four equations permit us to determine the values of E^x, E^z, T_d^x, and T_d^z.

The Distribution Branch determines what fraction of total income X and Z are to receive and provides for the required transfers or taxes. According to equation (2-6), the share of X in total earnings is given as a function of the allocation of the product between goods and services supplied to satisfy social and private wants. This function, here represented by the simple coefficients m and v, depends upon the resources supplied by X and Z and the production functions of goods supplied to meet the two types of wants. Equation (2-7) shows that the sum of factor earnings, including the shares of X and Z, is equal to income. Equation (2-8) shows the tax on X or the transfer to X needed to set his share at the desired fraction j. If a transfer is made, T is negative and the term $-T_d^x$ becomes a positive amount.

Since outlays for payments to the Allocation Branch are considered a use of income, the Distribution Branch does not deduct taxes paid to the Allocation Branch in defining income for distributive purposes. Taxes or transfers of the Stabilization Branch may be left out of consideration as well, since they are proportional to income as adjusted by the Distribution Branch. As shown in equation (2-9), the tax on X is equal to the transfer to Z, or vice versa, the budget of the Distribution Branch being again in balance.

The budget of the Stabilization Branch, finally, must meet these conditions:

$$Y = G + C + I \tag{2-10}$$

$$C = C^x + C^z \tag{2-11}$$

$$C^x = C^x\left[(E^x - T_d^x - T_s^x), \frac{p_a^x}{p_p} \right] \tag{2-12}$$

$$C^z = C^z\left[(E^z - T_d^z - T_s^z), \frac{p_a^z}{p_p} \right] \tag{2-13}$$

$$T_s^x = j(T_s^x + T_s^z) \tag{2-14}$$

Holding constant the values of G, p_a^x/p_p, and p_a^z/p_p as determined by the Allocation Branch, and the values of T_d^x and T_d^z as determined by the Distribution Branch, these five equations permit us to determine C, C^x, C^z, T_s^x, and T_s^z.

As shown in equation (2-10), full employment income Y is equal to the total of goods and service expenditures, including purchases by the Allocation Branch as well as private consumption and investment. According to equation (2-11), total consumption expenditures for the satisfaction of private wants equals the sum of consumption expenditures by X and Z. In equations (2-12) and (2-13), such expenditures are shown as functions of available income and of the relative prices of goods needed in the satisfaction of public and of private wants. Available income is defined again as earnings minus taxes paid to the Distribution and Stabilization Branches, plus transfers received from them. It is thus similar to the concept of available income used in equations (2-2) and (2-3), taxes of the Allocation Branch being again disregarded. Equation (2-14) shows that taxes or transfers of the Stabilization Branch must be in line with the proper distribution of income as determined by the Distribution Branch. The policy of the Stabilization Branch, as noted before, should be distributionally neutral.

Thus the substance of the budget determination is completed. We have, in all, fourteen equations that permit us to determine our fourteen unknowns, that is, G, $T_s{}^x$, $T_s{}^z$, $p_a{}^x/p_p$, $p_a{}^z/p_p$, E^x, E^z, $T_d{}^x$, $T_d{}^z$, C, C^x, C^z, $T_a{}^x$, and $T_a{}^z$.

Consolidation

There remains the more or less clerical task of consolidating these subbudgets into a single net budget plan. Adding together the various taxes and transfers, we obtain the following three equations:

$$T_n{}^x + T_n{}^z - G = B \qquad (2\text{-}15)$$
$$T_n{}^x = T_a{}^x + T_d{}^x + T_s{}^x \qquad (2\text{-}16)$$
$$T_n{}^z = T_a{}^z + T_d{}^z + T_s{}^z \qquad (2\text{-}17)$$

Equation (2-15) defines the balance ($+$ for surplus, $-$ for deficit) in the consolidated budget. This balance equals net tax receipts (tax receipts minus transfers) minus expenditures by the Allocation Branch. Equations (2-16) and (2-17) define net tax payments ($+$) or transfers ($-$) for X and Z as the sum of their respective taxes and transfers under the three subbudgets. Since all values except $T_n{}^x$, $T_n{}^z$, and B have been determined by our preceding set of equations, these additional unknowns may be found from equations (2-15) to (2-17).

Some Complications

The above model is based on highly simplified assumptions regarding not only the determination of social wants and distributional objectives but also the relationships by which income is determined. While nothing would be gained for present purposes from a more complex model, let us note briefly certain difficulties relating to the homogeneity of the G terms in equations (2-1), (2-6), and (2-10). The term G in equations (2-6) and (2-10) expresses goods and service expenditures of government as included in the national income accounts. The term G in equation (2-1) expresses the absorption of resources in the supply of goods and services for the current satisfaction of social wants. The two concepts may differ for various reasons.

Purchases by the Allocation Branch may involve existing assets rather than current output. In this case, they will not appear in the G term of equations (2-6) and (2-10), but they may be paid for by taxes and be included in the G term of equation (2-1). Further differences arise in the case of capital outlays by the Allocation Branch. Since the G term of equation (2-1) records the cost of public services consumed during the budget period, capital outlays must be spread over the lifetime of the asset. The G term of equation (2-1), therefore, may be smaller or larger than that of (2-6) and (2-10), where the capital outlay is included at the time when it is made. Further complications develop in the case of public subsidies. Subsidy payments by the Allocation Branch, or operation of government enterprise at a loss, involve the purchase of goods and services for the satisfaction of social wants and are properly included in the G term as used in equation (2-1) and (2-6); but they are not part of G as defined in connection with (2-10). These and other complications must be kept in mind; in a more elaborate model they would have to be taken care of.

Next, there is the more basic difficulty that the process of evaluation which applies to the case of public wants differs from that which applies to private wants. Yet, our model implies that the values of C and I, as measured in terms of market price, are homogeneous with the value of G, as measured by cost. Thus, there remains the general problem of valuation of public services in the social accounts—a problem that will be examined in some detail later on. Finally, the government may engage in adjustments, such as controls over imperfections in competition, where no transfer of resources to the satisfaction of social wants is involved and no corresponding value of G results. Such adjustments are not accounted for, or are recorded imperfectly, in the above system. Notwithstanding these omissions and simplifications, the system serves to bring out the essential problems to be met in connection with the different budget functions.

C. FISCAL EFFICIENCY AND FISCAL POLITICS

The administrative case for budget consolidation is self-evident, since it would be clumsy and wasteful to operate three separate sets of budget transactions when the very same objectives can be accomplished in consolidated form. But this consolidation is a matter of administrative expediency only; we must not lose sight of the basic principle that the consolidated budget has *no* rationale on its own and is nothing but a result obtained by the clearing of distinct subbudgets, each of which involves quite different considerations and planning objectives.

Consolidation, to be sure, presents no dangers in our imaginary model of efficient budgeting. It is an administrative device, an uninteresting clerical operation undertaken after each of the subbudgets has been formulated on its own merits. But in the real world the matter is regarded differently; there the tendency is to view the budget in consolidated terms from the outset, and thus to confuse the underlying issues in the planning stage.

Compensatory Adjustments and the Allocation Branch

In our normative model, expenditures of the Allocation Branch are taken as given for purposes of the Stabilization Branch, just as the condition of full employment and price-level stability is given for purposes of the Allocation Branch. The Stabilization Branch, accordingly, is restricted to tax and transfer operations; and the allocation of resources between the satisfaction of public and private wants must be planned on the assumption that all available resources are utilized fully.

In this efficient system, individual X, who places little value on the satisfaction of public wants and favors a small budget for the Allocation Branch, may consistently advocate compensatory action to check depression. Similarly, Z, who favors a large budget for the Allocation Branch, may consistently argue for vigorous compensatory action in a boom. By supporting antidepression action, X argues for transfer payments; he contemplates increased service programs only if, and to the extent that, there has been a bona fide increase in the demand for the satisfaction of social wants. By supporting anti-inflation action, Z favors higher taxes and no cutbacks in service programs unless justified by a reduced demand for the satisfaction of social wants. Putting it differently, there is no place in such a system for artificial ditch-digging programs. Such measures, to be sure, are better than unemployment, but they are inferior to transfer payments that lead to the employment of resources that satisfy the more important private wants. By the very same token, there is no excuse for cutting useful public services to curtail demand, since demand may be curtailed by raising taxes.

The reader will recognize readily that this is not precisely what happens in practice. The enthusiasm for budgetary measures to check depression in the thirties was considerably greater among those who emphasized the satisfaction of social wants; and the case for budgetary measures in the current inflation setting is argued with more enthusiasm by those who favor an incidental cutback in social services. These relationships are of great interest and are crucial to an understanding of fiscal politics, but they do not contribute to an efficient policy of budget determination.

Efficient policy must recognize the basic distinction between the satisfaction of social wants as a matter of allocation, on the one side, and the stabilizing action of budget policy as a transfer measure on the other. At the same time, situations may arise where countercyclical variations in goods and service expenditures of the government are justified. Countercyclical variations in the timing of public works may be desirable where unemployment is of a regional rather than a national character, or in order to avoid the waste of excess capacity caused by temporary dislocation. Moreover, we shall note that cyclical fluctuations may involve a countercyclical shift in the demand for services aimed at the satisfaction of social wants. For these and other reasons, the activities of the Allocation Branch may be influenced to some degree by the requirements of the Stabilization Branch, and some countercyclical fluctuation of public services will be in order. Nevertheless, the basic principle remains—that the stabilization function may be performed without inferior resource allocation—that is to say, without causing an excessive or a deficient level of public service.

Compensatory Adjustments and the Distribution Branch

Similar considerations apply to the relation between the Stabilization and the Distribution Branches. In the efficient system, the desired adjustments in distribution are applied to the distribution of earnings at a full-employment level of income, and the tax or transfer policies of the Stabilization Branch are distributionally neutral. This is the case, even though changes in the state of distribution may have repercussions upon the level of demand and upon the required budget of the Stabilization Branch.

Suppose that, under conditions of depression, regressive taxes are more deflationary per dollar of yield than progressive taxes. If it is desired to conduct compensatory policy with a minimum deficit, progressive taxes are required. Thereby compensatory action is rendered attractive to those who favor progression and unattractive to those who do not. Other objectives may lead to different pairings. In the efficient budget, such distortions are not permitted to occur. Distributional correctives are applied by the Distribution Branch without reference to Stabilization; and the Stabilization Branch makes its proportional transfers or imposes its proportional taxes at whatever level may be required, in view of the resulting level of private expenditures.

Again, we can recognize how the mixing of objectives may enter the politics of fiscal policy. The case against consumption taxes in the thirties was made with particular emphasis by those who not only favored compensatory policy but who sympathized with some degree of income redistribution. And the post-war case against progressive taxes is made with particular vigor by those who not only favor growth and price-level stability but whose distributional values are such as to oppose equalizing taxes.

Distributional Considerations and the Allocation Branch

Similar considerations, finally, apply to the relationship between the Allocation and the Distribution Branch. In our efficient system, the degree of income redistribution is determined independently of the scope of resource allocation for the satisfaction of social wants; and the distribution of taxes imposed by the Allocation Branch is a matter of income elasticity of social wants, not of redistribution. In practice, the two issues are mixed with each other. The degree to which distributional objectives are feasible to attain may depend upon the level of public services, and the level of public services may be determined by distributional considerations rather than by a bona fide demand for the satisfaction of social wants.

The direction of bias will differ with the state of fiscal development. When the budget is still small, relative to national income, the degree of equalization will be a direct function of the level of resource allocation to social wants—that is, a function of the level of public goods and service expenditures. The voters can expect new services to be financed by additional taxes on the "rich," and the voting coalitions will form accordingly. The poor will favor a large budget for the Allocation Branch, since little or no net cost is involved; the rich will oppose it, since the unit price of additional services is excessively high. In an early state of development, the poor will tend to outnumber the rich, and the bias will be toward a budget for the Allocation Branch which exceeds that permissible in the efficient system.

As this development continues and the relative weight of the budget increases, the high incomes are absorbed more and more in taxation. The tax base begins to extend downward; the marginal dollar in the tax base is now located at the lower rather than the upper end of the scale. The marginal cost of additional services becomes excessively expensive for the lower-income groups, while the higher-income groups tend to maintain their opposition to a large budget. The weight of voter opinion shifts, and we arrive at a situation where the bias tends to be towards an excessively small budget for the Allocation Branch.

Whatever the merits of this particular diagnosis, a proper separation of functions not only serves to classify the requirements of efficient budget planning but also offers a key to an understanding of the politics of fiscal policy. With all this, we do not wish to suggest that various issues of public policy may not be combined in the efficient system and voted upon in conjunction. On the contrary, we shall find that reaching an agreement on issues is facilitated precisely where the proper combinations can be devised; and that the constructive contribution of the politician lies in his ability to assemble such combinations. At the same time, this combining of inherently independent issues to secure agreement differs sharply from a linking of issues that is accomplished not by choice or bargaining but by failure to understand that, in fact, the issues may be handled independently. It is this latter practice that gives rise to the inefficiencies dealt with here.

CHAPTER 3

Problems of implementation

After the objectives of the budget plan are determined, the specific policies and legislation must be chosen that serve best to implement the objectives. On the expenditure side of the budget, it must be decided whether the goods and services needed to satisfy public wants should be produced by the government itself or purchased by the government from private firms. In the first case, the government must purchase factors of production; in the second, finished goods or services.

Taxes are needed to pay for these purchases. The taxes must be chosen so as to allocate the cost of public services in the desired fashion. More generally, the government must plan its tax and expenditure policies so as to obtain the desired end result *after* allowing for resulting interactions between the public and the private sector. Excess burdens must be avoided, and the budgetary capacity of the economy as a whole must be considered. In the present chapter, our introductory survey will be completed with a brief view of these issues.

A. PUBLIC PRODUCTION

The function of government as an entrepreneur or organization for production must be distinguished sharply from that of providing for the satisfaction of public wants. Indeed, it is related but loosely to our problem of budget policy.

Separation of Issues

After the Allocation Branch has decided which public wants should be satisfied, it must be determined whether the required goods and services should be purchased from private firms or produced under public management after governmental purchase of the factors of production.

Both techniques may be used.   And in both cases the finished product can be made available to the consumer free of direct charge but paid for by taxes.   The inapplicability of the exclusion principle refers to the demand, not to the supply, of the goods and services needed to satisfy public wants. Battleships may be produced in public or private shipyards; free education may be provided through public schools or by subsidies to private schools.   Moreover, the government itself may produce goods for sale at the market in response to the satisfaction of private wants.

As noted before, we can imagine an economy where a substantial part of the total resources goes to satisfy public wants but the government produces little.[1]   This would be the case in a private-enterprise economy in which a high value is placed on the satisfaction of public wants.   Or we can imagine an economy where public production is important, but only a small share of resources goes to satisfy public wants.   This would be true of a socialist economy in which a low value is attached to the satisfaction of public wants.   Indeed, we may have any of the four following combinations:

1. Goods and services provided free of direct charge and produced by the government

2. Goods and services provided free of direct charge and produced by private firms

3. Goods and services sold at the market and produced by the government

4. Goods and services sold at the market and produced by private firms

Since the scope of public production management is largely independent of that of public-want satisfaction, we may ask what the rules are that tell us when public production should be undertaken.   There are, however, no definite rules.   Many factors enter, ranging from technical considerations of relative cost, to the broader issues of social organization that transcend the limits of purely economic judgment.   Some brief observations may be made, however, on the more technical aspects of the matter.[2]

Public Goods

A first case for public production management arises in connection with certain goods and services whose inherent quality is such that they cannot be left to private suppliers.

Consider, for instance, the operation of military establishments or the

---

[1] See p. 15.

[2] For a succinct summary of the experience with public enterprise in the United States, see Clair Wilcox, *Public Policies toward Business*, Richard D. Irwin, Inc., Homewood, Ill., 1955, chap. 26.

administration of justice.   These are activities that technically could be leased out to private firms, as has occurred in colonial history.   However, such practice would be repugnant to democratic society as it is now understood.   The qualitative content of these services, or the wants which they are to satisfy, is such that they must be supplied through public office; even if supplied privately, they require such elaborate supervision that the situation is more or less equivalent to public production.

Somewhat the same situation applies to education.   The mere decision to provide free education is no reason why educational services should be supplied under public production management.   The objective of free education may be met as well through conditional transfer payments to parents or through subsidies to private schools.   If educational services are to be provided under public management, the reason must be found in the qualitative nature of the educational services desired.   Thus, public schools may be desired because they make for political and cultural tolerance, serve as a melting pot, and pass on a common cultural heritage. At the same time, public schools could be supplied on a fee basis and need not be linked with the idea of free education.   The case for supplying the services of public schools free of direct charge involves the twofold decision that education is considered a merit want and that it should be satisfied through a publicly controlled system.

Our concept of public wants may thus be supplemented by a concept of public *goods*—that is, goods the inherent quality of which requires public production.   While public goods are characteristically goods that satisfy public wants, not all goods that satisfy public wants must be public goods in this sense.   Indeed, the larger part of the outlays provided for by the Allocation Branch involves the purchase of more or less finished products from private firms.   While civil servants and sailors must be in government employ, pencils and battleships can be purchased from private firms.

Public Production as an Alternative to Public Control

Not all instances of public production management involve public goods.   A second case for public production management arises where such management serves as a convenient substitute for public control over resource allocation.

Consider, for instance, the case of monopoly control.   A need for control may arise under various conditions of closed entry and with industries subject to internal economies of scale.   This is the case of so-called natural monopolies, as illustrated by the postal service and railroads on the national level, and by light, gas, or city transportation on the local level.   Since the regulating forces of competition are absent, public control of some sort is needed.   In order to prevent inefficiencies in allocation in response to a given state of distribution, public control is particularly needed where (1) demand is elastic, and where (2) the wants in question are in the nature of merit wants, so that their satisfaction will be encouraged by public policy. In order to prevent distortions in the "proper" state of distribution, public control may be particularly needed where (3) demand is inelastic and where (4) purchases weigh heavily in the budgets of low-income families. The case of public utilities is typically one where considerations (2), (3), and (4) apply. At the same time, demand for the services of public utilities is usually inelastic, so that inefficiencies in allocation because of (1) will be of lesser weight.

Where controls over allocation are needed, the government may control the policies of private firms; it may replace private firms by public production or it may adopt various in-between forms of ownership and control. The most efficient solution in any particular case depends upon the degree of control necessary and on the complexity of the task. Where the need for intervention is slight, it may be readily manageable through external control. Where the need is extensive, public ownership could be the simpler course; this course may differ little from a comprehensive control of private firms.

Similar difficulties arise where controls are needed to cover divergences between social and private costs or benefits. The factory that causes a smoke nuisance may be required to raise the height of its chimney or to pay damages in the form of a tax used in turn to reimburse those who have suffered in the process.[1] Where external benefits occur, the collateral satisfaction of social wants, which the market fails to recognize, may be allowed for by a subsidy from the public budget. Where public and private time preference diverges, a subsidy may be paid to private owners of natural resources to reduce their rate of exploitation. A subsidy may also be paid in other situations in which divergences occur.

In some cases, the problem may be handled best by outside controls; in others, the task of administering a policy of subsidy or tax penalty, and of supervising the pricing policy of private firms becomes so formidable that outright public management offers the more efficient solution. Again, the difference between extensive control and outright public management may become nominal, so that the choice between the two is one of expediency in administration.

In the context of an efficiently operated Allocation Branch, the necessary degree of adjustment in resource allocation is one thing to be decided upon, and the choice of techniques to secure the adjustment is another. In this case as in others, the separation of issues becomes blurred when we move to the level of fiscal politics. The technique of public ownership

---

[1] As will be shown later, it is by no means a simple matter to determine just what the tax-bounty policy should be. (See p. 140.)

frequently may be expected to secure the required adjustment more thoroughly than external control does over private firms. Hence, one's choice of technique may depend upon how strongly one feels about securing the adjustment.

The choice of technique will frequently be a matter of judgment, not subject to a clear-cut decision on grounds of efficiency. The decision then hinges on a choice between the principle that production management should be private, unless specific circumstances prevail under which public management is called for, and the principle that production management should be public, unless special circumstances prevail under which private management is called for. A choice between these principles, or various in-between views, transcends considerations of economic efficiency. Political, social, and cultural aspects enter, as does the interrelation between economic organization and the state of individual freedom. These matters will not be examined here. Rather, we shall proceed on the assumption that public production should be limited to situations where it is clearly superior in efficiency to private production under public control. We are left, therefore, with a public household that operates within a largely private-enterprise system. The conduct of public finances in a socialist economy is an interesting problem, but it is not our present concern.[1]

B. PUBLIC MARKETING

We now turn to the behavior of the government as a party to transactions in the market. Such transactions arise primarily in implementing the budget of the Allocation Branch, where the government appears as a buyer, and in the operation of public enterprise where the government appears as a seller. Market transactions in liquidity incident to the management of the public debt are disregarded for the time being.

Public Purchases

Purchases by the Allocation Branch may be of products or of factors of production, depending on whether the goods in question are produced

---

[1] Assuming the socialist economy to be one where consumer sovereignty is recognized, the problem of the socialist Allocation Branch is very similar to that of our model. The bulk of the production plan dealing with the satisfaction of private wants may be tested against the judgment of the market, but that part of the plan which deals with the satisfaction of public wants cannot be so tested. It involves precisely the same difficulties as confront the Allocation Branch in our setting. The main difference between our case and that of the socialist budget relates to the interaction with the private sector. We must allow for effects on investment incentives, whereas the socialist budget need not do so, or must only to a much lesser degree.

under private or under public management. There are certain principles of purchase policy that must be followed.

In the normative system, these principles apply to the efficient allocation of resources to meet public as well as private wants. The objective of public policy is to see to it that all goods are produced so as to equate marginal cost and average revenue. When the government has established a perfect market, it may then proceed to pay the market price on its own purchases. This will be the efficient price from the point of view of the Allocation Branch, and it will be distributionally neutral in the sense of giving no undue gain or penalty to the seller.

In industries that operate under conditions of decreasing cost, a subsidy is required to secure efficient allocation, since the equating of average revenue and marginal cost leaves average cost in excess of average revenue. This is the case whether the product is purchased privately or by the government. For public purchases, the subsidy may or may not be counted as part of the price payment. This is a matter of terminology. At the same time, the subsidy payment must be distinguished from the payment at market price when comparing the relative costs of satisfying public and private wants. This must be done because the satisfaction of private wants is valued at market price.

Looking at the matter more realistically, let us take the case where the government purchases in an imperfect market. Here the government will be interested in the price it pays on its own purchases, even though it may not attempt to regulate private sales to private buyers. The government may use its bargaining position as a large buyer to obtain a proper price, or it may apply direct controls such as rationing or price ceilings. In either case there remains the problem of determining the relative prices upon which the allocation of resources between public and private wants should be based. More specifically, the question arises: Should the cost of goods provided for through the budget (but purchased in the market) be valued at a competitive price, even though the same goods may be valued in the market at a monopoly price? Or should the cost of publicly supplied goods be valued at whatever price the government pays, which price may be more or less than that paid by private buyers? Here, as in other situations, we are confronted with the difficulty of applying criteria of efficiency in a system that is only partially efficient.[1] Similar difficulties arise regarding the concept of distributional neutrality in public pricing, particularly in connection with debt management.[2]

These are the general principles of purchase policy, but there may be exceptions. Situations can arise, apart from the case of decreasing cost, where the government has an explicit intention to subsidize certain sellers.

[1] See p. 149.
[2] See p. 582.

Government contracts may be placed with small sellers, or with sellers in a particular location, even though their prices are higher. Here, purchase policy may reflect a combination of objectives involving distributional, social, or defense considerations, as well as considerations of efficiency in purchasing as such. As a result, the *net* budget may involve pricing policies that differ from those which would apply if no such supplementary objectives were involved.

Public Sales

Public sales are a less frequent phenomenon than public purchases. Nevertheless the government may find itself on the sellers' side of the market. This can involve either the sale of goods produced under public production management or the resale of goods previously purchased from private sellers.

The pricing policy for public sales is subject to the same general principles that apply to purchases. In the absence of special circumstances, considerations of resource allocation demand that public sales be at a uniform price. For goods produced under conditions of constant or increasing cost, the public price will equal that secured in a competitive market, where marginal (as well as average) cost and revenue are equated.[1] For goods produced under decreasing cost, the efficient level of output requires public operation at a loss. We may think of the government as subsidizing its own marginal-cost price. Not infrequently, public production will supply goods that go to satisfy private as well as public wants. Voluntary price payments at the market will account for a part of the cost, while the budget of the Allocation Branch will provide for the remainder. Here, difficult problems arise in allocating total cost between the part to be paid through the market and that to be paid through the budget process.

As in the case of public purchases, collateral objectives may enter price policy for public sales. The government may wish to penalize the buyer by selling at a monopoly price, as illustrated by profits from a tobacco monopoly; or, to put it differently, the government may impose an excise tax on its own sales. As a matter of administration, much is to be said for the excise-tax approach. The decision to charge a tax by monopolistic pricing, and how much, should not be vested with the manager of public enterprise. His function should be to produce efficiently and to sell at a competitive price, allowing for such excises as are imposed on his product. Taxation via monopolistic pricing is not compatible with the managerial role; and the amounts of excise implicit in monopolistic pricing for various industries may lead to a poor distribution of the tax bill. Finally, it may

---

[1] Qualifications similar to those noted in the case of public purchases may arise where the pricing of privately supplied goods is imperfect.

not be easy for the central budgetary authorities to extract monopoly profits from public enterprises that are wont to gain a status of semi-independence.

In other instances the government may wish to sell at a loss, not to meet the special problem of decreasing cost, but to subsidize the buyer of particular products. Such is the case with public operations in low-cost housing. Whether the policy is one of profit or loss, a recognized merit or demerit want must be involved in order to justify the practice in the efficient system. Indeed, a number of decisions are involved. In the efficient system, a loss operation in low-cost housing involves (1) a policy of distributional adjustment in favor of low incomes, since only *low*-cost housing is involved; (2) a recognition of *housing* as a merit want, since the distributional adjustment is not made in cash; and (3) a preference for *public* production management, since otherwise low-cost housing might have been provided by subsidies to private firms.

While situations arise where profit or loss pricing is called for, such policies must be justified in terms of specific penalty or subsidy objectives; in the absence of these objectives, the general rule of *price equals marginal cost* applies.

C. RESPONSE OF THE PRIVATE SECTOR TO BUDGET POLICY

While the public sector differs in its theoretical structure from the market sector, both are closely interdependent parts of one and the same working economy. This interdependence is an all-important feature of budget policy in a dual economic system.

Implementation of the Desired End Result

Policies undertaken to implement specific objectives of the budget plan must be designed to allow for the reactions they call forth in the market sector of the economy. Suppose that the government undertakes specific tax or expenditure measures. These may be looked upon as outside disturbances that call forth a chain of adjustments in prices, incomes, and other variables in the economic process. These adjustments affect the setting in which private households and firms operate, and react upon budget receipts and costs. Such adjustments must be allowed for in planning the policies by which various budget objectives are to be implemented.

All this goes without saying for the Stabilization Branch, whose tax or transfer measures are determined in their very nature by the relationships of the market sector. A similar if less obvious interdependence arises in the context of the other branches. The Allocation Branch may purchase a commodity produced by individual Y and intend to place the cost on individuals X and Z. Suppose, now, that the Branch levies a tax on the incomes of X and Z, who then reduce their purchases of goods produced by W. Depending on the adjustments that follow, the end result may be a worsening in the income position not only of X and Z but also of W, and a gain in the position of Y. This hardly complies with the intent of the tax policy, which was to place the cost of public services with X and Z. The concern of tax policy, therefore, must be with the ultimate end results and not the initial impact of fiscal measures. The reactions of the private sector must be taken into account to begin with; policies must be designed to beat the game and to obtain the desired result, after allowing for the adjustments that follow in the private sector.

Similar considerations hold for the tax-transfer plans of the Distribution Branch and for the taxes or transfers of the Stabilization Branch. Measures designed to obtain the "proper" state of distribution must be such as to realize this objective in the end result rather than in the initial impact of tax or transfer measures.

For these reasons, the formulation of budget policy does not end with the determination of budget objectives. Policies must be found that will implement them. Determination of these policies must be based on an understanding of how the private sector of the economy operates and what the responses to various policies will be. At this point, a normative or optimal theory of the public household becomes useless unless it can be put into practice by policies based upon a predictive theory of economic relationships that permits us to anticipate these responses.

Budget Policies as Exogenous Disturbances

When speaking of the economic effects of budget policies, we look upon such policies as more or less exogenous disturbances in the functioning of the market sector. In the case of the Stabilization Branch, there is no objection to this view; nor is there too serious an objection in the case of the Distribution Branch. However, the approach is puzzling when applied to the Allocation Branch.

To the extent that an adequate solution *can* be found to the satisfaction of social wants, the difficulties posed by the nonapplicability of the exclusion principle are overcome. The satisfaction of social wants then becomes a more or less endogenous part of the market mechanism. Tax payments, in this case, cannot be considered outside disturbances. Adjustments to expenditures and taxes of the Allocation Branch become similar in nature to those which follow changes in transactions by consumers or firms in the market. There is no problem of outside effects.

This line of reasoning has some merit, but it must not be carried too far. The budget of the Allocation Branch cannot be based on wholly voluntary action. Even in the normative model, it must be determined by a political process involving majority decision and compulsion of some sort. The expenditures and taxes of the Allocation Branch, therefore, cannot become a truly endogenous part of the market system; we shall do better, in tracing the effects of budget policy, to view the operation of the Allocation Branch as an exogenous factor.

Taxable Capacity versus Optimal Budget

The public and private sectors of the economy must be recognized as mutually interdependent parts of the same working economy. This disposes, or should dispose, of the fruitless debate as to whether the public sector diverts income produced in the private sector, or vice versa. There is no place for the goose-and-golden-egg doctrine in an objective view of the problem. The public sector of the economy, no less than the private, has important functions to perform, and neither sector can exist without the cooperation of the other. At the same time, it is important to investigate how budget policy affects the over-all performance of the economy, including that of the private sector.

Similarly, it is useful to inquire into the size and composition of what may be referred to as the optimal budget. This includes the problem of taxable capacity, but goes further. The very term *taxable capacity* invites bias. It limits the problem from the outset to the tax side of the budget, while disregarding the expenditure side; and by focusing attention on capacity, it suggests an upper limit to the size of the public household that the private sector can stand, while disregarding the need for a lower limit without which the private sector cannot exist. An unbiased view of the problem must consider the entire interrelationship between budget policy and the level of welfare; such a view must also allow for the contingency of an insufficient as well as an excessive level of social-want satisfaction. In other words, the concept of taxable capacity must be discarded in favor of a concept of optimal budget.

A different concept of taxable capacity arises in determining regional contributions to Federal finances, or the "fair" contributions of various countries to an international organization. Here the question is what sacrifice the community is able to sustain, a problem in the policy of the Distribution Branch transferred to an interregional or international plane. The greater the per capita and group incomes the greater, presumably, the taxable capacity or the ability to contribute.

Finally, the concept of budgetary capacity may be related to the desire of the public to sustain a certain absolute standard of public-want satisfaction. The absolute standard will be less in a poor than in a rich country; and, applying a modification of Engel's law, the nature of social wants may be such as to absorb an increasing share of outlays with a rising level of per capita income. This, apparently, was proposed by

Adolph Wagner in his famous law of "growing public expenditures." Although Wagner failed to specify whether expenditures grow in absolute or in relative terms, we may assume that he implied the latter.[1]

Gains and Losses from Budget Policy

The gains and losses incurred from budgetary activity reflect the operation of each of the three branches. First, there are the gains derived from the satisfaction of social wants. While this involves a reduced satisfaction of private wants, the transfer of resources to public use—if held within proper limits—brings a superior allocation and hence a net gain. Secondly, there is the gain derived from securing such improvements in the state of distribution as are held desirable. Thirdly, there is the gain derived from the maintenance of high employment and price-level stability. All these must be considered in determining the size and composition of the optimal budget. At the same time, care must be taken to determine *net* gains. Allowance must be made not only for the direct opportunity cost of resource transfer to public use but for the indirect and more or less hidden effects of budget operations upon the efficiency of performance in the private sector and upon the satisfaction of private wants.

Such effects are not identical with effects upon the level of output as measured in national product statistics. To begin with, output at full employment may be affected by resulting changes in the supply of *work effort*. With a given labor force, this supply depends on people's preferences between goods and leisure, and on the real wage rate. Budget policy bears directly upon these variables by affecting not only the price at which leisure may be traded for income but also the general environment in which a choice between income and leisure is made. We shall find that there is no a priori reason to expect that increased budget operations must reduce work effort. The opposite may be the case. However, there is some reason to expect that the level of work effort will be lower under a progressive than under a proportional or regressive tax structure. Thus, a distribution policy aimed at equalization may reduce the level of output at full employment.

[1] See Adolph Wagner, *Finanzwissenschaft*, 3d ed., C. F. Winter, Leipzig, Germany, 1883, part I, p. 76. Also see excerpts from Wagner in R. A. Musgrave and Alan T. Peacock (eds.), *Classics in the Theory of Public Finance*, International Economic Association, Macmillan & Co., Ltd., London, 1958.

For a discussion of taxable capacity with emphasis on political factors, see Colin Clark, "Public Finance and the Value of Money," *Economic Journal*, vol. 55, no. 220, pp. 371–389, December, 1945. Also see J. A. Pechman and T. Mayer, "Mr. Colin Clark on the Limits of Taxation," *Review of Economics and Statistics*, vol. 34, no. 3, pp. 232–242, August, 1952; and A. B. Prest, "Government Revenue and the National Income," *Public Finance*, vol. 6, no. 3, pp. 238–252, 1951.

In evaluating such results, note that a change in output due to a voluntary change in employment differs from a change in output due to changes in involuntary unemployment. A reduction in involuntary unemployment and a resulting increase in output is a net gain. This need not be the case for an increase in full-employment output that results from say, a tax on leisure or a subsidy to work income. Budgetary effects upon work effort, which result from a distortion in the choice between work and leisure, give rise to a burden; and this will be the case whether output increases or decreases as a result.

Output at full employment may be affected further through resulting changes in the rate of *capital formation*. Such changes may come about directly through the contribution of public capital formation, and indirectly through budgetary effects on the rate of private capital formation. The direct contribution of public capital formation plays a vital role in economic development. It may take the form of opening new areas through highway construction, or irrigation or flood-control projects; of improving labor productivity through public health and educational programs; or of industrial development for which the capital, know-how, or initiative is not available in the private sector. All these are of particular importance to undeveloped economies. Here there exists a special need for public capital formation, a need that arises because the types of investment required at the initial stages of development frequently fall outside the exclusion principle and thus involve social wants of various sorts. In the more advanced countries, the role of public capital formation differs. Here, emphasis may be on the conservation of resources, on special regional problems, express highways, and, especially, scientific development. In either setting, public investment may contribute significantly to economic growth.

The significance of budgetary effects on private capital formation, and the form these effects take, depends upon the nature of the economy. Consider first a classical setting where Say's law applies, and intended savings are always absorbed into private capital formation. Here, effects of budget policy on the level of private investment must operate through resulting changes in the level of private saving. Such resulting changes in the level of saving have no bearing on the level of prices or employment. They are important only in their effect on the division of output between consumption and capital formation and, hence, on the rate of growth.

This is not a realistic view of the modern economy, where intended savings may or may not be matched by investment, and vice versa. Here the effects of budget policy upon consumption, saving, and private capital formation assume a twofold significance. They continue to bear upon the *division* of the full-employment product between consumption and capital formation and, hence, upon the rate of economic growth; but they also come to bear on the *level* of expenditure in the private sector and, hence, upon the direction and scope of action to be taken by the Stabilization Branch.   Moreover, budgetary influences on private capital formation now come to operate primarily through the relative willingness of investors to invest available funds, rather than through changes in the available supply of funds.   Effects of budget policy upon the profitability of investment may be favorable or unfavorable.   Favorable effects may ensue from the expenditure side of the budget, and unfavorable effects may ensue from the tax side.   Effects upon the level and type of private investment will depend upon the level as well as the structure of taxation. Budgetary policies that raise the current share of capital formation out of full-employment output also raise the future level of such output.   Like changes in output due to changes in labor supply, a higher level of output need not reflect a gain, since it is purchased at the cost of reduced current consumption.   Again, the proper criterion is not whether output is increased or reduced but whether or not the allocation of resources is distorted.

Finally, budget policy may affect the level of output via other effects upon the efficiency with which resources are used in the private sector. Unless proper provision is made for the satisfaction of basic public wants, efficient operation of the private sector is impossible.   Security, enforcement of contract, and similar matters are necessary conditions without which the private sector cannot function at all.   Public services, such as education and research, render an important if indirect contribution; and we have seen that there are many situations where public regulation of the market is required.   At the same time, budget policy must avoid capricious interference with the satisfaction of private wants.   Budget policy should achieve its specific objectives, but beyond this it should be neutral. There should be no unnecessary interference with the choice between work and leisure, consumption and saving, different types of consumption, and different types of investment.   The ease with which such interference can be avoided depends on the structure of the budget and may become increasingly difficult as the level of the budget rises relative to total income.

Enough has been said to show that resulting changes in the gross national product are no precise indication of the effects of budget policy upon economic welfare.   Net gains that result from the satisfaction of social wants are not recorded, except where they reflect on the level of private output.   Resulting changes in the choice between goods and leisure, or consumption and saving, do affect the measure of output, but this may not be a proper index of the resulting change in welfare.   Gains from price-level stability are not recorded; other defects of the output measure may be added.

A Simple Model of the Optimal Budget

Granted that a precise and comprehensive measure of net gain from budgetary activity cannot be obtained, it may be useful nevertheless to illustrate the idea of an optimal budget in a simplified setting. We shall

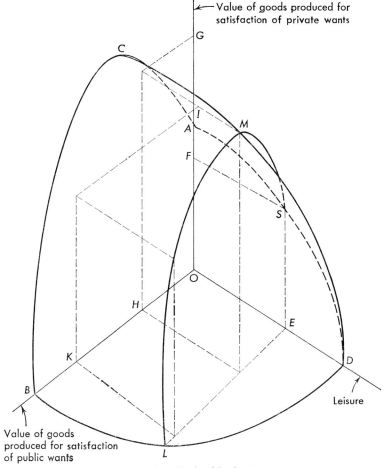

FIG. 3-1. Optimal budget.

assume for this purpose that a full-employment level of income and a given state of distribution prevail, and shall direct our attention to the function of the Allocation Branch.

In Figure 3-1 the value of goods produced for the satisfaction of private wants is measured along the vertical axis; the value of goods produced for the satisfaction of public wants, along the left axis; and leisure retained, on the right axis. The curve *BCA* in the left vertical plane shows the various possible combinations of goods that may be produced for the satisfaction of private and public wants, if leisure is at a minimum. Unlike the usual transformation curve, BCA is drawn so that an initial expansion of the Allocation Branch permits greater output for the satisfaction of private as well as public wants. After a certain point (indicated by C) is reached and the basic requirements of social organization are met, this relationship ceases, and further satisfaction of public wants is at the cost of private wants. The broken curve ASD in the right vertical plane measures available combinations between goods provided for the satisfaction of private wants and leisure, assuming the satisfaction of public wants to be zero. The curve BLD in the horizontal plane measures the corresponding relationship between the satisfaction of public wants and leisure, where the satisfaction of private wants equals zero. The surface $ACBLDSA$ describes possible combinations between the three components of welfare.

If leisure is held at OE, there is a choice between such combinations as OF of private wants and zero of public wants; OG of private wants and OH of public wants; or OI of private wants and OK of public wants. Of these possible combinations, it is evident that the second is preferable to the first because it involves more of both public- and private-want satisfaction. We may thus draw the ridge line CMD, which connects the high points of the curves BCA, LMS, and so forth, each corresponding to one particular level of leisure. The points on that part of the surface bordered by ACD are inferior and are disqualified from the optimal choice, which will be among points on the surface bordered by BDC.

In order to determine the best option, let us imagine a community preference surface involving the same axes but extending from above, down towards BDC. This preference surface in turn depends upon the way in which the cost of public services is distributed among individuals, and on what taxes are used. Given these two surfaces, the optimal choice is determined at that point on BDC where the community preference surface touches the transformation surface.

The problem is complicated further if the role of the Distribution Branch is allowed for. Measures to equalize income may expand or contract the transformation surface (so that more or less goods can be combined with a given amount of leisure), depending on whether the efficiency of the productive process is increased or reduced. Quite possibly, the surface will expand outward until some degree of equalization is reached, and contract as equalization is carried further. Finally, adjustments in distribution will change the preference surface. Thus, changes in the distributional adjustment lead to a new combination of goods and leisure as well as a new division of resources between the satisfaction of public and of private wants.

A concept of optimal budget may be developed along these lines that is more comprehensive and meaningful than the measure of budgetary effects on the level of net national product, as shown in Figure 3-1. Nevertheless, even a crude concept of optimal budget, relating budget policy to the size of the national product, is superior to the one-sided concept of taxable capacity, where no attention is paid whatsoever to the problem of lower limit and to the expenditure side of the budget.

PART TWO

The satisfaction of public wants

"*It would be strange if taxation by interest groups should not result in taxation according to interest.*" [KNUT WICKSELL, FINANZTHEORETISCHE UNTERSUCHUNGEN UND DAS STEUER-WESEN SCHWEDEN'S, JENA, GERMANY, 1896, P. 82]

CHAPTER 4

The benefit approach

We shall now examine more closely the way in which social wants are satisfied through the budget of the Allocation Branch, and how this relates to the adjustment in distribution prescribed by the Distribution Branch.

In tracing the development of thought on this matter, we find two distinct points of view. One may be referred to conveniently as the *benefit approach*. Its more modern formulation dates back to Adam Smith and leads up to the voluntary-exchange theory of Lindahl. The other may be referred to as the *ability-to-pay approach*. This also appears in Adam Smith and leads up to the later formulations of Pigou and Dalton. The benefit approach is considered in this chapter; the ability-to-pay approach will be discussed in the next.

A. BACKGROUND

Views on the principles of taxation may be found in the writings of innumerable authors—philosophers, economists, and political theorists—from the Middle Ages to date; and this for good reason: The duty to pay taxes, or the power to tax, is among the most tangible of all links between subject and sovereign, or citizen and society. The struggle to overcome arbitrariness in taxation was one of the early objectives of constitutional government; and the setting of tax maxims provided a means of defining the status of the individual in the social compact.

Two Major Approaches

We shall not attempt to review the endless succession of authors and pamphleteers who contributed to the theory of taxation.[1] Rather, we

[1] For a detailed yet cohesive and stimulating survey of this kind, see Edwin R.

shall trace the main divisions of thought under the two approaches, and how they came about. Not that taxation according to benefits received and taxation according to ability to pay have led to consistently different views on the proper scope of the public household or on the correct distribution of tax burdens; in either school, there were those who favored and those who opposed a wide range of public expenditures; and in either school, there were those who favored and those who opposed a progressive distribution of tax payments. The main distinction between the schools does not rest on these two points.

Rather, it rests on different views of the very nature of the public revenue-expenditure process. In the benefit approach, the relation of taxpayer and government is seen, as John Stuart Mill puts it, in quid pro quo terms.[1] Since the relation is one of exchange, the rules of the public household are taken to be more or less the same as those of the market. In the ability-to-pay approach, the proper contribution to public services is treated as an independent problem, quite separate from that of benefits received. Taxes are seen as compulsory payments, and the revenue-expenditure process is viewed as a planning problem not subject to solution by the automatic functioning of the market.

Both approaches have something to contribute and both have serious defects. The benefit approach, by its very nature, cannot solve the problem of the Distribution and the Stabilization Branches. However, in dealing with the Allocation Branch, this view has the great merit of tying the choice of public services to the preferences of the individual members of the community. As noted in Chapter 1, this is an essential requirement for a normative theory of budget determination in a democratic setting. Moreover, the benefit approach has the advantage of providing for a simultaneous determination of public services and tax shares, thus combining both sides of the budget process. This is an essential condition for any adequate theory of the public household. But here the usefulness of the traditional benefit approach ends.

If we look at the benefit principle as an equity rule, as the earlier

---

Seligman, *Progressive Taxation in Theory and Practice*, 2d ed., American Economic Association, Princeton University Press, Princeton, N.J., 1908, part II. Also see Gunnar Myrdal's brilliant discussion of fiscal theory in *The Political Element in the Development of Economic Theory*, trans. Paul Streeten, Routledge and Kegan Paul, Ltd., London, 1953, chap. 7. The first Swedish edition of this work appeared in 1930. Also see F. K. Mann, *Steuerpolitische Ideale, vergleichende Studie zur Geschichte der ökonomischen und politischen Ideen und ihres Wirkens in der öffentlichen Meinung 1600–1935*, Gustav Fischer Verlagsbuchhandlung, Jena, Germany, 1937.

[1] According to Seligman, *op. cit.*, p. 148ff., this expression was first used by Mill, although Mill is an outspoken opponent of the benefit view. See John Stuart Mill, *Principles of Political Economy*, ed. W. J. Ashley, Longmans, Green & Co., Ltd., London, 1921, p. 804.

writers did, there remains the vital question of just how benefits are to be determined. If we think of the benefit principle as implemented by a market mechanism, as the later writers did, we must make the unrealistic assumption that the exclusion principle and, hence, the principle of voluntary exchange are applicable to the satisfaction of public wants. Moreover, such a solution overlooks the difficulty of determining the optimal output in the case of social wants, even if true preferences are revealed.

The ability-to-pay approach has the merit of recognizing the compulsory nature of taxation and viewing the determination of the public household as a planning problem. In this setting, the problems of all three branches can be included. However, the ability-to-pay approach does not tell us just how the tax burden is to be distributed. Worse still, it disregards the expenditure side of the problem or, at best, provides us with the dictum that expenditures should be planned so as to maximize welfare. The ability-to-pay approach collapses completely if one accepts the hypothesis of the newer welfare economics, that interpersonal utility comparisons are inadmissible.

Some elements of both views will be drawn upon in our attempt to construct a more satisfactory approach. But first let us see in some detail what the two traditional views have to offer. We shall begin with the benefit approach.

General Setting

The benefit approach to taxation was accepted widely among the political theorists of the seventeenth century. Taxation as a price for services rendered seemed a natural complement to the contract theory of state. This view was held by German writers, including Grotius[1] and Pufendorf,[2] whose view of the contract was based on the moral precept of natural law; and it was accepted by writers such as Hobbes[3] and the physiocrats, who abandoned the concept of natural law and based the contract on observations of human behavior. The benefit view was also held by Locke,[4] who attempted to steer between the Aristotelian tradition of the social nature of man, as expressed in natural law, and the rising philosophy of extreme individualism, the war of man against man, as proclaimed by Hobbes. Subsequently, the benefit view was adopted by eighteenth-century writers such as Hume and Rousseau, who com-

---

[1] See Seligman, *op. cit.*, p. 160, note 4.

[2] *Ibid.*, note 5.

[3] *Ibid.*, p. 159, note 3.

[4] John Locke, "An Essay Concerning the True Original, Extent and End of Civil Government," reprinted in Ernest Baker (ed.), *The Social Contract*, Oxford University Press, London, 1946, book II, chap. 5, p. 120.

pleted the repudiation of natural law.[1]   But throughout, the notion of contract remained the basis of organized society, and protection appeared as a major, and at times the only, objective of the contract.   Taxes, accordingly, were considered a price to be paid for protection or for a membership fee in the association of organized society.

In the later part of the eighteenth century, when classical economics made its appearance, the protection principle of the contract theorists was replaced by the greatest-happiness principle of Bentham.   But the setting remained favorable to the benefit view, subscribed to by Bentham himself.[2]   Even though the foundation of natural law was discarded, the primacy of individual rights and the proposition of man's equality were retained.   These precepts, together with the rule that pleasure and pain must be judged by each for himself, again produced a view of society from which the benefit principle of taxation was but a logical extension. The registration and satisfaction of individual wants through the market were at the heart of Adam Smith's system of natural liberty; and the more the operations of government could be made a part of this system, the less objectional they were.

But to derive the benefit rule from the thinking of either Locke or Bentham, a further link in the argument was needed.   This was the assumption that there exists a given state of distribution that is to be accepted as the proper one.   Such an assumption is inherent not only in the protection theory of the contract but also in the utilitarian formula of maximizing happiness by noninterference.   Political theorists were not unaware of this, and dealt with the distribution problem at two levels.

First, there was the distribution of political power, the fundamental issue of how decisions are to be made under the social contract.   The basic hypothesis of man's equality before the law, which did *not* amount to saying that all people act and choose alike, led to a general acceptance of the rule that each man should be given one vote.   But this left the more difficult question of how decisions are to be made under the contract, a problem very much akin to certain issues raised by modern welfare economics.   Contract theorists of the seventeenth century, such as Grotius or Locke, drew a sharp distinction between the initial contract by which individuals combine to form a society, a contract that should be agreed upon voluntarily and unanimously, and subsequent actions of this society or its governing body, which may be based on majority decision.[3] Grotius, indeed, attempted to make the right of majorities a matter of

---

[1] Seligman, *op. cit.*, p. 184.

[2] *Ibid.*, p. 183.

[3] See J. W. Gough, *The Social Contract*, 2d ed., Clarendon Press, Oxford, 1957, for a compact discussion of the underlying political thought.

natural law, considering it unjust for the many to be detained by the few.[1] But his was not a convincing solution, and the rights of minorities remained a thorny problem in the contract discussion. This problem foreshadowed the recognition, arrived at only recently by economists, that conclusions of welfare economics, or any statements relating to the efficiency of society, must be preceded by a set of value judgments.

The second level at which political theorists treated the problem of proper distribution was property and income. This was dealt with most prominently by Locke, who argued that property is given in the natural state preceding the formulation of society.[2] The basic property of a man is his own person, and the fruits of his own labor. Since property is insecure in the state of nature, society must be formed to protect it. Indeed, this is the main function of the contract. In Locke we find not only the ethical foundation of a marginal-productivity theory of distribution but also a foundation for the differential treatment of so-called unearned or capital income, which came to play so prominent a part in the later treatment of taxable income.

Utilitarian writers from Bentham on have been less specific about what constitutes the proper state of distribution. Basically it must secure the greatest sum total of happiness; hence it depends on the comparison of the utility that various individuals derive from their incomes. On the whole, this points to an equalitarian solution and an ability-to-pay rather than a benefit view of taxation.

Most earlier writers who supported the benefit principle argued in terms of protection and concluded in favor of proportional taxation. Generally it was held that the need for protection should be measured in proportion to income or wealth or, in some cases, in proportion to expense. But not all shared this conclusion. Rousseau, for instance, maintained that the wealthy benefit more from protection. Sismondi argued that they must purchase the acquiescence of the poor; the need for protection increases more rapidly than income, and progressive taxation is called for. Others, including John Stuart Mill, interpreted the concept of protection more broadly and took the opposite view—that protection is needed more urgently by the poor. Indeed, Mill rejected the benefit view because it would lead to regressive taxation.

All these views may be held, and none can be proved correct.[3] While

---

[1] *Ibid.*, p. 81.

[2] *Ibid.*, p. 140.

[3] Writers who argued that the benefit theory leads to progression include Sir James Stuart and Bentham, who advocated a proportional rule of tax applicable over and above a minimum of subsistence, as well as Rousseau, Condorcet, and Sismondi, who advocated outright progression. As noted above, Mill interpreted the benefit rule

the equity view of the benefit rule was useful as an expression of political thought, it did not furnish an operational rule of tax policy. An attempt to interpret the benefit rule in an operational sense appeared only with the marginal-utility analysis of the 1880s.

The Classical Version

One hundred years prior to the appearance of *The Wealth of Nations*, Sir William Petty argued that "it is generally allowed by all that men should contribute to the public charge but according to the share and interest they have in the public peace; that is, according to their estates and riches."[1] Essentially the same principle, which includes both ability and benefit elements, reappears in Smith's first maxim of taxation.[2]

The subjects of every state ought to contribute toward the support of the government, as nearly as possible, in proportion to their respective abilities; that is, in proportion to the revenue which they respectively enjoy under the protection of the state. The expense of government to the individuals of a great nation is like the expense of management to the joint tenants of a great estate, who are all obliged to contribute in proportion to their respective interests in the estate. In the observation or neglect of this maxim consists what is called the equality of inequality of taxation.

In the first sentence of his maxim, Smith introduced ability as well as benefit considerations. This raises some doubt whether he should be placed in the benefit camp, but other passages in *The Wealth of Nations* clarify his position. Toward the end of Book V, there appears a clear-cut rule that the cost of public expenditures should be allocated, wherever possible, according to benefit; and that general contributions should be used only where expenditures cannot be allocated on a benefit basis.[3] At the same time, Smith's good judgment saved him from certain pitfalls common to many benefit theorists. He did not conclude that expenditures which must be financed from general revenue are, for this very reason, undesirable; nor did he confuse the benefit rule as a criterion of justice with the benefit rule as an operating guide to tax policy.

It is held frequently that Smith took a narrow-minded view of the expenditure functions of the state. The proposition is supported by

to require regression. The bulk of writers concluded in favor of proportional taxation, including the physiocrats Montesquieu, Adam Smith, McCulloch, Senior, and a host of Continental writers of the nineteenth century. (See Seligman, *op. cit.*, pp. 150ff.)

[1] Sir William Petty, "A Treatise of Taxes and Contributions," 1677, *The Economic Writings of Sir William Petty*, ed. C. H. Hall, Cambridge University Press, London, 1899, chap. 15, p. 91.

[2] Adam Smith, *The Wealth of Nations*, ed. E. Cannan, G. P. Putnam's Sons, New York, 1904, vol. II, p. 310.

[3] *Ibid.*, p. 300.

reference to a passage condemning taxes on capital because "they are all more or less unthrifty taxes that increase the revenue of the sovereign, which seldom maintains any but unproductive laborers; at the expense of the capital of the people, which maintains none but productive."[1]   Smith, however, has been misinterpreted.   The term *unproductive*, as he uses it, does not mean *useless* but merely *not for capital formation*.   There is ample evidence in Book V of *The Wealth of Nations* that public outlays can be highly useful, and indeed productive, in Smith's sense; in fact, they play an important and essential part in the system of natural liberty that orders economic affairs.   Following a lengthy discussion of expenditures for defense and justice, Smith shows how the sovereign must provide for "certain public works and certain public institutions, which it can never be for the interest of any individual, or small number of individuals, to erect and maintain; because the profit would never repay the expense to any individual or small number of individuals, though it may frequently do much more than repay it to a great society."[2]   Among these, there are public works such as canals and highways, and a case is made for public education.[3]

Furthermore, Smith was too realistic a thinker to overlook the difficulties of imputing to individuals the benefits that arise from general public services.   Everyone is benefited by such services and everyone should contribute to the cost of sustaining them.   But how is the individual benefit and cost contribution to be measured?   Since there is no practical way of doing this, a general rule of thumb is needed in place of individual imputation.   This rule, according to Adam Smith, is provided by taxing individuals "in proportion to their respective abilities; that is, the revenue which they respectively enjoy under the protection of the state."[4]   Smith thus shrewdly inserted an ability element into the weak link of the benefit rule.   Thereby, reliance on the protection theory of state was tempered.   The two approaches were joined in one, foreshadowing a similar solution in the modern version of the benefit doctrine.

While tax contributions should be in proportion to income, the income needed for the necessities of life ought to be exempted.   This should be so, not only as a matter of equity or, as Smith called it, "equality in taxation," but also as a matter of administrative expediency.   Since the income of the poor is needed to defray the basic cost of living, a tax on such income or on necessary commodities purchased with such income cannot be paid by the poor but must be passed on to others.[5]   It is only

[1] *Ibid.*, p. 347.
[2] *Ibid.*, p. 185.
[3] *Ibid.*, p. 270.
[4] *Ibid.*, p. 310.
[5] *Ibid.*, p. 355.

sensible, therefore, not to tax such income or such commodities in the first place.

Thus, the subsistence theory of wages led Smith to progressive taxation at the lower end of the income scale. At the same time, the exemption of a minimum standard also recommended itself on equity grounds, although here the argument shifted from a benefit to an ability-to-pay basis. Some such ability-to-pay element may be found among most of the writers who, while taking a benefit approach, favored some exemption at the lower end of the scale.

During the nineteenth century, the benefit approach came to be associated increasingly with a narrow insurance-premium interpretation of taxation, such as was held by McCulloch and Thiers.[1] Thereby the benefit theory tended to become an expression of bias against public expenditure. Since taxes are properly a premium for protection, so the argument ran, public services should be limited to those which serve protection. The constructive nucleus of the benefit principle, that the citizen must choose and pay for whatever public services he wishes to obtain, was lost in the narrow confines of an insurance theory of taxation. Ricardo, who considered taxation of sufficient importance to entitle his book *The Principles of Political Economy and Taxation*, evidently found public expenditures so wasteful that he did not feel it necessary to discuss them. He was satisfied to endorse "the golden maxim of M. Say, that the very best of all plans of finance is to spend little . . . ."[2]

No wonder, then, that by the end of the century it had become customary for many Continental writers of treatises in public finance, especially among French and German authors, to look at public finance as the science of taxation and to give scant attention to the expenditure side of the public-household problem.

B. RENAISSANCE OF THE BENEFIT APPROACH

This decay of the benefit discussion was halted only toward the end of the nineteenth century. Then another start was made. The proponents of the new theory assumed that efficient economic action must

[1] Seligman, *op. cit.*, p. 166.

[2] David Ricardo, *Principles of Political Economy*, E. P. Dutton & Co., Inc., New York, 1943, p. 159. Ricardo's quotation hardly does justice to Jean Baptiste Say. In *Treatise on Political Economy* (trans. C. R. Prinsep, Claxton, Philadelphia, 1869, chap. 6, p. 421, note), Say shows a less biased view than the above quotation suggests. In the following passage he explains why no comprehensive discussion of public expenditures is given: "A mere sketch is all that can be expected in a work like the present. A complete treatise on government would be equally appropriate with a survey of the arts, when it became incidentally necessary to touch upon the processes of manufacture. Yet, either would be a valuable addition to literary wealth."

conform to the rules of the market, and they were encouraged by the advance of subjective-value theory during the formative period of their doctrine. These later theorists proceeded to explain the revenue-expenditure process of government as a phenomenon of economic value and price, determined fundamentally by the same laws that govern market price in the private economy. Taxes were considered more or less voluntary payments rendered by the individual in exchange for services supplied by the government in accordance with personal evaluation of such services.

This renaissance of the benefit theory was closely related to the traditional doctrine, but with one important difference: Where the classical writers had postulated taxation according to benefit as a standard of justice, the new school interpreted the benefit rule as a condition of equilibrium. Taxation according to benefits received was to be formulated by determining tax shares according to subjective evaluation of public services. This was a fundamental change in approach. The construction of a normative model of public economy in terms of voluntary exchange established the first operational theory of the public household. While there was no quarreling with justice standards, this new model permitted objective appraisal.

Early Views

Early statements of the new approach included those of Pantaleoni, Mazzola, and de Viti de Marco in Italy, and of Sax in Austria.[1] Notwithstanding considerable differences in detail, the various authors joined in an effort to integrate the determination of taxes and expenditures with the allocation of resources in the market. Taxes came to be viewed as a price for public services, in line with taxpayer demand. Determination of the tax-price in accordance with benefits received came to be looked upon as a condition of efficient allocation; and beyond this, it was regarded as a condition of equilibrium brought about by either a political or a market process.

Perhaps the first statement of the new doctrine was advanced by

---

[1] M. Pantaleoni, "Contributo alla teoria del riparto delle spese pubbliche," first published in 1883 and reprinted in Pantaleoni's *Scritti varii di economia*, Milan, 1904, vol. II; U. Mazzola, *I dati scientici delle finanza publica*, Rome, 1880; A. de Viti de Marco, *Il carattere teorico dell'economia finanziaria*, Rome, 1888; Emil Sax, *Grundlegung der theoretischen Staatswissenschaft*, Vienna, 1887, and "Die Wertungstheorie der Steuer," *Zeitschrift für Volkswirtschaft und Sozialpolitik*, Neue Folge, vol. 4, 1924–1925.

For English translations from Pantaleoni, Mazzola, Sax, and other contributors to the early discussion, see R. A. Musgrave and Alan T. Peacock (eds.), *Classics in the Theory of Public Finance*, International Economic Association, Macmillan & Co., Ltd., London, 1958.

Pantaleoni. Pointing to the fact that public services involve the withdrawal of resources from private use, he argued that the tax and expenditure sides of the budget must be determined jointly. Unless this is done, there is no way of telling whether the benefits derived from public services are worth the losses that result as other wants become unsatisfied. The revenue-expenditure process, he insisted, must be made part of the Walrasian system. At the heart of this new approach was the recognition that the tax and expenditure sides of the budget must be determined in a simultaneous process and that the satisfaction of social wants must be traced to the preferences of the individual members of the group.

Mazzola, at the very outset, addressed himself to the nature of social wants. He attributed the specific problem in the satisfaction of social wants to the indivisibility of public services, which requires that the same amount must be consumed by all. Therefore, the pricing of public services must differ from the pricing of goods purchased privately in the market. If public services are sold at a single price, some consumers will find that this price exceeds the marginal utility derived from these services. If consumers are forced to contribute at this price, they will fail to maximize the satisfaction derived from their outlays. Yet, they cannot be excluded from the benefits rendered by such services. The difficulty is overcome if each consumer is called upon to pay a price equal to the marginal utility that he personally derives from the service.[1]

Like Pantaleoni, Mazzola did not expect this solution of the budget plan to come about as the automatic result of a voluntary market process. He noted that the actual budget plan must be determined by the agencies of government. However, he held that these agencies must act so as to satisfy the subjective preferences of the voters. Unless the agencies do this, the political equilibrium is disturbed and the government is overthrown. As the market equilibrates toward an efficient solution by the forces of competition, the budget process equilibrates toward an efficient solution by the forces of voter dissatisfaction.

Writing at about the same time, Sax distinguished between "personal collective wants," which can be met by voluntary payments of fees, and "collective wants proper," which cannot be satisfied in this fashion.[2] In dealing with the latter, relative tax shares are to be determined on the principle of equivalence, a mutual agreement among all taxpayers that

---

[1] Mazzola held that consumer surplus arises from single pricing in the market but is eliminated by multiple pricing in public services. This is incorrect. In order to avoid consumer surplus from the purchase of public services, the public price or tax must equal average rather than marginal utility.

[2] This summary follows the later version (1924) of Sax's doctrine. His original statement (1887) suffered from central emphasis on a distinction between public "services" and private "goods," which clouded the issue.

each is to contribute according to his value standards. This decision can be based on individual evaluation because each person can evaluate the marginal loss he suffers from the surrender of private income. For practical purposes, the principle of equivalence is said to be met by a proportional income tax.

The determination of the over-all level of taxation, according to Sax, cannot be based on individual preferences. Benefits from public services cannot be divided into individual benefit shares, and total benefits cannot be subjected to individual evaluation.[1] Determination of the over-all level of taxation, therefore, must be based on group decision and group preferences. The decision is in fact made by the governing elite, which is in a position to compare and rank individual needs. However, like Mazzola, Sax noted that the elite must adopt a program that will find more or less general acceptance lest the political equilibrium be disturbed and the governing group displaced.

Wicksell

Wicksell's main contribution to the debate is his emphasis on the political nature of the problem. He prefers the benefit to the ability-to-pay approach, not only because it is more suited to economic analysis, but because it is indicative of the spirit of modern democratic society. Since this society is based on the freedom of the individual, it would be unjust to force anyone to contribute to public services that he does not desire. Such a view is compatible with Mazzola's formal requirement that the individual should equate the marginal utility derived from his outlays on public and private services.

However, Wicksell holds that this requirement is useless.[2] The individual knows that his own contribution will be so small as to have no significant effect on the supply of public services. He will choose not to contribute. The individual consumer, therefore, cannot be expected to maximize satisfaction from public services. This is a task that must be undertaken through communication between the individual members of the group. Indeed, tax programs *are* determined by parliament, and "it would be strange if taxation by interest groups should not result in taxa-

---

[1] Sax appears to be confused in associating evaluation of *marginal* benefits with the determination of *individual* shares; and evaluation of *total* benefits with evaluation by the *group*. From his contention that evaluation by the group is needed, he concludes mistakenly that marginal evaluation alone will not do. Evidently, his exposition suffered from a block against the acceptance of marginal analysis, a phenomenon not infrequent in early responses to new doctrine.

[2] Knut Wicksell, *Finanztheoretische Untersuchungen und das Steuerwesen Schweden's*, Jena, Germany, 1896, p. 100. (English translation: Musgrave and Peacock, *op. cit.*)

tion according to interest."[1]   The problem, then, is how group decision can be arranged so as to secure maximum utility.

Since the will of the individual must be respected, Wicksell holds that the basic rule for budgetary decisions should be that of unanimity and voluntary action; but he then retreats from this stern position by calling for a rule of "approximate unanimity and approximately voluntary action."[2]   A set of majority rules are developed, designed to protect the minority.   These will be considered in more detail later on.[3]   Now we need only consider that Wicksell admits one important exception to his principle of approximate unanimity.   This principle, and indeed the entire concept of justice in taxation, requires that a just state of distribution should exist to begin with.   One cannot talk of a "just part in an unjust whole."[4]   Since redistributional adjustments may be impossible with even approximate unanimity, Wicksell admits that this principle may have to be suspended.   At the same time, he cautions lest distributional adjustments be abused.[5]   Nevertheless his distinction between (1) the problem of securing a just state of distribution and (2) of allocating the cost of public services in line with this distribution, is an important methodological step, and underlies much of the later discussion.

de Viti de Marco

Finally, mention may be made of de Viti de Marco's contribution.[6] The provision for general or tax-financed public services is considered an exchange relationship, where the citizen's duty to pay taxes is matched by the duty of the state to provide for general public services.   But, unlike the fee, the price-tax cannot be determined according to each person's actual consumption of public services.   Such services are not divisible into units of sales.   The individual consumption of such services, therefore, is an unknown quantity, and the problem consists of solving for this unknown.

The solution is based on two assumptions.   The first is that all members of the community are consumers of public services, though the esteem in which they hold these services—and, hence, their demand for them—differs.   The second assumption is that a person's income may be

[1] Wicksell, op. cit., p. 82.
[2] Wicksell, op. cit., p. 110.
[3] See text p. 127.
[4] Wicksell, op. cit., p. 143.
[5] Wicksell, op. cit., p. 144.
[6] See Antonio de Viti de Marco, Il carattere teorico dell'economia finanziaria, Rome, 1888, which is his first essay in this field; and the final statement in I primi principii dell'economia finanziaria, first Italian edition, 1932. (English translation: Edith Paolo Marget, First Principles of Public Finance, Harcourt, Brace and Company, Inc., 1936.)   See especially book II, chap. 2.

taken as an index of his demand for public services. Taxes may be looked upon as a subscription payment for the average consumption of public services over a period of time, analogous to a season ticket. Since almost all public services are instrumental in private production or necessary for private consumption, de Viti de Marco considers it permissible to assume that the consumption of general public services is proportionate to the income of each citizen. An element of arbitrariness remains, but it is said to be small, provided that taxpayers have the right to, and in fact do, approve tax legislation.

Even though de Viti de Marco assumes that each citizen uses public services in proportion to his income, he concludes that taxation should be progressive. This principle is referred to as the "economic" theory of progression, and is distinguished from the "political" principle of progression that follows if, for distributional reasons, a leveling of incomes is desired. The economic case for progression holds, says de Viti de Marco, because the tax dollar is worth less to the rich man than to the poor, the former's marginal income utility being lower. If charged the same price, the rich man would reap an "undeserved" surplus. Hence, the rule of single price cannot be applied in the market for public services, and a progressive rate of tax is required.

The determination of the expenditure plan, de Viti de Marco argues, must satisfy the voters. Unless they feel that their tax payments are put to good use, an economic and political reaction will set in to restore equilibrium. But even if a democratic process prevails, the minority will be compelled to consume public services in accordance with the supply decided upon by the majority. This involves a degree of partial unproductiveness not connected with the satisfaction of wants for price or fee payments.

C. THE VOLUNTARY-EXCHANGE APPROACH

If we disregard minor differences, confusions, and early errors in stating the doctrine, the preceding writers were in agreement on the essential point of their theory: The tax must be set as a price, designed to maximize the satisfaction that the consumer derives from his payments for public and private services. The equilibrating force by which this adjustment is secured is, in most cases, the political mechanism by which the agency of government is forced to represent the wishes of the voters.

We now turn to the final statement of the doctrine in the writings of Erik Lindahl.[1] Here we find not only a more precise formulation of the

[1] See Erik Lindahl, *Die Gerechtigkeit der Besteuerung*, Gleerupska, Lund, Sweden, 1919, which also contains a detailed survey of the literature, and "Einige strittige Fragen der Steuertheorie," in Hans Mayer (ed.), *Wirtschaftstheorie der Gegenwart*, Springer-

underlying principles of pricing but also a different and voluntary-exchange explanation of the equilibrating mechanism. As the final and most vigorous formulation of the doctrine, Lindahl's argument deserves more detailed consideration.

The Lindahl Solution

Following Wicksell's lead, Lindahl divides the requirement for justice in taxation into the "sociopolitical" problem of creating a just distribution of income (a problem corresponding to that of our Distribution Branch) and the "purely fiscal" problem of providing for the satisfaction of public wants while leaving the just state of distribution undisturbed (a problem corresponding to that of our Allocation Branch). Our present concern is primarily with the purely fiscal problem.[1]

Its solution in accordance with individual preferences, says Lindahl, involves three sets of decisions. We must determine (1) the total amount of public expenditures and taxes, (2) the allocation of total public expenditures among goods and services providing for the satisfaction of various social wants, and (3) the allocation of total taxes among various individuals. These decisions, which are all comprised in our Allocation Branch, are mutually interdependent and must be rendered jointly.

As a key to the solution, Lindahl points to an analogous pricing process in the market. This is the allocation of the total cost of two joint products, X and Y, to their respective supply prices. The allocation as shown by Marshall[2] is not made according to cost imputation but according to the demand for the two products. If A, the purchaser of X, is willing to contribute but a small portion of the total cost of producing both X and Y, then B, the purchaser of Y, will be called upon to contribute a correspondingly larger share.

According to Lindahl a similar situtation prevails with regard to goods

Verlag OHG, Vienna, 1928, vol. IV. (For an English translation of excerpts from these writings, see Musgrave and Peacock, *op. cit.*)

[1] The discussion of this section goes back to my first article, "The Voluntary Exchange Theory of Public Economy," *Quarterly Journal of Economics,* vol. 53, no. 2, pp. 213–237, February, 1938. However, the present discussion differs in one important respect. While I hold to my earlier critique of the *voluntary*-exchange assumption, I have reversed my original view (given on p. 233, note 9) that the theory of the public household need not concern itself with how social preference scales are determined. As I see it now, the theory of the revenue-expenditure process remains trivial unless these scales are determined. In determining them, and doing so on the basis of individual preferences, we are confronted by problems similar to those considered by Lindahl's formulation. The task, however, is to find a solution that does not involve the voluntary-payment assumption.

[2] Alfred Marshall, *Principles of Economics*, 8th ed., Macmillan & Co., Ltd., London, 1930, p. 791.

and services provided for the satisfaction of social wants. They will now be referred to as social goods.[1] To simplify matters, let us consider a community of two taxpayers, A and B, and one type of social goods only. Its supply furnishes benefits to both A and B, whose benefit shares may be considered joint products. Jointly A and B must contribute enough to cover the total cost of whatever volume of social goods is supplied; individually, each will have to pay less as the other contributes more. B's offer to contribute certain percentages of the total cost of various

DETERMINATION OF BUDGET LEVEL AND TAX SHARES

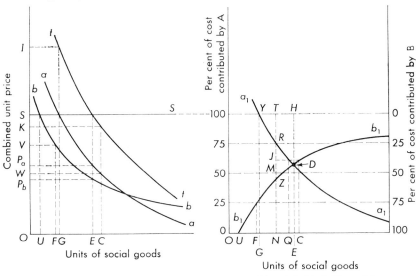

FIG. 4-1. Bowen model.   FIG. 4-2. Lindahl model.

amounts of social goods may be interpreted, from A's point of view, as a supply schedule of social goods; and A's offer may be interpreted similarly from the viewpoint of B.

The resulting price determination is shown in Figures 4-1 and 4-2. In Figure 4-1, the volume of social goods is measured on the horizontal axis. The combined unit price, including the contributions of both A and B, is measured on the vertical axis. Lines *aa* and *bb* show the demand schedules for social goods of taxpayers A and B respectively. Line *tt* shows the aggregate-demand schedule. Since both must consume the same amount of social goods, *tt* is obtained by vertical addition of the individual schedules and not by horizontal addition, as in the case of private wants, where various individuals may consume different amounts.

[1] Note that the term *social goods*, while used as a shortened form for *goods provided for the satisfaction of social wants*, is not used in the previously defined sense of public goods or goods produced by government. (See text p. 43.)

The aggregate-demand schedule tt thus shows the combined price per unit of social goods, offered for various amounts of jointly consumed public services.[1] SS is the supply schedule of social goods that we assume are produced under conditions of constant cost.[2]   The equilibrium output OE is determined where the tt and SS schedules intersect.   For this amount, the combined offers equal total cost.   Taxpayer A will pay unit price OP_a, while B will pay unit price OP_b.   For smaller amounts, the combined offer price exceeds unit cost.   At amount OG, for instance, the offer price exceeds unit cost by SI.   This, it is argued, leads to an increase in supply.   Not more than OE can be supplied, since for larger amounts the combined offer price falls short of unit cost.   At amount OC, for instance, the offer price falls short of unit cost by KS.   Supply will be reduced to OE where the cost is covered.   In this way, equilibrium output is said to be established at OE.

In Figure 4-2, the same argument is presented in Lindahl's terms.[3] On the horizontal axis, we measure the quantity of social goods as in Figure 4-1.   On the left vertical axis we measure the percentage of total cost contributed by A, and on the right vertical axis, we measure the percentage contributed by B.   The curve a_1a_1 is A's demand schedule transcribed from aa in Figure 4-1, price now being measured as a percentage of cost.   Taxpayer A is willing to pay 100 per cent for output OG, the amount at which his demand schedule in Figure 4-1 intersects the supply curve; he is willing to pay 50 per cent for OC, the output at which his offer price OW in Figure 4-1 equals one-half the unit cost OS, and so forth.   The curve b_1b_1 is a similar demand schedule for B, calculated from bb in Figure 4-1, use being made now of the inverted scale of percentage contributions on the right axis.   The schedule b_1b_1 may be viewed as B's demand schedule for social goods, or as a supply schedule of social goods to A.   Thus, B is willing to contribute 100 per cent of output OU, which amount is available free to A.   B is willing to contribute 75 per cent of OF, where OV in Figure 4-1 equals 75 per cent of OS in Figure 4-1.   This amount is available to A at 25 per cent of the cost, and so forth.

The equilibrium output remains at OE, where a_1a_1 and b_1b_1 intersect, and both shares add up to 100 per cent.   Here, A contributes ED, and B contributes DH per cent.   For any amount in excess of OE, the combined cost shares that A and B are willing to accept fall short of 100 per

---

[1] For this derivation of the demand schedule, see Lindahl, "Einige strittige Fragen der Steuertheorie," p. 294; and Howard R. Bowen, *Toward Social Economy*, Rinehart & Company, Inc., New York, 1948, p. 177.

[2] Both Figures 4-1 and 4-2 may be adapted to conditions of increasing cost without changing the principle of our argument.

[3] Figure 4-2 is an adaptation of a similar diagram used by Lindahl, *Die Gerechtigkeit der Besteuerung*, p. 89.   (English translation: Musgrave and Peacock, *op. cit.*)

cent. For output OC, for instance, the combined contribution falls short of the total by JM per cent. The amount OC cannot be supplied, and output must be reduced. For any supply below OE, both A and B are willing to offer better terms than the other demands. At ON, for instance, total offers exceed costs by RZ per cent. If A contributes fraction NR, supply ON will be available to B at TR, even though he would be willing to pay TZ if needed. If B contributes TZ, A will purchase this amount for NZ, even though he would be willing to contribute NR. If A contributes NJ and B contributes TJ, both pay less than they would be willing to contribute. From this Lindahl concludes that both parties will vote for larger amounts until OE is reached. Thus, the revenue-expenditure process for the satisfaction of social wants is determined by a competitive process similar to that which applies in the private market.

We may now drop the simplifying assumptions of a single type of social goods and two taxpayers only. As a variety of social goods becomes available, the goods will be valued differently by various taxpayers. Specific bids must be made for each social good. Recontracting must be permitted, since a taxpayer's bids for social good X will depend upon the price at which he may obtain social good Y. This complicates matters, but essentially the same problem arises in the satisfaction of private wants. Nor is the basic argument changed if a larger number of taxpayers is allowed for. Only the mechanical difficulty of determining expenditures and tax shares is increased. Each taxpayer must register his demand for each service. The government must solve for the equilibrium output for each social good and bill each citizen in accordance with his offer prices for these equilibrium outputs. This may be likened to a trial-and-error process of trading in the market, with continual recontracting until an equilibrium is reached. Actually, all this does not have to be done anew in each budget period. The process of choosing and providing for social goods is constant, and only marginal adjustments need be made from time to time.

Lindahl assumes that this entire process occurs against the background of a given proper state of distribution. His concern is with the problem of the Allocation Branch only. Given a proper distribution of income to begin with, Lindahl holds that the resulting equilibrium at OE is an optimum solution—one that complies with both the benefit and ability-to-pay principles. The benefit principle is met because each taxpayer equates his marginal rates of substitution between goods supplied for the satisfaction of social and of private wants with their respective price ratios.[1] On the basis of a given proper state of distribution, total utility

---

[1] Gunnar Myrdal, *The Political Element in the Development of Economic Theory*, trans. Paul Streeten, Routledge and Kegan Paul, Ltd., London, 1953, goes further and holds that the voluntary-payment solution equates the marginal benefits derived by

derived from public services is maximized thereby. If the general framework of this analysis is accepted, this conclusion follows.

The ability-to-pay principle is satisfied, according to Lindahl, because each taxpayer purchases social goods at a different price, reflecting his particular ability to pay. This seems to me a misleading interpretation. The factor of differential pricing cannot be looked upon as a distributional corrective, since the entire argument proceeds on the basis of a proper state of distribution. Rather, differential pricing is required to obtain optimal allocation in view of the effective demands that result from this distribution. The most that can be said is that this solution is compatible with the ability-to-pay principle, since the resulting set of prices is based upon the proper distribution. The crux of the ability-to-pay doctrine itself relates to the establishment of this distribution and not to the pricing of social goods.

Appraisal in Terms of Partial Equilibrium

We turn now to an appraisal of the voluntary-payment model. While this is an ingenious attempt to establish an economic theory of the public household, it hardly justifies the contention that the "basic outlines of the theory are by now fairly definitely established."[1] Indeed this conclusion is reminiscent of John Stuart Mill's dictum, voiced sixty years earlier, that "happily, there is nothing in the laws of value which remains for the present or any future writer to clear up; the theory of the subject is complete."[2] In 1928, as in 1848, a mere beginning had been made in formulating an adequate theory of the subject. And for that matter, little more can be claimed in 1958.

For the time being, let us accept the partial-equilibrium framework of the Lindahl model and assume that the demand for public services can

---

various individuals. Such a conclusion seems incorrect. All that can be said is that marginal benefits from outlays for the satisfaction of public and of private wants are equated for each individual. Unless marginal income utility is the same for all, different persons may be left with different marginal benefits from the purchase of social goods.

Myrdal holds further that an equality of *total* rather than *marginal* sacrifice is needed to make the voluntary-payment solution conform to the benefit principle. This seems inappropriate in the context where the proper state of distribution is given to begin with. The benefit principle merely requires that for each consumer the ratio of prices paid for public and for private goods must equal the ratio of marginal benefits derived from public and from private goods. There is no need for an interpersonal equality of either marginal or of total utilities from public services. Putting it differently, the proper distribution of income (and the resulting positions of real income) must be defined so as to allow for the resulting set of relative prices, including those of social goods.

[1] Lindahl, "Einige strittige Fragen der Steuertheorie," p. 284.

[2] John Stuart Mill, *Principles of Political Economy*, ed. W. J. Ashley, Longmans, Green & Co., Ltd., London, 1921, p. 436.

be determined independently of the demand for other goods.   The claim
for an optimal solution rests on the assumption that equilibrium will be
established at output OE in Figure 4-2, but it remains to be seen just how
this equilibrium is reached. Returning to the case of two taxpayers
only, we must have a solution analogous to the Cournot view of duopoly
pricing.   Each seller assumes his rival's price to remain constant and
increases his sales until a competitive supply is reached.[1]   The question
is whether a Cournot solution can be applied to the case of social wants.

We begin with a situation where output equals ON and assume that A
contributes NJ while B contributes TJ.   Following the Cournot case, we
suppose that A and B both disregard the effect of their votes upon the
other's cost share.   The position at J leaves both A and B with a price
below what they would be willing to pay.   Since A's share equals NJ, he
will vote to expand output to OQ.   Since B's share equals JT, he will
vote for OC.   Presently, B will find out that he cannot obtain OC at the
cost share TJ.   At output OC, A will contribute NM only, leaving MT
to B.   At this price, B will not agree to output OC.   Thus, B will vote
for a smaller supply, and the adjustment continues until output OQ is
reached and agreed upon by both A and B.   This is not Lindahl's optimal
output.   It is simply the most favorable position in view of the fact that
cost shares have been initially set at NJ/TJ.   The resulting output OQ is
arbitrary, since it depends entirely on the cost shares we assume to prevail at the outset.   Given the assumption that both disregard the effects
of their bidding on price, there is nothing in the mechanism of adjustment
that makes for a change in cost shares to ED/HD and a movement in
supply from OQ to OE.   The analogy to the Cournot solution does not
apply.

Moreover, it is hardly realistic to assume that each voter disregards
the effects of changes in quantity upon his price.   Once such effects are
allowed for, considerations of strategy enter.   The final solution becomes
the result of a bargaining process, and it need not be at OE.   Certain
points on or to the left of UDY will be preferred by *both* A and B to
certain others, and inferior solutions will be discarded.   Nevertheless,
there will remain a large number of points on or to the left of UDY,
movement between which involves a gain to either A or B and a loss to
the other.[2]   The solution will be at one of these points, but the specific
result will depend on the bargaining skills of the two voters.[3]

---

[1] See E. H. Chamberlin, *The Theory of Monopolistic Competition*, 5th ed., Harvard
University Press, Cambridge, Mass., 1948, pp. 34–46.

[2] Lindahl, *Die Gerechtigkeit der Besteuerung*, p. 89, holds that only the line UDY
constitutes the locus of possible equilibrium positions, but this need not be the case.
As long as total offers exceed cost, both may contribute less than their maximum offer.
Thus, the solution may be at J, where A contributes NJ and B contributes TJ per cent.

[3] Bargaining in this context cannot involve coalitions formed to obtain more favor-

Now, it might be suggested that these imperfections will vanish and output OE will be approached once larger numbers are introduced. Here the voluntary-payment model runs into a peculiar dilemma. In the private market, an increase in the number of sellers means that the demand schedule for the individual seller becomes increasingly elastic. Hence, he will be concerned less and less with the effect of his sales on price. The more efficient solution of pure competition is therefore approached as numbers increase. Such is not the case for social wants. Since all parties consume the same total of social goods, voter A cannot increase his purchases singlehandedly without calling others' attention to it. They will react by reducing their cost share and thus raise that of A. The introduction of large numbers, therefore, does not eliminate the strategy problem. Voter A may declare himself willing to pay x per cent of the cost of a given supply of social goods, if B is willing to pay y per cent. On this basis, an agreement might be reached to confront C, and so forth.

Finally, numbers may become so large that no practicable change in the contribution of any one individual can significantly affect the supply of social goods. Here our main objection comes to apply, and the entire assumption of voluntary contribution breaks down. Preferences will not be revealed, since the exclusion principle does not apply. Any one individual will find it profitable to understate his preference, knowing that this will have no significant effect on the total supply but result in a smaller assessment on himself.

The actual situation is not described quite accurately by either the large- or the small-number case. While the community comprises a large number of taxpayers or voters, they are represented by a small number of political parties. These parties constitute groups of people with more or less homogeneous preference patterns, who engage representatives to conduct their bargaining for them. If the representatives vote to reflect the preferences of the individual members of their party, the large-numbers case applies; preferences will not be revealed and voluntary bidding will not function. If we introduce independent judgment on the representatives' part, the case of small numbers applies; bargaining occurs and leads to an imperfect result.

Restatement in Terms of General Equilibrium

The preceding critique of the voluntary-payment model focused on the assumption that true preferences will be revealed. We now turn to a

___

able majority decision. It is ruled out because the present discussion is in a framework of voluntary agreement. Lindahl's interpretation of bargaining power as ability to *enforce* one's own preferences (see "Einige strittige Fragen der Steuertheorie," p. 295) seems to move outside his own framework.

second flaw, arising from the partial-equilibrium setting of the model, in which the satisfaction of social wants is considered independently of private wants. As pointed out by Samuelson, the problem must be restated in general-equilibrium terms.[1]

Optimal Solution with Known Preferences. In order to examine this aspect of the problem, let us assume that true preferences are revealed and known. How, then, can the government arrange for an optimal allocation of resources between private and social wants?

OPTIMAL ALLOCATION OF SOCIAL AND PRIVATE WANTS

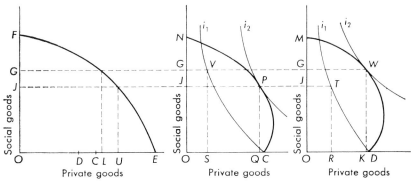

FIG. 4-3. Transformation sched- FIG. 4-4. Consumption   FIG. 4-5. Consumption
ule.   by A.   by B.

We begin with Figure 4-3, where the total output of social goods is measured on the vertical axis, and that of private goods, on the horizontal axis. The curve FE is a transformation schedule, showing what combinations of social and private goods may be produced. The combination to be chosen will depend upon the preferences of our two consumers, A and B, and upon the distribution of income between them. As before, we assume that the satisfaction of social wants is to be determined on the basis of a given proper distribution of income. In order to define this distribution, let us assume that only private goods are produced. We then specify that A's income in terms of private goods equals OC, and that B's income equals OD, where $OC + OD$ equals total output OE.[2] To simplify matters, we assume further that the distribution of factor income between A and B is similar for all compositions of output between

[1] Paul A. Samuelson, "The Pure Theory of Public Expenditures," *Review of Economics and Statistics*, vol. 36, no. 4, pp. 387–389, November, 1954, and "Diagrammatic Exposition of a Theory of Public Expenditures," *Review of Economics and Statistics*, vol. 32, pp. 350–356, November, 1955.

[2] Figures 4-3 to 4-6 are adapted from Samuelson's exposition, except for a difference in the treatment of income distribution. While we assume the state of distribution as given, Samuelson considers it as a part of the general problem of determining social wants. See text p. 84 for a further discussion of this point.

social and private goods; therefore their shares always equal OC/OE and OD/OE respectively.[1]

In planning for the satisfaction of social wants, it is assumed that the government proceeds on the premise of the "new" welfare economics, whereby arrangement X is to be preferred to arrangement Y, if a change from Y to X improves the position of either consumer without hurting the other. For consumer A, this means that no provision for social wants must be undertaken which would leave him in a worse position than he would be if he consumed OC of private goods.

Turning now to Figure 4-4, let us measure A's consumption of social goods on the vertical axis and his consumption of private goods on the horizontal axis. Now, let OC be A's income in terms of private goods and i_1C his indifference curve through C. No arrangement for the satisfaction of social wants can be made that places A on an indifference curve lower than i_1C, and he will be indifferent between various points thereon. At the same time, A's position on i_1C will not be of indifference to B. The latter's consumption of social and of private goods is defined by A's choice, and B will prefer certain locations of A to others.

B's consumption of social goods must be the same as A's; and B's consumption of private goods must equal the total supply of private goods (compatible with any given supply of social goods, as shown in Figure 4-3) minus A's consumption thereof. The curve DM in Figure 4-5 shows B's consumption of social and of private goods that results as A moves up along i_1C in Figure 4-4. If A is located at C in Figure 4-4, B is located at D in Figure 4-5. Neither receives social goods. The total output of private goods equals OE in Figure 4-3, of which A receives OC (Figure 4-4) and B receives OD (Figure 4-5), where $OE - OC = OD$. If A is located at V in Figure 4-4, B is located at W in Figure 4-5. Both receive OG of social goods. The total output of private goods equals OL in Figure 4-3, of which A receives an amount equal to OS (Figure 4-4), and B receives an amount equal to OK (Figure 4-5), where $OK = OL - OS$. Applying the same procedure to each level of social goods, we obtain the path DM in Figure 4-5.

Of all the combinations on this path, B prefers W, where DM is tangent to his indifference curve i_2. Here B retains OK of private goods and surrenders KD of potential private goods to obtain OG of social goods;

[1] This condition is met if A and B draw their respective incomes in equal proportions from various factors, in which case changes in relative factor earnings will not alter total income shares between A and B. If this assumption is dropped, we may still define the proper distribution of income with reference to a given product mix (e.g., a situation where only private goods are produced), and allow for changes in distribution as the product mix changes. In this case, the simple diagrammatical exposition breaks down, but the general nature of the argument does not change.

while A, located at V in Figure 4-4, retains OS in private goods and surrenders SC of potential private goods to obtain the same OG of social goods. The cost of social goods is divided between A and B in the ratio of KD in Figure 4-5 to SC in Figure 4-4, with A paying the larger share. On balance, A is as well off as in the absence of social goods since he has remained on i_1C, while B's position is improved since he has moved from i_1D to the higher indifference curve i_2W.

We now reverse the argument and obtain curve CN in Figure 4-4 as the path travelled by A, while B moves up along i_1D in Figure 4-5. Among all the points on CN, the point of tangency with an indifference curve or P will be best for A. Now A contributes QC of potential private goods to obtain OJ of social goods; and B, who is located at T in Figure 4-5, contributes RD of potential private goods to obtain the same OJ of social goods. B now contributes the larger share. His level of indifference is the same as it was in the absence of public goods, while A has moved to a higher indifference curve and his position is improved.

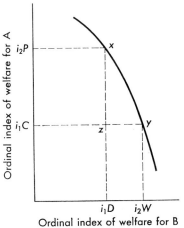

Fig. 4-6. Utility frontier with given income distribution.

We thus obtain the greatest gain that A can derive from the supply of social goods, provided that B's initial position is not harmed thereby; we also obtain the greatest gain that B can derive without harming A. Along the vertical axis of Figure 4-6, we measure an ordinal index of welfare for A, and along the horizontal axis, a similar index for B. If no public goods are produced, A is located at C in Figure 4-4, and his indifference level is given by i_1C; similarly, B is located at D in Figure 4-5, and his indifference level is given by i_1D. Both are at the lower limit of their respective welfare levels, as shown by point z in Figure 4-6. If the government decides to leave B's position unchanged, an arrangement for public services may be made that raises A to indifference level i_2P, indicated by x in Figure 4-6. This places A at P in Figure 4-4, and B at T in Figure 4-5. The supply of social goods equals OJ and that of private goods equals OU in Figure 4-3. If the government decides to leave A's position unchanged, an arrangement for public services can be made that raises B to indifference level i_2W. This arrangement, indicated by y in Figure 4-6, places B at W in Figure 4-5, and A at V in Figure 4-4. The output of social goods equals OG and that of private goods equals OL in Figure 4-3. The area zyx in Figure 4-6 shows the infinite number of possible solutions that leave A, B, or both better off than at z, where no public services are supplied. In choosing among them, the government will select a point on xy, since any point southwest thereof permits an improvement by moving towards the utility frontier.

This much can be concluded on the basis of the preceding assumptions: The choice among the infinite number of possible points on xy—all of which are optimal in the Pareto sense—cannot be decided on the basis of the simple condition that total welfare rises if the position of any person is improved without worsening that of another. As we move from y to x, A's position is improved and B's position is worsened. To choose among these solutions, a social-welfare function is required that permits us to evaluate the social gain or loss resulting when A's position is improved at the cost of B's, or vice versa. This need does not arise in the allocation of resources between various private wants where various individuals may consume different amounts of any one product. The simple welfare condition leads to a single solution and the optimal allocation of resources is determined uniquely on the basis of a given state of distribution.

The general-equilibrium view thus points to a second flaw in the voluntary-payment model. Even if all preferences are revealed, there is no single best solution analogous to the Pareto optimum in the satisfaction of purely private wants. Instead we are confronted with large number of solutions, all of which are optimal in the Pareto sense.

Separate Treatment of Income Distribution. The argument of the preceding section was based on the assumption that the proper distribution of disposable income is given to begin with. Thus, the discussion has been kept in line with the framework of our introductory chapter as well as with the Wicksell-Lindahl tradition.

We now find that the problem of distribution reenters the determination of social wants after all. The choice among the various points on the utility frontier affects the relative positions of A and B and involves distributional considerations. It may be asked, then, whether it remains meaningful to separate the determination of social wants by the Allocation Branch from the determination of the distribution of income available for private use by the Distribution Branch. In other words, can we determine the proper state of distribution independent of the effects on real incomes of the particular pattern by which social wants are satisfied? Following Samuelson's formulation, the entire state of distribution is determined along with the allocation of resources between social and private wants, thus combining the problem of the Allocation and the Distribution Branches into one.[1]

_____

[1] Returning to the diagrammatic exposition, Samuelson in "Diagrammatic Exposi-

This more general approach has its advantages, but I prefer to maintain the Wicksellian separation between the problems of the Allocation and the Distribution Branches. The kind of reasoning that deals with the efficient allocation of resources in terms of a given pattern of individual demand is not applicable to the problem of the Distribution Branch; the problem is ill-adapted to solution by the customary tools of economic analysis.[1] And the problem of the Allocation Branch, in so far as it deals with the choice among points on the utility frontier, similarly falls outside this line of reasoning; not, however, to the extent that we are unconcerned with reaching a solution that places the budget plan on the utility frontier.

Here we are on somewhat more familiar ground. In dealing with the preference system of the individual, we may readily conceive of preferences for the satisfaction of social wants as coordinate with preferences for the satisfaction of private wants. Were it not for the peculiar nature of social wants, which limits the revealing of consumer preferences, the individual's market basket could include goods to satisfy his social as well as his private wants. Thus the problem of determining the utility frontier involves some resemblance to that of determining allocation in the market. The problem is one of finding the political mechanism that will give us the same solution obtainable by the revealing of true preferences. No such as-if solution holds for the distribution problem.

The justification for retaining a separation between the two branches thus depends on how the problem of the Allocation Branch is viewed. The case for separation is weakened if the issue is considered primarily one of choosing among points on the utility frontier. The case is strengthened if emphasis is placed upon the task of reaching the frontier. While I am inclined to the latter view, Samuelson's argument shows that

---

tion of a Theory of Public Expenditures" determines the positions for B that result as A moves along A's entire set of indifference curves; and the positions for A as B moves along B's entire set of indifference curves. Samuelson thus obtains a curve similar to NC in Figure 4-4, showing A's positions for each of B's indifference curves, and vice versa for B. Plotting all these curves, he derives an envelope curve that is the utility frontier, containing one point on each of these curves. Each point on the utility frontier thus reflects a given combination of division of output between public and private goods, and of division of private goods (or of cost shares in public goods) between A and B. Samuelson's utility frontier includes two points on our utility frontier xy in Figure 4-6, corresponding to the two indifference curves that set the limits for our analysis.

[1] While Samuelson includes the general problem of income distribution in his analysis, note that the discussion centers around the feature of equal consumption. The diagrams in particular are directed toward the choice between social and private goods rather than toward the distribution of income available for private use.

the separation of the Allocation and Distribution Branches lacks the theoretical neatness it appeared to have in the earlier discussion. The political process, to put it differently, enters not only as a means to reveal preferences, but also to provide a different (nonmarket) rationale of decision making.

The Exclusion Principle Once More.   Restatement of the problem in general-equilibrium terms destroys the simple solution of the voluntary-payment model, even if we grant the assumption that preferences are revealed and known.   To this is added our earlier and perhaps more basic objection, which is directed against this very assumption.   Since the same amounts are consumed by all, the exclusion principle does not apply, and consumers will not reveal their preferences.[1]

In terms of the apparatus given in Figures 4-3 to 4-6, we cannot simply assume that the government has the information needed to derive the utility frontier.   This information must be provided for through either a market mechanism or a political process.   If we think in terms of the former, we encounter precisely the same difficulties noted in the preceding discussion of the Lindahl model.   There is no assurance that a solution on xy in Figure 4-6 will be reached.   What has been said about the case of small and large numbers again applies.   The final result depends upon the bargaining skill of the two parties.   The general-equilibrium view does not improve the workability of the voluntary-payment approach.

Alternatively, we may look at the problem as one of budget planning, based upon preferences revealed by a political process.   This is the more realistic view of the matter.   To obtain an efficient solution, the political mechanism and the inherent use of compulsion must be designed to induce people to reveal their true wants.   This we shall pursue further in Chapter 6.

D. THE SUBJECTIVE BASIS OF SOCIAL WANTS

Throughout this chapter we have argued that the satisfaction of social wants must be based on the preferences of individual consumers or voters. This, rather than the idea of voluntary exchange, is the essence of the benefit approach.   In concluding our discussion of this approach, let us note certain objections to the premise of individual evaluation.

One line of criticism is advanced by writers who feel that public wants differ basically from private wants and thus do not appear in the private preference schedules of individuals.   This view is taken by adherents of an organic theory of the state, who postulate the existence of group needs, or of needs that in some way or another are experienced by the "group

---

[1] Samuelson recognizes this second difficulty but does not deal with it at length in his discussion.   See "The Pure Theory of Public Expenditures," pp. 388 and 389.

as a whole."[1]   Since the group as such cannot speak, one wonders who is equipped to reveal group feelings.   Unless they are given by intuition or experienced by proxy by the leader, we are left with an authoritarian system of preference determination.   Whether such a system, or the organic view of society, is good or bad may be a matter of value judgment. All that need be said here is that the view is incompatible with a normative theory of public finances in a democratic setting.

More serious consideration should be given to critics who do not share the organic view yet want to reject a theory of the public household based upon individual preferences and anchored in the idea of consumer choice.   This is said to overlook the essentially political character of the budget process and the essentially social nature of its objectives.[2]   To point up the difference between the budget process and the satisfaction of private wants, Colm suggests (1) that the contribution-benefit relationship for any one individual depends upon the decisions of the responsible organs of government and not upon a market process, and (2) that there are political tasks in a democracy that are only indirectly related to such individual needs as are expressed in the market place.

On closer consideration, Colm's first point is readily reconciled with our approach.   We agree with Wicksell that budget determination is a political and not a market process.   This is the case because political action is needed to translate individual preferences for social wants into a specific budget program.   Since the responsible organs of government in a democratic society are the electorate and their representatives, budget determination by these responsible organs is determination through the democratic process.   This holds true even if allowance is made for the role of civil service and executive leadership.

Colm's second point introduces a difference in emphasis that may be more important.   He holds that the individual voter dealing with political issues has a frame of reference quite distinct from that which underlies his allocation of income as a consumer.   In the latter situation the voter acts as a private individual determined by self-interest and deals with his personal wants; in the former, he acts as a political being guided

[1] See, for instance, Albert Schäffle, *Das gesellschaftliches System der menschlichen Wirtschaft*, Tübingen, Germany, 1873, vol. I, p. 6.   Also see H. Ritschl, *Theorie der Staatswirtschaft und Besteuerung*, K. Schroeder, Bonn, Germany, 1925, chap. 1, and *Gemeinwirtschaft und kapitalistische Marktwirtschaft*, J. C. B. Mohr (Paul Siebeck), Tübingen, Germany, 1931, pp. 32–43.   For excerpts from Ritschl, see R. A. Musgrave and Alan T. Peacock (eds.), *Classics in the Theory of Public Finance*, International Economic Association, Macmillan & Co., Ltd., London, 1958.

[2] See text p. 11 and Gerhard Colm, *Essays in Public Finance and Fiscal Policy*, Oxford University Press, New York, 1955, pp. 32–33, and *Volkswirtschaftliche Theorie der Staatsausgaben: Ein Beitrag zur Finanztheorie*, J. C. B. Mohr (Paul Siebeck), Tübingen, Germany, 1927.

by his image of a good society. The two, Colm holds, are different things. Any theory of budget determination that is but an extension of the theory of consumer wants is said to overlook the essentially political nature of individual behavior in relation to the budget problem.[1]

In evaluating this critique, let us consider first those social wants that do not involve great issues of state but deal with individual needs quite akin to those satisfied through the market. Instances of this sort are provided by fire protection, street cleaning, and many of the services rendered by municipal government. Here Colm's fundamental objection does not apply. The problem is strictly that of dealing with wants that are consumed in equal amounts by the group in question. In principle, at least, the individual voter should be called upon to contribute according to the benefits he receives from the services rendered.

At the other end of the scale, we deal with social wants such as defense and education. Here the voter's attitudes and preferences may be conditioned by his image of the good society and by influences extending far beyond matters of his immediate environment. His choices may be determined by what he considers altruistic motivations rather than by the self-interest in the narrower sense that underlies typical consumer choices in the market.[2] All this is quite true, but it does not follow that the underlying preferences are any less subjective with social than with private wants. Various motivations overlap in both cases; and even where a difference in motivation exists, the hierarchy of total wants must still be measured against available income and scarce resources.

Finally, even if a separate determination of social wants were possible, it would still be necessary to derive the budget plan from individual preferences and to allocate the cost of the required services accordingly. The formal problem of decision making remains much the same, whether the underlying motivations are supposedly selfish or altruistic. Indeed, decisions on budgetary matters may be combined with others that relate to the content of public policy (foreign policy X versus foreign policy Y) and have no immediate opportunity cost in terms of private wants. The difference, perhaps, is one of semantics more than substance: By replacing the term *contribution in accordance with benefits received* with *contribution in accordance with evaluation of services rendered*, the policy criterion is made neutral with regard to motivation.

A further line of criticism directs itself at singling out the problem posed by goods consumed in equal amounts as the central issue in the

---

[1] This discussion of Colm's position draws upon personal discussion as well as his writings, but the responsibility for appropriate interpretation remains mine.

[2] See text p. 11 and G. Colm, "Comments on Samuelson's Theory of Public Finance," *Review of Economics and Statistics*, vol. 38, no. 4, p. 409, November, 1956.

theory of public wants.[1] It has been pointed out that a sizable part of budget activity does not deal with services consumed in equal amounts by all, but with services which are only partly of this sort. In considering this issue, it will be useful to classify wants as follows:

Degree to which consumer sovereignty applies	Degree of externality or per cent of benefit which is social		
	All	Part	None
Fully..................	1	2	3
Partially...............	4	5	6
Not at all..............	7	8	9

Case 1 is the 100 per cent social want, discussed previously, while case 3 is the 100 per cent private want. The objection is raised that, typically, both elements are present. The mixed situation of case 2 is illustrated by public education, which yields social as well as private benefits. We may grant that cases 1 and 3 describe polar situations, with reality falling somewhere between the two; but this does not invalidate the usefulness of our approach. The general reasoning underlying our theory of social wants may be applied also to case 2, thereby translating the argument from one of complete subsidy (full tax finance) to one of partial subsidy (partial tax finance).[2]

But though our approach covers situations 1 to 3, it does not cover the merit-want phenomenon which appears as we move below the first line. Here only two points may be raised in our defense. One is that the merit-want situation is not so frequent as is sometimes assumed; the case at closer inspection frequently proves to be one of social want.[3] The other is that a full theory of the public household requires multiple explanation. The allocation-branch problem posed by social (or mixed social-private) wants is more amenable to economic analysis than that posed by merit wants or that posed by the distribution-branch problem; and therefore it is proper for the economist to concentrate on this aspect.

[1] See Julius Margolis, "A Comment on the Pure Theory of Public Expenditures," *Review of Economics and Statistics*, vol. 32, no. 4, pp. 347–349, November, 1955.

[2] Suppose that a given public service satisfies both social and private wants. We obtain a total demand schedule for social wants by vertical addition of individual schedules for the social-want component, and a total schedule for private wants by horizontal addition of individual schedules for the private-want component. Assume further (though this is not essential) that the social and private product components are matched on a 1:1 basis. We then deduct the total demand schedule for the social component from the supply schedule. The intersection of the supply schedule thus adjusted with the total demand schedule for the private component shows the amount to be supplied (abscissa) and the part of the total unit cost to be paid for as price (ordinate). The vertical distance between the intersection and the unadjusted supply schedule shows the part of the unit cost to be provided for through the budget, i.e., by tax-financed subsidy. In the case of purely social wants (case 1 above), the subsidy is 100 per cent; while in the case of purely private wants (case 3), it is zero per cent.

[3] See p. 13.

CHAPTER 5

The ability-to-pay approach

Before turning to the political process of preference determination, let us trace the development of a second school of thought, referred to previously as the ability-to-pay approach. This approach denies the possibility of imputing benefit shares to individuals. Hence, a different principle must be substituted for the quid pro quo solution. The lines of development are less clear here because we deal with a heterogeneous group of writers who take quite different views of the ability principle. Three types of ability-to-pay approach may be distinguished and will be dealt with separately in this chapter.

A first view addresses itself to the distribution of tax payments only. The expenditure side of the budget is taken as given or determined according to principles which have nothing to do with tax shares. Tax shares are imposed by the state in an equitable or just fashion. The principles of taxation tell us how these requirements of equity are to be defined, and how they are to be translated into a specific schedule of tax rates.

A second view considers the distribution of the tax bill as a matter of welfare economics rather than justice but still omits the expenditure side of the picture. Taxes should be distributed so as to minimize the total sacrifice involved. This, in turn, is achieved by equating the marginal sacrifices of all taxpayers.

Though different in spirit, this welfare approach to tax distribution grew out of the equity view. The link was provided by an overlap of ideas in John Stuart Mill's formulation of the equity rule. Mill had argued that equity should be defined as the requirement that each taxpayer should suffer an equal sacrifice. To this he added that such a solution "is the mode by which least sacrifice is occasioned on the whole."[1]

[1] John Stuart Mill, *Principles of Political Economy*, ed. W. J. Ashley, Longmans Green & Co., Ltd., London, 1921, p. 804.

90

A few decades later, after marginal analysis had advanced further, it was shown that least aggregate sacrifice follows from equal treatment only if equality is defined as equal marginal sacrifice. This had hardly been Mill's understanding. Nevertheless, his argument was the first indication that the problem could be thought of in welfare rather than equity terms. The overlap between the equity and welfare view thus arose from the double role of equal marginal sacrifice as an equity rule and as a welfare condition; the relation between the two was strengthened further by the common bond of the "old" welfare economics; that is, the assumptions of similar, or at least comparable, utility schedules.

A third view, finally, retained the welfare approach to the determination of tax shares but extended the argument to the expenditure side of the budget. Thus the budget came to be seen as a more or less general plan to maximize welfare. This formulation, as advanced by Pigou and Dalton, closed the circle. Its problems, as we shall see, are not unlike those posed by the later versions of the benefit approach.

A. CONCEPTS OF ABILITY TO PAY

We shall begin with a brief review of how the idea of taxation according to ability to pay developed. Thereafter we shall examine various interpretations of the ability-to-pay concept.

General Setting

The requirement that the distribution of tax payments should be "just" is very old, as is the idea that just taxation is taxation according to faculty or ability to pay. The principle predates the benefit doctrine. The argument for progressive taxation, based on faculty, may be traced back to an essay by Guicciardini, published in the first half of the sixteenth century; a case for proportional taxation, based on faculty, was made towards the end of the same century by Bodin.[1] Since then, the principle has been restated and amended by numerous writers of widely differing philosophical backgrounds. We find in this group churchmen such as Bodin, humanists such as Rousseau, Utopians such as Sismondi, Manchester liberals such as Say or Mill, the *Katheder Sozialist* Adolph Wagner, and New Dealer Franklin Roosevelt. An evident lack of uniformity in social philosophy distinguishes this group from the writers of the benefit school, who commonly shared the foundation of natural law or social contract.

J. S. Mill, whose statement may be considered the classical version of

[1] See Edwin R. Seligman, *Progressive Taxation in Theory and Practice*, 2d ed., American Economic Association, Princeton University Press, Princeton, N.J., 1908, pp. 134ff., 228ff., and 239ff.

the ability doctrine, sharply rejected the benefit approach. Addressing himself to the then popular protection wing of the benefit school, he concluded that application of the benefit rule would lead to regressive taxation, as the poor are more in need of protection. This, he added, "would be the reverse of the true idea of justice." The protection theory of the state was unacceptable, he held, because the ends of government go much beyond those of protection. They include "things essentially indefinite, on which definite values cannot be set." Therefore, "government must be regarded so preeminently a concern of all that to determine who are most interested in it is of no common concern." A quite different principle of taxation is thus needed.

This new principle is furnished by the dictum that *all* should be treated equally under the law. "For what reason ought equality be the rule in matters of taxation? For the reason that it ought to be so in all affairs of government." And, so, the argument continues, "equality in taxation means equality of sacrifice."[1] Thus, the more or less objective concept of faculty, or ability to pay, as advanced by earlier writers was transformed into the strictly subjective concept of equal sacrifice. The just distribution of tax shares, according to Mill, prevails when all contribute to the common good so as to incur equal sacrifice.

Mill's emphasis on equal subjective sacrifice gave the ability-to-pay doctrine a distinctly individualistic flavor. In the interpretation of other authors, it involved a more collectivist view. The very proposition that public expenditures are for the "common good" and not subject to individual evaluation readily leads to some notion of a collective entity, as distinct from—and more than—the members of the group. The view that taxes must be imposed in accordance with some socially acceptable rules implies a planning view of the public household. The ability-to-pay idea, moreover, points beyond progressive taxation for the financing of public services towards the more general problem of income redistribution.

Considering these implications, it may seem surprising that the ability-to-pay approach should have been so popular among classical writers. For Adam Smith, the reason is simply that ability to pay was considered only as an adjunct to the more basic benefit rule. This cannot be said for later economists who, like J. S. Mill, rejected the benefit principle outright. To some extent, Mill's view can be explained by the influence of French reformers whose thoughts sprinkle his doctrine here and there. Also, emphasis upon equality of individual sacrifice might have overshadowed the collectivist implications of the ability-to-pay approach.[2]

---

[1] Mill, *op. cit.*, pp. 804ff.

[2] As suggested by Gunnar **Myrdal**, *The Political Element in the Development of Economic Theory*, trans. Paul **Streeten**, Routledge and Kegan Paul, Ltd., London, 1953, p. 165.

A more pertinent explanation of the popularity of the ability-to-pay approach among classical writers may lie on the expenditure side of the problem. Preference patterns under the benefit approach include public as well as private wants. Hence there can be no a priori judgment regarding the relative usefulness of the two. Benefit writers, such as Thiers, who wished to impose narrow limits on the public-expenditure function, had to defend their position by the argument, increasingly untenable, that protection was the only form of benefit that could be derived from the state.[1] We have seen how this position came to be replaced later on by a much broader and more constructive view of the benefit rule.

The ability-to-pay approach avoids the absurdity of the Thiers position as it bypasses the expenditure problem altogether. Thereby it permits *any* a priori judgment one wishes to make, including the Ricardian view that public expenditures are inherently wasteful, and the opposite view (held by German nineteenth century writers such as Dietzel[2]) that public expenditures are inherently highly productive.

Mill's treatment of public expenditures is a case in point. He considers at length the scope to which public expenditures should be extended. Entirely divorced from his discussion of taxation, the treatment is based on the precept, inherent in the system of natural liberty, that public expenditures should be at the narrowest compass possible. "Laissez-faire, in short, should be the general practice; every departure from it, unless required by some great good, is a certain evil."[3] While Mill mentions sufficient exceptions to the general rule to permit almost any type of public activity, the recurring theme is an a priori case for utmost restriction.[4] Indeed, the Manchester proposition that efficient economic activity must be in terms of free market transactions, and the recognition that taxes are compulsory and extraneous to such market forces, nicely combine to support the conclusion that public expenditures are inherently bad. Considering these implications, it is not so strange, after all, that

[1] See Seligman, *op. cit.*, p. 166.

[2] Carl Dietzel, *Das System der Staatsanleihen im Zusammenhang der Volkswirtschaft betrachtet*, Heidelberg, 1855.

Also see Walter Stettner, "Carl Dietzel, Public Expenditures and the Public Debt," in *Income, Employment and Public Policy: Essays in Honor of Alvin H. Hansen*, W. W. Norton & Company, Inc., New York, 1948, pp. 276–299.

[3] Mill, *op. cit.*, p. 950.

[4] Cases in which the good *may* outweigh the evil include (1) public education; (2) care of children and imbeciles; (3) protection of contracts in perpetuity; (4) supervision of joint stock companies, especially if in monopolistic positions; (5) public assistance; and (6) "important public services which are to be performed, while yet there is no individual especially interested in performing them, nor would any adequate remuneration naturally or spontaneously attend their performance." (*Ibid.*, p. 975.)

classical writers found the ability-to-pay approach acceptable, and in many cases preferable to, the benefit view.

In order to translate the equal-sacrifice principle into a specific pattern of tax distribution, a number of problems have to be faced. It must be decided by what objective index ability to pay can be measured; the term *equal*, in the equal-sacrifice principle, needs to be defined more precisely; and assumptions must be made regarding the slope of the income-utility curve so that individual sacrifice can be measured and any particular concept of equal sacrifice can be expressed in terms of a specific rate schedule. Let us consider these three points and then turn to reexamine the underlying hypothesis (which, for the time being, we will grant) that utility can be measured and that interpersonal utility comparisons can be made.

Index of Ability to Pay

In the later stages of the debate, it was taken for granted that the relative welfare position of individuals should be measured in terms of their income, and that sacrifice is a function of income surrendered. But the ability-to-pay doctrine in its earlier version was formulated in terms of faculty rather than income.

The term *faculty*, or *ability*, as used in the Elizabethan poor law, referred to property, and the same was the case in the early legislation of the American colonies.[1] With the progress of industrial society and the development of a pecuniary economy, there followed a successive shift in emphasis to income rather than property as an index of ability to pay. Adam Smith had already formulated his first maxim in terms of income only, and through the last century income came to be accepted more or less generally as the proper index of ability to pay. The personal income tax accordingly came to be considered the most equitable tax. Nevertheless, the problem still remains open to debate. It may be argued that income should be defined to include leisure, or that the index of ability to pay should be defined as consumption rather than income. Even if an accretion concept of income is accepted as the proper index of ability to pay, it is far from clear how accretion should be defined in concrete cases. Along with the growth of modern economic society and its increasing complexities, these difficulties have grown by leaps and bounds. The treatment of items such as retained earning of corporations, inventory profits, unrealized capital gains, or depreciation did not concern the classical writers, but today they are among the major issues of taxation.

These problems will be considered briefly in Chapter 8. Now we shall note only how the degree of arbitrariness involved in defining income

---

[1] See Edwin R. Seligman, *Essays in Taxation*, 9th ed., Columbia University Press, New York, 1921, chaps. 1 and 2.

permitted classical writers to compromise between the belief that more favorable treatment should be given to the poor and the fear that it might be dangerous to accept progression as a principle. Adam Smith admonished that wages and necessities which compose the real subsistence income should be exempted from taxation because taxes on the poor are bound to be shifted. Taxable income, therefore, should be defined as "clear" income, or as income above subsistence. This view came to be accepted widely among classical writers who favored progressive taxation implemented by exemptions at the lower end of the scale, while sticking to proportional taxation for the middle and upper income ranges.[1]

A further degree of progression was introduced through discrimination in favor of earned (wage) as against unearned (capital) income. Underlying this was the idea that sacrifice involves not only a loss of enjoyment from the use of income but also a pain of having suffered in vain the disutility of earning such income. Moreover, the basic philosophy of property, as developed by Locke, drew a distinction between property acquired by labor, to which man has a "natural" right, and other property, the rights to which are more questionable.[2] Pigou, among the more recent writers, specifically defined loss of satisfaction in net terms, thus allowing for changes in disutility of work that may result from a reduced work effort.[3] Indeed, the very development of the British income tax—the oldest of the personal income taxes—has been in terms of a family of taxes or schedules assessed upon various forms of income, rather than a single tax on all incomes.

Concepts of Equal Sacrifice

Let us assume, now, that the subjective sacrifice which each individual makes should be measured as a function of the income he surrenders in tax. The next step is to define what is meant by a state of "equal" sacrifice.

After considerable floundering in the earlier discussion, three distinct concepts of equal sacrifice were advanced by Cohen-Stuart and Edgeworth.[4] These included equal absolute, equal proportional, and equal

[1] Adam Smith, *The Wealth of Nations*, ed. E. Cannon, G. P. Putnam's Sons, New York, 1904, vol. II, p. 355; Seligman, *Progressive Taxation in Theory and Practice*, p. 151.

[2] John Locke, "An Essay Concerning the True Origin, Extent and End of Civil Government," reprinted in Ernest Baker (ed.), *The Social Contract*, Oxford University Press, London, 1946, book II, chap. 5.

[3] A. C. Pigou, *A Study in Public Finance*, 3d ed., Macmillan & Co., Ltd., London, 1951, p. 42, where net satisfaction is defined as satisfaction from income minus dissatisfaction of work.

[4] A. J. Cohen-Stuart, *Bijdrage tot de Theorie der progressieve Inkomstenbelasting*, Martinus Nijhoff, The Hague, Netherlands, 1889; and F. Y. Edgeworth, *Papers*

marginal (or least aggregate) sacrifice. To illustrate these concepts, we accept the necessary assumption that interpersonal utility comparisons are admissible. Without this assumption, the entire type of discussion now under consideration breaks down. Moreover, we begin with the convenient assumption of identical tastes, so that the same income-utility schedules (marginal and total) may be applied to all taxpayers.

On the horizontal axes of Figure 5-1 we measure income, where OZ and DC are the amounts required for subsistence. On the vertical axis from O up, we measure marginal utility, and from D up, we measure total utility of income, leaving the utility of subsistence income undefined. CE is the total, and CF is the marginal income-utility curve. Now, suppose that taxpayer A has income above subsistence equal to ZG, while taxpayer B has income equal to ZH. The total utility received by A equals IE, and his marginal utility equals GF. The total utility received by B equals JK, and his marginal utility equals HL.

An income tax yielding MG is introduced. Under equal absolute sacrifice, A will pay NG, and B will pay TH, where $NG + TH = MG$. The amounts NG and TH are obtained so as to equate the total loss of utility by A or EP with that by B or KQ. Under equal proportional sacrifice, A pays RG and B pays SH, where $RG + SH = MG$; the shares are arranged so that $EW/EI = KU/KJ$. Under equal marginal sacrifice, A pays VG, and B pays VH, where $VG + VH = MG$; the marginal sacrifice for both is equal to Vn. Aggregate sacrifice, or $EX + KY$, is at a minimum.

Stated mathematically the conditions are as follows:

Concept	Term (given as equal for all people, whatever their income)*
Equal marginal sacrifice	$\dfrac{dU(Y - T)}{d(Y - T)}$
Equal absolute sacrifice	$U(Y) - U(Y - T)$
Equal proportional sacrifice	$\dfrac{U(Y) - U(Y - T)}{U(Y)}$

* Y = income; T = amount of tax paid; $U(Y)$ = total utility obtained from income Y.

Thus, there are at least three possible concepts of equal sacrifice, and the question arises which should be used.

Adam Smith's dictum that the subjects "contribute in proportion to their respective abilities; that is, in proportion to the revenue which they

Relating to Political Economy, Macmillan & Co., Ltd., London, 1925, vol. II, pp. 100ff.

For excerpts from the writings of both authors, see R. A. Musgrave and A. T. Peacock (eds.), *Classics in the Theory of Public Finance*, International Economic Association, Macmillan & Co., Ltd., London, 1958.

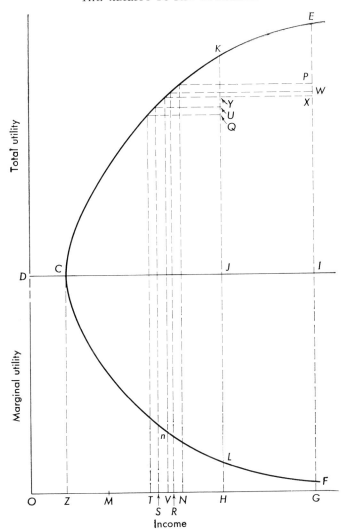

Fig. 5-1. Tax liabilities under various sacrifice formulas.

respectively enjoy . . . "[1] is not readily interpreted in this respect.
The expression "in proportion" might mean that all should contribute
in some proper relation to their income; or it could be interpreted strictly
to mean that all should surrender the same fraction of their income.
As we shall see presently, a proportionate structure will comply with
equal absolute sacrifice under certain conditions, and with *equal proportional* sacrifice under others. Moreover, there are passages in *The*

[1] Smith, *op. cit.*, p. 310.

Wealth of Nations that suggest a progressive rather than a proportional rate schedule. "

J. S. Mill, in advocating equal sacrifice, similarly failed to define the equality implied. While he was explicit in favoring a proportional rate of tax, it does not follow that he wished to define equality in terms of equal proportional sacrifice.[1] As shown below, conditions may be such that proportional taxation complies with the concept of equal absolute sacrifice.

Even after the three concepts of equal sacrifice were defined, there frequently remained some confusion between the initial problem of choosing between the various concepts of equal sacrifice and the subsequent problem of determining what rate schedule is required under the chosen concept.[2] More important, there remained a disagreement as to the merits of the various concepts even among those who recognized this distinction. Cohen-Stuart argued that there was a clear preference for equal proportional sacrifice because this would leave unchanged relative positions in terms of total utility.[3] Sidgwick[4] and Marshall[5] favored equal absolute sacrifice, while others such as Carver interpreted equality in terms of equal marginal sacrifice.[6] Edgeworth, and later Pigou, held that there was no logical or intuitive choice between the equity principles of equal absolute and equal proportional sacrifice. Arguing on welfare grounds, they considered equal marginal sacrifice the only proper rule, not as a matter of equity, but because it met the welfare objective of least aggregate sacrifice.[7]

B. TAX FORMULAS UNDER VARIOUS CONCEPTS OF EQUAL SACRIFICE

Whichever concept of equal sacrifice is chosen, the actual distribution of tax payments or rate structure required to implement it still depends

---

[1] Mill, *op. cit.*, p. 807, note 2. Also see Edgeworth, *op. cit.*, p. 236, who properly rejects Seligman's contention (*Progressive Taxation in Theory and Practice*, pp. 213 and 279) that Mill *must* have referred to proportional sacrifice.

[2] See, for instance, Seligman, *Progressive Taxation in Theory and Practice*, pp. 278ff.

[3] Cohen-Stuart, *op. cit.*, chap. 5. However, Edgeworth, *op. cit.*, p. 114, notes that the Manchester man might be satisfied with proportional sacrifice provided that the income-utility schedule is of the Bernoulli form, in which case progression will be moderate; but that he will hardly acquiesce therein if the income utility is more steeply inclined, thus requiring rapidly rising progression.

[4] Henry Sidgwick, *The Principles of Political Economy*, Macmillan & Co., Ltd., London, 1883, p. 562.

[5] Alfred Marshall, *Principles of Economics*, 8th ed., Macmillan & Co., Ltd., London, 1930, p. 135, note 1.

[6] T. N. Carver, "The Minimum Sacrifice Theory of Taxation," *Political Science Quarterly*, vol. 19, no. 1, pp. 66–79, March, 1904.

[7] Edgeworth, *op. cit.*, p. 117; and Pigou, *op. cit.*, p. 61.

on the income-utility curve that applies. This relationship differs for each of the three concepts.[1]

Formulas with Known and Identical Utility Schedules

For the time being, we shall retain the assumption that the same marginal- and total-utility schedule applies to all taxpayers, and that this schedule is known.

Consider first the case of equal marginal sacrifice. Provided that marginal income utility declines over the entire range when moving up the income scale, taxes must be allocated so as to level down income from the top until the necessary yield is obtained.[2] Returning to Figure 5-1, the entire tax will be paid by A as long as the yield is less than GH, which is the excess of A's income over B's. Successive yield increments will be divided equally between A and B, leaving them with equal incomes. Equal marginal sacrifice requires what might be called maximum progression, provided that the marginal income utility declines. If the marginal income-utility schedule is constant over the relevant range, any distribution of the tax bill will be equally good. If marginal income utility rises over the relevant range, yield requirements will be met by absorbing successive slices of income, moving from the bottom up.

Consider now the case of equal absolute sacrifice. If marginal income utility is constant over the relevant range, equal absolute sacrifice requires equal amounts of tax at different levels of income. This means a regressive rate schedule. Now suppose that the marginal income-utility schedule shifts and that marginal utility declines somewhat as income rises. The required tax on the larger income must be raised and that on the smaller income must be reduced. As a result, regression is lessened. This tendency continues as we assume the marginal income-utility schedule to become steeper. Eventually, regression disappears and a proportional rate of tax is required. This is the case where the slope of the income-utility schedule is such that marginal income utility declines at the same percentage rate at which income increases. This proposition was advanced over two hundred years ago by Daniel Bernoulli in his attempt to solve the so-called St. Petersburg problem on gains from

[1] For a general discussion, see E. D. Fagan, "Theories of Progressive Taxation," *Journal of Political Economy*, vol. 46, p. 457, August, 1948, later reprinted in R. A. Musgrave and Carl Shoup (eds.), American Economic Association, *Readings in the Economics of Taxation*, Richard D. Irwin, Inc., Homewood, Ill., 1958. Also, see the appraisal by Walter J. Blum and Harry Kalven, Jr., *The Uneasy Case for Progressive Taxation*, University of Chicago Press, Chicago, 1953.

[2] If the required yield falls short of the differential between the highest and the next highest income, the rule of equal marginal sacrifice is inapplicable. However, the least-sacrifice principle tells us that the tax be taken from the highest income. If the required yield exceeds this amount, the two principles give identical results.

gambling.[1] While this schedule has no particular justification in psychology, it is significant in the present connection because it defines the case where equal absolute sacrifice requires a proportional rate of tax. If the utility schedule becomes steeper, so that the percentage decline in the marginal utility of income is more rapid than the percentage increase in income, a progressive tax schedule applies. If marginal income utility falls off less sharply, regression is needed.[2]

The case of equal proportional sacrifice is more difficult. One is tempted to conclude that the rate structure must be progressive, provided that marginal income utility declines. If marginal income utility is constant, equal proportional sacrifice clearly calls for a proportional rate of tax. If the schedule now tips downward while tax payments remain unchanged, it would seem that the high-income taxpayer surrenders a lesser fraction of his total income utility than does the low-income taxpayer. Thus a progressive rate schedule appears to be called for. But

---

[1] Daniel Bernoulli, "Specimen theoriae novae de mendura sortis," *Commentarii academiae scientarum imperialis Petropolitanea*, Tomus V. Petrop, 1738, pp. 175–192. (German translation: A. Pringsheim, *Die Grundlage der modernen Wertlehre*, Duncker und Humblot, Leipzig, 1896, p. 46.)   The problem is: A coin is thrown by Peter until it shows heads.   If it shows heads the first time, Peter pays Paul 1 ducat.   If it shows heads only the second time, he pays 2 ducats; if it shows heads the third time, he pays 4 ducats, and so forth.   What is the expected value of this game for Paul?   The hypothesis of the Bernoulli-type income utility is introduced to show that the value is less than infinity.

[2] Following Paul A. Samuelson, *Foundations of Economic Analysis*, Harvard University Press, Cambridge, Mass., 1947, p. 227, the condition of equal absolute sacrifice requires that

$$u(y) - u(y - T) = \text{constant for all } y$$

where y is income, u is total utility, and T is the amount of tax paid.

Differentiating so as to determine the required change in T with respect to y, we have

$$\frac{dT}{dy} = \frac{u'(y - T) - u'(y)}{u'(y - T)} \tag{1}$$

where the term u' is a measure of the marginal utility of income.   This expression will be positive if marginal income utility is declining.   If we have a progressive tax rate, the elasticity of income after taxes, relative to income before taxes, must be less than 1. Thus

$$\frac{y}{y - T} \frac{d(y - T)}{dy} < 1 \tag{2}$$

But $d(y - T)/dy = 1 - dT/dy$, and by substituting for dT/dy from (1) we have

$$yu'(y) / (y - T)u'(y - T) < 1$$

The left-hand term of this expression is the elasticity of the marginal income-utility schedule.   Thus, progression will apply only if this elasticity is less than 1.   If it is equal to 1, as in the Bernoulli case, the left side of expression (2) as well must equal 1, and a proportional tax rate applies.

as Cohen-Stuart and Edgeworth have shown, such a conclusion is not valid. The mere condition of a declining marginal income-utility schedule does not always lead to progression.[1]

Equal proportional sacrifice requires a proportional rate of tax if the marginal utility decreases at the same percentage rate as the average utility; that is, a proportional rate of tax is required when for each point on the marginal-utility curve the product of abscissa and ordinate comprises the same portion of the total area between the ordinate, the axes, and the left portion of the curve. Cohen-Stuart shows that this condition for a proportional rate may be met by a variety of marginal income-utility schedules, including (1) a rising schedule represented by a straight line through the origin, (2) a horizontal schedule of constant income utility, and (3) a declining schedule of the usual type, convex to the origin and asymptotic to both axes but drawn so that the product of ordinate and abscissa for any level of income equals the same fraction of total utility derived from that income. Progression is required if marginal utility declines more rapidly than average utility; that is, if the utility curve descends more sharply than the line of proportion. Regression is required if marginal utility declines less rapidly than average utility; that is, if the utility curve descends less sharply than the line of proportion.

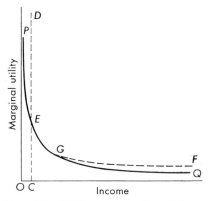

FIG. 5-2. Utility curves after Cohen-Stuart.

Let PQ be a line of proportion, so that a proportional rate of tax is required.[2] Suppose, now, that the ordinate is shifted to CD. The utility curve is then reflected by EQ, and progression will be called for,

[1] Cohen-Stuart, *op. cit.*, chap. 3. Also see Pigou, *op. cit.*, p. 86; Edgeworth, *op. cit.*, pp. 239ff.; and Seligman, *Progressive Taxation in Theory and Practice*, pp. 218–222. For excerpts from Cohen-Stuart and Edgeworth, see Musgrave and Peacock, *op. cit.*

[2] This curve is similar to curve PQ in Fig. 9 of Cohen-Stuart's discussion, *op. cit.* The equation for PQ is given by $U_{y_2} = (1/\sqrt{Y_2/Y_1})U_{y_1}$ where U_{y_1} and U_{y_2} are the marginal utilities of income for incomes Y_1 and Y_2. Edgeworth, *op. cit.*, p. 239, assumes the relationship $Z = H\sqrt{y/b}$, where Z is total utility, y is income, and H is a constant for incomes in amounts greater than b. Given such a utility function, equal proportional sacrifice requires proportional taxation, while equal absolute sacrifice requires regression. Given utility function $Z = He^w$, where $w = [(y - a)/b]^{\frac{1}{3}}$ for amounts of income greater than a and less than $a + 8b$, the rate structure must be regressive for both concepts. Both functions are subject to the condition that utility increases with income at a decreasing rate, i.e., that marginal income utility falls.

at least at the beginning of the scale. If the utility derived from a subsistence minimum, such as *OC*, is excluded, progression is needed even though a proportional rate may apply in the absence of such exclusion. The opposite case is shown by curve *PF*, where regression is required to the right of *G*. The special case of a marginal income-utility schedule that has unit elasticity throughout leads to a proportional rate schedule under equal proportional, as well as equal absolute, sacrifice. In this case the two formulas coincide.

Since intuition tells us little about the rate at which marginal income utility declines, we cannot presume that equal marginal sacrifice should require progression in the typical case.[1] Certainly, there is no reason to assume that it must always do so.

The Hypothesis of Declining Marginal Income Utility

The popular interpretation that the ability-to-pay doctrine requires progression is based on the assumption of declining marginal income utility. There is fairly general agreement among ability-to-pay writers that the marginal income-utility schedule declines when moving up from a very low to a medium income. There is less agreement for the higher income ranges. Mill, for instance, held that the sacrifice imposed by taxes which cut into subsistence outlays is "incommensurably" higher than that imposed by taxes which cut into superfluities. But once this range is passed, he considers the case for progression "too disputable altogether, and even if true at all, not true to a sufficient extent to be made the foundation of any rule of taxation."[2]

The hypothesis of declining marginal income utility differs from the principle of diminishing utility as applied to the consumption of any particular commodity.[3] It is reasonable to assume that successive units of commodity X become less useful relative to commodity Y, which is held constant; also, it is reasonable to assume that successive increments of X and Y should become less useful relative to leisure, holding leisure constant. Leisure, however, constitutes a third commodity and should be included in income. The proposition to demonstrate is that the marginal utility of income (defined to include all goods as well as leisure) declines with successive increments in income. This is a quite different matter. While the proposition seems sensible enough, there is no con-

---

[1] Such, at least, is the conclusion reached by Edgeworth and Cohen-Stuart. Seligman, *Progressive Taxation in Theory and Practice*, holds that the required rate schedule will be progressive, and Blum and Kalven, *op. cit.*, p. 43, refer to the case of other than progressive schedules as involving a somewhat "eccentric" marginal-utility schedule.

[2] Mill, *op. cit.*, pp. 806 and 807.

[3] See Pigou, *op. cit.*, p. 90.

clusive a priori reasoning that would establish it; nor has the matter been demonstrated successfully on an empirical basis.

The proposition of a declining marginal income utility has been criticized for a number of reasons. Rising needs develop with rising income, and a person's marginal income utility is said to shift upward as his income rises.[1] Let us grant this and suppose that the upward shift in the schedule will make marginal income utility constant in terms of the long-run schedule, though declining in terms of the short-run schedule. If reference is to the long-run schedule, the distribution of the tax bill becomes a matter of indifference under equal marginal sacrifice; it becomes regressive under equal absolute sacrifice, and proportional under equal proportional sacrifice. Throughout, reference to the long-run schedule renders the distribution of tax payments more favorable to large incomes.

This much is clear, but it is not evident just which schedule should be used. By the nature of the present assumptions where the same basic tastes apply to all, an upward shift in the schedule will be experienced by anyone whose income rises. If this is the case, reference to the long-run schedule leads to a perplexing situation. Suppose that A's taxes are reduced and B's taxes are increased. As a result, A's utility schedule moves up, and the shift in tax liabilities becomes justified. But the same may be accomplished by relieving B and raising A's tax. In the first case, A is given a tax credit for the satisfaction of his new wants, while B is penalized because A has developed new wants. This is done even though A's total utility is increased by the upward shift in the marginal utility schedule, and even though B would have been equally capable of developing new wants if the tax relief had been granted to him. Given a utility structure of this sort, we must either conclude that the sacrifice criteria are unworkable or proceed on the assumption of the short-run schedule.

A further complication results if the utilities derived by various income recipients are interdependent. In other words, satisfaction from income is partly a matter of keeping up with the Joneses. The bearing of this interdependence upon the appropriate rate schedule hinges on the weight of the Jones factor at various points in the income scale. Pigou makes much of this matter. He suggests that its importance as a determinant of satisfaction rises when moving up the scale. He then concludes that equal proportional sacrifice indicates continued progression at the upper end of the income scale, even though a Robinson Crusoe stranded on an isle of plenty might find that his marginal income utility is constant.[2]

[1] The factor of rising aspiration levels must not be confused with that of hidden costs to be incurred in securing a higher income. For purposes of this discussion, such costs are eliminated in defining net income.

[2] Pigou, op. cit., p. 91. A similar point was made much earlier by Sir William Petty,

While most people accept the hypothesis of declining marginal income utility, there is less agreement regarding the *rate* at which the marginal utility of income declines. The hypothesis of Daniel Bernoulli has been noted already. It is mathematically convenient and significant in this context, since it provides the dividing line between regression and progression under equal absolute sacrifice; but this is no reason why the hypothesis should be realistic. Others may do equally well. A view commonly found among ability-to-pay writers is that the actual marginal-utility schedule cuts across the Bernoulli curve from above. For equal absolute sacrifice, this means a declining degree of progression (referred to by earlier authors as *degressive progression*) changing eventually into regression, when moving up the income scale.[1] For equal proportional sacrifice, the degree of progression tends to decline and approach proportionality.

But these are assumptions only. Attempts to arrive at a statistical measure of income utility have been unsuccessful to date. Both Fisher and Frisch tried to derive utility schedules by comparing consumer budgets at different levels of income and by measuring utility with reference to changes in a standard budget pattern. This attempt serves to demonstrate the hypothesis of a common taste pattern, but it does not provide a cardinal measure of utility required for our purposes.[2] Other economists have tried to measure income utility in terms of effort;[3] more recently, experimental work has been done to measure utility in terms of reaction to risk.[4] These experiments involve the utility or disutility of risk taking as much as the utility or disutility of income. They are important in other connections; but they do not provide a primary

---

"A Treatise of Taxes and Contributions," 1677, *The Economic Writings of Sir William Petty*, ed. C. H. Hall, Cambridge University Press, London, 1899, chap. 15.

[1] For a definition of various measures of "degree" of progression, see R. A. Musgrave and Tun Thin, "Income Tax Progression, 1929–48," *Journal of Political Economy*, vol. 56, no. 6, pp. 498–514, December, 1948.

[2] Irving Fisher, "A Statistical Method for Measuring 'Marginal Utility' and Testing the Justice of a Progressive Income Tax," in Jacob H. Hollander, *Economic Essays, Contributed in Honor of John Bates Clark*, The Macmillan Company, New York, 1927; and Ragnar Frisch, *New Methods of Measuring Marginal Utility*, J. C. B. Mohr (Paul Siebeck), Tübingen, Germany, 1932.

[3] R. F. Harrod, "Progressive Taxation and Equal Sacrifice," *Economic Journal*, vol. 40, no. 160, pp. 704–707, December, 1930; and Lionel Robbins, "On the Elasticity of Demand for Income in Terms of Effort," *Economica*, vol. 10, no. 29, p. 123, June, 1930.

[4] See, among others, F. Mosteller and Philip Nogee, "An Experimental Measurement of Utility," *Journal of Political Economy*, vol. 59, no. 5, pp. 371–404, October, 1951, and literature given therein. Also, see the suggestions by J. von Neumann and O. Morgenstern, *Theory of Games and Economic Behavior*, Princeton University Press, Princeton, N.J., 1944, pp. 15–31.

measure of utility in the "absolute" sense in which this concept appears in connection with taxation according to ability to pay.

If the precise slope of the marginal income-utility schedule is not known over the *entire* scale, no specific schedule of tax rates can be derived from the equal–proportional-sacrifice principle; and unless the slope is known over the *relevant* range, no such schedule can be deduced from the equal–absolute-sacrifice principle. All that can be done is to apply one or the other principle *as if* some assumed form of the utility schedule were the correct one. The principle of equal marginal sacrifice requires less information than do equal absolute or proportional sacrifice. If the same utility schedule applies to all, the conclusion of maximum progression follows, once we assume that marginal income utility declines (regardless of rate) over the relevant range.

Reversing the line of reasoning, one can attempt to measure the schedule of income utility implicit in actual tax legislation on the assumption that this legislation is in accordance with one or the other equity concept.[1] This is of interest, but it does not reveal the true utility schedule unless we assume that the legislation was actually based on this schedule.

Formulas with Known but Different Utility Schedules

We now allow for the possibility that different people have different income-utility schedules, while retaining the assumption that income utilities are comparable and known. Since variations exist in all measurable physiological or psychological qualities of people, their ability to derive welfare from their income may be expected to differ as well. This circumstance does not invalidate the ability-to-pay approach, but it complicates matters.

If total-utility schedules are dissimilar, but marginal-utility schedules similar, over the relevant range, the previous conclusions still hold for the principles of equal marginal and equal absolute sacrifice, though not for equal proportional sacrifice. If both total and marginal schedules differ, strict adherence to any of the three definitions of equal sacrifice excludes application of the same tax schedule (expressing tax liability as a function of income) to all individuals. Rather, each individual must now be assessed according to his own utility schedule. While the slope of any one schedule may call for progression if applied to all individuals, some wealthy people whose utility curve lies at a low level will pay a lower rate of tax than some poor people whose schedule lies at a high

---

[1] See the paper by A. D. Preinreich, "Progressive Taxation and Sacrifice," *American Economic Review*, vol. 38, no. 1, pp. 103–117, March, 1948, for a measure of the schedules of income utility *implicit* in United States tax legislation, based on the assumption that this legislation has been predicated consistently on the principle of equal proportional sacrifice.

level. At the same time, the average rate of tax payable by people in various income brackets may still show a positive relation between income and tax assessment.

Formulas with Known but Unassigned Utility Schedules

A further situation is dealt with by A. P. Lerner who assumes that the marginal income-utility schedules for all individuals decline. He therefore allows for differences in the slopes and levels of the individual schedules. However, it is not known which schedule attaches to whom.

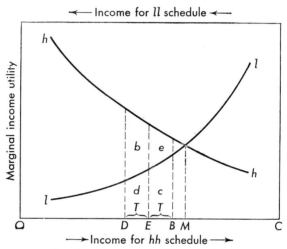

Fig. 5-3. Unassigned utility schedules.

Consider two individuals and two utility schedules. Both schedules are known to slope downward, and one is known to lie above the other. There is complete uncertainty as to who has the higher and who has the lower schedule. On this basis, Lerner concludes that any move toward a more equal distribution is likely to increase total welfare, while any move toward greater inequality is likely to reduce it.[1]

In Figure 5-3, let marginal income utility be measured on the vertical axis and income on the horizontal axis. There are two consumers, X and Y. One has a high marginal income-utility schedule *hh*, where income is measured from left to right, and one has a low marginal income-utility schedule *ll*, where income is measured from right to left. Schedule *hh* lies above *ll* for similar amounts of income.

Suppose that total income *OC* is divided equally, so that one has *OE*

[1] A. P. Lerner, *The Economics of Control*, The Macmillan Company, New York, 1944, p. 30. For expositional reasons this argument is included here, although it properly belongs to the welfare approach of section C further on.

and the other CE. If it were known that the hh schedule belongs to consumer X and the ll schedule to Y, total utility would be maximized by collecting a tax of EM from Y and paying it as a transfer to X. Since we do not know which schedule belongs to whom, it will be best to leave income divided equally. Any change from this position is likely to reduce total welfare. Suppose we reduce the income of X by an amount T and transfer this amount to Y. Two possibilities must be considered. If X is subject to the high-utility schedule hh, his income falls from OE to OD, and his loss of total utility equals areas $d + b$. A transfer of T is added to Y's income, which rises from CE to CD, and his gain in total utility equals area d. For both combined, there is a net loss of b. If X is subject to the low-utility schedule ll, his income declines from CE to CB and his welfare loss equals area c. At the same time, Y's income rises from OE to OB, and his welfare gain equals areas $c + e$. The net gain in aggregate welfare equals e. The possible net gain e is smaller than the possible net loss b. Since there is an equal chance for either result to occur, it is preferable to stay with the initial state of equal distribution. In the same way, it may be shown that adjustments from an unequal position to a position approaching equality are desirable because the probable gain is greater than the probable loss, the probability of either gain or loss being identical.

Putting the matter differently, let us suppose that all people are arranged into various groups, combining in each group all those with similar utility schedules.[1] Within *each* group, where the same utility schedule applies, welfare is maximized by an equal distribution. Now, let us assume that there exists a random relationship between the incomes received by various individuals and the level of their marginal income-utility curves. It then follows that the mean income will be the same for all groups of people with equal utility schedules. Hence, welfare is maximized by an equal distribution, which includes individuals in *all* groups.

If this argument is accepted, it follows that the concept of equal marginal sacrifice requires a tax formula of maximum progression, where the required yield is obtained by slicing off incomes above a certain amount. Similarly, we find that a differential system of tax rates tailored to individual utility schedules, in accordance with equal proportional or equal absolute sacrifice, leaves us with a positive relation between individual tax liabilities and incomes. If the set of individually tailored rates is to be replaced by a generally applicable schedule, such a schedule might be fitted to a mean of the individual marginal-utility schedules.

[1] See Milton Friedman, "Lerner on the Economics of Control," *Journal of Political Economy*, vol. 55, p. 409, October, 1947, reprinted in Milton Friedman, *Essays in Positive Economics*, University of Chicago Press, Chicago, 1953, pp. 301–322.

Putting it still differently, suppose that the marginal income-utility curves of all people are downward-sloping and different, and that there exists a random relationship between a person's ability to obtain income and the level of his utility schedule. The marginal income utility among all people with a given income will then form a more or less normal distribution.[1]   We may compute a mean value of marginal income utility for each level of income and thus obtain a marginal income-utility curve composed of these mean values. A schedule of tax rates fitted to this curve will be similar to one obtained by computing the tax liability for each individual on the basis of his particular utility schedule, and then computing a mean value of tax liabilities for any given level of income. Such a schedule of tax rates would be the best uniform schedule that could be devised.

This line of reasoning, though provocative, falls short of being convincing. Lerner's case for equal distribution rests on the uneasy assumption that there is an even probability that one or the other utility schedule attaches to X or Y; and that if it were known which schedule applied to which person, the conclusion would be different. The argument, not unlike the principle of insufficient reason, remains inconclusive. More or less the same holds for the construction of a mean-utility schedule. If the utility schedules of individuals (on which the mean schedule is based) were known, we would do better to disregard the mean schedule and to assign taxes in accordance with these individual schedules.

Doubtful Nature of Interpersonal Utility Comparisons

It is evident from all this that we lack the information needed to apply any one of the three equity concepts in an objective fashion. This holds in particular for the equal–absolute- and the equal–proportional-sacrifice rules, and the evidence on which application of the least–aggregate-sacrifice rule is based is dubious as well. Moreover, this entire discussion rests on the assumption that interpersonal utility comparisons can be made in a meaningful fashion. This assumption is basic to a subjective view of the ability-to-pay doctrine. Yet it is an assumption generally rejected by the "new" welfare economics. If such rejection is valid, the entire concept of equal sacrifice becomes so much nonsense and must be discarded—lock, stock, and barrel.

I hesitate to go this far. While we cannot assume that the utility schedules of individuals are known, the new welfare economics may have gone too far in its categorical rejection of interpersonal utility comparisons. Such comparisons are made continuously, and in this sense have operational meaning. Surely, there is such a thing as utility from

---

[1] For a similar construction, see Howard R. Bowen, *Toward Social Economy*, Rinehart & Company, Inc., New York, 1948, p. 181.

the receipt of income. Evidence on measurable characteristics of people—physical, mental or emotional—lends credence to the assumption that there is a fair degree of similarity among individuals living in a given society. If this is the case, it is not unreasonable to expect that a similar situation prevails with regard to satisfaction derived from income, or income utility. Since individual differences on measurable traits follow a more or less systematic pattern of distribution, it would not be surprising to find the same to hold with regard to satisfaction derived from income.

Nevertheless, this line of thought does not tell us how a workable measure of utility could be devised. Measurement must record a response to a given stimulus; the question is what experiment to conduct. If we measure income utility in terms of disutility of work or risk, we do not obtain the absolute measure of utility needed for this purpose. If we attempt to measure income utility directly by asking people what successive increments of income will increase their satisfaction by equal amounts, a host of difficulties arises in obtaining meaningful and comparable answers.

It remains to be seen whether a workable and reasonably meaningful measure of utility can be developed in time and whether thereby the subjective concept of ability to pay can be given an operational meaning. At this stage, we do not possess a universally accepted measure of utility by which to apply one or the other sacrifice formula.

This dearth of evidence on which to base the case for progression or regression must not be interpreted as evidence in favor of proportional taxation. If the one is questionable, so is the other. For purposes of policy formation in a democracy—or, for that matter, in a nondiscriminating dictatorship—the best solution may well be to follow Robbins' formula and to proceed as if individuals were alike.[1] Thereby, the concept of subjective utility is translated into one of social income utility. We may then postulate a marginal-utility schedule that seems proper as a matter of social policy and choose between the principles of equal sacrifice so as to derive a tax formula from this schedule. If we proceed along these lines, the principle of ability to pay ceases to be the subjective matter that J. S. Mill had thought it to be. It becomes a question of social value, and the problem is how the values can be determined. In a democracy they must be traced to the preferences of individuals, and a political mechanism must be designed by which this can be accomplished.

---

[1] See Lionel Robbins' nice statement in "Interpersonal Comparisons of Utility," *Economic Journal*, vol. 48, no. 4, pp. 635–641, December, 1938: "I do not believe and I have never believed that in fact men are necessarily equal or should always be judged as such. But I do believe that in most cases, political calculations which do not treat them as if they were equal are morally revolting."

The circle closes, and we are brought back to the problems of the preceding chapter.

C. BUDGET DETERMINATION AS A WELFARE PLAN

We now leave the approach to equal sacrifice in equity terms, and turn to those writers who wished to allocate taxes, or expenditures and taxes, so as to minimize aggregate sacrifice and maximize welfare. Thus, the emphasis is changed from equity to welfare.

Equal Marginal Sacrifice as the Ultimate Principle of Taxation

Edgeworth and later Pigou concluded that least aggregate sacrifice is the superior principle of tax distribution, not because it is equitable, but because it derives directly from the basic utilitarian principle of maximum happiness.

The political compact, according to Edgeworth, cannot be compared to a competitive bargain, since there is no rate of exchange at which marginal utilities can be equated.[1] Another modus operandi must be found. According to Edgeworth, this is given by the principle of maximum happiness. Self-interested parties, contracting in the absence of competition, must adopt that arrangement which conduces to the greatest sum of welfare to all, subject only to the condition that no one should lose by the contract. People will be willing to accept this arrangement because no party to the bargain can expect to obtain a share of total welfare which exceeds that provided by the maximum-welfare rule. Each party, therefore, realizes that maximizing aggregate utility will be to his own advantage. Supported by possible motives of good will to others, he will act accordingly. Presumably, a similar bargaining process might be applied to the determination of public services, but Edgeworth does not concern himself therewith.

It follows that taxation required to finance public services should be distributed in accordance with equal marginal or, which is the same, least aggregate sacrifice. The basic argument, however, applies over a wider range including the entire problem of the Distribution Branch. The principle making it desirable to finance the costs of the Allocation Branch so as to minimize welfare loss in private-want satisfaction also renders it desirable to arrange the residual-income distribution so as to maximize welfare in private-want satisfaction. Edgeworth accepts this broader implication of the welfare rule. Assuming a declining marginal income-

---

[1] F. Y. Edgeworth, *Papers Relating to Political Economy*, Macmillan & Co., Ltd., London, 1925, p. 102; and excerpts from Edgeworth in R. A. Musgrave and Alan T. Peacock, *Classics in the Theory of Public Finance*, International Economic Association, Macmillan & Co., Ltd., London, 1958.

utility schedule, he concludes that welfare is maximized by an equal distribution. Moreover, he proposes that the mechanism of bargaining, based on an equal distribution of votes, will in fact secure the equal distribution of income. This will come about because it is the only way out of what is otherwise a stalemate.

In other passages, Edgeworth takes a more realistic view and considers the least-sacrifice principle as a rule to be imposed by government rather than a state of affairs to come about as a compromise in the market place. Much is made of the point that implementation of the least-sacrifice principle will be more feasible than implementation of the equal–absolute- or equal–proportional-sacrifice rules. We need know only the fact that the common marginal-utility curve is downward-sloping and not the precise rate at which it declines.[1] This conclusion again falls or is qualified with the assumption of dissimilar utility schedules.

Pigou views least total sacrifice as a moral postulate rather than a working rule. It is said to follow from the principle that all government activity should be directed at the welfare of its citizens and that the welfare of all should be given equal weight. Hence, "the maximum aggregate welfare is everywhere accepted as the right goal of government." And "in the specific field of taxation, this general principle is identical with the principle of least sacrifice. Its validity appears to me given directly in intuition."[2] Introducing again the assumption of similar and declining marginal-utility schedules, Pigou says, " . . . it appears that a system of equal marginal sacrifice fully carried out would involve lopping off the tops of all incomes above the minimum income and leaving everybody, after taxation, with equal incomes."[3] Moreover, the principle of least aggregate sacrifice does not apply to distributional considerations only. It requires as well that taxes be such as to minimize excess burden.[4]

More generally, the effects of progressive taxation on output must be considered. Edgeworth as well as Pigou recognizes that extreme measures of equalization may have detrimental effects on total output and proposes that the rule of least total sacrifice be redefined to allow for such effects.[5]

The Social-welfare Principle of Taxation

We have noted that the ability-to-pay principle was advanced by a heterogeneous group of writers, including those with reformist and

---

[1] Edgeworth, *op. cit.*, pp. 234ff.

[2] A. C. Pigou, *A Study in Public Finance*, 3d ed., Macmillan & Co., Ltd., London, 1951, p. 43.

[3] *Ibid.*, p. 57.

[4] See text p. 149.

[5] Edgeworth, *op. cit.*, pp. 104–106; and Pigou, *op. cit.*, chaps. 4–6.

socialist leanings. To them the ability-to-pay principle seemed a promising base from which to advocate progressive taxation and to advance the general objective of income redistribution. This approach was taken by the more radical writers of the French Revolution as well as by early socialists such as Sismondi and Hall. In the 1880s, the role of distributional considerations was restated in more moderate terms by German reformers such as Adolph Wagner.

Wagner follows other equity theorists in considering the distribution of tax shares as independent of the expenditure side of the budget. Indeed, he argues rather pedantically that only the former problem is a matter of public finance, while the latter is one of general economics.[1] However, in his discussion of the tax problem, a sharp distinction is drawn between what he calls the "purely fiscal" and the "social-welfare" principle of taxation.[2] The purely fiscal principle is based on the assumption that the prevailing distribution of income is the proper one. The rule of taxation is equal treatment, or maintenance of the prevailing state of distribution. Thus proportional taxation is called for, according to Wagner. Accepting the proposition of a declining income-utility schedule, he maintains that this will result in a lesser proportional sacrifice for high- than for low-income taxpayers. He holds that this result is validated by the very assumption that the prevailing distribution of income is the proper one.[3]

The social-welfare principle (*das sozialpolitische Prinzip*, as Wagner called it) is based on the assumption that the state should correct the distribution of income as determined by market forces and by the institution of inheritance. Taxation according to ability to pay, in the context of the social-welfare principle, should result in equal sacrifice. While Wagner does not specify whether he refers to proportional or absolute sacrifice, he argues that progressive taxation is needed to obtain it.

Wagner's distinction between the purely fiscal and the social-welfare principle of taxation somewhat resembles that of Wicksell and Lindahl, and our distinction between taxation by the Allocation and the Distribution Branch. However, Wagner draws this distinction as a historical rather than analytical matter.[4] The tax problem is viewed as one.

[1] Adolph Wagner, *Finanzwissenschaft*, 3d ed., C. F. Winter, Leipzig, 1883, vol. I, p. 4. For a discussion of the proper scope of state activity, the reader is referred to Wagner's *Grundlegung der politischen Ökonomie*, 3d ed., C. F. Winter, Leipzig, 1892, part I, p. 892, where the problem is dealt with in rather sketchy historical terms. For translations from Wagner, see Musgrave and Peacock, *op. cit.*

[2] Wagner, *Finanzwissenschaft*, vol. II, pp. 372–455; and Musgrave and Peacock, *op. cit.*

[3] As we have seen, this is essentially a matter of how proper distribution is defined. See p. 78.

[4] Our distinction between the Allocation and Distribution Branches, while based on

Whether it is solved according to the fiscal or the social-welfare principle, or to what degree each enters, depends on the historical setting. The emphasis will vary according to time and place, but Wagner notes that the trend is towards the social-welfare view.

The Maximum-welfare Principle of Budget Determination

While the equity approach to taxation was limited to a just distribution of the given cost of public services, the welfare approach extended over a wider range, including the entire problem of income distribution. Yet both schools are equally narrow in that only the tax (and possibly transfer) aspects of the budget are considered. The determination of public services is left dangling in mid-air.

We now turn to a broader formulation that draws the determination of public services into the picture. This is but a logical extension of the welfare approach to taxation. Pursuing a line of reasoning advocated some fifty years earlier in Schäffle's principle of proportional satisfaction of public and of private wants,[1] Pigou and subsequently Dalton proposed two principles of budget policy. The first is that resources should be distributed among different public uses so as to equalize the marginal return of satisfaction for each type of outlay. The second is that public expenditures should be pushed to the point where the satisfaction obtained from the last dollar expended is equal to the satisfaction lost from the last dollar taken in taxes.[2] Thereby, the marginal satisfaction derived in the public and private sectors is equalized.

This approach is illustrated in Figure 5-4, where the size of the budget is measured horizontally, and marginal utility or disutility is measured vertically. Suppose that the marginal utility of successive dollars of public expenditures, allocated optimally between different public uses, is shown by line ee; and that the marginal disutility of taxes, imposed so as to cause least total sacrifice, is shown by tt. Since the marginal utility of both public and private outlays declines with successive increments, both schedules fall from the left to the right. The line nn is obtained by deducting tt from ee, and measures the net benefits derived from successive additions to the public budget. The optimum size of the budget is determined at OM, where marginal net benefits are zero.[3] In this way,

---

analytical considerations, does not exclude the historical factor. Indeed, fiscal history may be told in terms of varying emphasis on the different branches.

[1] Albert Schäffle, *Die Grundsätze der Steuerpolitik*, Tübingen, Germany, 1888, p. 17.

[2] Pigou, *op. cit.* p. 31. Also, cf. H. Dalton, *Principles of Public Finance*, 9th ed., Routledge and Kegan Paul, Ltd., London, 1936, chap. 2.

[3] The diagram of Fig. 5-4 will have come of age when this book appears. See my doctoral dissertation, "The Theory of Public Finance and the Concept of Burden of Taxation," Harvard University, Cambridge, Mass., 1938, p. 113.

the minimum-sacrifice approach to the allocation of taxes is matched by a maximum-benefit approach to the determination of public expenditures, and the two are combined in a general theory of budget planning.

This formulation can be accepted readily as a general statement of the planning problem for the Allocation Branch, that is, the problem of providing for the satisfaction of public wants. Transfers may be included in it, and the statement may be extended to include the problem of the

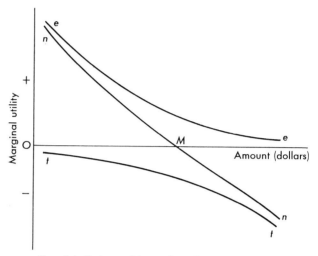

FIG. 5-4. Gains and losses from budget operation.

Distribution Branch. Since the social utility of public services is taken as given, taxation under the Allocation Branch may be combined with taxes and transfers of the Distribution Branch.[1] While the operation of the Stabilization Branch falls outside this framework, it provides us with a fair statement of the allocation and distribution problems. Since public expenditures are made an integral part of the solution, it is much superior to the equity view of taxation. At the same time, it is more general than the benefit approach, since it permits us to include the satisfaction of merit as well as social wants. Finally, the approach has the advantage of emphasizing the political or nonmarket nature of the problem.

However, the principle of budget determination in accordance with maximum welfare looks more helpful than it is. This becomes evident once we inquire just how the tt and ee schedules are determined. Pigou does not provide an answer. His *A Study in Public Finance*, brilliant though it is, contains only a brief chapter on the expenditure side of the budget. The treatment of divergencies between the private and social net product in *The Economics of Welfare* comes closer to the problem, but

[1] See p. 22.

it still leaves us short of the answer.[1]   A divergence occurs if costs, such as smoke nuisance, or benefits, such as increased real estate values due to local improvements, are not reflected in the calculations of the market; welfare may be increased by introducing an appropriate correction into the market mechanism.   Arguing on the basis of interpersonal utility comparisons and known preferences, Pigou finds no conceptual difficulty in determining the appropriate tax and bounty systems.   But this is too easy a solution.[2]

There remains the fundamental difficulty of determining the preferences on which the values of the ee and tt schedules are to be based, and the further problem of choosing between alternative solutions.   The mere principle of equal marginal benefit leaves us without a concrete standard by which the efficiency of various expenditure programs can be determined, just as the mere principle of least total sacrifice leaves us without an operational means of allocating tax shares.   In all, the "rules" of Figure 5-4 offer little more than a pious reminder that the budget should be planned efficiently.   If we are to determine the ee and tt functions, benefits from public services and losses from the withdrawal of resources in private use must be valued and related to each other. These valuations must be derived from individual preferences, or we must postulate a social-utility function that is imposed in an authoritarian fashion.   In the democratic model, the former approach must be taken, thus returning us to the problems posed at the close of the preceding chapter.

[1] A. C. Pigou, *op. cit.*, part I; and *The Economics of Welfare*, 4th ed., Macmillan & Co., Ltd., London, 1932, part II, chap. 9, pp. 172–203.   The argument in the latter is restated in part II, chap. 8, of *A Study in Public Finance*, but strangely enough Pigou fails to note that the case of social wants is the purest and most important instance of divergence.

[2] See p. 140.

CHAPTER 6

Budget determination through voting

The preceding sketches of the benefit and ability-to-pay theories leave us without a solution to our central problem. A technique must be found by which individuals are induced to reveal their preferences for social wants (even though the exclusion principle cannot be applied) and by which a choice can be made among all the solutions that are optimal in the Pareto sense. Without this, neither the benefit nor the ability-to-pay approach has much content. Moreover, a technique must be found to determine what merit wants are to be satisfied and what distributional adjustments are to be made. Since these problems cannot be solved by the mechanism of the market, we must turn to a process of political decision making. This may not be a problem in economics as it is usually conceived, but it is an inherent part of the theory of public economy.

A. NATURE OF THE PROBLEM

Determination of the budget plan through voting is a special application of the general problem of social choice—a problem that has received much attention in recent writings on welfare economics.[1] The discus-

---

[1] Among a large and rapidly growing literature on this subject, see Howard R. Bowen, *Toward Social Economy*, Rinehart & Company, Inc., New York, 1948; K. Arrow, *Social Choice and Individual Values*, John Wiley & Sons, Inc., New York, 1951, which contains extensive literature references; Duncan Black, "On the Rationale of Group Decision-making," *Journal of Political Economy*, vol. 56, no. 1, pp. 23–24, February, 1948, and "The Decision of a Committee Using a Special Majority," *Econometrica*, vol. 16, no. 3, pp. 245–261, July, 1948, and "Wicksell's Principle in the Distribution of Taxation," in J. K. Eastham (ed.), *Economic Essays in Commemoration of the Dundee School of Economics*, Culross & Sons, London, 1955; Clifford Hildreth, "Alternative Conditions of Social Ordering," *Econometrica*, vol. 21, no. 1, pp. 81–94,

sion, as formulated in the pioneering work of Arrow, has focused on the question of whether there exists in all cases a social ordering (that is, an order of social preferences expressed by the group) which meets certain fundamental requirements of collective rationality.   Our own focus is somewhat different.   We are concerned not only with finding a consistent solution on the basis of given data but with finding a technique by which individuals can be induced to reveal their true preferences on matters of budget policy.

Suppose again that the proper distribution of income has been established, so that we are concerned with the budget of the Allocation Branch only.   To begin with, we shall consider the satisfaction of social wants, leaving merit wants for later consideration.   We know that there exists a set of "true" demand schedules for the satisfaction of social wants, based upon the preference systems and incomes of the various individuals and unaffected by considerations of strategy.   The individual demand schedules dealt with in our discussion of the voluntary-payment system do exist; the problem is one of inducing people to reveal them and to determine the budget plan on such a basis.   The means to accomplish this is the voting process, followed by enforcement of the chosen expenditure budget and tax formula.   Thus, the voting process is both the hero and the villain in the piece.   It is the hero because it offers us a means by which individuals can be forced to reveal their preferences; it is the villain because the resulting budget will not satisfy everyone, except in Wicksell's unusual case of unanimous consent.[1]   Since the same public services are available to all, and since all are subject to the same tax formula, contributions will not be allocated according to the true evaluation of each and every member of the group.   Yet the use of such a formula and the inherent compulsion are the only means by which voters can be induced to reveal their preferences.   The trick, then, is to find the type of voting process that gives us the best approximation to a result based on the true evaluations.

Before dealing with various types of ordering under various voting processes, let it be noted that the final choice among the types rests upon value judgments.   To begin with, there is the basic choice between an ordering of social preferences that is authoritarian, to meet the personal preferences of a ruler, benevolent or otherwise; and an ordering that is

January, 1953; James M. Buchanan, "The Pure Theory of Government Finance: A Suggested Approach," *Journal of Political Economy*, vol. 57, no. 6, pp. 496–505, December, 1949, and "Social Choice, Democracy and Free Markets," *Journal of Political Economy*, vol. 62, no. 2, pp. 114–123, April, 1954.   For a discussion of the broader framework, see also R. A. Dahl and C. E. Lindblom, *Politics, Economics and Welfare*, Harper & Brothers, New York, 1953.

[1] See pp. 72 and 127.

democratic, to reflect the preferences of the constituent members of the group. Given our particular value judgment, the normative theory of budget planning must be democratic.

This may be readily agreed upon, but it is not enough. The term *democratic* comprises a large family of constitutions, ranging all the way from Plato's rule of philosophers proposed in the *Republic*, to the "all men are created equal" assumption of Jeffersonian democracy and the concomitant principle that everyone should be given an equal voice. In order to define what is meant by ordering social preferences on a democratic basis, it is necessary to specify the distribution of votes and, beyond this, to determine the particular conditions that the ordering should meet.

The obvious answer to the problem of vote distribution—obvious, that is, as a matter of inbred value judgment rather than logic—is that votes should be distributed equally. The social ordering arrived at on this basis should be determinate and independent of such arbitrary matters as the sequence in which issues are voted upon. The solution should be such as to approximate one of the points on the utility frontier, as determined on the assumption that true preferences are known.[1] But beyond this, a choice must be made between the many solutions that meet this criterion.[2]

Arrow's particular set of conditions for social ordering are based on norms that are met where majority voting leads to an unambiguous result. This is an interesting case because majority voting is widely used; but it is only one possible case, without claim to general validity. A system of ordering proper for judging athletic contests, for instance, may be quite out of place for selecting social wants.[3] It remains to be seen whether the results obtained under a system of qualified majority, plurality, or point voting might not be superior. Some do better in reaching the utility frontiers than others. Beyond this, there remains the choice between points thereon, which, again, is a matter of value judgment. Moreover, different systems of voting allow for different types and degrees of voting strategy, and thus serve in different degrees to reveal true preferences. While strategy is disregarded for the time being, it is an important factor in the total picture, and will be introduced at the end.

---

[1] See p. 83.

[2] For emphasis upon the distinction between the *process* of decision making and the *rule* that states the proper social ordering, see Buchanan, "Social Choice, Democracy and Free Markets."

[3] Arrow, *op. cit.*, p. 27, where it seems to be implied that the same system should do for all purposes.

B. MAJORITY RULE

According to Arrow,[1] the minimum conditions necessary for collective rationality are:

1. Between three alternatives, the social-welfare function must give rise to a unique social ordering, no matter how individual members of the group choose to order the three alternatives.

2. The social ordering must correspond positively, or at least not negatively, to changes in the ordering of any one individual.

3. The elimination of any one alternative shall not affect the ranking of the other alternatives in the social-welfare function.

4. Voters can choose freely among all alternatives.

These conditions do not specify that the social-preference function must depend on everybody's ordering, so that this argument may be applied to the whole family of democratic constitutions. But given more than two people who "count," the last condition means that the ordering between any two alternatives in the social-preference function must correspond to their ordering by the majority of voters.

The General Case

In a situation where only two alternatives are to be decided upon, the natural method of choice is that of majority vote. This will always yield a solution or, at the worst, a draw. If there are more than two alternatives, votes must be taken between pairs of alternatives, with successive pairings of the winners, until a final "best" solution is found. Suppose, for example, that there are three voters, X, Y, and Z, and three choices, A, B, and C. Suppose that A is the conservative, B the moderate, and C the radical policy. Let X prefer A to B to C; let Y prefer B to C to A, and let Z prefer C to B to A. In such a case, alternative B wins a majority vote over both A and C. Whatever sequence the alternatives are paired in, B wins. The outcome is determinate.

As a second case, let Z be one of those fatal people who like extremes per se, thus preferring C to A to B. We now find that A has a majority over B, B over C, and C over A. This time, the winner in the elimination voting depends upon the particular sequence in which the alternatives are paired. The outcome is arbitrary. There is no ranking that meets Arrow's conditions, and the system of majority rule breaks down.

Thus Arrow presents his possibility—or, better, impossibility—theorem. If there are at least three choices that the members of society are free to order in any possible way, then there can be no social-welfare function that always meets both the doctrine of voter's sovereignty and

[1] Arrow, *op. cit.*, chap. 3.

what Arrow considers the minimum conditions of collective rationality. Granted that there may be situations where these conditions are not met, let us note when they *are* met—when possible choices can be represented by a one-dimensional variable (choices, for example, ranging from small to big, or conservative to radical) and when preference patterns for all voters are single-peaked. This means that there are no extremists per se.

PREFERENCE RULINGS

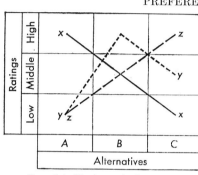 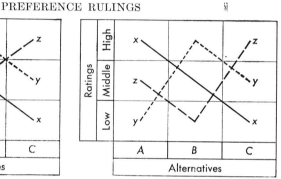

FIG. 6-1. Single-peaked system.   FIG. 6-2. Mixed single- and multiple-peaked system.

The majority to be obtained by successive pairings will then go to the median value, and results will be independent of the sequence of pairing.[1]

A situation involving three voters with single-peaked preferences is shown in Figure 6-1, where line xx indicates the ratings of voter X, yy indicates the ratings of voter Y, and zz indicates the ratings of voter Z. The ratings are those of our first case, and alternative B wins. A situation with a multiple-peaked preference pattern is shown in Figure 6-2. The ratings are those of our second case, and the result is arbitrary, depending on the sequence of voting.

Types of Budget Choice

Let us now consider whether preferences on budget policy tend to be single- or multiple-peaked. Much depends on the type of choice involved. On the expenditure side, we distinguish between choices regarding the level of expenditures and choices regarding the composition of expenditures. On the tax side, we distinguish between three types of tax.

The first type is a tax that imposes fixed shares at all levels of yield, so that the share in the tax bill assumed by various taxpayers is independent of the level of taxation. This is true in the case of a head tax and a

---

[1] We assume that there is an unequal number of voters. If there is an equal number, a draw will result. However, the draw will be between two alternatives that lie next to each other and at the middle of the scale. Thus, not much is lost if the choice between them is by lot.

proportional income tax. It is also true, though less obviously, in the case of a family of regressive or progressive income tax schedules constructed so that changes in yield are always accomplished by equal percentage changes in tax liability at various points in the income scale.[1]

Our second type of tax involves a rate formula of such a type that an increase in yield results in a continuous change in tax shares. In the case of a progressive income tax, this would be illustrated by an arrangement where a change in yield is accomplished by changing bracket rates by an equal number of percentage points. Thereby the distribution of shares is changed in favor of high incomes as yield rises.

The third type of tax is a variable-share tax of a self-reversing sort, where the pattern of change differs for various ranges of yield. Thus, as yield is increased, the change in rates may be such that the share paid by upper incomes rises for some range of increase in yield and then falls, or vice versa. The significance of these distinctions will become apparent presently.

Single-service Budget: Tax with Fixed Shares Given, Size of Budget to Be Determined

To begin with the simplest case, suppose that there is only one type of public service and that the budget is to be financed by a given type of fixed-share tax. If we assume that the total unit cost of public services is constant, this means that the unit cost of public services is constant (though not necessarily similar) for all voters. Each voter must decide how much public services he wishes to purchase at whatever constant unit price is assigned to him. Since there is only one type of public service, he may arrange his alternatives in one dimension, that is, from a small to a large budget. While there is no reason to expect that all or even a majority of voters will prefer precisely the same budget, there *is* reason to expect that the ordering of preferences will be single-peaked.

On the vertical axis of Figure 6-3, we measure goods to satisfy social wants, and on the horizontal axis, goods supplied to satisfy private wants. The picture applies to the individual voter. Since his unit cost of public services is constant, the price line AB is drawn as a straight line. Its slope will depend on the total unit cost of public services and on the particular tax formula that is used. The preferred size of the budget is

---

[1] In other words, the relationship between the various schedules is such that liability progression remains constant between any two points in the income scale. Liability progression between any two points Y_0 and Y_1 is defined as $\dfrac{T_1 - T_0}{T_0} \cdot \dfrac{Y_0}{Y_1 - Y_0}$ where T_0 and T_1 are the tax liabilities for income Y_0 and Y_1 respectively. See R. A. Musgrave and Tun Thin, "Income Tax Progression, 1929–48," *Journal of Political Economy*, vol. 56, no. 6, p. 504, December, 1948.

determined by the tangency between the price line and the indifference curve at *P*. Our voter chooses budget size *OC* and surrenders *DA* of private goods in tax. Any increase or decrease in the budget size will

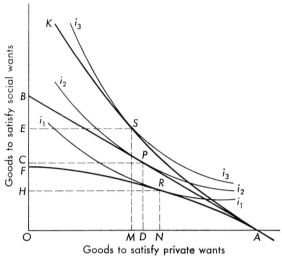

FIG. 6-3. Choice among budgets of various sizes.

successively worsen his position. His preferences are obviously single-peaked. The same holds for other voters, and majority rule gives a clear-cut solution.

Single-service Budget: Tax with Variable and Continuous Shares Given, Size of Budget to Be Determined

Let us now consider the same choice, but let the tax formula be of the flexible-share type. Suppose, for instance, that changes in yield are accomplished by equal point changes in all bracket rates. The share contributed by consumers with high incomes falls as the budget expands, while that contributed by consumers with low incomes rises, and the unit cost of public services changes accordingly. If the voter has an income above average, the price line now steepens as the budget increases, as is shown by *AK* in Figure 6-3. The new tangency point is at *S*, and his preferred budget size rises to *OE*. If the voter has an income below average, his price line flattens, as shown by *AF*. The new tangency is at *R*, and his preferred budget size falls to *OH*. Regardless of the voter's income, the principle of the matter is not changed. There will still be an optimal budget size and a single-peaked preference distribution.[1] Majority rule still gives a determinate solution.

[1] This will clearly be the case for the low-income voter whose price line is *AF*. The case of the high-income voter is somewhat troublesome, since, depending on the shape of the indifference pattern, there may be no tangency with *AK*.

Single-service Budget: Tax with Variable and Reversing Shares Given, Size of Budget to Be Determined

Let us suppose, now, that the variable-tax formula is not of the continuous but of the reversing type. The individual tax-payer may be confronted with a rising unit cost of public services for budget expansion up to some size, and a declining cost thereafter, or vice versa. In terms of Figure 6-3, the situation is one of a price line that wiggles, involving one or more turning points. In this case, there is no reason to expect that preferences will be single-peaked, and there may be a number of solutions that are equally good for any one voter. The results of majority rule become arbitrary.

Single-service Budget: Size and Tax with Fixed Shares to Be Determined

Let us now consider a situation where voters must determine the size of the budget as well as the type of tax. To begin with the simplest case, we shall stipulate that only fixed-share taxes are eligible. We assume that voters may choose between a small s, medium m, and big budget b. Also, they may choose between a head tax H (which is regressive), a proportional income tax P, and a progressive income tax formula R of the fixed-share type. Thus there are nine combinations to choose from. The choice is to be made by three voters: X, who has a low income; Y, whose income is just average; and Z, whose income is high.

TABLE 6-1. CHOICE OF BUDGET SIZE AND TYPE OF TAX

Budget size	Voter X Tax plan			Voter Y Tax plan			Voter Z Tax plan		
	H	P	R	H	P	R	H	P	R
s	5	8	9	4	2	6	4	3	1
m	2	6	7	8	7	9	7	6	2
b	1	3	4	3	1	5	9	8	5

In order to define the preference patterns of these voters, let us assume that they assign scores to each choice of tax type and budget size, in order of preference, with 9 the highest and 1 the lowest score. There are many possible patterns, but they must all meet certain conditions. A first condition is that for any one tax plan, preferences must be single-peaked. A second condition is that for any one budget size, voter X will prefer plan R to P to H, while voter Z will prefer H to P to R. Voter Y whose income is average, will be indifferent between M and P. His choice between either and R will depend upon the particular situation. We assume that he prefers R, but the principle of the matter is not changed if the positions of choice are reversed. A final condition is that for each voter the best solution under the best tax plan should provide for a larger budget than the best solution under the second-best tax plan; and that the second-best tax plan should provide for a larger budget than the best solution under the worst tax plan.[1] This will be the case because a better tax plan signifies a lower unit cost of public services.

The ratings shown in Table 6-1 meet these conditions. Beyond this, we picture X as a person who dislikes large budgets, Z as a person who likes large budgets, and Y as a person with more moderate tastes. We now have a set of majority votes, matching each of the nine possible pairs with all others. We find that not even one combination is eliminated in the first round.[2] While mR loses only against sP, sP in turn loses to sR, mH, mP, bH, bR. If we assume an arbitrary sequence of matches and proceed with a corresponding set of elimination votes, some result is arrived at, but it merely reflects this arbitrary sequence. Majority rule breaks down.

Inspection of Table 6-1 explains why this is the case. The nine vertical arrays are all single-peaked. The horizontal arrays are single-peaked for voters X and Z, but they are multiple-peaked for voter Y. Hence, the ambiguous result of the vote. Now, it would have been possible to construct a set of scores so that some one combination would win over all others, while complying with our conditions; but it is evident that this convenient outcome need not prevail. The finding will be the same for a choice that involves variable-share taxes, and difficulties will be compounded once variable and reversing-share taxes are introduced.

---

[1] In Table 6-1, where only three budget sizes are included, the requirement of *larger* is replaced by *equal or larger*.

[2] The voting matrix, with the winner in each case, is as follows:

	sH	sP	sR	mH	mP	mR	bP	bH	bR
sH		sH	sR	mH	mP	mR	sH	sH	bR
sP			sR	mH	mP	sP	sP	bH	bR
sR				mH	mP	mR	sR	sR	sR
mH					draw	mR	bP	mH	mH
mP						mR	mP	mP	mP
mR							mR	mR	mR
bP								draw	bR
bH									bR
bR									

Multiple-service Budget: Size and Fixed Tax Given, Composition to Be Determined

We shall now drop the assumption of a single-service budget and consider the choice between various types of public services. To simplify matters, we assume that the size of the budget is given and that it is to be financed by a given tax with fixed shares.

The choice between sizes of a single-service budget financed by a given fixed-share tax could be arranged in a single dimension. Barring the case of innate extremists, preferences were single-peaked, and a meaningful majority rule was possible. When it comes to the choice between types of services, there is no obvious sequence in which to arrange them. In some cases, it may be possible to array services in terms of benefit differentials by income size, or in others, in terms of benefit differentials by location. Some services may carry ideological implications and permit ranking from the political left to the right, and so forth. Where this is the case, preferences may be expected to be single-peaked. However, this is the exception rather than the rule. In most cases, no such simple arraying of choices is possible, and where it is, the underlying feature may be only a part of the total benefit picture to be considered. Thus, the sequences in which choices are lined up will be arbitrary, and individual rankings will be multiple-peaked. Majority decision leads to arbitrary results.

Evaluation

In evaluating these considerations, two points must be made. One is that the problem of arbitrariness is a matter of degree. The other is that even an unambiguous majority decision is not necessarily the best solution.

We have seen that preferences on budget policy may readily lead to arbitrary results under majority rule. This we found to be the case for the choice between various types of public expenditures and for variable tax plans of the reversing type. Matters are complicated further if choices on the tax side are combined with those on the expenditure side.

Yet observation of the political process, based on majority rule, suggests that the result is far from chaotic. Decision making by majority vote somehow leads to reasonably satisfactory results. While it is difficult in many cases to arrange matters of budget choice in a single dimension, the problem of choice is facilitated where a fair degree of similarity exists between the preference patterns of voters.[1] Studies of

---

[1] A similar assumption underlies Bowen's (*op. cit.*, p. 181) treatment of the single-service case with constant unit cost. Bowen postulates large numbers and a normal

family budgets show that budget patterns among people within a cohesive social group follow a fairly uniform pattern. Within certain limits, such similarity of tastes may be expected to hold as well for preferences with regard to public wants. In other cases, the choice of public services may be similar to the choice between red and blue hats rather than to the choice between hats and food; and here there is less reason to expect a uniformity of budget patterns.

Indeed, it may be well to reverse the line of reasoning. Democracy works well where considerable similarity in preference patterns exists, thus furnishing the necessary degree of cohesion; and where a sense of politics exists, thus making it possible to find combinations of issues (budgetary policy plus other aspects of public policy) on which agreement can be reached. As noted before, it is the function of the politician to be the catalyst in this process. Where there exists such social cohesion in preference patterns and political awareness, decisions reached by majority vote may still be arbitrary in a purist sense; but they will not be so highly arbitrary as to be intolerable. A reshuffling of votes and reconsideration of issues will continue until a more or less satisfactory solution is found. The task at any one time is not to determine the whole array of social wants but only to make marginal adjustments in the established budget pattern.

Let us now examine the sense in which majority rule gives an efficient solution in situations where the outcome is determinate and is independent of the order in which votes are taken. As far as the satisfaction of social wants is concerned, solution by majority vote is clearly not the perfect result. The decision by majority vote, though nonarbitrary as to sequence, remains inefficient in that the preferences of some voters are disregarded. Some may prefer the change in budget policy decided upon by majority vote to a situation where no change is made. Others may feel that they suffer a net loss. While some voting procedure and enforcement of the result is inevitable in order to induce people to reveal their preferences, the very process also leads to a result that is not a perfect reflection of the preferences of all concerned. The result of majority vote, even where nonarbitrary in Arrow's sense, need not place us on the utility frontier as defined above and it need not place us on the best point thereon.[1]

If majority rule does not provide a wholly efficient solution, it remains

---

distribution of prices offered by various voters for any given amount of public services. For any one amount, the modal-price offer obtains a plurality, and that amount is chosen at which the modal price equals cost. Given the assumption of a normal distribution, the mode and the median—and hence the results of the plurality and majority technique—coincide. (See p. 108.)

[1] See p. 83.

to be seen what sort of an approximation it provides. The result of majority voting is optimal in the sense that it is *the* solution agreed to by more people than any other. One way of interpreting this is to attach the same positive weight or utility to each person who agrees, and no negative weights or disutilities to persons who disagree. Or, the same result is obtained if the latter are assigned the same absolute weight, with a negative sign, as the former. On the basis of this calculus, the majority solution gives us a welfare maximum of greatest aggregate utility. An interpretation of this sort involves interpersonal utility comparison. Yet without some such rationalization, one is hard-pressed to explain why the right to vote should be uniform, or why the majority solution should be optimal. It appears that the premise of a social-welfare function, based on decision by majority vote, differs less from the assumptions of the old welfare economics than appears at first sight. In the latter case, it was argued that utilities *are* comparable and measurable. In the former, we proceed as if they were.[1]

In employing this kind of calculus, majority rule is similar to other voting procedures. However, the calculus of majority rule, which assigns to all winners the same weight of satisfaction and to all losers the same weight of dissatisfaction, is exceedingly crude compared to the calculus of other systems, where some attention is paid to the intensity of satisfaction or dissatisfaction of individual voters. Instead of considering the degree of arbitrariness of majority rule, we may consider the degree to which it gives rise to decisions that are tolerable in terms of a more refined procedure and type of ordering.

C. OTHER ORDERINGS

A particularly unhappy feature of simple majority rule is that no attention is paid to the views of the minority. We now turn to various systems that are more sensitive in this respect.

Wicksell's System of Qualified Majority

Wicksell is much concerned with the danger of abuse of minority rights, especially where the same group continues in power for a long time. We have noted before his initial suggestions that budget policies be made contingent on unanimous consent, and his subsequent but hesitating agreement to settle for a rule of "relative unanimity."[2]

---

[1] For a somewhat similar view, see Clifford Hildreth, "Alternative Conditions of Social Ordering," *Econometrica*, vol. 21, no. 1, p. 90, January, 1953.

[2] See text p. 72 and Knut Wicksell, *Finanztheoretische Untersuchungen und das Steuerwesen Schweden's*, Jena, Germany, 1896, pp. 116 and 122. English translation:

In developing his principle of relative unanimity, Wicksell suggests that proposals for increasing expenditures by various amounts should be combined with alternative proposals for new taxes to finance these expenditures. Each combination is to be matched with a policy of no change and a vote then taken. If some specified combination obtains the required majority, "perhaps of three-quarters, five-sixths, or even nine-tenths," it should be enacted.[1] If none does, the matter should be dropped for the time being.

The same procedure is to be used for adjusting the tax structure or for replacing one tax with another, but Wicksell proposes a different and rather complicated system for decisions to reduce expenditures.[2] The first step is to assign specific expenditure items to specific tax dollars. This may be done by simple majority. The second step is to decide by vote whether one or another of these tax-expenditure packages should be discontinued. The decision to discontinue may be reached with a minority of a "tenth, sixth or quarter" of the votes.[3] If others want to continue the expenditures in question, they must find a tax plan that makes these expenditures acceptable to the minority which voted to discard the old package.

These rules and the different levels of qualified majority needed for various purposes are designed to protect the interests of those who would otherwise be politically helpless.[4] To do this, Wicksell, the social nonconformist, notes that the initial problem may be one of protecting the interests of the lower against the upper classes; but he foresees the time when the dangers of abuse may turn in the other direction.

Wicksell's case for qualified majority has the advantage of protecting minorities and serving as a stabilizing factor. At the same time, it encourages a policy of inaction and interferes with the interests of the majority.

R. A. Musgrave and Alan T. Peacock (eds.), *Classics in the Theory of Public Finance*, International Economic Association, Macmillan & Co., Ltd., London, 1958.

Also see James M. Buchanan, "Social Choice, Democracy and Free Markets," *Journal of Political Economy*, vol. 62, no. 2, p. 118, April, 1954, who views the inconsistency of social choice as a safeguard for the minority; and the discussion of Wicksell's system by Duncan Black, "Wicksell's Principle in the Distribution of Taxation," in J. K. Eastham (ed.), *Economic Essays in Commemoration of the Dundee School of Economics*, Culross & Sons, London, 1955, p. 15.

[1] Wicksell, *op. cit.*, p. 117. Wicksell does not allow for the possibility that the results may be arbitrary, depending upon the sequence of voting. As in the case of simple majority, arbitrariness will tend to result unless preferences are single-peaked.

[2] *Ibid.*, p. 120.

[3] *Ibid.*

[4] *Ibid.*, p. 122.

Plurality Rule

A more subtle approach to the protection of minority views is provided by such systems as plurality and point voting. Under plurality rule each voter ranks the available policies, and the winning alternative is chosen on the basis of the total score, obtained by aggregating for each policy the rankings assigned by various voters. Returning to the illustration of Table 6-1, we find that combination mP wins with a total score of 20. Under the majority rule, mP lost to mR, which under plurality vote scores 18 only.

What is there to be said in favor of mP compared to mH and mR? For one thing, mP is the only possible solution under plurality rule, whereas mH and mR are arbitrary choices under the majority vote. By the very nature of the plurality rule, there must be either one winner or a draw between a number of winners, all of which have equal scores. Unless there is a random distribution of preferences, the combinations with equal scores will tend to include only a small part of possible alternatives; and though an arbitrary choice is made between them, the damage is likely to be less than it would be with an arbitrary majority vote.

Apart from this, we may explain the logic of plurality choice as follows: If we assume that each voter derives an equal dose of utility by moving up one notch anywhere in his rating, and that these doses of utility are equal among voters, the alternative with the largest total score leaves us with the largest aggregate utility. Based on this calculus, plurality rule gives the optimal solution. Such a rationale differs from that of the majority solution, which assigns an equal utility dose to each member of the majority. The question is which system better reflects the underlying pattern of individual preferences. Under plurality rule attention is paid to the minority, and the entire structure of preferences of various voters is allowed for. Neither of these considerations, however, enter with majority rule. The plurality rule, therefore, accounts more fully for individual preference patterns than does the majority rule.[1]

---

[1] This conclusion runs counter to Arrow's indictment of the plurality rule as inconsistent with collective rationality (*Social Choice and Individual Values*, John Wiley & Sons, Inc., New York, 1951). His charge is based on the claim that orderings under the plurality rule depend upon "irrelevant" alternatives.

To illustrate, let us consider the ratings of Table 6-2, where alternative A wins under either the majority or the plurality rule. Now, suppose that for some reason alternative B drops out of the running, e.g., a candidate dies or an issue is declared unconstitutional. Voters will reassign their scores as shown in Table 6-3. The majority decision still goes to A, but the plurality vote changes to C. This, Arrow says, is incompatible with collective rationality; the winning alternative should not change simply because an irrelevant (i.e., nonwinning) alternative has dropped out of the

Point Voting

While the plurality system is more responsive to the preferences of all voters than majority rule, it still fails to permit individual voters to express the intensity of their feelings. Ordering by rank is satisfactory in a situation where there is a continuous set of alternatives but quite unsatisfactory where alternatives are discontinuous, so that the difference in utility between any two consecutive items in the ranking varies greatly.

This rigidity may be overcome by point voting. Each voter is given a total number of points—say 100—and is permitted to allocate these points among the available alternatives. This leaves him with much greater flexibility than he has in plurality voting. Under the plurality system, the ratio of weights assigned to the best and the poorest alternatives will be as $n:1$, where n is the number of alternatives. With point voting, the ratio may be infinity, and the spacing between alternatives may be adjusted according to the pleasure of the voter. Thus, he may assign 100 to any one choice, and 0 to the rest if he so wishes. With given preferences, the alternative with the highest point score may not be that which wins under plurality rule.

A system of this sort, which permits the voter to express the intensity of his feelings, may again be rationalized in terms of an as-if rule in utility. The hypothesis now is that to each voter the utility values of various alternatives stand in the ratio of the points he assigns; and that

---

picture. The crux of the matter is whether we wish to consider a nonwinning alternative irrelevant. This may be an appropriate assumption for scoring athletic contests, but it does not belong here. To assert that any alternative that disappears is irrelevant merely stipulates that collective rationality must comply with majority rule. If the rationale underlying the plurality type of scoring is preferred, all alternatives, winning or not, are relevant. The result of majority rule may be said to contradict this type of collective rationality precisely because the outcome does not change, even though a previously available alternative drops out. As far as I can see, there is no inherent logical flaw in the plurality vote; nor does intuition reveal that the democratic process should be interpreted in terms of the majority rule.

| | TABLE 6-2 | | | | | TABLE 6-3 | | |
| Voter | Alternative | | | | | Alternative | | | |
	A	B	C	D	E	A	C	D	E
X	5	4	3	2	1	4	3	2	1
Y	5	4	3	2	1	4	3	2	1
Z	2	1	5	4	3	1	4	3	2
Total votes	12	9	11	8	5	9	10	7	4

the utility dose per point is the same for all voters. We may expect such a system to give determinate results over a wider range of cases than the plurality rule and to give a better reflection of underlying preferences. This holds for a comparison with plurality rule, and even more so for a comparison with majority rule.

D. STRATEGY

In the preceding discussion, we have compared the results of various voting systems based on given sets of true preferences, as shown in the ratings of Tables 6-1 to 6-3. We have assumed these ratings to reflect true preferences and have used them to determine the results for different voting methods. Voter strategy was disregarded.

Central Finance

The foregoing assumption must now be revised. The need for a voting process arises precisely because voters will *not* reveal their true preferences on a voluntary basis. Since the benefit of public services is obtained independently of contribution, it is good strategy not to reveal true preferences. A voting process combined with a compulsory application of the result is needed to force people into making their wants known. Depending upon the voting system, people may still choose not to reveal true preferences but to use strategies to obtain a preferred result.

To illustrate, let us turn to Table 6-1 and apply the plurality rule with strategy permitted. Voter Z may now announce a rating which assigns 4 to mP, 6 to sH, 9 to mH, and 7 to bH. Thereby he reduces the score of mP to 17, and mH becomes the winner with 19. He will prefer this to the solution without strategy, since his true score for mH exceeds that for mP, even though it does so by less than his rating with strategy would suggest. Similar efforts will be made by other voters, whose skills in assessing the situation may differ. Bargains will be made between voters or groups of voters on various issues, to improve their positions at the cost of a third group. When all is said and done, the final result may be a long way from that which would be obtained under our earlier assumption that voting proceeds independently and on the basis of true ratings.

The total score of the winning alternative under plurality and point voting will be less if strategy is present than without. In the preceding illustration, for instance, strategy resulted in a switch from mP, with a true score of 19, to mH, with a true score of 17. This follows from the very nature of our utility calculus or standard, which is in terms of true scores. Since the true orderings are not known, we cannot ascertain just where the gains and losses accrue, but we do know that the total true score is reduced by strategy. The kind of reasoning—the as-if argument in utility—which suggests that one or the other type of ordering should be preferred also suggests that the scope for strategy should be minimized.

Since various types of voting permit varying degrees of elbowroom for strategy and collusion, resulting differences in imperfection must be taken into account in choosing between voting systems. This is essential in a more extensive examination of the problem. Chances are that the scope for strategy will be greater with a sensitive system such as point voting than with a global system such as majority voting. On balance, majority voting may be the better system, even though point voting would be superior in the absense of strategy. Much depends on the degree of social cohesion and the basic similarity of preference patterns. Where preference patterns differ greatly, the finer adjustment of point voting would seem desirable. Yet this is precisely the setting where the results of strategy threaten to render the political process unworkable. Where preferences are reasonably similar, majority voting will do, even though society may be able to afford the results of point voting.

Other problems that should be dealt with in this connection can only be mentioned. Thus, it must be considered how various systems of voting are affected by the delegation of decision making from the individual voter to the elected representative; how decision making among representatives is affected by parliamentary procedure and party organization; and how imperfections in the decision-making process, for example, the two-party system versus proportional representation, may contribute to stability and more sensible results. History shows that parliamentary government works better where (as in the Anglo-Saxon countries) a rather crude system of representation is applied; and that the devisive forces of society are encouraged where constitutional arrangements provide for a highly representative system. These are enticing problems of political theory as the economist would like to see political theory approached, but they cannot be explored here.

A Special Problem of Local Finance

There remains to be noted a special problem posed by local finance. It arises where the individual has an option to leave one fiscal community and move to another rather than submit to the majority decision of any particular place.[1] To simplify matters, let us suppose that there are no transportation costs that enter into the choice of location. Let us now assume a situation where all people are in a similar position with regard to

[1] For the original discussion of this idea, see Charles M. Tiebout, "A Pure Theory of Local Expenditures," *Journal of Political Economy*, vol. 64, no. 5, pp. 416–424, October, 1956.

income, but some value social wants higher, relative to private wants, than others.   In this situation it will be advantageous for people to join up with others who have similar preferences.   Where social wants are concerned, a person stands to gain from having a preference pattern similar to that of others.   For private wants, the opposite tends to be the case: A person who prefers Florida vacations in August has an advantage over someone else who likes them in January.

Next, let us consider a situation where all people have similar preference for social wants but differ in income.   In this case, it will be advantageous for people with high incomes to associate with others with high incomes, while excluding people with low incomes.   At the same time, it will be desirable for people with low incomes to enter a community with as high an average income as possible.   This principle is reflected in the history of the poor laws as well as in the sociology of suburbia.   It applies if taxes are proportional and moreso if they are progressive.

The choice is less obvious if differences in income are combined with differences in preferences.   Moreover, transportation costs and other factors enter into location, and fiscal considerations may be more or less minor.   Nevertheless, the possibility of moving to other communities establishes something equivalent to a market mechanism in local finance. The determination of social wants within any one community remains a problem in social wants, but that of choosing among communities becomes a market problem.   Thereby a more homogeneous pattern of preferences tends to be established within any one community, and the task of finding a satisfactory solution is simplified.

E. SUMMARY

This brings us to the end of our exploration into the theoretical nature of budget determination.   While the results are inconclusive, the reader should not feel disheartened.   We have examined some central problems in the theory of public finance that no serious student of the subject can afford to disregard.

The basic precept of our analysis has been that public wants, the satisfaction of which is provided through the budget, are an inherent part of the preference patterns of the individual members of the community.   In this respect they do not differ from private wants, the satisfaction of which is provided through the mechanism of the market. As a conceptual matter, individual demand schedules for services supplied in the satisfaction of public wants may be derived from the indifference pattern of individual preferences—as demand schedules for services supplied in the satisfaction of private wants are derived.   The basic problem in the theory of public economy, therefore, is not that social wants are generated in some different and mysterious fashion; rather it is that the same amounts of services are consumed by all, so that (1) true individual preferences for such wants are not revealed at the market, and (2) there is no single solution that is optimal in the Pareto sense.

Of these two problems, the first is the most immediate. In the satisfaction of private wants, the market functions as an auction place, forcing individual consumers to reveal their true preferences: Unless I bid, I shall not be able to get what I want. In the satisfaction of social wants, this reasoning does not hold. The services supplied are not subject to the exclusion principle. Consumers will be able to obtain the benefits whether they contribute or not. Since the exclusion principle cannot be applied, there is no reason why consumers should reveal true preferences. The problem, therefore, is to find a way by which they can be induced to reveal these preferences so that the budget may be planned accordingly.

Neither the benefit nor the ability-to-pay theory offers an answer to this problem. The benefit approach has the advantage of tying the expenditure and tax sides of the budget together and relating both to individual preferences. Yet it fails in that it provides no way of ascertaining the true benefits. The voluntary-payment version furnishes no operational solution. The ability-to-pay approach to the theory of taxation proves even less satisfactory. It gives no clear-cut principle of tax distribution and fails altogether to answer the problem of expenditure determination. Later versions, categorizing the budget as a welfare plan, introduce the expenditure side of the budget and have the merit of emphasizing the planning aspects. However, these versions do not show how to determine the social preferences, without which determination the requirements of the welfare approach are an empty shell.

We are thus confronted with the necessity of examining the processes by which individuals may be induced to reveal their preferences. This requires a voting mechanism, together with a compulsory application of the budget plan thus decided upon. This very necessity for compulsory application of a general tax formula means that the resulting solution will not be optimal.

The definition of what constitutes an optimal solution leads to the second difficulty. Since the same supply of public services must be consumed by all, there is no single optimal solution for the amount supplied and the distribution of cost shares. Rather, there are a number of solutions falling along a utility frontier, all of which are optimal in the sense that there can be no improvement in the position of any one member of the group without damaging the position of someone else. Thus, even if the problem of revealing true preferences is disregarded altogether, and true preferences are assumed to be known, the economist's concept of efficiency permits us only to determine which solutions are on, and which are below, the utility frontier.   A more specific social-welfare function is needed to choose among the points on the frontier.   This again requires a political process.

In evaluating various voting systems, we must ask ourselves whether they will give a solution that comes close to the utility frontier, and what principles underlie the choice between various points on the frontier.   In comparing the rationale of various systems, we can hardly avoid reasoning *as if* interpersonal utility comparisons can be made, the difference between the old and the new welfare economics of this type being less than is frequently supposed.   Disregarding considerations of strategy, much is to be said in favor of the more sensitive orderings resulting from a system of point or plurality voting.   Allowing for considerations of strategy, the balance may tip the other way, and the results of the cruder system of majority voting may be the better choice.

The preceding discussion has been concerned primarily with that phase of the Allocation Branch which deals with the satisfaction of social wants. The problem of merit wants differs in that it falls outside the framework of consumer sovereignty.   Theoretical constructions of the benefit type— with or without implementation through voting—are inapplicable.   Yet the determination of merit wants is undertaken in the same voting process as that of social wants; and the considerations of the present chapter largely apply to both cases.

Determination of the "proper" state of income distribution is a further problem in social choice, and again more difficult than that of social wants.   Given the distribution of income, we can visualize that there exists a true set of demand schedules for the satisfaction of social wants. From this we know that there exists a set of optimal solutions to their satisfaction.   To be sure, the choice among these optimal solutions still involves distributional considerations.   Thus the problems of the Allocation and the Distribution Branches cannot be separated altogether.   At the same time, the determination of these optimal solutions can be handled more readily in economic terms than can that of proper distribution.   For these and other reasons, a separation of the Allocation and Distribution Branches remains advisable.

CHAPTER 7

Further problems in efficiency

We shall now turn to some remaining issues which have been dealt with at length in the theory of welfare economics and which have a direct bearing on the efficiency of budget policy. They include the use of subsidy and tax policies to secure an efficient output for decreasing-cost industries, similar budgetary corrections for industries involving important external economies or costs, and the much-discussed problem of excess burden in taxation.

A. SUBSIDY-TAX POLICY FOR DECREASING-COST INDUSTRIES

Efficient allocation of resources requires that the supply of any product or service should be carried to the point at which marginal cost MC and price or average revenue, AR, become equal. If less is supplied, price will exceed marginal cost. Consumers will be willing to pay more for an additional unit of output than the cost to produce it. Hence it is to the advantage of society that more should be produced.

The condition of $MC = AR$ is met by the market in the case of perfect competition. Under monopoly AR exceeds MC. Inefficient allocation results, and consideration must be given to public policies that force firms to produce at an optimal output where AR equals MC.[1]

The problem of adjustment is relatively simple in industries that operate under conditions of increasing cost and where monopoly is due to closed entry. Here the firm can be forced to produce optimal output and still cover its cost. Such is not the case with industries where maximum technical efficiency is reached at an output greater than the market can sustain. Here monopoly results, but the problem is not simply one of

[1] See p. 44.

enforcing a competitive output. Average cost AC will exceed AR at the level of output where AR equals MC. Production at the efficient level of output thus involves a loss to the producer. In order to obtain an optimal output, the private producer must be given a subsidy, or the goods must be supplied by a public enterprise that operates at a loss. The argument seems straightforward until we begin to inquire just how the subsidy should be collected and what level of capacity should be established in the first place.[1]

Consider the classical illustration of pricing the services of a bridge. The *short-run* aspect of the problem poses no particular difficulty. A bridge has been built in the past, and capacity is given. Thus marginal pricing involves variable cost only. To simplify matters, let us assume that no variable costs arise in the maintenance of the bridge.[2] Marginal

---

[1] Alfred Marshall, *Principles of Economics*, 8th ed., Macmillan & Co., Ltd., London, 1930, book V, chap. 13, p. 425, concluded that welfare, as measured by the total of consumer surplus, is increased if a tax is levied on an increasing-cost industry and the proceeds are paid as bounty to a decreasing-cost industry. This early version of the argument implies a constant marginal utility of money and comparability of income utility. (See text p. 108.) Thereby it avoids all the difficulties arising from the need to determine the amount and source of subsidy. See also H. Myint, *Theories of Welfare Economics*, Harvard University Press, Cambridge, Mass., 1948, chap. 9.

For a more modern formulation of the argument in terms of marginal-cost pricing, see Jules Dupuit, "On the Measurement of the Utility of Public Works," first published in *Annales des Ponts et Chaussées*, ser. 2, vol. 8, 1844 (English translation in *International Economic Papers*, no. 2, pp. 83–110, London, 1952); H. Hotelling, "The General Welfare in Relation to Problems of Taxation and Railway and Utility Rates," *Econometrica*, vol. 6, no. 3, pp. 242–269, July, 1938, and "The Relation of Prices to Marginal Costs in an Optimum System," *Econometrica*, vol. 7, no. 2, pp. 151–155, 1939, as well as "A Final Note," *Econometrica*, vol. 7, no. 2, pp. 158–160, 1939; Ragnar Frisch, "The Dupuit Taxation Theorem," *Econometrica*, vol. 7, no. 2, pp. 145–150, 1939, and "A Further Note on the Dupuit Taxation Theorem," *Econometrica*, vol. 7, no. 2, pp. 156–157, 1939. The initial contribution by H. Hotelling is reprinted in R. A. Musgrave and Carl Shoup (eds.), *Readings in the Economics of Taxation*, American Economic Association, Richard D. Irwin, Inc., Homewood, Ill., 1958.

Also see Melvin Reder, *Studies in the Theory of Welfare Economics*, Columbia University Press, New York, 1947, chap. 4; Howard R. Bowen, *Toward Social Economy*, Rinehart & Company, Inc., New York, 1948, chap. 17; A. P. Lerner, *The Economics of Control*, The Macmillan Company, New York, 1944, chap. 16; Nancy Ruggles, "The Welfare Basis of the Marginal Cost Pricing Principle," *Review of Economic Studies*, ser. 1, vol. 17, no. 42, pp. 29–46, 1949–1950, and "Recent Developments in the Theory of Marginal Cost Pricing," *Review of Economic Studies*, ser. 2, vol. 17, no. 43, pp. 107–127, 1949–1950.

In particular, see the compact treatment of the problem by A. M. Henderson, "The Pricing of Public Utility Undertakings," *Manchester School*, vol. 15, no. 3, pp. 223–250, September, 1947.

[2] Maintenance expenditures independent of the rate of use are, in effect, new investment expenditures. The problems raised by such outlays are those involved in the long-run aspects.

cost is zero, and the proper pricing requires that the services of the bridge be supplied free of charge. The more the bridge is used, the greater is the welfare derived from its services. At least, this is the case if there is no problem of "crowding." If there is, an auction is in order to ration out limited space. That is to say, tolls may be charged to those who wish to use the bridge without crowding, with the proceeds paid to those who in return are willing to stay away.

All this is simple enough, provided that the bridge is given to begin with. In the *long* run, such is not the case. Decisions must be made when to build a bridge. This is the more interesting part of the problem. *All* costs are now variable costs and must be allowed for, when deciding whether a bridge is worth building. It must be determined who is to pay for the structure. Let us assume, for present purposes, that the only benefits the bridge provides are those that accrue from its direct use. The rule might be proposed that the building project is worth undertaking if the total cost can be covered by subsequent toll proceeds.[1] The scale of output (number of bridges) will then be carried to the point at which the additional cost incurred will fall just short of the marginal toll proceeds. The general principle is clear enough, but the problem is how to implement it in an efficient fashion.

One policy is to build the bridge and then to defray the cost by toll finance. If the cost is not recovered, an investment error was made. If the cost *is* recovered, the bridge should subsequently be given over to free use. If crowding results, a new bridge can be built and the same test applied, and so forth. This policy has the advantage of providing ex post evidence of whether or not the investment was justified. It has the *dis*advantage of inefficiency in the charging of tolls on the latest bridge—because this restrains any additional use of the bridge that would be possible without crowding.[2] We have, then, a paradoxical situation where the exclusion principle *can* be applied (distinct from our case of social wants proper, where this is not feasible) but where such application (in the case of the bridge) results in an inefficient solution.

A second policy may be considered that avoids this inefficiency. This is to finance the bridge by either a lump-sum tax or from general revenue.[3]

[1] Henderson, *op. cit.*, suggests that the bridge is worthwhile if covered by toll proceeds, with tolls arranged so as to result in perfect price discrimination. Whether this is preferable to uniform pricing depends on how the proper state of distribution is defined. (See text p. 77, note 1.)

[2] Such a difficulty would not arise if the supply of bridges was sufficiently divisible to permit a precise adjustment to demand without crowding or excess capacity. The entire problem would vanish, since the market could resolve it by the usual mechanism of price or toll finance.

[3] In the case of a lump-sum tax, we avoid the imposition of an excess burden, which is likely to arise in the case of other taxes. This aspect of the matter will be considered shortly.

In both these cases, there need be no toll that restrains the use of existing capacity. This is all to the good, but we are left without any assurance whether the construction of the bridge was worthwhile in the first place; that is, whether it could have been financed by tolls, if tolls had been charged. Moreover, we are confronted with an arbitrary change in the state of distribution, since the people who pay the tax may not be the people who use the facilities.

The choice between the two policies of toll finance and tax finance is a matter of judgment, depending on the specific case. The first policy has the advantage of ex post justification (or rejection) of the investment and the avoidance of arbitrary distributional effects. The second policy has the advantage of a more efficient use of existing facilities. Under certain circumstances the latter advantage may carry greater weight; under others, the former may be decisive.

Some attempts can be made to compromise between the two policies. The tax used in the second case might be drawn from people who are most likely to use the facility; or the toll in the first case might be transformed into an initial admission charge prerequisite to any use of the bridge, plus a fee per unit of use equal to marginal cost. Since the marginal cost for the bridge would equal zero, we would be left again with the question of how to assess the general admission charge.[1]

However, none of these is a satisfactory solution. To obtain one, it must be shown that the investment is justified on the basis of consumer preferences. This can be done only if the facility is paid for in accordance with these preferences. Such payment is necessary for operational reasons, quite apart from the theoretical proposition (which to me seems eminently reasonable) that compensation must be paid if a welfare gain is to be established by the compensation principle.[2]

All this leads to the conclusion that the building of the bridge (and similar facilities) must be determined by the same political process that determines the satisfaction of social wants in the budget of the Allocation Branch. Even though the exclusion principle can be applied in the technical sense that barriers can be established, use of the principle is inadmissible because decreasing costs prevail.

---

[1] Henderson, *op. cit.*, refers to this plan as the "two-part tariff." Presumably less is lost by excluding those who do not pay admission than by restraining those who do.

[2] See W. J. Baumol, "Community Indifference," *Review of Economic Studies*, vol. 14, no. 35, p. 44, 1946–1947; and K. Arrow, *Social Choice and Individual Values*, John Wiley & Sons, Inc., New York, 1951, p. 38.

In this basic sense, Hotelling, "The General Welfare in Relation to Problems of Taxation and Railway and Utility Rates," p. 242, seems quite mistaken when he holds that there is no reason why "every tub must stand on its own bottom." It must, from the long-run point of view, where all costs are allowed for.

B. COLLATERAL BENEFITS AND COSTS

Let us suppose, now, that our bridge not only benefits the direct users but also results in collateral benefits to residents of the adjoining territory or other groups, independent of their use of the bridge.   Price payments for such benefits cannot be collected by toll finance, even if it is decided to charge a toll for direct use.   We have here an outright case of social wants.   Where such collateral benefits exist, construction of the bridge may be worthwhile, even though the cost cannot be recovered by toll finance.   The question is how to evaluate these benefits.[1]

Precisely the same problem arises whenever we encounter a divergence between social and private net product.   In the framework of the older welfare economics—which assumes preferences to be known and permits interpersonal utility comparisons—such situations may be readily remedied by designing the appropriate tax-bounty scheme.[2]   If this solution is discarded, we are left with the basic difficulties encountered previously in the satisfaction of social wants.   To begin with, there is the problem of inducing those who enjoy gains or suffer losses to reveal their evaluation of such gains or losses.   In addition, there is again the problem of choosing between points on the utility frontier that is established on this basis.

Resorting to the principle of compensation does not solve the problem.[3] There is no market mechanism by which collateral benefits or costs can be determined; hence there is no basis on which to assess those who enjoy the benefits or to compensate those who suffer the loss.   The principle of compensation can be applied only if we know how much should be paid in compensation; but to determine this, a political process is needed.   Where the required compensation is revealed, the exclusion principle applies, and the pricing system takes care of the problem.

C. AVOIDANCE OF EXCESS BURDEN

In our efficient system, the costs of public services provided by the Allocation Branch are imputed to the members of the community in line

---

[1] For a critical discussion of procedures followed in evaluating such benefits, see Julius Margolis, "Secondary Benefits, External Economies and the Justification of Public Investment," *Review of Economics and Statistics*, vol. 39, p. 284, August, 1957.

[2] See p. 115.

[3] For discussions of the principle of compensation, see A. Bergson, "A Reformulation of Certain Aspects of Welfare Economics," *Quarterly Journal of Economics*, vol. 52, no. 2, pp. 310–334, February, 1938; J. R. Hicks, "The Foundations of Welfare Economics," *Economic Journal*, vol. 49, no. 96, pp. 696–712, December, 1939; and N. Kaldor, "Welfare Propositions of Economics and Inter-personal Comparisons of

with their individual preference patterns. In approximating this ideal solution, the tax-expenditure plan is determined through the political process. Taxes are assessed according to certain objective criteria such as income, outlay, ownership, or simply existence. These criteria are chosen so as to allocate the costs in accordance with the intended pattern of burden distribution. This is the function of taxation in the Allocation Branch. Taxes should be designed so as to meet that function with greatest efficiency, but beyond this, taxes should be as neutral as possible. Unintended interference with the market mechanism may result in an excess burden that should be avoided.

Similar considerations apply to the efficient design of taxes in the context of the Distribution and Stabilization Branches. Taxes should accomplish their assigned objective, but beyond this, they should not interfere with the functioning of the market system. This is the principle of neutrality in taxation. As we shall see, the desire to avoid an excess burden is not always compatible with other objectives of budget policy, in which case a choice must be made. Recognition of the principle of neutrality in no way excludes the use of tax policy to accomplish *desired* objectives of economic control. Neutrality is efficient only in the avoidance of effects that are not an intended part of an efficiently determined set of policy objectives.

It follows from the principle of neutrality that taxes should be imposed so as to place the least burden upon whoever is to be taxed. There should be no excess burden that can be avoided.[1] The question is

---

Utility," *Economic Journal*, vol. 49, no. 195, pp. 549–552, September, 1939; Paul A. Samuelson, *Foundations of Economic Analysis*, Harvard University Press, Cambridge, Mass., 1947, chap. 8; and Melvin Reder, *op. cit.*

[1] The literature on excess burden is voluminous. For treatment of the problem in terms of the old welfare economics, involving interpersonal utility comparison, see Alfred Marshall, *op. cit.*, chap. 13; and A. C. Pigou, *A Study in Public Finance*, 3d ed., Macmillan & Co., Ltd., London, 1951, especially part II, chaps. 5 and 6. Pigou refers to excess burden as "announcement effects" to be considered in adapting taxes to the objective of least total sacrifice.

The framework of the new welfare economics excludes interpersonal utility comparisons. For the first round of contributions, formulated in partial-equilibrium terms, see M. F. W. Joseph, "The Excess Burden of Indirect Taxation," *Review of Economic Studies*, vol. 6, no. 3, pp. 226–231, June, 1939; A. M. Henderson, "The Case for Indirect Taxation," *Economic Journal*, vol. 58, no. 232, pp. 538–553, December, 1948; H. P. Wald, "The Classical Indictment of Indirect Taxation," *Quarterly Journal of Economics*, vol. 59, no. 4, pp. 577–596, August, 1945; and George J. Stigler, *The Theory of Price*, The Macmillan Company, New York, 1946, p. 81.

For a second round of contributions stated in a general-equilibrium setting, see Earl R. Rolph and George F. Break, "The Welfare Aspects of Excise Taxes," *Journal of Political Economy*, vol. 57, pp. 46–54, July, 1949; I. M. D. Little, "Direct vs. Indirect Taxes," *Economic Journal*, vol. 61, no. 243, pp. 577–584, September, 1951,

whether certain types of taxes are superior in this respect to others. Let us assume that the government wishes to obtain an amount of revenue from a particular taxpayer sufficient to secure a given resource transfer to public use. The required revenue may be obtained by various types of taxes including a head tax, a general income tax, a general sales or excise tax, and a selective excise tax. We are assuming that the general taxes are proportional, leaving progression for later consideration. The problem is to compare the burdens that result from the various taxes, the same yield being obtained in all cases.

Fixed Supply of Work Effort and Saving

Suppose, first, that the supply of work effort and saving are fixed. Also, suppose that pure competition prevails in all markets. It may be shown under these conditions that a head tax, general income tax, and general consumption tax of equal yields are equivalent in that they impose equal burdens, but that the selective excise tax is inferior because it imposes a greater burden.

This follows from the welfare conditions that must be met if the allocation of resources is to be optimum. Suppose we have an economy with two products, X and Y. Efficient allocation of resources requires that for X and Y the marginal rate of transformation (the rate at which they can be substituted for each other in production) should equal their marginal rate of substitution by the consumer. In competitive equilibrium, these two rates are equal. If they diverge, an adjustment can be made that will be to the advantage of both sellers and buyers.

When a head tax is imposed, the prevailing equilibrium is disturbed. Eventually a new equilibrium is reached, and this new equilibrium again meets the optimum condition of equality between the rates of transformation in production and of substitution in consumption. The head

---

reprinted in I. M. D. Little, *A Critique of Welfare Economics*, 2d ed., Clarendon Press, Oxford, 1957, pp. 294–300; Milton Friedman, "The Welfare Effects of an Income and an Excise Tax," *Journal of Political Economy*, vol. 60, no. 1, pp 1–24, February, 1952, reprinted in M. Friedman, *Essays in Positive Economics*, University of Chicago Press, Chicago, 1953, pp. 100–116; W. J. Corlett and D. C. Hague, "Complementarity and the Excess Burden of Taxation," *Review of Economic Studies*, ser. 1, vol. 21, no. 54, pp. 21–30, 1953–1954. The contributions of Little and of Rolph and Break are reprinted in Musgrave and Shoup, *op. cit.*

Also see Earl R. Rolph, *The Theory of Fiscal Economics*, University of California Press, Berkeley, Calif., 1954, chaps. 7–10; and Anthony Y. C. Koo, "Welfare and Direct Taxation," *Canadian Journal of Economics and Political Science*," vol. 21, no. 1, pp. 30–47, February, 1955. For a summary of the entire discussion, see David Walker, "The Direct-Indirect Tax Problem: Fifteen Years of Controversy," *Public Finance*, vol. 10, pp. 153–177, November, 1955.

tax is always a lump-sum tax, since it meets the condition that the amount of tax does not depend upon any variable in the system.   In the special case under consideration here, where the supply of effort and of saving are fixed, this condition is also met by a general income tax and a general sales or consumption tax.   Both are lump-sum taxes and equivalent to a head tax.   Whichever of the three is imposed, the condition of optimum will not be disturbed.

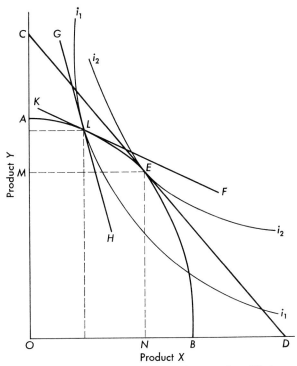

Fig. 7-1. Excess burden of excise tax in general equilibrium.

When a selective excise tax on product X only is imposed, the situation differs.   The consumer's rate of substitution between X and Y now equals the ratio of their market prices.   The producer, however, equates the rate of transformation to the ratio of their net (after tax) prices.   Since the tax enters as a wedge between the market price of X and its net price, these two ratios will not be the same.   Hence, the consumer's rate of substitution will differ from the rate of transformation in production. The optimum condition is not met, and an inefficient allocation of resources results.   Therefore, the partial excise tax is inferior to the other taxes.

In Figure 7-1, this argument is illustrated for consumers as a group.[1] We measure product X on the horizontal, and product Y on the vertical axis. The production-possibility curve AB shows the various combinations of X and Y that may be produced. Assuming the community to be composed of individuals with equal incomes and tastes, the community's position may be represented by any one individual. Now let his preference pattern be indicated by a set of indifference lines such as i_1 and i_2, so that equilibrium is established at E on indifference curve i_2. The

---

[1] This reasoning follows that of Little, Friedman, and Rolph. It differs from the partial-equilibrium argument presented initially by Joseph and repeated by Stigler, Boulding, and others. The earlier version of the argument is shown in the following figure:

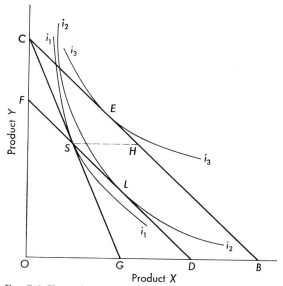

Fig. 7-2. Excess burden of excise tax in partial equilibrium.

Here a consumer divides his income between products X and Y. His total income in terms of X equals OB, and the initial equilibrium is at E on indifference curve i_3. An income tax equal to DB of X is imposed. The set of opportunities now available to him are shown by FD, and the new equilibrium is at L, on indifference curve i_2. The situation is precisely the same under a general consumption tax on X and Y. Now let the government obtain the same revenue by a tax on X only. As a result, the price line swings from CB to CG, and the new equilibrium is at S, on indifference curve i_1. The government's revenue is equal to SH, which is the same as the income tax revenue DB. The consumer is on a lower indifference curve, provided only that the curves are convex to the origin and do not intersect.

As noted by Little and others, this analysis is not conclusive. It is in partial-equilibrium terms, and neglects changes in cost. If the government's position under the income tax and the excise tax is to be the same, the government should be able to

product will be divided between X and Y in the ratio of ON to OM. The marginal rate of substitution in consumption is the same as the marginal rate of transformation in production. The price line CD is tangent to both the producer's transformation curve and the consumer's indifference curve.

Let us now introduce budget expenditures on goods and services that are financed by an income tax. If the production-possibility curve AB expresses the combination of products available for *private* use only, introduction of the budget will move the entire curve AB closer to the origin; whether or not this shift is parallel will depend on the nature of the public services for which resources are withdrawn from private use. To simplify matters, suppose that this shift has been allowed for already. In other words, let AB and the equilibrium at E depict a situation after adjustment to a given public expenditure and income tax.[1]

Now, let the income tax be replaced by an excise tax on X. Since the public use of resources is unchanged, the production-possibility curve AB remains the same. Again the new equilibrium must lie on this curve. And as before, it must lie on an indifference curve. Moreover, it must lie to the left of E, since at the new equilibrium the indifference curve must intersect the production-possibility curve from above. This follows because in the new equilibrium the slope of the production-possibility curve equals the ratio of prices net of tax, p_x^n and p_y^n, as received by the producer; the slope of the indifference curve equals the ratio of market prices, p_x^m and p_y^m, as paid by the consumer; but $p_x^m/p_y^m > p_x^n/p_y^n$.

Such a point is illustrated by L, where GH is the new market price or budget line, and the slope of KF shows the ratio of net prices. While our choice of the particular point L is arbitrary, we know that it must lie somewhere on AE, and that it must fall on a lower indifference curve than i_2. This will be true provided that the slope of the indifference curves is convex to the origin and that the curves do not intersect. An excess burden has been imposed by the use of the excise tax on X.

The excess burden arises only if X and Y can be substituted for each other. No substitution is possible if the consumption of X or Y is fixed in amount, or if X and Y are consumed in fixed proportions. In this case, the excise on X is equivalent to the other taxes, and no excess burden results. The degree of excess burden that results thus depends on the degree to which substitution is possible. At the same time, this relation-

---

obtain the same mix of X and Y in both cases. Since its revenue in both cases equals DB of X, and since it may purchase Y as well, obtaining the same mix will be possible only if the transformation curve of X and Y has the same slope at both the old and the new points of equilibrium. The same slope will not occur unless the transformation schedule is a straight line, both goods being produced under constant cost.

[1] This position is arrived at by the process shown in the following figure, where PR

ship cannot be expressed easily in terms of price and income elasticity. Substitution may exist where X is zero elastic to price but is not neutral to changes in real income.   Here X must be an inferior good since,

---

is the production-possibility schedule, ST is the price line, and U is the initial point of equilibrium, all before the government enters the picture.

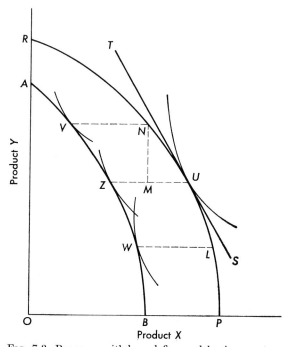

Fig. 7-3. Resource withdrawal financed by income tax.

Now, let the government purchase BP of product X.   The net production-possibility schedule BA shows the new combinations of X and Y available for private use. It is obtained by deducting BP horizontally from PR.   Assuming income tax finance, the new equilibrium will be where AB is tangent to an indifference curve.   This may be at point Z, in which case the slope of the price line remains unchanged; private buyers surrender X only, and the total output of X and Y remains as before.   But this is a very special case.   The new equilibrium may also be at a point such as V, where the total output of X is reduced by UM; that of Y is increased by MN; and p_x/p_y rises; or the new equilibrium may be at a point such as W, where the output of X is increased; that of Y is reduced; and p_x/p_y falls.   The outcome depends on the shape of the indifference pattern, the shape of the production-possibility curve, and the composition of government purchases.

Operationally, we may think of the income tax–financed budget as resulting initially in a parallel shift in the price line to the left, locating private buyers at point Z on the private production-possibility schedule.   If AB happens to be tangent to an indifference line at Z, this is the end of the adjustment.   If not, there follows a rearrangement of private purchases and a movement along AB to a point such as V or W, where AB is tangent to an indifference line.   The point E in Figure 7-1 represents such a point, reached after the entire adjustment is completed.

with a change in price, the price effect must be offset by an income effect. As an income tax is imposed, the purchase of X increases. As an excise on X is imposed, the purchase of X is unchanged, since the income effect is cancelled by the price effect. Nevertheless, the excise on X is inferior, since it results in a divergence between the consumer's rate of substitution and the seller's rate of transformation. The more X responds to income, the greater is this divergence and the resulting excess burden.

Similarly, substitution may be possible where X is zero elastic to income but elastic to price. In this case, imposition of an income tax leaves purchases of X unchanged, while imposition of an excise tax on X reduces such purchases. The excise tax is again inferior, since it disturbs the equality between the consumer's rate of substitution and the seller's rate of transformation. The more the demand for X is elastic to price, the greater is the degree to which substitution is possible and, hence, the greater the excess burden.

A general statement in terms of elasticities is difficult, however, if the product is elastic to both income and price. No simple rule can be given regarding the effects on excess burden either of varying degrees of income elasticity, with any given price elasticity greater than zero, or for varying degrees of price elasticity, with any given income elasticity greater than zero. Here the problem is stated better in terms of possible substitution than elasticity, the general rule being that excess burden varies positively with the degree of possible substitution.[1]

[1] Ursula Hicks, *Public Finance*, Pitman Publishing Corporation, New York, 1947, pp. 167–172, reaches the conclusion that excess burden varies directly with the elasticity of supply and demand of the taxed product or factor.

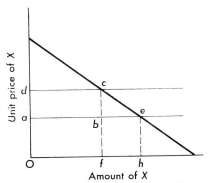

Fig. 7-4. Loss of consumer surplus.

It is assumed that perfect competition prevails; and that there are no closely related products or factors, so that a partial-equilibrium approach is justified; and that the tax in question is small, so that the marginal utility of money may be taken to be constant, and the demand curve may be looked upon as a marginal-utility curve.

The figure above shows supply and demand for a product assumed to be produced under conditions of constant cost equal to Oa. Imposition of a unit tax equal to ad results in a loss of consumer surplus, or S equal to bec and a gain in tax yield, or T

Multiple-excise System

The preceding conclusion rests on certain simplifying assumptions that must now be reconsidered. To begin with, we shall allow for the possibility of imposing more than one selective excise. Let us examine a situation where given expenditures are financed by an income tax and an excise on product X, with product Y tax-free. The situation may now be improved by curtailing or repealing the income tax and adding an equal ad valorem excise on Y. Matching an ad valorem excise on X with an equal rate excise on Y does, in fact, amount to repealing the excise on X and obtaining the total yield from a general ad valorem tax on sales. Under this general tax, the rate of substitution by consumers of p_x^m/p_y^m is equal in equilibrium to the rate of transformation or p_x^n/p_y^n, and the condition of optimum is met.

Now let us consider three products: X, Y and Z and begin with a situation where only X is subject to an excise tax. Will it still be an improvement to add an excise on Y (but not on Z) and reduce the income tax accordingly? Before adding a second excise, the rates of substitution and of transformation will be equal between Y and Z, but unequal between X and Y, and X and Z. After the tax on Y has been added, the two rates will be equal between Y and X, but unequal between X and Z, and Y and Z. No general conclusion can be drawn, therefore, whether the excess burden would be increased or reduced by the second excise. Nor can a ready answer be given for the more realistic case of expanding or contracting an excise system that already includes many partial excises. The answer cannot be found in counting product relations which involve excess burden and those which do not. The weight of excess burden in the case of any particular pair must be considered. While we *can* conclude that a general ad valorem tax is preferable to a system of selective excises imposed at differential rates,[1] we cannot say with assurance

---

equal to $bc \cdot ab$. If the demand schedule is a straight line over the relevent range, we have $\frac{S}{T} = \frac{1}{2}\frac{eb}{ab}$. Now $\frac{eb}{ab} = E_d\frac{bc}{cf} = E_d\frac{T}{N}$, where E_d is the elasticity of demand and N is consumer outlays including tax. We therefore obtain $S = \frac{1}{2}\frac{E_d}{N}T^2$. Thus, the excess burden varies directly with the elasticity of demand and with tax yield, but inversely with consumer outlay including tax.

Assuming increasing cost, and treating producer surplus accordingly, Mrs. Hicks obtains $S = \frac{1}{2}\frac{E_dE_s}{E_d + E_s}\frac{T^2}{N}$, where E_s is the elasticity of supply.

[1] This conclusion differs from Pigou's principle that the optimal solution will be one where different products are taxed at differential rates, set so as to reduce the production of all commodities in equal proportions.

See A. C. Pigou, *A Study in Public Finance*, 3d ed., Macmillan & Co., Ltd., London,

whether a somewhat more broadly based system of ad valorem excises is preferable to a somewhat more selective system.

Imperfections in the Market

Next, we shall abandon the assumption of pure competition but retain that of a fixed supply of effort and saving. This leaves intact the conclusion that a head tax, an income tax, and a general excise tax are equivalent; but we can no longer prove that a selective excise tax must be inferior. Such a tax may now be preferable to a general tax, provided that it moves the allocation of resources to a closer-to-optimal position.

Suppose that product X is produced under monopoly, while Y is produced under pure competition. The market produces too little of X and too much of Y. In order to remedy this situation, general revenue may be obtained by placing an excise on Y; or an excise may be placed on Y and the proceeds used to subsidize the production of X. An alternative approach is to impose an incentive tax on the producer of X to encourage him to produce at a closer-to-optimal scale of output. This, of course, will not be accomplished by a simple tax on total monopoly profits or even by an ordinary tax on excess profits. Rather, it requires a special tax, designed to render the exercise of monopoly power unprofitable.[1]

1951, p. 106; and Frank Ramsey, "A Contribution to the Theory of Taxation," *Economic Journal*, vol. 37, no. 145, pp. 46–61, March, 1927. In Pigou's as well as Ramsey's reasoning, the theorem is arrived at within the framework of the old welfare economics of interpersonal utility comparison. It belongs in the welfare view of the ability-to-pay approach and does not fit the context of the present argument.

Nevertheless, Pigou's theorem may be noted briefly at this point. Suppose that the government secures a given revenue to purchase goods previously bought by private buyers, or to finance services provided free of charge and unrelated to private demand for goods purchased at the market. Suppose further that the marginal utility of income is constant and equal for all; that resource allocation in the private sector is optimal; and that all demand and supply curves are straight lines. It may then be shown that the optimum system (the system involving least total sacrifice) of raising a given revenue by proportional taxes on the outlay on various goods is that which curtails the production of all commodities and services in equal proportions. This holds whether demands for various private products are independent or not.

The rates of tax required to secure proportional reductions in output depend on the elasticities of the demand and supply schedules for products that would be produced in the absence of taxation. The objective of equal proportional reduction in output is secured if $t_r/(1/s_r - 1/d_r)$ has the same values for all r, where t_r is ad valorem rate of tax, s_r is the elasticity of supply, and d_r is the elasticity of demand (defined as negative) in respect to pre-tax output of the rth commodity. Thus, the rate of tax will be larger, the less demand is elastic and the less supply is elastic (if positive). Only if all products are produced under constant cost, and if the total supply of labor is fixed, will all commodities have the same rate of tax.

[1] See Joan Robinson's proposal for a dual measure comprising (1) a subsidy per unit of output equal to marginal cost minus marginal revenue for the purely competi-

Since the assumption of pure competition is unrealistic, our earlier conclusions must be qualified accordingly. At the same time, allocation in the market is not altogether chaotic. Therefore, we are still well advised to prefer the general tax unless there is a clear case for correcting a specific imperfection.

Variable Supply of Effort

A further assumption underlying the conclusions of the simple case was that of a fixed supply of effort and saving. Let us now reinstate the assumption of pure competition and allow for a variable supply of effort. Saving is held fixed for the time being.

We must now consider the effects of various taxes upon the rate of substitution between leisure and product X, leisure and product Y, and products X and Y. The argument is similar to that of the preceding case, leisure being now like a third good, the consumption of which may be varied. For welfare to be maximized, the worker-consumer's rate of substitution of leisure for X or Y must be equal to the rate of transformation of leisure into X or Y, just as the rates of transformation and substitution must be equal between X and Y. The question is how these equalities are affected by various taxes.

Under a head tax, the tax liability does not vary with changes in the taxpayer's behavior. It is assessed in Sartre fashion—on the mere fact of existence. As before, this tax is a true lump-sum tax and free of excess burden. But imposition of an income tax now involves an excess burden. After such a tax is imposed and equilibrium is reached, the rate of substitution between leisure and X, as seen by the worker-consumer, equals the net (after tax) wage rate in terms of X. The rate of transformation, as seen by the producer-employer, equals the gross wage rate paid in the market. Introduction of an income tax renders the two rates unequal. The same applies with regard to leisure and good Y. The income tax now interferes with optimal allocation.[1]

---

tive output, and (2) a tax equal to supernormal profits, including subsidy (*Economics of Imperfect Competition*, Macmillan & Co., Ltd., London, 1933, pp. 164–165). For further discussion of this proposal, see Benjamin Higgins, "Post-war Tax Policy," *Canadian Journal of Economics and Political Science*, vol. 9, no. 3, part I, pp. 408–428, August, 1943, reprinted in Musgrave and Shoup, *op. cit.* For alternative approaches, see Arthur Upgren, Objectives and Guides to Policy, *American Economic Review*, vol. 35, no. 2, p. 77, May, 1945; and Kenneth Boulding, *Economic Analysis*, 3d ed., Harper & Brothers, New York, 1955, p. 622.

[1] The case may be illustrated again by Figure 7-1. We now measure leisure on the horizontal axis and good X on the vertical axis. AB, in this case, is the transformation curve of leisure into goods after imposition of a head tax, and E is the initial equilibrium. Now an income tax is substituted for the head tax. The transformation curve is unchanged, and the new equilibrium must again lie on it, as well as on

Since we have retained the assumption of a fixed supply of saving, precisely the same conclusions hold for a general sales tax. Like the income tax, the general sales tax is inferior to the head tax. The selective excise tax is also inferior. Like the income and general sales taxes, the selective excise tax reduces the real wage rate, whereas the head tax does not. This much is clear, but it remains to compare the excess burden under a selective excise tax with that under an income or a general sales tax.

It is tempting to argue—and, indeed, it was held for some time—that a selective excise is again inferior to an income tax. Both, it was said, distort the choice between goods and leisure, but the excise on X involves an additional distortion in the choice between goods X and Y.[1] This reasoning holds if the supply of effort is fixed, so that effort is the same under both taxes. If the supply is variable, effort may differ under the two taxes. Hence, we cannot conclude that the excess burden caused by distorting effects on the supply of leisure will be the same in both cases.

With labor supply variable, the comparison between an income tax and an excise on X is similar to the previously noted comparison between two selective excises.[2] We may think of leisure as a third good L, and of the income tax as an excise on the sale of L. A tax on income leads to inefficient allocation between L and X and between L and Y. It does not interfere with the allocation between X and Y. An excise tax on X leads to inefficient allocation between X and L and between X and Y. It does not interfere with the allocation between Y and L. In both cases, two relationships are disturbed and one is unaffected. There is no general way of telling the weight of the excess burden that results from each of the two types of interference under either tax; and there is no general way of telling which of the two taxes is superior.

The result in any particular case depends upon the rates of substitution and of transformation between X, Y, and L. Suppose, first, that no substitution is possible between L and X and between L and Y. This returns us to the case of fixed supply of effort. Only the relationship between X and Y remains open to distortion. The income tax or general sales tax is equivalent to a head tax, while a selective excise is inferior.

---

an indifference curve. The slope of the transformation curve will equal the gross rate of exchange between X and leisure, while the slope of the indifference curve will equal the net rate. Since the slope of the transformation curve is larger, the indifference curve again intersects it from above. The new equilibrium lies to the left of E at a point such as L, and on a lower indifference curve.

[1] See, for instance, A. M. Henderson, "The Case for Indirect Taxation," *Economic Journal*, vol. 58, no. 232, pp. 538–553, December, 1948.

[2] See I. M. D. Little, "Direct vs. Indirect Taxes," *A Critique of Welfare Economics*, 2d ed., Clarendon Press, Oxford, 1957, p. 296.

Next, suppose that there is no substitution between L and X and between X and Y. In this case, only the relationship between L and Y is open to distortion. Since an excise on X is neutral in this respect, it is equivalent to a head tax and superior to an income tax or an excise on Y. Finally, suppose that no substitution is possible between X and Y, but that both may be substituted for L. A selective excise on X may be superior to a general excise or income tax if the rate of substitution of X for L is lower than that of Y for L. Such will be the case where X is more or less complementary to leisure (tickets to watch a ball game, for example) while Y is rival to leisure (as with work clothing). In between these extremes lies the real world, where X, Y, and L are all more or less close substitutes for each other. In this case, there is no general presumption that one or the other tax is superior.[1] The only over-all conclusion that one may venture is that the best taxes are those on goods (including leisure) which have the lowest rates of substitution.

Variable Supply of Saving

We shall now allow for a variable supply of saving. The assumption of a fixed supply of effort is restored, and that of pure competition is retained.

To simplify matters, suppose first that there exists one product only. In this case, the only possible distortion is between present and future consumption of this single good. In the pre-tax equilibrium, the consumer's marginal rate of substitution between present and future consumption equals the producer's marginal rate of transformation between present and future goods. Introduction of a head tax does not interfere with the equality of these two rates, but introduction of an income tax does. Such a tax reduces the rate at which future consumption may be substituted for present consumption. Since interest income is subject to tax, the net rate of interest is reduced. The marginal rate of substitution by the consumer depends on the net rate of interest, while the rate of transformation by the producer depends upon the gross rate of

---

[1] W. J. Corlett and D. C. Hague, "Complementarity and the Excess Burden of Taxation," *Review of Economic Studies*, ser. 1, vol. 21, no. 54, pp. 21–30, 1953–1954, show that substitution of a selective excise for an income tax reduces the excess burden if it increases the supply of labor. While the consumer loses in adjusting to the changed price relationship between goods X and Y, this loss is negligible if we consider an infinitesimal tax change. It is outweighed by the gain derived from transferring the tax burden to the good that is more complementary to leisure. The tax change, in effect, involves imposition of a tax on the enjoyment of leisure, thus bringing the arrangement closer to that of a head tax which falls equally on the consumption of X, Y, and L. In the more interesting case of a finite change, effects on the rate of substitution between X and Y cease to be negligible, and the optimal combination of a direct and indirect tax now depends on the parameters of the particular case.

interest.   The two are rendered unequal in equilibrium, and the condition of optimal allocation is interfered with.

This interference is avoided if we impose an income tax under which interest income is not taxable.[1]   Interference is similarly avoided under a general consumption tax.   Both taxes leave the marginal rates of substitution between present and future consumption unaffected, as does a head tax.[2]

Let us now allow for two goods, X and Y, and consider a selective excise tax on X.   Reasoning as before, we find no clear preference between a general income tax and the selective excise.   The income tax introduces an inequality between the consumer's marginal rate of substitution and the producer's marginal rate of transformation in the matching of X_0 and X_1 and of Y_0 and Y_1, where subscripts 0 and 1 refer to present and future consumption.   The selective excise on X introduces an inequality in the matching of X_0 and Y_0 and of X_1 and Y_1.   There is no way of telling which excess burden is greater, the outcome depending again on the various conditions of substitution applicable in any particular case.   The general consumption tax does not disturb either set of equalities.

Variable Supply of Effort and of Saving

Next, let us return to the assumption of only one product X, allowing for a variable supply of effort as well as saving.   Let L indicate leisure, X_0 present, and X_1 future, consumption.   A head tax leaves the condition of optimum undisturbed.   A general income tax renders unequal the

---

[1] Note that the income tax, to be neutral, must exempt interest on old as well as new capital accumulation because the choice between present and future consumption involves not only the disposition of current income but also a decision whether to dissave old accumulation.

[2] Let income equal Y_0, and the rate of interest equal i.   *In the absence of a tax,* present consumption may equal $C_0 = Y_0$.   If consumption is postponed for a year, future consumption may equal $C_1 = (1 + i)Y_0$.   The ratio of C_1/C_0 equals $1 + i$. More generally, consumption for the second period equals $C_1 = (1 + i)Y_0 - (1 + i)C_0$ and $\partial C_1/\partial C_0 = -(1 + i) = -MRS_{01}$.

Now a *general income tax* is imposed.   This reduces possible present consumption to $C_0 = (1 - t)Y_0$.   If there is consumption after one year, we have

$$C_1 = (1 + i)(1 - t)Y_0 - ti(1 - t)Y_0$$

It follows that $C_1/C_0 = 1 + i - ti$, which is less than before tax.   Generally, we have $C_1 = (1 - t)(1 + i - ti)Y_0 - (1 + i - ti)C_0$, and hence

$$\partial C_1/\partial C_0 = -(1 + i - ti) = -MRS_{01}$$

Next, let us consider an *income tax with interest exempt.*   In this case, present consumption remains the same at $C_0 = (1 - t)Y_0$; future consumption now equals $C_1 = (1 + i)(1 - t)Y_0$, and $C_1/C_0 = 1 + i$, as in the pre-tax case.   More generally, we have $C_1 = (1 + i)(1 - t)Y_0 - (1 + i)C_0$, and $\partial C_1/\partial C_0 = -(1 + i) = -MRS_{01}$. Precisely the same holds for a tax that applies to present as well as future consumption.

respective marginal rates of substitution and transformation between X_0 and X_1, L and X_0, and L and X_1. A tax on present and future consumption does so between L and X_0, L and X_1, but not between X_0 and X_1. This does not establish a preference for the consumption tax over the income tax. The excess burden arising from interference in the choice between L and X_0 and between L and X_1 need not be the same under the two taxes, since the supplies of labor and saving may differ. All that can be said is that the head tax is superior to both the consumption and the income tax. A similar argument applies for the case of multiple goods and selective excises.

Progression and Other Complications

So far we have considered the problem of excess burden under a general and proportional income tax, a general and proportional consumption tax, and a selective excise. It remains to note the consequences of progression and of certain other complications that arise from unintended discriminations.

If the supply of effort and saving is fixed, the income tax remains without excess burden, even though progressive rates apply. If the supply of effort is variable, the excess burden placed upon a *given* taxpayer will be greater when he is called upon to pay a given amount under a progressive rate structure than when he pays under a proportional rate.[1] The degree of inequality between the worker's marginal rate of substitution and the producer's marginal rate of transformation between goods and leisure depends upon the marginal rate of tax; and this marginal rate of tax is higher under the progressive than under the proportional tax. Similar considerations apply to the comparison between a proportional and a progressive tax on consumption for the case of variable saving.

The term *general tax* as used in the preceding pages is a theoretical concept. In practice, the so-called general taxes frequently involve hidden elements of discrimination against certain industries, firms, or factor shares. Indeed, the complexities and varieties of modern economic society are such that it is extremely difficult to frame a tax law that proves truly general in its application. The problems posed by unintended discriminations of this sort are similar in principle to those dealt with here. They greatly add to the practical difficulties of devising an efficient tax system.

---

[1] The present argument relates to payment of a fixed amount by a given taxpayer under different tax formulas. As we shall see later, no ready conclusions can be drawn from this with regard to the effects on taxpayers as a group.

D. EXCESS BURDEN AND REQUIRED YIELD

Before leaving this problem, let us return briefly to the highly restrictive assumptions of the initial case, which provided for a fixed supply of labor and savings, a selective excise, and perfect markets.   In this setting, where the selective excise proved inferior to an income tax, let us now consider the relationship between the level of yield required to finance the same real purchases of government with different taxes, and the resulting level of excess burden.[1]   In particular, let us test the hypotheses that it is efficient to employ such taxes as minimize the yield requirement; and that it is efficient for the government to tax those products which it wishes to purchase.

Obviously the yield requirement cannot be defined in terms of the particular product purchased by government, because the product is held constant; nor can yield requirement be measured in money terms, since different taxes may lead to different prices and money incomes.[2]   This difficulty is avoided if yield requirement is measured by the ratio of tax yield to total income.   The question remains of how to define *total income*.   If we choose the national product at *market* price, we find that the yield-income ratio will be lower under an excise tax than under an income tax.   This is a trivial result that follows by definition.[3]   If the

---

[1] This interesting problem was brought to my attention by Amotz Morag, "Indirect Taxes, Inflation and Development: A Reappraisal of Indirect Taxation in Underdeveloped Countries," unpublished doctoral dissertation, Johns Hopkins University, Baltimore, 1954.   However, my formulation differs from Dr. Morag's.

[2] See pp. 212 and 364ff.

[3] This point may be illustrated readily for the one-product case.   Under income tax finance, the national product at market price equals $Y_m = pQ_c + pQ_g$ where Q_c and Q_g are the amounts bought by consumers and government, respectively.   The yield equals $T = pQ_g$, and the tax rate or yield requirement equals

$$t_1 = \frac{pQ_g}{pQ_c + pQ_g} = \frac{Q_g}{Q_c + Q_g}$$

Under excise-tax finance, and assuming the government purchases to be tax-free, the national product at market price equals $Y_m = (p + u)Q_c + pQ_g$, where u is the unit tax.   The yield equals pQ_g, and the tax rate or yield requirement is

$$t_2 = \frac{pQ_g}{(p + u)Q_c + pQ_g}$$

Assuming government purchases to be taxable, we have $Y_m = (p + u)(Q_c + Q_g)$. The yield equals $(p + u)Q_g$, and the tax rate or yield requirement is

$$t_3 = \frac{(u + p)Q_g}{(p + u)(Q_c + Q_g)} = \frac{Q_g}{Q_c + Q_g}$$

Thus we have $t_1 = t_3 > t_2$.   If we use the national product at factor cost as base, and defining yield requirement as net of taxes on government purchases, we have throughout $t = Q_g/(Q_g + Q_c)$.   The difference between t_1, t_2, and t_3 is definitional and of no particular interest.

yield requirement is measured by the ratio of tax payments to national product at *factor cost*, the change from an income tax to a general consumption tax leaves the yield requirement unchanged. Since the two taxes are equivalent under present assumptions, this is as it should be. Let us then adopt the foregoing definition of yield requirement.

Consider first a case of two products X and Y, which are produced under conditions of *constant* cost, and assume that the government buys X only. Transfer of a given amount of resources to public use is to be financed by an income tax. As the income tax is imposed, consumers reduce their purchases of both X and Y, assuming both to be superior goods. Since the government buys X, there results an increase in the output of X and a reduction in the output of Y. With constant costs, relative prices remain unchanged. The yield requirement or tax rate is independent of changes in the composition of output.

Now let the income tax be replaced by an excise on X. This tax enters as a wedge between the net price of X and its market price, the ratio of net prices being unchanged. The market price of X rises relative to that of Y, and consumer purchases shift from X to Y. Since relative net prices of X and Y are unaffected, the yield requirement remains unchanged.

The situation differs once *variable* costs are introduced. Let us suppose that both X and Y are produced under conditions of increasing cost. The government again enters the market and purchases X with income tax finance. A change in relative prices results. The government demand is directed entirely at X, and chances are that the output of X will rise. In this case, the ratio of net prices p_x^n/p_y^n will rise; and the more it rises, the higher will be the yield requirement (the ratio of yield to national product at market price) that must be met to secure the given resource transfer.[1]

Now, let the income tax be replaced by an excise tax on X, the product bought by government. The excise tax again enters as a wedge between the net and market price of X, thus raising p_x^m/p_y^m for any given ratio of net prices p_x^n/p_y^n. The tendency for p_x^m/p_y^m to rise is offset in part by the tendency of p_x^n/p_y^n to fall, as consumers move from X to Y in response to the substitution effect. On balance, production of X is less than under the income tax. We are left with some rise in p_x^m/p_y^m and some

---

[1] However, it is not certain that the output of X will rise. As the income tax is imposed, private buyers will reduce their purchases of both X and Y in response to the income effect; as the government purchases X, they will increase their purchases of Y and reduce those of X on account of the substitution effect. Thus, the output of x may either rise or fall depending on the weight of the various effects. If it falls or rises only slightly, the yield requirement will be reduced accordingly. (See page 147, note 1.)

fall in $p_x{}^n/p_y{}^n$. It follows that the yield requirement is smaller under the excise on X than under the income tax. This occurs even though the excise on X involves an excess burden that does not arise under the income tax. Indeed, the very ease of substitution of Y for X which makes for a large excess burden under the excise tax also makes for low yield requirement. Thus, the selective excise tax should be avoided precisely where it promises a lower yield requirement.

Let us consider now a situation where the excise tax is imposed on product Y, which is not bought by government. Following the same reasoning, we find that the yield requirement is larger under the excise tax than under the income tax. The same ease of substitution of Y for X which makes for a heavy excess burden under the excise tax now makes for a relatively lower yield requirement under the income tax. In this case, a low yield requirement and a reduction in excess burden are compatible objectives.

Finally, we compare financing by an excise tax on X with financing by an excise tax on Y. By similar reasoning as before, we find that the yield requirement is less if the excise is on X, the product purchased by government, than if it is on Y. But, this does *not* establish a presumption that the excise tax on X is preferable. The fact that the yield requirement is lower does not prove that the excess burden must be smaller. In a situation where more than two goods are involved, the excess burden under the tax on X will be larger if other goods are more readily substituted for X than for Y. The excess burden under the tax on Y will be greater if the opposite situation holds. While the yield requirement is always less if the excise tax is on the product purchased by government, there is no presumption that the excess burden will be less if such a tax is used.

E. THE RELATION OF NEUTRALITY AND EQUITY

After all qualifications are allowed for, there remains no simple way of rating taxes according to excess burden. Only the head tax can be given a categorical preference. For the other taxes, we are left with the common-sense view that the excess burden of more general taxes tends to be smaller than that of selective taxes; and with the formal conclusion that taxes on goods and services which have a low rate of substitution tend to be superior to taxes on those which have high rates of substitution.

This vagueness of result is unfortunate, the more so since the avoidance of excess burden is only one consideration among others in choosing between different taxes. Thus, tax A may involve a lesser excess burden than tax B, but it may be inferior on other grounds. To balance the two considerations, a more precise measure of excess burden is required.

Conceivably, the equity view of society may be such that the very tax which involves the least excess burden also proves the most equitable. But this is not the case. The head tax, that star performer in efficiency, ranks low on equity grounds; and the income tax, especially if progressive, involves an excess burden. Thus, the art of tax policy requires the finding of tax forms that are more or less acceptable on both grounds. If height were related to income, a tax on height would provide an opportunity to impose what is considered an equitable tax, and to do so without an excess burden. The problem is one of finding "handles" to which one may attach taxes that are neither inequitable nor burdensome.[1] But, unfortunately, such handles are hard to come by.

To a long line of writers, a happy coincidence between equity and efficiency seemed to apply to a tax on the rent of land. From the physiocrats, through Ricardo and Henry George, this appeared to be a tax that was not only efficient, since it did not distort the use of resources, but equitable, since the rent of land was unearned income par excellence.[2] Later it came to be recognized that ground rents were insufficient to meet yield requirements in the modern economy. Thus the argument was expanded to relate to all surplus income, whether from land or other factors.[3] Once this was done, the tax base was widened greatly.

However, there now arises the difficulty of identifying surplus income so that taxes can be assessed thereon. Surplus income, defined as income in excess of the minimum required to call forth a given service, cannot be determined in advance unless the supply schedule of the taxpayer's services is known. Thus an excess burden may result in the very process of finding a tax that will avoid it.

This difficulty aside, the underlying concept of equity, which centers on the distinction between earned and unearned—or functional and rent—income, does not agree with the widely accepted notion of taxation according to *total* income, regardless of its source. If the framework of equity is built around the proposition that equal treatment should be given to taxpayers with equal income, any tax that meets the requirement of horizontal equity also reduces the price of leisure. There is no way out of this dilemma, short of the Laputan system of self-assessment,[4] or the interesting but operationally impracticable suggestion of a tax on potential, as distinct from actual, income.[5] Moreover, if the equity

---

[1] See A. C. Pigou, *A Study in Public Finance*, 3d ed., Macmillan & Co., Ltd., London, 1951, p. 73.

[2] See Henry George, *Progress and Poverty*, Doubleday & Company, Inc., New York, 1914, book VII.

[3] See J. A. Hobson, *Taxation in the New State*, Methuen & Co., Ltd., London, 1919; and A. P. Lerner, *The Economics of Control*, The Macmillan Company, New York, 1944, p. 234.

[4] Jonathan Swift, *Gulliver's Travels*, Modern Library, Inc., New York, p. 217.

[5] Lerner, *op. cit.*, pp. 231–238.

concept of income is defined in terms of accretion, any tax that meets the concept of horizontal equity also reduces the rate of substitution of future for present consumption. The conflict is deepened where considerations of vertical equity suggest a progressive tax structure, with regard to either income or consumption.

What is commonly considered an equitable tax thus involves two types of excess burden. The one on saving can be avoided by replacing the general income tax with a tax on consumption; the one on leisure can be avoided by replacing the consumption tax by a head tax. If these solutions interfere with considerations of equity, a choice must be made between equity and the avoidance of excess burden. Society must ask itself what price, in terms of excess burden, it wishes to pay to secure certain equity objectives. In this sense, the narrow criterion of efficiency as avoidance of excess burden must be subordinated to a broader concept of efficiency under which conflicting objectives are reconciled.

While possible conflicts between efficiency (narrowly defined) and equity must be faced, the relation is not wholly one of conflict. Equity considerations suggest that income from different sources should be treated alike; efficiency considerations, except for primary taxation of rent incomes, suggest the same. These considerations apply to the requirement of uniform rates as well as a uniform definition of income for different industries, including the treatment of such controversial items as depreciation or depletion allowances.[1] Similarly, considerations of horizontal equity and efficiency both suggest that a general sales tax is to be preferred to a set of selective excises with differential rates; and that a uniform ad valorem tax is to be preferred to a set of unit taxes that are unequal in ad valorem terms.

[1] See p. 336.

CHAPTER 8

Equal treatment of equals

Perhaps the most widely accepted principle of equity in taxation is that people in equal positions should be treated equally. This principle of equality, or *horizontal equity*, is fundamental to the ability-to-pay approach, which requires equal taxation of people with equal ability and unequal taxation of people with unequal ability. Beyond this, the principle of equality is accepted by many who do not lay much store in the ability-to-pay approach. Indeed, it has been suggested that the rule of horizontal equity is valid, even though little can be said about the matter of *vertical equity* or about how the taxation of people in different positions should differ.

This is hardly justified. The requirements of horizontal and vertical equity are but different sides of the same coin. If there is no specified reason for discriminating among unequals, how can there be a reason for avoiding discrimination among equals? Without a scheme of vertical equity, the requirement of horizontal equity at best becomes a safeguard against capricious discrimination—a safeguard which might be provided equally well by a requirement that taxes be distributed at random. To mean more than this, the principle of horizontal equity must be seen against the backdrop of an explicit view of vertical equity.[1]

---

[1] Henry C. Simons, in his earlier work, *Personal Income Taxation*, University of Chicago Press, Chicago, 1938, chap. 1, treats the two principles as strictly coordinate. In his later work, *Federal Tax Reform*, University of Chicago Press, Chicago, 1950, p. 11, horizontal equity is considered of primary importance.

A. C. Pigou, *A Study in Public Finance*, 3d ed., Macmillan & Co., Ltd., London, 1951, p. 44, distinguishes nicely between the requirement that an equal sacrifice should be imposed on people in equal positions (which is the essence of horizontal equity) and Mill's principle that an equal sacrifice should be imposed on all people (which is but one among other interpretations of vertical equity).

An objective index of equality or inequality is needed to translate either principle into a specific tax system. While the earlier discussion of the ability-to-pay argument was in terms of faculty, the later discussion was increasingly in terms of income.[1] Nevertheless, there remains considerable disagreement on how the index of equality should be defined. In the present chapter, some points of disagreement are considered briefly. The chapter may be looked upon as a continuation of our earlier discussion of ability-to-pay, but it also bears on the problem of budget determination by voting. The vote on tax policy must be by reference to a specific tax formula; and the principle of equal treatment requires that this formula be in terms of a meaningful index of equality. Moreover, the index of equality and the equity principle of equal treatment bear upon the extent to which the efficiency principle of neutrality can be realized, and vice versa.[2]

A. THE INDEX OF EQUALITY

In choosing between various indexes of equality, two problems may be distinguished. The first is whether the proper index is given by income or by consumption; the second is just how income should be defined in this connection.

Consumption versus Income

Let us begin with the choice between income and consumption as an index of equality or inequality. Income is defined for this purpose as accretion, or increase in net worth plus consumption during a given period. To simplify matters, we shall assume that all income is realized, so that the distinction between realized and accrued income need not be considered for the time being. Consumption is defined to include outlays for current as well as for durable consumer goods, the difficulty of distinguishing between the latter and investment being disregarded at this point.

Strangely enough, it has been argued by a long succession of distinguished authors that a tax on income is inequitable because it is said to involve the double taxation of saving. Suppose that an income tax is imposed. Someone who wishes to consume pays a tax on his income and may apply the entire remainder to consumption. Someone who wishes to save also pays a tax on his income, thus reducing the capital that he can invest; and later on, he must pay an additional tax on his interest income out of this reduced investment. This subjects saving to double taxation.[1]   The double taxation, it is argued, will be avoided if saving is exempted and consumption only is taxed.

Now, there can be no question that a tax on income differs from a tax on consumption. The consumption tax is preferable to the saver, and the income tax to the consumer, the same yield being raised in both cases. Moreover, we have seen that under certain conditions the income tax imposes an excess burden, while the consumption tax does not.[2]   These differences exist, but it is a non sequitur to conclude that the principle of equal treatment, or horizontal equity, requires the exclusion of saving from the tax base.   Saving should be *excluded* if the concept of equity is such as to define the index of equality in terms of consumption.   Saving should be *included* if the concept of equity is such as to define the index of equality in terms of income or accretion.   In this case, the recipient's disposition over his income, whether for consumption, hoarding, or investment, does not matter.   Interest on accumulation is a further accretion, and the tax thereon is a new tax on new income.   If this view is taken, it is not the income tax that involves "double taxation," but the consumption tax that involves undertaxation of the saver.

Confusion is compounded if it is argued that the income tax should exclude saving because income is actually equal to consumption.   Now it might be useful for purposes of capital theory to define income as consumption,[3] but this is quite irrelevant in the present case.   What matters is that tax X, which taxes accretion, differs from tax Y, which taxes consumption.   To avoid semantic troubles, it might be well to refer to the income tax as an accretion tax.

Depending on the initial choice of proper index, the tax on accretion (income) will be more equitable than the tax on consumption, or vice versa.   Before a final choice is made between the two taxes, other considerations—involving differences in economic effects and possible excess

---

[1] See John Stuart Mill, *Principles of Political Economy*, ed. W. J. Ashley, Longmans, Green & Co., Ltd., London, 1921, pp. 814–817; Alfred Marshall, *Official Papers*, Macmillan & Co., Ltd., London, 1926, p. 338; Irving Fisher, "Double Taxation of Savings," *American Economic Review*, vol. 29, no. 1, pp. 16–33, March, 1939, and with H. W. Fisher, *Constructive Income Taxation*, Harper & Brothers, New York, 1942, which contains a comprehensive bibliography on this matter; Pigou, *op. cit.*, part II, chap. 10; C. W. Guillebaud, "Income Tax and Double Taxation," *Economic Journal*, vol. 45, no. 179, pp. 484–492, September, 1935; Simons, *Personal Income Taxation;* R. A. Musgrave, "A Further Note on the Double Taxation of Savings," *American Economic Review*, vol. 39, no. 3, pp. 549–550, September, 1939; and N. Kaldor, *An Expenditure Tax*, George Allen & Unwin, Ltd., London, 1955, especially pp. 54–78.

[2] It will be recalled that an absolute statement about the superiority of the income tax can be made only on the assumptions of flexible saving, pure competition, and fixed labor supply. See pp. 142ff.

[3] See Fisher, *op. cit.*, and his basic contributions to capital theory in *The Theory of Interest*, The Macmillan Company, New York, 1930.

burdens—are necessary. Considerations of equity need not be decisive; at the same time, a tax that involves an excess burden may be preferable on balance to one that does not.[1]

The only meaningful way in which the terms *double taxation* or *undertaxation* can be used in connection with equity is to indicate discrimination for or against particular taxpayers in terms of a given index of equality. It is this index that must be decided upon *first* to prove that double taxation or undertaxation occurs, rather than the reverse order.[2] By the same token, the concept of double taxation as *taxing a thing more than once* is fallacious. If three taxes on product X add up to an ad valorem rate which is less than that of a single rate on Y, X is undertaxed, not double-taxed.

All this is not to say that consumption lacks merit as an index of equality. It may be argued that a person should be taxed in accordance with what he takes out of the common pool and not in accordance with what he puts into it. This view may be found in Hobbes, and has recently been advanced by Kaldor.[3] In favor of income as a sensible index of equity, it may be argued that a person's economic capacity, and hence his ability to contribute, depends upon his wealth and not upon the way he chooses to use it. The advantages of accumulation in terms of social standing and security may be far from negligible even if no eventual consumption occurs. There are arguments on either side. The choice, as in all matters of equity, is essentially a matter of value judgment. The very fact that income has come to be accepted increasingly as the proper index is evidence that it has proven a superior expression of prevailing social philosophy; but this does not prove that income is *the* true index, or that social philosophy may not change.

Nor can it be argued that income is the appropriate index for those who desire progressive taxation and wish to reduce inequality, and that consumption is the appropriate index for those who wish to impose regressive taxation so as to increase inequality. As a matter of historical experience, we find that the income tax has been the vehicle of progressive

---

[1] See p. 158.

[2] The same view is taken by N. Kaldor, *op. cit.*, p. 81.

[3] *Ibid.*, p. 52, and Kaldor's references to Hobbes, *Leviathan*, chap. 30. Kaldor, in his spirited and imaginative book, attempts to marshal all possible, and some not-so-possible, points in favor of a spendings tax. Apart from the Hobbesian principle, he holds that the income tax in practice is so inefficient a measure of accretion that a spendings tax would be superior. In reaching this conclusion, insufficient attention it seems to me, is paid to the practical difficulties of a spendings tax. Kaldor's case is strongest when he holds that the spendings tax is desirable as a matter of economic policy. It serves to discourage dissaving and luxury consumption by people with large properties, if not high incomes, and thus raises the level of capital formation without reverting to regressive taxation.

taxation, and that the major sources of sales and excise taxation have been regressive. At the same time, there is no logical necessity for this. Once the transition is made from a tax on commodities to a personal tax on consumer expenditures, the spendings tax may be applied with progressive rates, no less than the income tax.

To be sure, a rate formula that involves a given progression in terms of absolute amounts of consumption will be less progressive, in terms of income, than an income tax that applies the same bracket rates to the income base.[1] However, the marginal rates of progression under a consumption or spendings tax may be raised readily above 100 per cent, whereas this cannot be done under the income tax. Disincentive effects on spending may be held desirable, whereas those on work effort are not. However, there is an inconsistency in comparing the progressivity of the spendings tax in terms of income with that of the income tax. If spending is the proper index of equality, then distributional considerations should be taken to apply to spending, and not to income.[2]

Viewed in terms of the Distribution Branch, the choice of the index of equality as well as the choice of the proper state of distribution are questions of social value. Let us now look at the matter in terms of the Allocation Branch. Following the spirit of the benefit rule, the tax formula should give equal treatment to people who would exert identical effective demand for public services, on the basis of true preferences. A tax formula that assesses taxes in relation to income is not without merit for this purpose. There is no reason to expect that goods provided for the satisfaction of social wants are inferior goods. Hence we may expect that a formula which involves a positive relationship between tax liability and income will give us a better approximation of the proper solution than one which imposes the same per capita tax on all. Similar considerations suggest that a tax based on spending gives an even better approximation, provided that the satisfaction of public wants primarily involves outlays on consumer goods; and that the income tax approach is superior where public services involve substantial capital outlays.

The Concept of Income

We shall now proceed on the assumption that income, and not consumption, is to be the index of equality. We must therefore consider the

---

[1] Greater progression in terms of income might be achieved by relating progression under the spendings tax to per cent of income spent. This requires determination of income as well as of spending.

[2] Kaldor, *op. cit.*, pp. 49, 238, and 241, recommends a progressive spendings tax with marginal rates up to 300 per cent, and defends the proposal by arguing that such a tax need not be less progressive in terms of income than the income tax. This comparison is not admissible in principle, if spending is considered the proper index of equality.

specific definition of income for this purpose.   The subject may be dealt with briefly, since it has been developed at length by Henry Simons and other authors;[1] little can be added as far as the principle of the matter is concerned.

The concept of taxable income which has gained increasing acceptance among fiscal theorists is that of total accretion.   Income is defined to equal consumption during a given period, plus increase in net worth. According to this concept, all accretions to wealth are included, in whatever form they are received or from whatever source they accrue.   Factor earnings such as rents, interest, profits, and wages are included along with gifts, inheritances, gambling profits, and any kind of windfall.   All of these accretions are included, independent of whether they occur at regular or irregular intervals, whether they are expected, and whether they are realized (translated into cash).   Similarly, all diminutions of wealth are allowed for, whether they take the form of wear and tear, technical obsolescence, decline in value due to change in the market, gambling losses, or what not.   Administrative considerations do not always permit drastic adherence to this general concept of accretion, but this does not obviate the need for a consistent theoretical concept.   Without such a concept as a normative standard, we have no basis from which to deal with each practical problem as it arises.[2]

Realization versus Accretion.   According to our broad definition, income is defined as accretion to wealth, equal to consumption plus increase in net worth during the period.   Increase in net worth is measured by comparing net worth valued at market price for the beginning and the end of the period.   All assets, including cash, debt claims, equity, and real property, are included, and all liabilities are deducted.   If a piece of real property rises in value from $1000 to $2000, there has been a corresponding accretion to wealth.   This will be the case whether the property was sold or not.   In other words, it is irrelevant to our measure of accretion

[1] Among Henry C. Simons's brilliant writings in this field, see *Personal Income Taxation*, and *Federal Tax Reform*.   For earlier statements of the central concepts of income, see Georg Schanz, "Der Einkommenbegriff und die Einkommensteuergesetze," *Finanz Archiv*, vol. 13, 1896; and R. M. Haig, "The Concept of Income: Economic and Legal Aspects," in R. M. Haig (ed.), *The Federal Income Tax*, Columbia University Press, New York, 1921.   For a later refinement, see William Vickrey, *Agenda for Progressive Taxation*, The Ronald Press Company, New York, 1947.   Also see Fritz Neumark, *Theorie und Praxis der modernen Einkommensbesteuerung*, A. Francke, Bern, Switzerland, 1947; and Royal Commission on the Taxation of Profits and Income, *Final Report*, Cmd. 9474, London, 1954.   For an excellent analysis of the income concept, see N. Kaldor, *op. cit.*, pp. 54–78.

[2] For a contrary opinion, see the majority report of the Royal Commission on the Taxation of Profits and Income, *op. cit.*, pp. 7–12, where it is held that attempts at a general definition of taxable income are unprofitable.   The more systematically reasoned minority report accepts the accretion concept.

whether gains have been transformed into cash, that is, realized, or whether appreciated assets are retained. Similarly, depreciation is taken care of automatically, as changes in the value of real assets, whether due to wear and tear or any other reason, will be reflected in accretion thus determined.

This view of the matter conflicts with the conventional accounting approach, according to which income is recognized only when gains are converted into cash.[1] At this time, a gain or loss will be recorded on the income statement. This is the general principle, but an exception is made with regard to depreciation charges. Here, a loss of value is charged against certain assets on the basis of a presumptive schedule, assumed to reflect their decline in value over the period of useful life. The charges appear as costs on the income statement and as additions to depreciation reserves on the balance sheet.

This procedure is designed essentially to record current costs and receipts and to measure profits from current business operations. The emphasis is on the income statement, and the balance sheet is adapted accordingly. Since the income statement is designed to show profits from current *operations* only, it does not record all changes in value during the period. Accordingly, assets must be carried at cost in the balance sheet. Gains or losses from changes in their value, other than wear and tear, which is allowed for by presumptive depreciation, cannot be recorded until they are realized.

From the economist's point of view, the resulting changes in the balance sheet may be quite misleading. In order to assess the position of a firm, we must determine the entire change in net worth, whatever the source. We must include not only gains and losses from current operations but also changes in net worth due to all other factors. To allow for these factors, including changes in the market value of all assets, income must be determined as the change in net worth as valued at the beginning and the end of the period. The criterion of realization becomes irrelevant.

While it seems impossible in principle to justify the requirement that income must be realized before it is taxed, a good defense of the realization rule may be made in pragmatic terms. It is the function of accounting rules to result in business statements that are as reliable and meaningful as possible in their practical application. Since valuation without

---

[1] See W. Paton and A. C. Littleton, *An Introduction to Corporate Accounting Standards*, American Accounting Association, Chicago, 1940, pp. 48–49. The authors note that earnings must not be confused with realization, and that revenue accrues and exists before it is realized. However, realization is held crucial as a basis for revenue recognition in the accounts. Revenue cannot be recognized and measured prior to completion and disposition of the product.

sale is a difficult matter, the inclusion of unrealized gains may involve a high degree of arbitrariness. The distortions which result from faulty evaluation may be worse than those which result if only realized gains are taken into account. Though realization is irrelevant in principle, in practice we may not be able to administer an income tax based on valuation.

Let us suppose, now, that valuation without realization is not feasible. Depreciation must then be charged on the basis of a presumptive schedule.[1] Gains or losses from other changes in the value of capital assets are disregarded until they are realized and then treated like other income at that time. This procedure discriminates in favor of people who enjoy unrealized accretion. Also, it offends the neutrality rule since it interferes with decisions to sell or buy capital assets.

To avoid such interference, capital gains and losses may be disregarded when realized, but only at the cost of even greater conflict with our index of horizontal equity. Since capital gains weigh more heavily in large than in small incomes, this policy, moreover, interferes with considerations of vertical equity. In view of these unpleasant alternatives, compromises are made in the tax law of the United States by providing for the taxation of gains at reduced rates together with only partial loss allowance. This special treatment, however, is reserved for gains or losses from the sale of assets that are not considered stock in trade. Gains or losses from the sale of assets that *are* stock in trade are taxed fully. Since they must be sold in the regular course of business, the flow of transactions will not be interfered with in this case.[2]

All these solutions are more or less unsatisfactory. As a compromise between an ideal and a practicable solution, it has been suggested that valuation be required, but at set intervals only. In this case, the problem of valuation without sale becomes more manageable. In the limiting case, one may apply a statutory presumption of realization at the time of the taxpayer's death. Thus it has been suggested by Henry Simons that capital gains should be treated as if realized at the time of death; and that an income tax be paid thereon, prior to the settling of the estate tax.[3] While proposals of this sort still encounter administrative difficulties, the latter hardly explain the lack of attention the proposals have received at the practical level. Rather, the explanation is found in an unwillingness to enforce the degree of progression that has been provided for in the nominal structure of income tax rates.

[1] See p. 338 for a discussion of the proper rate of depreciation.

[2] On the entire matter of capital gains taxation, see Lawrence H. Seltzer, *The Nature of Tax Treatment of Capital Gains and Losses*, National Bureau of Economic Research, Inc., New York, 1951.

[3] Henry Simons, *Federal Tax Reform*, p. 78.

Before leaving the problem of capital gains, let us note the proposition that capital gains which reflect a decline in the rate of interest should not be considered taxable income.[1] This view is correct if income is defined as potential earning power, but it is not correct if income is defined as potential spending power for consumption. In terms of our later discussion, the question is whether changes in the money value of net worth should be deflated by an index of capital-good or of consumer-good prices.[2] The choice between the two again depends on one's interpretation of the index of equality and the concept of horizontal equity.

Income in Real Terms versus Income in Money Terms. As a matter of principle, it is obvious that accretion as an index of equality should be measured in real terms. The value of net worth at the end of the period must be deflated in order to determine the change in net worth in real terms.

In practice, application of this principle has been urged primarily in two connections. One is the exclusion from taxable income of capital gains that reflect an increase in the general price level. This follows from our principle of real income, but the principle applies over a much wider range. Not only should the appreciation of real assets due to price inflation be excluded; but allowance should be made for losses suffered from the holding of claims (whether money or debt), and profits should be recognized from the gain that debtors experience when the real value of their obligations falls.

The other instance in which an adjustment in price level has been proposed is that of depreciation charges. After an inflationary period, when replacement cost has risen, depreciation at original cost does not permit the investor to recover the real value of his outlay. This argument is not without merit, but the principle of real value must be applied to the entire balance sheet. To illustrate, consider the balance sheet of a business that at the beginning of the period includes on the asset side, $80 million of real assets and $20 million of cash assets, and on the liability side $30 million of net worth and $70 million of debt. No operation occurs during the period, but the price level doubles. Revaluing real assets accordingly, the net worth at the end of the period equals $110. At the same time, the real value of net worth, in terms of the old price level, equals only $55. Thus accretion in real terms equals $25.* In such a system, depreciation is charged automatically, in accordance with the remaining market value of real assets, rather than in terms of original cost.

It now remains to determine the appropriate price index. In the case

---

[1] See Seltzer, *op. cit.*, pp. 8–18, and Kaldor, *op. cit.*, p. 44.

[2] See p. 381.

* This in turn equals the gain from reduced real value of indebtedness minus the loss from reduced value of claims.

of the individual taxpayer, an index of consumer prices seems in order, although difficulties arise in the treatment of saving. If saving is for purposes of potential consumption, it is proper to deflate by the prices of consumer goods. If saving is for purposes of continuous accumulation, it may be more appropriate to deflate by the prices of capital goods.[1]

For the balance sheet of the corporation, net worth might be deflated by the prices of such capital goods as comprise its real assets. This corresponds to the view of the corporation as an entity. If we look at the corporate net worth as assessed by the individual shareholders, an index of consumer prices may be more appropriate.

It is clear enough as a matter of principle that all assets and liabilities should be adjusted for changes in price level and that accretion should be measured in real terms. Yet it is hardly possible in practice to carry out all these adjustments. With minor exceptions such as inventory valuation, the income concept is, in effect, defined in money terms. In view of this, equity may be impaired rather than improved by piecemeal adjustments to allow for price-level change in selected parts of the system.[2]

Factor Earnings versus Transfers. The distinction between income which constitutes factor earnings and income which constitutes transfers is of fundamental importance to many aspects of economic analysis, but it is irrelevant in the present connection. An accretion occurs whether the addition to net worth is in the form of wages, profits, or other factor shares, or whether it is in the form of bequests, gifts, gains from gambling, or prizes. The origin of income does not enter the picture.

Given this broad concept of accretion, the total base of income as determined for tax purposes could exceed total income as measured in the national accounts.[3] For instance, gifts might be included as income to the recipient, but considered an income use (and hence not deducted) by the donor. Such conceptual differences need cause no concern. The concept of income in the context of horizontal equity is not the same as the concept of income as it appears in the national accounts or the theory of production. The one is a concept in social policy, whereas the other is a concept in production measurement. There is no reason why the two should coincide, as applied either to individuals or to the group as a whole.

Fluctuating versus Stable Income. According to the basic concept of income as accretion, it is irrelevant whether income is received period-

---

[1] See p. 381.

[2] See p. 334. On this general problem, see E. Cary Brown, *Depreciation Adjustments for Price Changes*, Harvard University Bureau of Business Research, Boston, 1952; and J. Keith Butters, *Inventory Accounting and Policy*, Harvard University Bureau of Business Research, Boston, 1949.

[3] We are disregarding here the many deductions, exclusions, and exemptions that in fact render taxable income very much smaller than net national product at factor cost.

ically or at irregular intervals. The occurrence of volatile income would raise no problem were it not for the fact that the rate structure of the income tax is progressive and that exemptions are allowed for. Because of this, recipients of fluctuating income may pay a higher rate of tax than recipients of stable income pay. This violates the principle of equal treatment. There is no particular reason why the index of equality should be defined in terms of income received over a one-year period rather than over several years. Indeed, a good case could be made for defining the index of equality in terms of lifetime income. Short of such an extreme solution, unequal treatment due to fluctuating incomes may be avoided by averaging devices designed at least to aid the more volatile types of income.[1] Or certain volatile incomes such as bequests could be given special treatment.

Expected versus Unexpected Income. Similar considerations apply to the distinction between expected and unexpected income, or income earned in the ordinary course of business and income obtained from an occasional source. Unless unexpected or irregular incomes give rise to problems of inequity because they are volatile, they do not pose a particular difficulty. An addition to net worth is an accretion, whether regular or irregular, expected or unexpected. It may be most important, as a matter of incentive, to distinguish between the taxation of expected and unexpected income; but it is not relevant in defining the index of equality in terms of accretion.[2]

Imputed Income. Not all accretion to wealth takes the form of income obtained in the market or of gains in the value of assets held. Food grown and consumed on farms constitutes an accretion to wealth just as wages used to purchase food are an accretion. Rent saved by owner occupancy constitutes an accretion to wealth no less than salary spent on rent or interest received on alternative investments. Services rendered by housewives constitute income as significant as wages spent on hired help or wages foregone by staying home. While a line must be drawn somewhere short of including all services rendered to oneself, the particular line of division remains arbitrary.

At the same time, failure to allow for imputed incomes leads to unequal treatment of people in essentially equal positions. Deductibility of mortgage interest without counting imputed rent on owner-occupied residences discriminates against the tenant; full taxation of the wife's wage income without adequate allowance for child-care expenses discriminates against employed mothers, and so forth. To avoid discrimi-

---

[1] See Henry C. Simons, *Personal Income Taxation*, pp. 153 and 212, and *Federal Tax Reform*, p. 40; Vickrey, *op. cit.*, pp. 164–198, and "Averaging Income for Income Tax Purposes," *Journal of Political Economy*, vol. 47, pp. 379–397, 1939.

[2] See p. 331.

natory results, the treatment of imputed income must be aligned carefully with the treatment of deductible costs.

Cost of Earning. By the nature of the accretion concept, income must be defined in net terms. Costs of acquiring income must be deducted, but these costs are not easily defined. The classical writers argued that consumption for subsistence should be deducted from income, regarding such outlays as a cost of production.[1] Others held that allowance should be made for the differences in hardship involved in obtaining various kinds of income. This led not only to the distinction between earned and unearned income and the recommendation that the latter be taxed more heavily but also to Pigou's formulation of sacrifice in which the disutility of work is allowed for.[2]

In the modern income tax, deductions are allowed for certain outlays that are considered costs of earning income, but the distinction between consumption and what constitutes cost of earning income is not clear-cut. The same outlay frequently serves both purposes. The problem is illustrated by the treatment of such cost items as work clothing, transportation to work, child care in the mother's absence, and insurance in hazardous work. All these points involve more or less arbitrary decisions. Even more far-reaching questions arise with regard to expenditures on education, which may be looked upon as costs of securing future income,[3] or expenditures for health, which may be regarded as costs of maintaining one's capacity to work.

The Tax-paying Unit

Suppose the structure of society is such that the composition of all tax-paying units is the same, consisting of, say, husband, wife, and two children. In this case, the problem of defining horizontal equity is solved by defining the index of equality. Since tax-paying units differ greatly, a further problem arises. This is the definition of the units between which equality shall be established.

[1] See Edwin R. Seligman, *Progressive Taxation in Theory and Practice*, 2d ed., American Economic Association, Princeton University Press, Princeton, N.J., 1908, p. 208.

[2] See A. C. Pigou, *A Study in Public Finance*, 3d ed., Macmillan & Co., Ltd., London, 1951, p. 64; also Lange's suggestion that to obtain a truly equal distribution of income, the socialist community would have to give all people an equal income but then require that part of this income must be paid back to the state in the purchase of jobs. The least desirable job would carry the lowest price and leave the highest income, and vice versa for desirable jobs. (One wonders whether teachers' salaries are determined on this basis!) See O. Lange and F. M. Taylor, *On the Economic Theory of Socialism*, ed. Benjamin E. Lippincott, University of Minnesota Press, Minneapolis, 1938, p. 102.

[3] See Seymour Harris, "Economics of Higher Education," *American Economic Review*, vol. 43, no. 3, pp. 344–357, June, 1953.

A family of six with a given income will be less well off than a unit of one with the same income, and so forth. This is recognized by granting exemption or tax credits in relation to family size. Similar consideration is given to groups subject to particular needs, such as the blind.[1] How these exemptions or credits should be scaled is another problem in social policy, along with choosing the index of equality that is to be applied.

The problem of the tax-paying unit, noted in the preceding paragraph, arises within the context of a proportional tax system. The definition of the tax-paying unit poses additional problems in the progressive system. This is particularly important regarding the treatment of income received by husband and wife. The current system in the United States of splitting the income raises the tax advantages enjoyed by the married taxpayer, compared with the single person, far beyond those given by an additional exemption. Since the benefits derived from income splitting differ with the size of income, the definition of the tax-paying unit poses problems not only in horizontal but also in vertical equity.

Deductions for Merit Wants

Before leaving the problems that arise in defining horizontal equity in terms of accretion, let us note briefly a major and increasingly popular infringement on this objective. This is the use of special deductions as a device to subsidize merit wants.

One type of deduction is illustrated by the allowance for medical expenditures, limited in amount and limited to outlays that are large, relative to income. The purpose here may be to recognize general need as well as to support particular uses of income. Another instance, more clearly dealing with a subsidy to merit wants, is the case of charitable contributions. Similar in effect to a matching grant, provision for charitable deductions reduces the opportunity cost of virtue as the tax rate rises. The social importance of the combination of high tax rates and liberal allowance for such contributions can hardly be overestimated. It permits quasi-budgetary finance of objectives that would not be supportable by legislative action. This provision can be looked upon as a serious offense against the principle of horizontal—or, for that matter, vertical—equity; or it can be looked upon as a splendid device for providing finance for such objectives.

In all, the possibility of adjusting the concept of taxable income so as to serve particular policy objectives both strengthens and weakens the

---

[1] Note in this connection the double role of exemptions. One role is to permit differentiation according to family size in lieu of applying different rates to tax-paying units having equal incomes but different family size. The other role is to serve as a device of progression where the term *exemptions* is applied to what in fact is a first bracket with a marginal rate of zero.

income tax.   On the one hand, the tax becomes a more flexible instrument of policy.   On the other, the granting of special provisions, once permitted for "worthy" purposes, now threatens to undermine the tax base by clauses favoring particular groups.[1]   Again, a clear view of the normative requirements of an equitable income concept is needed to stem such abuse.

B. THE COMPOSITION OF THE TAX STRUCTURE

Let us now turn to the role of various types of taxes in an equitable tax structure.   This may be looked upon first from the point of view of horizontal equity, with accretion as the basic index of equality.   Thereafter, certain considerations of benefit and of regulatory taxation will be added.

Tax Structure and Horizontal Equity

If accretion is accepted as the sole index of equality, there is no place for taxes on consumption, just as there is no place for an income tax if consumption is accepted as the basic criterion.   This much is clear, but the question remains whether certain other taxes—including the corporation income tax, the property tax, and death duties—are disqualified as well.

Taxes on Business Income.   We shall begin with income taxes on business firms, such as the corporation income tax.   The requirement of horizontal equity relates to the relative treatment of individuals.   People in equal income positions are to be treated equally, independent of their sources of income.[2]   The taxation of business income as such does not fit into this picture.   Businesses are owned by people, and business income should be taxed to the owners.

No difficulties arise in applying this principle to the case of proprietorships or partnerships, or to corporation income that is paid out as dividends.   A special problem arises only in the case of retained earnings of corporations.   Even here, the principle is clear.   A way must be found to tax such earnings to the shareholder as if they were distributed.   Various techniques have been proposed to deal with this matter.   Some of them provide a complete solution, including the so-called partnership method and the full-fledged taxation of unrealized capital gains.[3]   Other tech-

[1] See J. A. Pechman, "Erosion of the Individual Income Tax," *National Tax Journal*, vol. 10, no. 1, pp. 1–25, March, 1957.

[2] If a tax on business income *is* imposed, it should be designed to treat different firms equally.   This is a matter of neutrality in the efficiency of allocation rather than horizontal equity in the treatment of individuals.   It is essential that the two be distinguished clearly.

[3] If retained earnings are taxed as capital gains, the question arises whether there will be double taxation when the retained earnings are taxed as dividends at the sub-

niques are more practical but give a partial solution only. One provides for the exemption of dividends paid at the corporate level and formally resembles a tax on undistributed profits. The other provides for crediting at the personal level of tax payments by the corporation, and corresponds to source withholding of the personal income tax. Under either method, profits that are distributed are taxed at the appropriate rate applicable to each particular shareholder, but profits that are retained are taxed at an "average" rate that may exceed or fall short of the rates applicable to particular shareholders. The two methods give the same results, provided we start out with the same corporate profits before tax and assume that the same amount is retained in both cases. However, these assumptions may not be valid. Relief to the shareholder is justified only if the corporation tax is not passed on. Where the credit is given at the corporate level, that much less in tax is paid by the corporation, and that much less is passed on *if* shifting occurs. Where the credit is given at the personal level, part of the tax paid by the corporation may be shifted to begin with, while full deduction is allowed thereafter.

The problem of averaging and other difficulties involved in the various solutions cannot be considered here.[1] Our concern is only with the conclusion that considerations of horizontal equity do not justify an absolute corporation tax, that is, a tax that goes beyond the objective of extending the personal income tax to retained earnings. The principle of horizontal equity relates to equal treatment of *people* in equal positions and to the allocation of the tax bill between people. Corporations are important units of decision making. They have an existence independent of that of their shareholders, especially in the case of large "public" corporations. This separate existence plays a vital role in the functioning of the economy. It has considerable bearing on the reaction of business policy to the imposition of a profits tax. At the same time, corporations are not people. They do not have a tax-paying ability of their own, in the sense that the cost of public services may be placed on corporations instead of on people. If a corporation tax is imposed, somebody's wealth must be reduced, be it that of the owner, manager, worker, or consumer. Hence, there is no rationale for an absolute corporation tax in a system based on the equity concept

---

sequent time of distribution. The answer is no, because dividends will then be offset by capital losses, so that the shareholder's taxable income will not be increased on balance.

[1] In addition to the above references to Simons and Vickrey, see Richard Goode, *Corporation Income Tax*, John Wiley & Sons, Inc., New York, 1951; and H. M. Groves, "Preliminary Report of the Committee on the Federal Corporate Net Income Tax," *Proceedings of the 42d Annual Conference of the National Tax Association*, 1949, National Tax Association, Sacramento, Calif.

of accretion.[1] As will be seen presently, some forms of an absolute corporation tax may be highly desirable on other grounds; but they are not justified on the basis of horizontal equity or ability to pay.[2]

Property Tax. We now turn to a property tax. If all accretions to wealth are taxed under the income tax, any part of a person's net worth, whatever the particular form in which it is held, has been subject to tax at some past date when the accretion occurred. This being the case, there is no place for a further tax on the holding of property as such.

In the case of income-earning property, the property tax is equivalent to a supplementary income tax on property income. As such it results in unequal treatment between recipients of wage and capital income. With non-income-earning property, the property tax may be considered an income tax on imputed opportunity earnings. It is thus discriminatory unless other types of imputed opportunity earnings are taxed as well. As in the case of the corporation tax, a property tax may be called for on other grounds, but it is not justified in terms of horizontal equity based on accretion.

Death Duties. Finally, we may ask what reason there is, if any, for special tax treatment of accretion through inheritance. Since the receipt of bequests and gifts is a highly volatile form of accretion, proper provision for averaging is of special importance if accretion by bequests was made subject to progressive income tax rates. Moreover, it is necessary to provide for a payment period that is sufficiently long to avoid losses from forced liquidation. At the same time, this leaves intact the principle that bequests, along with other accretions, should be considered income. Viewed in this way, there is no case for differential taxation of accretion by inheritance at either higher or lower rates.

Now this may be too rigid a view. It may be argued that transfers at death, made among close members of the family, do not really add to the wealth of the survivor. If the tax-paying unit is defined in terms of the family group, no accretion has occurred. On this basis, transfers at

---

[1] For a different view, which defends the principle of an absolute corporation tax, see Gerhard Colm, "The Corporation and the Corporation Income Tax in the American Economy," *American Economic Review*, vol. 44, no. 2, pp. 486–501, May, 1954, reprinted in Colm's *Essays in Public Finance and Fiscal Policy*, Oxford University Press, New York, 1955, chap. 5. For a general appraisal of the corporation income tax, see Goode, *op. cit.;* and Richard E. Slitor, "The Corporation Income Tax: A Re-Evaluation," *National Tax Journal*, vol. 5, no. 4, pp. 289–309, December, 1952.

[2] The proposition that there is no case for introduction of an absolute corporation tax need not imply that the existing tax should be repealed. To the extent that the tax has been capitalized, its repeal will lead to windfalls and create a new inequity (in the absence of full taxation of capital gains) without removing an old one. This, however, is a more or less short-run argument that does not apply to future capital accumulation. (See p. 385.)

death may be treated more favorably than other accretions; and the logic of the argument points to the structure of the inheritance tax where progression is related to family status.

Stepping outside the framework of accretion, it may be held that the absolute nature of property rights applies to the living only but lapses wholly or partially at the time of death.   This view of property is in line with an interpretation of equality in terms of equality of opportunity, and the implicit view of distribution in terms of relative positions at the *beginning* of the race.[1]   For these reasons, a tax on estates may be held justified in the context of the Distribution Branch, prior to distribution of the estate and distinct from a possible inheritance tax on the recipients of the shares of the estate.[2]

Benefit Taxation

It is not surprising that a tax structure designed to provide equal treatment, with accretion as the index of equality, should point to the personal income tax as a single tax.   However, other considerations enter and qualify this result.

The case for equal treatment of equals, with income as index of equality, is persuasive enough, if examined in the context of the Distribution and the Stabilization Branches; but there may be instances where other types of taxes are called for in the context of the Allocation Branch. Here, finance by income tax is acceptable only where it serves as an approximation to the proper solution—a solution that involves equal treatment of people with equal levels of effective demand (if truly revealed) for public services.   A more direct approach to this proper solution is available where benefit taxes can be applied.

While specific benefit taxes cannot be applied over a wide range of social wants, there are areas where the use of such taxes is possible. Consider public services, the benefits from which are subject to spatial limitations.   This is illustrated by municipal services or regional developments of the central government.   In either case, such services are properly financed by the residents of the region, unless there is a specific intent of interregional transfer.   This leaves open the question whether finance should be by a regionally limited income tax or whether another

---

[1] Compare John Stuart Mill's conservative position regarding progression in income tax with his radical view on inheritance taxation.   According to the latter, bequests are to be allowed in amounts needed to provide for the education of younger children, while the remainder of the estate should be appropriated by the community.   John Stuart Mill, *Principles of Political Economy*, ed. W. J. Ashley, Longmans, Green & Co., Ltd., London, 1921, pp. 224–226.

[2] Under either principle, the treatment of accretion through gifts may be dealt with along similar lines and requires proper coordination with the treatment of death duties.

index should be applied.   For administrative reasons, the property tax lends itself more readily to taxation with regional differentials than does the income tax, and it is not too bad an index of equal treatment.   Thus, a case may be made for the property tax as a means of financing the cost of regionally limited services.

In other instances, specific benefits may be related directly to particular characteristics of an individual's position.   Specific benefit taxation in relation to property is illustrated by financing road improvements through special assessment, in accordance with road frontage of property; or, somewhat less neatly, by allocating the costs of fire protection on the basis of property values.   Specific benefit taxation in relation to consumption is illustrated by highway finance.   Toll finance, even if held desirable in principle, can be applied to a small part of the road and highway system only.   However, finance by motor-vehicle license or gasoline taxation may offer some approximation to benefit taxation by placing the cost of such services on drivers rather than nondrivers.[1]   The extent to which a gasoline tax will serve as an approximation to benefit taxation depends upon the degree of correspondence between the cost of highway services incurred on particular stretches of road and the taxes collected on gasoline consumed while traveling over these stretches.   Where such correspondence is weak, for example, down-state taxes go to finance up-state roads, the gasoline-tax approach has little merit on benefit grounds.   Taxation of highway users in one region to pay for highway facilities in another may be further removed from benefit taxation than finance by general revenue.   Benefit taxation relates to costs and benefits for the individual.   It cannot be replaced by a concept of group equity.[2]

Considerations of benefit taxation may also be applied to business taxation, although such considerations are limited in scope and may not lead to the customary type of corporation tax.   The benefit tax would apply to all business income rather than to corporations only, and its yield would be much less than that of the corporation tax.   It is frequently argued, in this connection, that the privilege of limited liability is of great advantage to corporations and that they should be called upon to pay for it.   This involves a misunderstanding of benefit taxation. Such taxation is justified only to the extent that the government incurs a

---

[1] The use of gasoline taxes is subject to the same advantages and disadvantages on grounds of efficiency as is the use of tolls.   License fees, in turn, are more or less similar to two-part tariffs.   They would be less objectionable if the proper fee could be determined at the outset.   See p. 139.

[2] On the problem of benefit taxation in highway finance, see James M. Buchanan, "The Pricing of Highway Services," *National Tax Journal*, vol. 5, no. 2, pp. 97–106, June, 1952; and O. H. Brownlee and Walter W. Heller, "Highway Development and Financing," *American Economic Review*, vol. 46, no. 2, pp. 232–251, May, 1956.

cost in granting the privilege. Thus, the yield should not exceed the cost of public control and supervision. Finally, there remains the question whether the benefit tax should be based on the net income of business as the proper index of benefits, or on either gross receipts or factor payments plus profits. In a competitive system, at least, public services to business are reflected in lower prices to the consumer rather than in higher profits to the owner. Thus the appropriate type of benefit tax may be a set of selective excises rather than a tax on profits.

Whatever the difficulties of obtaining an approximation to benefit taxation in each particular case, considerations like these modify the earlier conclusion that the good tax structure should include a personal income tax only. Where objective indices can be found to implement taxation according to benefit, supplements to the general income tax are in order. Notwithstanding much textbook opinion to the contrary, earmarking of taxes is a good procedure for the Allocation Branch, provided that a direct link to benefits can be established. At the same time, earmarking violates the rules of efficient budgeting where no such link exists.

Regulatory Taxation

Further qualifications of the income tax principle arise with regard to regulatory taxes—taxes that by definition are designed to interfere with the equal treatment of equals.

To begin with, there is the use of sumptuary taxes providing a negative case of merit wants. Just as society may wish to encourage certain uses of resources and provide subsidies to accomplish this, so it may discourage other uses and impose penalties for this purpose. Sumptuary taxes, such as discriminatory taxes against liquor and tobacco, are similar in principle to the use of expenditures to support free education or school luncheons. The economist can only note that both interfere with consumer sovereignty, but it is not for him to say that such an interference must always be inefficient if viewed in the broader framework of social values.[1]

Next, taxes may be used to improve the efficiency of resource allocation in the absence of pure competition.[2] Or, they may be used to secure a variety of structural changes that are considered desirable as a matter of public policy. If it is held that bigness is undesirable, whether for economic or other reasons, a progressive tax on business assets or income will be in order. Thus, an absolute tax on business income may be desirable as a means of control, even though it is not justified in terms of horizontal equity. If business is to be attracted to certain industries or regions, for reasons of national defense or to help retarded areas, differential income taxes can be used to accomplish this. Such measures are

[1] See p. 158.
[2] See p. 149.

objectionable from the point of view of horizontal equity, but this does not mean that taxes cannot be used for regulatory purposes. We must only note that the regulatory use of taxation involves a social cost in the form of lessened equity of the tax structure; and we must account for this cost when choosing between tax and other types of control.

C. MULTILEVEL FINANCE

So far, our discussion has been in terms of a fiscal system involving one level of government and one consistent tax plan only. It remains to consider briefly the complications that arise in a federal system where any given individual is a citizen of more than one level of government. The solution depends on what view of federalism we wish to take.

Pure Federalism

Let us begin with a case where state governments (a term here used for regional units) possess full autonomy. They differ from the central government only in area covered. Whereas the central government covers the entire area of the federation, each state government covers only its respective region.

Each state has a budget serving its Allocation Branch, as does the central government. To simplify matters, let us assume for the time being that all services are of such a type that they benefit either individuals in all states or individuals in one state only. The central government will then provide services whose benefits accrue to individuals in all States alike; and each State government will cover those services that benefit only the individuals within its particular boundaries.

Now let us assume further that preferences regarding the satisfaction of social wants are similar among all people with the same incomes. Taxpayers with a given income may then be expected to pay the same central tax in whatever state they live. The principle of equal treatment of equals applies to central taxation on a nationwide basis. At the same time, taxpayers with the same income may pay different state taxes, depending on the state in which they live. Not only may average incomes differ between states, but the citizens of different states may choose to provide for different levels or patterns of public services. The principle of equal treatment applies to state taxes among equals within any one state, but it does not apply on a nationwide level. By the same token, the principle of equal treatment of equals does not apply to total (state plus central) taxes on a nationwide level. This is nothing to object to. Indeed, it is as it should be. The very purpose of fiscal federalism, according to this approach, is to permit different groups living in various states to express different preferences for public services; and this, inevitably, leads to differences in the levels of taxation and public services.[1] The resulting differentiation in tax levels may interfere with the most efficient allocation of resources and location of industries for the region as a whole; but such is the cost of political subdivision, be it on an intranational or international level.

While the general principle is clear, some specific points remain to be noted. First, there is the question of how income that originates in one state and accrues to someone residing in another should be divided between the states. The answer differs for the finance of final and intermediate expenditures of government. Where the finance of final expenditures is concerned, income is properly imputed to the recipient in his state of residence, whether it originates from the outside or not. Where the finance of intermediate expenditures is concerned, income is properly taxable in the state where it originates, since it is here that the benefit is derived.[2]

Next, there is the question of how any one government should treat taxes paid to another government. In the perfect system, no deduction of taxes from taxable income should be permitted. In the ideal solution to the problem of the Allocation Branch, taxes must be considered uses of income aimed at the satisfaction of social wants; thus they would be similar in principle to other uses of income for the satisfaction of private wants. There is no more reason, in principle, for deducting taxes than for deducting private outlays. At the same time, it must be recognized that taxes of the Allocation Branch are determined by voting rules that may leave the minority dissatisfied. Failure to allow deduction of taxes paid to other governments may compound the hardships imposed on minorities and may lead to rates of tax in excess of 100 per cent. In view of this, some allowance may have to be made for taxes paid. The question remains whether the allowance should be at the state or central level, or whether it should be on a mutual basis. For reasons of fiscal discipline at the state level, a good case can be made for limiting deduction to central taxes in computing taxable income for purposes of state taxation; but this is a consideration in fiscal politics rather than in principle. Mutual deduction, moreover, complicates the entire process of budget determination, even though the problem remains determinate at a theoretical level.

Finally, let us drop the assumption that all public services can be divided between those which benefit all citizens of the federation inde-

---

[1] See p. 132, where it was argued that people with similar tastes will tend to move together.

[2] The problem of tax allocation between states is relatively simple if taxes are assumed to stay put, but it becomes exceedingly complicated once the possibility of tax shifting between the residents of various states is introduced.

pendent of the state in which they live, and those which benefit the citizens of one state only.   Allowance must be made for services whose benefits accrue to citizens of states A and B alike but not to citizens of state C; and for services whose benefits accrue in different degrees to citizens of states A, B, and C.   The former case might be handled by establishing a structure of federations, including combinations between A and B, B and C, and A and C; the latter case may be dealt with in the framework of the over-all federation.   Even if we retain the assumption that people with equal incomes have similar preferences regarding public wants, this system leads to unequal treatment of equals in the central tax structure, since the quantity of services received becomes a function of the state where the taxpayer resides.   For any particular service, the greater the differential in benefit levels among residents of various states, the more the service becomes one that is more properly supplied at the state level.

So much for the problem of the Allocation Branch.   The situation differs for the budgeting of the Distribution Branch.   Let us begin with a system where the Distribution Branches of the various state budgets apply their distributional adjustments first, and where the central adjustment is applied after the state adjustments have been made.   In this case, the central adjustment will be applied to incomes adjusted by the states.   As a result, the final distribution will conform with what is considered proper at the central level.   The preceding adjustments at the state level will have a bearing on the required patterns of central taxes and transfers, but they will not affect the final result.   The opposite holds if we assume that the central adjustment comes first and that state adjustments follow.   A situation in which both the state and central governments insist upon their particular patterns of proper distribution as the final result is not feasible: It would lead to a continuous set of adjustments and readjustments without a final equilibrium being reached.

Since one or the other level of government must be given priority, there is much to be said, in the federal system, for permitting this adjustment to be made at the central level.   Unless this is done, distributional adjustments at the state level may come to be nullified by interstate movement, and serious barriers to an optimal location of economic activity may be imposed.

The function of the Stabilization Branch, finally, must be performed largely at the central level.   While some degree of coordination may be attained between the levels, the compensatory function must be coordinated for the nation as a whole, and this requires central action.   The heart of fiscal federalism thus lies in the proposition that the policies of the Allocation Branch should be permitted to differ between states, depending on the preferences of their citizens.   The objectives of the

Distribution and Stabilization Branches, however, require primary responsibility at the central level.

Horizontal Equity in Combined Budgets

We now turn to a somewhat different view of fiscal federalism. It might be held desirable, as a matter of efficiency or equity, to apply the principle of horizontal equity with regard to the total tax bill, including all levels of government. Thus, people in equal positions should pay the same total tax bill in whatever state they live. To accomplish this, the federal tax for a taxpayer living in state A and receiving income Y must consist of a standard amount *minus* that amount by which the state A's tax on income Y exceeds (or *plus* that amount by which state A's tax on income Y falls short of) the average of the state taxes imposed on income Y.

Such a formula would enable a state to vote additional services while assuming only a fraction of the increased cost, since increased state taxes would be offset largely by reduced federal taxes. Fiscal irresponsibility would result. Indeed this is the case to some degree whenever state taxes may be offset against income subject to central tax. This difficulty is avoided if the principle of equal tax treatment of equals is replaced by a new rule, according to which people with equal incomes should experience the same *fiscal residue* or *net* benefit derived from budget operations.[1] The principle requires that benefits from public services must be imputed to individuals in order to measure the fiscal residue; let us assume that this can be done. Thus the equalizing function of the central budget does not induce fiscal irresponsibility. The citizens of different states may provide for varying levels of state services at their cost. If financed by taxes in accordance with benefits, such an arrangement will not affect the fiscal residue that various taxpayers enjoy. Under these conditions, the plan would be more or less similar to that of permitting differentials in the tax structures of the Allocation Branches for the various states while concentrating distributional adjustments at the federal level.

Assurance of a Minimum Level of Public Services

The preceding views of fiscal federalism were based on the proposition that the function of the central-government Allocation Branch should be limited to services whose benefits are nationwide; while the state-government Allocation Branch should supply services whose benefits are limited to citizens of the state, which citizens should be free to determine the

---

[1] See the original contribution by James M. Buchanan, "Federalism and Fiscal Equity," *American Economic Review*, vol. 40, no. 4, pp. 583–599, September, 1950. Also see J. A. Maxwell, *The Fiscal Impact of Federalism*, Harvard University Press, Cambridge, Mass., 1946.

level of public services. This philosophy of fiscal federalism was essentially one of independent units joined only to accomplish overlapping objectives.

We now turn to an entirely different view, according to which it is the obligation of the federation to see to it that the citizens of each state can enjoy a given minimum level of public services. If any one state is too poor to provide this minimum level, even though a required minimum degree of tax effort is made, the federation steps in. It calls for a transfer from wealthy states where the minimum level of public services is provided while tax rates are below the stipulated minimum level. If, however, the citizens of any one state fall short of the required tax effort, no claim for support can be established. Thus the citizens of wealthy states are assured that transfers will be made only where justified by the basic criteria of fiscal deficiency.

This approach contains an element of regional equalization of income, since transfers are made from wealthy to poor regions; and it contains an element of provision for the satisfaction of merit wants, since the equalization refers to minimum standards of social rather than private wants. Inasmuch as the concern is with a minimum level of social wants in general, the appropriate transfer to state budgets is made in a general cash grant.

An alternative view of this approach is an interpretation of fiscal federalism as an assurance to each citizen of the federation that specific social wants, such as elementary education, will be provided for adequately in all states. The social wants covered by this proviso may include those on the border line between nationwide and regional benefit. Or they may include social wants belonging to the state level but recognized as merit wants at the national level. Here we have the rationale for earmarked grants and for matching grants from the central to the state level.

If the considerations of the two preceding paragraphs are combined, redistributional elements may be attached to a specified grant, as is the case if the matching ratio is rendered a function of state need and fiscal ability.

The problems of fiscal federalism are complicated further if the levels of government are expanded beyond two, if overflows of public services from one state to another are allowed for, and if the possibility of mutual taxation (domestic tariff) is considered. The choice between the various suggested approaches as well as other patterns, is not a matter of fiscal analysis only. It is basically a matter of how to interpret the nature of the federation, thus involving political no less than economic considerations.

CHAPTER 9

Budget items in the social accounts

No attempt will be made here to examine in detail the many problems, theoretical and practical, that enter into the construction of social accounts. However, brief consideration will be given to certain major issues posed by the treatment of budget items.[1] These will be considered first with regard to the product and then with regard to the national income approach.

A. BUDGET ITEMS IN THE NET NATIONAL PRODUCT

The social accounts may be thought of as a set of sector accounts, including households, firms, government, and the rest of the world. In each sector account we record expenditures by final buyers on currently produced goods and services, and income earned in the process of current production. By aggregating the expenditure sides of these sector accounts, we obtain a measure of market value of currently produced goods and services. The purpose of this measure, and the reason for undertaking this aggregation, is to obtain a measure of total output, or economic performance. Indeed, the very structure of the sector accounts is designed to yield such an aggregate measure.

---

[1] See *National Income*, 1948 and 1954, supplements to *Survey of Current Business*, U.S. Department of Commerce. For comments dealing largely with the treatment of governmental terms, see Simon Kuznets, "Discussion of the New Department of Commerce Income Series: National Income, a New Version," *Review of Economics and Statistics*, vol. 30, no. 3, pp. 151–179, August, 1948; M. Gilbert et al., "Objectives of National Income Measurement: A Reply to Professor Kuznets," *Review of Economics and Statistics*, vol. 30, no. 3, pp. 179–195, August, 1948; T. C. Schelling, "National Income, 1954 Edition," *Review of Economics and Statistics*, vol. 37, no. 4, pp. 321–335, November, 1955.

Since we are concerned with a measure of total output, two adjustments must be made. The first is to allow for the wear of capital, so as to obtain a measure of net product. The second is to translate the measure of output in money terms into a measure in real terms. This cannot be done meaningfully for any one year, but deflation for price-level change leaves us with a measure of change in real output over time. The main application of the national-product concept, therefore, is to serve (in deflated form) as a measure of change in real output. This must be kept in mind when considering the proper treatment of budget items.

Final Expenditures

On the expenditure side of the budget, a distinction arises between goods and service expenditures and transfer payments. The former are purchase payments for current output. The latter are payments not made in the purchase of currently produced output. Transfer payments, therefore, must be excluded from the measure of current output.

Let us leave for later consideration the location of the dividing line between goods and service expenditures and transfer payments, and consider first how goods and service expenditures should be treated. Here a further distinction must be drawn between expenditures which provide for consumer goods, whether they are current or durable, and expenditures which provide for goods that in turn, as free factors, enter into the production of private firms. The former are referred to as *final* and the latter as *intermediate* expenditures.

Final expenditures are not reflected in private expenditures for consumption and capital formation. They must thus be included in the measure of total output. This much is clear, but there remains the problem of valuation. Privately purchased goods are always valued at market price, reflecting the double sanction of cost on the supply side and consumer preference on the demand side. Goods and services supplied by government are valued at cost when the government purchases resources and itself acts as an agent of production; or by market price when the goods are purchased from private firms. In both cases, consumer evaluation on the demand side is replaced by the more complex mechanism of the political process. This difference in valuation establishes no presumption that recording of government purchases at cost under- or overstates their true value compared with recording of private purchases at market price; but it points to a certain heterogeneity in net national product as a measure of output.

Moreover, sales to government may carry different profit margins from sales to private buyers. If proper deflators are applied, this will not disturb changes in net national product as a measure of changes in total output. At the same time, changes in the ratio of public to private expenditures may not be a proper measure of change in the composition of the real product.[1]

Intermediate Expenditures

Intermediate expenditures of government go to purchase goods and services that do not appear as distinct items in final output. Rather, the expenditures are reflected in the privately produced goods and services into whose production they enter. If we think of the net national product for any one year as the bulk of goods and services that have been produced, it would be double counting to include both the intermediate goods supplied by government and the private goods into which the intermediate goods have entered. The argument is quite analogous to that involved in counting the value added at various stages of production in the private sector, but not the gross value at each stage.

This view of the matter seems sensible, but it is not the basic problem. The purpose of measuring net national product, as noted before, cannot be to measure output for any one year in an "absolute" sense, but to measure changes in real output over a period of years. This being the main purpose of aggregating net national product from the sector accounts, the problem of double counting must be interpreted accordingly. Double counting must be excluded, not so much to provide a better measure of total output for any one year—such measure being unobtainable in the first place—but to prevent capricious changes in the deflated value of net national product.[2] In other words, the product must be defined so as to be invariant to purely structural and financial changes that leave real output unaffected.[3]

A measure of gross payments for production, including gross outlays by business at *all* stages of production, would function as a basis for measuring changes in total output if vertical integration remained unchanged from year to year. Since it does not, gross expenditures cannot be relied upon as a measure of change in economic performance. The concept of

---

[1] See Gottfried Haberler and Everett E. Hagen, "Taxes, Government Expenditures, and National Income," in *Studies in Income and Wealth*, National Bureau of Economic Research, Inc., New York, 1946, vol. VIII, p. 21.

Haberler and Hagen note that the prices of privately produced products include costs plus profits or minus losses, whereas government-produced products are valued at cost alone. Since profits tend to decline more rapidly than costs when income falls (and vice versa when income rises), cyclic changes in the ratio of money expenditure on publicly and privately produced goods are not an accurate reflection of changes in the composition of the real product.

[2] The Department of Commerce discussion (*National Income*) of the product concept is concerned largely with the figures for any given year, with little emphasis on the essential aspect of change.

[3] This principle of invariance is emphasized by Haberler and Hagen, *op. cit.*

net product in terms of final output is to be preferred, since it is invariant to changes in vertical integration.

A further problem of invariance arises in the treatment of intermediate expenditures of government. Here, two consistent approaches are conceivable. The first is to include such expenditures in computing the money value of the net national product, and to obtain changes in real value by deflating with an index of market prices, raised to include the cost of intermediate expenditures. The second is to exclude intermediate expenditures of government and to deflate the money value of the net national product by a simple index of market prices. Both methods would leave our measure of change in real output invariant to changes in the structure of production, involving a substitution of intermediate expenditures for private cost payments.

Both these methods are conceivable, but only the second can be applied. An index of market prices adjusted for the cost of intermediate goods is not available, nor can it be computed. Even if the cost of intermediate expenditures could be added, the weights for the adjusted index do not exist. Weights can only be derived from actual purchases, and these are allocated in response to unadjusted market prices. Since it is inconsistent to apply an index of market prices to the money value of a product that includes intermediate expenditures valued at cost, only the second approach is available. The net national product must be deflated by an index of market price, and intermediate expenditures must be excluded. The product will then be invariant to the substitution of intermediate expenditures for private cost payments.[1]

To illustrate, let us suppose that the government provides increased police protection. Guards previously on the payroll of a private firm are transferred to the public payroll. As a result, the private firm need not engage guards, and its cost of production is reduced. If it lowers prices accordingly, the money value of output is reduced, provided that public expenditures on guards are excluded. Prices are reduced as well, and the measure of market output in real terms remains constant. If the firm does not lower prices, the money value of output remains the same, prices are constant, and real output is unchanged. The principle of invariance is complied with in either case. If public expenditures on guards are included, the measure of output goes up, which is wrong.

---

[1] While changes in vertical integration and changes in intermediate expenditures of government both pose problems of invariance, note that these problems are not the same. In the latter case, the problem is one of consistency in the measure of money output and of the price deflator. In the former case, the price index is not involved. The view of the two problems posing the same issue of double counting (see *National Income*, 1954, p. 39) reflects what seems to me a mistaken preoccupation with national product as an absolute measure of output for any *one* year.

While the principle is clear enough, it is difficult to apply. Services rendered by intermediate expenditures of government are not recorded on the books of business firms. Rather, they appear as reductions in cost that are given no explicit recognition. Data on factor earnings similarly include earnings of factors engaged in the rendering of intermediate services. Thus there is no simple solution to the problem.[1] The only way in which goods and service expenditures of government can be divided between expenditures for final and for intermediate products is through a qualitative analysis of each expenditure item in the budget.[2] This is a difficult undertaking. A few expenditures fall clearly into one or the other category. Thus outlays for a playground may be considered a final expenditure and outlays for production advice to farmers may be considered as an intermediate expenditure. More frequently, the same expenditures benefit both consumers and business firms, thus containing elements of both final and intermediate products. Highways are used for pleasure driving and business transport; education provides consumer satisfaction and raises productivity, and so forth. For this reason, government statisticians should not be blamed too much for failing to exclude intermediate expenditures.[3]

---

[1] Kuznets, in his earlier writings, proposed that business tax payments should be assumed to equal intermediate expenditures, while personal tax payments should be taken to measure final expenditures. See Simon Kuznets, *National Income and Its Composition*, National Bureau of Economic Research, Inc., New York, 1941, vol. I, p. 44, and (with others) *National Product since 1869*, National Bureau of Economic Research, Inc., New York, 1946, p. 23. This assumption is completely arbitrary, and was later discarded by Kuznets himself. See Kuznets, "Discussion of the New Department of Commerce Series," p. 156. Another rule-of-thumb procedure, followed in Sweden (see Erik Lindahl et al., *Wages, Cost of Living and National Income in Sweden, 1860–1930*, P. S. King & Staples, Ltd., London, 1933–1937, vol. I, p. 227), is less arbitrary but still far from satisfactory.

[2] See Gerhard Colm, "Public Revenue and Public Expenditures in the National Income," in *Studies in Income and Wealth*, National Bureau of Economic Research, Inc., New York, 1937, vol. I, p. 210; and references by Haberler and Hagen, *op. cit.*, p. 13, and notes 18 and 19.

[3] Kuznets, "Discussion of the New Department of Commerce Series," p. 156, criticizes the Department's procedure of classifying all goods and service expenditures of government as final products, and notes that intermediate products should be excluded.

Gilbert et al., *op. cit.*, p. 185, in their rejoinder not only defend this procedure on grounds of feasibility, which is understandable, but go further and attempt to defend it in principle. They maintain that the inclusion of intermediate expenditures involves no duplication in estimating the value of the national product for any given year. This is correct if the national product is defined as total expenditures on the purchase of current output, excluding purchases for resale. But, as Kuznets correctly asks, what is the meaning of such a total, and why should it be of interest? Here, as in the discussion in *National Income*, the primary concern of the Department of Commerce is with a measure of output for any one year. However, Gilbert et al. recognize briefly

Remedial Expenditures

Further problems arise in the case of government expenditures that must be undertaken to meet adverse changes in environment. Such expenditures may be referred to as *remedial* expenditures. Here a distinction must be drawn between expenditures caused by environmental changes due to exogenous factors and expenditures caused by environmental changes due to the production process.

The first case is illustrated by emergency measures to meet natural catastrophes or by war finance.[1] Can a $1 billion increase in production for war be considered the equivalent of a $1 billion increase in production for peace? The answer depends on what we wish to measure. If we are concerned with changes in output as a matter of economic performance, changes in the pattern of wants are not relevant. Clearly there is an increase in output in both cases. If we wish to measure changes in welfare, the two situations differ. In the case of war, adverse changes occur that reduce the level of welfare vis-à-vis a given level of output. Welfare may be reduced while output is increased. In the other case, there has been no such change in needs. The increase in output now reflects a gain in welfare. Thus war expenditures are properly included in the national product as a measure of output, but care must be taken not to identify changes in output with net changes in welfare.[2]

The second case refers to changes in environment that are called forth by the process of production itself. To illustrate, the emergence of the modern corporation permits capital accumulation and more productive techniques; but it dissociates ownership from control and requires that the investor be protected against fraud by the supervisory function of governmental agencies. The agencies' services are designed to forestall a disutility or social cost not reflected in the market prices of the products produced by the corporation. Development of the automobile industry requires increased policing of traffic, the cost of which does not reflect a product carrying separate utility.

---

the theoretical problem of devising a measure of change in output. As a second line of defense, they hold that intermediate expenditures are stable over "short" periods and are (contrary to Kuznets' view) of small quantitative importance.

[1] See in this connection Kuznets, "Discussion of the New Department of Commerce Series," p. 156, and the rejoinder by Gilbert et al., *op. cit.*, p. 188. The latter correctly chide Kuznets for failing to distinguish between changes in output and changes in wants.

[2] A further difficulty of output measurement during war arises from the large-scale introduction of new products, not reflected in the base period on which the weights of price deflation are predicated. This difficulty is similar to that of adjusting weights in an index of physical production.

A reasoning similar to that of intermediate expenditures applies. There we argued that the wages of public guards should not be counted because the value that they contribute to output is not reflected in the market price. Now, similar reasoning shows that public expenditures for the services of the Securities and Exchange Commission or for traffic patrols should not be counted, since their exclusion merely corrects an overstatement arising because the market does not record these social costs when pricing private output. The extent to which national-product data overstate the growth of output by disregarding social costs of this sort is an interesting problem. Certainly, the phenomenon extends far beyond the range of cases where remedial public expenditures are applied, and it can be answered only in part by excluding public expenditures of this sort.[1] In other instances the remedy would have to be found by excluding certain private expenditures, or by adjusting the price index so as to allow for social costs.

Capital Outlays and Public Assets

A measure of output as an index of economic performance involves changes in the net rather than the gross product. Wear of capital must be allowed for. This holds for public no less than private capital assets.[2]

Final expenditures of government may provide for current consumption or for the purchase of durable consumer goods. In either case, the entire expenditure must be recorded in output in the period during which the goods are produced. If durable consumer goods are acquired, consumption is made possible free of direct charge in subsequent periods. The subsequent flow of services may then be included as imputed income in future years, while depreciation is charged to allow for the corresponding wear of the asset. These two entries will offset each other in determining net output in subsequent periods. However, the division of the net product between consumption and capital formation will be distorted in future years unless imputed income and capital consumption are recorded.

Intermediate expenditures of government may enter into private production in current or future periods. Our earlier rule that intermediate expenditures should be excluded must now be limited to the current type. Intermediate expenditures to acquire capital assets that aid private pro-

---

[1] See Kuznets' proposition that expenditures reflecting the "cost of membership in our business civilization" should be excluded from the national product ("Discussion of the New Department of Commerce Series," p. 156). Gilbert et al., *op. cit.*, p. 185, note correctly that exogenous changes in needs should be dissociated from a measure of output and should be distinguished from a failure to allow for social costs not recorded in the market.

[2] Failure to allow for depreciation of capital assets in the Department of Commerce accounts is criticized by Schelling, *op. cit.*, p. 327.

duction in the future must be included in the product of the period in which the assets are produced. In later years, when the resulting flow of services is reflected in the output of private firms, depreciation must be charged to allow for the wear of capital. Unlike the case of final expenditures, no imputed income will be charged. Unless this procedure is followed, real output will be overstated, the services of intermediate goods being reflected in the output of private firms without adding to their cost.

Transfer Payments

Public expenditures not directed at the purchase of currently produced goods and services are referred to as *transfer payments*. They may be payments for the purchases of existing assets, or they may be nonpurchase payments. They may go to consumers or firms, be available on a more or less restricted basis, be made with or without conditions as to the use of the income, and so forth. Whatever their particular characteristics, all transfer payments are similar in that they do not constitute a direct demand for current output. While they may add to the recipient's demand, such addition is reflected in private outlays for consumption or capital formation. It is evident, therefore, that transfer payments must be excluded from the measure of net output.

The principle is simple enough, but the practical dividing line between transfers and goods and service expenditures is not clear-cut. Payments are classified as transfers if they go to purchase secondhand goods, and as goods and service expenditures if they go to purchase currently produced goods. The burden of proof is thus shifted to the distinction between currently produced and secondhand goods, which is a matter of accounting convention. Government purchases of existing assets that are not the stock in trade of sellers are considered transfers; and purchases of goods drawn from inventory are considered goods and service expenditures, accompanied by dissaving in the private sector. While the value of total output is not affected by the particular point at which a dividing line is drawn, output is affected thereby.

Perhaps the most intriguing problem in the definition of transfers relates to the treatment of *interest on public debt*. The official view since 1947 has been that such payments are not to be counted as goods and service expenditures in computing the national product.[1] Some still hold, however, that interest on public debt should be included, and this for various reasons. One argument is that interest payments reflect the

---

[1] See *National Income*, 1954, pp. 97 and 149. Since their demotion in 1947, interest payments are "not considered income arising in current production," and are excluded from national income. At the same time, the Department of Commerce avoids outright classification of interest payments as transfers by listing them as a separate item.

imputed earnings of government assets. This view is clearly inapplicable where public debt is incurred to furnish services for current consumption, or where public assets of the durable–consumer-good type are used up before the debt is retired. Where such assets are in use, an income in kind should be imputed to them, and depreciation should be charged. However, this is better done directly, and not on the unwarranted assumption that the amount involved is equal to interest on public debt. Moreover, the situation would be worsened if imputed income were counted in terms of interest while depreciation were neglected. Present practice is consistent, at least in that both are disregarded, thus leaving the value of total output unaffected. For public assets of the intermediate type, depreciation should be charged without including income in kind. Inclusion of interest in this case would only add to the distortion that results from the failure to allow properly for depreciation.[1]

A better view of the matter may be obtained by relating interest to the various functions of public debt. In considering these functions we shall draw a distinction between what may be called the classical and the liquidity functions of public debt; and in dealing with the classical functions, we shall draw a further distinction between internal and foreign debt.[2] The function of domestic debt in the classical context is primarily to provide a public form of consumer credit, or to secure intertemporal allocation of costs between various generations. These adjustments may be valuable to society and worthwhile even though they draw upon a scarce supply of saving or upon a willingness to postpone consumption. Interest payments may be considered to reflect the imputed value of securing these adjustments; and as such, they may be judged a payment for current services.[3]

Foreign debt, in the classical context, serves the function of securing an intertemporal transfer of resources for the group as a whole. Interest on

---

[1] Contrary to the view here given, Kuznets, "Discussion of the New Department of Commerce Series," p. 159, holds that those who wish to exclude interest insist upon an undue identification of public debt with a specific tangible capital good. Suppose, for instance, that war debt is matched by the intangible value of national survival after a war, and that this survival is valued (if absurdly so) to equal interest on war debt. We may then conclude that an imputed income equal to interest should be added to post-war income. But, if this is done, we must either depreciate the intangible asset created by past defense outlays, in which case total output will not be affected; or we must conclude that the initial product furnished when the expenditures were made was undervalued at that time, and that the value of this past output is transferred to later years.

[2] See p. 575.

[3] These services are not the current utilities derived from the use of durable facilities, the treatment of which has been examined before. Rather they are the utilities derived from financing the cost of such durable goods in this particular fashion. (See p. 558.)

foreign debt measures the cost of this transfer. Suppose that a foreign loan was used to finance current consumption. Interest payments are the cost incurred to postpone repayment and thus maintain current consumption. They absorb part of current output as net export, and as such are included in the product. No reduction in the availability of domestic saving is involved, and no additional entry for interest payments is called for. A similar argument applies to borrowing for capital formation.

The role of domestic debt in a compensatory setting is quite different.[1] Here, public debt is maintained because its replacement by cash would result in excessive liquidity. Interest payments, if determined efficiently, are a necessary reward for a useful service, the surrender of liquidity. At the same time, this service cannot be considered output in the usual sense because it does not involve an opportunity cost of resource use. No postponement of consumption is involved. The gain of liquidity restriction lies in the avoidance of alternative measures of stabilization. These alternative measures may differ in their distributional implications and in their effects upon the efficiency of resource allocations. Thus the results secured by using liquidity restriction in place of other means of stabilization are useful, but they can hardly be considered an addition to output. The willingness to accept illiquidity cannot be considered a scarce resource in quite the same way as the supply of saving in the classical system. Thus, the exclusion of interest payments seems the better solution for the compensatory case. However, the problem posed by the treatment of interest is far from simple and the solution not so clear-cut as is frequently thought.

Another important category of transfer payments is provided by subsidies. Subsidies of all kinds are properly excluded from the net national product. Such is the case whether they go to consumers or to firms. Cash subsidies to business may or may not be reflected in a change in price. In either case, net national product in real terms will be invariant if the subsidy is excluded. The situation is precisely the same as in the case of intermediate expenditures. The latter may be thought of simply as subsidies in kind.

Receipts

The treatment of budget receipts in the net national product poses no problems. The net national product deflated by market price is invariant to changes in the sources of finance, whatever they may be. A change in tax structure, say, the substitution of a sales tax for an income tax, may or may not raise the price level.[2] If it does, the money value of output

[1] See p. 581.
[2] See p. 365.

rises accordingly, and the net national product is unchanged in real terms. If the tax substitution leads to an increase in real output at stable prices, the money value of the net national product rises, as will its deflated value. In either case, the measure of output is invariant to financial changes that leave real output constant. We need not concern ourselves in this connection with any distinction between taxes which stay put and others which are added to price. Whatever happens in this respect, the changes in the value of net national product as deflated by market price are the proper measure of changes in real output.

The same holds if taxes are replaced by borrowing.[1] The net national product in real terms is again invariant to the substitution of debt for tax finance.

Profits and Losses of Public Enterprise

Public enterprises are treated like private firms—as part of the business sector.

If public enterprises choose to operate at a loss, prices will be lower. Since output in money terms is deflated by an index of market prices, real output remains unchanged. If public enterprises choose to operate at a profit, prices will be higher and a corresponding adjustment occurs. In either case, private expenditures for such services are properly included at market price.

Public services sold for fee are similar in principle to those sold by public enterprise. Where the fee falls short of cost, the case is analogous to that of enterprise losses; and where costs are exceeded, the case is analogous to that of profits. In either case, the services in question must be valued at market price.

---

[1] Kuznets at one time held that government expenditures should be included only to the extent that they are tax-financed (*National Income; A Summary of Findings*, National Bureau of Economic Research, Inc., New York, 1946, p. 133, and further references there given). The argument was based on a strange analogy between public borrowing and business losses. Since the valuation of private services excludes losses, the same rule should be applied to public services that are not paid for by taxes.

The analogy is untenable. When private firms cut prices and incur losses, the real value of the net national product as deflated by market price remains unchanged. Precisely the same is the case when the government cuts taxes and substitutes loan finance. Whatever changes in the money value of output result, they will be offset by changes in price level. Exclusion of government expenditures would reduce the measure of real output and distort the picture.

The argument has been stated here on the assumption that real output remains constant as the budget policy changes, but the principle remains the same if a substitution of loan for tax finance is assumed to lead to an increase in real output. The national product as deflated by market price rises if output increases. The rule of invariance is satisfied in either case.

B. BUDGET ITEMS IN NATIONAL INCOME

We now turn to the treatment of budget items in the income, as distinct from the product, approach.   This is a more controversial matter because the nature and purpose of the national-income concept itself is ambiguous.

Suppose, first, that we have an economy without a government sector and with a stable price level.   Measurement of the net national product from the expenditure side may be supplemented by a measure of net national income from the income side.   The latter is obtained by adding the incomes of the factors of production that have been earned in the process of producing current output.   Since the value of goods at market price equals costs plus profits, the value of income thus arrived at must equal the value of the net national product as measured from the expenditure side.

The income and expenditure (product) measures thus represent two ways of looking at the same thing, each reflecting one side of the underlying sector accounts.   The product approach is more useful for some purposes, such as an analysis of output by types of products; the income approach is more useful for other purposes, such as a study of factor shares in income or contributions to output.   Still other problems, such as a breakdown of total activity by industries, are studied usefully in both product and income terms.

Difference between the money values of the net national product and net national income may arise from inventory gains or losses incurred in the process of price-level change, but this is adjusted when the money values are translated into real terms.   For an economy without a budget, there is no difficulty in reconciling the income and product approaches.

Public Expenditures

No difficulties will arise from the introduction of budget expenditures. To show this, let us assume first that all revenue is obtained by personal income tax.

Earnings from the production of final products purchased by government are to be included in net national income, just as final expenditures by government were included in the net national product.   Similarly, earnings from the production of intermediate goods purchased by government should be excluded, just as intermediate expenditures were excluded. This, at least, is the proper procedure if we look upon national income as a measure of economic performance in terms of income, analogous to net national product as a measure of economic performance in terms of output.

To obtain a measure of real income, we must deflate.   If earnings from the production of intermediate goods were included, we would have to deflate by an index of prices adjusted to allow for the additional cost of intermediate goods. This cannot be done because the proper weights for such an index are not available, purchases being made according to recorded market price. Earnings from intermediate expenditures should thus be excluded, and the value of money income should be deflated by market price.

At the same time, a measure of national income thus defined does not give a proper view of factor shares. These shares depend on total output, including that of intermediate goods. Returning to the previous illustration, the contribution of guard services (as a particular type of labor) to output is not reduced because guards were switched from the private to the public payroll. As a base for determining factor shares, the broader concept of factor earnings is needed, including earnings from intermediate goods.[1] Since we are dealing with shares, there is no need to deflate by changes in price level. At the same time, earnings from intermediate expenditures must be excluded, and the money value of output must be deflated if we wish to measure changes in economic performance.

Transfer payments should be excluded from national income, just as they are excluded from the national product, whether we look upon national income as a measure of output or as a base for determining factor shares.

Tax Receipts

So far, the argument is straightforward. Difficulties arise only when we introduce so-called indirect taxes, and with them the troublesome distinction between national income at factor cost and national income at market price.

As long as expenditures are financed by a personal income tax, and changes in inventory valuation are disregarded, national income and net national product will be equal in both money and real terms. The same total that is used to measure economic performance can be also used as a base for measuring factor shares. Now suppose that the personal income tax is replaced by a general ad valorem tax on sales. The sales-tax payments are inserted as a wedge between market price and the sum of cost payments to factors plus profits. This sum is referred to as net national

---

[1] In this sense Gilbert et al., *op. cit.*, are correct when they suggest that one may think of factor income as a concept distinct from output. Kuznets' concept of factor income ("Discussion of the New Department of Commerce Income Series," p. 160) as the sum of disposable income plus income in kind from final services in government necessarily equals his concept of total output as measured from the product side. As such, it cannot serve as a base for determining factor shares in the context of productivity analysis.

product at factor cost, or *national income*, in the Department of Commerce sense. It falls short of net national product at market price by the amount of sales-tax receipts.

National income thus defined cannot serve as a measure of change in economic performance or output. In order to obtain such a measure, we must deflate. Consistent with the nature of national income at factor cost, the proper procedure would be to deflate by an index of factor cost. The appropriate weights for such an index are not available, since purchases are made at market price.[1] Therefore, net national product at factor cost cannot serve as a measure of change in output or income. For this purpose, we must choose net national product at market price.

Nor does national income at factor cost express the total that is to be divided up when we wish to examine changes in the relative welfare of individuals who supply various factors. In this case, we must consider shares in disposable income, excluding all taxes (personal income taxes no less than sales taxes) and including all transfers.

It remains to consider whether national income at factor cost is the proper basis on which to determine factor shares, that is to say, the contributions of various factors to total output. The excise tax enters as a wedge between factor cost and market price. It may be looked upon as a diverting of part of the output produced by factors, no less than as an addition to factor cost.[2] Viewed as a slice of the total value of output that the factors produce, the tax must be included when determining how shares in the total output may be imputed to the various factors. This is necessary even though the term *factor income* is popularly applied to what is left after the sales tax is deducted from gross receipts.

If we are dealing with a general ad valorem sales tax, which applies at a uniform rate to all products, either one of two procedures may be followed: We may determine factor shares as shares in national income at factor cost; or we may determine shares in the net national product (or income at market price) by multiplying payments to factors by $1/(1 - t)$, where t is the rate of ad valorem tax. Since the sales tax is general, the same rate t applies in all cases, and the pattern of shares will be the same for both procedures. The concept of national income at factor cost is acceptable as a base for determining factor shares, but we can do just as well without it.

The two methods give different results if we deal with a partial sales

---

[1] See Gottfried Haberler and Everett E. Hagen, "Taxes, Government Expenditures, and National Income," in *Studies in Income and Wealth*, National Bureau of Economic Research, Inc., New York, 1946, vol. VIII, p. 14; and J. R. Hicks, "Valuation of Social Income," *Economica*, vol. 7, no. 26, pp. 105–124, May, 1940.

[2] For a similar view, see Earl R. Rolph, *The Theory of Fiscal Economics*, University of California Press, Berkeley, Calif., 1954, pp. 68ff.

tax, or a sales tax with unequal ad valorem rates. Suppose that factor A is employed largely in a taxed industry, while factor B is employed largely in a tax-free industry. As before, we may determine factor shares by the division of the national product at factor cost between payments to A and B; or we may impute taxes to factors employed in the taxed industry by applying the multiplier of $1/(1 - t)$, and determine factor shares in the net national product at market price. Since factor A derives a larger fraction if its income is in the taxed industry, A's share will be larger if we use the net national product at market price as a base; B's share will be larger if we use national income at factor cost as the base. If we are concerned with measuring changes in the productivity of the two factors, the determination of shares should clearly be based on market price, that is to say, taxes should be included.[1] Again, it appears that the national-income concept serves no essential purpose. Its role is that of an accounting total, arrived at in the process of computing the net national product at market price from the income side.

The same considerations apply to the treatment of the corporation income tax. This tax enters as a wedge between the share of proceeds that accrues to capital and profit income after tax. If we think of changes in national income as a measure of economic performance, the corporation tax, like all other taxes, should be included. If we wish to measure the welfare of income recipients, the corporation income tax, like all other taxes, should be excluded. If we wish to allocate total output among the contributions of the various factors, such allocation should again be made prior to deduction of the corporation income tax or any other tax.

Note that this entire argument has been conducted without any reference to the question whether taxes are shifted. The issue of shifting is indeed quite irrelevant in this connection. Where we deal with a measure of economic performance, our concern is with changes in real output; and the deflated value of the net national product or income at market price will be invariant to whatever price-level changes may result in the adjustment to various tax substitutions. Shifted or not, all taxes must be included. Where we deal with changes in the relative position of people receiving various types of factor income, the ex post data of income after tax will record the shifting that has occurred; all taxes must be *excluded*, whether shifted or not. Where we wish to impute shares in total output to the various factors, imputation to either base reflects such adjustments in the composition of output and in changes in relative factor prices that have resulted from the imposition of the tax. The question whether to

---

[1] Note that the determination of shares on either base will reflect changes in factor prices that may have occurred as the result of the tax.

allocate shares in income at market price or income at factor cost, therefore, is not a matter of shifting at all. Income at market price is the proper base, whether shifting has occurred or not.[1]

C. DISPOSABLE AND PERSONAL INCOME

Finally, we turn to the treatment of budget items in both disposable and personal income.

In computing *disposable income*, we must include all government expenditures, including goods and service expenditures of the final and the intermediate type, as well as transfers. All must be added when moving from net national product to disposable income. There is no need in this case to distinguish between final and intermediate expenditures, or between goods and service expenditures and transfers.

A problem arises only in drawing the line between government payments which are considered transfers and others which are not. The

---

[1] This view of the matter differs considerably from that taken by the U.S. Department of Commerce. The Department defines national income as a measurement of "output in terms of the costs or incomes of the factors of production." Therefore, national income "should change only if either the volume of factor services or their unit remuneration changes, and not because of a mere change in tax rates" (*National Income*, 1954, p. 33, supplement to *Survey of Current Business*, U.S. Department of Commerce).

Next, it is assumed that the property tax and excises are generally shifted forward, while the corporation income tax is not. On this basis, it is concluded that the former taxes should be excluded, while the latter should be included in national income, this being the method by which the money value of national income is held invariant.

Given these assumptions on shifting, the conclusion follows, provided we accept the criterion that the *money* value of national income should be invariant to tax substitutions. As I see it, this criterion has little merit. If we wish to use national income as a measure of change in income or output, and it is this measure of *change* that matters, rather than the absolute level for any one year, the test of invariance must surely be in *real* terms. In this case, the measure of income or output as a measure of economic performance must include all taxes, whether they are shifted or not. Substitution of a tax which is shifted for one which is not will be reflected in offsetting changes in money income and price level. Since an observable price index can be obtained in terms of market prices only, income at market price is the only proper measure of economic performance from the income side.

The assumption in shifting, underlying the Department of Commerce position, involves the proposition that sales taxes are passed on to the consumer, whereas corporation income taxes are not. The Department assumes further that shifting is done by increasing absolute prices by the amount of tax. As shown on page 380, this second conclusion does not follow from the first. However, the main difficulty here does not lie with assumptions as to shifting. Rather it lies with the criterion that national income should be invariant in *money* terms and with the resulting involvement in the question of shifting.

underlying principle is that payments received on income account are transfers, while those received on capital account are not. Thus, interest payments are included in disposable income, while redemption payments are not. At the same time, payments for the purchase of existing assets are treated as transfers, even though such payments are really on capital account.[1] As usual in such matters, the line of distinction is more or less arbitrary; the proper procedure depends on the use to which the resulting concept of income is to be put.

The treatment of budget receipts in disposable income is very simple. When moving from net national product to disposable income, all taxes must be deducted, no matter on whom they are assessed, or whether or not they are shifted. In the case of loan finance, no taxes are paid and no deductions are made.[2] Whether or not a substitution of loan for tax finance leads to a change in price level, the real value of disposable income as deflated by market price is invariant to such changes.

A problem in the treatment of taxes arises only in the case of *personal income*, obtained by adding the so-called personal taxes to disposable income. According to Department of Commerce practice, these include the personal income tax and the estate tax but not the property tax on residential property. The concept of personal income thus defined reflects the take-home pay of households, but it has little economic

---

[1] *National Income*, 1954, p. 59.

[2] Approaching the measure of total output from the income side, all taxes must be added to disposable income in order to obtain the net national product at market price. (See Haberler and Hagen, *op. cit.*, p. 9.) Disregarding retained earnings and depreciation, we have

$$Y_d + T_i + T_s - R = Y$$

where Y_d = disposable income, Y = total income, T_i = income taxes, T_s = sales taxes, and R = transfer payments.

But

$$T_i + T_s - R = G$$

where G = governmental goods and service expenditures, assumed to be on final goods. By substitution, we obtain $Y = Y_d + G$. In other words, total income may be derived by adding goods and services expenditure of government to disposable income.

In the case of loan finance, we have

$$Y_d + T_i + T_s - R = Y$$
But $$G - B = T_i + T_s - R$$
Hence $$Y_d + G - D = Y$$

where D is the budget deficit. In other words, total income may be obtained by adding goods and service expenditures to disposable income and deducting the deficit. The deduction of D is not called for if personal rather than disposable income is taken as the starting point. Using Y_p = personal income, we now have $Y_p + T_s - R = Y$. Since $Y_p = Y_d + T_i$, and $T_i + T_s = G + R - D$, this new definition of Y may be reconciled readily with the preceding formulation in terms of disposable income.

purpose that is not served more adequately by the concept of disposable income. In particular, the division between personal taxes and business taxes must not be taken to suggest that the former only bear on the position of households by affecting disposable income, or that the latter only operate by affecting the use of income. More will be said about this in the following chapters.

PART THREE

Adjustments to budget policy: classical aspects

"*Political Economy, when the simple principles of it are once understood, is only useful as it directs Governments to right measures in taxation. We very soon arrive at the knowledge that Agriculture, Commerce and Manufactures flourish best when left without interference on the part of Government, but the necessity which the state has for money to defray the expences of its functions, imposes on it the obligation to raise taxes, and thus interference becomes absolutely necessary. It is here then that the most perfect knowledge of the science is required. . . . *" [DAVID RICARDO, WORKS AND CORRESPONDENCE, VOL. VIII (1952), LETTERS, ED. P. SRAFFA, CAMBRIDGE UNIVERSITY PRESS, NEW YORK, 1951–1955.]

CHAPTER 10

Incidence and output effects
of budget policy

Through most of Part 2 we have dealt with certain basic differences in the normative theory of the public and the private sector. This involved a view of the budget plan as more or less distinct from the market system. We shall now leave these normative matters and turn to the problems that arise in implementing given budget objectives. If a given tax or expenditure measure is put into effect, what will be the resulting changes and adjustments in the private sector? Or, allowing for these adjustments, what fiscal measures must be put into effect to reach the desired objectives? To answer these questions, we must recognize that the operations of the private and public sectors are interdependent; both operate within the same economy and are parts of the same general-equilibrium system.

Public and private demand draw on the same total endowment of resources and share in the same output. Thereby they jointly determine relative prices of products and factors, the uses to which resources are put, and the way in which income is distributed. Similarly, the flow of public and private expenditures and receipts join to determine aggregate demand and hence the state of employment and the general level of prices.

When taxes are imposed, the statute places the legal liability upon particular consumers or firms. When public expenditures are made, they go to purchase specific resources from specific markets or involve gifts to particular people. There is a clearly defined point of impact at which the public-revenue or -expenditure flow is inserted, but the eventual distribution of costs or benefits may differ greatly from the way in which the initial liabilities or outlays are placed. The final results depend not only on how budget payments are inserted into the system but also on how the economy adjusts thereto.   Only if we can predict these adjustments can we determine what policies are needed to accomplish given objectives.

This is the task to which we now turn.   In the present chapter, some preliminary problems of measurement are considered.   This is followed by a series of chapters tracing the reactions to budget policies on the part of consumers, workers, business firms, and investors, all considered in a partial-equilibrium setting.   Thereafter we turn to the more difficult problem of adjustment in a general-equilibrium setting.   In dealing with the general-equilibrium view, we shall begin with the highly simplified case of an economy that involves the production of consumer goods only. Subsequently, capital formation is allowed for, but the discussion is held within the context of a classical system of income determination.   The incidence of alternative patterns of stabilization and problems of compensatory finance will be examined in Part 4.

A. ECONOMIC CONSEQUENCES OF BUDGET POLICY

We cannot meaningfully discuss the general economic consequences of budget policy at large; we must define specifically just what type of economic consequence we wish to measure and what type of change in budget policy we wish to examine.   For purposes of this chapter, let us overlook all the empirical difficulties that arise in implementing any such measures.   In order to deal with these difficulties at a later stage, we must define first what we would like to measure, if we can.   At the same time, our measure must be operational, that is, based on observable data.

Total versus Partial Effects

Let us suppose that the economy is in equilibrium and that this equilibrium is disturbed by a change in budget policy.   As a result, a set of interdependent adjustments occur and proceed throughout the economy until a new equilibrium is reached.   Following the method of comparative statics, we may then compare the state of affairs under the initial position with that which prevails after the new equilibrium is reached.   The difference reflects the economic consequences of the change in budget policy.

Note that this procedure leads us to deal with the *total* change that results.   If we focus on the changes in relative prices or earnings that come about as the result of the disturbance and adjustment, all such changes are included.   Suppose, for instance, that the initial disturbance involves imposition of a tax on product X, and purchase of product Y.   In the total adjustment, the relative prices of X and Y will change.   But the relative prices of products W and Z may change as well, and the final outcome will be affected by the entire set of price adjustments throughout the economy.

In order to determine the end result, we must consider the total change, no matter in what part of the system it occurs, or whether it was reached by a direct or an indirect path.   Budget planning, similarly, must be designed to equate the objectives of budget policy with this total change. As the architect designs his beams to allow for the settling of a building, so the budget planner should allow for resulting adjustments.   He should aim at equating his objectives with the results obtained after these adjustments are allowed for.

Major Aspects of Change

While we must consider the result of the total adjustment process, it is permissible and helpful to distinguish between various aspects of this total result and to apply distinct measures to these separate aspects.   The same procedure is applied in other fields.   As the result of a given medical treatment, a child may gain in height and weight.   These are inter-dependent results of the same treatment.   Yet they may be measured and recorded as distinct aspects of the over-all result.   Certain aspects of the total result of budget policy are of particular interest and are singled out here.   Others could be added.

Resource Transfer.   We shall begin with the transfer of resources from private to public use.   Assuming a given level of employment, resource transfer occurs whenever the level of public expenditures on goods and services is changed.   If the public absorption of resources is increased, whether through public purchases of factors or products, resources available for private use are reduced.   It is this withdrawal of resources that constitutes the opportunity cost of satisfying public wants.

Assuming a state of full employment, resource transfer comes about whether the additional resources are requisitioned or paid for; and it comes about whatever the sources of finance, be they taxation, borrowing, or the printing press.   The choice of finance is important in determining how the cost will be allocated among individuals; but it is the goods and service expenditures as such that cause the resource transfer.   In other words, the occurrence of the resource transfer is a consequence of the expenditure, and not the revenue, side of the budget.   More specifically, resource transfer may occur without taxes, and taxes may be imposed without resource transfer.[1]

Incidence.   Next, let us consider the resulting change in the distribution of income available for private use, a change here referred to as

---

[1] See Earl R. Rolph, *The Theory of Fiscal Economics*, University of California Press, Berkeley, Calif., 1954, p. 120.

incidence.[1]   Changes in this distribution, and hence incidence, may occur as the result of budget policies that involve resource transfer.   Suppose, for instance, that public expenditures on goods and services are increased. In the full-employment system, this will involve a resource transfer and a reduction in real income available for private use; but the distributional impact will differ, depending on the source of finance.   If finance is by credit creation and inflation, the price level will rise, but some prices and earnings will lag.   The distributional result will differ from that obtained if finance is by an income tax or by excises.   Thus, a given resource transfer may be associated with different distributional results, depending on the source of finance.

Similarly, distributional changes and incidence may result from changes in budget policy that do not involve changes in resource transfer to public use.   Thus, let us suppose that new money finance, whether by printing press or bank credit, is substituted for tax finance, while real expenditures of government are held constant.   Assuming an initial position of full employment, the price level will rise, as will the government's outlays in money terms.   Since all prices do not change at the same rate, there will be distributional changes, even though resource transfer to public use and total resources available for private use are not changed.   This is the incidence of inflation.   The same reasoning applies to an increase in taxes, with a resulting decline in price level; and to substitutions between taxes of equal yield, which leave the price level unaltered.   In all these cases, distributional changes occur without a change in resource transfer to public use.

Output Effects.   Finally, changes in budget policy may lead to changes in the level of output or real income.   These we shall refer to as output effects.   When associated with resource transfer, they may cushion or increase the resulting change in real income available for private use; and they may give rise to such changes even in the absence of resource transfer.

Various types of output effects may be distinguished.   In the context of the classical system, where full employment is assured, changes in output may be due to resulting changes in technique, voluntary changes in labor supply, changes in saving and capital formation, or in the efficiency of resource use.   Such changes may be referred to as Ricardian output effects.   Again, care must be taken to distinguish between a measure of change in output as an index of economic performance and a measure of change in welfare.[2]   Increased production due to increased labor supply, for instance, will not indicate a gain in welfare if the increased labor

---

[1] This differs from the more common usage of the term *incidence* to denote *ultimate resting point of the tax burden,* whatever that may mean.   (See p. 227.)

[2] See pp. 52ff.

supply reflects a less efficient allocation of resources between goods and leisure.[1]

In the context of a compensatory system, additional changes in output may result from changes in the level of involuntary unemployment.[2] These may be referred to as Keynesian output effects. Gains in output that reflect a reduction in involuntary unemployment always indicate a gain in welfare.

More will be said later on about these distinctions. Now we need only note that the various types of change—resource transfer, incidence, and output effects—are interdependent parts of the total change. Output effects bear upon the distribution of income and, hence, incidence. Distributional changes or incidence bear on the level of output. Both affect the steps required to secure a given resource transfer, and so forth. While it is helpful to distinguish between these various aspects of the end result, they are all part of one and the same adjustment process.

Adjustment over Time

In the framework of comparative statics, incidence and output effects are determined by comparing the initial equilibrium position of the economy (prior to the change in budget policy) with the new equilibrium position (reached after all adjustments to the change in budget policy are completed). Time does not enter, and the adjustment is assumed to be instantaneous. This is helpful for certain purposes, but unrealistic.

The actual adjustment process takes time. Successive transactions or income-expenditure circuits are needed to produce the final result. Different lags will be involved as various parts of the system adjust to the change. Consumers may not adjust their budgets at once to changes in incomes and prices, and workers may not be prepared to move immediately in response to changes in relative wages. Business firms may not recognize the need for sudden alterations in their policies. Moreover, it may take time to implement all these modifications once they have been decided upon. Adjustments in variable cost can be undertaken quickly, while changes in plant can be implemented only slowly. The distinction between short and long run, as related to the time dimension in the adjustment of fixed and of variable costs, is most pertinent to an analysis of the adjustment process. Even the very-long period,[3] so important to the

---

[1] In the following discussion of distributional change, real income will be defined to include leisure. To be consistent, the measure of change in output could be adjusted accordingly.

[2] The term *compensatory system* is used to describe a system in which full employment and price-level stability are not maintained automatically in the private sector. Whether this is due to liquidity preference, price rigidities, or other factors need not be considered now. (See p. 411.)

[3] See p. 388.

population factor in classical incidence theory, regains importance in conjunction with budget effects upon economic growth.

The effects of budget policy, which have resulted at a specified date after the budget change, depend upon the length of time that has been permitted to elapse. Instead of comparing the initial position of the economy with that after an infinite period of adjustment has passed, we may compare it with the position after a month or a year. For policy purposes, the results achieved over a limited period may be more important than those reached in the long run. Thus, the analysis may be limited to effects over a finite period, provided only that all changes up to that particular point of time are allowed for.

Nevertheless, this requires us to consider the particular time path along which the adjustment travels. We are thus confronted with the necessity of looking at the problem in dynamic terms. In the very-long run, the result may be the same as that reached by comparative statics, but it need not be. The disturbance caused by the initial change in budget policy may set into motion a chain of adjustments leading to continuous fluctuation rather than a new equilibrium position. Ultimately, a dynamic theory of the adjustment process will be called for.[1] However, the difficulties are formidable, and as yet the simpler method of comparative statics cannot be dispensed with.

Other Disturbances Allowed For

At this point, a further complication enters the picture. While it is helpful to study the results of budget policy on the assumption that no other disturbances will occur, such an assumption is not likely to be the case in the real world. Adjustments to changes in budget policy typically proceed in the framework of an economy that is subject to new disturbances, calling forth new adjustments. Changes that result from given budget adjustments will differ, depending on the nature of concurrent changes due to other causes. Imposition of a tax or a change in expenditure policy may lead to certain price adjustments in the upswing of the cycle or in an inflation period and to other adjustments in a period of cyclical decline and deflation. While the ceteris paribus assumption cannot be discarded in dealing with the incidence and output effects of fiscal measures, generalizations based thereon may be unrealistic.

Moreover, the distinction between old and new tax or expenditure policies loses much of its sharpness, as does the venerable saying that "Old taxes are good taxes." Where new taxes or expenditure policies create a disturbance and lead to change, old policies, that is, tax statutes in existence, constitute part of the environment that determines the out-

---

[1] See Chap. 20 for a brief excursion into the dynamics of the adjustment process in the compensatory model.

come.   The same holds for the disturbances caused by budgetary factors. Not only will the effects of new budget measures depend upon economic conditions at the time the measures are introduced, but also the effects of old measures will be subject to change with economic conditions.

Among other changes that may occur, we must include those in public policy, particularly in other forms of stabilization policy, as well as changes originating in the private sector.   As our discussion proceeds, the interplay of alternative stabilization policies will prove of considerable interest.

B. TYPES OF BUDGET ADJUSTMENT AND CONCEPTS OF INCIDENCE

Our measures of resource transfer, incidence, and output effect all record strategic aspects of economic change due to a specified change in budget policy.   It is essential, therefore, that we define clearly just what budget policy it is whose results we wish to measure in any particular case. This problem is viewed here in terms of incidence, but an analogous argument applies to output effects.   We assume, to begin with, that the budget change occurs within a classical system, where full employment is maintained automatically.   Thereafter, the problem is reconsidered in the context of a compensatory system.

Changes in Tax Policy

We shall begin with changes in tax policy while holding public expenditures constant in real terms.[1]   This adjustment involves no change in resource transfer to public use.

One way of dealing with modifications in tax policy is to examine a change in a particular tax function, such as a change in the rates of personal income tax.   The resulting alterations in distribution may be referred to as *specific tax incidence*.[2]   Suppose that income tax rates are cut.   As a result, income tax yield falls, in both real and money terms. Private expenditures increase, the price-level rises and public expenditures must be increased in money terms in order to maintain real purchases.[3]   In response to rising incomes, tax yields rise, but the initial losses are recouped in part only.   We thus face an inflationary process

[1] As another type of change, we may assume that expenditures are held constant in money terms, thus involving a possible change in resource transfer.   This may be the relevant formulation for some purposes, but it is of less general interest than that of constant real expenditures.

[2] I have referred to this previously as absolute incidence, but this proved misleading since it suggested a real cost of resource transfer.   See my paper "On Incidence," *Journal of Political Economy*, vol. 61, no. 4, p. 306, August, 1953.

[3] We assume that the additional means of finance are provided by a printing press, thus leaving the incidence of debt policy for later consideration.   (See p. 612.)

leading to a rising deficit in each round.   The best we can do is compare the initial state of distribution with that at any given later point of time. This distributional change depends upon the initial pattern of tax adjustment but also records the distributional results of the inflation process. The apparently simple case of specific incidence turns out to be a rather complex mixture of the combined incidence of tax reduction and inflation. Similar difficulties apply when considering an upward adjustment in tax function and the resulting process of deflation.

These difficulties are avoided if we consider a balanced-budget operation and compare the incidence of alternative methods of tax financing a given level of real expenditures.   The distributional changes that result as one such tax is substituted for another are referred to as the *differential tax incidence.*   In the context of the classical system, this would seem to require the comparison of taxes with equal money yield.   All income is spent, so that the aggregate level of private demand remains unaffected by the tax substitution.   On first consideration, we may expect that the same level of money expenditure by government will continue to secure the same transfer of real resources.   This, however, is not quite correct. Different taxes may involve different transaction demands upon a constant money supply and thus involve price-level changes.   These in turn will require changes in yield in money terms to finance the same level of real expenditures.[1]   More interesting, the substitution of one tax for another may affect relative prices via changes in private demand and may thus alter the yield in money terms that is required to purchase the particular product the government wishes to obtain.[2]

For these reasons it will be well to define differential incidence as the difference in the distributional results of two tax policies that provide for equal yield in real terms; or, to put it differently, that provide for money yields adequate to finance a given set of real expenditures of government under such absolute or relative prices as prevail under each type of tax. Substitution of equal yield taxes thus defined will be a balanced budget operation: Such changes in the level of money expenditures as are necessary to hold real expenditures constant will be matched by equal changes in the level of money yield.[3]

The concept of differential incidence has the advantage of not being inherently associated with an inflation or deflation process, whereas, specific incidence is.   At the same time, the new concept may seem

---

[1] See p. 365.

[2] See p. 155.

[3] If the reader prefers to define differential incidence in terms of substitution between taxes of equal *money* yield, he may do so; but in this case, the adjustment may involve deficit or surplus finance with inflation or deflation, or else a change in the level of real expenditures by government.

objectionable because it involves the analysis of changes in two tax functions rather than in one tax only.   Actually, this is no disadvantage. Tax policy does not deal primarily with a comparison between the incidence of inflation and that of any particular tax.   The basic policy problem is not one of specific incidence.   Rather, tax policy is concerned with alternative methods of financing a given expenditure program within the requirements of stabilization policy.   The main problem, therefore, is one of differential incidence.   This formulation furnishes much the most useful approach.   It will be used extensively in our discussion.[1]

Changes in Expenditure Policy

We now turn to the incidence of changes in public expenditures, while holding taxes constant.   The term *holding taxes constant* needs further interpretation.   An assumption of constant yield in money terms is ambiguous unless we specify just how tax functions are changed to maintain the yield in money terms as the tax base changes.   An assumption of constant yield in real terms involves the same difficulty, and raises the further question of which expenditure budget should be used to define constant yield.   Finally, we may specify that tax functions are held constant where the term tax function is used to describe both the assessment formula and rate structure.   This is the only unambiguous interpretation, and therefore has been adopted here.

We begin with a change in expenditure policy requiring that expenditures are increased in money terms at the initial prices.   Resource transfer to public use is also increased.   The distributional consequences of such a change may be referred to as *specific expenditure incidence*.   While the tax yield derived from constant tax functions increases in money terms as public expenditures are raised, the gain in yield falls short of what is needed.   An inflationary process results.[2]   Specific expenditure incidence therefore, involves the distributional effects of the inflation process as well as of the expenditure increase; in the case of expenditure reduction, it involves the distributional effects of the deflation process as well as of the

---

[1] The concept of differential incidence was used first by Knut Wicksell, *Finanztheoretische Untersuchungen und das Steuerwesen Schweden's*, Jena, Germany, 1896, pp. 6–7.

Wicksell was well aware of the requirement that the results of the entire budget adjustment must be allowed for.   Thus, tax changes cannot be considered unless we specify what happens on the expenditure side of the budget.   Confronted with the difficulty of linking particular parts of the tax yield with particular parts of the expenditure budget, Wicksell proposed differential incidence as a means of holding the expenditure side of the budget constant while considering tax changes.

[2] As before, we assume that the requirements of deficit are met by new money finance, leaving the incidence of debt policy for later consideration.

expenditure decrease.   The concept has the same disadvantages as that of specific tax incidence.

Proceeding in the same way as before, the difficulties are avoided if we consider changes in expenditure policy that can be met in the framework of a balanced budget while holding tax functions unchanged.   This we may refer to as *differential* expenditure incidence.   As does differential tax incidence, it permits us to separate expenditure incidence from the incidence of inflation or deflation.   Nevertheless, the concept of differential expenditure incidence is less interesting than that of differential tax incidence.   The problem of incidence is, by its very nature, of greater interest in changes in tax or transfer policy than in changes in public expenditures on goods and services.   While the benefits derived from public services may have distributional significance, especially in the case of merit wants, these benefits are not part of incidence as here defined. The term as we use it is limited to changes in the distribution of income disposable for *private* use.[1]

Goods and service expenditures of government do enter into the determination of relative factor and product prices, and hence of the distribution of income available for private use.   However, in the usual case these effects are only a by-product of expenditure policies.   They are not an independent policy objective.[2]   If the government wishes to purchase certain goods, they should be secured as a matter of purchase policy where they can be purchased most cheaply, and not where certain distributional results occur.   Situations may arise where distributional or other structural considerations are best expedited through purchase policy, but these are exceptions to the rule.   Decisions of tax and transfer policy, on the other hand, involve distributional matters as a primary policy consideration.   Therefore, problems of distributional change or incidence are of primary interest with regard to tax-transfer policy.

Changes in Tax and Expenditure Policy

It now remains to consider changes that involve adjustments in both tax and expenditure policy.   Among various possible combinations, consider that which involves a change in the level of resource transfer or real expenditures, combined with such change in tax functions as will furnish the required change in (real and money) yield.   The resulting changes in distribution may be referred to as *balanced-budget incidence.*

---

[1] It may be desirable to supplement the picture of distributional change in income available for private use by a picture of the distribution of income in kind provided by public services.   This distribution of income in kind may be highly important, but the problem involved in imputing benefits is quite different from that of determining incidence as here defined.

[2] See p. 47.

This formulation, similar to that of differential tax or expenditure incidence, has the advantage of excluding the distributional effects of inflation or deflation.   Moreover, it comes closest to the common-sense meaning of incidence as allocating the cost of public services among the members of the group.   At the same time, it has the disadvantage of involving the combined incidence of tax and expenditure policy.   It is not possible in this case to determine which elements of distributional change are due to the change in tax policy and which are due to the change in expenditure policy.

The concept of balanced-budget incidence may be readily applied where certain public services are actually added or dropped, accompanied by a specific tax change.   It cannot be applied easily in the absence of such a change, short of assuming removal or introduction of the entire budget. If we wish to apply the concept to a marginal change in expenditures, we do not know just what tax should be "thought away."   If the same real expenditures are paired with alternative taxes of equal yield, we return to the case of differential tax incidence.   It is precisely this sort of difficulty that led Wicksell to the differential approach.[1]

Finally, one may consider various combinations of tax and expenditure measures that involve unequal changes or changes in opposite directions. These leave us with various combinations of specific tax and expenditure incidence and combine their respective difficulties.

Among all these formulations, that of differential tax incidence should be the most useful, and that of balanced-budget incidence is next.   Other formulations are possible but of lesser significance.   The main point to be made is not that one or the other formulation is the best.   Any one of these cases, or many others not noted here, may be considered.   What is essential is to make clear at the outset just which case is under consideration and to allow for the total consequences of any particular change, including such inflationary or deflationary effects as may result.

Concepts of Incidence in the Compensatory System

The preceding applies to the incidence of alternative budget policies in a classical system, where planned saving and investment are equal and full employment is maintained automatically.   We now turn to a compensatory system, that is, a system where changes in aggregate demand may originate from changes in the desire to spend available funds, and where such changes may give rise to changes in the level of employment as well as in prices.

The concept of specific tax incidence in the classical system involves the distributional changes which result from particular tax or expenditure

---

[1] Wicksell, *op. cit.*

measures, as well as those which are caused by the resulting process of inflation or deflation. In the compensatory system, changes in tax or expenditure functions may not only affect the level of prices, but may give rise to changes in the level of employment. Thus, output effects of the Keynesian type, that is, changes in the level of involuntary unemployment, and their distributional implications come to be associated with the concept of specific incidence. A cut in tax rates may raise output available for private use even though resource transfer to public use is held unchanged, and an increase in tax rates may have the opposite result. Similar considerations apply to changes in public expenditures. An increase in goods and service expenditures may now raise rather than lower the actual (as distinct from the potential) level of resource use for the satisfaction of private wants; and the resulting changes in the level of employment and output again bear on the state of distribution.

Let us now consider what happens to the concept of differential incidence in this setting. In the classical case, differential tax incidence was defined as the change in the state of distribution resulting from the substitution of tax X for tax Y, where both taxes produce the same real yield, and public expenditures are held constant in real terms. Such substitution may involve changes in the level of yield in money terms, but with real expenditures constant, these will be matched by equal changes in the level of expenditures in money terms. Whatever the tax substitution, the budget will remain balanced.

This concept of differential incidence is of questionable value in the compensatory system. A substitution among taxes of equal yield may now change the level of aggregate demand and hence the level of employment and/or prices. This may be the case whether yield is held constant in real or in money terms. In either case, differential incidence thus defined includes the distributional changes that result from output effects of the Keynesian type or from price-level change. Such being the case, this concept of differential incidence is unsatisfactory, as was that of specific incidence in the classical setting.

In a properly run system of budget and stabilization policy, the contingencies of unemployment as well as of price-level change are to be avoided or minimized. The concept of differential incidence, therefore, must be re-defined to relate to tax substitutions that are compatible with the objective of stabilization. In the classical system, this purpose was served by exploring the substitution of taxes with equal real yield. In the compensatory system, we must examine instead the distributional consequences of tax substitutions that leave the level of private expenditure unchanged in money terms.[1] Tax substitutions that meet this

---

[1] Another possibility is to specify that private expenditures must remain constant in real terms. With extensive unemployment of all resources, the two concepts are

condition may change the level of yield, whether in real or money terms. Since the resource transfer to public use is to be held constant, differential incidence may now involve changes in the level of deficit or surplus finance. Further assumptions must be made with regard to monetary and debt policy, the incidence of which now gains in importance.

Once differential incidence is redefined in this fashion, the entire problem of incidence appears in a new light. Incidence now deals with the distributional consequences of alternative bundles of stabilization policies.[1] These bundles may involve alternative packages of taxes; or they may involve alternative mixes of tax and monetary restriction; or still other combinations may enter. Just as we can measure the distributional implications of substituting tax X for tax Y, we may measure those of substituting monetary restriction for either tax X or Y. The problem of tax incidence thus assumes a much broader meaning. It must not only be dissociated from resource transfer through public expenditure but recognized as a special case within a much broader range of problems, involving the differential incidence of alternative mixes of stabilization policy, be they tax or otherwise.[2]

C. A MEASURE OF INCIDENCE

Having interpreted incidence as the change in distribution that results from particular changes in budget policy, it remains to define precisely what is meant by change in distribution. We begin with measuring changes in the position of a particular individual and proceed to a measure of distributional change as applied to the group.

Measure of Change in Real Income of Individual

In an exchange economy, each individual is linked with the market in two ways. He is affected on the *sources* side through the price he obtains from the sale of his services; and he is affected on the *uses* side through the price he must pay for the products he buys. When a change in budget policy is made, he may find his position changed on both sides of his accounts. Depending on the particular case, one or the other change

---

more or less similar. With unemployment and flexible prices, the two concepts differ, and it may become more useful to specify constant private demand in real terms.

[1] A similar concept of incidence may be found in Bent Hansen, "Ett bidrag till incidenslaran," *Ekonomisk Tidskrift*, vol. 56, no. 3, pp. 195–213, 1954. Also see Bent Hansen, *Finanspolitikens ekonomiska teori*, Almqvist & Wicksell, Uppsala, Sweden, 1955, pp. 97–101.

[2] See p. 611.

may be more important. Both must be considered in order to account for the complete change in his position.

Changes on the Sources Side.   On the sources side, the individual may find that the market value of his services or his rate of personal tax has changed.   In both cases, the net return obtainable for his services is altered, and he will adjust his supply accordingly.   To simplify matters, let us assume that labor is the only factor.   If w is the net wage rate, we have $w = w_g(1 - t)$, where w_g is the gross rate and t is the rate of personal tax.   Now let the tax be reduced so that w_1 increases from w_1 to w_2, where subscript 1 refers to the position prior to the change in budget policy, and 2 refers to the position after the change.   As a result, let hours worked or W, change from W_1 to W_2.   The resulting change in the money income of our individual equals $w_2W_2 - w_1W_1$.   In order to measure the change in real income, and disregarding changes in product prices for the time being, we must allow for the fact that hours worked, and hence the retention of leisure, have changed in the process.   We must deduct $w_1 \Delta W$ or $w_2 \Delta W$, depending on which base we choose.   If the gain in the wage rate is valued at hours worked in the *first* period W_1 (or the loss of leisure is valued at w_2), the change in real income equals

$$\Delta R = w_2W_2 - w_1W_1 - w_2 \Delta W = \Delta wW_1 \qquad (10\text{-}1f)^*$$

If the gain in the wage rate is valued at hours worked in the *second* period W_2 (or the loss of leisure is valued at w_1) the change in real income equals

$$\Delta R = w_2W_2 - w_1W_1 - w_1 \Delta W = \Delta wW_2 \qquad (10\text{-}1s)$$

The two measures will differ unless the supply of labor is fixed, so that $W_1 = W_2$.   The choice between them is arbitrary.   Let us assume that the supply of labor increases with the net wage rate.   In this case, ΔwW_1 understates the true gain for an increase in w in that it falls short of the lump-sum payment that the individual would accept in place of the increase in wage rate.   This follows because, as w_1 changes to w_2, the individual moves from W_1 to W_2.   Also, we know that ΔwW_2 overstates the true gain for an increase in w, in the sense that it exceeds the lump-sum payment that the individual would demand in its place.   This follows because as w_2 changes to w_1, the individual moves from W_2 to W_1.   By the same token, ΔwW_1 overstates and ΔwW_2 understates the loss from a decline in w.   The bias in all these cases is reversed if hours worked move inversely with the wage rate.   The choice between the two measures poses a more or less insoluble problem in index numbers, and an arbitrary choice must be made.

---

*f after an equation number indicates first-period base; s indicates second-period base.

Changes on the Uses Side.   On the uses side, the individual may find that product prices have changed.   This may be because their factor costs have risen, because they are in increased demand, or because an excise tax has been inserted between factor costs and market price. Whatever the reason, he finds that a given amount of money income is worth more or less in real terms than before.   To simplify matters, let us assume that there are two consumer goods, X and Y only, and that all income is spent thereon.   Saving will be allowed for later on.   Suppose now that money income after tax has remained unchanged at $M = w_1W_1$, but that the prices of products X and Y have changed.

If the change in price is valued according to the quantities of the *first* period, the net gain equals

$$\Delta R = \Delta p^x Q_1{}^x + \Delta p^y Q_1{}^y \qquad (10\text{-}2f)$$

where $\Delta p = p_1 - p_2$ and hence is positive for a decline in price.   Equation 10-2f may be written as

$$\Delta R = \left(1 - \frac{P_2}{P_1}\right) M \qquad (10\text{-}3f)$$

where P_1 and P_2 are price indices weighted by first-period quantities.[1]

If the change in price is valued according to the quantities of the *second* period, we have

$$-\Delta R = \Delta p^x Q_2{}^x + \Delta p^y Q_2{}^y \qquad (10\text{-}2s)$$

where $\Delta p = p_2 - p_1$ and hence is negative for a decline in price.   This may be written as

$$-\Delta R = \left(1 - \frac{P_1}{P_2}\right) M \qquad (10\text{-}3s)$$

where P_1 and P_2 are price indices weighted by second-period quantities.[2]

The two formulations again differ, and neither gives the true picture. Using the first-period weights overstates the true loss from price rise in the sense that it exceeds the amount of lump-sum tax at unchanged prices that the individual would be willing to pay instead; and it understates the

[1] Equation (10-2f) may be rewritten as:

$$\Delta R = p_1{}^x Q_1{}^x - p_2{}^x Q_1{}^x + p_1{}^y Q_1{}^y - p_2{}^y Q_1{}^y$$

or $\qquad \Delta R = (p_1{}^x Q_1{}^x + p_1{}^y Q_1{}^y) \left(1 - \dfrac{p_2{}^x Q_1{}^x + p_2{}^y Q_1{}^y}{p_1{}^x Q_1{}^x + p_1{}^y Q_1{}^y}\right)$

Since money income M is held constant, this reduces to (10-3f).

[2] Equation (10-2s) may be rewritten as

$$-\Delta R = p_2{}^x Q_2{}^x - p_1{}^x Q_2{}^x + p_2{}^y Q_2{}^y - p_1{}^y Q_2{}^y$$

or $\qquad -\Delta R = (p_2{}^x Q_2{}^x + p_2{}^y Q_2{}^y) \left(1 - \dfrac{p_1{}^x Q_2{}^x + p_1{}^y Q_2{}^y}{p_2{}^x Q_2{}^x + p_2{}^y Q_2{}^y}\right)$

which reduces to (10-3s).

true gain from price decline, or the lump-sum subsidy that he would demand. Thus, ΔR is understated on both counts. Using second-period weights understates the loss from price rise and overstates the gain from price fall, so that ΔR is overstated on both counts.

Total Change.   We now drop the assumption of a constant value of M and combine the changes experienced on both sides of the individual's market position, thus obtaining the total change in real income or ΔR.

Using *first*-period quantities for weights throughout, we combine equation (10-1f) and (10-2f) to obtain

$$\Delta R = -\Delta w W_1 + \Delta p^x Q_1^x + \Delta p^y Q_1^y \qquad (10\text{-}4f)$$

This may also be written as[1]

$$\Delta R = w_2 W_1 - p_2^x Q_1^x - p_2^y Q_1^y \qquad (10\text{-}5f)$$

or, in index form as[2]

$$\Delta R = \left(\frac{w_2}{w_1} - \frac{P_2}{P_1}\right) w_1 W_1 \qquad (10\text{-}6f)$$

where P_1 and P_2 are price averages with first-period quantities as weights.

Using *second*-period quantities as weights, we combine equations (10-1s) and (10-2s) to obtain

$$-\Delta R = -\Delta w W_2 + \Delta p^x Q_2^x + \Delta p^y Q_2^y \qquad (10\text{-}4s)$$

which may also be written as[3]

$$-\Delta R = w_1 W_2 - p_1^x Q_2^x - p_1^y Q_2^y \qquad (10\text{-}5s)$$

or, in index form as

$$\Delta R = \left(\frac{P_1}{P_2} - \frac{w_1}{w_2}\right) w_2 W_2 \qquad (10\text{-}6s)$$

where P_1 and P_2 are price indices with second-period quantities as

---

[1] Equation (10-5f) follows by substituting

$$-\Delta w W_1 = w_2 W_1 - w_1 W_1$$

and $\qquad \Delta p^x Q_1^x + \Delta p^y Q_1^y = p_1^x Q_1^x - p_2^x Q_1^x + p_2^y Q_1^y - p_2^y Q_1^y$

in eq. (10-4f).

[2] We have

$$\frac{P_2}{P_1} = \frac{p_2^x Q_1^x + p_2^y Q_1^y}{p_1^x Q_1^x + p_1^y Q_1^y} = \frac{p_2^x Q_1^x + p_2^y Q_1^y}{w_1 W_1}$$

hence $\qquad\qquad p_2^x Q_1^x + p_2^y Q_1^y = w_1 W_1 \dfrac{P_2}{P_1}$

Equation (10-6f) follows by substituting the right term into (10-5f).

[3] Equation (10-5s) follows by substituting

$$-\Delta w W_2 = -w_2 W_2 + w_1 W_2$$

and $\qquad \Delta p^x Q_2^x + \Delta p^y Q_2^y = p_2^x Q_2^x - p_1^x Q_2^x + p_2^y Q_2^y - p_1^y Q_2^y$

in eq. (10-4s).

weights.[1]   In either case, the gain in real income will vary directly with the increase in the wage rate and inversely with the change in prices.

As noted before, the use of first-period weights understates the gain or overstates the loss that an individual experiences from the combined changes in wage rate and in prices.   It does not allow for the burden that may be avoided or the additional gains that may be made by adjusting the quantities supplied or purchased.   Thus it is excessively pessimistic on all counts.   The opposite holds for the use of second-period weights, where net gains will be overstated and net losses understated.   Since there is no logical preference between the two sets of measures, an arbitrary choice must be made.

Theoretically, a true measure could be obtained by presenting the taxpayer with the following question: What amount of lump-sum tax would you be willing to pay in order to cancel the given changes in w, p^x and p^y?   A true answer to this question would leave us with the correct solution, but it cannot be observed in the market and hence is not an operational concept.   While our definition of income change is only an approximation of the correct result, it can be measured from observable data.

Some Complications

We may now remove some of our simplifying assumptions.   Additional products may be added without difficulty, and earnings from factors other than labor may be introduced.   If income from capital is considered a rent income, the quantities corresponding to W_1 and W_2 may be set equal, as there is no counterpart to the surrender of leisure.   However, a reservation demand arises if risk is allowed for.

A further complication arises with allowance for saving.   So far, we have assumed that $wW_n = p_n{}^x Q_n{}^x + p_n{}^y Q_n{}^y$ for any one period.   As saving is introduced within the classical model, it is assumed that capital goods are purchased.   This raises the problem of how to interpret the position of the investor if there occur relative changes in the prices of consumer and of capital goods.[2]   Further difficulties arise if changes in tax policy differ in their effects on the prices of previously purchased and new capital goods.   Finally, the holding of balances or claims must be introduced, and the effects of price changes on their real value must be

---

[1] We have

$$\frac{P_2}{P_1} = \frac{p_2{}^x Q_2{}^x + p_2{}^y Q_2{}^y}{p_1{}^x Q_2{}^x + p_1{}^y Q_2{}^y} = \frac{w_2 W_2}{p_1{}^x Q_2{}^x + p_1{}^y Q_2{}^y}$$

hence

$$p_1{}^x Q_2{}^x + p_1{}^y Q_2{}^y = w_2 W_2 \frac{P_1}{P_2}$$

Equation (10-6s) follows by substituting the right term into (10-5s).

[2] See p. 381.

allowed for. These and other complicating factors are disregarded for the time being, but will enter the picture as our discussion proceeds.

Individual Income before and after Change

We must now go beyond this measure of change in the real income of any one individual and determine changes in the state of distribution among a group of individuals who have different levels of initial incomes and are subject to different changes in income.[1]

A first step is to expand the measure of change in individual income to permit a determination of income levels before and after the change. In other words, we must define not only ΔR but also the initial level of real income R_1 and the final level R_2.

Let us assume the change in income or ΔR to be measured in terms of *first*-period quantities. We then define R_1 as

$$R_1 = p_1{}^x Q_1{}^x + p_1{}^y Q_1{}^y + (\bar{W} - W_1)w_1 \qquad (10\text{-}7f)$$

where $\bar{W}$ is the individual's potential supply of work hours, W_1 is amount worked and $\bar{W} - W_1$ is the reservation demand for labor. While $\bar{W}$ is not a readily observable variable, we may assume it to equal, say, eight hours per day for everyone. Some such assumption is needed to define real income for any given period. Adding ΔR as defined by equation (10-5f), we obtain

$$R_2 = w_1\bar{W} + \Delta p^x Q_1{}^x + \Delta p^y Q_1{}^y + \Delta w W_1 \qquad (10\text{-}8f)$$

where $\Delta p = p_1 - p_2$ and hence is positive for a decline in price. In other words, income after the change in budget policy equals the potential money income prior to the change, minus losses or plus gains from a rise or fall in prices, and from a rise or fall in the net wage rate.[2] The change

---

[1] Our measure of incidence deals with measurable changes in real income. We leave open the question whether equal changes in real income, experienced by different individuals, do or do not imply equal changes in welfare. However, the very fact that we consider resulting changes in distribution a matter of interest suggests that interpersonal utility comparisons are possible in some sense, whether in terms of a social or an individual utility concept. (See p. 109.)

[2] Alternatively, we may measure ΔR in terms of *second*-period weights. In this case, we begin with the postchange income based on R_2 where

$$R_2 = Q_2{}^x p_2{}^x + Q_2{}^y p_2{}^y + (\bar{W} - W_2)w_2 \qquad (10\text{-}7s)$$

Deducting therefrom the income change ΔR as defined by eq. (10-4s) above, we obtain

$$R_1 = w_2\bar{W} + \Delta p^x Q_2{}^x + \Delta p^y Q_2{}^y - \Delta w W_2 \qquad (10\text{-}8s)$$

where $\Delta p = p_2 - p_1$ and hence is negative for a decline in price. In other words, the initial real income equals the potential money income after the change, plus losses or minus gains from a rise or fall in prices, and from a fall or rise in the net wage rate. The change in the wage rate is applied to hours of work in the final period and the price changes are applied to quantities purchased in that period.

in the net wage rate is applied to the initial hours of work, and the price changes are applied to quantities of products purchased in the initial period.

A Global Measure of Incidence

In a community composed of two people, the incidence of various budget changes may be measured simply by comparing the resulting values of ΔR or of R_2/R_1. In a community composed of many individuals it is neither feasible nor necessary to develop a measure of change in the state of distribution that allows for changes in the position of each individual. Some groupings must be made. The question is how to define relevant groups.

In the analysis of the classical economists, this grouping was by "distributive shares" or type of factor incomes. Thus, the discussion of tax incidence was in terms of incidence on wages, profits, and rents. For classical economists this scheme was doubly attractive. For one thing, it was an analytically convenient grouping, the pricing of various factors being subject to different principles.[1] For another, it was a socially relevant grouping, as the division of society into capitalists, landlords, and workers gave a fair picture of social stratification in the England of the early nineteenth century.

While textbooks continue to refer to the theory of factor pricing as *the* theory of distribution, the significance of the classical approach has been reduced in various ways. With the development of a more generalized theory of factor pricing, the distinction between particular shares has lost much of its analytical sharpness. At the same time, the social significance of distribution by factor shares has declined. It no longer can be maintained—if it ever could—that all workers live on subsistence levels, while landlords enjoy the windfall of ever-increasing rents.

Incomes from various factors, especially labor broadly defined, accrue to recipients at high and low points in the income scale, and there is a growing tendency for people to receive incomes from a variety of sources. Thus the focus of the distribution problem has shifted to a size distribution of total income independent of its source. Accordingly, incidence as here defined refers to changes in the distribution of income by size brackets and not by factor shares. At the same time, there remains the significant fact that wages as a source of income decline in weight when moving up the income scale, while capital income rises.

This switch in emphasis from incidence by factor shares to incidence by income brackets complicates matters in some respects but helps in others. Where we are concerned with changes in income positions that result from

[1] See p. 385.

the sources side, we must still work with the theory of factor shares. Since factor services supplied by people in any one size bracket are not homogeneous, they cannot be so determined by price theory. As a first step, we must take the classical view and determine how changes in budget policy affect the distribution by factor shares. Only then can we translate such changes into alterations in the distribution of income by size brackets. This second step may be based upon observed relationships between the composition of income sources and the size brackets of income. A tax that reduces the wage share, for instance, will tend to fall more heavily on low than on high income brackets; and vice versa for a tax that falls on the profit share.

Where we are concerned with changes in income position that result from the expenditure or uses side, we need not argue through the theory of factor shares. Rather, we may proceed directly to the study of incidence by size brackets of income, based in this case on observed budget patterns in relation to income. A tax that falls on necessities, such as work clothing, weighs more heavily on consumers in the lower brackets, and the opposite holds for a tax on luxuries.

Since incidence is to be defined in terms of change in the distribution of income by size brackets, use may be made of the familiar concept of the coefficient of equality. Let us suppose that income recipients are arranged in the order of income size, as defined by equation (10-7f). We may now compute the percentage of income recipients receiving incomes in excess of certain amounts as well as the percentage of total income accruing to income recipients with incomes above certain amounts. The resulting Lorenz curve may be plotted as shown in Figure 10-1, where the cumulative per cent of income is measured on the vertical axis and the cumulative per cent of income recipients on the horizontal axis.

Let the curve ODB express the initial distribution of income so that the lowest OF per cent of income recipients obtain ON per cent of the income, the lowest OE per cent of income recipients obtain OM per cent of the income, and so forth. A change in budget policy is made, and OGB indicates the state of distribution after the change. The coefficient of equality prior to the change in budget policy may be expressed as the ratio of two areas $ODBA/OBA$, and the coefficient after the change as $OGBA/OBA$. The ratio of the two coefficients or $OGBA/ODBA$ measures the incidence or distributional change that results. If the ratio exceeds 1, the over-all incidence is progressive; if it equals 1, it is proportional or neutral; if it falls short of 1, it is regressive.[1]

---

[1] This measure of incidence may also be looked upon as a measure of progression. As such it differs from the usual measures of progression (see p. 121), which are functions of the rate structure only. The present measure depends not only on the structure of statutory rates but also upon the level of yield, the distribution of income, and

This general approach may now be applied to our previously defined concepts of income before and after the budget change. If E_1 is the coefficient of equality applicable to the distribution of income in terms of R_1 as defined by equation (10-7f), and E_2 is the coefficient of equality applicable to the distribution of income in terms of R_2 as defined by equation (10-8f), the change in distribution or incidence may be measured by the ratio $0 < E_2/E_1 \lessgtr 1$. This global measure applies to the change in

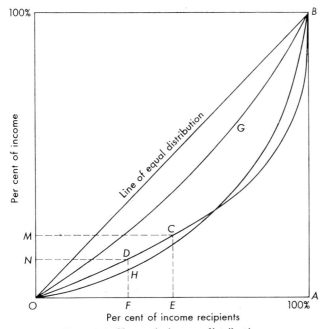

Fig. 10-1. Change in income distribution.

the *over-all* state of distribution. The measure may not be enough. Alterations in budget policy may leave the over-all index of equality unmodified but still cause significant changes between various ranges in the income scale. For instance, the state of distribution reflected by *ODB* may be replaced by one reflected by *OHB*. It may then be necessary to apply a finer set of measures, showing changes in distribution between various sections—say, deciles—in the income scale. Given the information needed for the global measure, the more detailed measures may be derived without difficulty.

the entire adjustment process that results. See also R. A. Musgrave and Tun Thin. "Income Tax Progression, 1929–48," *Journal of Political Economy*, vol. 56, no. 6, p. 510, December, 1948.

Incidence and Output Effects

The preceding measure of incidence deals with changes in the distribution of income available for private use. It does not concern itself with changes in the *level* of income thus available. Or, more correctly, it is concerned with alterations in the level only to the extent that they give rise to distributional alterations.

Suppose that tax X is substituted for tax Y, without change in real yield and in resource transfer to public use. Yet a change may result in output and hence in income available for private use. In the classical system, this may come about through effects on technique or through the efficiency of resource use. If output is defined as consistent with our concept of income, the resulting gains will be recorded in the values of R or R_2/R_1 for particular individuals. Depending on the relative levels of R_2/R_1 at various points in the income scale, the coefficient of equality may rise, fall, or remain unchanged. Whatever happens, our concept of incidence might be applied without difficulty to a situation where changes in output occur.

A complication arises in the compensatory system, where the budget change may affect the state of involuntary unemployment. By the nature of our concept of income, changes in labor supply at a given wage rate do not increase real income or output, since leisure is valued at the current wage rate. This approach is valid in the absence of involuntary unemployment but does not account for gains or losses resulting from changes in involuntary unemployment in the compensatory system. Thus we must adjust our measure to account for gains and losses from Keynesian output effects; or we must deal in terms of differential incidence defined so as to hold aggregate demand and employment constant.

These adjustments may be made, and our measure of incidence may be applied in a situation where output changes. The total change, which results from budget policy, may then be described by a consistent set of measures involving change in distribution or incidence and change in output. Apart from this, a more basic difficulty remains in relating these two measures. Let us suppose that there results no change in leisure or technique, nor in resource transfer to public use. This would seem to be a situation in which output remains unchanged. Yet it need not be a situation where the sum of individual gains just equals the sum of individual losses as measured in the preceding pages. In other words, our procedure of measuring individual gains and losses, though adequate for purposes of measuring distributional changes, does not permit a ready transition to a satisfactory measure of change in total output. By the same token, the excess of individual gains over losses, as measured in the preceding pages, does not constitute a satisfactory measure of over-all gain or change in output.   The inherent difficulty of the problem does not permit a simple solution.

D. OTHER CONCEPTS OF INCIDENCE AND SHIFTING

It now remains to compare our formulation with certain other interpretations of the terms *incidence* and *shifting*.   While no attempt is made at an extensive review of the literature, a brief comparison will help to place our usage within the general discussion of the subject.

Concept of Incidence

Without wishing to claim too much for our particular formulation of the concept of incidence, we cannot but note the great dearth of other attempts to assign a precise meaning to the concept.   The term *incidence* as commonly used refers to the location of the "ultimate" or the "direct" money burden of the "tax as such."[1]   It is said to occur whenever a particular piece of the tax comes to "rest" with the "final" payee, whether at the point of impact or farther down the direct line of subsequent transactions in the taxed product or service.   *Effects* are referred to as all "other" income changes that result in the course of the adjustment process.   Thus effects are defined as a residual, including both changes in output and those changes in distribution which are not considered a part of the direct money burden.

[1] See Edwin R. Seligman, *The Shifting and Incidence of Taxation*, 4th ed., Columbia University Press, New York, 1921, chap. 1.   Seligman's chapter is reprinted in R. A. Musgrave and Carl Shoup (eds.), *Readings in the Economics of Taxation*, American Economic Association, Richard D. Irwin, Inc., Homewood, Ill., 1958.   Seligman distinguishes between the incidence and the pressure of taxation.   Incidence is defined as "the settlement of the tax burden on the ultimate taxpayer" (p. 1), while pressure is defined as the "incidental burden which may rest on the shifter" (p. 11).   Otto von Mering, *The Shifting and Incidence of Taxation*, Richard D. Irwin, Inc., Homewood, Ill., 1942, p. 3, provides us, in his book, with the definition of incidence as the locale of the final burden of the tax.   The "further effects . . . which may follow the placing of the ultimate burden of a tax on certain persons or groups are not part of the theory of shifting."   For a more or less similar approach see also H. Dalton, *Principles of Public Finance*, 9th ed., Routledge and Kegan Paul, Ltd., London, 1939, p. 51; Harold Groves, *Financing Government*, 3d ed., Henry Holt and Company, Inc., New York, 1951, p. 102; and others.

This type of distinction between incidence and effects is rejected as arbitrary by E. Cannan, *Memorandum Relating Chiefly to the Classification and Incidence of Imperial and Local Taxation*, Royal Commission on Taxation, London, 1899, p. 166; and Duncan Black, *The Incidence of Income Taxes*, Macmillan & Co., Ltd., London, 1939, p. 123.   Both authors prefer to discard the concept of incidence and to deal with general effects only.   This is throwing out the baby with the bath.   As shown above, it remains useful to distinguish between various aspects of the over-all effects, and one of these is resulting changes in distribution or incidence as we define it.

This terminology is not easily interpreted, but the main difficulties seem to me as follows:

1. The traditional distinction between direct incidence and indirect effects involves an arbitrary separation between various elements of the total change that are neither separately identifiable nor of separate significance as matters of policy. When examining the distributional consequences of any particular budget change, all factors bearing on it must be considered. No special significance attaches to changes that come about in the direct path of transactions in the taxed product or service, compared with those which come about in the indirect path of subsequent adjustments. The changes must all be considered as interdependent parts of the adjustment, proceeding in one and the same system of general equilibrium.

Our distinction between resource transfer, distributional change, and output effects is not open to this objection. The three aspects are distinctly measurable and significant components of the over-all change. Whether the element of distributional change should be given the label of incidence is a matter of taste. Some readers may prefer to call it merely the distributional effect of budget policy.

2. The concept of incidence as locating *the* ultimate burden of a tax starts from the false premise that a tax as such has an ultimate burden. Taxes may be imposed, removed, and substituted for each other, without involving resource transfer to public use. A clear distinction must be drawn between the combined consequences of increased resource transfer to public use as financed by a given tax and the consequences of a change in methods of financing alone with unchanged resource transfer to public use. The distributional results of the former type of change are here referred to as budget incidence, and those of the latter as tax incidence. With regard to tax incidence, the problem of differential incidence is of particular interest. It is defined as the distributional change that results as one tax is substituted for another tax of equal yield; the term *equal yield* is defined differently in the classical and in the compensatory system.

3. When examining resulting changes in the real income of individuals, all such changes must be allowed for. This includes those which result from the income sources side, caused by changes in the net (after tax) prices of the services they have to sell, as well as those which result from the income uses side, caused by changes in the gross (after tax) prices of the products they have to buy.[1] This was recognized fully in the inci-

---

[1] For a different view, see Earl R. Rolph, *The Theory of Fiscal Economics*, University of California Press, Berkeley, Calif., 1954, pp. 124–126. Here the analysis of incidence is limited to changes on the income sources side. This is a partial concept of incidence, and seems to me quite insufficient for policy considerations. A second and less important difference between Rolph's analysis and ours is that he prefers to look at

dence analysis of Ricardo, whose discussion of a tax on land nicely distinguishes between the effects on the landowner as a recipient of rent and as a consumer of corn.[1]

Whether we look at incidence from the point of view of public policy or of particular individuals, it is a matter of indifference how the final distributional changes are arrived at. They must all be allowed for, whether they are due to price changes in taxed or in tax-free items, in products or in factors; whether they are arrived at in a direct or an indirect way; and whether they occur on the sources or the uses side of the household budget.[2]

4. In determining the distributional changes that result from an adjustment in budget policy, we must trace both losses and gains that may occur to particular individuals. This runs counter to the notion that imposition of a tax imposes a loss and that it is the problem of incidence to locate this loss. The latter is clearly *not* the problem, if we measure the results of a tax change or tax incidence, while holding constant the resource transfer to public use. Here no reduction in resources available for private use occurs, and the losses to some will be accompanied by gains to others.

Even in the case of budget incidence, where a resource transfer to public use is involved, we cannot limit our analysis to merely tracing the occurrence of losses in income available for private use. The net result of the adjustment will be to reduce total income available for private use; but this does not mean that all individuals suffer a reduction in such income. Some may find their positions improved, even though full employment prevails at the outset; and there may be a gain for the group as a whole if unemployment prevails at the outset.

In any case, we can never point to particular items of loss and identify these with the burden of the new tax or the cost of the new resource transfer, while reducing other gains or losses to the status of indirect effects.

---

the matter in terms of what we have called *specific* incidence, whereas we prefer the *differential* formulation.

[1] See p. 389.

[2] For an attempt to distinguish between "true" incidence and "horizontal price movements," see H. P. B. Jenkins, "Excise Tax Shifting and Incidence: A Money Flow Approach," *Journal of Political Economy*, 63, no. 2, pp. 125–149, April, 1955. Jenkins concludes that, for the excise tax, resulting changes in relative prices are horizontal price movements, which are not part of true incidence because such movements may be avoided by changes in the individual's expenditure patterns. This distinction is relevant for the problem of excess burdens, but it does not seem useful in the definition of incidence. The essence of the incidence problem, as I see it, is that different people possess different factor endowments and preferences and that they are in different positions to adjust to various taxes.

Rather, we must consider the entire change in distribution, including all individual gains as well as losses.

Concepts of Shifting

The term *shifting*, in the conventional usage, refers to the process by which the direct money burden is pushed along through price adjustments, from the point of impact (where the statutory liability is imposed) to the final "resting" place. We have seen that it is impossible in a general-equilibrium system to isolate this particular chain of events; and even if the direct burden could be located, its significance would not differ from that of other and indirect changes. The traditional concept of shifting, therefore, must give way to that of the general adjustment process in response to a change in budget policy, involving all effects that result. While we may separately measure various aspects of this end result, such as changes in distribution or in output, we cannot distinguish between one chain of adjustment that leads to changes in output and another that leads to changes in distribution.

Perhaps the concept of shifting may be rehabilitated by endowing it with a somewhat different meaning. Instead of relating it to the process of adjustment, let us relate it to the result. Consider (1) the actual change in distribution that results as a given tax is imposed or tax substitution is made; and consider (2) the change that would result if the income position of a new taxpayer were reduced by the amount of tax addition, or the income position of a former taxpayer were improved by the amount of tax remission, while the positions of all others remained unchanged. Change (1) may be referred to as *effective incidence*, and corresponds to the concept of incidence developed in the preceding pages. Change (2) may be referred to as *impact incidence*, while the difference between the two may be referred to as the result of shifting.

Impact incidence is on whoever is liable for payment under the law, whether it be the income recipient under our income tax, the shareholder under a corporation profits tax, or the seller at the particular stage at which the tax is imposed under an excise tax. If the seller can raise his price or cut other factor payments, effective incidence differs from impact incidence, and shifting has occurred. Thus indirect taxes are taxes that are meant to be shifted, and direct taxes are taxes that are meant to stay put.[1]

---

[1] De La Riviere argued that the land tax is *the* direct tax because it takes the tax directly where it is, thus avoiding shifting and repercussions. See C. F. Bastable, *Public Finance*, 3d ed., The Macmillan Company, New York, 1928, p. 347.

Similar definitions are used by John Stuart Mill, *Principles of Political Economy*, ed. W. J. Ashley, Longmans, Green & Co., Ltd., London, 1921, p. 837, who defines indirect taxes as those "which are advanced by one person to be, as is expected and intended,

This definition of shifting (or, rather, its results) is conceptually clear-cut, and may come fairly close to the popular interpretation of the term. What people want to know, when they ask whether this or that tax is shifted, is precisely whether there exists a difference between the statutory or impact distribution and the actual distribution of liabilities.   At the same time, this concept of shifting is conditioned by the artificial nature of *impact incidence*, a term that merely reflects the legal placing of the tax liability.[1]   Perhaps a more useful concept of shifting may be secured by measuring the difference between the actual change in distribution (or effective incidence) and the incidence of legislative intent.   Shifting thus defined is an index of frustration, as it measures the failure of tax policy to achieve its distributional objective.

---

reimbursed by another"; and Leon Walras, *Elements of Pure Economics*, trans. W. Jaffe, George Allen & Unwin, Ltd., London, 1954, p. 450, who defines indirect taxes as taxes on products, "it being clearly understood that the entrepreneurs will reimburse themselves by adding the amount of tax to the prices of the products."

For a historical discussion on opinions concerning the early use of the terms, see C. J. Bullock, "Direct and Indirect Taxes in Economic Literature," *Political Science Quarterly*, vol. 13, 1898, pp. 442–476, reprinted in C. J. Bullock, *Economic Essays*, Harvard University Press, Cambridge, Mass., 1936, pp. 1–35.

[1] Mrs. Hicks's distinction between *effective* and *formal* incidence should be noted in this connection.   See Ursula Hicks, *Public Finance*, Pitman Publishing Corporation, New York, 1947, p. 158, and "The Terminology of Tax Analysis," *Economic Journal*, vol. 56, pp. 38–50, March, 1946, reprinted in Musgrave and Shoup, *op. cit.*

Mrs. Hicks's concept of effective incidence is more or less analogous to our use of the term, as it allows for the entire adjustment process.   But her concept of formal incidence differs from our concept of impact incidence.   She defines formal incidence as measuring "the proportion of people's incomes which goes not to provide incomes of those who furnish them with goods and services, but is paid over to governing bodies to finance collective satisfaction."   According to this concept, the formal incidence of an income tax is on the income recipients, while the formal incidence of excises is on the buyer of the product.

Mrs. Hicks holds that the concept of formal incidence tells us nothing about the resulting adjustment process, but I wonder whether this is the case.   Does not the allocation of formal excise incidence to the consumer involve a hypothesis of shifting or an assumption that incidence operates through the income-uses rather than the earnings side of the budget?   While I consider it reasonable to assume that excise taxes are borne by the consumer, such a hypothesis relates to the *results* of the adjustment process.   The distinction between formal and impact incidence is thus blurred. (See text p. 379.)

CHAPTER 11

Adjustments in work effort

The final determination of incidence and output effects must be viewed in general-equilibrium terms, allowing for the interaction of all adjusting units, be they individual workers, consumers, financial investors, or business firms. As a steppingstone toward this general view, the specific reactions of these units will be examined first in a partial-equilibrium setting. Thereafter, we shall turn to a general-equilibrium setting.

A. A PROPORTIONAL TAX ON WORK INCOME

Let us start on the taxation side of the budget and leave the effects of public expenditures for later consideration. The first tax to be considered is a proportional tax on work income. Subsequently, a progressive tax will be examined, and capital income will be allowed for. Finally, other taxes will be introduced into the picture.

The Formal Argument

To simplify matters, we assume that all income is in the form of work income, that labor input may be measured in terms of hours worked, and that individual workers are free to adjust their labor input.

The formal argument is straightforward.[1] The individual who supplies

[1] See Enrico Barone, "About Some Fundamental Theorems on the Mathematical Theory of Taxation," *Giornale degli Economisti*, ser. 2, vol. 4, pp. 201–210, 1899; and Lionel Robbins, "On the Elasticity of Demand for Income in Terms of Effort," *Economica*, vol. 10, no. 29, pp. 123–124, June, 1930, and reprinted in *Readings in the Theory of Income Distribution*, American Economic Association, Richard D. Irwin, Inc., Homewood, Ill., 1946, pp. 237–244; Duncan Black, *The Incidence of Income Taxes*, Macmillan & Co., Ltd., London, 1939, chap. 12; Otto von Mering, *The Shifting and Incidence of Taxation*, Richard D. Irwin, Inc., Homewood, Ill., 1942, pp.

services is endowed with a given total of hours that he may take in leisure or may trade against income at the prevailing wage rate.[1]   On the basis of his given preference pattern between work and leisure, he will choose the optimal combination of income and leisure at the going wage rate.   Now a tax is imposed.   As a result, the net wage rate declines, and the worker adjusts his position accordingly.[2]   Whether leisure is increased or reduced in the process depends on the circumstances of the particular case, including the shape of the underlying preference pattern.

Assumptions for the shape of this pattern may be derived from, or expressed in, hypotheses regarding the slopes of the taxpayer's marginal utility of income and leisure curves.   Throughout we assume that a loss of leisure must be compensated by a gain in income (or vice versa) if the worker is to remain equally well off.   Both income and leisure carry positive utilities, and the surrender of either is a disutility.   To make this point, we need not argue that work is painful.   We must merely assume that the pleasure of work is outweighed by the opportunity pleasure of leisure.   Plotting income on the vertical axis and leisure on the horizontal axis, it follows that indifference curves will fall when moving from the left to the right.

This is plausible enough, but it is not sufficient to draw any conclusions. In order to determine what happens as the wage rate changes, we must know more about the marginal rate of substitution between income and leisure.   Here various assumptions may be entertained.

Marginal Utility of Both Income and Leisure Constant.   Suppose, first, that the marginal utilities of both income and leisure are constant.   In this case, the indifference pattern consists of a set of parallel straight lines rising up to the left.   Such a pattern is shown by i_1, i_2, and i_3 in Figure 11-1.   The individual will choose to retain his entire time in leisure if the slope of the wage line is less than that of the indifference line.   If the initial leisure endowment equals OA and the wage line equals AB, he will

---

100–116, and "A Note on Planning and Inducement to Work," *National Tax Journal*, vol. 9, no. 1, pp. 69–74, March, 1956; Richard Goode, "The Income Tax and the Supply of Labor," *Journal of Political Economy*, vol. 58, no. 5, pp. 428–437, October, 1949; Gershon Cooper, "Taxation and Incentive in Mobilization," *Quarterly Journal of Economics*, vol. 66, no. 1, pp. 43–66, February, 1952.   Also see the subsequent comments by Harry S. Schwartz and Otto von Mering, *Quarterly Journal of Economics*, vol. 66, no. 4, pp. 600–613, November, 1952.   The papers by Goode, Barone, von Mering, and Cooper are reprinted in R. A. Musgrave and Carl Shoup (eds.), *Readings in the Economics of Taxation*, Richard D. Irwin, Inc., Homewood, Ill., 1958.

[1] Complications that arise from the need for subsistence income and subsistence leisure are disregarded for the time being.   (See p. 239, note 1.)

[2] We assume here that imposition of the tax will not lead to an upward shift in the demand for leisure.   For a different situation, see p. 251.

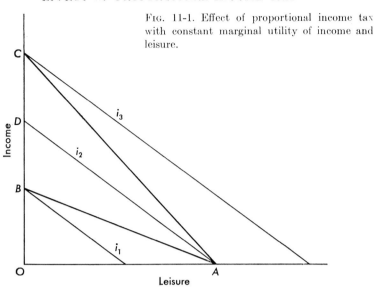

FIG. 11-1. Effect of proportional income tax with constant marginal utility of income and leisure.

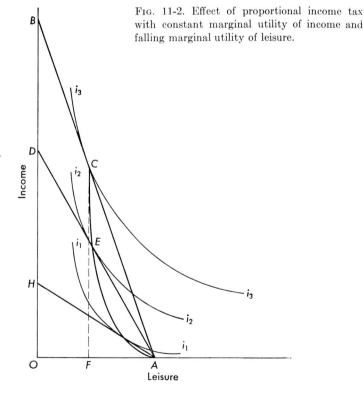

FIG. 11-2. Effect of proportional income tax with constant marginal utility of income and falling marginal utility of leisure.

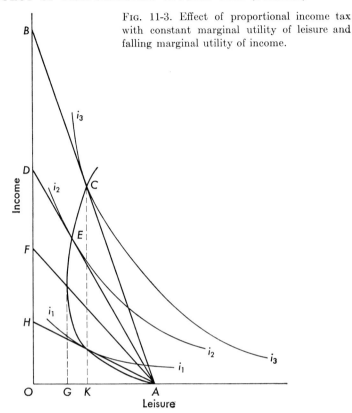

FIG. 11-3. Effect of proportional income tax with constant marginal utility of leisure and falling marginal utility of income.

remain at point A, since i_2 is the highest possible indifference level. Similarly, he will choose to retain no leisure and trade all available hours for income if the slope of the wage line is greater than that of the indifference line. Thus, if the wage line equals AC, he will obtain OC of income, i_3 now being the highest available level of indifference.

Suppose that the wage line before tax is given by AC. As a tax is imposed, the *net* wage line swings down towards AD. As long as the rate of tax falls short of DC/OC, work effort remains unaffected, as work hours remain at the maximum. Once the tax rate exceeds DC/OC, and the net wage line swings below AD, work will stop entirely. Evidently this is an absurd set of alternatives.

Marginal Utility of Income Constant and Marginal Utility of Leisure Decreasing. Suppose, next, that the marginal utility of income is constant, while that of leisure decreases. The indifference curves will then be convex to the origin. Measuring leisure along the horizontal axis and income along the vertical axis, the slope of successive lines remains constant as we move along a vertical line and decreases as we move right, along a horizontal line.   Such a pattern is shown in Figure 11-2, where OA is again the leisure endowment, AB is the wage line and C is the initial equilibrium.   As an income tax at rate DB/OB is introduced, the net-wage line falls to AD, and the new point of equilibrium is at E.   This point must be to the right of C, since the slope of indifference curves is constant along FC, but falls when moving to the right.   As the tax rate is increased, the position of equilibrium moves along a trading curve such as CEA.   The labor-supply schedule, which may be derived readily from the trading curve, is uniformly upward-sloping, and the income tax is adverse to work effort.[1]

Putting it differently, the substitution effect of the income tax is adverse to work effort.   Since the marginal utility of income is held constant, leisure is a neutral good, and there is no offsetting income effect.[2]   In equilibrium, the ratio of marginal utility of leisure to marginal utility of net income must equal the net-wage rate.   Introduction of the tax reduces the net-wage rate.   Since the marginal utility of income is assumed constant, the ratio of the two marginal utilities must be reduced by lowering the marginal utility of leisure.   This means that leisure must be increased.   The smaller the slope of the marginal leisure-utility schedule over the relevant range, the greater the required increase in leisure and reduction in work effort.

Marginal Utility of Leisure Constant and Marginal Utility of Income Decreasing.   Now let us suppose that the marginal utility of leisure is constant while that of income decreases.   The indifference curves will again be convex to the origin.   But now the slope of successive curves remains constant while moving along a horizontal line and rises while moving up a vertical line.   Such a pattern is shown in Figure 11-3, where OA is again the leisure endowment, AB the wage line, and C the initial equilibrium.   Now let an income tax be imposed.   The net-wage line falls to AD, and the new equilibrium is at a point such as E.   Since the slope of successive indifference curves is constant along any horizontal line, but rises when moving up a vertical line, the new equilibrium may be either to the right or to the left of C.   The adjustment now involves an income

---

[1] To derive the labor-supply schedule from the trading curve in Fig. 11-2, deduct leisure retained at various wage rates from potential leisure OA, and plot against the wage rate.

[2] If we lower the level of well-being while holding the wage rate constant, the individual surrenders income but not leisure.   As the wage line is shifted parallel to the left, the successive points of equilibrium fall along the vertical FC in Fig. 11-2.

effect favorable to work and a substitution effect favorable to leisure. Depending on which is stronger, the supply of work increases or decreases.

As the tax rate rises, the equilibrium travels along a trading curve such as CEA. For tax rate DB/OB, the new equilibrium is at E, and work effort is increased. As the tax rate is raised further to FB/OB, work effort reaches its maximum of GA. If the tax rate is increased even more, work effort begins to decline. At rate HB/OB work effort drops back to the pre-tax level KA. Thereafter a further increase in tax rate leads to a decline in work effort below that of the pre-tax equilibrium. The corresponding labor-supply schedule slopes upward until wage rate OF/OA and labor supply GA are reached and then turns back. The result of the tax in any particular case depends on the applicable range of the trading curve or labor-supply schedule.

In the pre-tax equilibrium, the ratio of marginal utility of leisure to marginal utility of income again equals the wage rate. Imposition of the tax lowers the net wage rate. Since the marginal utility of leisure is assumed constant, the equilibrium remains undisturbed and leisure unchanged, if the marginal utility of net (after tax) income rises by the same per cent as the net-wage rate declines. This will hold true if the marginal income-utility schedule has unit elasticity. If its elasticity is less, the resulting percentage rise in marginal utility of income is greater than the percentage decline in the wage rate. Thus the ratio of marginal utility of leisure to marginal utility of net income at the old hours of work falls short of the wage rate. Effort must be raised in order to reduce the marginal utility of income and to restore equality between the net-wage rate and the ratio of marginal utility of leisure to marginal utility of income.[1]

---

[1] Following Cooper, *op. cit.*, p. 46, we write the utility function $u = \phi(L,y)$, where u is utility, L is leisure, and y is disposable income. Disposable income equals $y = (1 - t)g$, where g is gross income and t is the tax rate. Hence,

$$y = (1 - t)[w(k - L)]$$

where w is the wage rate and k is the number of hours available. If the individual maximizes his utility, we have $[\phi_L(L,y)]/[\phi_y(L,y)] = (1 - t)w$. The ratio of the marginal utility of leisure to the marginal utility of disposable income is equal to the net-wage rate. As t is increased, the ratio of marginal utilities must fall, to maintain the required equality. This may require an increase or a decrease in hours of work. If utility is maximized, we have the condition (see Cooper, *op. cit.*, p. 65) that $[\phi_y + y\phi_{yy} - (k - L)\phi_{Ly}] \, dL/dt > 0$, where ϕ_y is the marginal utility of disposable income, $y\phi_{yy}$ is disposable income times the rate at which marginal utility of income changes as income increases, $(k - L)\phi_{Ly}$ is hours worked times the rate at which the marginal utility of leisure changes as income increases, and dL/dt is the change in leisure due to a small increase in t. The first term ϕ_y is positive. If the marginal utility of leisure is constant, the third term is zero. Hence dL/dt will be positive, and hours worked will decrease if $y\phi_{yy}$ is positive, i.e., if the elasticity of the marginal

Marginal Utility of Both Income and Leisure Decreasing. Finally, consider the more sensible hypothesis that the marginal utilities of both income and leisure decrease. The slope of successive indifference curves rises when moving up a vertical line and rises when moving left, along a horizontal line. As before, work effort may either rise or fall, depending on the weights of the income and substitution effects. The general form of the equilibrium path remains similar to that of Figure 11-3.

Imposition of a tax again reduces the net-wage rate as well as the ratio of marginal utility of leisure to net income at the old hours of work. If the elasticity of the marginal income-utility schedule is unity, equilibrium is maintained again at the old hours. If elasticity is less than unity, work effort must be raised; and if elasticity is greater than unity, work effort must again be reduced. If work effort falls, it will do so less than in the preceding case, since we now encounter a decline in the marginal utility of leisure as well as an increase in the marginal utility of income. Similarly, if work effort increases, it will increase less than in the preceding case, since we now encounter an increase in the marginal utility of leisure as well as a decrease in the marginal utility of income. As before, the direction of change in work effort is determined by the shape of the marginal income-utility schedule alone. The shape of the marginal leisure-utility schedule only enters in determining the magnitude of the change.[1]

The formal argument thus leaves us with the conclusion that there is no a priori reason to expect that an income tax will either decrease or increase work effort. The result depends upon the shape of the preference pattern over the relevant range, and this is a matter for empirical investigation to establish.

Secular Evidence

Pending the availability of such results, let us see whether a clue is not provided by the historical record regarding the aggregate–labor-supply schedule for workers as a group. The economic development of the last century or more shows a great increase in productivity, which was channelled into increased leisure as well as goods. In this secular sense, workers as a group have, in fact, operated on the backward-sloping part of the total–labor-supply schedule. This is not surprising, since techno-

---

income-utility schedule is less than unity. Similarly, dL/dt will be negative, and hours worked will increase if the elasticity of the marginal income-utility schedule is greater than unity. If the elasticity of the marginal income-utility curve equals unity, $y\phi_{yy}$ will be zero, and work effort will remain unchanged.

[1] For the same point, see Cooper, *op. cit.*, p. 50.

logical progress has been such that great gains in both goods and leisure were possible.

In viewing the historical record, it is well to distinguish between the short- and the long-run shape of the labor-supply schedule. In the long run, aspiration levels in terms of goods and/or leisure may rise. As new goods become available, the worker may be willing to surrender more leisure, which shifts the labor-supply schedule to the right. However, the new goods may be complementary to leisure, as is usually the case with rising standards of living; this may push the schedule to the left. Provided that the net shift has been to the left, the historical result of increased leisure remains compatible with the commonly held hypothesis that the short-run labor-supply schedule slopes upwards to the right.

Considerations of this sort may also help to explain why, in underdeveloped countries, a gain in productivity tends to be absorbed initially in increased leisure. Cultural barriers must be overcome (by observing Western standards of others) to permit rising aspiration levels in terms of goods. Until this occurs, and induces a shift of the labor-supply schedule to the right, a slight rise in wages pushes workers onto the backward-sloping part of their labor-supply schedule even though, in comparative terms, wages are still very low.[1]

Returning to industrially developed countries, note also that the secular rise in leisure has not been a simple expression of individual choices in the use of additional income. It has been the product of a complex set of social forces such as the movement to curtail child labor, the rise of mass education, and unionism.[2] The growth of leisure has been institutionalized in many ways and has become a more or less fixed factor in the environment in which individual choices are made. All this suggests that a reduction in the net-wage rate from W_2 to W_1 may produce a result quite different from that which was obtained in the past when the wage rate first reached W_1.

The time factor enters not only in the historical perspective but also in dealing with current changes. Where a decline in wage rates leads to a reduction in effort, the reduction will tend to be less in the short run than

---

[1] An alternative explanation for a backward-sloping labor-supply schedule at low wage rates has been suggested to me by Mr. David Cole. It may be derived from the assumption that workers will only work whatever hours are needed (within limits set by minimum requirements for leisure) to obtain a subsistence income. This leads to a labor-supply schedule of unit elasticity until a given wage rate is reached. Only thereafter will the worker respond to a further increase in the wage rate by trading leisure for income. Thus the labor-supply schedule resembles a rectangular hyperbola at the lower end of the scale. After the wage rate has risen above a certain level, the worker begins to substitute income for leisure; the labor-supply schedule turns and slopes upward to the right.

[2] See Richard Goode, *op. cit.*

in the long run. Since income commitments are more rigid than leisure commitments, work effort might be increased at first and reduced later. Sudden changes in the net-wage rate are felt more keenly and may be expected to have a sharper substitution effect than gradual adjustments have, and so forth. For all these reasons, no simple conclusions can be drawn from the historical experience.

Spite Effect

So far, we have assumed that a worker's reaction to a tax-induced change in wage rates is the same as his reaction to an equal change in the net-wage rate caused by market forces. This may not be the case. Taxes, especially those considered unfair, may meet with a *spite effect*. Imposition of a tax may call forth a feeling of anger, a desire, as it were, to hit back and inflict losses on the government by reducing one's work effort and hence one's tax base. Such a demonstration, to be sure, is costly to the worker. But the satisfaction of revenge may compensate the taxpayer for his loss; or he may hope that the government can be intimidated by such action.[1] Where a spite effect is present, the resulting reduction in work effort will be greater, or the increase will be less, than would otherwise be the case.

The hypothesis of a spite effect is supported by the widely accepted view (explained alternatively by considerations of money illusion) that hidden taxes are less harmful than open taxes; that the use of a wide variety of taxes is desirable because such taxes are less apparent than a larger single tax; or that income taxes withheld to begin with are less damaging (since less noticed) than income taxes paid by direct assessment. What may be an advantage of hidden taxes in this respect is a disadvantage in another. Taxes that are not noticed as such will create the illusion of costless public services, and thus invite faulty budget determination.

The factors involved in the spite effect can also operate in the other direction. The worker may view his tax payment as a purchase of public services that he desires. A reduction in wages due to tax, if related to public services received, involves a lesser reduction in the price of leisure than an equivalent wage reduction in the market. Such at least would be the case if a voluntary-exchange solution could be applied to the problem of the Allocation Branch. While this can be done as a matter of degree only, the spite effect may turn into a support effect, depending on the attitude of the public. In the case of war finance, in particular, the severity of possible disincentive effects will be related inversely to the intensity of patriotic feeling and the imminence of danger.

[1] Similar considerations may arise with regard to investment effects.

B. A PROGRESSIVE TAX ON WORK INCOME

We now turn to a progressive income tax. Concerning the effects of progression upon the work effort, a distinction must be drawn between the effort of any particular individual and the effort of the group as a whole. We retain the assumption that all personal income is in the form of work income.

Adjustment by Individual

Consider the case of a worker who receives an income of $10,000 and pays a tax of $5,000. This might have been obtained by a proportional tax of 50 per cent or by a progressive tax providing for, say, an exemption of the first $2,000, a rate of 40 per cent on the next $2,000, 60 per cent on the next $4,000, and 90 per cent on the final $2,000. Both rate formulas give a liability of $5,000 for an income of $10,000. Thus, it would seem a matter of indifference to our taxpayer which formula is used.

This way of putting the matter overlooks the fact that effort and income before tax may differ in the two cases. To put it properly, let us begin with a person who receives an income of $10,000 prior to the imposition of either tax. We now wish to impose a $5,000 income tax liability on him. In one case, we shall do this by imposing a flat rate. We know from the preceding argument that imposition of the tax may induce the taxpayer to increase or to reduce his effort. Let us assume that he reduces his effort by one-tenth, so that his income before tax declines to $9,000. A flat rate of approximately 55.5 per cent is needed to obtain the required $5,000. Now it can be shown that work effort will be reduced more, and income before tax will fall to below $9,000 if the same yield is obtained under a progressive formula.

This is demonstrated in Figure 11-4. The leisure endowment again equals OA, the wage line is AB, and pre-tax equilibrium is at C. Our worker receives OE of income, retains OD of leisure, and works DA hours. Now a proportional tax is imposed that swings the net-wage line to AF and places the new equilibrium at G. Leisure is increased from OD to OH. Income before tax equals HK, with GK paid in tax.

Now let the same yield GK be obtained with a progressive rate structure. Many different rate schedules can be used for the purpose. Under one such schedule, the net-wage line may be as shown by AL. Since the rate schedule is progressive, the slope of AL declines when moving to the left. The new tangency point lies at M, where the net-wage line intersects NP, a parallel to AB drawn through G. It is here that the tax yield MR is equal to the required amount GK. At the new equilibrium M, leisure retained equals OS. Both G and M may be to the right or left of C. Either tax may reduce or increase work effort. However, it follows from the shape of the indifference curves that M must lie to the right of G.[1] Leisure must be greater under the progressive tax. Note also that the new equilibrium M lies above the trading line AGC, which shows the points of equilibrium that result in response to various rates of proportional tax. Just as leisure will be greater under a progressive tax with the same yield, so the yield will be greater under a proportional tax with the same leisure.

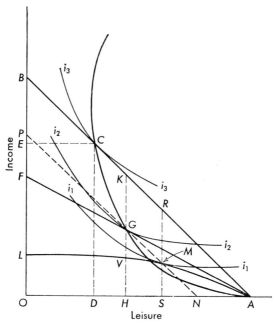

FIG. 11-4. Effect of progressive income tax.

This is as might be expected. The progressive tax involves a higher marginal rate than does the proportional tax; hence it involves a stronger substitution effect, adverse to work effort.[2] More generally, we find that work effort will increase if the average rate of tax is raised while the marginal rate is reduced or left unchanged; that work effort will decline if the average rate is reduced while the marginal rate is left unchanged or

---

[1] The slope of AL at V, its intersection with a vertical through G, must be flatter than the slope of AF at G. Since the marginal rate of tax must be higher, the marginal (net) wage rate must be lower. Provided that the marginal utility of income declines, the point of tangency between AL and an indifference curve must lie below G; provided that the marginal utility of leisure declines, the tangency point must lie to the right of G. Either or both assumptions will do, since the point of tangency for a progressive tax of equal yield must lie on PN.

[2] See Tibor Scitovsky, Edward S. Shaw, and Lorie Tarshis, *Mobilizing Resources for War*, McGraw-Hill Book Company, Inc., New York, 1951, p. 67.

increased; and that work effort may either rise or fall if both the average and marginal rates are raised or reduced.[1]

When a proportional tax reduces work effort, a progressive tax of equal yield reduces work effort further; and when a proportional tax increases work effort, the increase is less under a progressive tax. By the same reasoning, it may be shown that a regressive tax leaves us with a higher level of work effort than a proportional tax of equal yield. If we impose a 100 per cent tax on the slice of income in excess of $5,000 and nothing on the slice below $5,000, the disincentive effects on work effort are greatest; if we impose a 100 per cent tax on the first $5,000 and nothing on the remainder, the disincentive effects are least. Indeed, imposition of such a tax has no substitution effect, and is certain to increase effort unless income is an inferior good.

Adjustment by Group

The level of work effort is less for any one worker, if he pays a given amount of tax under a progressive rather than a proportional or a regressive rate schedule. Since progressive taxation for the group requires that a progressive formula be applied to each individual,[2] a conflict is suggested between a policy of distributing the tax bill progressively and a policy of leaving the total supply of effort unaffected or of increasing it. However, closer consideration shows that the problem is more complex. The results that apply to the individual cannot be transferred mechanically to the group.[3]

Suppose, now, that a proportional income tax is replaced by a progressive tax of equal yield, while public expenditures are held constant. As a result, both average and marginal rates of tax will be increased for people with high incomes and decreased for people with low incomes. But the changes in marginal rates will be sharper than the changes in average rates.

Without presenting a complete picture of the resulting patterns of change, the nature of the problem is illustrated in Figure 11-5. Low-income recipients in range A find that both their marginal and average rates of tax are reduced. They may either increase or decrease work effort. At the top of the scale are the people in group D, who find both their marginal and average rates of tax increased. As do members of the bottom group, they may either reduce or increase work effort. Workers

[1] See Cooper, op. cit., p. 63.

[2] This is inevitably the case. The statement by Scitovsky et al., op. cit., p. 182, that "unless special precautions are taken, highly progressive rates also imply high marginal rates of tax" is a contradiction in terms.

[3] This aspect of the matter is usually overlooked, even in the otherwise excellent paper by Cooper, op. cit.

with low to middle incomes in range *B* find that their marginal rate of tax is unchanged, while their average rate is reduced. They will reduce work effort. Workers in the middle to high income group, or range *C*, find their marginal rate increased and their average rate reduced. They will have a twofold reason to reduce work effort.

There is no simple way of predicting what the net result for the groups as a whole will be. Let us suppose that workers in group *A* raise work effort, while those in group *D* reduce it. The net result then depends on the amount of increase in group *A* as against the amount of decrease in groups *B*, *C*, and *D*. These changes in turn depend upon the distribution of income as well as the particular change in the rate structure.

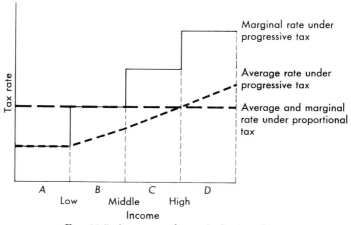

FIG. 11-5. Average and marginal rates of tax.

Moreover, marginal rates of substitution may differ at different points in the income scale. Opposite changes in work effort in groups *A* and *D*, for instance, may differ in degree. Thus, no simple conclusions can be drawn from the hypothesis of a backward-sloping supply schedule of labor and from the assumption that people with low incomes are subject to low wage rates while people with high incomes are subject to high wage rates. Substitution of the progressive schedule cannot be interpreted as a mere change in wage rates. Since the change in the marginal rate differs from that of the average rate, the adjustment is not along the normal labor-supply schedule or trading line applicable to the case of a proportional tax.[1] If the marginal rate of substitution of leisure for income is high for people with large incomes and low for people with small incomes, the substitution of a progressive rate structure will be least favorable to work effort; and it will be most favorable if this relationship is reversed.

[1] See p. 234.

The argument is complicated further if we allow for qualitative differences between the work effort of different groups. From the point of view of output effects, resulting changes in wage income may be of greater interest than resulting changes in hours worked. Thus hours worked may remain unchanged or rise, while the value of output is reduced or vice versa. Moreover, all workers may not be free to adjust their supply of effort. Observation of labor markets suggests that people commanding high salaries tend to be self-employed or in supervisory positions and hence less subject to work discipline. At the same time, they may be motivated more largely by nonpecuniary factors, so that their supply of effort is relatively inelastic. Recipients of lower wages are typically subject to contract, and may have to choose between working a required amount or not at all. Where this is the case, a tax on low income leaves work effort more or less unaffected. Moreover, imperfect market conditions may permit some income recipients to recover the tax by demanding an increased wage rate at the given labor supply. Such may be the case with the executive who sets his own wage rate.[1]

A special problem arises in the effects of high tax rates upon executive mobility. While recent studies show that there is little evidence that taxes reduce work effort at this level, it appears that high marginal rates reduce the interbusiness mobility of executives.[2] This results from high tax rates combined with provisions in the law that grant preferential treatment to certain incomes, such as income invested in retirement funds or income received in the form of stock options. By granting relief if income is received in these forms, the law imposes a penalty on movement. The remedy here is to do away with tax provisions that discriminate against movement. If it is desired to grant tax relief for executive incomes, more neutral measures such as income averaging, rate reduction, or special credits may be enacted.

Finally, let us note that people are concerned with their relative positions in the income scale as well as their absolute incomes. The desire to maintain one's relative status, or to improve it, may be a major factor in determining the marginal utility of income and hence in surrendering leisure at given wage rates.[3] Much depends on how relative position is defined. Suppose that it is defined as the ratio of one's income to the

---

[1] See p. 362.

[2] See T. H. Sanders, *The Effects of Taxation: On Executives*, Harvard University Bureau of Business Research, Boston, 1951; and C. A. Hall, Jr., *Effects of Taxation: Executive Compensation and Retirement Plans*, Harvard University Bureau of Business Research, Boston, 1951.

[3] A. C. Pigou, *A Study in Public Finance*, 3d ed., Macmillan & Co., Ltd., London, 1951, pp. 86–91, applies this type of consideration in justifying progression under equal sacrifice. (See text p. 103.)

average or to the income of one's rival. Substitution of a progressive for a proportional tax now involves a status effect leading to increased work effort by recipients of high incomes and reduced work effort by recipients of low incomes. If, however, relative position is defined in terms of rank order, the net result of the tax substitution does not involve a status effect. If relative position is defined in terms of absolute differences, even a proportional tax has a status effect. Thus it appears that the differential effects of alternative tax schedules on the *total* labor supply are a much more complex matter than such effects on the work effort of the individual taxpayer.

C. INCOME TAXES WITH CAPITAL INCOME

We shall now introduce capital income to the picture. A distinction must be drawn between taxes on wage income, taxes on capital income, and taxes that fall upon both sources of income alike. As before, we shall begin with the effects of income taxes upon the work effort of the individual worker, and thereafter consider effects on the group as a whole.

Adjustment by Individual

In determining the effects of a tax on wage income, the same principles apply, whether or not the wage earner also has capital income. However, the presence of capital income affects his choice between income and leisure, and it may affect the balance between the income and substitution effects that result from the tax. The presence of capital income will reduce the disincentive effects of a wages tax if it strengthens the income effect relative to the substitution effect—a condition that may well be met in most cases.

Turning now to a tax on capital income, suppose that this tax applies only to income from previously accumulated capital. There will be no substitution effect in favor of leisure. Since the income effect is adverse to leisure, assuming throughout that the latter is not an inferior good, leisure will be reduced and work effort will be increased as the result of the tax.[1] The level of work effort will be higher if a given yield is obtained from a tax on income from old capital than from a tax on work income.

Next, suppose that the tax applies to income from new capital only, that is, to future earnings from the investment of current work income. Such a tax discriminates in favor of leisure compared to future consumption. It is neutral between leisure and present consumption, and

---

[1] We assume that imposition of a tax on income from old capital will not call forth anticipations that income from new capital will be made taxable at a later time. This is the same assumption underlying the proposition that a capital levy does not affect investment incentives. (See p. 328.)

discriminates in favor of present compared to future consumption. There is a substitution effect in favor of leisure and an income effect adverse to leisure. The net result depends on the weight of the two effects. The level of work effort under such a tax may well be higher than under a tax on wage income; the latter tax discriminates in favor of leisure, compared with both present and future consumption, but is neutral between present and future consumption. However, we cannot be certain that work effort will be lower under the tax on wage income. The result depends on the various rates of substitution between present consumption, future consumption, and leisure.

The results of a tax on both types of capital income combine those of the tax on income from old capital and the tax on income from new capital. Comparison with the effects of a tax on wage income now depends on the size of the tax base provided by income from old capital. If this base is large, a relatively low rate of tax on total and, hence, new capital income will suffice, and adverse substitution effects will be small.

It now remains to compare the effects of a tax on capital income with the effects of a tax on capital. Provided that all capital is income-earning, and that capital values are obtained by capitalizing income at a uniform rate, the two taxes are the same. The distinction between old and newly accumulated capital now replaces the distinction between earnings from old and new capital. A difference arises only if we allow for the possibility that capital may be held in non-income-earning form. This possibility may be overlooked here, but will be dealt with in a later connection.[1]

Adjustment by Group

As before, the problem is more complex if we consider effects upon the work effort of taxpayers as a group.

Beginning with a tax on wage income, the presence of capital income affects the difference in the level of work effort under a proportional and a progressive tax. The weight of capital income increases when moving up the income scale, so that larger wage incomes tend to be matched by even larger capital incomes. The result may well be to subdue detrimental effects of progression on work effort, or to strengthen favorable effects.

We turn next to the comparison between a proportional tax on wage income and a proportional tax on capital income. Since the ratio of capital to wage income rises when moving up the income scale, the tax on capital income will be distributed more progressively in terms of total income than the tax on wage income. Thus, differences in the response of high- and low-income recipients are added to differences in the response of any one taxpayer to a tax on wage income and a tax on capital income.

[1] See p. 327.

Similar considerations apply to the comparison between a progressive tax and a proportional tax on total income.   Since the share of capital income rises when moving up the income scale, the progressive tax implies higher marginal rates of tax on the average dollar of capital income and lower rates on the average dollar of wage income.   Thus, differences in response to a tax on capital income and a tax on wage income are added to differences in response between taxpayers with high and low incomes.   If we assume that taxation of capital income is more favorable to work effort than the taxation of work income, the substitution of progressive for proportional rates will be less unfavorable, or more favorable, to work effort than it was in the absence of capital income.

Succession Duties

Succession duties, including estate and inheritance taxes, may be thought of as delayed income taxes payable at the time of death.   They may be translated into a current income tax, equal in amount to the premium payments needed to purchase an annuity with which to pay the tax at the time of death.[1]

A discount factor may be applied to allow for the difference in the current value of present and of future tax liabilities, but the annuity approach remains an oversimplification.   The distinction between taxes payable currently and taxes payable after death is not one in time only. The opportunity to accumulate a fortune for oneself may well be a more important motivating factor in work effort than the opportunity to leave a fortune to one's heirs.   The taxpayer, therefore, may discount the burden of estate taxes more heavily than is suggested by the time factor alone.   If a progressive income tax reduces work effort, an equivalent set of death duties will do so to a lesser degree.[2]

Corporation Income Tax

The corporation income tax, provided that it is not passed on, may be considered a special case of a tax on capital income.   If the shareholder identifies himself with the corporation, the result will be the same as with a direct tax on capital income.   If the shareholder is interested in divi-

---

[1] See N. Kaldor, "The Income Burden of Capital Taxes," *Review of Economic Studies*, vol. 9, no. 2, pp. 141–151, 1942.   Essentially the same considerations apply to an estate-tax type of succession duty as to an inheritance tax, but the latter may be of more concern to the testator.

[2] By the same reasoning, disincentive effects may best be avoided by a succession duty of the Rignano type, where property is taxed at increasing rates when passing to successive generations.   See E. Rignano, *The Social Significance of the Inheritance Tax*, Alfred A. Knopf, Inc., New York, 1924.

dend income only, while disregarding capital losses, effects on work effort will differ, depending on whether the tax is reflected in reduced dividends or reduced retained earnings.

D. TAXES ON CONSUMPTION

The taxation of consumption may take the form of a spendings tax on the consumer or a tax on the sale of consumer goods imposed on the firm. For purposes of this discussion, the two approaches are considered equivalent.[1]

General Tax on Consumption

The question arises how the level of work effort under a general and flat-rate tax on consumption or spending compares with that under a general and flat-rate tax on income. We assume that both taxes provide for the same yield.

To answer this, we shall begin with adjustments by the individual tax-payer and compare his levels of work effort if he is called upon to pay equal amounts under the two taxes. A tax on income discriminates in favor of leisure against present consumption, and more strongly so in favor of leisure against future consumption. Moreover, it discriminates in favor of present against future consumption.[2] A tax on consumption discriminates equally in favor of leisure against present and future consumption, and is neutral between present and future consumption. According to the earlier view of excess burden, one is tempted to argue that work effort is higher under a tax on consumption because an income tax imposes an excess burden. However, we have seen that this conclusion follows only if the supply of work effort is assumed to be fixed; it does not apply in the present case, where work effort is variable. Depending on the circumstances, one or the other tax may be more adverse to work effort. Work effort will be higher under the consumption tax if future consumption and work are complementary while present consumption and work are rival; and it will be higher under the income tax if these relations are reversed.[3]

We now turn to effects upon the work effort of taxpayers as a group. Since spending falls as a per cent of income when moving up the income scale, a proportional spendings tax is regressive in terms of income. If we accept the hypothesis that work effort is higher under a regressive than under a progressive income tax, it suggests that work effort will be higher

[1] See p. 349.
[2] See p. 263.
[3] It is assumed that all saving is for purposes of future consumption. The case is complicated further if saving for perpetual accumulation is allowed for.

under a proportional spendings tax than under a proportional income tax.[1] Such at least will be the case if the rate of substitution between leisure and present consumption is the same as the rate of substitution between leisure and future consumption.

So far, the comparison has been between taxes of equal yield. In a compensatory setting, an alternative concept of differential incidence is more relevant, providing for a comparison between taxes that reduce current levels of consumption by equal amounts. While this runs ahead of our story, the point must be considered briefly in this connection. Since the income tax discriminates in favor of present consumption, while the spendings tax does not, the required yield is less under the spendings tax. The required rate of the spendings tax may now fall below that of the income tax. Assuming equal-rate taxes to have the same adverse effect on work effort, the level of work effort will now be higher under the spendings tax. This result becomes the more likely if the spendings tax is considered temporary. Such a tax discriminates in favor of both future consumption and leisure against present consumption, and is neutral between leisure and future consumption. The required rate of tax is likely to fall well below that of an income tax, which hits both present and future consumption. Work effort will be greater. This is why a temporary spendings tax is an ideal tax for preventing wartime inflation. Similar considerations apply to the wartime use of refundable taxes or compulsory lending.[2]

Partial Tax on Consumption

Similar principles apply to a partial tax on consumption. To simplify, let us assume that all income is spent on the consumption of products X

---

[1] N. Kaldor, *An Expenditure Tax*, George Allen & Unwin, Ltd., London, 1955, pp. 134–136, argues that work effort will be higher under a proportional spendings tax than under an equal-*rate* income tax. This will be so because the discounted value of future consumption per unit of work is larger under the spendings tax. The rate at which leisure can be converted into real income is more favorable. Hence, Kaldor concludes that work effort will be higher. At the same time, the *yield* will be less under the spendings tax. To equalize yields, the rate must be higher. For the average taxpayer, this just offsets the advantage of a more favorable rate of conversion of leisure into real income. Thus the results, Kaldor holds, are the same for equal-yield taxes. However, he adds that the spendings tax will result in a higher level of work effort after all, provided that the worker values the holding of funds set aside for future tax payment during the interim period.

[2] The difference in incentive effects between a refundable proportional income tax and a temporary proportional spendings tax is slight, relating merely to the treatment of interest, but the refundable tax has the advantage of reducing postwar liquidity. The ideal solution may be found in a spendings tax combined with absorption of savings (voluntary absorption, if possible) into securities whose maturity is subject to later policy decision, depending upon the postwar outlook. See J. M. Keynes, *How to Pay for the War*, Macmillan & Co., Ltd., 1939.

and Y, so that an income tax and a general tax on consumption are alike. We then compare the effects on work effort of a tax on X and Y with those of equal-yield taxes imposed on X or Y only.

The tax on X and Y discriminates in favor of leisure for both products, and is neutral between X and Y. The tax on X discriminates in favor of leisure compared to X; and since the rate of tax on X must be higher than the rate of tax on X and Y, the discrimination against X is increased. Also, the tax on X discriminates in favor of Y compared to X, remaining neutral between Y and leisure. Corresponding relationships apply for a tax on Y. The results depend on the prevailing rates of substitution between X, Y, and leisure. Let us assume that X is rival to leisure while Y is complementary to leisure. Thus X may represent work clothing while Y represents camping equipment. In this case, the level of work effort will be highest if the tax is imposed on Y, and lowest if it is imposed on X.

Reasoning along similar lines, it has been suggested that a tax on luxuries provides a lesser disincentive to work effort than a tax on necessities, the presumption being that luxury goods are associated with the enjoyment of leisure.[1] These considerations apply to a comparison between taxes of equal yield imposed upon any one individual. At the same time, necessities weigh more heavily in the budget of consumers with low incomes, while luxuries weigh more heavily in high-income budgets. In assessing differences in the effects upon the work effort for the group as a whole, possible differences in the reaction of low- and high-income recipients must again be accounted for.

E. PUBLIC EXPENDITURES

We shall now turn to expenditure effects on work effort, disregarding taxation effects for the time being. The nature of the problem differs between transfer payments and goods and service expenditures. As in all problems of this sort, both sides of the budget must be considered. Unless this is done, a one-sided and distorted picture of the public economy is obtained.

Transfer Payments

It is frequently said that transfer payments are simply negative taxes and thus pose no additional problem. This is correct in some cases but

---

[1] See I. M. D. Little, "Direct vs. Indirect Taxes," *Economic Journal*, vol. 61, no. 243, p. 584, September, 1951; W. J. Corbett and D. C. Hague, "Complementarity and the Excess Burden of Taxation," *Review of Economic Studies*, ser. 1, vol. 21, no. 54, p. 21, 1953–1954; David Walker, "The Direct-Indirect Tax Problem: Fifteen Years of Controversy," *Public Finance*, vol. 10, no. 2, p. 164, November, 1955.

too simple a view when considering incentive effects. The assessment formula and rate structure of transfers differs from that of taxes.

Income Transfers. Income transfers are transfers that are a function of income. A proportional income transfer is the opposite in sign to a proportional income tax. The latter has an income effect which is favorable to work effort (provided again that leisure is not an inferior good) and a substitution effect which is adverse. The proportional income transfer has an income effect which is adverse to work effort and a substitution effect which is favorable to it.

Now, consider rate schedules that are not proportional. In the case of a tax, marginal rates may range from zero to 100 per cent. While a progressive tax can reduce the marginal net wage to zero (when the marginal rate of tax becomes 100 per cent), it cannot render it negative. In the case of a transfer, the marginal rate can begin at above 100 per cent at one end of the scale and fall below minus 100 per cent at the other.

The same equalitarian philosophy that renders the income tax progressive also calls for transfer payments with declining marginal transfer rates as income rises. As long as the marginal transfer rate remains positive, the substitution effect remains favorable to work effort but declines as we move up the income scale. An illustration of such a transfer schedule is provided by general-revenue contributions to retirement pensions, where the subsidy rate declines with the size of the pension.

In other cases, the marginal transfer rate may not only decline towards zero but become negative. The substitution effect then becomes adverse to work effort. While the marginal transfer rate falls toward minus 100 per cent, the marginal net wage rate falls toward zero, as it does when the marginal rate of tax approaches plus 100 per cent. Such a situation arises with a means-test type of relief formula, where the amount of transfer is determined as the difference between actual earnings and some set amount of subsistence income. Here the marginal gain obtained from the surrender of leisure is zero for any level of earnings below the statutory amount. The substitution effect is the same over this range as that of a marginal tax of 100 per cent.

This is the kind of transfer formula that is required for a policy of complete income equalization. The statutory minimum income is defined as the community's average income, and the transfer formula is supplemented by a tax imposing a marginal rate of 100 per cent in excess of the average income. Thus the price of leisure would be zero for both taxpayers and transfer recipients, and nonpecuniary incentives, be they rewards or threats, would have to be relied upon to induce work effort.

Finally, the transfer formula may be such that the marginal rate falls below minus 100 per cent. This is the case with a relief formula that provides for a fixed subsidy, subject to the condition that earnings do not exceed a given amount. Thus the formula may provide for a transfer of $1,000, subject to the condition that other earnings do not exceed $1,000. In this case, the price of leisure is unaffected as far as the first $1,000 of earnings are concerned. But if earnings are increased by an additional dollar, total income (including transfers) will fall from $2,000 to $1,001; that is to say, the transfer provision is equivalent in its substitution effect to a marginal tax rate of 100,000%. For larger increments of earning, the marginal rate declines; it reaches 100 per cent for an increment in earnings of $1,000. For $2,000 it falls to 50 per cent, and so forth, approaching zero for larger additions to earnings.

Where the marginal transfer rate is negative and where leisure is not an inferior good, both substitution and income effects work toward reducing work effort. Disincentive effects on work effort may become severe if the transfer rate falls off sharply, especially if it drops below minus 100 per cent. At the same time, these effects may be dampened by certain other considerations. A dollar of relief may not be considered the full equivalent of a dollar of income, since most people will be eager to trade involuntary leisure for the recovery of independence. Moreover, the limit set by the support formula may be so low that people will be willing to push through the threshold of a negative wage rate, in order to obtain a higher income.

The problem thus posed is especially acute in the case of unemployment relief. However, more or less similar situations arise where free public services are made available, subject to the condition that incomes do not exceed a given amount, as is the case with charity hospital services or public subsidies to housing for low-income tenants. Again, similar considerations apply regarding the limited allowance of current earnings for people receiving old-age retirement benefits, where excess earnings will result in reduced benefit payments.

Other Transfers. Not all transfer payments are related to income. They may be related to age, infirmity, past military service, and so forth, thus corresponding to lump-sum taxes. Unlike the minor role of such taxes, lump-sum transfers play an important part in the transfer structure. Like lump-sum taxes, these transfers do not carry a substitution effect, but their income effect is adverse to work effort. However, note that lump-sum transfers are usually directed at the aged, the blind, invalids, young children, and other groups not in the labor force, or serve to rehabilitate temporarily disqualified workers.

Subsidies to business may be thought of here as negative excise taxes. Their effects upon work effort as noted in the preceding discussion of such taxes, depend on the marginal rates of substitution between the subsidized products and leisure.

Goods and Service Expenditures

We now turn to the effects of goods and service expenditures. Such effects may arise from changes in relative factor earnings that result as public purchases enter the market. Nothing need be added here. However, let us consider the effects on work effort resulting from the "free" supply of goods and services provided for through the budget.

Public services for education, health, and similar programs may increase labor productivity and real wages. While the income effect is adverse to work effort, the substitution effect is favorable, and the net result may go either way. The effect will be similar to that of an income transfer with a positive marginal rate and opposite to that of an income tax.

Other goods and services provided for through the budget benefit the individual consumer independent of his work effort. Effects on his work effort here depend on whether the "free" good is rival, complementary, or unrelated to privately purchased goods and to leisure.

The supply of free goods that are rival to privately purchased goods will reduce work effort if the free goods are independent of, or complementary to, leisure, and the outcome will be uncertain if the free goods are rival to leisure. The supply of free goods that are complementary to private goods will increase work effort if the free goods are independent of, or rival to, leisure, and the outcome will be uncertain if the free goods are complementary to leisure. The supply of free goods that are independent of privately purchased goods, finally, will increase or reduce work effort, depending on whether the free goods are rival or complementary to leisure.

Unfortunately, it is difficult to allocate major expenditure categories to these empty boxes. To begin with, it is difficult to say whether particular free goods are, on balance, rival or complementary to privately purchased goods. Police services, for instance, are rival to private goods in that they reduce necessary expenditures for locks; and they are complementary in that they make the acquisition of real property more attractive. Highway improvements reduce the need for tire replacement but make it more worthwhile to have cars. Similar arguments apply to expenditures on education, housing, and so forth. Moreover, it is not always clear whether a particular service is rival or complementary to leisure. Public camping grounds would be one extreme and transportation facilities for commuters another, but in most cases both leisure and work may be benefited to some extent. Expenditures for defense, as usual, offer particular difficulties in interpretation. Thus, it is evident that no simple generalization is permissible.

Combined Tax and Expenditure Effects

In order to obtain a complete view of budgetary effects upon work effort, the partial effects resulting from the tax and expenditure sides of the budget must be combined into a single picture.

On the tax side, we find an income effect throughout that is favorable to work effort, provided always that leisure is not an inferior good; and for most taxes, including those which furnish the bulk of revenue produced in the modern tax structure, we find substitution effects that are adverse to work effort. On balance, work effort may be increased or decreased.

On the expenditure side, we find some situations where the net effect is adverse to work effort, including certain transfers and the supply of free goods that are rival to privately purchased goods but not to leisure. Similarly, we find some situations where the net effect is favorable to work effort, such effects including the supply of free goods that are complementary to privately purchased goods but rival to leisure. In addition, there are situations where expenditure effects may go either way, including some transfers; and situations where work effort may not be affected in either direction. Expenditures that increase productivity, finally, may increase or reduce work effort.

Considering these manifold possibilities, it is difficult to say whether, on balance, the modern budget has gone to reduce or increase work effort, or what the implications of future developments will be. Looking at the expenditure side, there is reason to expect that future expansion will be aimed primarily at the satisfaction of social wants proper. Outlays on public health, education and highways, all promise to have a favorable effect on work effort; and outlays on national defense, though they may not be directly complementary to the satisfaction of private wants, are at least not rival to such satisfaction. Looking at the revenue side of the picture, increased reliance may come to be placed on taxes that do not involve a highly restrictive substitution effect on work effort. Thus, future budget expansion need not have a restrictive effect on work effort; the opposite may well be the case.

Finally, note that the growth of the budget must be seen in the context of an expanding economy. Efficient use of resources in such an economy involves growth in the satisfaction of public wants as well as private wants and leisure. There is no reason to assume that public services are an inferior good, or that the income elasticity of public goods or services is less than that of privately purchased goods or services. Indeed, it is not unreasonable to expect that certain public services, such as public health and education, may demand a rising share as total output grows. There is no a priori reason to expect that such budget expansion will be detrimental to work effort.

Significance of Changes in Work Effort

In concluding, let us return briefly to the significance of changes in work effort. They are important as one vehicle of change in the course of the adjustment process, and thus, have an important bearing on incidence. Beyond this, resulting changes in work effort enter into output effects; but as noted before, changes in output, as commonly measured, must not be confused with changes in welfare.[1] The criterion of efficiency in budget policy is not related to changes in work effort but to noninterference with the choice between work and leisure. A policy that avoids interference may result in either a higher or a lower level of work effort. The former is the case if we compare the effects of a lump-sum tax and an income tax, and the latter holds if we compare the effects of a lump-sum transfer and an income transfer. A high level of work effort per se is not an indication of a high level of welfare. A proper measure of welfare must allow for leisure as well as goods. Situations may arise where a high level of work effort is a valid policy objective, as in war economy, but this is an exception to the rule. Generally the proper criterion of efficient budget policy is noninterference with the choice between work and leisure, rather than maximization of work effort.

[1] See p. 52.

CHAPTER 12

Adjustments in consumption and saving

We now turn to the effects of budget policy on the use of consumer income. These adjustments may involve shifts between the consumption of different products, between present and future consumption, and between consumption and accumulation. Unless noted otherwise, we shall assume throughout this chapter that the supply of effort is fixed.

A. ADJUSTMENTS IN THE COMPOSITION OF CONSUMPTION

Assuming that all income is consumed, let us begin with adjustments in the composition of consumption.

In Figure 12-1, units of product Y are measured on the vertical axis, and units of product X on the horizontal axis. We assume that the consumption of both X and Y is subject to decreasing marginal utility. The indifference curves are convex to the origin, and the slope of successive curves rises when moving up on a vertical line and when moving to the left on a horizontal line. Let OA be an individual consumer's initial income in terms of X, and OB/OA the price ratio p_x/p_y. The initial equilibrium will be at a point such as C.

General Tax on Income. Now, suppose that the government imposes a general tax on income. Since saving equals zero, this is the same as a general tax on consumption. Assuming relative prices to remain unchanged, the price line shifts parallel to the left. For a tax equal to $DA/OA = EB/OB$, the new equilibrium will be at F, which must be below and to the left of C. Since X and Y are both superior goods, the consumption of both is reduced by the income effect of the tax. Since relative prices are unchanged, there is no substitution effect. As the rate of tax is increased further, the price line proceeds to the left, and successive points of equilibrium follow a path such as CFO.[1]

Partial Excise Tax.   Next, let this tax be replaced by a partial excise tax on Y.   With an ad valorem rate of HB/OB, the price line swings to AH, and is tangent to an indifference curve at a point such as K.   As the tax rate is increased to MB/OB, the price line swings to MA, and a new equilibrium is obtained at N.   A further increase in the tax rate, swinging

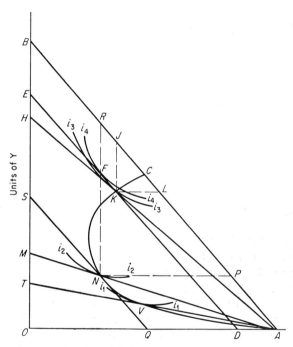

Fig. 12-1. Choice between consumer goods.

the price line to AT, gives an equilibrium at V, and so forth.   We thus obtain an equilibrium path as shown by CNA.

Initially, imposition of an excise on Y results in reduced purchases of both X and Y.   The income and substitution effects both make for reduced purchases of Y; the substitution effect makes for increased purchases of X but is outweighed by the income effect.   As the tax rate increases and the ratio of p_y/p_x rises, the substitution effect gains in

[1] This path, which declines at an increasing rate, is drawn on the assumption that X is a luxury, while Y is a necessity.   If this assumption is reversed, the equilibrium path is swung around the OC axis, and declines at a decreasing rate from C to O.

weight.   Eventually it outweighs the income effect, and any further rise in the tax rate leads to increased purchases of X.   The equilibrium path bends back and leads to A, the entire income being spent on X when the rate of tax on Y becomes infinitely large.

We may now compare the adjustment to a general tax on income or total consumption with the adjustment to a partial tax on consumption of equal yield.   Let the government obtain DA of X under the general tax. If the same yield is to be obtained by an excise on Y, the tax rate imposed must be such that the new price line at its intersection with ED is tangent to an indifference curve.   This is the case for tax rate HB/OB, which intersects ED at K.   The yield here equals KJ of Y, which in turn equals KL or DA of X.   The new equilibrium K must lie below C but may fall either to the left or right of it.   This must be the case because both substitution and income effect are adverse to the purchase of Y, while the two forces oppose each other with regard to X.   For similar reasons, K must lie below and to the right of F.[1]

The largest yield obtainable under the selective tax is derived at rate MB/OB, where yield equals NR of Y or NP of X.   This yield is matched by a general income or consumption tax at rate $QA/OA = SB/OB$.   As the rate of income tax is increased, larger yields may be obtained.   Since the supply of effort is assumed to be fixed, a 100 per cent rate will furnish a yield equal to OA.[2]   In contrast to this, the yield of the partial excise on Y will fall if the rate is increased beyond MB/OB.   Thus, each yield up to QA (in terms of X) may be obtained by two rates of excise tax.   To minimize the excess burden or remain on a higher indifference curve, it will evidently be desirable to employ the lower-rate solution.

Note that the exposition of Figure 12-1 is in strictly partial-equilibrium terms.   This may be valid for the individual consumer but not for consumers as a group.   Once a general approach is used, introduction of the budget with general income or consumption-tax finance need not result in a parallel shift of the price line.[3]   However, substitution of the excise on Y for the general tax still leads to increased private purchases of X.

B. ADJUSTMENT IN CONSUMPTION AND SAVING BY INDIVIDUAL

We now introduce saving and, to simplify matters, shall assume that there is only one homogeneous consumer good.   Also, we shall retain the

---

[1] As before, these conclusions simply follow from the assumed shape of the preference pattern.   (See p. 233.)

[2] If the supply of effort is variable, it becomes possible that the maximum yield may be larger under the partial excise on Y.   Such may be the case if Y is complementary to leisure while X is rival to leisure.

[3] See p. 146.

earlier assumption of fixed effort supply. The adjustment between consumption and saving will be examined first with regard to the individual consumer and then with regard to the group.

Saving for Consumption Only: Standard Case

The adjustment depends on the underlying motivation for saving. Let us suppose, first, that all saving is undertaken to postpone consumption and will eventually be dissaved and consumed. Saving for accumulation's sake is excluded.

Consider a two-period model where, in period 1, the consumer has a given wage income that may be consumed during that period or saved for consumption in period 2. Depending upon the available rate of interest, smaller consumption in period 1 may be traded against larger consumption in period 2. We are assuming that no further wage income will be received in period 2 and that all income carried over from period 1, plus interest thereon, will be consumed during period 2.[1]

In Figure 12-2, period 1 consumption is measured on the horizontal axis, and period 2 consumption on the vertical axis. The shape of the indifference curves between present and future consumption depends on the objective time distribution of needs and their subjective evaluation. Whatever the particular situation, we may assume that both present and future consumption are subject to declining marginal utility of income. Thus the indifference curves are convex to the origin, and the slope of successive curves rises when moving up on a vertical line and to the left along a horizontal line.[2] This we refer to as the standard case, leaving certain special cases for later consideration.

Let OA in Figure 12-2 be the initial income of period 1. Our householder may consume this income in period 1, or he may invest it. If the rate of interest i equals $(OB - OA)/OA$, period 1 consumption of OA may be traded against period 2 consumption of OB. The slope of the price line, or OB/OA, equals $1 + i$. The initial equilibrium may then be at C, where OD is consumed in period 1 and DC in period 2.

We shall now examine how various taxes affect present and future

---

[1] The principle of the argument remains the same if further wage income for period 2 is introduced. For an exposition of consumption theory along such lines, see Kenneth Boulding, *Economic Analysis*, 3d ed., Harpers & Brothers, New York, 1955, pp. 826ff.

Similarly, the principle of the argument is unchanged if the first-period income includes interest income from past accumulation. What matters in the case of the income tax is whether or not *future* interest income will be taxed.

[2] Assuming equal objective needs for both periods and no impatience factor to overvalue present needs, the indifference pattern is such that consumption would be divided equally between the two periods at a zero rate of interest. With unequal needs over time, and the possible influence of impatience, this need not be the case.

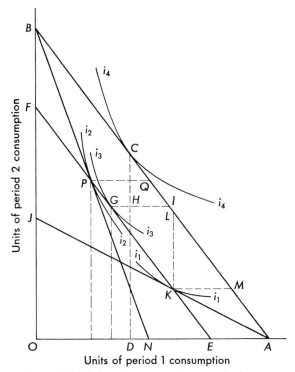

FIG. 12-2. Timing of consumption: standard case.

consumption. The substitution effects of various taxes are listed in Table 12-1.

Tax on Income Excluding Interest. A tax on income excluding interest does not affect the choice between present and future consumption. If the tax rate equals EA/OA, disposable income of the first period is reduced to OE. The price line shifts parallel to the left, as

TABLE 12-1. SUBSTITUTION EFFECTS ON PRESENT AND FUTURE CONSUMPTION

Tax base	Substitution effect
Income excluding interest Present and future consumption	None
Future consumption Saving Interest Total income	In favor of present consumption
Present consumption	In favor of future consumption

shown by EF, and the new equilibrium is at G.[1]   The yield equals EA in terms of present consumption.   Given our assumptions regarding the indifference pattern, G must lie below and to the left of C.   Provided that present and future consumption are not inferior goods, they are both reduced by the income effect.   There is no substitution effect in this case.

Tax on Present and Future Consumption.   The same result is obtained if the same rate of tax EA/OA is applied to both present and future consumption.   The government now collects GH of period 1 consumption in period 1, and HC of period 2 consumption in period 2.   This is equivalent to HI in terms of period 1 consumption, and GH plus HI equals EA.   A tax on consumption, present and future, is thus equivalent to a tax on income excluding interest.   This equivalence holds true provided there is no saving without subsequent consumption and no consumption from past balances without current saving.   These complications will be considered later on.

Tax on Future Consumption.   A tax on future consumption reduces the rate at which future consumption may be substituted for present consumption.   The slope of the price line declines.   Suppose that the government again wishes to obtain a yield equal to EA in terms of present consumption.   It imposes a tax on period 2 consumption at the rate JB/OB, set so that the new price line AJ intersects EF at a point where AJ is tangent to an indifference curve.   The new equilibrium is at K.   The yield is obtained in period 2, and equals KL in terms of period 2 consumption.   This is equivalent to $KM = EA$ in terms of period 1 consumption.

The position of K must be below and to the right of G, the equilibrium for the tax on income excluding interest.   This follows from the substitution effect of the tax on future consumption and the assumed properties of our indifference pattern.   At the same time, K may lie to the left or right of the pre-tax equilibrium C.   The substitution effect favorable to period 1 consumption may or may not outweigh the income effect.   As the rate of tax is increased, the path of equilibrium will be similar to CNA in Figure 12-1.[2]

Tax on Saving.   In the present model, where consumption in period 2 equals saving in period 1 plus interest, a tax on saving at rate t is equivalent to a tax on period 2 consumption at the same rate t.   The yield of the tax on saving equals tS, and is obtained in period 1.   The yield of the tax on period 2 consumption equals $t(1 + i)S$ and is obtained in period 2.

---

[1] Viewed from the standpoint of general equilibrium, this implies that introduction of the tax and resource withdrawal by the government does not affect the interest rate. The transformation schedule is a straight line. If the interest rate changes, the shift in the price line will not be parallel. (See p. 146.)

[2] See, however, p. 258, note 1.

The present value of this yield equals tS, which is the same as for the tax on saving.

Tax on Interest.   Now let us compare a tax on interest with a tax on saving that provides the same yield.   Since the tax on saving is due in the first period, the corresponding rates are such that $t_i = [(1 + i)/i]t_s$, where t_i is the tax rate applicable to interest and t_s is the tax rate applicable to saving.[1]   Imposed at corresponding rates so as to provide for equal yields in terms of present value, a tax on future consumption is thus equivalent to a tax on saving or a tax on interest.

General Income Tax.   The general income tax is a composite of a tax on wage income and a tax on interest income.   While it discriminates against future consumption, the required rate of tax—and hence the degree of discrimination—is less than for interest income only.

After a general income tax of equal yield is imposed, the price line in Figure 12-2 starts between E and A, and its slope falls between that of AB and AJ.   The new equilibrium again lies on EF.   It must lie to the right of G, the position under the tax on wage income only, since period 2 consumption is now discriminated against; and it must lie to the left of K, the position under the tax on period 2 consumption, since discrimination on period 2 consumption is now less severe.

Tax on Present Consumption.   A tax on present consumption increases the rate at which future consumption may be substituted for present consumption.   The slope of the price line is steepened.   Let a tax on period 1 consumption be applied so as to yield EA in terms of period 1 consumption.   Still referring to Figure 12-2, the required rate is NA/OA, set so that the new price line BN intersects EF at a point where BN is tangent to an indifference curve.   The new equilibrium is at P.   Tax yield is $PQ = EA$ in terms of period 1 consumption. P must lie above and to the left of G, since we now have a substitution effect adverse to period 1 consumption; P must also lie to the left of the pre-tax equilibrium C, since period 1 consumption will be reduced as the result of the tax.   However, P may be either below or above C, as period 2 consumption is subject to the opposing forces of a favorable substitution and an adverse income effect.

The potentially powerful substitution effect of a tax on present consumption is of great practical importance.   It is of particular significance for the case of war finance.   Here, a temporary tax on consumption may provide a powerful incentive to postpone consumption.   In our two-period case, imposition of tax on consumption in period 1 at rate t raises

---

[1] The yield from the tax on saving is obtained in the first period, and equals t_sS. The yield of the tax on interest is obtained in the second period, and equals t_iiS.   Its value in terms of period 1 consumption equals $t_i[i/(1 + i)]S$.   It follows that for taxes of equal yield $t_i = [(1 + i)/i]t_s$.

the effective rate of interest from i to $(i + t)/(1 - t)$.* With a market rate of interest of 5 per cent and a tax rate of 50 per cent, the effective rate of interest becomes 110 per cent. A temporary tax on consumption, or spendings tax, therefore furnishes a much more powerful deterrent to present consumption than could be provided by any practicable monetary policy. Moreover, the rate of tax needed to secure a given reduction in consumption will be lower under the tax on present consumption than under any other taxes. This proves an important consideration in cushioning the impact of war finance on work incentives.[1]

Effects of Progression. The preceding discussion has been in terms of proportional taxes. Where substitution effects are present, these will be accentuated if a given yield is obtained from any particular taxpayer under a progressive rate schedule. As noted before, the income effect is a function of the average rate of tax, while the substitution effect is a function of the marginal rate. Under a progressive formula, the marginal rate is higher relative to the average rate than it is under a proportional tax.[2]

Saving for Consumption Only: Special Cases

These general results may now be modified to meet certain special cases of consumer behavior. The assumption of zero net saving for both periods as a whole is retained for the time being.

Target Saver. We shall begin with a householder who sets a fixed target for his future level of consumption. He saves whatever part of period 1 income is needed to secure a given consumption for period 2. This is the hypothesis behind the familiar speculation that saving may be related inversely rather than directly to the rate of interest.

The indifference pattern of the target saver consists of a series of rectangular lines, such as BCD, GMD, and EHD in Figure 12-3, where OC is the fixed amount of period 2 consumption. With a pre-tax income of OA and a rate of interest equal to $(OB - OA)/OA$, the price line equals AB, and the equilibrium is at H. Present consumption equals CH, and future consumption equals OC. Now, a tax is imposed, designed to yield FA in terms of period 1 consumption. With a tax on income excluding interest, the price line shifts parallel to the left, as shown by FL, and the new equilibrium is at M. Period 2 consumption remains unchanged at

---

* If Y is income, the effective rate of interest is

$$i_e = \frac{(1 + i)Y - (1 - t)Y}{(1 - t)Y}$$

[1] See p. 250. See M. Friedman, "The Spendings Tax as a Wartime Measure," p. 50, and K. E. Poole, "Problems of Administration and Equity," p. 63, both in *American Economic Review*, vol. 23, no. 1, March, 1943.

[2] See p. 241.

OC, while period 1 consumption is reduced to OW. The same result is obtained with equal-yield taxes on future consumption, saving, or interest, in which cases the price line shifts to AN; or by a tax on present consumption where the price line shifts to BR. The marginal rate of substitution of present for future consumption equals zero, and the result is the same in all cases.

Residual Saver. Next let us consider a householder with a fixed level of present consumption. This residual saver uses whatever part of his income is needed to meet a given consumption requirement in period 1 and saves what is left.

His indifference pattern consists of a series of rectangular lines such as EHD, EMS, and ETA in Figure 12-4, where OT is the fixed amount of

TIMING OF CONSUMPTION: SPECIAL CASES

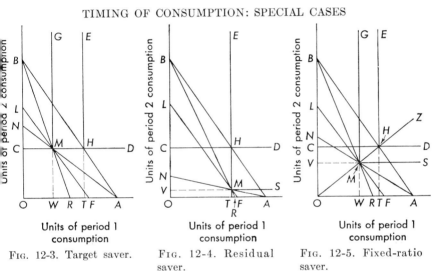

Fig. 12-3. Target saver.   Fig. 12-4. Residual saver.   Fig. 12-5. Fixed-ratio saver.

period 1 consumption. The initial equilibrium is now at H. A tax on income excluding interest shifts the price line to FL and the equilibrium to M. An equal-yield tax on future consumption, saving, or interest moves the price line to AN, and a tax on present consumption moves it to BR. The marginal rate of substitution of future for present consumption is again zero, and the outcome remains the same under all taxes. The entire adjustment now is in period 2 consumption, just as in the previous case it was in period 1.

Fixed-ratio Saver. Finally, consider a householder who spreads his total consumption in a fixed ratio over the present and the future period. His indifference pattern consists of a series of rectangular lines such as GMS and EHD in Figure 12-5, whose corners are located on a straight line through the origin, such as OZ. The initial equilibrium is now at H, and the new position under all the tax alternatives is again at M. As before, the marginal rate of substitution between present and future consumption is zero, and it is a matter of indifference which type of tax is used.

So far, we have assumed that the individual proceeds rationally and fixes his time pattern in terms of consumption net of taxes. The results differ if he operates under a tax illusion and insists upon saving a given amount or a given fraction of his period 1 income without allowing for the effect of various taxes upon the net (after tax) value of present or future consumption.[1] Suppose that he saves a given fraction s of period 1 income Y_1. Under a tax of given yield on period 1 consumption, his consumption in period 1 equals $(1 - s)Y_1 - T$, and his consumption in period 2 equals $(1 + i)sY_1$. The entire tax comes out of period 1 consumption. Under a tax of equal yield on period 2 consumption, his consumption in period 2 equals $(1 + i)sY_1 - (1 + i)T$, and in period 1 equals $(1 - s)Y_1$. Here the entire tax comes out of period 2 consumption. The results of a tax on income excluding interest now differ from the results of a tax on present and future consumption, but are similar to the results of a tax on present consumption. Given this tax illusion, the effects simply depend on whether the tax is collected in period 1 or in period 2.

Saving for Consumption and Accumulation

We shall now drop the assumption of zero saving for the two periods as a whole and consider a householder concerned not only with arranging his time stream of consumption between periods 1 and 2 but also with perpetual accumulation as such.[2]

The comparative effects of the various taxes now depend on the taxpayer's marginal rates of substitution between future consumption and present consumption, accumulation and present consumption, and accumulation and future consumption; and upon the way in which the various taxes affect the rates at which these three alternative uses of income may be exchanged for each other.

In considering this more complex situation, let us return to the standard pattern of behavior; but let us think in terms of a preference surface involving accumulation as well as present and future consumption. A

---

[1] These cases cannot be shown in terms of the preceding diagram, where the decision between present and future consumption is in net terms.

[2] The significant point in this connection is motivation, i.e., whether the taxpayer saves with the intent of future consumption or for accumulation's sake. The fact that estates are left is not necessarily a proof of saving for accumulation's sake, since death may have occurred sooner than expected. Moreover, accumulation of an estate to provide for the future consumption of heirs may be interpreted as saving for future consumption rather than for accumulation.

tax on income excluding interest is now the only one among our taxes that involves no substitution effect.[1]   The tax on present and future consumption that was previously in this category now discriminates in favor of accumulation.   Thus, saving will be increased if this tax is substituted for the tax on income excluding interest.   The same is true, and to a greater degree, if a tax on total consumption is substituted for a tax on total income.

A tax on interest or saving was shown previously to discriminate in favor of present against future consumption.   Thus the substitution effect was adverse to saving.   We can now add that the tax also discriminates in favor of present consumption against accumulation.   The negative substitution effect on saving is reinforced.

Similarly, a tax on present consumption was shown previously to discriminate in favor of future against present consumption.   The substitution effect was favorable to saving.   We can now add that the tax also discriminates in favor of accumulation against present consumption. The positive substitution effect on saving is reinforced.

Also a tax on future consumption was shown previously to discriminate in favor of present against future consumption.   Here the substitution effect was adverse to saving.   Now, as accumulation is introduced, we find that the tax discriminates against future consumption compared to accumulation.   Thus, saving for accumulation may be substituted for saving for future consumption, and the net impact of the substitution effects depends upon the circumstances of the case.

Since accumulation is allowed for, let us note the effects of a property tax.   This tax may be translated again into a tax on property income.[2] Its effects on saving and consumption are similar to those of a tax on interest.   The distinction between old and new capital income from old and new capital proved of considerable importance in dealing with taxation effects upon work effort, but it is not relevant in the present connection (if we disregard friction in the rearrangement of portfolios).   A tax on interest from an old investment or a property tax thereon constitutes an inducement to dissave, just as a tax on interest from a new investment or a property tax thereon constitutes a deterrent to save.   At the same time, a tax on total property or property income results in a higher level of net saving (or a lower level of dissaving) than a tax on the increment only.   Since the base will be larger, the marginal rate of tax on saving, and hence the negative substitution effect will be less.

Other taxes can be fitted into this pattern and further motivations for

---

[1] It will be recalled that the supply of labor is assumed to be fixed, so that substitution effects on leisure may be disregarded.

[2] If the holding of non-income-earning property is allowed for, the two taxes will be dissimilar.   (See p. 325.)

saving allowed for. Thus, death duties may be introduced and allowance made for saving designed to provide for one's heirs. Other simplifying assumptions of the preceding model might be removed. The two-period setting could be replaced with one allowing for the allocation of consumption and income over the expected life span. Removal of the assumption that there is only one consumer good opens the possibility for selective excises. Their effects on saving will vary, depending on differences in the rates of substitution between present and future consumption of various commodities. Finally, removal of the assumption of fixed effort supply introduces the further choice between leisure, consumption (present and future), and accumulation. With this change, the income tax on income other than interest joins the group of taxes with substitution effects, and only the head tax remains to claim the distinction of neutrality.

C. ADJUSTMENTS IN CONSUMPTION AND SAVING BY GROUP

We now turn to the effects of taxation on consumption and saving by the group as a whole. Such effects are important in terms of aggregate demand, capital formation, and so forth. But setting aside these broader considerations for the moment, let us turn to the aggregate level of saving and consumption that results if alternative taxes of equal yield are applied to a given level of income. The present discussion thus remains in partial-equilibrium terms, even though tax effects on the group's saving and consumption level are considered.

When exploring these effects for the group as a whole, we must allow for the fact that different types of taxes are paid by different people and that different people react in different ways to any particular tax. This applies to effects on consumption and saving no less than to effects on work effort.

Income Effects

All taxes have an income effect, but they may or may not have a substitution effect. As a result of the income effect, all taxes tend to reduce consumption, saving for future consumption, and saving for accumulation. This holds true since we may assume that present consumption, future consumption, and accumulation are all superior goods. However, the extent to which one or the other use of income is cut back differs with different people. More specifically, we know from the study of family budgets that the marginal propensity to save rises as we move up in the income scale. In the absence of substitution effects, a dollar paid by a taxpayer with a larger income tends to be reflected more heavily in reduced saving than a dollar paid by a taxpayer with a smaller income.

This principle permits us to draw certain conclusions regarding the comparative impact of various taxes on consumption and saving in the absence of substitution effects. Thus, a progressive income tax reduces saving more and consumption less than does a proportional tax. The same holds for a proportional tax on income compared with one on consumption. We find from observation that consumption declines as a fraction of income when moving up the income scale. Hence, a general tax on consumption is regressive in terms of income. Similarly, it follows from the composition of consumer budgets that a tax on necessities falls more heavily on consumption than does a tax on luxuries. Analogous conclusions apply regarding income taxes that differentiate between different types of income. A proportional tax on wage income tends to fall more heavily on consumption than a similar tax on capital income. We learn through observation that the ratio of wage to capital income falls when moving up the income scale. Therefore a proportional tax on wage income is regressive, and a proportional tax on capital income is progressive, if the ratio of tax to total income is considered.

These conclusions may be subject to qualification or reversal after substitution effects are allowed for, but let us disregard such possibilities for the time being. The significance of differences in the consumption impact of various taxes then depends upon the degree to which the marginal propensity to save rises as we move up the income scale. While available data bear out the impression that the average propensity to save rises sharply as we move up the income scale, the marginal propensity shows a higher degree of stability than might be expected in view of substantial differences in the average propensity.[1] On the basis of these data, one may attempt to estimate the "initial" changes in consumption and saving that result from various adjustments in the tax structure. As noted before, subsequent multiplier effects or other effects on the level of income before tax are disregarded for the time being.

To illustrate, we may compare the initial changes in consumption and saving that would result from a $1 billion cut in the yield of the Federal income tax secured, first, by a 3 per cent cut in all bracket rates and, secondly, by a cut in rates so as to make the allocation of yield similar to the estimated distribution of the tax burden under a general sales tax.[2]

[1] See, for instance, the findings of the Annual Survey of Consumer Finances conducted by the Survey Research Center of the University of Michigan for the Board of Governors of the Federal Reserve System. The last year for which this particular data has been published is 1950. See *Federal Reserve Bulletin*, September, 1951.

[2] The underlying data refer to 1954, and may be found in my paper on "The Incidence of the Tax Structure and Its Effect on Consumption," *Federal Tax Policy for Economic Growth and Stability*, Joint Committee on the Economic Report, 84th Cong., 1st Sess., Nov. 9, 1953, pp. 96–113. Also see R. A. Musgrave and M. S. Painter, "The Impact of Alternative Tax Structures on Personal Consumption and Saving,"

Assuming sales taxes to be paid by the consumer, the tax relief under the second policy is much more favorable to small incomes than under the first policy.   Yet the estimated gain in consumption is $825 million under the second policy and $750 million under the first policy, the difference being only 7.5 per cent of the total change in yield.[1]   From this and similar estimates, it appears that the importance of the relationship between degree of progression and division of the tax bill between consumption and saving is easily overstated.

As noted before, this is true because the marginal propensity to save, as evidenced by available budget studies, rises only slightly when moving up the income scale.   The coexistence of a fairly constant marginal propensity to save with a sharply rising *average* propensity to save is explained by the phenomenon of dissaving at the lower end of the income scale.

The persistence of dissaving at this end of the scale is a rather puzzling piece of information.[2]   Recent budget studies suggest that it can be explained in considerable part through dissaving by individuals who are *temporarily* in lower-income brackets.   Such dissaving by "temporary losers" occurs throughout the income scale, but it is only in the lower brackets that their dissaving outweighs the positive saving of others who are more permanent inhabitants of these particular brackets.

The important question arises whether the results would differ—more specifically, whether the quantitative importance of progression would be increased—if the analysis could be based on data (as yet unavailable) in which households with relatively stable incomes were separated from

---

Quarterly Journal of Economics, vol. 62, no. 4, pp. 475–499, August, 1948; and H. Lubell, "Effects of Income Redistribution on Consumer Expenditures," *American Economic Review*, vol. 37, no. 1, pp. 157–170, March, 1947.

[1] In arriving at this estimate, substitution effects are disregarded.   An income tax paid on interest income is assumed to affect consumption in the same way as an income tax paid on wage income, provided the incomes are of the same size.   A sales tax paid by the consumer is assumed to affect consumption in the same way as an equal amount paid in income tax, provided, again, that both consumers have the same income.

Moreover, the estimate is based on certain hypotheses with regard to incidence. In particular, it is assumed that the sales tax is borne by the consumer and that no money illusion arises.   Some degree of justification for these hypotheses will be found in the following pages, especially with regard to the incidence of excise taxes.   However, they are hypotheses only.   For an optimistic view, see R. A. Musgrave et al., "Distribution of Tax Payments by Income Groups: A Case Study for 1948," *National Tax Journal*, vol. 4, no. 1, pp. 1–53, March, 1951.   For a skeptical appraisal, see A. R. Prest, "Statistical Calculations of Tax Burdens," *Economica*, New Ser., vol. 22, no. 87, pp. 234–245, August, 1955.

[2] The following discussion is based on suggestions by my colleague, Professor J. Morgan.

others with relatively unstable incomes.   General considerations suggest that this would not be the case.

Suppose that dissaving by income units at the bottom of the scale is less for units with stable incomes than for the combined group.   The hypothetical savings schedule for the stable group, therefore, lies higher at the bottom of the scale than does the observed schedule for the combined group.   It does not follow from this that the marginal propensity to save rises more sharply for the stable group when moving up the income scale. While stable units are likely to have a higher propensity to save at low-income ranges, they may also have a lower propensity to save at high-income ranges.   Income uncertainty, which is one of the inducements to save, is not present.   Thus, separating out the stable group may result merely in a pivoting of the savings schedule; the slope of the schedule may change, but it may remain more or less a straight line.   The marginal propensity to save may again be fairly constant.   There is no a priori reason, therefore, why application of the observed savings schedule (derived from the combined groups) to the stable group should either over- or understate the differential in the savings impact of alternative tax structures.

Turning now to spending units with fluctuating incomes, let us adopt the hypothesis that consumption depends not only on present income but also on the preceding income high.[1]   Those who have dropped temporarily to low-income brackets consume more and save less (or dissave more) than do stable units at the same income level.   But this will not be true for units with temporarily high incomes.   Differences in the marginal propensity to consume at various points in the income scale will be less, therefore, for the unstable group than for the stable group.   These speculations suggest that application of the combined schedule to the unstable group tends to exaggerate rather than understate the differences in the savings impact of alternative tax structures.

Substitution Effects

Substitution effects must now be reintroduced.   Considering these effects on total saving for the group, we now have two reasons to expect that a proportional tax on capital income will fall more heavily on saving than will a tax on wage income.   Not only is the former distributed more progressively in terms of total income, but it also has a disincentive effect. Comparison between a progressive tax and a proportional tax on capital income leaves us with a doubtful result, since we are dealing with similar sets of opposing forces, as noted previously in connection with the effects

[1] See James S. Duesenberry, *Income, Saving and the Theory of Consumer Behavior,* Harvard University Press, Cambridge, Mass., 1949, especially chap. 5.

of income taxation on work incentives.[1]   However, allowance for sub-stitution effects gives added reason to expect that a progressive tax on total income will bear more heavily on saving than a proportional tax. This will be the case because under a progressive tax a larger part of the total yield is drawn from capital income.[2]   Similarly, allowance for the substitution effect gives additional reason to expect that savings for the group will be reduced more under a proportional tax on income than under a proportional tax on present and future consumption.

While the direction of the substitution effect is clear in most cases, its magnitude is not easily assessed.   It would seem to be of minor impor-tance if we compare a flat-rate tax on income with a flat-rate tax on consumption, and it may well remain of modest importance, even if progression in the income tax is allowed for.   At the same time, the substitution effect may become most powerful in the case of a temporary tax on consumption or a tax on present consumption only.[3]

In concluding, we may note an important analytical difference between the income and substitution effect.   If the tax results in an income effect only, any one taxpayer will reduce both consumption and saving. Assuming the labor supply to be fixed, the sum of both reductions equals his change in income or tax paid.   Thus we can speak of the yield as being divided initially between reduced consumption and reduced saving.   If a substitution effect is present, consumption may rise and saving may fall (or vice versa).   Combining both effects, the sum of changes in consump-tion and saving (which may move in opposite directions) still equals yield, but the decrease in consumption or in saving taken by itself may exceed yield.   Indeed, substantial (if equal-sized) changes in consump-tion and saving may occur with a zero yield.   The concept of yield, being divided between consumption and saving, must be replaced by that of taxation effects upon consumption and saving.

D. EFFECTS OF PUBLIC EXPENDITURES

As in the case of work incentives, consumer behavior may be affected from the expenditure as well as from the tax side of the budget.   This is of particular importance in connection with transfer payments but may also apply in the case of goods and service expenditures.

Transfer Payments

In a formal sense, transfers may again be looked upon as negative taxes. Transfers that subsidize or match wage income are neutral with regard to

---

[1] See p. 248.   For purposes of the present discussion, the labor supply is held fixed.

[2] This conclusion is supported further by the hypothesis that, within any income group, people with high capital incomes will also be high savers.

[3] See p. 264.

the choice between present consumption, future consumption, and accumulation. Transfers that subsidize or match interest income are neutral as between future consumption and accumulation, but discriminate against present consumption. This is the case if the government offers debt at terms more favorable than the market demands.[1] Transfers that subsidize or match present and future consumption discriminate against accumulation, and so forth.

Thus, the preceding analysis of taxation effects may be repeated in reverse for the case of transfers. More interesting, however, is the fact

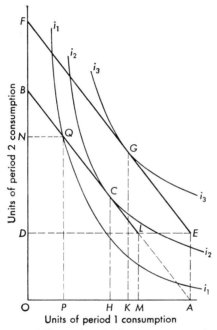

FIG. 12-6. Effects of social insurance on saving.

that the typical transfer structure differs from that of taxes. The bulk of transfers in the modern budget are part of the social security system.[2] These transfers provide for needs under certain contingencies such as old age, ill health, or unemployment. They reduce the need for saving in order to provide for future consumption in such contingencies, but they do not change the terms of saving for purposes of accumulation.

Let us return to our two-period model. In Figure 12-6, OA is period 1 income, $(OB - OA)/OA$ is the rate of interest, AB is the price line, and C is the initial equilibrium. Now let us assume that certain benefit pay-

[1] See p. 583.

[2] I am indebted to Professor Elizabeth Liefman-Keil, with whom the following problems have been discussed on various occasions.

ments are introduced, providing for future consumption of OD. The possible combinations available to the individual are now indicated by EF, and the new equilibrium is at a point such as G. Period 1 consumption rises from OH to OK, and saving is reduced from HA to KA. This is the typical case of noncontributory social security benefits, where private saving is reduced not by raising the rate at which present consumption may be traded for future consumption but by providing for future consumption free of direct charge. The new equilibrium G lies to the right of the pretransfer equilibrium C, provided that present and/or future consumption is/are subject to decreasing marginal utility.

Now let us allow for the financing of benefit payments and assume, first, that the operation is financed on a strictly contributory basis. Let us also assume that the same rate of interest applies to both public and private insurance.[1]   In this case, the government imposes a tax on income (interest excluded) at the rate of MA/OA, and the opportunities available to the individual are now shown by LB. The individual will return to the initial equilibrium at C. Private saving will equal HM, saving through social insurance will equal MA, and total saving will remain unchanged at HA.[2]

There is the possibility that the saving provided for under the public plan exceeds the private target. Thus, suppose that the public plan provides future consumption ON, requiring an income tax rate of PA/OA. The consumer must now choose among positions on QB, and will place himself at Q, where private saving is zero. However, total saving, now all in the form of saving through social insurance, is raised to PA.

Finally, we must reconsider the assumption, implicit in the preceding argument, that all saving is homogeneous. The consumer may find that compulsory saving (under insurance) falls short of his own target for one type of saving (such as old age) while exceeding it for another (such as illness). Unless savings for various purposes can be readily substituted for each other, compulsory saving may force him to increase his total saving. Thus it would not be surprising if a strictly contributory social security system increases total saving by the group as a whole.[3]

---

[1] The term *rate of interest* as used here involves the yield of investment as well as the actuarial cost of insurance.

[2] If the public plan involves economies of scale not available to private finance, a lesser rate of tax will do, and the new equilibrium will be between C and G. Total saving will be increased. This, at least, will be true for our earlier assumptions of the "standard case." For the special problem of the target saver the opposite result applies.

[3] Lord Keynes, in a lecture presented at the Federal Reserve Seminar in Washington in 1945, expressed the hope that the growth of social security would lead to a substantial decline in private saving, thus helping to avoid secular underemployment without heavy reliance on deficit spending by government.

Finally, let us consider a mixed system that is not on a strictly contributory basis. For a person who is subsidized on balance, the rate of income tax required to finance OD of future consumption will be less than MA/OA. The new equilibrium will lie between C and G, and his total saving will decrease. The opposite holds for a person who loses on balance. The net effects of tax-transfer systems upon consumers as a group thus depend upon the direction of the redistributional change and upon differences in the reactions of consumers at various points in the income scale. The role of progression again enters the picture. Assuming a progressive tax to fall more heavily upon saving than a proportional tax, a mixed system with an equalitarian element of redistribution will raise total saving less than a contributory system, and may even reduce it.

One other aspect of the matter must be noted. Whatever the effect upon the total level of saving, social insurance schemes—unless on a strictly pay-as-you-go basis—involve a transfer of investible funds from the private to the public sector, thus rendering public institutions a governing factor in the capital markets.[1]

Goods and Service Expenditures

The effects of goods and service expenditures on consumption and saving in the private sector may be explained in terms similar to those previously applied to effects on work incentives.[2] Public expenditures that increase productivity may affect private saving via resulting changes in the return to capital. Public expenditures that result in a free supply of consumer goods may affect the division of income between present and future consumption, depending on the relationship (complementary, neutral, or rival) of these goods to privately purchased goods that are consumed at present and in the future. The free supply of old-age homes will affect savings patterns differently from the free supply of elementary schools, for example. The approach to the problem is similar to that used in the preceding chapter and need not be pursued again.

[1] See p. 527.
[2] See p. 254.

CHAPTER 13

Adjustments in price and output

We shall now turn to adjustments on the part of the business firm. Taxes payable by the firm may be assessed on net receipts, gross receipts, or cost payments—involving variable, fixed, or total cost. The firm's adjustments may take the form of short-run changes in price and output with a given plant capacity, or they may lead to long-run changes in capacity. Similar adjustments may result in response to subsidies. In the present chapter, we are concerned primarily with the short-run aspect of adjustments and with adjustments in a partial-equilibrium setting. The long-run aspect is taken up in the following chapter, and adjustments in the general equilibrium will be examined thereafter.

A. TAX ON NET INCOME

We shall begin with a tax on business net income or profits. In the United States tax structure, this means primarily the corporation income tax, although the same principles apply to the taxation of income from unincorporated business under the personal income tax.

Possible Types of Adjustment

Suppose that a tax on business profits is imposed. The firm may find it profitable to maintain its price and output at pre-tax levels. A loss of profits, proportional to the rate of tax, is accepted in the short run and allocated in some fashion between dividends and retained earnings. This may be followed in the long run by adjustments in the level and type of capital investment. Or the firm may find it profitable to curtail output at once and to raise price. A third alternative is for the firm to pay less for the materials or services it purchases. Each of these adjustments will give rise to further change. The final incidence and output effects will differ, depending on what move is made initially.

The very nature of a tax on profits hinges on this initial adjustment. To the extent that profits are cut, the tax on business profits belongs to the family of taxes on capital income. It remains to be seen, in this case, how the recipients of profits will adjust themselves, how investors will react to the fall in profits, and how capital formation and the profit share are affected in the long run. To the extent that prices are raised, the tax on business profits is more or less similar in effect to a tax on gross receipts or on consumer expenditures. Subsequent adjustments will take a different path and lead to different results. To the extent that wages are reduced, the consequences of the profit tax are more or less similar to those of a payroll tax, and further adjustments depend on the reaction of the wage recipient. Unless the nature of the initial adjustment is known, little can be said about the merits of a profits tax as a major component of the tax structure, or about the merits of various proposals for integrating the personal and the corporation income tax.

The Traditional Argument

Unfortunately, there is little empirical evidence on incidence of a profits tax. With few exceptions, economists have argued that a tax on profits cannot be shifted in the short run. Edgeworth,[1] for example, says, "That taxation upon the profits of a monopolist cannot be shifted is universally acknowledged." Yet businessmen have maintained stubbornly that they consider the tax a cost that is added to price.

The traditional argument has been that it is not advisable in the short run to counter the imposition of a profits tax by adjustments in output and price so as to absorb the tax in higher profits.

In order to maximize profits, the individual firm determines price and output to equate marginal revenue and marginal cost. A tax on profits does not change the position of the marginal revenue and cost schedules; hence, it does not change the position of optimum price and output. This will be the case, whatever the state of competition.

[1] F. Y. Edgeworth, *Papers Relating to Political Economy*, Macmillan & Co., Ltd., London, 1925, vol. II, p. 97; also see A. Cournot, *Researches into the Mathematical Principles of the Theory of Wealth*, ed. I. Fisher, The Macmillan Company, New York, 1938, p. 68 (first published 1838); Knut Wicksell, *Finanztheoretische Untersuchungen und des Steuerwesen Schweden's*, Jena, Germany, 1896, pp. 11–20; Edwin R. Seligman, *Studies in Public Finance*, The Macmillan Company, New York, 1925, pp. 59–84; H. Dalton, *Principles of Public Finance*, 9th ed., Routledge and Kegan Paul, Ltd., London, 1936, pp. 81–85; Richard Goode, *Corporation Income Tax*, John Wiley & Sons, Inc., New York, 1951, pp. 47–54. Also see the *Report of the Commission on National Debt and Taxation* (Colwyn Report), H. M. Stationery Office, London, 1927, Hansard 2800.

Under pure competition, a profits tax is without yield.   The marginal firm incurs no profits of any kind.   Superior firms, whose cost of production is lower than that of marginal firms, do obtain efficiency earnings, but these are in the nature of differential rents and, hence, costs to the firms.   Even if efficiency earnings were taxed as profits, no change in supply would result.   Being differential rents, such earnings are determined by, and are not determinants of, costs or price at the margin.

The monopolist as well does best to leave his price and output unchanged and to surrender whatever fraction of his profits is taken from him.[1]   This will be desirable whether the tax is proportional or progressive, provided that the marginal rate falls short of 100 per cent.

Qualifications

The logic of the conventional argument is compelling if the underlying assumptions are accepted.   But they need be qualified in various ways.

Cost Elements in Tax Base.   The traditional argument implies that taxable net income under a profits tax excludes all cost items.   This will be the case only if the tax law permits deduction of all costs, taxable profits being computed as gross receipts minus costs.   Without entering into the technical aspects of income definition, let us consider briefly the role of normal profits.

D. H. Robertson and others have suggested that the profits tax may be shifted because it does not allow for such profits.[2]   This group has argued

---

[1] Given the demand function for the monopolist $p = p(q)$ and the average cost function $c = c(q)$, total revenue is given by

$$R = pq = p(q)q$$

and total cost is given by

$$C = cq = c(q)q$$

In equilibrium, $R - C$ must be a maximum, so that equilibrium output is given by

$$\frac{dR}{dq} - \frac{dC}{dq} = p(q) + qp'(q) - c(q) - qc'(q) = 0$$

After a profits tax at rate t is imposed, the monopolist maximizes $(1 - t)(R - C)$, which leaves us with the same condition for equilibrium output as before.

[2] D. H. Robertson, "The Colwyn Committee, the Income Tax and the Price Level," *Economic Journal*, 37, no. 142, December, 1927, pp. 566–581, reprinted in R. A. Musgrave and Carl Shoup (eds.), *Readings in the Economics of Taxation*, American Economic Association, Richard D. Irwin, Inc., Homewood, Ill., 1958.   Also see Duncan Black, *The Incidence of Income Taxes*, Macmillan & Co., Ltd., London, 1939, chaps. 1–3.

Robertson's argument was directed primarily at Coates's statistical thesis before the Colwyn Committee that wide variations of cost among firms within an industry prove that price is determined by marginal (no-profit) firms; and that, *therefore*, the tax is not shifted.   See W. H. Coates, "Incidence of the Income Tax," *Appendices to the Report of the Commission on National Debt and Taxation*, H. M. Stationary Office, London, 1927, pp. 65–113.

that the Marshallian concept of normal price, defined as the price required to keep output unchanged, allows for normal profits, including a return to capital as well as to wages of management. These returns, it is claimed, are not rents. They are not determined by price but are cost payments to factors, the supply of which is more or less elastic. They enter into the cost schedule of the representative firm and are determinants of price. Putting aside the somewhat ambiguous concept of the representative firm, the argument says that a normal-profit component is included in the cost schedule of all firms whose supply enters at the margin, and that a tax thereon is a tax on cost.

Consider first the normal return to capital. In so far as fixed capital is concerned, this is a long-run matter, as is Marshall's doctrine of normal price. If necessary returns, such as rewards for waiting, the surrender of liquidity, or risk are reduced by the tax—and it remains to be seen in the following chapter how and whether this may be the case—the supply of capital and risk taking will be curtailed. If the tax is partial, some firms will leave the industry and move into fields that are not subject to tax, thus equalizing returns net of tax. If the tax is general, this adjustment is not needed. In either case, a restriction in the return to capital may reduce the capital stock or may slow down its growth. This in turn may affect real wages as well as profits. Such adjustments may come about in the long run and must be distinguished from the proposition that profits are reduced in the short run.

In the short run, the plant is given, and there is no normal return to fixed capital. A return to capital must be paid only with regard to working capital.[1] Thus, the tax affects cost in the short run, if no allowance is made for a normal return to working capital. Such is the case when short-run capital is in equity form, since imputed interest may not be deducted. Depending on the industry in question and on the financial structure of the firm, the imputed return to working capital may be a factor of some importance.

Another possible component of normal profits is wages of management. Since the demanders and suppliers of such services are frequently the same people, we deal here with a highly administered price. Returns to management, though wages by nature, are not easily distinguishable from profits. On the whole, the definition of taxable profits in the United States tax laws is such that ample allowance is made for this kind of wages. Where allowance is not made, wages of management are

[1] See E. Cary Brown, "The Corporate Income Tax in the Short Run," *National Tax Journal*, vol. 2, no. 3, p. 240, September, 1954. A similar point is made by Shoup; see note on p. 280. Also see Diran Bodenhorn, "The Shifting of the Corporation Income Tax in a Growing Economy," *Quarterly Journal of Economics*, vol. 70, no. 4, p. 563, November, 1956.

reduced by the profits tax, and the problem becomes one of effort supply. If the tax is partial, management may move to tax-free industries unless its wages are raised. If such movement is possible without much delay, the tax may raise cost in the short run. If the tax is general, the total supply of entrepreneurial effort may go up or down, with corresponding adjustments in the firm's output and price.[1] This may enter in the short run, where entrepreneurial effort relates to the degree of capacity utilization, and in the long run where such effort relates to investment decisions. In either case, wages of management are a highly administered price, and a tax thereon may be absorbed by other cost or profit components.[2]

Restraint in Profit Maximization. The conventional argument is based on the assumption of profit maximization as the guiding objective in the determination of price and output. This requires qualification.

Profit maximization by the monopolist may not be a short- but a long-run objective. A firm may forego current profits or incur losses in order to obtain control over a market by undercutting competitors or building up good will. But this has no immediate bearing on our problem, provided that the profits tax is permanent. If profits are postponed, so are taxes. If both are subject to the same discount, the decision to postpone will not be influenced by the tax factor, provided that the tax rate is expected to remain constant. The case differs where a change in tax rate is expected. The profitability of foregoing profits now may be increased by the expectation of a declining tax rate; or the importance of preserving good will may be lessened by the expectation of rising rates.

Moreover, a monopolist may exercise restraint in exploiting available market opportunities. He may fear antitrust action if his profits, or the size of his business, become too large; he may feel that excessive profits are incompatible with his concept of a just price or socially responsible profit margins; he may wish to forestall undesirable effects on wage policy; or he may wish to fend off potential rivals. With administered prices based on considerations of this kind, a tax on profits may lead the monopolist to raise prices in order to restore profits to the proper level, as he sees it—provided that this level of profits after tax determines the desired degree of restraint. How far the monopolist can go in recouping profits prior to imposition of the tax will depend upon the structure of cost and demand[3]

---

[1] Assuming the scale of output to be related inversely to entrepreneurial leisure, Boulding shows that a profits tax may either reduce or increase output. In this argument, the tax on profits is treated essentially as a tax on wages. See Kenneth Boulding, "The Incidence of a Profits Tax," *American Economic Review*, vol. 34, no. 3, pp. 567–572, September, 1944.

[2] See p. 362.

[3] In this connection, see Carl Shoup, "Incidence of the Corporation Income Tax: Capital Structure and Turnover Rates," *National Tax Journal*, vol. 1, no. 1, pp. 12–17,

and upon the extent to which previous restraint kept him from making full use of his profit potential.

The proposition that a tax on the seller is more likely to be shifted in a seller's market than in a buyer's market is usually interpreted in terms of various elasticities of supply and demand. As such it is applicable to a tax on gross receipts rather than on profits. However, the argument may be restated in terms of restraint in price policy. Suppose that price is set so as to secure a limited profit net of tax. An increase in the rate of profits tax in the boom will be passed on in full, since there exists an ample margin of unused profits; and a reduction in the rate of tax will be passed on in lower prices so as to avoid excessive profits. An increase in the tax rate under conditions of depression will not affect price. Maximum profits after tax fall short of the limit set by restraint, and price cannot be raised. Nor is a reduction in the tax passed on, provided that the increment does not raise profits beyond the permissible limit. In a position where maximum profits after tax just equal the permissible amount, an increase in tax rate will not be reflected in a change in price, but a reduction in tax rate will lead to a cut in price.

Monopolistic Competition. Further exceptions to the conventional reasoning may arise from market structures that involve various types of imperfections.

In a market characterized by a small number of sellers supplying a standardized product, price will be set somewhere between the competitive price and the monopoly price, but there is no way of telling just where it will come to rest. The solution depends on the strategy pursued by the participating firms. If they are fully aware of each other's reaction, they may agree to set a monopoly price and share the profits. If they pay no attention to each other, a competitive price may result. Or there may be no stable solution, and price may continue to oscillate.

Imposition of a profits tax will leave unaffected the two limiting price positions. If our oligopolists acted like competitors, they would reach the competitive price that is unaffected by the tax; if they acted as a single monopolist, they would remain at the initial monopoly position. Therefore, if the tax is to have an effect on oligopoly price, it must affect the particular in-between position at which the various sellers choose to settle. Imposition of a tax may do this if the tax acts as a signal to individual firms that price can be raised without retaliatory action by competitors. And removal of a tax may act as a warning that others will

---

March, 1948, reprinted in Musgrave and Shoup, *op. cit.* Shoup assumes that the firm attempts to recover the tax by raising price and that its ability to do so depends on the percentage increase in gross receipts required to restore the absolute level of pre-tax profits. This increase in turn depends on the rate of turnover and the composition of capital between equity and borrowed capital.

reduce their price, thus forcing any one seller to conform. Again, there is a distinct possibility, quite within the framework of conventional price theory, for a profits tax to lead to price adjustments.

No such exception arises in the case of product differentiation with a large number of firms.[1] Monopoly profits are absent in this case, and the argument is similar to that which was used for the competitive industry. No profits are reaped, and no tax will be due. The presence of advertising costs does not change the situation. The margin up to which such costs prove worthwhile remains unchanged by the tax.

Where product differentiation is combined with a small number of firms, monopoly profits may prevail. As in the case of pure oligopoly, the tax does not change the limits between which the price can be set. The only way in which the tax can affect price determination is to act as a signal that a price increase can be introduced with impunity or that a decrease in the rival's price is in the offing.

Collective Bargaining.   Let us now consider possible effects of a profits tax on the wage bargain.   In a purely competitive labor market, the wage rate equals the marginal-revenue product of labor at the optimum output. If this output is not changed by the imposition of the tax, the wage rate remains unchanged as well.   In a situation where the employer occupies a monopolistic position in the labor market, labor may be paid less than its marginal-value product, but the optimal wage rate and output are again unaffected by the tax.   Nor will the wage rate be affected if the union occupies a monopoly position in labor supply but carries on a conditional bargain.   Thus, the union may set the wage rate, while leaving it to the firm to set output and employment.   Introduction of the tax will not change the volume of employment offered by the firm at any given wage rate, and hence it will not affect the union's choice among available combinations.

Now consider a union policy that not only sets the wage rate but also demands that an annual bonus equal to a given fraction of profits should be added to the annual wages bill.   If this bonus is defined as a fraction of profits *after* tax, an increase in the rate of tax will reduce the bonus.   In this case, the tax is partially shifted backward.   If the bonus is defined as a fraction of profits *before* tax,[2] an increase in the tax will leave the bonus unaffected.   However, the increase in tax rate permits the firm to recoup a larger part of the bonus in the form of tax savings.   In neither case does the demand for such a bonus change optimum price; and in

---

[1] See E. H. Chamberlin, *The Theory of Monopolistic Competition*, 5th ed., Harvard University Press, Cambridge, Mass., 1948, especially chap. 5.

[2] This is the plan proposed by the United Auto Workers in January, 1958, subject to the further qualification that the "tax" which the union imposes applies to excess profits only.

neither case does the existence of such a bonus permit the firm to pass the tax on to the consumer.

The situation is changed if the union presents the firm with a package proposal that specifies both wage rate and level of employment. Bargaining on an all-or-nothing basis, the union demands that the firm accept this package or shut down.[1] In such a case, the firm is reduced to an agent of the union, which determines output as well as factor prices.

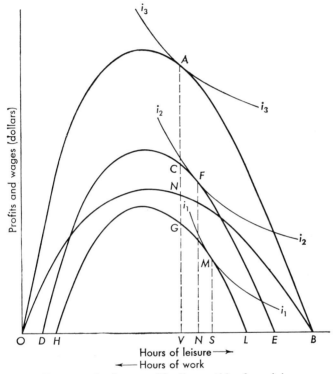

FIG. 13-1. Profits tax with all-or-nothing bargaining.

Such a situation is shown in Figure 13-1.[2] Total profits and/or wages are measured vertically, while leisure is measured horizontally. Assuming a given total leisure in the absence of work, the leisure axis may be translated readily into an employment axis, hours worked being measured from the right to the left. The revenue curve OAB shows the total

[1] On the problem of all-or-nothing bargaining, see W. Fellner, *Competition among the Few*, Alfred A. Knopf, Inc., New York, 1949, chap. 10, and especially appendix 1; and W. Leontief, "Pure Theory of the Guaranteed Annual Wage Contract," *Journal of Political Economy*, vol. 59, no. 1, pp. 76–79, February, 1946.

[2] The figure is similar to the diagram that Boulding uses in explaining entrepreneurial behavior. (See text p. 280.)

return, available for profits and wages (after deducting other shares), which is obtained at various levels of leisure; the indifference curves show the union's preference between income and leisure.

Suppose, first, that the union wishes to exploit its position to the utmost, leaving the firm without profits. If OAB shows the wages-plus-profits bill available at various levels of employment and output, the best choice is at A. No profits accrue to the firm. This however, is hardly a possible position for the union to take, since the firm would then shut down. Thus the union will find it necessary to leave the firm with some profits.

Suppose that the firm is to be left with a given *amount* of profits, say, AC. The wage bill at different levels of output or leisure is shown by curve DFE, derived by deducting AC from OAB. The wage rate at the old level of output is reduced. The union now chooses a point such as F as the best available position. Depending on whether a reduction in the wage rate increases or reduces work effort, F will lie to the left or to the right of A.

Now let a profits tax of $\frac{1}{3}$ be imposed. Had it been possible to remain at A, introduction of the tax would not have mattered. Profits and, therefore, the tax would be zero. Since AC of profits remain, imposition of the tax calls for reconsideration of union policy. Let us suppose, now, that the union wishes to maintain net profits for the firm at AC. In this case, gross profits must be raised to $GA = \frac{3}{2}AC$. The reduced wage bill available at various levels of output or leisure is shown by HGL, obtained by deducting GA from OAB. The best available combination will now be at a point such as M. If preferences are such that F lies to the right of A, then M lies to the right of F. Imposition of the tax leads to a reduction in work and a corresponding increase in leisure. Output is reduced, and the price of the product is increased. The opposite result of an increase in output and a reduction in price occurs if we assume that a reduction in the wage rate raises work effort. Under this assumption the indifference curves are such that F falls to the left of A, and M to the left of F. Either result is possible.

An alternative union policy may be to set permissible profits as a *fraction* of wages plus net profits. If the ratio of profits to wages plus profits is set at NA/VA, the available levels of the wage bill prior to tax are given by ONB. In this case, the union will respond to the imposition of the tax by reducing ONB by one-third, so as to maintain a constant ratio of net profits to net profits plus wages. Whatever the particular union policy, it is evident that short-run changes in price may result.

To be sure, the case of all-or-nothing bargaining is too extreme a position. Strikes are costly, and the union is not all-powerful. There may be some competition in labor supply and less-than-perfect competition among employers. The situation may be one of bilateral monopoly, where the firm is able to counter the union with its own demands, thus involving a compromise solution. Ability to pay will be but one among other considerations in the determination of wage demands, and its weight will vary. Nevertheless, considerations of this sort are frequently present. Where they apply, a profits tax may give rise to adjustments in price and output.

Average-cost Pricing. The preceding considerations go far in qualifying the conventional conclusion that the corporation tax cannot lead to price adjustments in the short run. Yet they are wholly compatible with the basic principles of profit maximization and with what may be referred to as the academic theory of the firm. We must still note, however, a quite different approach, which rejects the conventional conclusion of shifting because the entire framework of underlying price theory is held to be unrealistic. This is the "practical" man's view. Businessmen, it is argued, do not know their marginal-revenue and cost schedules. Hence, they cannot set their price where MR equals MC. What is more, they do not attempt to do so but follow a procedure of setting price so as to cover average cost, with allowance for a proper profit margin. As far as the profits tax is concerned, this margin is likely to be net of tax, so that the tax is considered as a cost and is added to price.[1]

This argument, at least in its cruder form, involves a misunderstanding rather than a critique of conventional price theory.[2] The proposition that profits are maximized where MR equals MC is not so much a description of intended behavior as a statement of the condition of successful behavior. The question is not whether actual business calculations are based on just this formula, but whether actual pricing policies lead to a result approximating that obtained by the profit-maximization formula.

Obviously, the average business man does not have at his disposal a neat set of marginal-cost and -revenue data. There is considerable uncertainty involved. Bench marks and rules of thumb, rather than

---

[1] Richard Goode, *Corporation Income Tax*, John Wiley & Sons, Inc., New York, 1951, p. 50, quotes from *Accounting for Income Taxes*, American Institute of Accountants, Committee on Accounting Procedure, Accounting Research Bulletin 23, 1944, as follows: "Income taxes are an expense which should be allocated when necessary and practicable to income and other accounts, as other expenses are allocated."

[2] See R. L. Hall and C. J. Hitch, "Price Theory and Business Behaviour," *Oxford Economic Papers*, no. 2, pp. 12–45, May, 1939; E. A. G. Robinson, "The Pricing of Manufactured Products," *Economic Journal*, vol. 60, pp. 771–781; December, 1950; A. Silbertson, "The Pricing of Manufactured Products," and E. A. G. Robinson, "Rejoinder," both in *Economic Journal*, vol. 61, no. 242, pp. 426–433, June, 1951; E. H. Chamberlin, "Full Cost and Monopolistic Competition," and Joan Robinson, "A Comment," both in *Economic Journal*, vol. 62, no. 246, pp. 318–326, June, 1952.

For an attempt to rationalize the businessman's view, see W. J. Eiteman, *Price Determination*, Bureau of Business Research, Report no. 16, University of Michigan Press, Ann Arbor, Mich., 1949, and the bibliography there given.

precise calculations, apply.   The outcome is an approximation only, but there is little evidence to think that it is not an approximation to maximum profits.   The process of approximation may involve a "customary" profit margin to be added to average cost; but average cost may not differ greatly from marginal cost over the relevant range, and the customary margin is not fixed for all time and every occasion.   It depends, in turn, on market factors.   While sluggish and discontinuous in adjustment, the margin is likely to adapt itself to drastic changes in the condition of the market.   In other words, it is an approximation to the optimum price.[1] If it were not, one would have to reconsider the claim that the market mechanism is an efficient allocation device.

The preceding conclusions regarding the effects of a tax on price are not qualified greatly.   As long as the cost-plus price is an approximation of optimum price, firms would be foolish to raise the margin by including the tax.   If the margin happens to be in agreement with the optimum price— and, a fortiori, if it is above the optimum price—such inclusion would only reduce profits net of tax.   Only if the margin is below the optimum price is there a gain in raising it.   In this case, the widening of the margin is desirable with or without tax.   It would come about sooner or later, and introduction of the tax merely speeds up the timing of the adjustment.

Conclusions

The traditional rule that a profits tax cannot give rise to short-run adjustments in price remains a good point of departure, but hardly more. Without falling back upon the "practical" argument that businessmen do not act this way, we find a variety of situations where the tax may lead to adjustments in price and output.   These include the return to working capital, monopoly pricing under restraint, oligopoly pricing, and situations of collective bargaining where the firm's ability to pay is taken into consideration.   Possibilities such as these throw considerable doubt on the conventional position that price policy remains unaffected in the short run.   In addition, there are the long-run considerations where the tax may act upon the supply of capital and entrepreneurship.   On balance, the theoretical argument lends more support to the moderate conclusions that short-run adjustments in price (1) play a significant role, and (2) that a part of the tax is passed on, than it lends to the extreme position that no such adjustments occur.[2]

[1] See Tibor Scitovsky, *Welfare and Competition*, Richard D. Irwin, Inc., Homewood, Ill., 1951, especially chaps. 11 and 13.

[2] Thinking along these lines, I have assumed in other connections that approximately one-third of the tax is shifted.   This, to be sure, is rather arbitrary, but less extreme than the usual hypothesis that the entire tax falls on profits.   See Musgrave et al., "Distribution of Tax Payments by Income Groups: A Case Study for 1948," *National Tax Journal*, vol. 4, no. 1, pp. 1–53, March, 1951.

However, the theoretical case is far from conclusive. There remains a crying need for empirical investigation.[1] Historically, while periods of high tax rates have most often been periods of high profits after tax— witness the forties and fifties—this is no proof that shifting has occurred. Yet we know that much the larger part of the yield of the corporation tax is derived from industries in which administered prices prevail in both the product and the labor markets. We know that business executives in large enterprises are not unaware of the social and political implications of excessive profit margins, and we know that union policy is aware of considerations of ability to pay. The conditions in which shifting of this type might occur are widely met, and probably some of it does occur.

B. TAXES ON UNIT OF OUTPUT AND GROSS INCOME

The second type of business tax to be considered is the tax on gross receipts and its cousin, the tax per unit of sale. These taxes are usually treated under the joint heading of sales or excise taxes. Both drive a wedge between price and factor payments, but they differ as to base. One is assessed on gross receipts, and is a function of price, while the other is assessed on the unit of output, and constitutes a constant addition to variable costs.

Economists have paid a good deal of attention to these taxes. "There is scarcely any economic principle," observes Marshall, "which cannot be aptly illustrated by a discussion of the shifting of the effects of some taxes . . . ."[2] And, one might add, there is scarcely any tax which offers so inviting a playground for price theory as the sales tax. No wonder, then, that the adjustment of individual firms to such taxes has been discussed at great length by price theorists. This sport was resumed with new vigor in the 1930s as price theory was restated in terms of imperfect and monopolistic competition. Nevertheless, the matter is not so clear as it might be, and a survey of the major issues is in order.[3] Our discussion

[1] For beginnings in this direction see W. N. Coates, appendix A, *Report of the Commission on National Debt and Taxation*, H. M. Stationery Office, London, 1927, Hansard 2800; Eugene M. Lerner and Eldon S. Hendrickson, "Federal Taxes on Corporate Income and the Rate of Return on Investment in Manufacturing, 1927–52," *National Tax Journal*, vol. 9, no. 3, pp. 193–202, September, 1956; M. A. Adelman, "The Corporate Income Tax in the Long Run," *Journal of Political Economy*, vol. 65, no. 2, pp. 151–157, April 1957.

[2] Alfred Marshall, *Principles of Economics*, 8th ed., Macmillan & Co., Ltd., London, 1930, p. 413.

[3] For the first intensive treatment, see A. Cournot, *Researches into the Mathematical Principles of the Theory of Wealth*, ed. I. Fisher, Macmillan, 1938, chap. 6 (first published in 1838); also see F. Y. Edgeworth, *Papers Relating to Political Economy*, Macmillan & Co., Ltd., London, 1925, pp. 14–21; and Knut Wicksell. *Finanztheoretische Untersuchun-*

is limited, for the time being, to the *partial*-equilibrium aspects of the problem, dealing with adjustments to a tax imposed on a particular industry or firm.   General-equilibrium aspects of sales taxation will be examined later on.

Diagrammatic View

By way of introduction, let us look at the problem briefly in diagrammatic terms.[1]   To simplify the interpretation, all demand and cost schedules in Figures 13-2 to 13-5 are drawn as straight lines, but the diagrams may be adjusted readily for nonlinear schedules.

ADJUSTMENT TO UNIT TAX

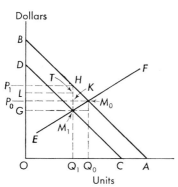

Fɪɢ. 13-2. Competitive industry.   Fɪɢ. 13-3. Monopoly.

Unit Tax.   When a unit tax is imposed, unit cost rises by a constant amount for all levels of output.   The tax, therefore, may be thought of as causing a parallel upward shift in the average-cost schedule; or it may be looked upon as causing a similar downward shift in the average-revenue schedule.   The diagrams follow the latter interpretation.

The adjustment to a unit tax by a competitive industry is shown in Figure 13-2.   Let AB be the industry demand schedule before tax, and CD the industry demand schedule after tax.   The vertical distance between the two, or B minus D, is the unit tax. EF is the supply schedule for the industry.[2]   The pre-tax price is at P_0, and the post-tax price is

gen und das Steuerwesen Schweden's, Jena, Germany, 1896, pp. 10–21.   For excerpts from these authors see Musgrave and Shoup, *op. cit.*   For more recent treatments, see Otto von Mering, *The Shifting and Incidence of Taxation,* Richard D. Irwin, Inc., Homewood, Ill., 1942, chaps. 3 and 4; and John F. Due, *The Theory of Incidence of Sales Taxation,* King's Crown Press, New York, 1942, where an extensive bibliography is given.

[1] For an intensive diagrammatic treatment, see Due, *op. cit.*

[2] This supply schedule may be looked upon as the sum of the marginal-cost schedules of individual firms if we consider the short run; or as an average–total-cost schedule if we consider the long run.

at P_1. The increase in price P_1 minus P_0 depends on the slopes of the supply and demand schedules. This will be seen by rotating the two schedules around M_0. In the case of constant cost, the increase in price equals the unit tax. In the case of increasing cost, shown in Figure 13-2, the increase in price falls short of the tax. This reflects the cushioning effect of the reduction in unit cost with declining output. The increase in price due to tax rises as the absolute slope of the demand schedule is increased and as the absolute slope of the supply schedule is decreased. For decreasing cost, these relationships are reversed.

The corresponding adjustment for a monopolist is shown in Figure 13-3, where AB and KB are the average- and marginal-revenue schedules before tax, CD and HD are the corresponding schedules after tax, and EF is the marginal-cost schedule. The pre-tax price is P_0. After the tax is imposed, the monopolist equates marginal net revenue with marginal cost, and the new price is at P_1. As before, the resulting increase in price depends upon the slopes of the cost and demand schedules. Changes in the slopes of these schedules affect the increase in price in the same direction as they do in the competitive case. For changes in the slope of the marginal-cost schedule, this effect is again readily seen by rotating the schedule around M_0 in Figure 13-3. The increase in price now falls short of the tax for both constant and increasing cost; and it may fall short of, or exceed, the tax for decreasing cost. Regarding changes in the slope of the demand schedule, the diagrammatic case is less easily interpreted.[1] As will be shown presently, the increase in monopoly price throughout equals one-half that obtained under pure competition.

Ad Valorem Tax.   The ad valorem tax is a constant fraction of price. The value of the tax per unit of output varies with price. Diagrammatically, this tax cannot be expressed as a change in the cost schedule, but appears as a pivoting down to the left of the demand schedule.

The resulting adjustment for a competitive industry is shown in Figure 13-4. The industry demand schedule before tax equals AB, and the net demand schedule, after imposition of a 50 per cent ad valorem tax, equals AD. If EF is the supply schedule, pre-tax price equals P_0, and post-tax price equals P_1. The effects of changes in the slopes of the two schedules upon the changes in price are similar in direction to those indicated for the unit tax, but the intercepts of the two schedules now enter as additional determining factors. For conditions of constant cost, the increase in price again equals the tax per unit at the post-tax level of output; and the

---

[1] If the slope of AB in Fig. 13-3 is steepened at M_0, that of KB will be steepened at N, and the intersection of the new net marginal-revenue line with EF must be to the right of R. The ordinate of this intersection thus increases. Since the post-tax price equals $Z/(1-r)$ where r is the tax rate and Z is the ordinate of the intersection with EF, the post-tax price P_1 must increase as the slope of AB is steepened.

.increase in price varies with unit cost. The increase in price falls short of this amount for increasing cost and exceeds it for decreasing cost.

ADJUSTMENT TO AD VALOREM TAX

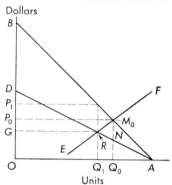

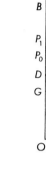

FIG. 13-4. Competitive industry.   FIG. 13-5. Monopoly.

The corresponding adjustment for a monopolist is shown in Figure 13-5, and similar observations apply. The effects of changes in the slopes of the marginal-cost schedule upon price are similar in direction to those which applied under the unit tax. For conditions of constant and increasing cost, the increase in price, or P_1 minus P_0, falls short of the amount of tax paid per unit at the new output, or P_1 minus G; and for decreasing cost, the increase in price exceeds this amount. The interpretation of changes in the demand schedule is again difficult to undertake in diagrammatic terms.[1] Throughout, the increase in monopoly price again equals one-half that of the competitive case. The general results are similar to those for the unit tax, but the underlying relationships are more complex.

Algebraic Treatment with Linear Functions: Unit Tax

While the general story can be told in diagrammatic terms, not all these conclusions can be drawn with sufficient precision. A more precise statement of the underlying relationships is needed. In the case of linear demand and cost functions, a statement may be given algebraically in terms of finite differences—an approach not without its advantage. A more general formulation follows the linear treatment.

Pure Competition. We shall begin with a unit tax, to be applied first to an industry operating under pure competition, and then to monop-

[1] If the average-revenue schedule AB is rotated around M in Fig. 13-5, we experience a change in the pre-tax price and output no less than in the post-tax price and output. If, instead, we think of the marginal-revenue schedule KB as being rotated around N, pre-tax output remains unchanged, but pre-tax price is changed. Thus, no simple determination of changes in price is possible from the diagram.

oly. Given the demand function $p = a + bx$ and the supply function $s = d + ex$, let us assume that a unit tax of amount t is imposed. We readily obtain the expression

$$\Delta p = \frac{b}{b - e} t \tag{13-1}$$

which describes the relationship between change in price Δp and unit tax t.*

Note that Δp depends upon the slopes of the demand and supply functions only. The intercepts a and d do not appear as determinants of Δp, whose value is the same for revenue and cost schedules of given slopes, independent of their intercepts and the pre-tax price. For constant cost, we have $e = 0$ and

$$\Delta p = t \tag{13-2}$$

For increasing cost, we have $b < 0$ and $e > 0$, hence $0 < [b/(b - e)] < 1$, and $\Delta p < t$. The value of Δp will vary directly with $|b|$ (the absolute value of b independent of sign) and inversely with e. For decreasing cost, we have $b < 0$ and $e < 0$, as well as the stability condition $|b| > |e|$. It follows that $[b/(b - e)] > 1$, and $\Delta p > t$. The value of Δp now varies directly with e and inversely with $|b|$.

The values of b and e define the slopes of the demand and supply functions. They must not be confused with elasticities. However, for the present case the one may be translated readily into the other. As the demand schedule in Figure 13-2 is rotated around the initial equilibrium M_0, an increase in the slope implies a decrease in elasticity for outputs slightly below Q_0. The direct relationship between the slope of the demand schedule and Δp reflects an inverse relationship between elasticity and Δp. Similarly, the inverse relationship between Δp and the slope of the supply schedule under increasing cost implies a direct relationship between Δp and elasticity.

The ratio of unit tax to price increase, or $(P_1 - G)/(P_1 - P_0)$ in Figure

---

* The initial equilibrium output for the industry is given by the condition

$$a + bx = d + ex,$$

which, by solving for x and substituting into the demand equation, gives us the initial price $p_0 = a + b \dfrac{a - d}{e - b}$. After the unit tax is imposed, the net revenue schedule becomes $AR = a + bx - t$, where t is the unit tax. The new equilibrium is given by $a + bx - t = d + ex$. Solving for x, we obtain the new output, and substituting into the demand equation, we obtain the new price $p_1 = a + b[(a - d - t)/(e - b)]$. Finally, we obtain the change in price as $\Delta p = p_1 - p_0 = [b/(b - e)]t$. If we deal with a change in the rate of tax rather than with the introduction of a new tax, we may substitute Δt for t.

13-2, equals $(e_s + e_d)/e_s$, where e_s is the elasticity of supply and e_d is the elasticity of demand. This follows, since $e_d/e_s = (P_0 - G)/(P_1 - P_0)$.*

Monopoly. Turning now to the case of monopoly, we begin with the demand function $p = a + bx$ and the cost function $c = d + ex$. As a unit tax t is introduced, the resulting change in monopoly price is defined by

$$\Delta p = \frac{b}{2(b - e)} t \qquad (13\text{-}3)$$

which equals one-half the change for the competitive case.[1]

* A similar approach is taken by Dalton, whose concern is with the ratio

$$\frac{P_1 - P_0}{P_0 - G} = \frac{e_s}{e_d}$$

Interpreting $P_1 - P_0$ as the buyers' share in the tax burden, and $P_0 - G$ as the sellers' share, Dalton concludes that the burden is divided between buyers and sellers in the ratio of the elasticity of supply to the elasticity of demand. See H. Dalton, *Principles of Public Finance*, 9th ed., Routledge and Kegan Paul, Ltd., London, 1936, p. 73.

The interpretation of $(P_1 - P_0)/(P_0 - G)$ as indicating the way in which the burden of the tax is divided must be handled with care, since it applies to a strictly partial-equilibrium setting only. On the buyers' side, loss of consumer surplus and changes in other prices are disregarded. On the sellers' side, factors engaged in the taxed industry may move to other industries, and the loss of proceeds equal to $P_0Q_0 - GQ_1$ is offset in part by gains from employment in tax-free industries.

[1] Let the monopolist's average-revenue schedule before tax be $AR = a + bx$. His total-revenue schedule is $R = ax + bx^2$, and his marginal-revenue schedule is

$$\frac{dR}{dx} = a + 2bx$$

Similarly, we have the average–unit-cost schedule $AC = d + ex$, and the marginal-cost schedule $dC/dx = d + 2ex$. For the present case of linear schedules, the slope of the marginal schedule is twice that of the average schedule.

Output at the pre-tax equilibrium is determined by equating marginal revenue and marginal cost, so that

$$a + 2bx = d + 2ex$$

which, solving for x and substituting into the demand equation, gives us the pre-tax price p_0 as

$$p_0 = a + b\left[\frac{a - d}{2(e - b)}\right]$$

The equilibrium output after imposition of a unit tax t is determined by

$$a + 2bx - t = d + 2ex$$

which, solving for x and substituting into the demand equation, gives us the new price, p_1 as

$$p_1 - a + b\left[\frac{a - d - t}{2(e - b)}\right]$$

The change in price is obtained as

$$p_1 - p_0 = \Delta p = \frac{b}{2(b - e)} t$$

For conditions of constant cost, we have $e = 0$, so that

$$\Delta p = \tfrac{1}{2}t \qquad (13\text{-}4)$$

For conditions of variable cost, Δp depends upon the value of e/b. This will be seen readily if we rewrite equation (13-3) as

$$\Delta p = \frac{1}{2[1 - (e/b)]}\, t$$

In the case of increasing cost, we have $b < 0 < e$, so that $e/b < 0$. Hence $\Delta p < \tfrac{1}{2}t$. The value of Δp varies directly with $|b|$ and inversely with $|e|$. In the case of decreasing cost, we have $b < 0 > e$, so that $e/b > 0$. Hence, if $e/b = \tfrac{1}{2}$, then $\Delta p = t$; if $\tfrac{1}{2} < e/b < 1$, then $\Delta p > t$; and if $0 < e/b < \tfrac{1}{2}$, then $\Delta p < t$. The value of Δp now varies directly with $|e|$ and inversely with $|b|$.

The position reached after adjustment to the tax may be one where the monopolist suffers losses but continues in operation. Such will be the case in the short run, provided that average net revenue at the optimum output does not fall short of average variable cost. If it does, losses will be minimized by ceasing operation.

Algebraic Treatment with Linear Functions: Ad Valorem Tax

Pure Competition. Using the same demand and supply function as before, the resulting change in price for the competitive industry is now given by

$$\Delta p = b\left[\frac{r(bd - ae)}{(e - b)^2 + r(eb - b^2)}\right] \qquad (13\text{-}5)$$

where r is the rate of ad valorem tax.[1] The change in price for the case of

[1] As shown in the starred footnote on page 291, the pre-tax price is

$$p_0 = a + b\,\frac{a - d}{e - b}$$

After the imposition of the tax, equilibrium output is determined by the condition

$$(1 - r)(a + bx) = d + ex$$

and the new price is

$$p_1 = a + b\left(\frac{a - ra - d}{e + rb - b}\right)$$

By deducting p_0 from p_1 we obtain

$$\Delta p = b\left[\frac{r(bd - ae)}{(e - b)^2 + r(eb - b^2)}\right]$$

If we deal with an increase in tax rather than the introduction of a new tax, we obtain

$$\Delta p = b\left[\frac{\Delta r(bd - ae)}{(e - b)^2 + (eb - b^2)(r_0 + r_1) + r_0 r_1 b^2}\right]$$

where r_0 is the old rate of tax and r_1 the new rate.

constant cost is

$$\Delta p = \frac{dr}{1 - r} \qquad (13\text{-}6)$$

the increase in price varying directly with average cost. This differs from the case of the unit tax, where we found that Δp is independent of d. However, the increase in price is again equal to the tax per unit at the new output.[1] For conditions of variable cost, Δp now depends on the intercepts as well as on the slopes of the two schedules. The former did not enter in the case of the unit tax. For conditions of increasing cost, we have $b < 0$ and $e > 0$. The increase in price varies directly with a, d, and $|b|$ and inversely with $|e|$. We have $\Delta p < rp_1$, the increase in price falling short of the tax per unit at the new output.[2] For conditions of decreasing cost, we have $b < 0$, $e < 0$, and $|b| > |e|$. The increase in price varies directly with d and $|e|$, and inversely with a and $|b|$. We now have $\Delta p > rp_1$, the increase in price exceeding the tax per unit at the new output.[3]

Monopoly. For the case of monopoly, the increase in price due to ad valorem tax is

$$\Delta p = \frac{b}{2} \left[\frac{r(bd - ae)}{(e - b)^2 + r(eb - b^2)} \right] \qquad (13\text{-}7)$$

and is again one-half that of the competitive solution in equation (13-5).[4]

---

[1] The tax per unit at the new output is

$$rp_1 = r \left(a + b \, \frac{a - ra - d}{rb - b} \right) = \frac{dr}{1 - r} = \Delta p$$

[2] The difference between tax per unit of output and increase in price is now

$$rp_1 - \Delta p = r \left(a + b \, \frac{a - ra - d}{e + rb - b} \right) - b \left[\frac{r(bd - ea)}{(e - b)^2 + r(eb - b^2)} \right]$$

Under conditions of increasing cost, where $e > 0$, this expression will be > 0.

[3] We have $e < 0$ and $|b| > |e|$, so that $rp_1 - \Delta p$, as defined on p. 293, note 1, becomes negative.

[4] The pre-tax price as shown on p. 292, note 1, is

$$p_0 = a + \frac{b}{2} \left(\frac{a - d}{e - b} \right)$$

The equilibrium output after imposition of the tax is now given by

$$(1 - r)(a + 2bx) = d + 2ex$$

so that the post-tax price is

$$p_1 = a + \frac{b}{2} \left(\frac{a - ra - d}{e + rb - b} \right)$$

and

$$\Delta p = \frac{b}{2} \left[\frac{r(bd - ae)}{(e - b)^2 + r(eb - b^2)} \right]$$

The effects of changes in the slopes and intercepts of the two schedules are similar in direction to those noted in the preceding discussion of equation (13-5). Under conditions of constant cost, we obtain

$$\Delta p = \frac{1}{2} \frac{dr}{1 - r} \tag{13-8}$$

The tax per unit at the new output now exceeds the increase in price, and the excess varies directly with the intercept of the demand schedule.[1] Under conditions of variable cost, the relation between Δp and changes in the slopes and intercepts of the two schedules are again the same in direction as for the competitive case. For conditions of increasing cost, the increase in price again falls short of the tax per unit of output.[2] For conditions of decreasing cost, the tax per unit of output may again exceed, equal, or fall short of the increase in price.

The General Case: Unit Tax

We shall now drop the assumption of linear demand and cost functions and restate the problem in general terms.

Pure Competition. Let us begin with the adjustment of a competitive industry to a unit tax. If $p = p(q)$ is the demand function, and $c = s(q)$ the supply function, we obtain

$$\frac{dp}{dt} = \frac{p'(q)}{p'(q) - s'(q)} \tag{13-9}$$

where t is the unit tax.[3] This corresponds to the linear formulation of

---

[1] The difference between tax per unit of output and increase in price is

$$rp_1 - \Delta p = r\left(a + \frac{b}{2}\frac{a - ra - d}{rb - b}\right) - \frac{1}{2}\frac{dr}{1-r} = \frac{ar}{2} > 0$$

[2] The difference between tax per unit of output and increase in price is now

$$rp_1 - \Delta p = r\left(a + \frac{b}{2}\frac{a - ra - d}{e + rb - b}\right) - \frac{b}{2}\left[\frac{r(bd - ea)}{(e - b)^2 + r(eb - b^2)}\right]$$

If $rp_1 - \Delta p > 0$ for the competitive case (see p. 294, note 2), then it must hold also for the present case, since the positive a in the first term remains unchanged, while the other terms are halved.

[3] The industry will be in equilibrium after imposition of a unit tax t where

$$p(q) - s(q) - t = 0$$

Differentiating with respect to t, we obtain the change in equilibrium output as t changes:

$$\frac{dq}{dt} = \frac{1}{p'(q) - s'(q)}$$

Differentiating the demand function $p = p(q)$ with respect to t, we obtain the change

equation (13-1) above, where $p'(q) = b$ and $s'(q) = e$.* In the case of constant cost, $s'(q) = 0$ so that $dp/dt = 1$. In the case of increasing cost, we have $p'(q) < 0 < s'(q)$ and the stability condition $\dfrac{s'(q)}{(\partial p/\partial q) - s'(q)} <$ 0.† Hence, dp/dt varies directly with $p'(q)$ and inversely with $s'(q)$, and $dp/dt < 1$. In the case of decreasing cost, we have $p'(q) < 0 > s'(q)$ and $|p'(q)| > |s'(q)|$. Hence, dp/dt varies directly with $|s'(q)|$ and inversely with $|p'(q)|$, and $dp/dt > 1$.

Monopoly. We now turn to the case of monopoly. If $p = p(q)$ is the monopolist's demand function, and $c = c(q)$ is his cost function before imposition of a unit tax, we obtain

$$\frac{dp}{dt} = \frac{1}{2\left[1 - \dfrac{c'(q)}{p'(q)}\right] + \dfrac{q}{p'(q)}\,[p''(q) - c''(q)]} \tag{13-10}$$

where t is again the unit tax.[1] Whereas dp/dt in the competitive case depended on the slopes of the revenue and cost schedules only, the

---

in price as t changes:

$$\frac{dp}{dt} = p'(q)\frac{dq}{dt}$$

and by substituting for dq/dt from the preceding equation:

$$\frac{dp}{dt} = \frac{p'(q)}{p'(q) - s'(q)}$$

* In the linear formulation, we have dealt with the introduction of a new tax so that $t = \Delta t$ in eq. (13-1).

† See Paul A. Samuelson, *Foundations of Economic Analysis*, Harvard University Press, Cambridge, Mass., 1947, p. 18. In the linear case, this condition reduces to $\dfrac{|e|}{|b| - |e|} < 0.$

[1] Given the demand function for the monopolist

$$p = p(q)$$

and the average-cost function, after imposition of a unit tax,

$$c = c(q) + t$$

total revenue is given by

$$R = pq = p(q)q$$

and total cost by

$$C = cq = c(q)q + tq$$

In equilibrium, $R - C$ must be at a maximum, so that equilibrium output is given by

$$\frac{dR}{dq} - \frac{dC}{dq} = p(q) + qp'(q) - c(q) - qc'(q) - t = 0$$

Differentiating with respect to t, we obtain the change in equilibrium output with a

monopoly case involves second-order terms as well.   The simple relationship between the competitive and the monopoly solution—according to
which the increase in price for the latter is one-half the increase for the
former—holds for the linear case only.

In the linear case, the second-order terms vanish so that

$$\frac{dp}{dt} = \frac{p'(q)}{2[p'(q) - c'(q)]} \tag{13-11}$$

which corresponds to equation (13-3) above.   For conditions of constant
cost, $c'(q) = 0$ so that $dp/dt = \frac{1}{2}$.   For conditions of increasing cost,
$\frac{c'(q)}{p'(q)} < 0$, hence $dp/dt < \frac{1}{2}$.   For conditions of decreasing cost, $\frac{c'(q)}{p'(q)} > 0$.
In this case, we obtain $\frac{dp}{dt} = 1$ if $\frac{c'(q)}{p'(q)} = \frac{1}{2}$, $\frac{dp}{dt} > 1$ if $\frac{1}{2} < \frac{c'(q)}{p'(q)} < 1$, and
$\frac{dp}{dt} < 1$ if $0 < \frac{c'(q)}{p'(q)} < \frac{1}{2}$.

The General Case: Ad Valorem Tax

Pure Competition.   We now turn to the adjustment of a competitive
industry to an ad valorem tax.   Given the demand function $p = p(q)$
and the supply function $c = s(q)$, we obtain

$$\frac{dp}{dr} = \frac{p(q)}{(1 - r) - s'(q)/p'(q)} \tag{13-12}$$

where r is the ad valorem rate of tax.[1]   This corresponds to the linear

---

change in t as

$$\frac{dq}{dt} = \frac{1}{2[p'(q) - c'(q)] + q[p''(q) - c''(q)]}$$

Differentiating the demand function with respect to t, we obtain the change in price
as t changes:

$$\frac{dp}{dt} = p'(q) \frac{dq}{dt}$$

and by substituting for dq/dt from the preceding equation:

$$\frac{dp}{dt} = \frac{1}{2\left[1 - \frac{c'(q)}{p'(q)}\right] + \frac{q}{p'(q)} [p''(q) - c''(q)]}$$

[1] The equilibrium condition after imposition of an ad valorem tax at rate r is given
by

$$p(q)(1 - r) - s(q) = 0$$

The change in the equilibrium quantity with respect to r is

$$\frac{dq}{dr} = \frac{p(q)}{(1 - r)p'(q) - s'(q)}$$

The change in equilibrium price with respect to r is

formulation of equation (13-5).*   In the case of increasing cost, $s'(q) > 0 > p'(q)$ so that dp/dr varies directly with $|p'(q)|$ and inversely with $|s'(q)|$.   In the case of decreasing cost, $s'(q) < 0 > p'(q)$ so that dp/dr varies directly with $|s'(q)|$ and inversely with $|p'(q)|$.   In the case of constant cost, equation (13-12) reduces to

$$\frac{dp}{dr} = \frac{p(q)}{1 - r} \tag{13-13}$$

which corresponds to the linear solution of equation (13-6).†

Monopoly.   In the case of monopoly, we have the demand function $p = p(q)$ and the cost function $c = c(q)$.   We obtain

$$\frac{dp}{dr} = \frac{p'(q)[p(q) + qp'(q)]}{2[p'(q)(1 - r) - c'(q)] + q[p''(q)(1 - r) - c''(q)]} \tag{13-14}$$

for the general case.[1]   In the linear case, the second-order terms drop out,

$$\frac{dp}{dr} = p'(q)\frac{dq}{dr}$$

Substituting for dq/dr from the preceding equation, we obtain

$$\frac{dp}{dr} = \frac{p(q)}{(1 - r) - s'(q)/p'(q)}$$

* Substituting $p(q) = a + [b(a - d)]/(e - b)$, and $s'(q) = e$, and $p'(q) = b$ into eq. (13-12), we obtain the linear solution of eq. (13-5) above.

† Substituting $p_0 = a + [b(a - d)/(e - b)]$ into (13-13) and setting $e = 0$, we obtain the linear solution of eq. (13-6).

[1] Given the demand function before tax $p = p(q)$, we now have the net revenue function after tax $n = p(q)(1 - r)$.   The cost function again is $c = c(q)$.   Total net revenue is $N = p(q)(1 - r)q$, and total cost is $C = c(q)q$.   In equilibrium, $N - C$ must be at a maximum so that equilibrium output is determined by

$$\frac{dN}{dq} - \frac{dC}{dq} = p(q)(1 - r) + q(1 - r)p'(q) - c(q) - qc'(q) = 0$$

Differentiating with respect to r, we obtain the change in equilibrium output with a change in r:

$$\frac{dq}{dr} = \frac{p(q) + qp'(q)}{2[p'(q)(1 - r) - c'(q)] + q[p''(q)(1 - r) - c''(q)]}$$

We now turn to the determination of dp/dr.   Rewriting the net revenue function as $n = n(q,r)$, we have $p = [1/(1 - r)]n(q,r)$.   Differentiating for p with respect to r, we obtain

$$\frac{dp}{dr} = p'(q)\frac{dq}{dr}$$

Substituting the above value for dq/dr, we obtain

$$\frac{dp}{dr} = \frac{p'(q)[p(q) + qp'(q)]}{2[p'(q)(1 - r) - c'(q)] + q[p''(q)(1 - r)c''(q)]}$$

so that

$$\frac{dp}{dr} = \frac{p(q) + qp'(q)}{2\left[(1 - r) - \dfrac{c'(q)}{p'(q)}\right]} \tag{13-15}$$

which is similar to equation (13-7).[1] For increasing cost, dp/dr again varies directly with $|p'(q)|$ and inversely with $|c'(q)|$; and for decreasing cost, it varies directly with $|c'(q)|$ and inversely with $|p'(q)|$. For constant cost, we now have

$$\frac{dp}{dr} = \frac{p(q) + qp'(q)}{2(1 - r)} \tag{13-16}$$

corresponding to equation (13-8).[2]

Monopolistic Competition

Similar principles may be applied to market structures other than pure competition and monopoly. Consider first a group of firms selling a differentiated product under conditions of free entry. The equilibrium position will be one where $AR = AC$, the group-demand schedule being tangent to the average-cost curve of the individual firm. Now suppose that a unit tax is imposed. Assuming the old output for the group to be maintained, the net (after tax) demand schedule for the individual firm will shift to the left. Each firm will contract output, and some may cease operation. As output for the group is reduced, the net demand schedule for the individual firm rises, permitting it to recover part of the previous decline. Eventually, a new equilibrium is reached where, for each firm, a new net average-revenue schedule is again tangent to the new average-cost schedule.[3] Assuming constant cost for the group and a parallel shift in the demand schedule for each firm, the price for each firm will rise by the amount of tax.[4] If the group operates under conditions of variable cost, the increase in price may exceed or fall short of the tax. Moreover, cost conditions may differ between firms, and individual firms

[1] Substituting $p(q) = a + b\dfrac{d - a}{2(b - e)}$, $q = b\dfrac{d - a}{2(b - e)}$, $c'(q) = e$, and $p'(q) = b$ into (13-15), we obtain the formulation of (13-7).

[2] Substituting as in the preceding note, eq. (13-16) reduces to the earlier formulation of eq. (13-8).

[3] See E. H. Chamberlin, "*The Theory of Monopolistic Competition*, 5th ed., Harvard University Press, Cambridge, Mass., 1948, p. 84.

[4] See Otto von Mering, *The Shifting and Incidence of Taxation*, Richard D. Irwin, Inc., Homewood, Ill., 1946, pp. 71–77. See also John F. Due's treatment of excise taxes in monopolistic competition, *The Theory of Incidence of Sales Taxation*, King's Crown Press, New York, 1942, reprinted in R. A. Musgrave and Carl Shoup (eds.), *Readings in the Economics of Taxation*, American Economic Association, Richard D. Irwin, Inc., Homewood, Ill., 1958.

may be confronted with different changes in demand. The price may rise by more than the tax for some firms and by less than the tax for others.

The difficulty of predicting the outcome is increased further when we consider a combination of small numbers and product differentiation. As noted before, the solution for the case of closed entry is affected by the tax only to the extent that the tax itself changes oligopoly behavior, that is, acts as a signal for concerted action for a revision of prevailing price positions.

Special Cases

A number of special problems in price adjustment to excise taxes arise in the case of particular demand or supply situations, and may be noted here.

ADJUSTMENT TO UNIT TAX: SPECIAL CASES

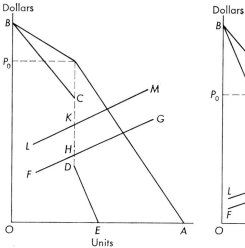
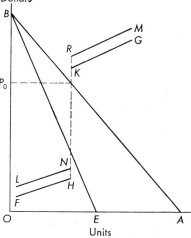

FIG. 13-6. Unit tax with kinked demand schedule.

FIG. 13-7. Unit tax with kinked supply schedule.

Kinked Demand Schedule. Let us first consider the case of a monopolist confronted with a kinked demand schedule, leaving the marginal-revenue schedule undefined over a range bounded by the two extreme values.[1] Now suppose that the marginal-cost schedule intersects marginal revenue within the undefined range.

Such a situation is shown in Figure 13-6, where AB and $BCDE$ are the

[1] See Paul M. Sweezy, "Demand under Conditions of Oligopoly," *Journal of Political Economy*, vol. 47, no. 4, pp. 568–573, August, 1939, reprinted in, *Readings in Price Theory*, American Economic Association, Richard D. Irwin, Inc., Homewood, Ill., 1952, pp. 404–409.

average- and marginal-revenue schedules before tax, and FG is a monopolist's marginal-cost schedule. P_0 is the pre-tax price. As a unit tax of
HK is imposed, the marginal-cost schedule shifts to LM, but price remains
at P_0. The same result is obtained with an ad valorem tax.

Inelastic Supply. A similar situation arises where the average-cost
schedule is kinked and supply is wholly inelastic over the relevant range.

Such a situation is shown in Figure 13-7, where AB and EB are the
average- and marginal-revenue schedules, $FHKG$ is the monopolist's
marginal-cost schedule before tax, and $LNRM$ is the marginal-cost schedule after unit tax HN. The tax again leaves price and output unchanged.
This explains why an excise on scarce articles, imposed in a situation of
acute shortage, might be equivalent in effect to a tax on profits.[1]

"Peculiar" Cases of Value. Edgeworth, in his discussion of excise
incidence, reaches the usual conclusion that such taxes tend to impose a
burden on both sides of the market, under either competition or monopoly.
The extreme instances of wholly inelastic demand or supply are considered
limiting cases rather than exceptions to the rule.

Edgeworth's main contribution rests with the treatment of special
cases—"peculiar" or "anomalous," as Mill called them—which provide
significant exceptions to the general rule. These are the cases of products
with correlated demands or costs. Under competition, two propositions
are advanced. If the demand for product X is independent of the
demand for Y, a tax on X will raise the price of X and reduce the price
of Y, provided that they are rival in production; a tax on X will raise the
price of both X and Y, provided that the two are complementary in
production. Similarly, if X and Y are independent in production, a tax
on X will raise the price of X and reduce the price of Y, if the two are
complementary in demand; a tax will raise the price of both, if they are
rival in demand.

Under monopoly, Edgeworth notes that "if a monopolist supply two
commodities for which the demand is correlated, that is either rival or
complementary, then a tax on one commodity may benefit the consumers
of both."[2] If the products are rival in demand, this result may come
about regardless of cost conditions. This is the famous Edgeworth
paradox. A small ad valorem tax imposed on the gross receipts obtained
from first-class passenger traffic may lead the railroad to reduce the fares
for both first- and third-class traffic.[3] The case of independent demand

---

[1] See von Mering, *op. cit.*, p. 34; and *Economic Report of the President*, January,
1951, p. 106. Also see F. Y. Edgeworth, *Papers Relating to Political Economy*, vol. II.
Macmillan & Co., Ltd., London, 1925, p. 90.

[2] Edgeworth, *op. cit.*, vol. II, pp. 93 and 399.

[3] As first-class fares are raised initially, passengers will shift to third class. This
drives up third-class fares. Management will provide then more third-class facilities,

but correlated production similarly leads to special results. If X and Y are independent in demand but rival in production, a tax on X will raise the price of X; but unlike the competitive case, the tax need not reduce the price of Y. If X and Y are independent in demand but complementary in production, a tax on X will raise the price of X; but unlike the competitive case, the tax need not raise the price of Y.

In fact, all products are more or less interdependent in production as well as in demand, and it is this interdependence which determines the relative changes in factor and product prices that result from the imposition of a discriminatory tax. More will be said about this when the general-equilibrium aspects of incidence are considered.

Comparison of Unit and Ad Valorem Taxes of Equal Yield

Suppose that a given yield is to be obtained from an excise on a particular product. The question is whether this should be done by way of a unit tax or an ad valorem tax. In practice, the choice may be determined largely by considerations of administrative feasibility, but let us suppose that both means of taxation are possible. On grounds of economic efficiency, we prefer that tax which obtains the desired yield with a lesser increase in price.[1] This calls for a comparison in the increase in price that results from an ad valorem and a unit tax of equal yield.[2]

---

which drives down third-class fares. Suppose that third-class fares fall, on balance. This will call for a downward reduction in first-class fares. At the end of the adjustment process, both fares *may* be below their original level.

For a restatement of the argument and an attempt to define the conditions under which it holds, see H. Hotelling, "Edgeworth Taxation Paradox and the Nature of Demand and Supply Functions," *Journal of Political Economy*, vol. 40, no. 5, pp. 577–616, October, 1932. In his review of the Edgeworth paradox, H. Hotelling concludes that the same result may be obtained under competition, provided that the two products are rival in production. He concludes that "there is no basis known at present for denying that Edgeworth's phenomenon may pertain to a large proportion of ordinary situations, or for affirming that it is, in his language, 'a mere curiosum' " (p. 583). Also see Martin J. Bailey, "Edgeworth's Taxation Paradox, and the Nature of Demand Functions," *Econometrica*, vol. 22, no. 1, pp. 72–76, January, 1954.

[1] This conclusion is subject to certain conditions noted in our earlier comparison between an income and an excise tax. (See p. 142.)

[2] The argument of this section follows D. B. Suits and R. A. Musgrave, "Ad Valorem and Unit Taxes Compared," *Quarterly Journal of Economics*, vol. 67, no. 4, pp. 598–604, October, 1953.

The comparison between equal-yield taxes is discussed with similar conclusions by Knut Wicksell, *Finanztheoretische Untersuchungen und das Steuerwesen Schweden's*, Jena, Germany, 1896, p. 20. It must be distinguished from the less significant comparison between taxes that impose the same burden at the initial price. This latter comparison is emphasized by John Due, *The Theory of Incidence of Sales Taxation*, King's Crown Press, New York, 1942, pp. 13–21, note 19.

Competition. In the case of competition, a pair of unit and ad valorem taxes that provide the same yield also result in the same final price. In both cases, price exceeds cost by the tax per unit at the new output. In equilibrium, average revenue minus tax per unit must be the same for both types of tax if the yield is to be the same. Hence, output and price must be the same as well.

This is seen readily in Figure 13-8. A unit tax of FE is imposed, which shifts the net average-revenue schedule from AB to GH. The price rises from P_0 to P_1, and the yield is equal to $DEFP_1$. To obtain the same yield from an ad valorem tax, the new net revenue schedule AC must intersect the marginal-cost schedule at the same point E.

COMPARISON OF UNIT AND AD VALOREM TAX UNDER COMPETITION

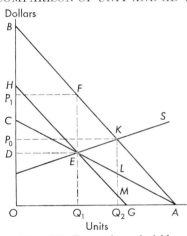 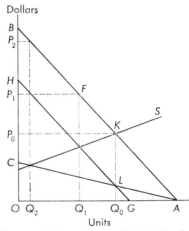

FIG. 13-8. Taxes of equal yield.   FIG. 13-9. Taxes of equal initial burden.

Moreover, it is evident that a unit and an ad valorem tax that provide the same yield involve a higher burden at the initial price under the unit tax. At the initial price P_0, the unit tax equals MK, whereas the ad valorem tax equals LK, which is less. This holds true because the unit tax involves a parallel shift in the demand schedule, whereas the ad valorem tax involves a pivoting of the schedule.

If we compare a unit tax and an ad valorem tax that impose the same burden at the initial price, the resulting increase in price will be larger under the ad valorem tax. This is illustrated in Figure 13-9. The revenue and cost schedules are the same as in Figure 13-8, and the same unit tax is applied. The ad valorem tax is adjusted so as to impose the same burden at the initial price. For this purpose, the net revenue schedule AC is drawn so as to intersect HG at L. The price now rises to P_2 and exceeds P_1, the price reached under the unit tax. The rise in price follows from the difference in the slopes of the two net revenue schedules.

Monopoly. For the case of monopoly, the yield from any given unit tax is always smaller than the yield from an ad valorem tax that results in the same final output and price.

Let AB and DB in Figure 13-10 be the average- and marginal-revenue schedules before tax, with MC the marginal-cost schedule. After imposition of a unit tax equal to BV, the net average- and marginal-revenue schedules become FV and TV, respectively. The equilibrium output after tax equals Q_1, and the price is P_1. The tax yield Y_t equals the area $KLMP_1$. For an ad valorem tax to result in the same price and output, the marginal-revenue schedule net of ad valorem tax must pass through point N. The schedule is shown by DS. The corresponding net average

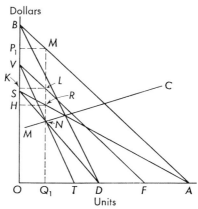

FIG. 13-10. Comparison of equal-yield taxes under monopoly.

revenue schedule is AS. The equilibrium output after tax is unchanged at Q_1, and the price unchanged at P_1, but the tax yield Y_r is the area $HRMP_1$. This is larger than the unit tax yield, as it includes the area $KLMP_1$.*

The maximum yield that may be obtained from a unit tax is smaller than the maximum yield possible from an ad valorem tax. This follows directly from the preceding proposition. Since for every unit tax the ad valorem tax leading to the same price has a higher yield, the higher yield must also be obtained from that unit tax which gains the maximum possible unit yield.

Finally, if the same yield is obtained from a unit tax and an ad valorem

---

* To state the matter in general terms, suppose that a tax of t dollars per unit has been imposed, with the result that the monopolist maximizes profits at output x_t and price p_t. At this output, marginal cost equals marginal revenue net of tax:

$$MC(x_t) = MR(x_t) - t$$

Now let the unit tax t be replaced by an ad valorem tax at rate r (fraction of gross revenue), which tax results in the same final price and output. Therefore, the mar-

tax, the new price will be higher (and the output smaller) under the unit tax.   This is true because, up to a maximum yield, any increase in yield is accompanied by an increase in price.   If an ad valorem tax results in a given yield, the unit tax that results in the same price and output gives a lesser yield.   To obtain the same yield with a unit tax, the resulting price must be higher.[1]

We conclude, therefore, that the choice between the two taxes is a

---

ginal-revenue net of tax still equals marginal production cost at output x_t:

$$MC(x_t) = MR(x_t) - rMR(x_t)$$

Equating the right-hand sides of the two equations and solving for r, we obtain

$$r = \frac{t}{MR(x_t)}$$

The yield of the unit tax is given as

$$Y_t = tx_t$$

while the yield of the ad valorem tax is

$$Y_r = rp_tx_t = \frac{t}{MR(x_t)} p_tx_t$$

The difference between the ad valorem yield and the yield of the unit tax will then be

$$Y_r - Y_t = tx_t \left[\frac{p_t}{MR(x_t)} - 1 \right]$$

Since the yield of the unit tax (tx_t) is positive, and since price exceeds marginal revenue, the right side of the last expression is positive, and the yield of the ad valorem tax exceeds that of the unit tax.   This proof also applies to the competitive case.   If price equals marginal revenue, the right side of the last expression is zero, and the yields are equal.

The ad valorem tax rate r is here defined as a per cent of gross revenue.   Instead, tax laws may define a rate that applies to gross revenue net of tax.   If s is such a tax rate, we simply substitute s for r, where $s = r/(1 - r)$.   The above propositions hold whether the tax is defined by s or r, and the proofs are similar.

[1] Instead of comparing taxes of equal yield, we may compare an ad valorem tax and a unit tax imposing the same burden at the initial price.   Let us denote the final price achieved under the two taxes as p_r and p_t, respectively.   Given a matched pair of rates r (the ad valorem rate) and t (the unit rate) so that $r = t/p_0$, we find that $p_t = p_r$ under pure competition.   Under monopoly there is always a matched pair of rates for which $p_t > p_r$; but there are matched pairs of rates for which $p_r \geqq p_t$ only if there is some point on the demand schedule where the corresponding value of the marginal revenue equals or exceeds p_0.

With linear revenue and cost schedules, the rate of unit tax at which yield is a maximum will be that at which marginal revenue is equal to p_0.   If the rate is increased further, yield falls.   Therefore, given linear marginal-cost and average-revenue schedules, and assuming rates not to be pushed beyond the maximum yield, p_t will always exceed p_r; that is to say, the final price will always be higher under the unit tax.   See Suits and Musgrave, op. cit., p. 603.

matter of indifference under competition but that the ad valorem tax is the more efficient approach in the case of monopoly.   If a general tax on a number of products is considered, the ad valorem tax may be preferable in the competitive case as well, since the ratio of tax per unit to price will be uniform.

C. TAXES ON COST PAYMENTS

The third family of taxes that may be imposed on the firm consists of taxes on cost payments.   Such taxes may be applied to total cost, variable cost, or fixed cost; and they may be general or restricted to costs arising from the purchase of certain factors only.

Ad Valorem Tax on Total Unit Cost

Competition.   We shall begin with a general ad valorem tax on total unit cost and long-run adjustments thereto.   Under competition, an

GENERAL AD VALOREM TAX ON COST PAYMENTS

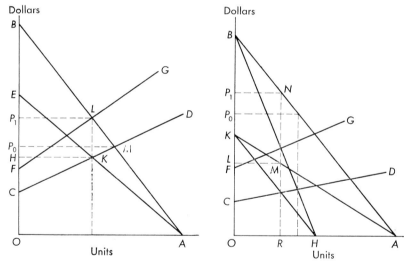

FIG. 13-11. Competitive industry.   FIG. 13-12. Monopoly.

ad valorem tax on total unit cost must result in the same price as an ad valorem tax on revenue of equal yield.   The difference between average revenue before tax and average cost before tax must be the same for both types of tax if the yield is to be the same.   Hence, output and price must also be the same.   If the rate of tax on revenue or demand equals r_d, the equivalent rate of tax on cost is given by $r_c = r_d/(1 - r_d)$.   This follows because under the tax on revenue at rate r_d, we have in equilibrium

$(1 - r_d)AR = AC$, and under the tax on cost at rate r_c, we have $AR = (1 + r_c)AC$.

The result is illustrated in Figure 13-11. Let AB be the industry demand schedule and CD the long-run supply schedule before tax, with price at P_0. An ad valorem tax on average revenue is imposed, swinging the net average-revenue schedule to AE and moving price to P_1. Next, let an ad valorem tax on cost be imposed, raising the supply schedule to FG. The price is again at P_1, and yield in both cases equals $HKLP_1$.

For conditions of increasing cost, the increase in price due to an ad valorem tax on cost becomes larger as the demand schedule is rotated around M and its slope is increased, and as the supply schedule is rotated around M and its slope is reduced. These relationships are similar to those which applied to the ad valorem tax on revenue. Given the average-revenue function $p = a + bx$ and the supply function $s = d + ex$ as before, we obtain

$$\Delta p = b\, \frac{r_c(db - ae)}{(e - b)^2 + r_c(e^2 - eb)} \tag{13-17}$$

as the change in price in response to a tax on cost at rate r_c.[1] By substituting $r_d = r_c/(1 + r_c)$ this may be converted into the ad valorem case of equation (13-5).

For the general case we now obtain[2]

$$\frac{dp}{dr_c} = \frac{s(q)}{1 - (1 + r_c)[s'(q)/p'(q)]} \tag{13-18}$$

Equation (13-18) may be reconciled similarly with the ad valorem tax on revenue presented in equation (13-12). The relationships between changes in the slope of the two schedules and changes in price are similar to those noted in the case of an ad valorem tax on revenue.

[1] As shown in the footnote on p. 291, the price before tax for the linear case is

$$p_0 = a + b\,\frac{a - d}{e - b}$$

After the ad valorem tax on cost is imposed, the new equilibrium output is determined by

$$a + bx = (1 + r_c)(d + ex)$$

which, by solving for x and substituting into the demand equation, gives us the after-tax price

$$p_1 = a + b\,\frac{a - d - dr_c}{er_c + e - b}$$

We thus have

$$\Delta p = b\left(\frac{a - d - dr_c}{er_c + e - b} - \frac{a - d}{e - b}\right)$$

or

$$\Delta p = b\,\frac{r_c(db - ae)}{(e - b)^2 + r_c(e^2 - eb)}$$

[2] The change in the equilibrium quantity with respect to r is

Monopoly.   Turning now to the monopolist, the change in price subsequent to an ad valorem tax on cost is

$$\Delta p = \frac{b}{2} \frac{r_c(bd - ea)}{(e - b)^2 + r_c(e^2 - eb)} \qquad (13\text{-}19)$$

for the linear case.[1]   The change is again one-half that obtained under competition.

As in the case of competition, a tax on cost at rate r_c results in the same price as a tax on gross receipts at rate r_d, where $r_c = r_d/(1 - r_d)$.*   This is illustrated in Figure 13-12, where AB and HB are the average- and marginal-revenue schedules, CD is the marginal-cost schedule, and P_0 is the price before tax.   After an ad valorem tax of 50 per cent on revenue, the marginal-revenue schedule swings to HK, and price rises to P_1.

$$\frac{dq}{dr_c} = \frac{s(q)}{p'(q) - (1 + r_c)s'(q)}$$

The change in price with respect to r is

$$\frac{dp}{dr_c} = p'(q) \frac{dq}{dr_c}$$

and by substitution

$$\frac{dp}{dr_c} = \frac{s(q)}{1 - (1 + r_c)[s'(q)/p'(q)]}$$

[1] The price before tax is

$$p_0 = a + b\left[\frac{a - d}{2(e - b)}\right]$$

After adjustment to an ad valorem tax on cost, the new equilibrium output is determined by

$$a + 2bx = (1 + r_c)(d + 2ex)$$

so that

$$p_1 = a + \frac{b}{2}\left[\frac{a - d(1 + r_c)}{e(1 + r_c) - b}\right]$$

and

$$\Delta p = \frac{b}{2} \frac{r_c(bd - ea)}{(e - b)^2 + r_c(e^2 - eb)}$$

* In equilibrium, marginal cost plus tax equals marginal revenue:

$$MC(x_t)(1 + r_c) = M_r(x_t)$$

Now let the cost tax be replaced by an ad valorem tax on revenue of rate r_d, which results in the same final price and output x_t.   We then have

$$MC(x_t) = MR(x_t)(1 - r_d)$$

Solving the first equation for $MC(x_t)$ and equating with the second, we obtain

$$r_c = \frac{r_d}{1 - r_d}$$

After a corresponding ad valorem tax of 100 per cent on cost, the marginal-cost schedule rises to FG, and price is again at P_1.

Unlike the case of competition, the yields of the two taxes now differ.[1] The yield of the tax on demand or revenue equals $Y_d = r_d AR_d$, where AR_d is the price obtained after adjustment to the tax. The yield of the tax on cost equals $Y_c = r_c ATC_c$, where ATC_c is the total unit cost after adjustment to the tax. If the prices are to be the same for both taxes, we have $r_c = r_d/(1 - r_d)$ and $Y_c = [r_d/(1 - r_d)]ATC_c$. It follows that $Y_d > Y_c$ if $AR_d > [1/(1 - r_d)]ATC_c$. This holds in the case of equilibrium, provided that profits remain. Only if profits after tax are zero are the yields equal. Thus a tax on the gross receipts of the monopolist tends to be more efficient, subject to certain earlier qualifications, than a tax on total unit cost.

Ad Valorem Tax on Variable Cost

Now let us consider an ad valorem tax that applies to variable cost only, while excluding fixed cost. In the long run, this distinction may be disregarded, since all cost becomes variable. In the short run, the two taxes differ.

Under competition, a tax on variable unit cost results in the same increase in price over the short run as does an equal-rate tax on total unit cost. This is true because the tax on total cost applies at the same rate to variable cost. The fact that fixed cost is taxed in the one case but not in the other has no bearing on short-run changes in price. At the same time, the yield of the tax on total unit cost will be larger. An ad valorem tax on variable cost is less efficient in the short run than a tax on total cost or an ad valorem tax on revenue imposed at a corresponding rate.

The same principles apply under monopoly. A tax on variable cost again results in the same rise in price as an equal-rate tax on total cost. Since the base is smaller, the yield will be smaller as well.[2] The same holds a fortiori for the comparison between a tax on variable cost and a tax on revenue imposed at a corresponding rate.

Ad Valorem Tax on Fixed Cost

An ad valorem tax on fixed cost has no bearing on output in the short run. In this respect it is superior to taxes on revenue, total cost, or variable cost. However, the situation differs for the long run.

In Figure 13-13 we see the adjustment to an ad valorem tax on fixed

---

[1] This cannot be seen readily from Fig. 13-12, since CD is the marginal-cost function while the tax on cost applies to average cost.

[2] The yield from a tax on marginal cost equals $Y_{mc} = r_c MC$. For the yield of the tax on gross receipts to be larger, we must have $r_d AR > r_c MC$, or $AR > [1/(1 - r_d)]MC$. This holds true in equilibrium.

cost by a firm operating in a competitive industry. Let AFC_0, AVC_0, and ATC_0 be the average fixed- , variable- , and total-cost curves before tax. With the average-revenue schedule given by AR_0, the price is at P_0. Now, a tax on fixed cost at rate EF/FQ_0 is imposed. The average fixed-cost schedule shifts up to AFC_1, and the average total-cost schedule rises to ATC_1. The increase in total unit cost is equal for each output to that in fixed unit cost. In the short run, the MC schedule is not affected. The firm will continue to produce output Q_0 and suffer a loss per unit equal to KL. Whereas a tax on variable cost leads to zero output in the short run if variable cost plus tax exceeds average revenue at the optimal

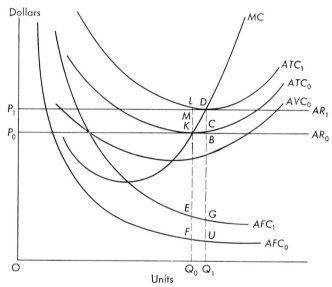

Fig. 13-13. Ad valorem tax on fixed cost under competition.

(least-loss) output, a tax on fixed cost, no matter how high, cannot have this result.

In the long run, some firms will leave the industry. Assuming constant cost for the industry as a whole, there will be no further change in the ATC schedule. The average-revenue schedule for the remaining firms rises to AR_1, and the new price is at P_1. The increase in price, or BD, exceeds the average tax, or DC, by the increase in average variable cost, or CB. Thus, a tax on fixed cost increases the scale of operation and reduces the number of firms that remain in the industry.

Now let us impose a tax that raises variable cost—say, a unit tax equal in amount to MK. The ATC and MC schedules both shift upward in a parallel fashion, and the new equilibrium is reached at M. The price and output for the industry as a whole will be the same as with the tax on fixed cost, but the tax per unit equals KM. Yield will be larger than under the tax on fixed cost. Thus, the tax on variable cost is more efficient.

A franchise tax may be looked upon as a lump-sum addition to fixed costs and may be treated accordingly.

Partial Taxes on Selected Factors

While a general tax on all factor payments may not be found in the usual tax structure, taxes on cost payments to particular factors are widely used. A payroll tax imposed on the employer is a tax on the purchase of labor; a tax on business property is a tax on the employment of capital, and so forth.

If the production function is such that it requires fixed proportions of factor inputs, there is no difference between a tax on total cost payments and a tax on cost payments to certain factors only. If factor proportions are variable, imposition of a tax on the purchase of certain factors will lead to substitution of tax-free factors for taxed factors, until an equality between gross factor prices (including tax) and marginal-value products is restored. Depending upon the supply elasticities of the various factors and the production function, the resulting upward shift in the cost schedule may be more or less severe.

CHAPTER 14

Adjustments in investment

Let us now turn to the long-run adjustments to a tax on investment income. As in the preceding chapters, our immediate concern is with the reactions of the individual investor to the imposition of such a tax. The important macro implications of resulting changes in investment are considered later on.

Though not passed on in the short run by changes in price and output with a given plant, a tax on profits may affect the direction and level of future investment. In the case of a truly general tax on investment income, the problem is how the tax affects the investor's choice between holding cash and investing, and between investing at various degrees of risk. In the case of a tax that applies differentially to earnings in various industries, the adjustment involves a further transfer of capital from discriminated to favored industries. While our present concern is with the effects of a general tax imposed on all capital earnings alike, it remains to be seen just what is meant by *alike*. Inclusion of earnings from all industries in the tax base is not a sufficient condition for a truly general tax. A proper treatment of losses, depreciation, and other items in the determination of income is required to design a nondiscriminatory tax.

Taxation effects upon investment behavior will be looked upon first in terms of a *financial* investor, who chooses among the purchase of various assets and/or the holding of cash. Thereafter, we shall consider effects on business firms purchasing primarily *output assets*. While the two problems are basically similar, they differ in certain respects.

A. ADJUSTMENTS IN FINANCIAL INVESTMENT

In dealing with financial investment, let us begin with taxation effects upon the investor's willingness to invest available funds. Effects on the availability of funds will be considered briefly thereafter.

312

For an investment to be undertaken, the present worth of the expected income stream must exceed the cost of the initial outlay.[1] This general principle is simple, but its application is not. Much depends on just what kinds of return are to be included in this income stream, how the investor formulates his expectations, what investment characteristics he is primarily concerned with, and how his preferences are determined. This is a complex process, but it must be reduced to manageable terms before we can determine how the investor reacts to one or another budget policy.

Investment Choice in Absence of Tax

Let us begin with a simple situation where a given amount of investible funds are available to the investor, who endeavors to allocate them in what he considers an optimum fashion.[2] The choice before him is between the prospect of income and the avoidance of losses. Such a choice is similar in some respects to that between income and leisure or consumption and saving. The investment yield obtainable at the market sets the rate at which the assumption of risk, or parting with the assurance of zero loss, may be traded against the prospect of income. As before, an indifference analysis may be applied to determine this choice.

Nevertheless, the present problem is more complex. While the worker knows precisely (or nearly so) what wage rate he can obtain, the investor must appraise the market outlook for various investment opportunities in his own terms. He must assign quantitative values to what he considers desirable or undesirable characteristics of various investment opportunities. This appraisal is based on observation of more or less objective market conditions, but the interpretation of these observations is a highly subjective matter.

Consider first how the merits of any one investment may be appraised. The investor will examine the probabilities of obtaining various net income streams from a particular investment; or, expressing the present

[1] The argument up to p. 322 is largely a summary of an earlier paper by Evsey D. Domar and R. A. Musgrave, "Proportional Income Taxation and Risk-taking," *Quarterly Journal of Economics*, vol. 58, pp. 387–422, May, 1944. Also see E. Cary Brown, "Business-income Taxation and Investment Incentives," in *Income, Employment and Public Policy: Essays in Honor of Alvin H. Hansen*, W. W. Norton & Company, Inc., New York, 1948, pp. 300–316. Both papers are reprinted in R. A. Musgrave and Carl Shoup (eds.), *Readings in the Economics of Taxation*, American Economic Association, Richard D. Irwin, Inc., Homewood, Ill., 1958. For a further development of the approach, see Paul Streeten, "The Effect of Taxation on Risk-taking," *Oxford Economic Papers*, vol. 5, pp. 271–287, October, 1953.

[2] We assume that the investment market is atomistic so that the investor can disregard the effects of his decision on yields, and that investments are divisible into small units. This points to a first difference between the case of financial investment and that of real investment.

value of these net income streams as a percentage of cost, he will consider the probability of obtaining various yields. Income is defined to include changes in capital value as well as realized cash income; to obtain *net* income, all monetary costs of investment are deducted.

Having determined the probabilities of obtaining various yields (positive or negative) from a particular investment, the investor then proceeds to assess its merits in terms of this probability distribution. While all the characteristics of the distribution may be of interest to him, he will want to focus on certain key features, if only to facilitate comparison with the characteristics of other investments. For purposes of the present analysis, we assume that the investor will focus his attention on the mathematical expectation of the percentage yield y, which is the average amount that he expects to win in the long run. In addition, he is interested in y's positive or gain component g and its negative or risk component r.* Let us also assume, for the time being, that the investor is certain with regard to the underlying probability distribution.

Having determined the characteristics of each asset in terms of y, r, and g, the investor must decide what combination of assets he wishes to hold. His objective is to obtain the most desirable investment mix, consisting of various investments and of cash.

Let us first disregard cash and consider a choice between two noncash assets X and Z. In the southwest quadrant of Figure 14-1, we measure vertically the yield of any given combination of X and Z. On the horizontal axis, we measure the fraction of total holdings of X plus Z, which is held in X. The origin indicates a position where Z only is held, while the weight of X increases as we move out to the left. At combination a, the entire portfolio is in X, the yield being equal to the ordinate of a. At combination b, only Z is held, the yield being equal to the ordinate of b. Investment Z has the greater yield. The yields of various combinations

---

* If $q_1, q_2 \ldots q_k, q_{k+1} \ldots q_n$ are the expected rates of return to the extent that $q_i < q_{i+1}$ and $q_k = 0$, and if the probability of the occurrence of q_i is p_i, so that $\sum_{i=1}^{n} p_i = 1$, we arrive at the following definitions:

$$r = -\sum_{i=1}^{k} q_i p_i$$

$$g = \sum_{i=k+1}^{n} q_i p_i$$

$$y = \sum_{i=1}^{n} q_i p_i = g - r$$

Since the values of all q's from the beginning to q_k are negative, r is positive.

of X and Z are located on a straight line from a to b; since the yield of each combination equals the weighted average of the yield of the two component assets.

In the northwest quadrant of the figure, the risk of any given asset combination is measured vertically, and the mix is again measured horizontally. If only Z is held, the risk is measured by the ordinate of b, and

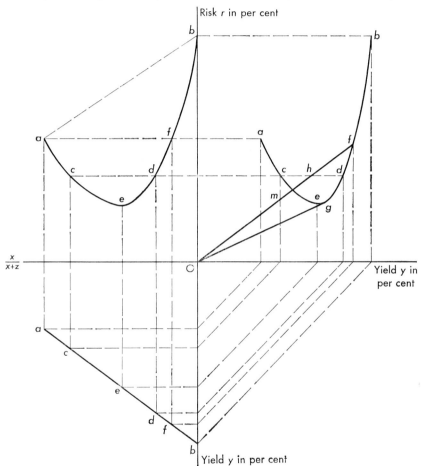

Fig. 14-1. Derivation of optimum-asset curve.

if only X is held, the risk is measured by the ordinate of a. Investment Z, which carries the higher risk, also offers the larger yield. As the holding of X is reduced and some Z is added, the risk of the portfolio declines, reflecting the principle that diversification of the portfolio among independent assets of equal risk narrows the dispersion of the distribution and reduces risk. But Z is the investment with higher risk, and as successive doses of Z are added, the risk of the portfolio will eventually rise. We thus obtain a line such as aeb, showing the risk of portfolios containing a decreasing fraction of X.

Finally, the risks and yields of the various asset combinations are recorded in the northeast quadrant, where risk is measured on the vertical axis and yield is measured on the horizontal axis. We thus obtain the curve aeb, which shows the available combinations. Those to the left of e may be ruled out as inferior, since each is matched to the right of e by a superior combination with the same risk but a higher yield. The curve eb thus gives the locus of the highest-yield–lowest-risk combinations of non-cash assets from which our investor may choose.

But what if the investor wishes to hold cash? The holding of cash is assumed to carry zero risk, price-level changes being ruled out for the time being. As various combinations of X and Z are deleted by the addition of cash, let us suppose that risk and yield are reduced at the same rate.[1] Let cash be added to the asset mix indicated by f in the northeast quadrant. The risk and yield of a portfolio containing one-half of mix f and one-half of cash is indicated by m, lying at the mid-point on a straight line from f to the origin. Results obtained by mixing other asset combinations with cash similarly fall on straight lines connecting various points on curve eb with the origin. Of all the combinations involving cash, only those on Og are of interest, since the investor always prefers to combine the same risk with the highest possible yield. The locus of the best possible combinations, including cash, is thus indicated by the line Ogb, which is referred to as the optimum-asset curve.

---

[1] As an alternative and perhaps more realistic assumption, it might be argued that the initial addition of cash to any given portfolio will reduce risk at a sharper rate than yield, thus allowing for reduced danger of forced sale and for Hart's principle of linkage of risks. See A. G. Hart, *Money, Debt and Economic Activity*, Prentice-Hall, Inc., Englewood Cliffs, N.J., 1948, pp. 198ff.

Such an approach was followed in an earlier paper, Domar and Musgrave, *op. cit.*, p. 399, where the optimum-asset curve is derived as an envelope to risk-income lines pertaining to mixtures of given combinations of non-cash assets with varying degrees of cash. This may be the more realistic view, but it does not permit us to determine precisely to what extent a change in risk taking involves a change in the riskiness of non-cash assets and to what extent it involves a change in the fraction of the portfolio that is held in cash. The approach of Fig. 14-1 permits us to determine precisely the fraction of cash included at each point on Ogb. For a similar approach see James E. Tobin, "Liquidity Preference as Behaviour towards Risk," *Review of Economic Studies*, ser. 2, vol. 25, no. 67, pp. 65–87, February, 1958.

The shape of the optimum-asset curve in Fig. 14-1 is convex to the abscissa, similar to the shape obtained in my earlier paper with Domar, *op. cit.* Streeten, *op. cit.*, p. 275, notes that the optimum-asset curve may be concave to the abscissa because an individual investor may benefit from the fact that the market-opportunity curves of other investors are unduly convex, and because the risk aversion of others reduces the number of people who compete in risk taking.

This optimum-asset curve is repeated in Figure 14-2. The investor's choice among all points on OGB is determined by his preference between risk r and income y. The indifference map of Figure 14-2, which expresses this preference, is based on the assumption that the size of the asset portfolio is given; thus the values of y and r may be defined in percentage terms rather than in dollar amounts.[1] The indifference lines are drawn on the assumptions that the marginal utility of income falls with rising income and that the marginal disutility of risk rises with increasing risk.[2] The slope of the indifference curves, being equal to the ratio of marginal utility of income to marginal disutility of risk, must thus be positive. Moreover, it follows that (1) the slope of any indifference curve decreases

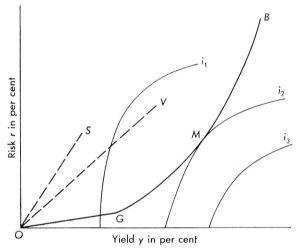

FIG. 14-2. Choice of optimum-asset combination.

upward and to the right, (2) the slopes of successive curves fall when moving along a horizontal line to the right, and (3) the slopes of successive curves fall when moving up a vertical line. In the following argument (3) is not made use of, but (1) and (2) are. They are satisfied by the condition of declining marginal utility of income.

On the basis of this preference pattern and the optimum-asset curve OGB, the investor will choose that combination which places him at the highest possible indifference curve. In Figure 14-2, this is at M, where our investor's portfolio includes a mixture of X and Z but no cash. Another investor might interpret the market outlook differently or have

[1] The preference pattern thus defined will change with the size of the investor's portfolio. See Fig. 14-5 for a preference pattern in dollar terms, independent of the size of the portfolio.

[2] The marginal utility of income is assumed to be independent of risk, and vice versa. For a different view see p. 329.

a greater risk aversion, leading to a tangency point on the linear part of the optimum-asset curve. He will then include cash in his portfolio.

Taxation without Loss Offset

Let us see, now, how investment decisions are affected by a tax. We shall consider the effects of a proportional tax on *net* income, allowing for the deduction of all money costs of investment, including depreciation or tax-free recovery of the initial investment and of wages of management.[1] However, we must distinguish two different situations with regard to the treatment of losses:[2] first, a situation where losses suffered in any one investment cannot be offset by gains made in another investment; second, a situation where it is *always* possible to offset losses against other income.

By imposing a tax without loss offset, the Treasury shares in the investor's gains, while leaving his losses unchanged. Let us now consider the effects of the tax on the magnitudes of y and r, and then the investor's reaction to this change.

Prior to the tax, we have for any one investment combination the actuarial value of

$$y = g - r \qquad (14\text{-}1)$$

which, after tax, becomes

$$y_t = (1 - t)g - r \qquad (14\text{-}2)$$

Since losses cannot be deducted, the positive component g is reduced, while the negative component r remains unchanged. Also, it is evident from equations (14-1) and (14-2) that y_t is smaller than $(1 - t)y$, which is to say that the yield is reduced by a greater percentage than the rate of the tax. The percentage reduction in y that will occur with any given tax rate is equal to

$$\alpha = \frac{y - y_t}{y} = \left(1 + \frac{r}{y}\right)t \qquad (14\text{-}3)$$

The degree of tax sensitiveness or α of a particular investment depends upon the ratio of r/y rather than on r alone. Note that there is no particular reason why investments with a high r should have a high α as well. However, between points on the optimum-asset curve, an increase in r necessarily entails an increase in α.[3]

[1] See Domar and Musgrave, *op. cit.*, p. 403, note 9, for the implications of alternative assumptions.

[2] Credit for recognizing the crucial importance of the loss-offset problem goes to Henry C. Simons, *Personal Income Taxation*, University of Chicago Press, Chicago, 1938, p. 21, note 2; and to A. P. Lerner, "Functional Finance and the Federal Debt," *Social Research*, vol. 10, pp. 38–51, February, 1943, and *The Economics of Control*, The Macmillan Company, New York, 1944, p. 238.

[3] The value of α varies directly with the value of r/y. For any particular asset combination, the value of r/y is the slope of the line connecting it with the origin. In

The shift in the optimum-asset curve, due to imposition of a tax, is shown in Figure 14-3. OGB is the position of the optimum-asset curve before tax, and the equilibrium is at M. When a tax is imposed, each point of the asset curve suffers a reduction in y in accordance with its degree of tax sensitiveness. Since the risk remains unchanged, each point moves to the left along a horizontal line. Thus, if a 25 per cent tax is imposed, the new optimum-asset curve becomes $OG_{25}B_{25}$; if a 50 per cent tax is imposed, the curve becomes $OG_{50}B_{50}$, and so forth. Because the tax sensitiveness of points on the asset curve rises with r, the upper part of the optimum-asset curve (after tax) bends to the left, and yield becomes negative if the rate of tax is sufficiently high.

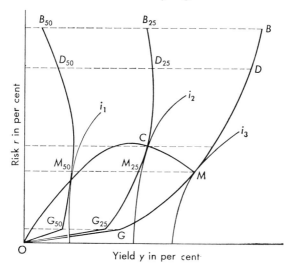

Fig. 14-3. Income tax without loss offset.

Consider an investor located at M prior to the tax. He finds himself at M_{25} after a 25 per cent tax is imposed, assuming the identical portfolio to be retained. This point is not an equilibrium position. He can improve his position by moving up along $G_{25}B_{25}$ until tangency with an indifference curve is reached at C. The line MCO traces the equilibrium path as rates of tax are increased.

When moving from M to the left, the level of r first rises and then falls. The resulting adjustment is determined by an interaction between the income effect and the substitution effect. The income effect pushes the investor toward taking more risk in an attempt to recover his income, as income from the old combination is reduced. The substitution effect

---

Fig. 14-2, the value of r/y is higher for combination S than for combination V, even though S is the less risky investment. Moving up along OB, r/y remains constant from O to G but rises thereafter.

pushes him toward taking less risk as the reward for risk taking falls. The net result may be either an increase or a decrease in risk.[1]   Initially, the income effect tends to outweigh the substitution effect.   The investor is induced to take more risk as the result of the tax.   Sooner or later, the situation is reversed, leading to an all-cash position when a 100 per cent rate of tax is reached.   The net result thus depends on the particular conditions that apply.   If the investor is more optimistic, the optimum-asset curve lies farther down to the right, and the tax will be more favorable or less detrimental to risk taking.

Taxation with Full Loss Offset

Let us suppose, now, that losses can be offset completely.   Where the investor has at his disposal a sufficient amount of income derived from other sources, full loss offset may be assured by adequate provision for carry-over of losses in the tax law.   This, in effect, is accomplished in the United States income tax for well-established and diversified investors but not for new firms which may go bankrupt and which have insufficient past income.   To some extent, losses may be recovered by tax sales, but the market is imperfect and favors the buyer.   To assure complete loss offset for all firms, let us assume that the Treasury actually refunds losses at the rate of tax applicable to gains.   This does not change the status quo for firms that can use the present carry-over of losses, but it does extend the privilege to firms that cannot do so.   The Treasury then becomes a partner who shares equally in both losses and gains.[2]

Under these conditions, expected losses as well as gains are cut by a percentage equal to the tax rate.   We now have

$$y_t = (1 - t)g - (1 - t)r \qquad (14\text{-}4)$$

Substituting equation (14-1) into (14-4), we obtain

$$y_t = (1 - t)y \qquad (14\text{-}5)$$

---

[1] If marginal income utility is constant, there is no offsetting income effect, and risk taking is reduced.   For alternative assumptions, including that of increasing marginal utility of income, see Streeten, *op. cit.*, p. 273.

[2] The idea of positive loss refunds sounds shocking.   Will not provision for perfect loss offset open the gate to wild speculation and cause an inefficient allocation of resources?   If so, the remedy is simple.   Partial refunds may be substituted, and risk taking depressed to the desired level.   In any case, there remains the question whether the present limitation of effective loss offset to certain types of firms involves the most efficient pattern of discrimination; if not, generalized loss offset improves the situation by rendering the tax neutral.   Moreover, differential treatment may be given to certain types of risk taking.   Gambling gains may be taxed, and refunds disallowed, if gambling is to be discouraged.

The actuarial value, or yield, is now reduced by the same percentage for all asset combinations, whatever their initial value of r or of r/y.

The shift in the optimum-asset curve that results from a tax with full loss offset is shown in Figure 14-4. When such a tax is imposed, the values of r and y are both reduced at the same rate. Each point on OGB, the pre-tax optimum-asset curve, moves towards the origin along a straight line. If a 50 per cent tax is imposed, the optimum-asset curve after tax becomes $OG_{50}B_{50}$; if a 75 per cent tax is imposed, the optimum-asset curve becomes $OG_{75}B_{75}$, and so forth.

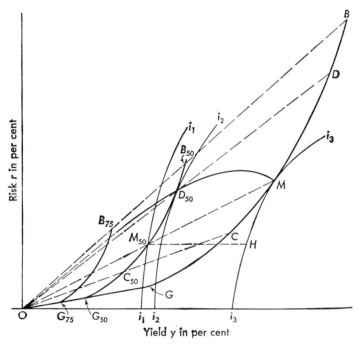

FIG. 14-4. Income tax with full loss offset.

The pre-tax equilibrium is again at M. Now a 50 per cent tax is imposed. The investor, while retaining the same asset portfolio, finds his position moved from M to M_{50}, but M_{50} is not an equilibrium point. He will move up the post-tax optimum asset curve $OG_{50}B_{50}$ until tangency with an indifference curve is reached at D_{50}. The path $MD_{50}O$ again traces the locus of the optimum positions under various rates of tax.

Since losses are fully offset, the tax has no substitution effect. It involves an income effect only. The investor will want to recover at least a part of the risk removed by imposition of the tax. Depending on the circumstances, D_{50} may be below or above M, and the investor may

take more or less risk than before the tax.   However, his new position at
D_{50} involves a greater risk than he would have incurred had he remained
at M_{50}.*   The significance of this becomes evident once we distinguish
between *total* yield and *private* yield, and between *total* risk and *private*
risk.   The imposition of the tax reduces the private yield and private risk
inherent in the initially held asset portfolio M, from the coordinates of
point M to those of M_{50}.   But the total yield and the total risk inherent
in this particular asset combination are entirely unaffected by the tax,
and remain those of point M.   Similarly, the coordinates of point D_{50}
register the private risk and the private yield of the new asset combination
only.   The total risk and yield of this new asset combination are regis-
tered by the coordinates of point D.   Since D_{50} must lie above M_{50}, D
must lie above M because $r = r_p/(1 - t)$, where r_p is the private risk of
any given point on the optimum-asset curve after tax, and r is the total
risk of the corresponding point on the optimum-asset curve before tax.

Thus, total risk taking is increased by the tax, although private risk
taking may be reduced.   The higher the rate of tax, the larger the increase
in total risk.   From the point of view of the economy as a whole, it is the
total risk that matters and not only the amount of private risk.   In
interpreting the concept of total risk, it should be kept in mind that the
government is a sleeping partner.   The decisions that give rise to public
sharing of risk are made entirely by the private investor.

The Size of the Portfolio

In the preceding analysis, the size of portfolio was assumed given.
The problem was how to allocate this given portfolio between cash and
other assets.   Let us now allow for the possibility of borrowing and
confront the investor with the additional problem of determining the gross
size of his portfolio.   To simplify matters, we shall assume that he can
borrow any desired amount at the market rate i.   This eliminates from
consideration a possible increase in the cost of borrowing as the investor's
ratio of borrowing to net worth rises or the riskiness of his investments
increases.

* The conclusion that D_{50} must lie above M_{50} follows from two propositions: The
first is that the slope of indifference curve i_1 at M_{50} must be greater than the slope of i_3
at M.   This proposition, in turn, follows from the fact that at M the slopes of OMB
and i_3 are equal, and both are smaller than the slope of i_3 at H; and that the slope of i_1
at M_{50} must be equal or greater than the slope of i_3 at H.

The second proposition is that the slope of $OG_{50}B_{50}$ at M_{50} is equal to the slope of
OGB at M.   This is true because r and y are both reduced by the rate of tax.

From these two propositions, it follows that at M_{50}, the slope of i_1 will exceed that
of $OG_{50}B_{50}$.   Since the slope of $OG_{50}B_{50}$ increases when moving upward and to the
right, while the slope of any one indifference curve decreases, the new equilibrium
point D_{50} must be to the right and above M_{50}.

The dollar yield Y of any particular portfolio combination without borrowing is given by

$$Y = (g - r)N \qquad (14\text{-}6)$$

where Y is yield in dollar terms, g and r are the rates of gain and loss, and N is net worth in dollar terms, or the available amount of investor-owned capital. With borrowing allowed for, we have

$$Y_b = (g - r)(N + B) - iB \qquad (14\text{-}7)$$

where B is borrowing in dollar terms. Setting $B = bN$, equation (14-7) may be rewritten as

$$Y_b = [(g - r)(1 + b) - ib]N \qquad (14\text{-}8)$$

Dividing by N, we have

$$y_b = y(1 + b) - ib \qquad (14\text{-}9)$$

where $y_b = Y_b/N$ is the net yield or income rate of the portfolio with borrowing, and $y = g - r$ is the yield in the absence of borrowing. The risk R_b of a portfolio with borrowing equals

$$R_b = r(1 + b)N \qquad (14\text{-}10)$$

where R_b is the risk in dollar terms. Dividing again by N, we have

$$r_b = r(1 + b) \qquad (14\text{-}11)$$

where $r_b = R_b/N$ is the risk rate of the portfolio with borrowing, and r is the risk rate in the absence of borrowing. If $i = y$, we have $y_b = y$, but $r_b > r$. Borrowing will not be worthwhile. Where $i < y$, we have $y_b > y$. Borrowing may be worthwhile, but the extent of borrowing will depend on the increase in yield that the investor demands if he is to assume increased risk.

The investment choice with borrowing is shown in Figure 14-5. The expected yield and loss are measured in dollar terms, and OGB is the optimum-asset curve available with a given net worth in the absence of borrowing. The indifference curves refer to risk and yield in dollar terms. Now, the investor considers the possibility of borrowing. Suppose that the rate of interest equals the value of yield y corresponding to combination C, so that $i = OA/N$. If the investor chooses to borrow in order to purchase more of combination C, he finds that Y remains unchanged, while R is increased. He moves up vertically along the borrowing line CK. Since this places him on a lower indifference curve, he will not borrow while holding the portfolio mix C. If we consider mix F, we have $i < y$. Borrowing is more attractive as both Y and R are increased when moving up the borrowing line FL. However, borrowing with mix F

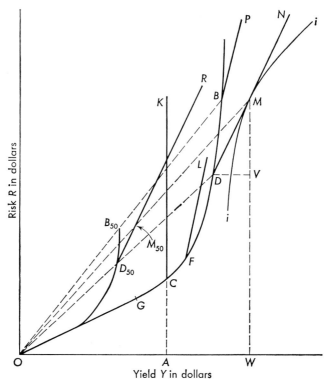

Fig. 14-5. Investment choice with borrowing.

remains less attractive than riskier portfolio mixes without borrowing. Borrowing will not be considered until a mix is reached where the slope of the borrowing line equals that of OFB.[1]   For this and riskier investments,

---

[1] Note that the slope of the borrowing line is vertical to begin with; then it decreases and finally increases again.   According to eq. (14-8) we have, for any given point on the optimum-asset curve,

$$Y_b = g(1 + b)N - r(1 + b)N - ibN$$

Differentiating with respect to bN, we obtain

$$dY_b = gdbN - rdbN - idbN$$

Similarly, we have from eq. (14-10)

$$R_b = (1 + b)rN$$

where R is the dollar amount of risk, and $dR_b = rdbN$.   Dividing, we obtain

$$\frac{dY_b}{dR_b} = \frac{g - r - i}{r} = \frac{y - i}{r}$$

which is the slope of the borrowing line at the point given on the curve.

For $y = i$, we have $dY_b/dR_b = 0$, and the borrowing line is vertical.   As we move

borrowing may be considered, since borrowing moves the investor to a higher indifference curve. The investor now seeks his new equilibrium at the tangency point of this and higher borrowing lines with the highest indifference curve, and the equilibrium may be reached at a point such as M, where asset combination D is held and the amount of borrowing is such that $b = MV/VW$.*

We may now introduce a tax into this system. Choosing the case of perfect loss offset and assuming contractual interest cost to be deductible from taxable income, the dollar yield after tax Y_{bt} is given by

$$Y_{bt} = (1 - t)(g - r)(N + B) - iB + tiB \qquad (14\text{-}12)$$

Substituting $B = bN$ and dividing by N, we obtain

$$y_{bt} = (1 - t)[(g - r)(1 + b) - ib] \qquad (14\text{-}13)$$

As before, yield as well as risk is reduced by the rate of tax. Neither risk taking nor borrowing are discriminated against.

Returning to Figure 14-5, let us suppose that a 50 per cent tax is imposed. The optimum-asset curve, applicable to the portfolio without borrowing, swings from OGB to OD_{50}, B_{50}. The investor finds that his private risk and yield is reduced by the rate of tax. If his pre-tax position was at M, his position after a 50 per cent tax is at M_{50}. As before, he will improve his position by recovering part of the income that has been lost. Since full loss offset prevails, we are dealing only with an income effect and not a substitution effect. Recovery of income may now take the form of increased borrowing, or a shift to a riskier asset combination, or both.[1] Total risk taking is increased in either case.

Tax on Capital

A tax on capital is the same as a tax on capital income, if it applies to income-earning assets only, and if such assets are valued by capitalizing the income stream. However, capital taxes may take forms that differ significantly from a tax on capital income.

Tax on Total Capital. Let us begin with a tax on capital that is assessed on the value of the taxpayer's assets at the beginning of the period. Cash

---

up the optimum-asset line, $y - i$ may rise at a faster rate initially than r, so that dY_b/dR_b increases. Eventually, however, the optimum-asset line becomes asymptotic to some value of Y. Thus dY_b/dR_b turns down and approaches zero.

* At point M we have $R_b = MW$ and $rN = VW$. From eq. (14-10) we have $R_b = (1 + b)rN$. Substituting, we obtain $b = (MW - VW)/VW = MV/VW$.

[1] As will be seen from p. 324, note 1, the slope of the borrowing line at D_{50} is parallel to DN.

assets are included as well as earning assets.   The question may be raised
of how the effects of this tax on risk taking compare with the effects of an
equal-yield tax on capital income.[1]

  OPZ in Figure 14-6 represents the optimum-asset curve before tax; *A*
is the pre-tax equilbrium.   An income tax at rate BA/OA is imposed, and

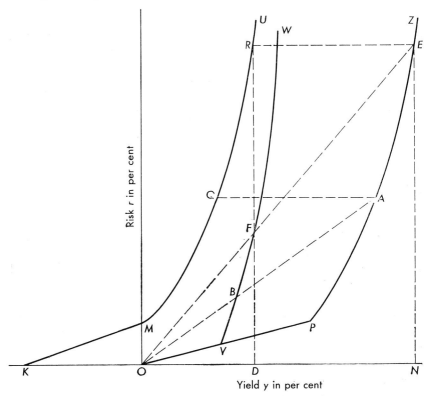

Fig. 14-6. Comparison of income tax and capital tax.

full loss offset is assumed.[2]   The optimum-asset curve after income tax
equals *OVW*, and the new equilibrium is at a point such as *F*.   Private
risk equals *DF*, total risk equals *NE*, and the yield of the income tax (or

---

[1] N. Kaldor, *An Expenditure Tax*, George Allen & Unwin, Ltd., London, 1955,
p. 117, holds that risk taking will be higher under the capital tax.   As noted by E.
Cary Brown, this does not appear to be a valid conclusion.   (See Brown's "Mr.
Kaldor on Taxation and Risk Bearing," *Review of Economic Studies*, vol. 25, no. 1,
pp. 49–52.)   Our argument is an adaptation of that presented by Brown.

[2] If loss offset is imperfect, the attractiveness of the income tax suffers.   Imperfection of loss offset does not raise the burden of a capital tax including cash, since a
loss in this case reduces the future tax burden.   A capital tax that includes cash thus
provides for a built-in loss offset.

the government's share in y) equals DN.   Now let a capital tax of equal yield be substituted for the income tax.   The new equilibrium is established where KMU is tangent to an indifference curve.   If this point of tangency is at R, which lies vertically above F, risk will be the same under both taxes.   If the tangency point is below R, risk will be higher under the income tax; and if it is above R, risk will be higher under the capital tax.   The result depends upon our particular assumptions regarding the shape of the indifference pattern.   Returning to our earlier assumptions, three cases may be considered:

1. The slopes of successive indifference curves fall when moving to the right along a horizontal line, and are constant when moving along a vertical line.   In this case, the equilibrium after capital tax is at R, and risk is the same under both taxes.   This follows because the slope of KMU at R is the same as that of OVW at F, both being equal to that of OPZ at E; and because the slope of the indifference curve through R is the same as that of the indifference curve through F.

2. The slopes of successive indifference curves fall when moving up a vertical line, but are constant along any horizontal line.   In this case, the equilibrium cannot be at R, since here the slope of MRU exceeds that of the indifference curve.   This inequality is increased if we move up from R, since the slope of MRU rises while the slopes of successive indifference curves fall at their intersections with MRU.   The inequality is reduced and eventually eliminated if we move down from R, since the slope of MRU falls while that of successive indifference curves rises.   Equilibrium is reached at a point below R, and risk is greater under the income tax.

3. The slopes of successive indifference curves fall when moving to the right along a horizontal line, and up along a vertical line.   The argument is the same as in the preceding case, but equilibrium is reached sooner (the difference between the two taxes is less marked), since the equilibrating adjustment in the slopes of successive indifference lines is now supported by both assumptions.   However, the income tax again leaves us with the higher level of risk taking.

Since (3) seems the most reasonable assumption, we may expect risk taking to be greater under the income tax.

Tax on Hoards.   The situation is quite different if we consider a tax that applies to cash holdings only.   Such a tax increases the attractiveness of noncash assets relative to that of cash assets.   Where an easy-money policy may be unable to break through the interest floor, a tax on hoards, if sufficiently severe, may reduce the effective interest rate to zero or push it to a negative level.   As noted previously for the case of a temporary spendings tax, tax policy may serve to produce a far more powerful change in effective rates of interest than can be obtained through monetary policy.[1] It is not surprising, therefore, that a tax on hoarding was given much attention in fiscal discussions during the thirties.[2]

Capital Levy. The preceding discussion has dealt with taxation effects upon the decision to undertake new investment. A profits tax limited to earnings from old investments or a capital tax on such investments has no effect on earnings from new investment. Such is the case of the capital levy, discussed so much in the aftermath of World War I. Provided that it is considered a once-and-for-all tax, it will have no substitution effects on new investment.

Similar considerations apply to stimulation of investment by tax reduction. If a profits tax is such that it deters new investment, investment will be stimulated more effectively per dollar of revenue loss if the tax reduction is restricted to earnings from new investments. This may take the form of reducing the rate applicable to new investment or of shortening the depreciation period. Since it is administratively simpler to limit accelerated depreciation to new assets than to limit a rate reduction to earnings from new investment, tax reduction by accelerated depreciation is often a considerable advantage.

Qualifications

The preceding discussion leads to the conclusion that taxation with perfect loss offset will not reduce, and may well increase, the total level of risk taking in the economy. This result is not incompatible with evidence in the historical experience of the United States. Periods of high-profit taxation have typically been periods of high-level investment; and corporations and partnerships took more risk than single proprietorships seemed able to take. At the same time, our argument is subject to a number of qualifications that must be remembered before extensive policy conclusions are drawn.

Theory of Investment Behavior. Conclusions on the taxation effects of investment can be no better than the underlying theory of investment behavior, and this theory is far from satisfactory.

While retaining our general framework, it might be argued that the investor is not concerned only with g and r, but considers as well certain other aspects of the probability distribution. Two asset combinations that carry the same g and r may differ significantly in other respects.

---

[1] See p. 264.

[2] While administrative difficulties may interfere with the feasibility of such a tax, the idea has much theoretical appeal. For a discussion of various schemes, including those of Sylvio Gesell and Arthur Dahlberg, see David McCord Wright, *The Creation of Purchasing Power*, Harvard University Press, Cambridge, Mass., 1942, chap. 5. Also see Gerhard Colm, "Full Employment through Tax Policy," *Social Research*, vol. 7, pp. 447–467, 1940, where a similar principle is applied to a corporation income tax.

One combination may involve a high probability of moderate gains and a slight probability of large gains or losses, while another may involve a substantial chance of large gains but a less pronounced assurance of even moderate gains and a substantial probability of losses. The investor may well be interested in these further characteristics. If so, the merits of a particular asset portfolio may be affected differently by the imposition of a tax, depending on what characteristics of the distribution are considered. Suppose, for instance, that the investor considers y as defined here but substitutes r' for r, where r' is the standard deviation of the probability distribution. In this case, a tax with a perfect loss offset again leaves r'/y unaffected, and the conclusions are essentially the same as for our case. However, a tax with imperfect loss offset now reduces r', and investment will be reduced less, or increased more, than if r is used.[1] The result will be changed more drastically if a measure of variance is used or if the investor concerns himself with a limited set of most probable values only.[2] While there is no ready presumption that such additional factors will reverse our results, they may greatly complicate the picture.

Most important, perhaps, is the objection that attitudes toward risk and income are not independent of each other, but that both refer to the single objective of maximizing utility. Instead of assuming that the investor chooses between various investments in terms of yield and risk as here defined, let us consider the following approach: The investor values probable gains and losses to be derived from any investment in terms of a utility index. He thus obtains an expected yield weighed in terms of this utility index, and he chooses that combination which carries the highest rating. Thus we dispense with an indifference pattern between risk and yield. We derive the resulting investment choice directly from the investor's market outlook as defined by the probability distributions for various investments and the investor's index of income utility. Risk aversion as such, or joy of gambling, do not enter the picture. Our approach in the preceding pages is not incompatible with this alternative formulation, but it does involve an oversimplification of it.[3]

[1] See James E. Tobin, "Liquidity Preference as Behaviour towards Risk," *Review of Economic Studies*, ser. 2, vol. 25, no. 67, pp. 65–87, February, 1958.

[2] See text p. 331 , note 1, the reference to G. L. S. Shackle, *Expectation in Economics*, Cambridge University Press, New York, 1949.

[3] Note that our conclusions do not require the assumption that the marginal disutility of risk rises with risk, provided that the marginal utility of income falls with increasing income. The reader may wonder how the indifference pattern of Fig. 14-2 would look for an investor whose only concern is with utility maximization. Actually, there would be no such pattern but merely a rating of various combinations in terms of the utility values of their expected yields.

In some cases, results may be obtained from the utility approach by assuming that

Next, one cannot dismiss the fact that the market outlook is uncertain, and that this uncertainty applies to the very probability distribution on which the values of r and g are based.   The degree of uncertainty differs for different ranges within the basic probability distribution for any one asset combination as well as for the distributions pertaining to different combinations.   These differences in uncertainty can hardly be disregarded by the investor.[1]   Between two investments for which the values of r and y are the same, he may be expected to prefer the one for which the probability distribution seems more certain.   This factor has not been allowed for in our analysis, and there is some question whether taxation effects on the return for uncertainty bearing can be handled in the same terms as taxation effects on risk taking.

Qualifications of this sort may well be in order, but they remain within the general framework of a probability analysis.[2]   Nor need we be too concerned over the objection that it is not feasible to compute the probabilities for all the available alternatives.   The answer here is much the same as for the marginal-cost controversy.[3]   More serious is the contention that the probability approach is inapplicable for logical reasons: To make use of probable values, the player must have a large number of

the marginal utility of income falls as income rises, without any further assumptions regarding the rate at which marginal utility falls.   Thus, if the choice is between holding cash and a risk asset, it may be shown analytically that imposition of a tax will induce the investor to increase the ratio of risk asset to cash in his portfolio. More specifically, I am indebted to Professor Tobin, op. cit., for a demonstration that the elasticity of the demand for the risk asset with respect to the tax rate is unity.

In terms of the preceding analysis, this means that the investor wishes to hold private risk constant, thus finding it necessary to increase his holding of the risk asset accordingly.   The optimum-asset curve in this case is a straight line.   As a 50 per cent tax is imposed, the investor finds his private risk reduced by one-half. His position is moved half-way toward the origin.   However, the point of tangency remains unchanged at the initial equilibrium.   In order to move back to this point, the investor must choose a combination whose distance from the origin is twice that of the original equilibrium position.   Thus private risk remains constant while total risk is doubled.   The proposition of unit elasticity, while applicable to the choice between cash and a given risk asset, does not apply, however, if a choice between combinations of various risk assets is considered.

[1] Our distinction between risk and uncertainty follows the terminology used by Knight, Hart, and others.   A. G. Hart, *Anticipations, Uncertainty, and Dynamic Planning*, University of Chicago Press, Chicago, 1940, has pointed out that the problem of uncertainty cannot be solved by boiling down into a single superdistribution the set of probability distributions applicable to any one asset combination; such a superdistribution would conceal relevant characteristics of the underlying distributions.   See Evsey D. Domar and R. A. Musgrave, "Proportional Income Taxation and Risk-taking," *Quarterly Journal of Economics*, vol. 58, p. 395, note 6, May, 1944.

[2] See also the discussion by Streeten, *op. cit.*, p. **277.**

[3] See p. 285.

tries, but the investor who loses cannot continue to play. Though this objection is well taken, it is hardly conclusive. By observing the market, the individual investor may learn from the large numbers of similar tries made by others. Moreover, there appears to be no alternative to the probability approach.[1]

Progressive Tax Rates. The preceding argument has been stated in terms of a proportional tax. The results must be qualified for a progressive tax. A tax that is progressive by size brackets of profit income will reduce expected gains at a higher rate than losses, even though full loss offset may be assured. This will be true especially when the size of the portfolio (including borrowing) is large, so that there is a wide spread between marginal rates of tax applicable to potential gains and losses. The resulting discrimination may be reduced by a general provision for averaging of income, in addition to the carry-over of losses, but it will hardly be eliminated. To avoid all discrimination, the rate of refund must be set to equal the rate of tax applicable to the expected yield. Since the expected yield has a subjective magnitude, this procedure is not feasible.

Next, consider an excess-profits tax where progression relates to the rate of return on the invested capital.[2] Here the size of the portfolio does not matter. However, the risky investment will remain at a disadvantage unless the principle of progression is extended downward into the range of negative yields, or risk differentials are allowed for in defining excess profits in various industries.

Significance of Income Effect. Our conclusions on imperfect loss offset have depended on the relative weights of the income and substitution effects; while for perfect loss offset our conclusions have depended on the absolute weight of the income effect. Since investment decisions in the modern economy are made largely by corporations and institutional investors, one may speculate how well the concept of income effect can be applied to such organizations.

On the one extreme, suppose that the executives of corporations act as

---

[1] Shackle's suggestion that the investor is concerned with certain focus values rather than with the entire distribution offers a novel application of the probability approach, but it does not give a truly different view. Some sort of probability distribution is needed to determine the focus values. See G. L. S. Shackle, *Expectation in Economics*, Cambridge University Press, New York, 1949.

Shackle concludes (chap. 5) that incentive effects of taxation will be minimized if the tax is relatively low within, and relatively high outside, the focus range. While he gives no explicit treatment of loss offset, the role of loss offset is the same as it is in our approach, provided that the lower focus value extends into the loss range.

[2] For a general discussion of the nature of the excess-profits tax, see Roy Blough, "Measurement Problems of the Excess Profits Tax," *National Tax Journal*, vol. 1, no. 4, pp. 353–365, December, 1948.

perfect representatives of the shareholders. The executives will proceed on the basis of a preference pattern more or less reflecting a weighted average of the preferences of the shareholders. This will tend to be the case for an investment trust, and nothing need be added. On the other extreme, suppose that the policies of corporations are determined by their existence as independent units. Considerations that apply to the individual investor may not apply in this case. The operation of the income effect as an offset to the substitution effect is based on the hypothesis that the marginal utility of income rises as income falls. This seems sensible for the individual investor, but the same reasoning does not hold for a business organization. Where the income effect is weak or lacking, the proportional tax without loss offset may be expected to reduce risk taking; and the tax with perfect loss offset may be expected to leave total risk more or less unchanged.

Investment Effort. So far, the nature of investment income has been interpreted wholly as a return to risk taking. This is not realistic. A distinction must be drawn between the function of risk taking, which is assumed by the owner of capital, and the truly entrepreneurial function of rendering a superior investment choice. Both functions may be performed by the same person, but they tend to be increasingly divided. The entrepreneur is the person who estimates or intuitively assesses the optimum-asset curve and fits it to the investor's preference pattern. This is a service that requires special qualifications as well as effort. The return which accrues to it may be defined as the difference in earnings that may be obtained with or without the benefit of superior investment decisions.

Suppose that, prior to the imposition of a tax, an investment of $100 promises a return of $10 with an inferior investment choice and $50 with a superior investment choice. The superior investment is made, and $40 out of the earnings of $50 are imputed to the entrepreneurial service. Now, let a tax of 50 per cent be imposed and assume that the entrepreneurial wage is not deductible. Assuming that full loss offset is assured and that the tax is neutral in other respects, the return on both investments will be reduced equally, that is, to $5 and $25. Nevertheless, the absolute differential—which is the entrepreneurial return—is reduced to $20. The entrepreneurial return, in other words, is curtailed by the rate of tax. As a result, the supply of entrepreneurial effort may decline. If it does, investment decisions may become inferior, and high tax rates may have a deteriorating effect on investment choices, even though full loss offset is assured.[1] These consequences disappear if the reward for entrepreneurial service is deductible. The taxable income for the superior

[1] On the supply of entrepreneurial effort, see p. 245.

investment will then be $50 minus $40, or $10.   Imposition of a 50 per cent tax will reduce this amount to $5, but it will not affect the entrepreneurial return of $40.

While the tax law can hardly be accused of inadequate provision for the deduction of entrepreneurial wages, it is difficult to allocate investment income between such wages and the return for risk taking.   There remains here a source of potential disincentive effects for the quality of investment choice.   Similar considerations apply to the personal income tax.

The Supply of Funds

The profits tax may not only affect the profitability of investment but also change the initial distribution of net worth and the terms at which funds are available to the would-be borrower.   An income tax, unless reflected in reduced consumption, goes to curtail the taxpayer's net worth. Now it is a matter of indifference whose savings are reduced if all investors have the same preferences between risk and income and if all potential borrowers have access to loanable funds at the same terms.   In these cases, the only relevant factor is the effect upon the *level* of available funds.

In reality, neither situation occurs.   Potential investors differ in their asset preferences, owing to differences in tastes, needs, or restrictions imposed by the nature of their balance sheets.   Some investors want to hold cash, others prefer secure investments, and still others seek larger returns at greater risk.   Thus the supply of funds to various types of investment outlets differs, depending on whose savings are reduced.   On the demand side for funds, some borrowers have ready access to the capital market, while others do not.   Moreover, some potential investors are willing to undertake equity investments if they can do so out of their own funds, such as retained earnings, but they are unwilling to go to the market.   The capital market is far from being a common pool, and the supply of funds is far from being homogeneous.   Because of this the pattern, as well as the level of investment, may depend greatly on just whose savings are reduced by taxation.

Progressive taxes, which reduce funds made available by the well to do, may differ greatly in their qualitative impact on investment (per dollar of reduction in available funds) from proportional or regressive taxes, which reduce funds supplied by the small investor.   Taxes that absorb retained earnings of business will be less harmful to new enterprise than taxes that absorb personal savings.   Similar considerations apply to the structural effects of changes in the supply of bank credit, especially in the restrictive phase of monetary policy.   In credit as in tax restriction, a realistic view of the problem must go beyond the general case of a perfect credit market. The institutional characteristics of the given setting must be allowed for.

Changes in the Price Level

So far, we have assumed the holding of cash to be without risk and yield. This assumption falls once price-level changes are allowed for. Losses and gains must now be measured in real terms, and the holding of cash may be risky or profitable.

Taxation effects on the investor's choice between equity (real assets) on the one side and cash or claims on the other, now depend upon the definition of taxable income.[1] In particular, the outcome depends on whether taxable income is defined in money terms or in real terms, and on how capital gains are treated. Various possible approaches are indicated by number in Table 14-1.

TABLE 14-1. TAXATION AND CHANGES IN THE PRICE LEVEL

Terms in which income is defined	Capital gains and losses		
	Not taxed	Taxed when realized	Taxed when accrued
Real terms..............	1	2	3
Money terms............	4	5	6

Let us suppose that our investor expects prices to rise. In the absence of an income tax, he will be induced to shift from claims into equity.[2] How does the imposition of an income tax affect this tendency?

Under policies 1 and 4, capital gains and losses are disregarded, and the choice between cash and equity is not affected. Under policies 2 and 3, appreciation in the money value of equity capital is not taxed, but depreciation in the real value of claims is met by a refund or loss offset. The Treasury shares in the loss, which results from staying in claims, and the inducement to purchase equity is reduced. If we assume that a decline in the real value of cash is realized when it occurs—the alternative being a reversed concept of realization with purchase—policies 2 and 3 are equivalent.

Under policies 5 and 6, gains in the money value of equity capital will be taxed, while losses in the real value of claims will not be refunded. Again, less can be gained from the purchase of real assets than can be gained in the absence of the tax. This effect will be stronger under policy 6, where the tax becomes due when the gain accrues, than under policy 5, where it becomes due only when the gain is realized. If the tax applies

---

[1] For a consideration of these problems in terms of horizontal equity, see p. 168.

[2] See Chap. 22, p. 544.

only to gains, while losses are disregarded, policies 2 and 3 do not affect the advantage of shifting into equity, while policies 5 and 6 still reduce the advantage to be derived from such a shift.

A similar analysis might be made where the investor expects a decline in price level, thus tending to substitute claims for equity. Imposition of a tax with loss offset again diminishes the advantages to be derived from such shifts under policies 2, 3, 5, and 6, whereas policies 1 and 4 are neutral. Failure to allow for losses now renders policies 5 and 6 neutral, whereas 2 and 3 still discourage a shift into claims.

If perfect loss offset is assured, a tax on capital gains thus reduces the advantage of shifting between equity and claims in anticipation of price-level changes; this is the case whether income is measured in real or in money terms. If losses are disallowed, taxation in money terms discourages shifts in anticipation of inflation, whereas taxation in real terms discourages shifts in anticipation of deflation. These considerations, to be sure, apply to the substitution effect only. The income effect may work in the opposite direction.

Expenditure Effects

A direct expenditure effect on private investment may be exerted through subsidies to business firms or investors. Such subsidies may be thought of in terms of negative taxes, and their effects may be dealt with accordingly. Thus, a general subsidy to investment returns may be treated analagously to a tax on investment income. The effects of an income subsidy will differ, as will those of an income tax, depending upon the treatment of losses. A subsidy that adds to income without enlarging (that is, imposing a tax on) losses may be considered similar to a tax that permits loss offsets at a higher tax rate than applies to income. In both cases, the return on risk is increased. The substitution effect on investment is favorable.

Furthermore, government lending may be used to provide investment funds at favorable terms. This may be done by way of direct lending, the reverse of refundable taxes,[1] or by insuring the risk of private lenders at rates below those given by actuarial considerations, thus inducing private lenders to make funds available to private investors. While the insurance approach is in the nature of subsidies to risk taking, it has the advantage of reducing the extent to which the government is responsible in selecting each individual investor.

---

[1] For a direct lending program to be effective in this sense, the governmental credit agency must be willing to undertake risks that the market is unwilling to assume. This may involve a more optimistic appraisal of the outlook on the government's part or a difference in social and private risk, justifying an explicit policy of incurring losses.

Less direct in its effect upon private investment, but no less important, is provision for social overhead capital. The productivity of private enterprise depends upon governmental functions such as the guarantee of private property, the enforcement of contractual obligations, or the functioning of the monetary authority. Beyond this, there exist many specific expenditure programs that create a structure of cost and demand such as to render private investment profitable.

Certain social wants may have to be met before the conditions for profitable private investment exist. Highways and transportation facilities are needed to establish markets that are sufficiently large to permit large-scale production; flood-control projects and irrigation may be required before private farming can be profitable; large public outlays may be needed to advance technological innovation to the point of practicable application, and so forth.

The provision for social overhead capital is of special importance to underdeveloped economies. Here the approach to development through private capital formation is frequently blocked by the lack of certain external economies that must be provided by the public sector. It is this feature, no less than the frequently mentioned lack of private capital or entrepreneurial talent, that explains the primary role of government in the early stages of development.

Not all expenditure effects on private investment are positive. Conflicts and competing interests may arise where public enterprises operate in a market so as to compete with private enterprises. Strictly self-liquidating investments, that is, public investments that can be serviced and amortized out of fee proceeds, tend to be in this class. Where such investments replace private expenditure, they do not add to aggregate demand. The role of self-liquidating projects, therefore, belongs in the framework of the Allocation rather than the Stabilization Branch.

B. REAL INVESTMENT AND DEPRECIATION

We now leave the financial investor and turn to the underlying problem of real investment. This is the employment of capital in production and its marginal efficiency, which determines the yield on financial investment.

Significance of Depreciation

Let us consider the case of a manager of a producing firm who contemplates the addition of various types of capital equipment. The effects of an income tax enter his decision in two ways. One is the statutory rate of tax applied to taxable profits, and the other is the schedule at which recovery of capital may be deducted in computing taxable income. Both affect the rate at which profits are reduced by the tax, and both are reflected in the level of the tax rate t as used in the preceding discussion. These two elements must now be distinguished.

The rate at which an initial cost may be recovered or written off for tax purposes is significant for a number of reasons. Among them, the following may be noted:

1. Shortening of the depreciation period results in postponing the tax payment, thus reducing the present value of the tax and hence the effective burden.

2. Shortening of the depreciation period provides the investor with an immediate increase in liquidity. This is important in the absence of a perfect credit market. Moreover, it provides an immediate supply of equity capital without diluting control.

3. Over a period during which the taxpayer expects fluctuations in tax rates, flexibility in the timing of depreciation charges permits him to take depreciation during times of high rates and thus reduce his tax liability for the period as a whole.

4. In a period of rising prices, fast write-off increases the real value of the depreciation allowance and the opposite holds if prices fall.

5. A shorter depreciation period renders the depreciation allowance more valuable if the investor attaches a penalty discount to more distant returns due to increasing uncertainty.

6. The investor may not be certain, in the absence of tax refunds on losses, that there will be sufficient future income from which to deduct the depreciation allowance at the permissible time. The sooner he can deduct depreciation, the more certain he is that he will be able to deduct at all.

For the time being, let us focus on point 1 only. Here we assume that tax rates and price levels are expected to remain stable, that loss offsets as well as credit markets are perfect, and that no additional uncertainty discount attaches to more distant returns. While point 1 is not necessarily the most important from a practical standpoint, it is the most basic to the general problem of depreciation theory.[1]

---

[1] Among a large literature on the tax treatment of depreciation, see the basic article by E. Cary Brown, "Business-income Taxation and Investment Incentives," in *Income, Employment and Public Policy: Essays in Honor of Alvin H. Hanson*, W. W. Norton & Company, Inc., New York, 1948, reprinted in R. A. Musgrave and Carl Shoup (eds.), *Readings in the Economics of Taxation*, American Economic Association, Richard D. Irwin, Inc., Homewood, Ill., 1958, and "The New Depreciation Policy under the Income Tax: An Economic Analysis," *National Tax Journal*, vol. 8, no. 1, pp. 81–97, March, 1955; Richard Goode, *Corporation Income Tax*, John Wiley & Sons, Inc., New York, 1951, especially pp. 124–127, and "Accelerated Depreciation Allowances as a Stimulus to Investment," *Quarterly Journal of Economics*, vol. 69, no. 2, pp. 191–220, May, 1955, with literature references on p. 192; Evsey D. Domar, "The Case for Accelerated Depreciation," *Quarterly Journal of Economics*, vol. 62, no. 4, pp. 493–519, November, 1953, and "Depreciation, Replacement and Growth,"

Depreciation Policy in a Neutral Profits Tax

Let the tax rate be 50 per cent; now suppose that a particular investment, costing $1,000, may be depreciated in equal installments over a period of ten years. The taxpayer can look forward to ten annual tax savings, due to depreciation, of 0.5 times $100, or $50. Given an interest rate of 5 per cent, the present value of this income stream of $50 per year over a period of ten years equals $386. Now suppose that the law is changed and the investment may be written off more rapidly, say over a five-year period. In this case, the tax saving equals the present value of an income stream of $100 per year over five years, or $432.94. The position of the taxpayer is improved by the shortening of the depreciation period. If he is permitted to deduct the entire amount at once, the present value of the tax saving rises to $500. Thus, the burden imposed by a tax depends not only upon t_s, the statutory rate of tax, but also upon d, the length of the depreciation period. If we wish to design a tax system that is neutral between different investments, we must apply, in each case, a combination of the statutory rate and the depreciation period, which will give the same effective rate for all investments. This is the key to the problem.

Condition of Neutrality. To state this condition of neutrality more specifically, suppose that we have an investment, the present cost of which is C, and which is expected to yield an income stream of R per year for a period of n years. We may write

$$C = RA \qquad (14\text{-}14)$$

where A is the present value of an annuity of $1 for n years, discounted at the rate of interest i.[1] The rate i, at which the present value of the income stream becomes equal to cost, may be referred to as the internal rate of discount, or yield inherent in this particular investment.[2] It corresponds to our earlier term y. The concept of a market rate to which this internal rate is equated at the margin does not enter our discussion for the time being. Replacing A by the formula for the present value of an

---

Economic Journal, vol. 63, pp. 1–32, March, 1953, both reprinted in Domar's *Essays in the Theory of Economic Growth*, Oxford University Press, New York, 1957; S. P. Dobrovolsky, "Depreciation Policies and Investment Decisions," *American Economic Review*, vol. 41, no. 5, pp. 906–914, December, 1951; and M. Kalecki, "Three Ways to Full Employment," in *The Economics of Full Employment*, Basil Blackwell & Mott, Ltd., Oxford, 1947, pp. 45–46; George Terborgh, *Dynamic Equipment Policy*, McGraw-Hill Book Company, Inc., New York, 1949, and *Realistic Depreciation Policy*, Machinery and Allied Products Institute, Chicago, 1953.

[1] The term A may also be written as a_n.

[2] From the actuarial point of view, i should be referred to as a rate of interest rather than a rate of discount.

annuity of $1, we have

$$C = R \left[\frac{1 - (1 + i)^{-n}}{i} \right] \qquad (14\text{-}15)$$

as defining the relationship between cost, income stream, and internal yield.

Now a profits tax at the rate t is imposed, and the taxpayer is required to spread his amortization charges in equal annual installments over d years. Straight-line depreciation is assumed. The value of d may be equal to n, but it need not be. Holding C and R constant, equation (14-14) now becomes

$$C = (1 - t)RA_t + t\frac{C}{d}B_t \qquad (14\text{-}16)$$

where $(1 - t)RA_t$ is the present value of the income stream after tax, as it would be if the tax law did not allow for depreciation; and $t(C/d)B_t$ is the present value of tax savings obtained because the law does permit the deduction of depreciation charges.[1] A_t measures the present value of $1 over a period of n years, the value of $1 being discounted now by the new (after tax) internal rate of discount i_t. B_t measures the present value of $1 over a period of d years, discounted at i_t. Equation (14-16) may be written as

$$C = (1 - t)\, R \left[\frac{1 - (1 + i_t)^{-n}}{i_t} \right] + t\frac{C}{d} \left[\frac{1 - (1 + i_t)^{-d}}{i_t} \right] \quad (14\text{-}17)$$

where i_t is the new internal rate of discount, or yield net of tax. We may now define the effective rate of tax as the resulting percentage change in yield, that is

$$t_e = \frac{i - i_t}{i} = 1 - \frac{i_t}{i} \qquad (14\text{-}18)$$

A firm will be indifferent between a change in t and a change in d as long as the resulting change in t_e is the same. A neutral tax plan, similarly, will be one that imposes the same effective rate of tax on all investments. Using subscripts x and z to indicate two investments, our definition of a neutral tax must meet the condition

$$\frac{i_x}{i_{xt}} = \frac{i_z}{i_{zt}} \qquad (14\text{-}19)$$

In other words, the effective rate of tax is the same if the internal rate of discount is reduced by the same fraction in all cases.

[1] Equation (14-16) resembles that used by Brown, "Business-income Taxation and Investment Incentives," p. 304. However, Brown's argument is based on discount by a market rate of interest (see note on text page 342), and it refers to the special case where $d = n$.

Suppose, now, that the same statutory rate t_s is to be applied to all investments, involving different pay-off periods (or values of n) and carrying different rates of internal discount. The problem is to determine the value of d for each investment so as to meet our criterion of neutrality. Given the value of t_e and t, equations (14-15), (14-17), and (14-19) define the resulting values of i, i_t, and d for any investment with specified values of C, R, and n. While the problem does not lend itself to a simple mathematical solution in solving for d or t, the results of various policies may be tested by computing sample cases on the basis of actuarial tables.

Comparison between Investments of Different Length. In Table 14-2 we compare investments that pay $R = \$1$ a year, and have the same internal rate of discount of $i = 0.05$. They vary in the length of the pay-off

TABLE 14-2. EFFECTIVE TAX RATES FOR INVESTMENTS WITH EQUAL YIELDS
AND DIFFERENT PAY-OFF PERIODS*
($i = 0.05$; $t_s = 0.5$; straight-line depreciation)

		$d = \infty$		$d = 5$		$d = n$		Required values for $t_e = 0.475$ of	
n	C	i_t	t_e	i_t	t_e	i_t	t_e	d	d/n
(1)	(2)	(3)	(4)	(5)	(6)	(7)	(8)	(9)	(10)
1	0.9524	$r < 0$	$t_e > 1$	$r < 0$	$t_e > 1$	0.0250	0.500	$d < 0$	$d/n < 0$
2	1.8594	$r < 0$	$t_e > 1$	0.0000	1.000	0.0252	0.496	1.6	0.800
5	4.3295	$r < 0$	$t_e > 1$	0.0255	0.490	0.0255	0.490	4.5	0.900
10	7.7217	$r < 0$	$t_e > 1$	0.0325	0.350	0.0260	0.480	9.5	0.950
20	12.4622	$r < 0$	$t_e > 1$	0.0384	0.232	0.0265	0.470	20.0	1.000
32	15.8027	$r = 0$	1.000	0.0412	0.176	0.0273	0.450	36.0	1.125
50	18.2559	0.0131	0.738	0.0437	0.126	0.0280	0.440	63.0	1.260
85	19.6836	0.0211	0.578	0.0442	0.116	0.0284	0.432	132.0	1.565
100	19.8479	0.0225	0.550	0.0444	0.112	0.0282	0.436	168.0	1.680
200	19.9988	0.0250	0.500	0.0450	0.111	0.0274	0.452	255.0	1.275
∞	20.0000	0.5000	0.000	0.0500	0.000	0.0025	0.475		

* Simple inverse interpolation was used to estimate i_t in those cases where i_t fell between tabular entries in the tables. For col. 7, where $d = n$, it was necessary to calculate i_t by trial and error, inserting alternative values of i_t into eq. (14-17) and computing the right-hand member until its value equaled the required value of C.

period n, as shown in column 1. The corresponding initial costs of investment C are shown in column 2. The same statutory rate of tax $t_s = 0.5$ is applied in all cases, and the resulting values of net yield after tax i_t and effective rate of tax t_e are computed for different values of n and depreciation periods d.

In the absence of any depreciation allowances (see columns 3 and 4, where $d = \infty$), we find that i_t rises and t_e falls as n increases; that is, short investments are discriminated against. If straight-line depreciation over some finite period is permitted for all investments (see columns 5 and 6, where $d = 5$), short investments are still discriminated against, though to a lesser degree than previously. Retaining straight-line depreciation but depreciating over the entire life of the asset for all investments (see columns 7 and 8, where $d = n$), i_t rises and t_e falls as n increases. This continues up to some value of n, beyond which the relation is reversed.[1] While the degree of discrimination over the relevant range is less than before, a significant degree of discrimination remains. In order to obtain a neutral tax, the ratio d/n must be increased for rising values of n up to some fairly high level of n, and must be reduced thereafter. This is shown in columns 9 and 10, where d is adjusted so as to obtain $t_e = 0.475$ for all cases.

TABLE 14-3. EFFECTIVE TAX RATES WITH VARIOUS DEPRECIATION SCHEDULES*
$(i = 0.05; t_s = 0.5; d = n)$

n	Straight-line		Annuity		Declining-balance		Sum-of-the-year's-digits	
	i_t	t_e	i_t	t_e	i_t	t_e	i_t	t_e
1	0.02500	0.5000	0.02500	0.5000	0.02500	0.5000	0.02500	0.5000
5	0.02544	0.4919	0.02520	0.4960	0.02779	0.4442	0.02867	0.4266

* The straight-line case is taken from Table 14-2; for $n = 5$, depreciation for each year equals 20 per cent. For the declining-balance case, the per cent of C allowed as depreciation over successive years equals 0.4, 0.24, 0.114, 0.108, and 0.108, respectively. For the sum-of-the-year's-digits method, the respective fractions are 0.333, 0.267, 0.200, 0.133, and 0.067.

Under the annuity method, the amount permitted each year expressed as a per cent of asset cost equals $D_n = (1 + i)^{-d+n-1}$, where $d = n = 5$. For purposes of estimation, we assume $i = 0.05$, the internal rate of discount before tax. The respective amounts of depreciation for the five years are 0.82367, 0.844263, 0.85637, 0.88700, and 0.90918, adding to $C = 4.32948$ for the period as a whole. To be theoretically correct, we should use i_t instead of i, where i_t itself is a function of the depreciation pattern. Since $i_t < i$, the approximation here used involves a less rapid depreciation than would apply in the true case. Hence, discrimination would be reduced further under the true solution.

In Table 14-3, certain other depreciation patterns are compared with the straight-line method. The comparison is made for the $n = d$ case, using $n = 1$ and $n = 5$. The degree of discrimination against short investments is increased under the declining-balance method, and even

---

[1] The lower the i, the higher the n at which the turning point occurs. For $i = 10$ per cent the turning point is at $n = 50$.

more so under the sum-of-the-year's-digit method. The degree of discrimination is reduced and becomes very slight under the annuity method. The latter thus offers a close approximation to a neutral tax, provided that income accrues on a straight-line basis.[1]

Comparison between Investments of Different Yield. In Table 14-4 we compare investments that pay $1 a year for a length of twenty periods but have different internal rates of discount (and, hence, costs, as shown in columns 1 and 2).

TABLE 14-4. EFFECTIVE TAX RATES FOR INVESTMENTS WITH
EQUAL PAY-OFF PERIODS AND DIFFERENT YIELDS*
($n = 20$; $t_e = 0.5$; straight-line depreciation)

i	C	$d = \infty$		$d = n$		$d = 5$		Required values for $t_e = 0.475$ of	
		i_t	t_e	i_t	t_e	i_t	t_e	d	d/n
(1)	(2)	(3)	(4)	(5)	(6)	(7)	(8)	(9)	(10)
0.01	18.0456	$r < 0$	$t_e > 1$	0.0051	0.490	0.0078	0.220	$d < 0$	$d/n < 0$
0.03	14.8775	$r < 0$	$t_e > 1$	0.0156	0.480	0.0232	0.227	3	0.15
0.05	12.4622	$r < 0$	$t_e > 1$	0.0266	0.468	0.0384	0.232	20	1.00
0.08	9.8181	0.0018	0.978	0.0436	0.455	0.0605	0.244	80	4.00
0.10	8.5136	0.0160	0.840	0.0550	0.450	0.0754	0.246	200	10.00
∞	0.0000	∞	0.000	∞	0.000	∞	0.000		

* See note to Table 14-2.

As before, we impose the same statutory rate of tax $t_s = 0.5$ throughout and apply different depreciation policies, or values of d. If depreciation charges are disallowed (see columns 3, and 4, where $d = \infty$), the tax now discriminates against low-yield investments. If we apply straight-line depreciation over a finite period, discrimination is reduced. The case of $d = n$ (see columns 5 and 6) is now a special case of equal finite depreciation, where $d = 20$. Discrimination is slight, but low-yield investments

[1] For a similar conclusion, though in a somewhat different context, see E. Cary Brown, "The New Depreciation Policy under the Income Tax: An Economic Analysis," *National Tax Journal*, vol. 8, no. 1, pp. 81–98, March, 1955.

Brown defines true depreciation as that which matches the rate of decrease in the usefulness of an asset. Thus, if the asset decreases in usefulness by equal annual amounts, annual depreciation allowances should be such that their present values are equal. This calls for the annuity method and, hence, rising absolute amounts of depreciation.

While the annuity method is to be preferred in both cases, Brown's condition for true depreciation is not quite the same as our condition for neutral depreciation. The neutral depreciation rate as here defined depends upon the statutory rate of tax, the internal rate of discount, and the length of the pay-off period. Brown's concept depends upon the rate at which capital is used up and upon the market rate of interest.

still suffer a higher rate of tax. As the value of d is reduced further, this pattern is reversed, and low-yield investments come to enjoy the benefit of a smaller effective rate of tax.

If we combine variations in both i and n, the task of formulating a truly neutral-depreciation policy becomes exceedingly complex. Nevertheless, our approach supplies the conditions for a truly neutral policy and thus suggests a direction in which analysis may proceed.

Instantaneous Depreciation. The shorter the depreciation period, the greater the benefit to the owner of the depreciable asset. In the extreme case, we may visualize a system where depreciation is permitted once the investment is made. Since no income is received yet, this means that a loss is incurred. Under a system of perfect loss offset, the loss will be refunded at once, provided it cannot be offset against other income. Such a system is, in fact, equivalent to a zero-tax situation. We can now define

$$C = (1 - t)RA_t + tC \qquad (14\text{-}20)$$

but $C = RA$, so that $RA = RA_t$ and hence $i = i_t$. A tax that permits instantaneous depreciation leaves the internal rate of discount unchanged. It is a perfectly neutral solution—so neutral, in fact, as to be a zero tax.

To illustrate, let us suppose that our investor purchases an asset at an initial outlay of \$100. He expects an income stream of \$10 for twenty years, the yield being approximately 7.45 per cent. A tax of 50 per cent is imposed, together with a depreciation period of twenty years, and the net yield falls to about 4.25 per cent. Next, consider a situation where the investor is permitted to take instantaneous depreciation. When making his initial investment of \$100, the investor will register an immediate loss of \$100, since this amount of depreciation is charged, prior to the receipt of any income. With a perfect loss offset, the investor will obtain a refund of \$50.[1] This refund, when reinvested, will lead to a further refund of \$25, thus giving rise to a series of refunds and reinvestments totaling \$100. The total investment now equals \$200.[2] Assuming constant returns, receipts now equal \$20 per year for twenty years. Since the investor has taken depreciation already, this entire amount is subject to tax, leaving him with an annual income stream of \$10. After tax, the investor is left in precisely the same position he was in prior to the tax. What happens, in effect, is that the Treasury advances him an interest-free loan sufficient to increase his earnings by the amount of tax. Thus, in our illustration, the investor receives additional funds of \$100

---

[1] In order to make instantaneous depreciation effective, perfect loss offset (including provision for immediate refunds) *must* be assumed.

[2] If C is the initial outlay and t the rate of tax, total refunds equal $[1/(1 - t) - 1]C$, and the total amount invested equals $[(1/1 - t) - 1]C$.

for twenty years, this being precisely the sum returned to the Treasury as tax.[1] The investor, therefore, is indifferent to the imposition of such a tax-refund arrangement.

Now consider the position of the Treasury. While it gains in tax revenue, it incurs the cost of advancing the capital when making the initial refund payment. Provided that the Treasury itself could have invested in an asset of equal yield, the gain in tax revenue and the opportunity cost of lost earnings cancel each other out.[2] An investment of $100 for twenty years (assuming a 50 per cent rate of return) gives the Treasury precisely the same income stream as it obtains from the tax. The Treasury is indifferent to having such an arrangement. We are left with the somewhat ironic result that the search for the perfect tax leaves us with a solution that involves, in effect, a zero tax.[3] Given perfect loss offset, we must have $d > 0$ in order to obtain $t_e > 0$. At the same time, the value of d can be adjusted (depending on differences in i and n) to obtain equal values of t_e for diverse investments.

This argument, to be sure, relates to the case of a tax on new investment only. A profits tax (limited to old investment) or a capital levy, are different matters. Where depreciation has been taken in the past, while current profits continue to accrue, the tax involves a loss to the investor and a gain to the Treasury, even though instantaneous depreciation is permitted for new investment.

Tax Treatment of Interest Cost

Thus far no reference has been made to the existence of a market rate of interest. Our discussion has been entirely in terms of the internal rates of discount applicable to particular investments. In such a framework,

---

[1] A similar argument applies if we assume that investment proceeds are continually reinvested. The sequence of taxes paid in returning the initial advance of $100 is then matched by a sequence of new refunds. These refunds are made to account for losses incurred when instantaneous depreciation is claimed on the reinvestment of current earnings. The two streams of tax payments and refunds cancel, and the net effect is to leave the initial advance with the investor as long as earnings are reinvested. In other words, the investor has unilateral control over the period for which the Treasury loan is extended. Only when reinvestment of earnings is discontinued must a tax be paid, thus returning to the Treasury the initial loan plus earnings thereon.

[2] This assumes that the Treasury, in the absence of a "refund loan," would have been able to invest its funds at the same terms. If this possibility does not exist, the Treasury gains from the tax.

[3] Brown, "Business-income Taxation and Investment Incentives," notes that instantaneous depreciation plus perfect loss offset renders the investor indifferent to the tax, but Brown does not conclude the same for the Treasury. A proposal for instantaneous depreciation was made by M. Kalecki, "Three Ways to Full Employment," in *The Economics of Full Employment*, Basil Blackwell & Mott, Ltd., Oxford, 1947, p. 46; but again the Treasury's cost of advancing funds is not considered.

the internal rate of discount is *the* capital income: There is no appropriate place for interest as a cost that may be deducted from taxable income. A tax that permits deduction of interest at the computed internal rate would leave no income. However, let us assume that the law provides for deduction of interest at some uniform statutory rate.

Suppose, first, that the investor may charge and deduct interest against the entire cost of his investment, with the interest computed at some statutory rate i_s. Equation (14-16) then becomes

$$C = (1 - t)RA_t + t\frac{C}{d}B_t + ti_sCA_t \tag{14-21}$$

where the last term is the gain or saving in tax from the interest deduction. To simplify, let us set $d = n$, so that

$$C = RA_t - tA_t\left(R - \frac{C}{d} - i_sC\right) \tag{14-22}$$

If the annual depreciation charge C/d plus the annual interest imputation i_sC equals the annual income R, no taxable income is left. We then have $C = RA_t$. Since $C = RA$, it follows that $A = A_t$ and $i = i_t$. If $i_sC < R - (C/d)$, the tax is positive, and $i_t < i$. However, the effective rate of tax t_e is smaller than it would be in the absence of interest deduction. The lower i is, the greater the reduction in t_e due to interest deduction, since a low i makes for a high ratio of i_s/i. Deductibility of interest at a uniform imputed rate thus discriminates in favor of low-yield investments.

Next, suppose that the investor can charge and deduct interest on borrowed funds only, computed at the particular contractual rate. In this case, equation (14-21) becomes

$$C = (1 - t)RA_t + t\frac{C}{d}B_t - i_cbCA_t + ti_cbCA_t \tag{14-23}$$

where i_c is the contractual rate of interest and b is the fraction of cost met by borrowing. Thus, i_cbCA_t is the annual repayment of loan, and ti_cbCA_c is the new term for tax saving due to interest deduction. Setting $d = n$, we now have

$$C = RA_t - i_cCA_t - tA_t\left(R - i_cC - \frac{C}{d}\right) \tag{14-24}$$

The general argument is the same as before, but discrimination now favors investments with a high b, or ratio of debt to equity finance, and with a low ratio of i_c/i. In both connections, risk investment is likely to be discriminated against.

An Alternative Framework

Throughout the preceding discussion, we have assumed that the investor determines the profitability of an investment in terms of the internal rate of discount and makes his investment decision on the basis of profitability and inherent risk. As an alternative framework, let us consider a system where the investor maximizes profits by investing up to the point where the present worth of the income stream, discounted at prevailing market rate of interest on government bonds i_m, equals cost.[1] Now a proportional tax on profits with full loss offset is imposed.

We assume first that interest on government bonds is not taxable. The loss in the present value of the income stream due to tax will exceed the present value of tax savings from the depreciation deduction, both being discounted at the market rate. Some previously profitable investments now become unprofitable, compared to the yield of bonds. Funds will be shifted into bonds. Assuming the money supply to be infinitely elastic, the market rate is unchanged. The level of real investment declines. If depreciation is charged on a straight-line basis over the life of the asset, the present value of tax savings from depreciation will be a declining fraction of cost as the investment becomes longer. Thus, long investments are discriminated against.[2]

Now consider the opposite case of a tax that applies only to interest income on government bonds and not to profits from real investment. As before, we assume that the supply of funds is infinitely elastic so as to maintain the yield of bonds (before tax) at i_m.* As the tax is imposed, the net return on investment in bonds is reduced to $(1 - t_s)i_m$. Earnings from real investment are now discounted at this lower rate. The tax on the interest from government bonds is similar in effect to a reduction in the market rate. Real investment is increased, and long investments benefit relative to short investments.

Finally, there is the case of a general tax that applies to both interest from government bonds and profits from real investment. This combines the opposing effects of the two preceding cases.

---

[1] This is the approach taken by E. Cary Brown, "Business-income Taxation and Investment Incentives," in *Income, Employment and Public Policy: Essays in Honor of Alvin H. Hansen*, W. W. Norton & Company, Inc., New York, 1948.

[2] This result seems to run counter to our earlier conclusion for a policy of $d = n$. However, the earlier comparison of Table 14-2 related to investments with equal rates of internal discount, and the internal rate itself was reduced by the tax. In the present case, the market rate is assumed to be unchanged.

* For a discussion of this dubious assumption, see p. 543.

CHAPTER 15

Incidence in the all-consumption model

In the preceding chapters we have dealt with partial equilibrium adjustments to changes in budget policy by various decision-making units of the economy, such as the worker, the consumer, and the business firm. These partial adjustments are strategic elements in the over-all change, but nothing more. They have repercussions upon the market setting within which any adjusting unit operates, thus giving rise to a chain of adjustments until a new equilibrium is reached. The final result of the adjustment process is the product of the interaction of these individual moves. As the student of macro economics knows only too well, this interaction has its own logic. It may produce results far removed from the intent of the individual unit of adjustment.

It is necessary, therefore, that we push beyond the partial equilibrium view and consider the general adjustment process as a whole. This is a difficult task. One may readily understand the general interdependence of the pricing system as a concept or as a formal statement within the framework of the Walrasian equilibrium system.[1] But it is quite another matter to formulate the problem so as to obtain specific results. To make matters worse, an adequate analysis must allow for changes in the level of employment and prices and for effects upon the long-run aspects of growth. A workable system of this sort remains to be devised before it can be applied to the determination of incidence.

In order to make some inroads into the problem and still maintain our bearings, we shall do well to proceed step by step, moving from a very

---

[1] For attempts at general statements of incidence theory in a complete system, see Ronald W. Shepard, "A Mathematical Theory of the Incidence of Taxation," *Econometrica*, vol. 12, no. 1, pp. 1–18, January, 1944; and J. E. Meade, "The Effects of Indirect Taxation upon the Distribution of Income," *Trade and Welfare*, vol. II, sec. 4, Mathematical Supplement, Oxford University Press, London, 1955.

simple to a more complex model. Let us begin, therefore, with the simplest type of economy, where only consumer goods are produced. Thus, all the complications that arise from the presence of saving, capital formation, and economic growth are avoided for the time being. In this setting, we shall explore the basic problem of changes in *relative* prices that result as general or discriminatory taxes are imposed. Thereafter, we shall examine the relationship between incidence and *absolute* price change. The next chapter discusses a more complex setting where saving and capital formation are allowed for. Incidence in an economy that combines growth with the need for compensatory policies will be considered in the concluding chapter.

A. RELATIONSHIP BETWEEN GENERAL AND DISCRIMINATORY TAXES

In our all-consumption economy there is no saving. No cash balances are held beyond those required to meet transaction needs. Available factors of production, including labor and raw materials, are provided by householders in their capacity as workers and owners of resources. These factors, the supply of which may be more or less elastic, are purchased by firms, transformed into products in a single stage of production, and sold to householders in their capacity as consumers. We assume for the time being that both factor and product markets are perfectly competitive, so that factor shares exhaust the total product and factor prices equal the value of the marginal product of the factor.

In this system, the distribution of income depends on the distribution of ownership of factors including labor, the production functions of factor inputs required to produce various products, and the preference patterns of individuals for these products. From these basic data, relative product and factor prices are determined by the market, as are relative levels of real income.[1] A money equation may be added to obtain the absolute levels of money prices and incomes. Little is gained thereby, since money in this system is a veil and has little bearing on the essential problem of incidence.

General versus Discriminatory Taxes

The crux of incidence analysis, in the general equilibrium context, lies in determining whether, and in what respect, any given tax is general or discriminatory. Any one tax may be general in some respects and discriminatory in others, depending on the type of transaction upon which the tax is imposed. We shall disregard, for the time being, taxes other than those on transactions—such as lump-sum taxes or taxes on the holding of property.

[1] Such a system is given in eqs. (1) to (12) of Meade's system, *ibid.*, pp. 34–37.

Transactions, in our simple system, involve either products or factors. Households sell factors and buy products, while firms buy factors and sell products.   Thus, a tax may be imposed on transactions either in products or in factors; the tax may be applied on the buyer's or the seller's side of the market.   In each of these four cases, the tax may be general and apply to all the transactions in the indicated category; or it may be discriminatory and apply to certain transactions only.   A simple schema outlining by numerical designation the resulting types of tax is shown in Table 15-1.

TABLE 15-1. GENERAL AND DISCRIMINATORY TAXES

Tax imposed on transactions by–	Tax on transactions in–			
	All		Some	
	Products	Factors	Products	Factors
All:				
buyers............	1	3	5	7
sellers.............	2	4	6	8
Some:				
buyers............	9	11	13	15
sellers.............	10	12	14	16

There are four types of truly general tax, shown as cases 1 to 4 in the table.   Case 1 is a general spendings tax on households, case 2 a general sales tax on firms, case 3 a general factor-purchase or cost-payment tax on firms, and case 4 a general income tax on households.   Of the four, 2 and 4 are familiar forms of taxation, 1 is receiving increasing attention, and 3 is of somewhat academic interest.

Turning now to possible types of discrimination, consider first a group of taxes that apply to all transactors but only to some transactions. These are listed as cases 5 to 8 in the table.   In this group we have a spendings tax on consumers that applies at differential rates to various products bought, or case 5; a sales tax on firms that applies at differential rates to various products sold, or case 6; a tax on cost payments of firms applicable to selected factors only, or case 7; and a tax on receipts from the sale of factors applicable to particular factors only, or case 8.   Case 6 is encountered widely as a selective excise or sales tax.   Case 8 is encountered in the form of income taxes that apply with differential rates to various types of factor incomes, for example, penalty rates on unearned income or employee contributions to payroll taxes.   Case 7 is illustrated by the employer contribution to payroll taxes and, after capital formation is allowed for, by property taxes on business plant.

A second group of discriminatory taxes apply to all transactions but only to some transactors. These are listed as cases 9 to 12 in the table. Discrimination of this type may be based on a variety of criteria. Thus, case 9 may take the form of a spendings tax that discriminates against people with large incomes or large amounts of spending. Case 10 may take the form of a tax limited to foreign firms, for example, a flat tariff on all imports from a given country; or of a tax limited to domestic firms with certain organizational characteristics such as corporations or chain stores. Case 12 may take the form of a progressive income tax or an income tax that discriminates between steady and volatile incomes.

A third group of discriminatory taxes, which combines both types of discrimination, appears as cases 13 to 16 in the table. In case 14, we have discrimination by seller and product, illustrated by a classified tariff; in case 15, we have discrimination by buyer and factor, illustrated by a payroll tax applicable to large firms only; in case 13, we have discrimination by buyer and product, illustrated by a spendings tax differentiated by product, size of outlay, and so forth. Further classifications and subcases may be readily developed, but this will suffice for our purposes. Our specific concern is with cases 1 to 8, in which the basic problems of adjustments are covered.

The Equivalence of General Taxes

The relationship among the truly general taxes, or cases 1 to 4, may be pictured by noting their location in the circular flow, shown in Figure 15-1.

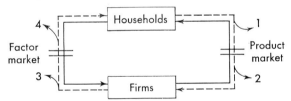

Fig. 15-1. General taxes in the circular flow.

On the left, we note the flow of factors (solid line) from households to firms and the reverse flow of factor payments (broken line), both traversing the factor market. On the right, we note the flow of products (solid line) from firms to households and the reverse flow of expenditures (broken line) from households to firms, both traversing the product market. As we have stated, households are sellers of factors and buyers of products, while firms are sellers of products and buyers of factors. A tax on the buyers of factors, or case 3, is a purchase tax on the firm, its impact falling on the firm's side of the factor market. A tax on the sellers of factors, or case 4, is a personal income tax, its impact falling on the household side of this market. The buyer's tax on products, or case 1, is a purchase tax on households, its impact falling on the buyer's side of the product market. The seller's tax on products, or case 2, is a sales or excise tax assessed on the seller's side of the market. These four taxes are equivalent in this simple model. Not only is their differential incidence neutral in the previously defined sense of leaving the size distribution of income unchanged, but substitution between these four taxes leaves the position of each individual household and firm unaffected.[1] The following propositions or rules of equivalence hold for this model:

First, *it is a matter of indifference whether a general tax on transactions is assessed on the seller's or on the buyer's side of the market.* In the product market we have, on the seller's side (case 2), a tax on the gross receipts of firms, or an ad valorem sales tax at rate t_r; on the buyer's side (case 1), a tax on expenditures by consumers, or a spendings tax at rate t_e, where $t_e = t_r/(1 - t_r)$.* In case 2, a fraction of the firm's gross receipts is diverted into taxes and is not available for factor payments; in case 1, the same fraction of consumer payments is diverted into taxes and does not reach the firm. In both cases, the same wedge is driven between gross expenditures of consumers and net receipts of firms. In both cases there occurs the same decline in the *net* revenue schedule relative to the *gross* revenue schedule of business firms. This is what counts, and not whether the decline reflects a statutory tax obligation on the seller's or the buyer's part. Cases 1 and 2 are thus equivalent.

In the factor market we have, on the seller's side (case 4), a tax imposed on the proceeds from factor sales, or a personal income tax at rate t_p; on the buyer's side (case 3), a tax imposed on the cost payments for the purchase of factors at rate $t_c = t_p/(1 - t_p)$.† In both cases, the same wedge

---

[1] It is assumed throughout this discussion that there is no money illusion or spite effect. (See p. 240.) The worker is indifferent to whether a change in the net wage rate occurs due to change in tax or due to change in the gross wage rate; and the consumer is indifferent to paying a spendings tax versus a higher price.

* The yield of the tax on consumer expenditures equals

$$T_e = t_e(p_p Q_p - T_e)$$

where T_e is the yield, t_e is the rate, and p_p and Q_p are the price and quantity of products bought. The yield of the tax on gross receipts is

$$T_r = t_r p_p Q_p$$

where T_r is the yield and t_r the rate. By setting $T_e = T_r$, we obtain

$$t_e = \frac{t_r}{1 - t_r}$$

† The yield of the tax on the cost payments of the firm equals

$$T_c = t_c(p_f Q_f - T_c)$$

where T_c is the yield, t_c is the rate, and p_f and Q_f are the price and quantity of factors

is driven between the outlay made by the firm and the income received by the supplier of the factor.   Part of the firm's outlays do not go into factor payments, or part of the payments to factors do not become available as disposable factor income.   In both cases there occurs the same decline in the *net* demand schedule relative to the *gross* demand schedule for factor inputs.   Cases 3 and 4 are thus equivalent.

The second proposition is that *it is a matter of indifference whether a general tax is assessed on the product or on the factor transactions of any particular transactor*.   Where the tax is assessed on the firm, a general tax on gross receipts or sales (case 2) at rate t_r is equivalent to a general tax on factor purchases or cost (case 3) at rate $t_c = t_r/(1 - t_r)$.*   Both drive the same wedge between sales receipts and funds available for net factor payments; and substitution of the one for the other will not affect the combination of factors.   Prior to tax, the value of the marginal product will be the same in a competitive market for any one factor in all its uses. The price of each factor will be equal to the value of its marginal product; and the prices of various factors will stand in the ratio of the value of their marginal products.   After a general tax on product sale and/or factor purchase is introduced, the *net* value of the marginal product must be the same for any one factor in all its uses, net value being defined to exclude product tax.   The gross price of each factor will equal the net value of the factor's marginal product, gross price being defined to include factor purchase tax; and the gross or net prices of various factors will stand in the ratio of the gross values of their marginal products, which will also equal the ratio of net values.   Cases 2 and 3 are thus equivalent.

Where the tax is imposed on the household, this equivalence refers to a general tax on factor sales or personal income tax (case 1) at rate t_p, and a general tax on product purchases or consumer expenditures (case 4) at rate t_e, where $t_e = t_p/(1 - t_p)$.†   In our simplified system, earnings from factor sales equal outlays on products, so that cases 1 and 4 are equivalent, as are cases 2 and 3.

We now combine the conclusion that case 2 is equivalent to 3 and case 1

---

bought.   The yield of the tax on personal income is

$$T_p = t_p(p_f Q_f)$$

where T_p is the yield and t_p is the rate.   By setting $T_c = T_p$, we obtain

$$t_c = \frac{t_p}{1 - t_p}$$

* This expression is obtained by equating T_r and T_c as defined in the preceding footnotes.   This may be done because gross receipts equal factor payments on the assumption of pure competition.

† This expression is obtained by equating T_e and T_p as defined in the preceding footnotes.   This may be done because saving is assumed to equal zero.

is equivalent to 4 with the previous conclusion that case 1 is equivalent to 2 and case 3 is equivalent to 4.   This gives us the third proposition—that in this simple model *there is an equivalence between a personal income tax (case 4) and a general sales tax (case 2)*.   Similarly, there exists an equivalence between a general tax on the factor payments of firms (case 3) and a spendings tax on households (case 1).   In other words, there exists an equivalence between all four types of truly general tax.

The proposition of equivalence between a general and proportional income tax and a general and proportional sales tax does *not* imply that the former leads to a proportional change in all factor prices, while the latter leads to a proportional change in all product prices.   A general proportional income tax may—and most likely will—result in a change in relative factor prices, depending upon differences in the elasticity of supply for various factors; and the subsequent adjustment will involve changes in relative product prices as well.   Similar changes result from a general and proportional sales tax.   The proposition of equivalence implies only that resulting changes in relative product and factor prices will be the same for both taxes.

These conclusions must be qualified as the simplified setting of the present model is abandoned.   Nevertheless, an understanding of this basic equivalence among the general taxes in this simplest type of model is the gateway to an understanding of the more complex cases.   We shall see not only how discriminatory taxes tend to be nonequivalent in this simple model but how apparently general taxes become discriminatory in a more realistic setting, allowing for imperfect markets and capital formation.

Equivalent Sets of Discriminatory Taxes

The rules of equivalence that apply to nondiscriminatory taxes may be applied also to certain types of discriminatory taxes.   However, considerations of administrative feasibility limit the choice among various ways in which a given discrimination can be applied.

Let us begin with a selective sales tax on product X.   As before, this tax is equivalent to a tax on consumer purchases of X, and can be applied readily in either form.   It is equivalent also to a purchase tax on factors that enter into the production of X or to an income tax on the sale of such factors.   However, the latter taxes are not practicable, since it would be necessary to classify factor transactions by the products into which the factors are destined to enter.

Next, suppose that a selective income tax is imposed on earnings from factor Z.   Such a tax is equivalent to a tax on firms on the purchase of Z, and can be applied readily in either form.   It is equivalent also to a sales tax on products assessed at differential rates in proportion to that part of the market price which reflects cost payments to Z; and it is equivalent to a corresponding spendings tax on consumers.   While such a construction is conceivable, the latter taxes are again impracticable, since it would be necessary to classify gross receipts or consumer outlays by the factors to which they are to accrue.   In cases such as these, the tax may be imposed on the seller's or the buyer's side of the market; but a tax that discriminates by products must be applied in the product market, and one that discriminates by factors must be applied in the factor market.

Moreover, the type of discrimination may be such that considerations of feasibility determine the side of the market as well as the market in which the tax must be imposed.   Thus a progressive income tax cannot be administered readily as a factor-purchase tax.   Source withholding without individual returns is feasible only with a flat-rate tax.   A progressive tax on corporation income cannot be readily administered as a tax on the shareholder; a progressive tax on consumer spending cannot be readily administered as a tax on the gross receipts of the firm; and so forth.   As a matter of administrative convenience, it is therefore wise to assess the tax at that side of the market at which the discrimination is directed.   At the same time, the theoretical construction of equivalent groups of taxes remains useful even when discrimination is involved.

Distributional Equivalence

So far we have used the concept of equivalence to apply strictly to taxes among which substitution leaves all relative prices and individual incomes unchanged.   Following our earlier definition of incidence as change in the distribution of income by size brackets, we may redefine equivalent taxes as taxes among which substitution leaves the size distribution of income unchanged.

A progressive income tax might then be matched by some pattern of excise taxes applying higher rates to luxuries than to necessities.   Such a pair of taxes could be neutral in differential incidence as defined previously, yet result in changes in relative product and factor prices and in the relative positions of particular individuals.   Under either approach, the general equilibrium adjustment to the tax substitution must be considered. In testing distributional equivalence, we must allow for the distributional effects of resulting changes in incomes and prices before tax, as well as for changes in tax payments as such.   Nevertheless, the requirement of distributional equivalence is less severe.   Taxes that have equivalence in the strict sense will be equivalent also in distributional terms; but pairs of taxes may be found that are more or less equivalent in their distributional effects, yet will be far from equivalent in the strict sense of the term.[1]

[1] The concept of distributional equivalence might be defined in terms of a single over-all coefficient of distribution or in terms of a set of coefficients applicable to various interdecile distributions.   See p. 225.

Both concepts of equivalence are useful and will be applied in the following discussion. Absolute equivalence is a helpful analytical tool, while distributional equivalence is the more relevant concept for purposes of tax policy.

B. THE INCIDENCE OF GENERAL AND DISCRIMINATORY TAXES

We now turn to the incidence of general and discriminatory taxes. By the nature of the problem, our concern is with changes in the *relative* prices of products and of factors of production only. Changes in price level will be considered in the concluding section of this chapter.

The Incidence of a General Tax

Let us now examine the incidence of a general tax such as a proportional tax on income, or case 4 of Table 15-1. The argument used for case 4 holds for cases 1, 2, and 3.

Since this is the first tax to be considered, its incidence cannot be examined in differential terms. A point of reference must first be established, against which the differential incidence of other taxes can be measured. For this purpose, we shall examine the budget incidence that results if the government increases goods and service expenditures, financed by a general income tax.[1]

It is conceivable that the introduction of the budget will leave relative factor and product prices unchanged—but only if factor supplies are fixed and no change occurs in product mix, with the government purchasing precisely the same goods that private consumers drop off their list as disposable incomes decline. Though this is a conceivable result, it is one that is quite unlikely. There is every reason to expect that relative product and factor prices *will* change. The basket of goods demanded by government and the factor inputs these goods require will differ from the goods that the private sector chooses to surrender (in response to the tax) at the old set of prices. The revenue and expenditure sides of the budget will not be negatively equivalent, in the sense of complete cancellation. However, it remains to be seen whether incidence may not be neutral in our sense of leaving the equality of income distribution unchanged. In exploring this, and throughout the following discussion of discriminatory taxes, separate attention must be given to changes that result from the uses and the sources side of the individual's income position.

Changes on the Sources Side. We shall begin with changes in relative positions that result from the income sources or earnings side. We may expect the introduction of the budget to result in an increase in the prices of factors that are specific to goods purchased by government, relative to

[1] See p. 214.

the prices of factors that are specific to goods purchased privately.   In order to determine the significance of this change, we must establish the distributional characteristics of the two types of factors.   In a budget not weighed down by military expenditure—one that would have been considered normal some decades ago—products purchased by government tend to be more labor-intensive and less capital-intensive than products purchased privately; and personal income paid by government tends to be distributed more equally than wage and salary incomes paid by private firms.   Therefore, the substitution of government demand for private demand will tend to equalize the distribution of factor payments.[1]   Budget incidence will tend to be progressive from the income-sources side. This presumption disappears with the modern budget, characterized by the predominant weight of defense expenditures.   Here public purchases from private industry occupy a large part of total expenditures, and they are for highly capital-intensive products.   Thus no ready conclusion can be drawn regarding the impact of government expenditures from the income-sources side.[2]

Furthermore, we may expect the introduction of the budget to result in an increase in the prices of factors that are specific to products for which the private demand is inelastic to income, relative to the prices of products for which the demand is elastic.   As the disposable income of the private sector is reduced, the prices of necessities will rise relative to those of luxuries.   However, there is no reason to expect that factor earnings from the production of necessities will accrue to recipients of low incomes, while those from the production of luxuries will accrue to people with large incomes.   Indeed, let us apply the hypothesis that this is a random relationship and assume the distributional characteristics of resulting changes in factor prices to be neutral.

Finally, we may expect an increase in the prices of factors that are elastic in supply, relative to the prices of factors that are inelastic in supply.   The distributional implication of such changes may relate to differences in the elasticity of labor supply at various points in the income scale, a matter on which little can be said that is definite.[3]   Or, distributional changes may result from differences in the elasticity of the supply of labor compared to the elasticity of other factors.   The introduction of

---

[1] Bent Hansen, "Ett bidrag till incidenslaran," *Ekonomisk Tidskrift*, vol. 56, no. 3, pp. 195–213, 1954, uses the assumption that all government expenditures are wage payments to conclude that budget incidence with a proportional income tax is progressive.

[2] We are not concerned here with certain transfer programs designed to be highly unneutral in incidence.   Since transfers are in the nature of negative taxes, such programs are excluded from the present case, which allows for general and defense expenditures in the form of goods and service expenditures only.

[3] See p. 245.

such influences is complex because a reduction in labor supply involves a gain in leisure that must be included in income, whereas there is no corresponding reservation price for certain other factors such as land.[1]

Changes on the Uses Side. A similar set of considerations applies to changes in relative position that result from changes in relative prices of products bought.

Introduction of the budget will result in an increase in the prices of goods that are rival in production to goods bought by government, relative to the prices of goods that are complementary. Government demand, if directed heavily at military equipment, will compete with automotive products and other durables and thus burden the purchasers of such products. Since expenditures on durable goods rise when moving up the income scale, the incidence is progressive. However, this conclusion is based on a postulate of increasing cost that may be outweighed by economies of scale, and it fails to account for the impetus to technological advance that results from government programs. Thus there is no ready presumption regarding the immediate distributional impact of public expenditures.

This leaves changes in relative prices due to shifts in the pattern of private demand. As disposable income declines, the prices of products bought by high-income recipients may be expected to fall relative to those purchased by low-income recipients. As a result, there will be a tendency for incidence to be regressive. However, this is a rough approximation only, and may be qualified by allowance for differences in the cost conditions under which various types of goods are supplied.

Conclusions. The preceding discussion suggests an approach and poses problems for empirical investigation, but it does not provide a conclusive answer. In the absence of special considerations to the contrary, we shall proceed on the hypothesis that budget incidence with finance by a proportional income tax is more or less neutral.[2] While this conclusion has not been demonstrated in a rigorous form, the hypothesis is not based on a plea of complete ignorance. It is reasonable in view of the various factors involved, and it must *not* be confused with the old diffusion doctrine. Indeed, the very considerations that point to a more or less neutral incidence for the general tax also point to progressive or regressive patterns of incidence for discriminatory taxes.

Simple Discrimination in Products

We are now ready to examine the incidence of various discriminatory taxes. Since the general tax has been dealt with, the incidence of discriminatory taxes may be approached in differential terms.

---

[1] See p. 221.

[2] For a definition of budget incidence see p. 214.

Let us consider taxes on product transactions, applicable to transactions in selected products only.   While discriminatory between products, such taxes remain general, since they apply to all sellers or all buyers who transact in certain products.   Applicable at either side of any particular market, they may take the form of gross-receipts taxes on sellers or of purchase taxes on buyers, reflecting cases 6 and 5, respectively, of Table 15-1.   As noted before, the incidence will be the same, provided that both taxes impose equivalent discriminations.

Suppose, now, that a sales tax on product X is substituted for a general income tax or sales tax on all products, including X, Y, and Z.   Real expenditures of government are unchanged, and yield is adjusted to purchase the same goods at the new set of prices.[1]

Changes on the Uses Side.   Resulting changes in the relative prices of products may be of two types: First, there is a rise in the price of X relative to the prices of Y and Z.   The magnitude of change will be great if the elasticity of substitution of Y and Z for X is low on the part of the consumer and high on the part of the producer.   If the tax is broadly based, consumers will find it more difficult to switch to tax-free products, and factors will find it more difficult to seek employment in tax-free industries.   Moreover, consumers will find it more difficult to escape the tax if it applies to basic goods and seminecessities than if it applies to optional outlays.   The bulk of discriminatory taxes is derived precisely from such items, for example, cigarettes, liquor, and gasoline.   Finally, the increase in the relative price of the taxed product will depend upon the time allowed.   Adjustments in consumer budgets take time, and the mobility of labor and capital is greater in the long run.   In some cases, transferability of factors may be difficult even in the long run.   Thus, land primarily suited for tobacco production may continue to absorb a substantial part of a tax on tobacco products.

The resulting process of adjustment may give rise to a second type of change in relative prices, applicable to various tax-free products.   Thus, the price of Y will fall relative to that of Z, if Y is complementary to the taxed product X in consumption and rival to it in production; the opposite holds for Z.

Changes in relative product prices may be translated again into changes in distribution or incidence by reference to the place of various products in the budget pattern of consumer households.   If the taxed product is a luxury, purchases of which increase in importance as we move up the income scale, consumers with large incomes will lose, relative to consumers with small incomes.   Differential incidence will be progressive, just as the differential incidence of a tax on necessities will be regressive.   Since

[1] See p. 212.

taxed articles may be allocated in this fashion, it will be possible in our particular case to determine the implications for incidence that result from the first type of price change. Those which follow from the second type of price change are more difficult to interpret. Suppose that X and Y are luxuries, while Z is a necessity, X being again the taxed product. This suggests the hypothesis that Y is more rival, or less complementary, in consumption to X than is Z. Hence, the price of Y will tend to rise relative to that of Z. As a result, the progressive nature of differential incidence is confirmed. However, no particular hypothesis claims priority regarding rivalry or complementarity in production, thus leaving the end result open.

Thus, we may adopt the working assumption that the second type of price change is distributionally neutral. On this basis, we can conclude that the nature of incidence from the uses side depends on the importance of the taxed product in consumer expenditures at various levels of consumer income.

Changes on the Sources Side. Changes in relative product prices are accompanied by corresponding changes in relative factor prices. The prices of factors that are specific to the production of the taxed product X will tend to fall, relative to those which are specific to Y and Z, depending upon the respective elasticities of factor supply. This much may be stated unequivocally; but the distributional implications of the changes are difficult to interpret.

The assumption that X is a luxury while Z is a necessity permits no conclusion regarding the size distribution of the income earned in the production of X compared with that of the income earned in the production of Z. Poor people may produce luxuries, and rich people may produce necessities. Again using the assumption that there is a random relationship between the size distribution of earnings from any particular product and the distribution of income among its consumers, we arrive at the hypothesis that the incidence of a selective excise tax will be neutral from the income-sources side.

This hypothesis may be adjusted in any particular case where the nature of the taxed industry calls for exceptional treatment; and it is subject to empirical investigation as a general proposition. Pending such investigation and the substitution of a better hypothesis, the present formulation will have to do. Indeed, some such simplification seems essential if we are to build a bridge between the formal universe of the complete Walrasian system and the exigencies of empirical work in this field. For the time being, we are left with the conclusion that the differential incidence of the selective excise depends largely upon the consumption characteristics of the taxed product.

Simple Discrimination in Factors

Let us now turn to a discriminatory tax imposed on transactions in selected factors, or items 7 and 8 in Table 15-1. Suppose that a general income tax or factor purchase tax on factors U, V, and W is replaced by a tax on the income of factor U only. Real purchases of government are again held constant.

Changes on the Sources Side. Applying similar reasoning as before, two types of changes in relative factor prices may be distinguished. First, we can expect that the net return of factor U falls relative to that of factors V and W. Secondly, changes may result in the relative returns of V and W.

Suppose that factor supplies are inelastic. Disregarding possible changes in the pattern of demand, the gross rate of return to U will remain unchanged relative to that of V and W; and the net rate of return to U will fall relative to that of V and W. This reflects the removal of the tax wedge between the market prices and net prices of V and W, and the widening of the wedge for U. Differential incidence now depends on the distributional characteristics of the taxed factor. If income from the taxed factor declines as a per cent of total earnings when moving up the income scale, differential incidence is regressive, as it is with a tax on wage income; if the per cent rises, differential incidence is progressive, as it is with a tax on capital income.

This result is qualified if we allow for elastic factor supplies. Assuming upward-sloping supply schedules, the supply of taxed factors declines, while that of tax-free factors rises. Thus the gross rate of return of the taxed factor rises relative to that of the tax-free factors; and the relative decline in the net rate of return of the taxed factor is lessened. A higher rate of tax will be required to obtain the given yield, and the burden on the taxed factor will be increased.[1]

Changes in the relative prices of tax-free factors V and W may result from further changes in the pattern of demand that came about in the general adjustment process. Proceeding as before, we apply the hypothesis that such changes have no systematic effect on the size distribution of income and hence are neutral in incidence. The outcome thus depends primarily upon changes in the relative net prices of taxed and tax-free factors. These changes result in progression or regression, depending on the factor that is taxed. Substitution of a tax on unskilled-labor income for a general tax on factor transactions will be regressive in differential incidence; substitution of a tax on capital income for a tax on labor income will be progressive; and so on.

---

[1] See the earlier discussion (p. 221) regarding the inclusion of leisure in income and the inapplicability of a reservation price to certain other factors.

Changes on the Uses Side. Turning now to product prices, there will be an increase in the relative prices of products involving heavy inputs of taxed factors and a decrease in the prices of products drawing primarily on tax-free factors—particularly if factor supplies are elastic. These changes may increase the prices of necessities relative to those of luxuries, or vice versa. However, the distributional characteristics of the taxed factor with regard to income sources are unrelated to the distributional characteristics of the resulting outputs with regard to income uses. Following our earlier procedure, we shall adopt the hypothesis that the substitution of a discriminatory factor tax will be distributionally neutral from the income-uses side. In the absence of special evidence to the contrary, this hypothesis is reasonable; and as noted before, it is subject to empirical verification.

Whereas changes in the relative *market prices of products* provide the strategic element in the incidence of discriminatory *product* taxes, changes in the relative *net prices of factors* are the strategic element in the incidence of discriminatory *factor* taxes. In the one case, the strategic change results from the ways in which the income recipient may use his income. In the other case, the strategic change occurs in the terms at which income may be obtained.

A similar line of reasoning may be applied to taxes involving discrimination against groups of buyers and sellers rather than factors and products; and to taxes involving various patterns of multiple discrimination. As the pattern of discrimination is expanded, the complexity of the problem is increased accordingly.

Market Imperfections

So far, the adjustment to various tax substitutions has been examined on the assumption of a perfectly competitive market. Additional problems arise once imperfections in the market are introduced.

Rules of Equivalence. Our first rule of equivalence applies to taxes imposed upon the buyer's and the seller's side of a particular transaction. This equivalence may not hold for imperfectly competitive markets. Consumers who are subject to a money illusion may react differently toward an open product tax, such as a purchase tax, and a hidden product tax, such as a tax on the gross receipts of firms.[1] More important, unions subject to a tax illusion may react differently in collective bargaining, depending on whether a tax on factor transactions is imposed on the

---

[1] In Chamberlin's terms, the preceding discussion referred to markets that are perfect as well as purely competitive. Some of the difficulties now considered involve not only lack of purity but also other imperfections. See E. H. Chamberlin, *The Theory of Monopolistic Competition*, 5th ed., Harvard University Press, Cambridge, Mass., 1948.

employer or the employee. The legislative intent of splitting payroll taxes into an employer and an employee share would be futile in a perfectly competitive market, but it may have some bearing on wage and price policy in an imperfect market.

Our second rule of equivalence applies to a general tax on the gross receipts of firms and a general tax on their cost payments to factors. This equivalence disappears under conditions of monopoly where gross receipts of the firm are divided between payments which enter into cost and profits which do not. Suppose that a tax at rate t_r is imposed on the average revenue of the monopolist, leading to a certain change in output and in price. Now let this tax be replaced by a tax on cost at rate t_c, applicable to average cost excluding tax. Output and price after tax will be the same if we set t_c to equal $t_r/(1 - t_r)$. At the same time, yields will differ. The yield of the receipts tax will be larger if profits remain, and that of the tax on cost payments will be larger if losses are incurred.[1]

The existence of monopoly profits destroys the equality between receipts and cost payments by the firm, and the tax on monopoly profits enters as a third category of tax, to be distinguished from a tax on gross receipts and a tax on cost payments. The distributional implications of a tax on profits, like those of a tax on factor transactions, lie primarily on the earnings side of the household position. Considering monopoly profits as a rent income, the profits tax may be likened to that of a discriminatory tax on a factor transaction, where the factor is inelastic in supply.

Our third rule of equivalence, applicable to a general income and a general consumption tax, is not affected by the introduction of imperfect competition, since it is based on the assumption of zero saving.

Budget Incidence of General Income Tax. Allowance for market imperfections calls for qualifications in our earlier appraisal of budget incidence with a general and proportional income tax. These qualifications apply to changes that result from the sources side.

Where factor prices are determined in an imperfect market, demands may be affected by a change in tax rates. Executives who supply and demand their own services may set salaries with allowance for prevailing tax schedules. An increase in tax might be compensated for by an increase in pay so as to maintain earnings net of tax. The same situation might arise with regard to professional fees, where the seller is in a monopolistic position but has not charged what the market will bear prior to tax. This is a reasonable assumption in many cases. The salary level for top executives or the fee level for highly paid professional services is usually an administered price, and may be subject to compensatory adjustments when tax rates rise. Moreover, high marginal tax rates

[1] See p. 308.

reduce the net (after tax) differential between earnings at various levels of a business firm's hierarchy. If it is customary to maintain certain differentials in living standards, top salaries may move up with an increase in progression.[1] Quite possibly, the steepening of income tax progression over the last decades has been a factor in widening salary spreads in this fashion.

Corresponding adjustments are less likely to be found at the lower end of the scale. Not only are tax rates lower and carry less weight in the picture, but individual bargaining positions tend to be weaker. Union policy may allow for personal income tax payments as a factor in wage demands, but this has hardly been a major factor to date.

Discrimination in Products. In the competitive setting, we arrived at the hypothesis that the distributional results of a discriminatory tax on product transactions are determined largely by changes in relative product prices, that is, from the side of income use. Changes resulting from the sources or earnings side were considered a minor factor in determining the distribution of income by size.

However, this may not hold in an imperfect market. Owing to the occurrence of monopoly in the product market, a discriminatory tax on product transactions may have important distributional repercussions from the earnings side; and the importance of repercussions from the side of income use may be reduced. In the extreme case where the supply of the taxed product is wholly inelastic, a discriminatory product tax is equivalent to a tax on monopoly profit.[2]

In less extreme cases, the major distributional changes may still come about from the side of income uses, that is, through changes in relative product prices; but these may now be supplemented by significant and systematic changes from the earnings side. If the product tax goes to curtail monopoly profits, changes from the earnings side will be similar to those which result from a discriminatory tax on capital income; if these changes curtail the wages share in profits, the results will be similar to those of a wages tax, and so forth.

Discrimination in Factors. Similar qualifications arise for discriminatory taxes on factor transactions. In the competitive setting, we arrived at the hypothesis that distributional changes will be determined primarily from the earnings side; and that changes which result from shifts in relative product prices will have little systematic importance. The results may differ for the imperfect market.

A tax on wages, paid in an imperfect factor market, is of particular interest. Consider a situation of monopoly, where labor is paid less than its marginal value product. A tax on wage payments may now be

---

[1] See pp. 103 and 245.
[2] See p. 301.

reflected in reduced profits on the part of the producer, as well as in a changed position of the wage earners, including the possible results of reduced hours of work and a reduced wage bill.   The strategic factor of distributional change still occurs on the earnings side, but the earnings that are changed will not be the same as in the competitive case.

Next, consider a situation of monopoly on the seller's side of the factor market.   Suppose that the unions bargain on an all-or-nothing basis and successfully appropriate a share in the profits reaped by the producer from his monopoly position in the product market.   If the bargaining policy of the union has been unrestrained prior to tax, it may now have to absorb the tax.[1]   If the pre-tax policy was one of restraint, imposition of a wages tax may lead to increased wage demands.   In other situations, imposition of a wages tax may lead the union to demand increased wages, even though this reduces employment under conditions of incremental bargaining.

A more elaborate analysis would require us to combine various assumptions regarding competitive structures in the product and factor markets, but little would be gained by a mere cataloguing of possible results. What is needed is a framework of simplifying assumptions, sufficiently realistic to be of empirical interest and sufficiently simple to permit the development of hypotheses for testing—in other words, a counterpart to the Keynesian revolution applicable to the problems of price and distribution theory.   In the meantime, reasoning on incidence will lead to unverified hypotheses rather than to results that may be relied upon without qualification.   However, considerations of incidence play an important part in the immediate needs of tax legislation, and properly so; this being the case, the social scientist, unlike the astronomer, cannot postpone judgment until a wholly conclusive proof can be given.   Short of the limiting case of complete ignorance, the economist is called upon to produce as good a hypothesis as may be developed, even though it be less than perfect.[2]

C. ADJUSTMENTS IN ABSOLUTE PRICES

Thus far we have dealt with changes in *relative* product or factor prices, brought about by various changes in tax structure.   Nothing whatsoever has been said about changes in *absolute* prices.   This is as it should be. The essence of the incidence problem, as a problem in distribution, lies in the analysis of changes in relative prices regardless of the changes in absolute prices through which the relative changes occur.   The direction of change in absolute prices will be considered briefly in the remainder of

[1] See p. 282.
[2] See p. 270, note 1.

this chapter.[1]   Thereafter, we shall resume the main thread of our argument, which is in terms of relative prices.

Monetary Considerations

For the time being, we shall retain our simple setting of an all-consumption economy but shall inquire into the absolute changes in price and income that result from budget adjustments.   This is essentially a monetary problem and, more specifically, an exercise in quantity theory. We may assume that money in the all-consumption model is in the form of transaction money only, no cash being held as a part of asset portfolios. Moreover, we may assume that the velocity of transaction money is fixed, so that a given money supply expedites a fixed total volume of payments within a given period.   Finally, let us assume that payments to or by the government involve the same claim on transaction money as do payments between private parties.[2]

Since the total volume of payments is set by the money supply, our problem is merely to determine what changes in absolute prices and earnings will implement the necessary changes in relative prices, while providing for the total of required payments.   Or, if we wish to obtain certain changes in absolute prices, the problem is one of determining which changes in money supply are needed so as to obtain the necessary adjustment in relative prices while meeting the set condition of absolute price change.

Adjustment to General Taxes

To simplify matters, let us reinstate the assumption of perfect competition.   In dealing with the case of general taxes, we may consider consumer households as a group and assume that there is only one factor, say labor, going into the production of one single product X.   Let us suppose that 100 units of X are produced per year, and that 100 hours of labor are required.   Setting the product price per unit as $1, the hourly wage will also be $1.   The value of total output, or gross national product, equals $100.   Total payments, including wage payments of $100 plus purchase payments of $100, equal $200.   Assuming further that the average dollar

---

[1] For a discussion of quantity-theory approaches to incidence, see O. Engländer, *Allgemeine Steuerlehre und Steuerüberwälzung*, Rohrer, Brünn, Germany, 1935; and G. Schmölders, "Monetäre Theorie der Steuerüberwälzung," *Finanzarchiv*, Neue Folge, vol. 4, pp. 280–290, 1936.

[2] If the reader wishes to assume that transactions with the government involve a smaller or larger transaction velocity, the subsequent argument may be adjusted readily to fit alternative assumptions.   Compare, for instance, Ricardo's clever assumption (see p. 390) that tax- and government-purchase payments are cleared against each other, thus involving no actual transactions and no claim on transaction money on either the tax or the expenditure side of the process.

TABLE 15-2. PRICE ADJUSTMENTS TO GENERAL TAXES*

Sector accounts	Before tax (1)	Income tax — Money supply held constant (2)	Income tax — Price level held constant (3)	Sales tax, Gov. purchases taxable — Money supply held constant (4)	Sales tax, Gov. purchases taxable — Money wage held constant (5)	Sales tax, Gov. purchases tax-free — Money supply held constant (6)	Sales tax, Gov. purchases tax-free — Public price held constant (7)	Sales tax, Gov. purchases tax-free — Private price held constant (8)
Consumer sector:								
1. Wage bill	$100.00	$83.33	$100.00	$60.00	$100.00	$71.40	$100.00	$60.00
2. Wage rate	1.00	0.83	1.00	0.60	1.00	0.71	1.00	0.60
3. Income tax		33.33	40.00					
4. Purchase payments	100.00	50.00	60.00	60.00	100.00	71.40	100.00	60.00
5. Price per unit	1.00	0.83	1.00	1.00	1.66	1.19	1.66	1.00
6. Units bought	100	60	60	60	60	60	60	60
Business sector:								
7. Receipts from consumers	100.00	50.00	60.00	60.00	100.00	71.40	100.00	60.00
8. Receipts from government		33.33	40.00	40.00	66.66	28.56	40.00	24.00
9. Wage payments	100.00	83.33	100.00	60.00	100.00	71.40	100.00	60.00
10. Gross-receipts tax				40.00	66.66	28.56	40.00	24.00
11. Units sold	100	100	100	100	100	100	100	100
Public sector								
12. Income tax		33.33	40.00					
13. Gross-receipts tax				40.00	66.66	28.56	40.00	24.00
14. Expenditures		33.33	40.00	40.00	66.66	28.56	40.00	24.00
15. Price per unit		0.83	1.00	1.00	1.66	0.71	1.00	0.60
16. Units bought		40	40	40	40	40	40	40
All sectors:								
17. Gross national product (6 + 7)	100.00	83.33	100.00	100.00	166.66	100.00	140.00	84.00
18. Total payments (2 + 6 + 7 + 8 + 9)	200.00	200.00	240.00	200.00	333.33	200.00	280.00	168.00
19. Average product price per unit	1.00	0.83	1.00	1.00	1.66	1.00	1.40	0.84
20. Money supply	10.00	10.00	12.00	10.00	16.66	10.00	14.00	8.40
21. Transaction velocity	20	20	20	20	20	20	20	20

* In dollars except for items 6, 11, 16, and 21.

is paid out twenty times a year, we require a total money supply of $10. This is the situation shown in column 1 of Table 15-2. We shall now introduce a public budget designed to permit the government to purchase 40 per cent of the product. We assume that real output remains unchanged.

Income Tax. Let government purchases be financed by an income tax on households. Introduction of such a budget results in a more elaborate structure of payments. The part of the product purchased by government is now paid for twice—once through income tax payment by households and again through purchase payments by government.[1] Previously, 200 units (of product and labor) were purchased once. Now, 40 units of the product are paid for twice, so that 240 units are purchased altogether. Since the money supply is assumed constant at $10, total payments remain constant at $200. The average price per unit (product and labor) falls to $\frac{200}{240} = 0.83$. The income tax on households leaves unaffected the equality between receipts and factor payments by the firm. Hence the unit prices of product and labor both decline at the same rate. This result is shown in column 2 of the table.[2]

Since the assumption of a constant money supply leads to a reduction in prices and wages, an increase in money supply is required if prices and wages are to remain constant. This case is shown in column 3.*

[1] If we assume source withholding of income tax, there may be no net extension of the payment stream, as income tax payments by the employer take the place of wage payments and public-purchase payments take the place of private payments. Hence, the price level remains unchanged.

[2] Where A = aggregate volume of payments
$\quad\quad U$ = units of product
$\quad\quad L$ = units of labor
$\quad\quad W$ = wage payments
$\quad\quad T_i$ = income tax payments
$\quad\quad C$ = consumer-purchase payments
$\quad\quad G$ = government-purchase payments
$\quad\quad p$ = unit price of product
$\quad\quad w$ = unit price of labor
$\quad\quad g$ = fraction of product bought by government
we have seven equations:

$$A = W + T_i + C + G$$
$$T_i = G$$
$$C = W - T_i$$
$$G = \bar{g}p\bar{U}$$
$$G + C = p\bar{U}$$
$$W = w\bar{L}$$
$$A = \bar{V}\bar{M}$$

Given $\bar{g}$, $\bar{U}$, $\bar{L}$, $\bar{V}$, and $\bar{M}$, these equations permit us to determine A, W, T_i, C, G, p, and w. Column 2 of Table 15-2 shows the results for $g = 0.4$, $\bar{U} = 100$, $\bar{L} = 100$, $\bar{V} = 20$, $\bar{M} = 10$.

* In this case, M becomes an unknown, and $\bar{w} = \$1$ is given.

General Sales Tax with Government Purchases Taxable.   Next, let us assume that the budget is financed by a general sales tax applicable to both private and public purchases.   Government purchases are now paid for once by tax payments by the firm and again by government outlays. As before, total purchases include 100 units of labor and 140 units of products, or 240 units in all.   With a constant money supply, total payments in dollar terms remain constant at $200, the average price (including product and labor units) must again fall to 83 cents.   The tax now enters as a wedge between product price and factor payment.   Hence the wage rate falls relative to the product price.   As shown in column 4, the product price remains at $1, while the wage rate falls to 60 cents.[1]   In brief, the sales tax payment takes the place of wage payments, and government-purchase payments take the place of reduced private payments.

The assumption of a constant money supply leaves product prices unchanged while reducing money wages; it follows that money supply must be increased if wages are to remain unchanged while, at the same time, price is increased by the amount of tax.   This result is shown in column 5.*   In this case the tax is added to price, while factor payments are held constant.   The direction of adjustment differs, but the real value of the hourly wage, or real wage rate, is reduced equally in both cases.   In column 4, the money wage rate is 60 cents, while the product price is $1; whereas in column 5, the money wage is $1 while the product price is $1.66.   The real incidence of the tax, or the division of the product between the consumer and government sector is unchanged.   This can be seen also by comparing lines 6 and 16 of the table.

General Sales Tax with Government Purchases Tax-free.   The result differs if government purchases are exempted from tax payment.   As before, wages decline relative to the price payable by private buyers; but in addition, the price charged to private buyers now exceeds the price payable by government.

The resulting picture for a constant money supply is shown in column 6.

---

[1] Using T_s = sales tax payments, we now have the following system of equations:

$$A = W + T_s + C + G$$
$$T_s = G$$
$$C = W$$
$$G = \bar{g}p\bar{U}$$
$$G + C = p\bar{U}$$
$$W = w\bar{L}$$
$$A = \bar{V}\bar{M}$$

Given g, $\bar{U}$, $\bar{L}$, $\bar{V}$, and $\bar{M}$, we again determine A, W, T_s, C, G, p, and w.   Column 2 of Table 15-2 shows the results assuming the same constants as before.

* In this case M becomes an unknown, and $w = \bar{w} = \$1$.

Money wages again fall, though less than in the previous case. The product price payable by private buyers now increases, and that payable by government falls. The average product price, including prices paid publicly and privately, remains unchanged.[1]

Again we may adjust the money supply so as to hold product prices constant, but now there are two possibilities. In column 7 of Table 15-2, the price payable by government is held constant. Since the government pays the cost price free of tax, and since wage costs must be the same for products purchased by government or privately, the wage rate will be unchanged. The price payable by private buyers now increases by the amount of tax; total payments rise sharply, and a substantial expansion in money supply is required.[2]

In column 8, we assume that the price payable by private buyers is held constant, which means that the price payable by government must fall by the amount of tax. The money wage rate that is equal to the net price must fall accordingly. A contraction in the money supply is required.[3]

Notwithstanding these differences in the pattern of changes in prices and wage rates in dollar terms, the resulting changes in the real income of consumers and government are the same throughout. Moreover, this result is precisely the same whether the budget is financed by a general income tax or a general sales tax. Differential incidence between the two is neutral, whatever the monetary adjustment be.

Adjustment to Discriminatory Taxes

A similar analysis may be applied to the case of discriminatory taxes, such as taxes on transactions in selected products, or on transactions in selected factors. The same principles apply. A discriminatory tax on product transactions leads to an increase in the relative price of the taxed

---

[1] Where p_g = price paid by government, and p_p = price paid by consumer, we have the following system:

$$A = W + T_s + C + G$$
$$T_s = G$$
$$C = W$$
$$G = \bar{g} p_g \bar{U}$$
$$C = (1 - g) p_p \bar{U}$$
$$p_c - p_g = \frac{T_s}{\bar{g}\bar{U}}$$
$$W = w\bar{L}$$
$$A = \bar{V}\bar{M}$$

Given $\bar{g}$, $\bar{U}$, $\bar{L}$, $\bar{V}$, and $\bar{M}$, we may determine A, W, T_s, C, G, p_g, p_p, and w. The results of column 6 use the same numerical values for the constants as before.

[2] In the above system, we now have $p_g = \bar{p}_g = \$1$, and M becomes a variable.

[3] The adjustment of the preceding footnote is now replaced by $p_p = \bar{p}_p = \$1$, with M again variable.

product. This may take the form of an increase in the price of the taxed product, a decrease in the price of the tax-free product, or a mixture of both. A discriminatory tax on factor transactions may reduce the net money rate of return to the taxed factor, raise the net money rate of return to the tax-free factor, or be a mixture of both. Resulting changes in the distribution of real income will be independent of the particular pattern of change in absolute prices. *Incidence is not a function of changes in absolute prices but of changes in relative prices.* The latter are determined by the structure of the tax and the prevailing market forces. Changes in relative prices may be implemented through various sets of changes in absolute prices, but the direction of change in absolute prices as such does not tell us what incidence will be.[1]

Alternative Monetary Assumptions

The preceding argument was based on the simplifying assumption that all money is in the form of transaction money. This assumption will do for the simplified case of an all-consumption economy, but it is hardly adequate for a more realistic model.

Alternative assumptions may be made regarding the demand for money. Consumers may wish to hold a fixed amount of asset money or an amount of money equal to a fixed fraction of their income, either before or after tax. Such assumptions can be built readily into our model, and the results adapted accordingly; the basic principle remains the same. As long as the reasoning is based on a full-fledged classical system, the resulting change in price level is set by the simple requirements of transaction velocity, while the resulting change in relative prices is given by the shape of supply and demand functions for the various factors and products. The structural changes in transaction needs that result from the substitution of various taxes will affect the price level but not relative prices.[2]

As liquidity preference is allowed for, the demand for money comes to be determined by a more complex set of forces. Changes in the supply of asset money, resulting from changes in transaction needs due to tax substitution, may affect the rate of interest and the level of investment. Depending on the nature of the system, this may be of significance only for the level of prices and the composition of the product between consumption and capital formation; or it may affect the level of output as well.[3] Moreover, the change in price level associated with a given change

---

[1] For a somewhat similar type of discussion, though in a different context, see D. H. Robertson, *Banking Policy and the Price Level*, 2d ed., Staples Press, Ltd., London, 1926, chap. 3.

[2] See p. 365.

[3] See p. 470.

in relative prices may assume distributional importance, once the holding
of claims (money and debt) is allowed for.   Where money illusion is present, the change in relative prices may come to depend on the direction of
absolute change.   Some of these more complex situations will be dealt
with later on.   They introduce important qualifications but do not
invalidate the principle that the problem of incidence is primarily one of
changes in relative rather than absolute prices.   This stands out most
clearly in the all-consumption model, where the direction of absolute
price change is a monetary veil, without importance in real terms.

CHAPTER 16

Incidence in the capital-formation model

We now return to the more important matter of changes in relative product and factor prices, to be reexamined in a setting that allows for saving and capital formation. At the same time, we shall retain the classical framework of equality between planned saving and investment. Prices and factor shares are flexible, and full employment of capital and labor is maintained automatically.

In this setting we may distinguish two aspects of the incidence problem. First, there is the question of how budget policies may affect growth, and how resulting changes in growth may affect factor shares, and hence distribution. Secondly, there is the question of how various budget policies may affect the state of distribution with given factor shares.

A. EFFECTS ON GROWTH AND FACTOR SHARES

The first problem is one about which one can say little in categorical terms.

Let us consider a system with a constant supply of labor and natural resources and an annual investment equal to a given fraction of income that is saved. The path of income depends on the supply of resources and labor, the initial capital stock, the propensity to save, and the production function. Following the principle of diminishing returns and holding technique constant, the gain in income declines with successive increments in capital stock. As investment proceeds, the ratio of capital to labor increases, and the marginal productivity of capital declines. At the same time, the capital stock grows. Depending on the balance between these two tendencies, the share of capital in total income may decline, but this need not be the case. The production function, while meeting the

372

assumption of diminishing returns, may be such that the capital share remains constant as the capital stock increases. This will occur if the production function is of the Cobb-Douglas type, where factor shares are independent of factor proportions;[1] or the production function may be such that the capital share rises or falls as output grows. Even the classical hypothesis that the capital share approaches zero does not assure a declining capital share. No generalization can be made on a priori grounds about changes in factor shares in the process of growth. By the same token, no categorical statement can be made about the distributional effects of budget policies that expand or retard growth.

To simplify further, let us suppose that the capital-output ratio is the same for public as for private investment. In this case, introduction of a balanced budget will raise growth if the government's marginal propensity to invest (government investment as a fraction of government expenditures) exceeds the taxpayers' marginal propensity to save; it will reduce growth if the opposite is the case. If growth is retarded, the capital share will rise or fall, depending on whether growth leads to a falling or rising share, and vice versa if growth is speeded up.

If propensities to save differ among taxpayers, effects upon growth depend upon the government's propensity to invest, compared to the taxpayers' weighted marginal propensity to save. Since the marginal propensity to save tends to rise as we move up the income scale, substitution of a progressive for a regressive tax retards growth. If the capital share declines with growth, substitution of a progressive tax increases the capital share before tax. Since capital income accrues more largely to the upper-income groups, this curtails the equality of income distribution. At the same time, it raises the share of the tax that must be paid by recipients of large incomes. The share of upper-income groups in disposable income may rise, fall, or remain unchanged. If factor shares are independent of growth, or if the capital share rises with growth, both effects work in the same direction, and differential incidence is progressive.

Similar considerations apply to a more complex system involving growth of labor as well as capital.[2] Suppose that the structure of the system is such that it tends towards an equilibrium rate of growth. After this rate is reached, factor shares as well will be at equilibrium levels. The equilibrium rate of growth and the corresponding equilibrium level of factor shares depend on the propensity to save. Thus, differing budget policies, by affecting s, may affect not only the equilibrium rate of

---

[1] See Paul Douglas, *The Theory of Wages*, The Macmillan Company, New York, 1934, pp. 145–158; and R. G. D. Allen, *Mathematical Analysis for Economists*, St. Martin's Press, Inc., New York, 1950, pp. 284–289.

[2] See Robert M. Solow, "A Contribution to the Theory of Economic Growth," *Quarterly Journal of Economics*, vol. 70, no. 1, pp. 65–94, February, 1956.

growth but the equilibrium level of factor shares. As before, one cannot conclude on an a priori basis whether a tax policy that raises s, and hence the equilibrium rate of growth, will reduce or raise the equilibrium level of the capital share. Either result may occur.[1]

Not only does a priori reasoning fail to answer the problem, but it is difficult to interpret the historical record. Past evidence shows that factor shares have remained rather stable, but this does not prove that the underlying production function is of the Cobb-Douglas type. What the data show is the combined result of capital accumulation, growth in labor supply, and changes in technique. The net result of constant shares therefore, does not reveal how factor shares would have changed, had accumulation occurred without changes in technique.[2] More might be learned by comparing current capital shares between countries with different capital-income ratios, but such comparisons are beset with difficulties of their own.

Once changes in techniques are involved, effects of budget policy upon technological change must be allowed for. The problem here concerns not only effects on growth but the particular types of innovations called forth, which differ in their effects on factor shares.[3] Thus the effects of growth on factor shares, and hence on incidence, are exceedingly complex. The effects of budget policy on growth itself can be handled more readily, and will be explored in a later chapter.[4]

B. DIFFERENTIAL INCIDENCE WITHOUT GROWTH EFFECTS

Let us now turn to the effects of alternative taxes upon the distribution of net income with a given rate of growth. For this purpose, we shall assume that all taxpayers have the same marginal propensity to save, so that the substitution of one tax for another cannot affect saving and the rate of growth. Effects of alternative taxes upon the willingness to invest available funds are ruled out by the assumption of equality between ex ante saving and investment.

To simplify matters, let us suppose that there is one type of consumer good only, so that gross factor shares remain unchanged as various taxes are substituted for each other. We must now examine what happens to the relative position of various groups in the economy as one tax is replaced by another of equal yield. In order to have a standard of comparison,

[1] *Ibid.*, p. 84.

[2] See Francis M. Bator, "On Capital Productivity, Input Allocation and Growth," *Quarterly Journal of Economics*, vol. 71, no. 1, pp. 80–106, February, 1957.

[3] See J. R. Hicks, *The Theory of Wages*, Macmillan & Co., Ltd., London, 1935, chap. 6; and W. Fellner, *Trends and Cycles in Economic Activity*, Henry Holt and Company, Inc., New York, 1956, part III.

[4] See p. 483.

let us assume that each of the alternative taxes is introduced as a replace-ment for a general and proportional income tax.[1]

Comparison of Income Taxes and Product Taxes

For purposes of this discussion, let us classify individuals according to the nature of their income source, depending on whether their ratio of wage income to capital or interest income Y_w/Y_k exceeds, equals, or falls short of the national average; and according to the nature of the income uses, depending on whether the propensity to save $S/(Y_w + Y_k) = S/Y$ exceeds, equals, or falls short of the national average. We thus obtain the nine groups shown in columns 1 and 2 of Table 16-1, and may examine how their relative position is changed if various taxes are substituted for a proportional and general income tax.

TABLE 16-1. DIFFERENTIAL INCIDENCE IN CAPITAL-FORMATION MODEL*
(Gross factor shares assumed constant)

Sources and uses of taxpayer's income		Tax replacing proportional income tax			
Uses	Sources	Tax on wages	Tax on interest	Sales tax on consumer goods	Sales tax on capital goods
(1)	(2)	(3)	(4)	(5)	(6)
1. S/Y < average		+ or −	+ or −	−	+
2. S/Y = average	Y_w/Y_k < average	+	−	0	0
3. S/Y > average		+	−	+	−
4. S/Y < average		−	+	−	+
5. S/Y = average	Y_w/Y_k = average	0	0	0	0
6. S/Y > average		+	−	+	−
7. S/Y < average		−	+	−	+
8. S/Y = average	Y_w/Y_k > average	−	+	0	0
9. S/Y > average		+ or −	+ or −	+	−

* + indicates net gain in relative position.
− indicates net loss in relative position.
0 indicates no change in relative position.

Suppose that the general income tax is replaced by a tax on wages. To maintain equal yield, the new rate of the wages tax must be higher than the old rate of the income tax. On the sources or earnings side, this is to the advantage of those for whom Y_w/Y_k < average, and to the dis-advantage of those for whom Y_w/Y_k > average. People for whom

[1] To permit this comparison, the yield of the income tax must be such that it does not exceed the yield obtainable from the other taxes.

Y_w/Y_k = average are indifferent as between the two taxes.   On the side of income use, repeal of the income tax means that henceforth savings may be invested, and the subsequent interest income enjoyed free of income tax.   The discounted value of these future tax omissions constitutes a gain to the advantage of people for whom S/Y > average, relative to those for whom S/Y < average.   People for whom S/Y = average are indifferent between the two taxes.   Combining both considerations, the results are as shown in column 3.   For the cases shown in lines 1 and 9, the changes resulting from the sources and uses side differ in direction, and the net result may involve either a gain or a loss.

Now suppose that the income tax is replaced by a tax on interest, applicable to capital income from old and new investment alike.   Since wages are excluded from the tax base, the new tax rate must again be higher than that of the income tax.   Changes on the sources side are now to the advantage of those for whom Y_w/Y_k > average, and to the disadvantage of those for whom Y_w/Y_k < average.   On the uses side, future income from savings will be taxed at a higher rate.   This is to the disadvantage of those for whom S/Y > average, relative to those for whom S/Y < average.   The results shown in column 4 are opposite in direction to results of the wages tax, with the outcome for lines 1 and 9 again depending on the particular circumstances of the case.

Let us now replace the general income tax by a sales tax on consumer goods, or a spendings tax on consumers.   If an equal yield is to be obtained, the new tax rate must again be higher.   On the sources side, this substitution affects the recipients of wage income and capital income alike.   Gross shares before tax are assumed to remain unchanged, and removal of the proportional income tax leaves shares in disposable income unchanged as well.   Relative positions are unchanged on the sources side.   On the uses side, the repeal of the income tax increases the return obtained from savings, and the consumption tax reduces the amount of consumption obtained from current income.[1]   The substitution, therefore, is to the advantage of those whose ratio S/Y is above the average, relative to those whose ratio S/Y is below the average.   The results are shown in column 5.   The change in relative position is clear-cut for all groups.   The current composition of income sources is irrelevant, the outcome depending only on whether the S/Y ratio is above or below the average.

Let us now examine the sales tax on capital goods.   On the sources side, the repeal of the income tax leaves the relative position of wage

---

[1] We are concerned here merely with the fact that substitution of a sales tax on consumer goods for a general income tax improves the *relative position* of the saver. We are *not* concerned with evaluating this change, with regard to either excess burden or a definition of equitable income.   (See pp. 140 and 162.)

earners and interest recipients unchanged. The tax is removed for recipients of wage income as well as for recipients of interest income from previously acquired capital assets. Unlike a general tax on interest income, the sales tax on capital goods applies to new acquisitions. It is equivalent to a tax on interest income from newly acquired capital. On the uses side, substitution of the tax on capital goods is to the disadvantage of those for whom $S/Y >$ average, and to the advantage of those for whom $S/Y <$ average. This follows since the tax rate on capital goods must again be higher than the tax rate on general income. The result, as recorded in column 6, is opposite to that of the tax on consumer goods. In the course of time, all old capital goods depreciate, and the entire capital stock is in the form of new capital goods. Thus, in the long run, the sales tax on capital goods becomes equivalent to a general tax on all interest income.

We therefore arrive at the following results:

1. Replacement of the proportional income tax by a tax on wage income is unfavorable to wage earners and consumers, and favorable to recipients of capital income and savers. On both counts, differential incidence is regressive.

2. Precisely the opposite holds, on all points, for the tax on interest. It favors wage earners and consumers and hurts recipients of capital income and savers. On both counts, differential incidence is progressive. People who look forward to saving a great deal but have mostly wage income, and people who consume a great deal but have mostly interest income, may be affected either way under both taxes.

3. Replacement of the income tax by a sales tax on consumers is to the disadvantage of consumers and the advantage of savers. The division of present earnings between wage and capital income has no relevance in this case. Differential incidence is regressive.

4. Substitution of a sales tax on capital goods is to the advantage of consumers compared to savers, and differential incidence is progressive.

We may now interpret the categories of Table 16-1 in terms of some typical situations. Line 7 tends to reflect low-income families, while line 3 tends to reflect high-income families. Low-income families should gain from replacement of the income tax by a tax on interest and lose from replacement of the income tax by a tax on wages or consumption. High-income families will be affected inversely. The heavily taxed widow is reflected by line 1, which, oddly enough, she shares with the playboy who disperses inherited wealth. Both stand to gain if the income tax is replaced by a sales tax on capital goods, and to lose from a tax on consumer goods. The young man who makes his way in the business world in the Horatio Alger tradition is reflected by line 9. He gains from the substitution of a tax on consumer goods, and is hit hardest by a sales tax on capital goods. The average man, line 5 is sublimely indifferent to what happens.[1]

While this exercise yields a fair amount of relevant information, it must be recalled that the argument rests on the assumption that factor shares before tax remain unchanged. In practice, such will rarely occur. The supply of labor may change, and resulting changes in the rate of growth may alter factor shares before tax. These changes may alter the picture, but as shown above, the direction of this influence cannot be predicted in general terms.

Equivalence between Taxes

We return briefly to the problem of equivalence between various taxes, considered previously for the all-consumption model.[2] Introduction of consumer saving does not affect the equivalence between taxes imposed on different sides of the same transaction; and it does not affect the equivalence between a tax on business receipts and cost, the assumption in both cases being that perfect competition prevails. However, introduction of consumer saving suspends the equivalence between a general income tax and a spendings tax on the consumer, or between a general income tax and a sales tax on consumer goods.

The general income tax is now equivalent to a combination of other taxes. A general income tax may be said to comprise a tax on wage income, a tax on interest from past investment, and a tax on interest from future investment, all imposed at the same rate t. On the earnings side, removal of the income tax will benefit recipients of wage income and of old capital income alike. The composition of present income sources does not matter. On the uses side, the saver benefits more by the removal of the tax than does the current consumer. The introduction of a sales tax on consumer goods similarly imposes a lesser burden on the saver than on the current consumer. In order to adjust for this, we must supplement the sales tax on consumer goods with a tax on interest from future investment. Thereby, equivalence with the general income tax is restored. Wage income and interest from old investment are treated alike as before. They are now both subject to a zero rate, while previously they were subject to the same rate $t > 0$. Since interest on future investment is taxed, the saver is in the same position, relative to the current consumer, as he was under the income tax.

If the combination of a sales tax on consumer goods and an income tax on interest from future investment is equivalent to the general income tax, so is the combination of a sales tax on consumer goods and a sales tax

---

[1] See Adolphe Quetelet's theory of the *homme moyen* in *Sur l'homme*, Paris, 1835, trans. R. Knox, Edinburgh, 1842.

[2] See p. 350.

on capital goods. This is the case because the sales tax on capital goods is equivalent to a tax on interest from future investment. The former is a tax on the use of capital in production. Since the imposition of the tax leaves the production function unchanged, disregarding possible changes in the supply of capital, the tax must be charged against the return on new capital.[1]

Finally, it should be noted that a tax on interest income from old and new investment is equivalent to a sales tax on capital goods if a sufficiently long period is considered, as all investment in the long run will be new investment. We thus have, in the long run, a further equivalence between the general income tax and (1) a sales tax on consumer goods plus a tax on all interest income, or (2) a tax on wage income plus a sales tax on capital goods.

Incidence of Sales Tax on Consumer Goods

We have shown that the substitution of a sales tax on consumer goods for an income tax of equal yield is to the advantage of the saver and to the disadvantage of the consumer.[2] This is in line with the traditional view that a sales tax on consumer goods is borne by the consumer. However, the argument must be stated carefully if misunderstanding is to be avoided.

The usual line of reasoning has been that the consumer bears the tax because the market price of consumer goods rises in absolute terms when the tax is imposed. This involves a double fallacy: First, there is no necessity for the price of the taxed product to increase in absolute terms,[3] certainly not if the problem is viewed in a general-equilibrium setting.[4]

[1] See p. 376.

[2] For a critique of this view see H. G. Brown, "The Incidence of a General Output or a General Sales Tax," *Journal of Political Economy*, vol. 47, no. 2, pp. 254–262, April 1939, reprinted in R. A. Musgrave and Carl Shoup (eds.), *Readings in the Economics of Taxation*, American Economic Association, Richard D. Irwin, Inc., Homewood, Ill., 1958; and Earl R. Rolph, "A Proposed Revision of Excise Tax Theory," *Journal of Political Economy*, vol. 60, pp. 102–117, April 1952. Also see Rolph's *The Theory of Fiscal Economics*, University of California Press, Berkeley, Calif., 1954, chap. 6. While my conclusions differ from Rolph's in important respects, his stimulating work has been most helpful in formulating my own ideas.

[3] How imbedded the assumption of increase in price has been is illustrated nicely by Walras's statement that it is "clearly understood that [entrepreneurs] will reimburse themselves by adding the amount of tax to the prices of the product." See Leon Walras, *Elements of Pure Economics*, trans. W. Jaffe, George Allen & Unwin, Ltd., London, 1954, p. 450. Brown, *op. cit.*, and Rolph, "A Proposed Revision of Excise Tax Theory," note correctly that there is no need for prices to rise; however, I do not think that these economists are justified in assuming that prices must be reduced if competition prevails. Either may happen, depending on the monetary circumstances of the case.

[4] See p. 358.

As the tax is imposed, the prices of consumer goods may rise, cost payments to factors may fall, or there may be various combinations of the two.   What happens to the price level depends on our monetary assumptions, and does not matter in the present case.[1]

Second, and more important, the *direction* of the adjustment, or the absolute price change, does not in itself matter.   If in a given situation the absolute price of consumer goods rises by the amount of tax, this does *not* prove that incidence is on the consumer.   If in another situation factor payments fall by the amount of tax, this does *not* prove that the incidence is on factor incomes.   What matters is the resulting changes in *relative* prices, not in absolute prices or price level.   Such, at least, is the case if we assume perfect competition and absence of money or tax illusion, and if we disregard the effect of changes in price level on the real value of claims held by various people.   In a complete system, these factors must be allowed for, but it is well to disregard them at first.   Only in this fashion can we get at the heart of the incidence problem, which is one of relative prices.

Let us return to the substitution of a sales tax on consumer goods for a general income tax.   The sales tax may be thought of as a general charge against all cost payments entering into the production of consumer goods. If we assume that the inventory of consumer goods in process remains unchanged during the period, total cost payments on consumer goods account for total income.   As the tax on consumer goods is substituted for the income tax, we merely remove the income tax wedge between factor earnings and disposable income, and replace it by a sales tax wedge between firm receipts and factor payments.   Both wedges are non-discriminatory and chargeable equally against all earnings or cost payments.   It follows that relative disposable earnings remain unchanged. Differential incidence is neutral on the earnings or income-sources side.

But, this is not the entire picture.   When we say that the incidence problem is one of relative prices, we must insist that product as well as factor prices be considered.[2]   While relative earnings remain unchanged in the present case, relative positions with regard to income use do not. The prices of consumer goods subject to tax rise relative to the prices of capital goods that are tax-free.   This follows from the basic relationship

[1] See p. 368.   The same quantity-theory reasoning applies in the capital-goods model of the present chapter, since we continue to exclude liquidity preference and changes in the holding of idle balances.

[2] The major difference in the conclusions reached by Rolph, "A Proposed Revision of Excise Tax Theory," and myself appears to stem from a disagreement on this point. If I understand it correctly, Rolph defines incidence as change in position on the earnings side only, whereas I follow the Ricardian tradition and consider both sides.

between the prices of consumer goods and capital goods in our simple system.[1]   If we deflate the incomes of consumers by an index of consumer-good prices and that of savers by an index of capital-good prices, the consumers find their relative position worsened, while the savers find theirs improved.   As before, the essence of the argument is one of change in relative prices, but it may be translated readily into change in absolute prices.[2]

Readers who find it awkward to deflate the income of savers by the prices of capital goods may look at the matter in terms of changes in future net income.   Relative positions with regard to present earnings are unchanged by the tax substitution, but relative positions in terms of future earnings are improved for the saver, who receives his future interest income free of tax.

The magnitude of the gain that the saver derives depends upon his future budget pattern.   If he saves now in order to dissave later, the consumption tax will become due at a later time.   The gain consists

[1] Let us refer to an economy where there is one type of consumer good only.   We may think of the "unripened" capital good as being produced instantaneously by a given labor input.   The unit of this capital good may be defined in terms of a given input of labor hours, labor being taken as homogeneous.   Consumer goods are obtained through the "ripening" of capital goods over a certain period, plus the addition of some direct labor input added at the end of the ripening process.   The value of the unripened capital good equals the wage cost of labor input.   At the same time, it equals the present value of the quantity of consumer goods that result, net of the wage cost of the direct labor input added at the end of the ripening process.   The price of the resulting quantity of consumer goods equals the value of the unripened capital good plus the earnings of capital and the wage cost of the direct labor input. The price of capital goods thus equals the discounted value of what remains after the market price of consumer goods is reduced by the cost of direct labor input.

After a product tax is imposed on consumer goods, the price of capital goods equals the discounted value of what remains after the market price of consumer goods is reduced by the tax and by the cost of direct labor input.   Since relative factor earnings (or wage and interest cost) remain unchanged, the price of capital goods remains unchanged relative to the price of consumer goods *net* of tax.   But the market, or *gross*, price of consumer goods exceeds its net price.   Hence, the market price of consumer goods rises relative to that of capital goods.

[2] Let us assume that the *net* price of consumer goods remains unchanged while the market price rises by the amount of the tax.   Total cost payments are unchanged and continue to be split in the same ratio between the suppliers of labor and saving. Accordingly, the suppliers of both factors find their dollar earnings unchanged. Since the proportional income tax is removed, both suppliers find that their disposable money incomes are increased at the same rate.   But the prices of consumer goods have risen by the amount of tax while those of capital goods have remained unchanged.

Alternatively, we may assume that the *market* price of consumer goods remains unchanged and that factor prices fall by the amount of tax.   In this case, the gap between the market prices of consumer and of capital goods is widened by an absolute decline in the price of consumer goods.

merely in a postponement of the tax liability.[1]   The saver receives, as it were, an interest-free loan from the government.   If dissaving never occurs, the gain is greater, since the saver escapes the tax forever.

The distributional implications of these two types of gain may differ. The distribution of gains from tax postponement, which result where saving is for later consumption, depends on the relationship between transfer of income over the life cycle and lifetime income.   If the fraction of income thus transferred (saved and dissaved) rises when moving up the (life) income scale, the ratio of interest gain to income rises accordingly, and differential incidence of our tax substitution is regressive.   If this fraction falls, differential incidence is progressive.   It is by no means obvious which of the two hypotheses hold in practice.[2]

The distribution of gains from tax remission, which result when saving is for permanent accumulation, depend on the way in which accumulation till death is related to lifetime income.   Empirical evidence shows that the fraction of income thus accumulated rises when moving up the (life) income scale.   Therefore, the gain from our tax substitution accrues more largely to the higher incomes.   Differential incidence on this count is regressive.   It seems reasonable to assume that the gain from permanent accumulation weighs more heavily in the total picture than the gain from tax postponement.   Differential incidence, therefore, tends to be regressive.

C. DISCRIMINATORY INCOME TAX AND CAPITALIZATION

Finally, let us allow for more than one consumer good and consider a discriminatory income tax applicable to all factors but covering earnings in certain industries only.   For instance, let the general income tax be replaced by a tax on the earnings of capital and labor employed in the production of a particular consumer good X, while exempting earnings in

---

[1] The question arises how to treat people who save in order to have their children consume.   Are they to be considered subsequent consumers or perpetual accumulators?   In other words, are we to define the taxpayer as a given individual for the duration of any one year or for his entire life span; or are we to go further and think of the taxpayer as part of a family that includes successive generations?   There is no answer to this in theory.   The gain in interest grows with time but can hardly be assessed at infinity.   Common sense suggests that a cutoff must be made somewhere.

[2] The fact that the average propensity to save rises when moving up the income scale does not prove that the fraction of income saved for later dissaving increases as well.   Rather, it may reflect a higher rate of accumulation over the life span.   On a priori grounds, there is no reason to expect that the incentive to equalize lifetime consumption will be greater for large incomes than small ones.   Indeed, the opposite may be the case.   At the same time, the relation between the time patterns of income accrual and income need may differ for the two groups, and the facilities for income transfer will be greater for the larger income.

the production of consumer good Y. Such a partial income tax will be equivalent under perfect competition to a tax on factor purchases by industry X.

As in the all-consumption model, the substitution of a partial tax leads to a transfer of factors from the taxed to tax-free industries, until the net (after tax) rate of return to factors is equalized in all uses. In the process the price of X rises relative to that of Y, and the consumers of X lose, while those of Y gain. Moreover, the price of factors used specifically in the production of X falls relative to that of factors used specifically in the production of Y. Depending on whether more is to be gained from capital intensive production in Y or in X, the capital share will rise or fall. As in the case of the all-consumption model, we may expect that incidence, that is, systematic changes in the equality of income distribution, will be determined primarily from the side of income use.

The basic argument is the same as for the all-consumption model, but certain additional considerations enter. The tax substitution may now lead to changes in the rate of saving and hence in growth, which in turn may lead to changes in factor shares. Moreover, the time element now becomes of crucial importance. The movement of capital and the equalization of net returns in taxed and tax-free industries takes time. In the short run, the supply of capital to any particular industry is more or less inelastic. Plant and equipment are given, and the return to capital is a quasi rent.[1] As a tax is imposed on one particular industry, the return to mobile factors such as labor or materials cannot be reduced below the rate paid for such factors in other (tax-free) industries. Capital, in the short run, is more or less fixed in supply to the taxed industry.[2] Hence, the return to such capital can be reduced. Where capital is fixed and labor can be readily moved, a tax on income earned in a particular industry must be absorbed by capital invested in that industry. Labor, for the time being, escapes the tax, and the burden on capital is concentrated on the taxed industry.

A tax on capital income in a particular industry thus falls on the owners of the capital at the time the tax is imposed. These owners are unable to rid themselves of the tax by disposing of the taxed asset. Suppose, for example, that individual A owns land X prior to imposition of a tax. A tax is imposed on earnings from X, but it does not apply to earnings from other similar pieces of land, such as Y and Z. As a result, the price of X

---

[1] See Alfred Marshall, *Principles of Economics*, 8th ed., Macmillan & Co., Ltd., London, 1930, book V, pp. 431–439. For an attempt to discuss the factors that determine the period of adjustment, see M. Fasiani, "Materials for a Theory of the Duration of the Process of Tax Shifting," *Review of Economic Studies*, vol. 1, no. 2, pp. 81–101, February, 1934, and in vol. 2, no. 2, pp. 122–136, February, 1935.

[2] An exception is provided by working capital. (See p. 279.)

falls, giving the same yield net of tax as Y and Z.   Therefore, if A wishes to sell X, he will be able to do so at a reduced price only.   B, who purchases X, obtains the same yield on X as he would if he purchased Y or Z. This is the so-called phenomenon of tax capitalization.   It consists of the revaluation of relative capital values that occurs when an income-earning property has been subject to a discriminatory tax on earnings.

Capitalization may occur as the result of a tax on capital income in a selected industry or group of industries, or as the result of a general income tax on earnings from selected industries.   Moreover, it can come about as the result of a partial sales tax, leading to a reduction of earnings from capital in a particular industry.[1]   Indeed, even a supposedly general income tax may involve imperfections in the definition of taxable income and reduce capital yields in various industries unevenly.   Thus, capitalization is a widespread phenomenon.[2]

At the same time, the process of capitalization does not arise in connection with a truly general tax.   Suppose that all real investments are subject to tax, but that income from a government bond at rate i is tax-free.   In this case, the reduced earnings from real investment will be capitalized at i, and all capital values will fall relative to that of bonds. Capitalization still occurs.   Now, suppose that the interest on the government bond is taxable as well, while its gross yield remains unchanged. The market rate of interest at which earnings from other investments are capitalized is reduced by the same fraction as these earnings, and capital values remain unchanged.   In the long run, this may lead to a decline or increase in the supply of capital, with resulting changes in yield of new assets.   These, in turn, give rise to a revaluation of existing assets, and may involve changes in the relative yields and capital values of various assets.   If one wishes, one might refer to all these resulting changes in capital value as *capitalization*.   However, I find it preferable to reserve this term for the changes in relative capital values that are due to the discriminatory nature of a tax.

Once a tax is capitalized, its existence becomes a matter of indifference to the buyer and rests on the seller, who owned the property at the time at which the tax was imposed; or the tax rests on the seller's heirs.   The property may change hands during the course of time and come to be owned by others than the original owner.   Thus, the burden of a partial tax on capital or capital income becomes dissociated from the ownership of the taxed property, and the benefit of subsequent repeal may constitute

---

[1] See J. A. Stockfisch, "Capitalization-Investment Aspects of Excise Taxes under Competition," *American Economic Review*, Vol. 44, no. 3, pp. 287–300, June, 1954.

[2] See Luigi Einaudi, "Capitalization and Amortization of Taxes," *Encyclopedia of the Social Sciences*, The Macmillan Company, New York, 1937, vol. III, pp. 211–213, reprinted in Musgrave and Shoup, *op. cit.*

a windfall to the new owner who holds the property at that time.[1] Some writers, including Walras, have gone so far as to argue that this process leads to a situation where eventually the tax is borne by no one.[2] But such a situation does not occur. The pre-tax owner or his heirs suffer a permanent reduction in income stream, which continues even after the tax is repealed.

D. HISTORICAL REVIEW

Before turning to an analysis of public finances in the more realistic setting of a compensatory system, let us sample some classical and neo-classical contributions to a general-equilibrium theory of incidence.[3]

A general-equilibrium view of incidence is as old as the vision of an economic system as such. Its first appearance, in the tableau of the physiocrats, was suited admirably to solve the incidence problem. As agriculture is the only source of income, all taxes must be paid by agriculture. Hence, it is only efficient to assess taxes on agricultural produce from the outset. This neat solution was qualified subsequently in the classical doctrine, where the contributions of labor and then of capital were admitted in addition to land. Still, the theory of incidence remained a direct application of the theory of factor shares.

Ricardo

Fortunately for us, the main architect of the theory of factor shares was very much interested in incidence. Indeed, if Ricardo's own testimony can be relied upon, it was his very desire to solve the puzzle of incidence that confronted him with the necessity of formulating a general theory of distribution.[4] Ricardo's incidence theory, in many ways, is based on the

[1] These considerations bear on the problem of integrating the corporation tax with the personal income tax. (See p. 173.) It has been pointed out that the inequity of past overtaxation cannot be remedied by repeal, since the benefit would not go to those who suffered the initial loss; rather, it would give windfalls to new owners. As a result, nothing can be done to improve the tax structure, it is argued. I feel uneasy about this application of original sin to taxation. If we assume that an absolute corporation tax contradicts considerations of horizontal equity, the short-run inequity of windfall will hardly outweigh the long-run gains in more equitable taxation of new capital. The basic problem is not solved by pointing to the inequities of transition, which might be avoided or limited by taxing the windfalls to new owners at a special rate of capital-gains taxation.

[2] Walras, *op. cit.*, p. 453, holds that a fraction of the property equal to the rate of tax is appropriated by the government when the tax is imposed, and that no one pays the tax thereafter.

[3] For a history of incidence theory, see Edwin R. Seligman, *The Shifting and Incidence of Taxation*, 4th ed., Columbia University Press, New York, 1921, pp. 1–218.

[4] See our quotation at the beginning of Part 3, drawn from a letter by Ricardo to Trower, in Ricardo's *Works and Correspondence*, vol. VIII (1952, p. 131), *Letters*, ed. P. Sraffa, Cambridge University Press, New York, 1951–1955; and David Ricardo,

discussion contained in Book V of Adam Smith's *The Wealth of Nations*, and is improved upon in minor details by later writers such as J. S. Mill. Nevertheless, it must be considered the classical statement of the doctrine.

Having determined the theory of factor shares, Ricardo considered the incidence of taxes on wages, rent, and profits, as well as of various kinds of product taxes. In each case, incidence is determined by the principle that determines the particular factor share. Contrary to the usual pattern of Ricardian analysis, there is a primary emphasis on the short-run aspects of the adjustment.

Tax on Wages. The level of wage rates is, in the long run, determined by the cost of subsistence.[1] The supply of labor is homogeneous so that there is only one wage rate, applicable to all units of labor. This rate, measured in real terms, must suffice to pay for the cost of producing labor. In equilibrium, it must provide subsistence to the worker, but no more. In an advancing economy, population adjustments may lag, and wages may rise above this level. Eventually, population will expand, the labor supply will increase, and wages will be returned to subsistence. If wages drop below subsistence, population shrinks and wages rise.

Given this theory of wage determination, it follows that a tax on wages cannot, in the long run, be reflected in a reduction in the real wage rate net of tax. The tax must come out of profits. "The principle of the division of the produce of labor and capital between wages and profits," writes Ricardo, "appears to me so certain, that excepting in the immediate effects, I should think it of little importance whether the profits of stock, or the wages of labor, were taxed."[2] The underlying principle, of course, is that whatever reduces net wages must reduce profits; profits equal the excess of output at the margin of cultivation over what is needed to sustain the labor that produces that output.

Ricardo's emphasis, somewhat surprisingly, is on the short rather than the long-run adjustment; and it is framed in terms of budget rather than tax incidence.[3] As the tax is imposed, so argues Ricardo, there will be no change in the wage bill after tax. The private demand for labor remains unchanged, and government demand is added to it. As a result, the money wage rate before tax rises so that the wage bill net of tax remains unchanged. If we assume further that prices remain unchanged, the real

---

On the Principles of Political Economy and Taxation, ed. P. Sraffa, Cambridge University Press, New York, 1951. Also see Carl Shoup, "Ricardo on the Taxation of Profits," *Public Finance,* vol. 5, no. 2, pp. 1–18, 1950, and his forthcoming *Ricardo on Taxation,* Columbia University Press, New York, 1959.

[1] See Ricardo, *On the Principles of Political Economy and Taxation,* chap. 16.

[2] *Ibid.,* p. 226.

[3] The argument given in the text represents my interpretation of what Ricardo says. His discussion in chap. 16 is far from clear-cut.

wage bill remains unchanged as well.   Since the real wage bill remains unchanged, the requisite population needed to consume this wage bill at a subsistence wage remains unchanged.   With population unchanged, the employer cannot recompense himself for the increase in wage rates by raising prices; if he were to attempt this, the subsistence requirements of the fixed population would necessitate an increase in the net money wage rate.   Thus, the increase in wage rates must be absorbed in reduced profits.   Rent remains unchanged since population and the reward for agricultural produce is constant.

Let us consider more closely the assumption that introduction of the tax leaves unchanged the wage bill net of tax.   This, one might expect, reflects the idea of a given wage fund in real terms, consisting of consumer goods advanced to the workers—goods the supply of which cannot be reduced at once or transformed into other goods.[1]   But such is not Ricardo's explanation.   Money wage rates and the gross-wage bill are said to increase because aggregate demand for labor rises.   This comes about because the public demand for labor is added to a presumably unchanged level of private demand.   Ricardo's case is evidently one of budget incidence rather than of specific or differential tax incidence. There is no complaint about this, but it remains to be explained why insertion of the budget should raise total expenditures on labor.   For this result to come about, insertion of the circuit of taxes and public expenditures must be assumed to increase velocity of circulation.   More specifically, Ricardo's case implies the assumption that the transaction demand of the budget circuit equals zero.   It is interesting to note this early, if dubious, version of a balanced-budget theorem.[2]

Ricardo's monetary assumption only clouds the issue.   The essence of his argument is the assumption of an inelastic labor supply demanding that the wage bill in real terms remain constant.   Since rent remains unchanged as well, the decline in disposable real income must be absorbed by profits.   This result follows whether we assume total expenditures to increase, or whether we allow for transaction needs by government.   If the wage bill before tax remains unchanged in money terms, this implies a resulting decline in money wages after tax and a fall in the prices of consumer goods so as to maintain the real income of the wage earner. Here the cut in profits comes about by a decline in price, whereas in Ricardo's case it comes about by a rise in the money wage rate.

Whichever interpretation is applied, the crucial assumption, from which all the rest follows, is that of a fixed labor supply.   If this assumption is

[1] See text p. 392 for a similar assumption by Wicksell.

[2] There is, of course, a basic difference between this and later versions that involve a marginal propensity to spend of less than one in the private sector and finance by dishoarding.   (See text p. 432.)

relaxed, producers may at once begin to reduce real wages (by cutting money wages and/or raising prices) to protect their profits, thus forcing a decline in population.

Ricardo's long-run argument allows for a decline in population, but for a different reason. The curtailment of profits results in an impairment of real capital and a reduction in growth. Eventually this will reduce circulating as well as fixed capital and bring about a reduction in the demand for labor. Population declines, the price of corn falls, and wages tend to rise by less than the full amount of tax.[1]

As cultivation is reduced, rent falls and the landlord assumes a part of the burden. At first some decline in wages may be suffered without decline in population, as wages may be above subsistence in an expanding economy; and there is occasional recognition of the possibility that subsistence itself is a flexible concept.[2] But neither of these exceptions is given much weight. To the extent that accumulation *is* reduced, an eventual drop in population follows.

Ricardo does not consider the very long-run case of the stationary state, where profits have declined to zero; but we may readily conclude what happens in terms of his system. Here, a tax on wages must result in a reduction in population, thus reducing the margin of cultivation, raising gross wages, and curtailing rent. Once the stationary state is reached, little difference remains between the Ricardian and the physiocratic doctrine.

Taxes on Agriculture. Ricardo's treatment of agricultural taxes is a straightforward application of his rent doctrine. The principle of rent determination is the very opposite to that of wage determination. Whereas the supply of labor is infinitely elastic (in the long run) at the subsistence wage, the supply of land is wholly inelastic. No rent is obtained at the margin of cultivation or on the marginal land, where the product of labor just suffices to provide subsistence. Rent is a differential return, not a cost. Thus it does not enter into price but is determined by price.

Various types of taxes on land or its products are distinguished.[3] First, there is a unit tax on raw produce. Such a tax applies at the margin of cultivation and is added to price. Ricardo repeats the assumption, so crucial in his discussion of a tax on wages, that population is fixed, so that

---

[1] Ricardo, *On the Principles of Political Economy and Taxation*, p. 222.

[2] *Ibid.*, p. 215. Ricardo, in apparent agreement with Adam Smith, quotes him as follows: "The demand for labor, according as it happens to be either increasing, stationary or declining, or to require an increasing, stationary, or declining population, regulates the subsistence of the laborer, and determines in what degree it shall be either liberal, moderate or scanty." See Adam Smith, *The Wealth of Nations*, ed. E. Cannan, G. P. Putnam's Sons, New York, 1904, p. 348.

[3] Ricardo, *On the Principles of Political Economy and Taxation*, p. 157.

the demand for raw produce is inelastic.[1]   Accordingly rent is unaffected, and the price of raw produce rises by the amount of tax.   While money rent remains unchanged, rent in terms of corn declines in proportion to the increase in price.   Landlords are unaffected by the tax as recipients of rent, but they suffer as purchasers of agricultural products.   Again, we have here a nice illustration of Ricardo's awareness of the need for recognizing changes in real income positions from both the income sources and uses sides.[2]   To the extent that agricultural products are necessities consumed by workers, money wages must be raised to maintain real wages at subsistence levels.   The tax thus becomes similar to a tax on wages, and it falls on profits.

The incidence of the tithe, a tax on land based on the value of its raw produce, is essentially similar to that of a direct tax on raw produce.   A tax per acre of land also follows the same principle, as it raises the cost of production on the marginal land more sharply than on the superior land.   In addition, such a tax will increase the rent of superior land.   The price of corn per bushel rises by an amount equal to tax per marginal acre, divided by bushels produced on the marginal acre.   As the superior acre produces more bushels, the cost differential is increased.[3]

A tax on the pure *rent* of land, finally, falls on the landlord.   This readily follows from the very nature of rent.   However, a tax on rent is likely to include in its base the profits on capital invested in land.   To the extent that this is the case, the tax is similar to a tax on profits in certain trades only.

Tax on Profits.   The incidence of a tax on profits differs, depending on whether the tax is selective or general.

The burden of a general tax on profits, so argues Ricardo, must fall on profits.   Manufacturers or farmers cannot raise prices relative to wages, since wages are at subsistence level and the supply of labor is inelastic in the short run.   The farmer cannot reduce rent, since the tax applies to profits on capital in manufacture as well as in farming.   Hence, profits net of tax will be cut.   As with the wages tax, such reduction in profits will reduce real capital and, eventually, the demand for labor.

The mechanism by which profits are reduced differs, depending on whether or not the tax applies to the mining of precious metals.   If the tax so applies, the relative profitability of mining remains unchanged.   The money supply will not be increased.   As a result, prices in general cannot rise, and each producer must give up an equal proportion of his profit income.   If the mining of precious metals is not taxed, capital will flow into mining; the money supply will be increased; and all prices,

[1] For a criticism of this assumption, see Alfred Marshall, *op. cit.*, pp. 833–837.
[2] See pp. 217 and 380, note 2.
[3] Ricardo, *On the Principles of Political Economy and Taxation*, p. 182.

including wages and rent, will rise.   Profits after tax remain unchanged in money terms.   This does not mean that all prices will rise at the same rate.   If profits are to remain unchanged in money terms, prices must rise more sharply in the case of products that have a low turnover rate.[1]

Somewhat as an afterthought, Ricardo queries his earlier judgment that increased prices *will* require increased circulation.[2]   No increase in circulation is required if the government purchases products from the same sellers from whom it collects the tax, so that the tax and purchase payments may be taken to cancel out.   As a result, consumers will be able to purchase the smaller amount available to them at higher prices, without requiring an increase in money supply.   In any case, Ricardo adds that a general rise in prices is possible in the closed economy only.   If the mining of precious metals is carried on abroad, all prices cannot rise.   Or, to say the least, no permanent rise in prices can occur since this would result in an adverse balance of trade and an outflow of bullion.

In the case of a partial profits tax, which applies to some industries only, the price of the product must rise for the taxed industry in order to restore the level of profits to that of tax-free industries.   Ricardo does not seem to allow for recovery of profits due to reduction of supply and reduced unit cost in the taxed industry, thereby neglecting the spillover effect of a partial tax on profits at large.[3]

A distinct and ingenious argument applies to the landlord's attitude with regard to a tax on profits.[4]   If the tax on profits excludes profits on capital invested in agriculture, the price of corn does not rise.   Money rent and rent in terms of corn remain unchanged.   The landlord, however, loses from such a tax as a consumer of nonagricultural products.   Now, let the profits of agricultural capital be included in the tax base.   The tenant (who invests the capital in the land he rents from the landlord) is indifferent to such a tax, since he recoups the tax by raising the price of raw produce.   The landlord gains, since money rents rise at the

---

[1] See Ricardo, *On the Principles of Political Economy and Taxation*, p. 207.   See also text p. 280, note 3; and Shoup, *op. cit.*

[2] Ricardo, *On the Principles of Political Economy and Taxation*, p. 213, note *.   See also Ricardo's discussion with Trower, *Letters*, p. 321.   On text p. 367, we concluded that introduction of a budget with income tax and a constant money supply will result in a reduced price level, but we added that the price level will remain unchanged if source withholding is assumed.   Ricardo goes one better by assuming not only that tax payments are substituted for income payments, as is implied in source withholding, but also that the public expenditure itself involves no drain on transaction funds. If this assumption is made, introduction of the budget with constant money supply leads to Ricardo's result of a rising price level.

[3] Ricardo, *On the Principles of Political Economy and Taxation*, pp. 205 and 213.

[4] *Ibid.*, pp. 210ff.

same rate as the price of raw produce.[1]   Hence, Ricardo's intriguing conclusion that "by taxing profits of the farmer you do not burden him more than if you exempted his profits from the tax, and the landlord has a decided interest that his tenants' profits should be taxed, as it is only on that condition that he himself continues really untaxed."[2]

Tax on Manufactured Products.   The incidence of a tax on products has already been dealt with under the tax on raw produce.   The principle is the same for a tax on manufactured products.   As the tax is imposed, the price of the taxed product is increased.   Where the product is in the luxury class, the tax is borne by the consumer.   Where it is a necessity consumed by the laborer, the tax is equivalent to a tax on wages and, hence, to a tax on profits.   In order to maintain wages at subsistence, the wage rate must be increased and profits reduced accordingly.

The Ricardian theory of incidence is unique in elegance and positiveness of result.   Especially impressive is the consistent view of the problem in general-equilibrium terms and the allowance for changes on both the sources and uses side of income positions.   Yet the results can be no better than the underlying theory of distribution.[3]   The most serious deficiency, of the latter lies in the theory of wages.   The Malthusian doctrine has proven false as a principle of wage determination in the Western world. The underlying assumptions as to population behavior are incorrect, and steady gains in technique have far outstripped the pressure of a growing population on resources.[4]   Ricardo's subsistence theory of wages, therefore, had to be replaced by an entirely different principle of wage determination, based on the product of labor rather than its cost of production. With this restatement of wage theory, Ricardo's argument on the incidence of a tax on wages becomes untenable in both the short- and the

---

[1] The argument is similar to the argument for the tax on land.   The increase in the price of produce must be sufficient to restore profits on the marginal dose of labor and capital.   Since the intramarginal doses produce a larger amount of product, the increase in price provides for more than is needed to restore these profits to the level of profits earned on the marginal dose.   Since the return must be the same in all doses, the excess goes to the landlord in the form of increased rent.

[2] Ricardo, *On the Principles of Political Economy and Taxation*, p. 213.

[3] See on this point Schumpeter's uncharitable judgment that Ricardo's theory is an excellent one which can never be refuted and lacks nothing but sense.   I am tempted to say that the theory is a sensible one which has been disproven by history. See Joseph Schumpeter, "Review of the Troops," *Quarterly Journal of Economics*, vol. 65, no. 2, p. 161, May, 1951.

[4] In undeveloped countries—indeed, for areas containing the larger part of the world's population—the population problem is still of great importance, and the Malthusian doctrine cannot be written off so readily.   However, even in this setting, the Ricardian argument is hardly tenable.   There are degrees of subsistence or star- vation wages, providing a range of adjustment that may well shield profit until pop- ulation adjustments occur.   Political attitudes may be such as to exclude a tax on already excessively low wages, but this is a different matter.

long-run version; the same holds for the incidence of a product tax on necessities, agricultural or otherwise.

Similarly, Ricardo's argument on the incidence of a general tax on profits becomes shaky as his theory of determination of profits as a residual is replaced by a productivity theory of capital income. Only the rent principle is salvaged unharmed from the Ricardian toolbox; and even this must be reinterpreted as a general principle, applicable to all factors that are inelastic in supply. Ricardo's attempt at a general and determinate theory of incidence, beautiful and heroic though it was, had to make way for a more complex, if less manageable and determinate, formulation of the problem.

Wicksell

A second attempt at a general-equilibrium theory of incidence was made some seventy years later by Wicksell. As in the Ricardian case, it reflected the structure of a very specific model of distribution theory.[1]

While the Ricardian system still lacked an explicit theory of capital income, Wicksell developed such a theory along Böhm-Bawerk's lines: Capital renders a productive service because the advancing of capital permits the employment of labor in roundabout production, thereby raising total output obtained from a given labor input. Wicksell focused primary attention on the relationship between output and the degree of roundaboutness or, to put it somewhat differently, on the length of the investment period. In order to explore this relationship, the supply of free capital that constitutes the subsistence fund is taken as given. The problem is to determine the average length of the investment period that makes for the most efficient employment of this fund. While Wicksell emphasized the nature of this fund as a wage and rent fund, let us consider here the simpler case where the services of land are forthcoming free of charge, in which case the subsistence fund is a wage fund.

Wicksell's line of reasoning took an important step toward a marginal-productivity theory of factor shares. However, the marginal-productivity tool was still crippled by the limitations resulting from the arbitrary assumption of a fixed wage fund. A satisfactory theory of interest, and hence wages, could be developed only after the supply of capital itself became a dependent variable, to be determined by the system.[2] Wicksell's analysis preceded this break-through in distribution theory; and his

[1] I am indebted to Dr. H. Geyer and Dr. W. P. Yohe for help in arriving at this interpretation of the Wicksellian case.

[2] Lutz, in his analysis of this development, shows how a proper formulation of the problem could not be achieved without making the wage fund a dependent variable. If this is done, the problem becomes one of saving and investment (with or without liquidity preference), and the wage-fund concept is rejected. See Friedrich A. Lutz, *Zinstheorie*, Polygraphischer Verlag, Zurich, 1956, especially chaps. 1-7.

results on incidence still reflect the peculiar assumption of a fixed wage fund.

System without Tax.   Wicksell's basic system is given by four equations.[1]   The first of these is the production function

$$P = f(t) = at^m \qquad (16\text{-}1)$$

where P is the product per worker, t is the average period of investment, and $a > 0$ and $m < 1$ are given parameters describing the relationship between P and t.   The shape of this relationship is such that output per worker increases at a decreasing rate as t rises.

The second equation of the system is definitional and divides the product into factor shares:

$$P = L + ZLt \qquad (16\text{-}2)$$

where L is the wage income per worker, Z is the rate of interest, and Lt is the investment per worker.   Thus, the product per worker is divided between wage income per worker received by the worker and capital income per worker received by the capitalist.

The third equation is given by the wage-fund relation

$$LA = \frac{K}{t} \qquad (16\text{-}3)$$

where A is the number of workers and K is the capital stock.   The equation tells us that the wage fund, or the available wage bill per period, must equal the product of wage per worker and number of workers employed. In other words, the entire wage fund must be employed in the purchase of labor.   As Wicksell points out, the wage fund cannot be used in any other way.[2]

The fourth equation is given by the profit-maximizing condition

$$\frac{dZ}{dt} = 0 \qquad \text{with} \qquad \frac{d^2Z}{dt^2} < 0 \qquad (16\text{-}4)$$

which tells us that the capitalist, who controls the wage fund, lengthens the period of investment up to a point where the rate of interest reaches a

---

[1] A brief statement of the system is given in Wicksell's *Finanztheoretische Untersuchungen und das Steuerwesen Schweden's*, Jena, Germany, 1896, pp. 21–75.   For a more detailed presentation, see Wicksell's *Value, Capital and Rent*, originally published 1893, trans. S. H. Frowein, George Allen & Unwin, Ltd., London, 1954.   For a critical discussion and evaluation, see George J. Stigler, *Production and Distribution Theories: The Formative Period*, The Macmillan Company, New York, 1941, chap. 10; and K. G. Landgren, "Wicksell och gränsproduktivitetsläran," in *Twenty-five Economic Essays in Honour of Erik Lindahl*, Ekonomisk Tidskrift, Stockholm, 1956, pp. 186–203.

[2] Wicksell, *Finanztheoretische Untersuchungen und das Steuerwesen Schweden's*, pp. 21–42.

maximum for any given value of L.   Given a, m, A, and K, the system permits us to determine P, L, t, and Z.

A diagrammatic view of the system is given in Figure 16-1.*   Let us measure P on the vertical axis and t to the right of O on the horizontal axis.   The curve OS is the production function as defined by equation (16-1).   Now let us assume some value of L so that OD of the product goes

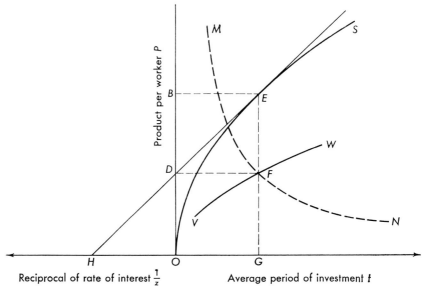

FIG. 16-1. Wicksellian equilibrium without tax.

to labor.   Capitalists will choose that value of t at which Z is maximized. This value of t is found for the given value of L by drawing a tangent to OS through D.   We thus obtain $t = OG$ and $1/Z = HO$.†   For any value

* The figure is similar to Wicksell's in *Finanztheoretische Untersuchungen und das Steuerwesen Schweden's*, p. 40, with the addition of the VW and MN curves, which may be found in Ursula K. Webb (Hicks), "Taxation and Production: The Wicksell Analysis," *Review of Economic Studies*, vol. 2, no. 1, pp. 18–30, October, 1934.

† We have $HO/DF = OD/EF$ from similar triangles; and since $DF = OG$ and $OD = GF$, we obtain

$$HO \cdot EF = OG \cdot GF \text{ or } HO = \frac{OG \cdot GF}{EF}$$

or

$$HO = \frac{OG \cdot GF}{GE - GF}$$

Since $OG \cdot GF$ is equal to $K/A = tL$, and since $GE - GF$ equals the capital share or $Z(K/A)$ we have

$$HO = \frac{K/A}{Z(K/A)} = \frac{1}{Z}$$

of t larger or smaller than OG, we find that $1/Z = HO$ is increased, and hence Z is reduced. We may now undertake the same experiment for other assumed values of L and derive corresponding optimal values of t. Let the locus of these points be described by the line VW. This much we may derive from equations (16-1), (16-2), and (16-4) of the system.

In order to determine which combination of t and L will be chosen, we must draw upon equation (16-3). Since K and A are given, the value of Lt is given. Measuring L on the vertical axis, we obtain the rectangular hyperbola MN, which shows the possible combinations of L and t. The solution is found at F, the intersection of VW and MN. If we were located at point W, the value of tL would exceed the available capital per worker, or K/A. Hence, some workers become unemployed, and wages would be bid down. If we were at a point such as V, part of the wage fund would be unemployed, and wages would be bid up. F is the only possible solution. Here the product per worker $P = GE$. The wage per worker $L = GF$. The capital income per worker is $KZ/A = FE$. The average period of investment or $t = OG$, and $Z = 1/OH$.

Leaving the diagrammatic view, we may determine the equilibrium value of t analytically. Setting the right sides of equations (16-1) and (16-2) equal to each other, substituting equation (16-3) for L into this expression, and solving for Z, we obtain

$$Z = \frac{aAt^m}{K} - t^{-1} \qquad (16\text{-}5)$$

Differentiating for t, we obtain

$$\frac{dZ}{dt} = \frac{maAt^{m-1}}{K} + t^{-2} \qquad (16\text{-}6)$$

and by setting equal to zero, we can solve for t. This is as far as the matter need be carried for our purposes, since equation (16-6) may be compared with the corresponding expression if a tax applies.

System with Income Tax. Now suppose that an income tax is imposed and that part of the product is purchased by the government. Equation (16-1) remains unchanged, it being assumed that there is only one product or that total output is independent of the composition of the product. Equation (16-2) may now be written as

$$P = (1 - r)(L + ZLt) + r(L + ZLt) \qquad (16\text{-}2i)$$

where r is the tax rate. Total factor earnings equal to P now comprise the part retained by the recipients, or $(1 - r)(L + ZLt)$, and the part they pay in tax, or $r(L + ZLt)$. Equation (16-3) is unchanged, owing to the assumption that introduction of the tax must not be permitted to reduce the wage fund.   Equation (16-4) may be rewritten as

$$\frac{dZ}{dt}(1 - r) = 0 \qquad \text{with} \qquad \frac{d^2Z}{dt^2} < 0 \qquad (16\text{-}4i)$$

since the capitalist tries to maximize interest net of tax, although the same result is obtained if we leave equation (16-4) unchanged.   Proceeding as before, we obtain

$$\frac{dZ}{dt}(1 - r) = \left(\frac{maAt^{m-1}}{K} + t^{-2}\right)(1 - r) \qquad (16\text{-}6i)$$

Since $(1 - r)$ cancels out, we again have equation (16-6).   The value of t is the same as in the absence of tax.   Output is unchanged, and the recipients of wage and capital income find their disposable income reduced by the rate of tax.   Given inelastic factor supplies, the same result is obtained if factor shares are determined by a marginal-productivity theory.   The wage-fund doctrine, in this case, leaves the outcome unaffected.

System with Production Tax.   The wage-fund doctrine affects the outcome, however, if we deal with a tax on production or gross receipts. If we impose a production tax at rate r, we have

$$p = (1 - r)P \qquad (16\text{-}7)$$

where p is the net product.   Or, substituting from (16-1),

$$p = (1 - r)at^m \qquad (16\text{-}1p)$$

becomes our first equation, now defined in terms of *net* product.   Since only the net product is available for distribution to factors, we may rewrite equation (16-2) as

$$p = L + ZLt \qquad (16\text{-}2p)$$

Equation (16-3) is unchanged, since the wage fund is assumed to remain intact.   Substituting as before, we obtain

$$Z = \frac{(1 - r)aA}{K} t^m - t^{-1} \qquad (16\text{-}5p)$$

and differentiating for t

$$\frac{dZ}{dt} = \frac{m(1 - r)aA}{K} t^{m-1} + t^{-2} \qquad (16\text{-}6p)$$

We may now compare the right term in equation (16-6p) with the corresponding expression in the absence of tax, as given in equation (16-6). The term maA/K is the same in both cases, but it is multiplied by $(1 - r)$ in the case of the production tax.   Since both expressions are set equal to zero, the value of t must be larger with the production tax. Thus, the production tax leads to a lengthening of t. With the increase in t, we have an increase in P, as shown by equation (16-1); a decrease in L as shown by equation (16-3); and a decrease in Z as shown by equation (16-5p), where $M < 1$. The extent to which L and Z are decreased, respectively, depends on the slope of the production function.[1]

The case of the production tax is shown diagrammatically in Figure 16-2. As a 50 per cent tax is imposed, the product available for allocation to factors at various levels of t is reduced from OS to OR. The latter is the net production function as defined by equation (16-1p). The

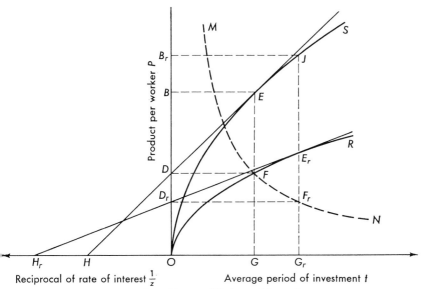

FIG. 16-2. Wicksellian equilibrium with product tax.

wage-fund equation, and hence the curve MN, are, by assumption, unchanged. Thus the new equilibrium F_r must again lie on MN, but wages are reduced to D_r, the rate of interest has fallen from $1/OH$ to $1/OH_r$, and output has risen from OB to OB_r. In the new equilibrium, tax payments per worker are equal to E_rJ, wages per worker, or L, are equal to G_rF_r and the capital income per worker equals F_rE_r. Given the parameters assumed for the diagram, capital income is reduced more sharply than wage income. If the OS schedule had been drawn with a more nearly constant slope to the right of E, then t would have been lengthened further and L would have been reduced more sharply.

We thus obtain the strange result that a tax on production leads to a

[1] See Wicksell, *Finanztheoretische Untersuchungen und das Steuerwesen Schweden's*, p. 41.

change in the structure of production and possibly unequal reductions in factor shares; whereas an income tax leaves production unchanged and merely reduces the disposable income of both factors proportionately. According to marginal-productivity reasoning, this cannot be the case. If a product tax is introduced, it enters as a wedge between gross and net product, and is charged equally against both factors. Output and gross earnings of factors remain unchanged, net earnings are reduced by the rate of tax, and the outcome is similar to that of an income tax. This, of course, assumes that factor supplies are inelastic in both cases.

A result similar to that of marginal-productivity reasoning is obtained from the four basic equations if we assume that the wage fund is reduced by the rate of the production tax, in which case t will remain unchanged.[1]

---

[1] We again have, as in eq. (16-1p),

$$p = (1 - r)at^m$$

where p is the net product. Equation (16-2p) is now written as

$$p = l(1 + zt)$$

where l and z are net wage and interest, respectively. Now, we may write

$$L(1 - x) = l$$

where L is the gross wage paid out of the gross-wage fund K, and l is the net wage that remains after a tax at rate x is charged against it. Note that the wedge between gross and net wage is defined as x, since it remains to be seen whether or not $x = r$. Substituting into eq. (16-3) we obtain

$$l = \frac{K(1 - x)}{At}$$

This equation, it will be noted, relates net wages received by workers to a net wages fund curtailed by a tax at rate x. It differs from the previously used eq. (16-3), according to which the entire wages fund K remains tied up in the employment of workers.

Substituting as before and solving for z, we obtain the following equation corresponding to (16-5p):

$$z = \frac{(1 - r)aAt^m}{(1 - x)K} - \frac{1}{t}$$

and

$$\frac{dz}{dt} = \frac{ma(1 - r)At^{m-1}}{(1 - x)K} + t^{-2}$$

corresponding to eq. (16-6p). If $r = x$, the value for dz/dt as defined by the preceding equation is the same as defined by the pre-tax eq. (16-6). Hence t remains unchanged. An independent consideration, based on marginal-productivity reasoning, tells us that x must be equal to r because in a competitive market the tax must be shared by the factors in proportion to their marginal productivity. Thus, we find that the production tax leaves t unchanged.

While the argument of this footnote may help the reader to understand the Wicksellian problem, it should be kept in mind that this line of reasoning is not permissible in the Wicksellian system since it mixes the logic of marginal-productivity reasoning with the apparent setting of a wage-fund doctrine.

The production tax and the income tax then become equivalent in their effect on output and disposable incomes.   This result makes sense, but a reduction in the wage fund is not permissible in the spirit of the Wicksellian system.   Once the determination of the wage fund is made part of the system, rather than taken as fixed, the entire concept of the wage fund might as well be discarded.   In the Wicksellian system, K must remain unchanged.   The capitalist cannot recoup possible losses in capital income by reducing the wage fund that he advances to labor. The only way in which he can meet the tax is by raising P via an adjustment in t.   Such an adjustment becomes profitable because the tax has reduced dZ/dt at the old value of t, as shown by comparing equations (16-6) and (16-6p).   As t is lengthened, L is cut.   Labor is made to carry part of the burden by having payments out of the fixed wage fund spread over a longer period.   This the capitalist can do, even though he is not permitted to curtail the total wage fund that he advances to labor.[1]

Thus the Wicksellian treatment of incidence makes an interesting case study of the wage-fund doctrine, but, as in the Ricardian approach, the conclusion can be no better than the underlying theory of distribution.

Walras

Walras devotes the closing lesson of his *Elements* to an analysis of incidence.   He considers an economy of landowners, workers, and

---

[1] In discussing the Wicksellian model, Erik Lindahl, *Die Gerechtigkeit der Besteuerung*, Gleerupska, Lund, Sweden, 1919, p. 177, note 1, observes correctly that Wicksell's peculiar result is arrived at because the wage fund is assumed to remain constant.   He interprets this to mean that real capital is increased, in the sense that the capitalist is willing to advance the *entire* amount of tax out of his capital income.   Lindahl adds that it is more reasonable to assume that the capitalist will reduce the wage fund by the rate of tax, which returns us to the case of the preceding footnote.

This interpretation, as well as that of Mrs. Hicks, *op. cit.*, focuses on the question of finance during the interim period of adjustment to the tax.   But this is hardly the basic problem.   Let us assume that the producer, once the tax is announced, makes all the correct adjustments and compares the new with the old equilibrium position. Since Wicksell's model is static, this is permissible.   The basic objection to the assumption of a constant wage fund, in this case, is quite independent of the problem of transition finance.   It arises because the fund itself is not determined as a part of the system.

For the same reason, it does not seem legitimate to postulate, as a possible alternative behavior assumption, that the capitalist will reduce his wage fund by the rate of tax. If he did so, the determination of the fund would be based on an economic calculus that is incompatible with the essence of the wage-fund theory.   Moreover, such adjustment might be made in response to the income tax as well.   In brief, there is no way of retaining the wage fund while arguing in terms of a marginal-productivity doctrine.

A dynamic element compatible with the wage-fund doctrine might be added with the capitalist's propensity to save and a relating of the wage fund to his disposable income; but if this is done, the fund, and hence t, may change under both types of tax.

capitalists.[1]   The government can collect its taxes directly by cutting into the income received by these three groups.   Or it may collect the tax in advance from the entrepreneurs prior to the distribution of earnings to the factors, "it being clearly understood that they [entrepreneurs] will reimburse themselves by adding the amount of the tax to the prices of the products which they sell to landowners, workers and capitalists.   In this way, the reduction in rent, wages and interest is made indirectly.   Direct taxes are levied on services, and indirect taxes are levied on products."[2]

A personal tax on wage income cannot change the price obtained for a given supply of labor in the market.   As a result of the tax, the supply of labor may rise or fall; but which will be the case we do not know.   Nor do we know whether the wage bill will rise or fall with any given change in labor supply.   If these eventualities are disregarded, and we assume labor supply unchanged, the burden of the tax will fall entirely on the workers. An exception arises where wages are at the subsistence level and the tax is passed on to consumers through a reduction in the labor force.

A tax on rent falls on the income of the landowner.   If the tax is levied in perpetuity, it is equivalent to a confiscation of a part of the land. Thus, if the tax rate equals 50 per cent, the owner of the land when the tax is introduced loses half of his income as well as half of his capital. After the land has changed hands, the tax, as noted before, is said to be paid by no one.[3]   This phenomenon of capitalization cannot arise in the case of labor, since labor can be sold only as a service, and the worker himself cannot be sold as a capital asset.

If a tax is imposed on the income from all capital goods, the income of capitalists is reduced.   As a result, so argues Walras, savings may rise or fall.   If we assume them to remain unchanged, we must conclude that the tax falls on the capitalist.   The situation differs if the tax is imposed on income from selected capital goods only.   If capital only in industry Y is taxed, the supply of capital to this industry will decrease, the price of product Y will rise, and the consumers of Y will bear the tax.   However, a portion of the tax will be borne by the capitalists.   Capital will flow to other industries, resulting in a general decline in capital income and a reduction in the prices of other goods, thus enabling consumers to recover part of the loss suffered from the rise in the price of Y.   While Walras recognizes the spillover effect of a tax on capital earnings in a particular industry, he does not conclude, as he should, that there is no a priori reason why a selective tax on capital income should be more or less detrimental to the consumer and more favorable to capitalists as a group

[1] Leon Walras, *Elements of Pure Economics*, trans. W. Jaffe, George Allen & Unwin, Ltd., London, 1954.

[2] *Ibid.*, p. 450.

[3] See p. 385, note 2.

than a general but equal-yield tax on capital income.[1]   With this exception, the Walrasian lesson on incidence is unobjectionable, but unfortunately, it presents a rather sketchy treatment of the problem.

[1] It may be noted that prior to the third edition Walras, like Ricardo, made no allowance whatsoever for the spillover effect, but concluded that the entire tax was to be borne by the consumer of the product supplied by the industry in which capital is taxed.   See Walras, *op. cit.*, p. 609.

PART FOUR

Compensatory finance

CHAPTER 17

Income determination and the theory of stabilization

Let us now turn to the problems of the Stabilization Branch, involving the effects of budget policy upon employment, price level, and growth. Here we shall deal with systems where the simple classical relationship between money supply and money expenditure is broken by liquidity preference, and where money wages or prices may be rigid in the downward direction. For these and other reasons, the economy may deviate from full employment and price-level stability, and public policy must concern itself with preventing or discouraging such deviations. This is by no means a matter of budget policy or of budget and monetary policy alone. At the same time, the modern budget takes up a large share of total income, and budget policy is bound to have a major effect upon output and prices. Budget policy, accordingly, must play a major role in stabilization policy. Since the mid-thirties, this role has been explored extensively in the literature on fiscal policy and compensatory or functional finance—all terms that are more or less synonymous with the function of our Stabilization Branch.[1]

The vital importance of this function must be recognized. Yet the classical functions of budget policy, involving matters of allocation and distribution, must not be forgotten in the process. Stabilization policy is an additional, not an alternative, consideration. In the following discussion of stabilization, we shall ask repeatedly how the objectives of the Stabilization Branch may be pursued best without conflict with those of the other branches.[2]

[1] See p. 22.
[2] See pp. 37 and 517.

A. OBJECTIVES

By way of introduction, let us take a brief look at the major objectives of the Stabilization Branch, that is, the maintenance of price-level stability and full employment.

The objective of price-level stability needs no lengthy defense. To be sure, there are times when some increase in price level may be desirable to induce entrepreneurial optimism, or a more substantial rise may be needed to speed up transition to a war economy; and there are other times when a decline in price level may be useful, for example, in order to adjust to world markets, to release an excessive margin of profits, or to pass on technological gains where rising money wages cannot be secured. Short of these special situations, price-level stability is desirable.

Changes in the price level involve arbitrary changes in relative prices and distribution, hardly in line with the objectives of the Distribution Branch. They also introduce uncertainties into the economic scene that should be avoided in an orderly economy.

Similarly, we may take it for granted that the objective of full employment is desirable. While there will always be a number of people who are in transition between jobs, it is only reasonable to demand of an orderly economy that people should not be exposed to the calamity of involuntary unemployment beyond such transitional situations. What is more, the prevention of unemployment is a condition for the social stability of the economic system itself. These are elementary facts, which must not be overlooked in the search for details on just how unemployment should be measured and how full employment should be defined at the technical level.[1] While full employment and price-level stability may not be readily compatible, this does not void the proposition that both are desirable as such.

The dual objective of price-level stability and full employment is referred to usually as stabilization. This is somewhat misleading, since stabilization of full employment does not imply stabilization of output. With a growing capital stock, labor force, and technique, maintenance of full employment and price-level stability requires maintenance of an equilibrium rate of growth. Thus the problem of growth becomes an integral part of stabilization policy.

This much is clear; but growth as a third policy objective raises more difficult problems. While it is obviously desirable to secure any given rate of growth at a minimum cost, this is not to say that one should secure

---

[1] For a compact discussion of the problem of measuring unemployment and of defining full employment, see the paper and references given by Albert Rees, "The Meaning and Measurement of Full Employment," in *The Measurement and Behavior of Unemployment*, National Bureau of Economic Research, Inc., New York, 1957.

a maximum rate of growth, whatever its cost.   In the classical system, the rate of growth is determined in the market, involving the time preference of consumers on the one side and the efficiency of investment on the other.   The rate of growth thus determined may be considered optimal in the sense of being sanctioned by the effective time preference of consumers with a given distribution of income.   This happy solution is lost in a system where Say's law does not hold, and compensatory measures of public policy are required to assure stability.[1]

In the process of maintaining price-level stability and full employment, public policy also influences the rate of growth.   But various patterns of stabilization policy may lead to different rates of growth, and the choice between them becomes a matter of public policy rather than determination by the market.   It is for this reason that the neoclassical system cannot return us to the benign state of the classical case, even if we assume that full employment and price-level stability can be assured.[2]

Moreover, it remains to be seen whether any particular growth objective is compatible with the objectives of full employment and price-level stability; and there may be conflicts between the desired rate of growth and the policies pursued by the Allocation and Distribution Branches. Throughout the following chapters, this multiplicity of objectives and their interdependence must be kept in mind.

B. THE STRUCTURE OF INCOME DETERMINATION AND THE ROLE OF MONETARY AND FISCAL POLICY

The theory of stabilization policy—fiscal or monetary—cannot be developed in a vacuum.   It must be defined with reference to the system of income determination that applies in the economy under consideration. Thus it will be well to introduce the more detailed discussion of compensatory finance by a general view of the relationship between income theory and the theory of stabilization.

The Classical System

It has become customary to distinguish between the classical system, the Keynesian system, and various combinations of the two.[3]   Let us

---

[1] See p. 483.

[2] See p. 553.

[3] For similar discussions, see Gottfried Haberler, *Prosperity and Depression*, 3d ed., League of Nations, Geneva, 1941, chap. 8; Lawrence R. Klein, *The Keynesian Revolution*, The Macmillan Company, New York, 1947, pp. 199ff; Franco Modigliani, "Liquidity Preference and the Theory of Interest and Money," *Econometrica*, vol. 12, no. 1, pp. 45–88, January, 1944, reprinted in Friedrich A. Lutz and Lloyd W. Mints (eds.), *Readings in Monetary Theory*, American Economic Association, Richard D. Irwin, Inc., Homewood, Ill., 1951, pp. 186–239; Don Patinkin, *Money, Interest, and Prices,*

begin with the so-called classical system. The system described in equations (17-1) to (17-8) differs slightly from what is usually understood by the classical system, since saving here is made a function of income as well as interest. Thus the system is made somewhat more realistic without affecting its essential properties. Also, it will be noted that classical writers were more intelligent in their understanding of income theory than their system suggests. They were much concerned with the importance of capital formation and growth, and they were by no means unaware of the possibility of hoarding and dishoarding.[1]

The modified classical system here used is composed of the following equations:

$$S = S(i,Y) \tag{17-1}$$
$$I = I(i) \tag{17-2}$$
$$S(i,Y) = I(i) \tag{17-3}$$
$$Y = Y(N) \tag{17-4}$$
$$N = N(W) \tag{17-5}$$
$$W = Y'(N) \tag{17-6}$$
$$Y_m = \bar{V}\bar{M} \tag{17-7}$$
$$Y_m = PY \tag{17-8}$$

Given $\bar{V}$ and $\bar{M}$, the system of eight equations permits us to determine $S, I, i, Y, N, W, Y_m,$ and P. To this we may add the definitional equation

$$Y = C + I \tag{17-9}$$

to determine consumption.

All equations, with the exception of (17-7) and (17-8), are in real terms. The level of real output, or income Y, is determined as a function of labor input N, as shown in equation (17-4). The labor supply N, is a function of the real-wage rate W, as shown by equation (17-5). The real wage W equals the marginal product of labor which, for a given capital stock, is a function of N. This is shown by equation (17-6). Together, these three equations determine Y, W, and N. Saving S is a function of the rate of interest i and Y, as shown by equation (17-1). Investment I is a function of the rate of interest i as shown by equation (17-2). Saving and investment, as determined by these functions, are equated in equilibrium, as shown by equation (17-3). Given Y, these three equations determine S, I, and i. Consumption C follows from the budget equation (17-9).

Row, Peterson & Company, Evanston, Ill., 1956; and Challis A. Hall and James E. Tobin, "Income Taxation, Output and Prices," *Economia Internazionale*, vol. 8, no. 3, pp. 527–532, August, 1955, also vol. 8, no. 4, pp. 751–755, November, 1955, and vol. 9, no. 1, pp. 1–8, February, 1956.

[1] See Jean Baptiste Say, *Treatise on Political Economy*, trans. C. R. Prinsep, Claxton, Philadelphia, 1869, p. 133. Also see Jacob Viner, *Studies in the Theory of International Trade*, Harper & Brothers, New York, 1937, especially pp. 185ff.

The level of employment and output, as well as the division of the product between consumption and investment, are determined by a system that is altogether in real terms.   Given the functional relationships involved, equations (17-1) to (17-6) permit us to determine $Y, I, S, i, N,$ and W, all defined in real terms.   Addition of equation (17-9) permits the determination of C.

While the interesting properties of the system are determined independently of money, the system does not apply to a barter economy only. Given the money supply $\bar{M}$ and the income velocity $\bar{V}$, the level of money income Y_m is determined by equation (17-7), and the price level

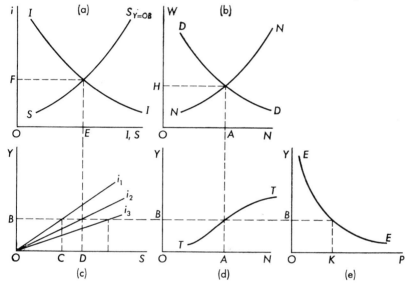

FIG. 17-1. Income determination in the classical system.

P by (17-8).   Given P, the money values C_m, S_m, and I_m may be determined readily from C, S, and I.   In other words, the real values of the system may be translated into money values by adding the equation of exchange, where $\bar{V}$ is given by the structure of existing payment institutions.   This can be done because there is no liquidity preference, and all money is in the form of transaction money, the velocity of which is determined by institutional factors.   Thus the monetary part of the system is added to the real part but has no bearing on the real issues involved.   This procedure has been criticized in recent years as leaving us with an inconsistent system, but I am not at all persuaded that such is the case.[1]

The system is shown diagrammatically in Figure 17-1. NN in Figure 17-1b is the labor-supply schedule as defined by equation (17-5) and DD is

[1] See p. 427.

the demand schedule for labor as defined by equation (17-6). The equilibrium level of employment equals OA, and the real-wage rate equals OH. Let TT in Figure 17-1d show real output as a function of employment N, as defined in equation (17-4). With employment at OA, output equals OB. In Figure 17-1c we plot the relationship between saving, income, and the rate of interest, as defined by equation (17-1). Each line shows saving at various levels of income and a given rate of interest. Assuming a positive relationship between i and S, we have $i_1 < i_2 < i_3$. At income OB, saving with $i = i_1$ is OC; saving with $i = i_2$ is OD; and so forth. These results are plotted in Figure 17-1a, where SS shows the level of saving out of income OB at various rates of interest. II shows investment as a function of interest as defined in equation (17-2). We know from equation (17-3) that saving and investment thus defined must be equal, which is the case at OE. The rate of interest accordingly is $OF = i_2$. Note that the determination of output and employment in Figure 17-1b and d must precede the determination of investment in Figure 17-1a and c. A causal link in the reverse direction can come about only if the model is expanded to allow for the effects of capital accumulation on the production function.

All these variables are in real terms. The translation into money terms is given in Figure 17-1e. With $\bar{V}$ and $\bar{M}$ given, total money income is constant. As shown by equations (17-7) and (17-8), the relationship between price level and output is given by the constant expenditure line EE. With output or real income equal to OB, the price level equals OK, and money income equals OB times OK.

It is usually said that the classical model is one which must equilibrate at a full-employment level of output. Such is the case for the system just described. Note, however, that this is so only if the relationships expressed in equations (17-1) and (17-2) are such that the savings schedule out of a full-employment level of income, as plotted in Figure 17-1a, *will* intersect the I schedule at a feasible rate of interest.[1] If this is the case, there can be no involuntary unemployment. Workers can work the number of hours they wish to work at the real-wage rate paid for various levels of labor input.

Consider the effects of monetary and fiscal policy in such a system. Let us suppose that the government increases the money supply.[2] Since

[1] See p. 413 for what happens if these conditions are not met.

[2] The question arises just how the money supply is increased. This may be accomplished by open-market operations or, if fractional-reserve banking is assumed, by reduction of reserve requirements. Alternatively, we may assume that monetary policy takes the form of "money rain," an additional supply of bills dropped from airplanes. This assumption causes no difficulty in the classical system, but complicates the distinction between monetary and fiscal policy in the Keynesian system. See p. 415, note 1, and p. 528.

total output is fixed by the real part of the system, it cannot be affected. The entire change in money supply will be reflected in a change in transaction money. With constant V, the change in money supply results in a proportional change in the level of money expenditure or income. With output constant, this means a proportionate change in the price level. The quantity theory of money holds in the narrow sense of the term.

Turning to the effects of budget policy, consider what happens in the case of an equal expansion in government expenditures and tax receipts. Real output and employment cannot change, nor can the total level of money payments. Whether the level of product prices rises or not depends on the type of tax used and its relation to the structure of payments.[1] Since the propensity to spend on consumption and investment equals unity for the private sector, there is no difference, in the short run, between the price-level effects of tax and loan finance. Budget expansion financed by an increase in money supply, finally, raises the price level as does monetary expansion proper, that is, the case of money rain.

At the same time, note that the various policies may have different effects upon the division of the private product between consumption and capital formation in the private sector. If we adjust the model to allow for growth as a function of capital formation, different rates of growth will result. Assuming the marginal propensities of consumers to differ, growth effects will depend on resulting changes in distribution. In the case of money rain, the result will differ depending on who finds it. In the case of tax increase, the result will differ depending on who pays it. Substitution of loan finance for proportional income tax finance will reduce private capital formation as loanable funds are diverted into public debt. The choice of revenue policy remains of importance in its effects on price level and growth, even though full employment prevails.

The Keynesian System

We now turn to the other extreme, provided by the so-called Keynesian system. Again, the emphasis is on *so-called* because the system does not quite reflect what is to be found in *The General Theory*. In particular, the dependence of the rate of interest on transaction demand for money, and hence on the level of income, is allowed for. The system consists of the following equations:

$$S = S(i,Y) \qquad (17\text{-}1)$$
$$I = I(i) \qquad (17\text{-}2)$$
$$S(i,Y) = I(i) \qquad (17\text{-}3)$$
$$M_a = M_a(i) \qquad (17\text{-}10)$$
$$Y = Y(N) \qquad (17\text{-}4)$$
$$N = N(W_m) \qquad (17\text{-}11)$$

[1] See p. 365.

$$W = Y'(N) \tag{17-6}$$
$$M_t = (1/V_t) Y_m \tag{17-12}$$
$$M = M_a + M_t \tag{17-13}$$
$$Y_m = PY \tag{17-8}$$
$$W_m = PW \tag{17-14}$$

To this may again be added the equation

$$Y = C + I \tag{17-9}$$

in determining consumption.

Equations (17-1) to (17-3) remain the same as before, and are stated again in real terms.[1] Now we depart sharply from the classical model. The rate of interest is now determined not by simply equating the saving and investment schedules but by meeting the liquidity preference of investors as well. The demand for money as an asset becomes an important part of the system. As shown in equation (17-10), the demand for asset money, or M_a, is a function of the rate of interest and is expressed in money terms.[2] Given the supply of asset money to be held, equation (17-10) sets the rate of interest that prevails in the market. The larger the supply of asset money to be held, the lower the rate of interest will tend to be, until a possible floor has been reached. Equation (17-4) remains the same as before, stated in real terms. In equation (17-11) we depart again from the classical system. The supply of labor is now a function of the money-wage rate W_m. Moreover, we assume the shape of this function to be such that the money-wage rate cannot fall below a fixed level, even though an additional labor supply would be available at the prevailing real wage. The significance of this will be considered presently. Equation (17-6) is the same as before, stated again in real terms. Equations (17-12) and (17-13) take the place of equation (17-7), where V_t is the income velocity of transaction money. M_t is the amount of transaction money, and M is the total money supply. Equation (17-14) establishes a relationship between money wages, real wages, and the price level. Equations (17-8) and (17-9) remain unchanged. Given the total money supply M, velocity of transaction money V_t, as well as the functional relationships of the system, our twelve equations permit us to determine Y, C, I, S, i, W, W_m, N, Y_m, M_a, M_t, and P.

[1] While the formal expression of eq. (17-2) remains the same, note that the investment schedule of the Keynesian system relates to subjective market expectations rather than to objective facts of the market as generally assumed in the classical system.

[2] If the precautionary motive is introduced, we may replace eq. (17-10) by

$$M_{as} = M_{as}(i) \tag{17-10a}$$
$$M_{ap} = M_{ap}(Y_m, i) \tag{17-10b}$$

where M_{as} is speculative and M_{ap} is precautionary demand. The latter may be in real terms and hence becomes a function of money income Y_m. (See p. 428.)

The level of employment and real output, as well as the division of the product between consumption and capital formation, are now linked with the monetary part of the system.   For any money-wage rate, we have a certain level of money income for each level of employment and output. With a given velocity of transaction money, this defines the amount of transaction money required at various levels of employment at the assumed money wage.   With a given total money supply, we thus have specified amounts of asset money available for various levels of employment.   For any amount of asset money, we have a corresponding amount of saving.   Income then must be established at that level where the amount of planned saving matches the amount of investment.

If the level of income leaves some workers unemployed, they will bid down the money-wage rate, provided that it is above the floor level. This releases transaction money at any level of employment and increases the supply of asset money.   If the rate of interest is still above the floor level, this leads to an increase in investment (provided that the I schedule is not wholly inelastic) and raises employment.   Suppose, however, that the lower limit of the money-wage rate is reached before full employment is restored; or suppose that we have the special Keynesian case where an interest floor is reached prior to arriving at the wage floor.   In either case, equilibrium leaves us with involuntary unemployment.   People would be willing to work at a real wage below the one that prevails, but have no chance to do so.

The determination of the equilibrium income in such a system is shown in Figure 17-2.[1]   We assume that the wage rate has been bid down to the floor level.   Thus prices are given by the system, and all variables may be plotted in money terms.   We shall begin with Figure 17-2d, although any other starting point would do as well.   The level of money income Y_m is measured on the vertical axis and asset money, or M_a, on the horizontal axis.   Now, let AB indicate the relationship between Y_m and M_a for given values of total money supply M and transaction velocity V_t.   This relationship is given by equations (17-12) and (17-13).   Suppose, now, that income equals OC so that M_a equals OD.   Moving up to Figure 17-2b, i is measured on the vertical axis and M_a on the horizontal axis. LL is the liquidity-preference schedule given by equation (17-10).   Since the supply of asset money equals OD, the corresponding rate of interest equals OE.   Moving left to Figure 17-2a, the value of i is measured again on the vertical axis and investment expenditure I_m on the horizontal axis. II is the investment schedule as defined in equation (17-2).   With $i = OE$, we have $I_m = OF$.   Moving down to Figure 17-2c, saving S_m

---

[1] For the first use of a four-quadrant approach see Tord Palander, "Keynes' allmänna teori och dess tillämping inom ränte-, multiplikator- och pristeorien," *Ekonomisk Tidskrift*, vol. 44, no. 4, pp. 233–273, December, 1942.

is measured on the horizontal axis and Y_m on the vertical axis. SS is the savings function given in equation (17-1).* According to equation (17-3), I_m as determined by II must be matched in equilibrium by S_m as determined by SS. This is the case where $I_m = S_m = OF$. With $S_m = OF$, we find from Figure 17-2c that $Y_m = OC$. This is the level of income that we assumed at the beginning in Figure 17-2d. If the initial point of departure had been chosen for an income smaller or larger than

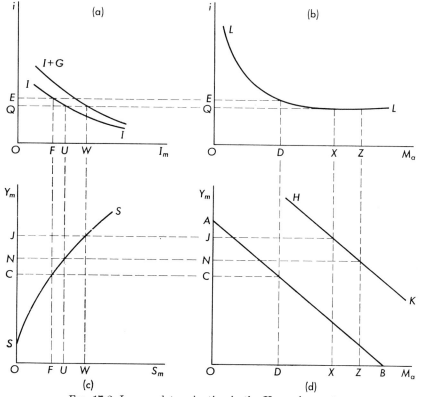

FIG. 17-2. Income determination in the Keynesian system.

OC, the path around the graph would not have returned us to the point of departure. A larger income will result in a decline, since planned saving exceeds investment, and a smaller income will lead to an increase, since investment exceeds planned saving. Thus, the level of income is uniquely determined.[1]

* To simplify matters, we shall now disregard the effect of i on S.

[1] Since I is assumed to be independent of Y, the equilibrium will be stable if $0 < (ds/dY) < 1$. If the investment function is written $I = I(Y,i)$, we must have $0 < (dc/dY) + (dI/dY) < 1$. The latter form is more widely used, but I see no particular reason, for purposes of a static model, why I should be a function of Y.

Consider, now, the role of monetary policy in this system. Suppose that we are in a position of underemployment equilibrium and that the money supply is increased.[1] At the prevailing level of money income, the increment will be an addition to the supply of asset money. Within some limits, this may be expected to reduce interest and raise investment. In the special Keynesian case, interest cannot continue to fall forever; the liquidity-preference schedule becomes infinitely elastic, thus setting a floor to the rate of interest. Once this floor is reached, further additions to the money supply will not reduce i and, hence, will have no effect on I and Y. This is the characteristic case of the Keynesian model. Monetary policy is totally helpless and without bearing on either real or monetary magnitudes in the system.

Fiscal policy now has its day. We shall find that an increase in government expenditures combined with an equal increase in tax yield may raise income and output by an equal amount, prices being assumed constant. An increase in public expenditures with tax yields constant increases income by a larger amount. This result will now be the same, whether the deficit is financed by new money or by the sale of public debt. Debt policy, like monetary policy, has no effect on aggregate demand. Such, at least, will be the case so long as the drain to transaction money from asset money does not reduce the supply of asset money to below the point at which the liquidity-preference schedule ceases to be infinitely elastic.

Returning to Figure 17-2d, let us suppose that income OC leaves the economy with unemployment, and that income OJ is required for full employment. As we increase the money supply, the supply schedule of asset money shifts to the right. As a result, i falls. Tracing the result through Figures 17-2b, a, and c, we get a rise in I and Y_m. This process can continue until the interest floor OQ is reached in 17-2b. Let this be the case with an increase in money supply by an amount that the supply schedule of asset money rises to HK in 17-2d. In the process, investment rises to OU and income to ON, but monetary policy can go no further towards the goal OJ. Only fiscal policy can do this. To simplify matters, let us suppose that initially there was no government budget. Government expenditures G equal to the horizontal distance between the II and $I + G$ schedules in Figure 17-2a are now introduced. Income then rises to the desired full-employment level of OJ. The rise in income,

---

[1] Again, there is the question of how the increase in money supply is implemented. If we apply the assumption of money rain, there will be an initial income effect. The finders experience a temporary increase in income and spend part of it on consumption. This temporary effect may be disregarded for purposes of long-run analysis, but it is more convenient to assume that the increase in money supply is secured through open-market operations or a reduction in reserve requirements.

or NJ, exceeds the increase in government expenditure, or UW. The values of I and i are not affected, since the resulting drain on the supply of asset money from OZ to OX leaves M_a within the range of infinitely elastic liquidity preference.[1]

Mixed Systems without Wealth Effects on Consumption

Let us now turn to the effectiveness of fiscal and monetary policies in mixed systems, that is, systems that combine certain characteristics of the classical and the Keynesian models. A set of such systems, though by no means a complete one, is included in Table 17-1. Possible wealth effects on consumption are disregarded for the time being, but will be introduced later.

TABLE 17-1. SYSTEMS OF INCOME DETERMINATION WITHOUT WEALTH EFFECTS ON CONSUMPTION

Liquidity preference	Money-wage rate	
	Flexible	With floor
No liquidity preference	a	d
Liquidity preference:		
I and S schedules intersect at a feasible rate of interest. . .	b	e
I and S schedules do not intersect at a feasible rate of interest.	c	f

Cases a and f will be recognized as the classical and Keynesian models, respectively, and need not be reconsidered. The other cases present us with new situations.

Case b. First, we shall adjust the classical model [equations (17-1) to (17-9)] to allow for liquidity preference. Accordingly, we add equation (17-10), which defines the demand for asset money as a function of the rate of interest, independent of price level;[2] and we replace equation (17-8) by (17-12) and (17-13). Thus we have two additional equations, matched by two additional unknowns, M_a and M_t. We assume the shapes of the liquidity-preference, investment, and savings schedules to be such that we can obtain whatever amount of investment is required to match saving out of a full-employment income. In other words, the liquidity-prefer-

[1] This assumes that the increase in the supply of asset money to OZ was somewhat larger than needed to exhaust the effectiveness of monetary policy. Otherwise an offsetting effect on investment would result—unless the increase in public expenditures is financed, at least partially, by increasing the money supply. (See p. 456.)

[2] Such demand for real balances as arises from the precautionary motive is assumed to be independent of interest and is incorporated into the demand for transaction money. This does not do full justice to the matter (see p. 427), but it will suffice for present purposes.

ence schedule must be less than infinitely elastic over the relevant range, and the investment schedule must have an elasticity greater than zero.[1]

Given these conditions, the level of employment is determined by the real part of the system. Full employment is established automatically, as in the classical model. If unemployment exists, money wages are bid down. Less transaction money is needed to finance a given real income, and the supply of asset money is increased. As a result, the rate of interest falls and investment rises. This process continues until full employment is restored. Indeed, the real part of the system determines not only the level of employment but also the division of the product between consumption and capital formation, as well as the rate of interest. Liquidity preference is of significance only in determining the price level. With the rate of interest set by the real part of the system, people wish to hold a certain amount of asset money, depending upon the shape of the liquidity-preference function. The remainder is used as transaction money, the supply of which, together with the velocity factor, determines the price level.

Consider, now, the role of monetary and fiscal policy in such a system. An increase in money supply—implemented by our previous policy of money rain—leaves the level of output unchanged.[2] In this case, the division of the product between consumption and capital formation remains unchanged as well. Since the rate of interest is unchanged, the demand for asset money is also unchanged, and the entire increase in money supply becomes transaction money. The increase in price level, therefore, will be more than proportionate to the increase in total money supply. A proportionate increase would be obtained only if the demand for asset money were defined in real terms.

Turning to budget policy, suppose that government expenditures and taxes are raised by equal amounts. Depending upon resulting changes in the structure of payments, a larger amount of transaction money may be required to finance the given real income at prevailing prices. This suggests a decline in price level. At the same time, the increase in tax yield will reduce saving and investment in the private sector. Assuming government outlays to be on consumption, net investment will fall, and the rate of interest will rise. Money will be released from the asset sphere. This release may match the increased demand for transaction funds owing to changes in the structure of payments, and thus may leave the price level unchanged; or we may be left with some net rise or fall in the price level.

---

[1] We need not specify here whether such a solution can be found at a positive or only at a negative rate of interest, provided that interest can fall to a sufficiently low level.

[2] Initial income effects on the finders are again disregarded.

Deficit finance out of newly created money will be similar in effect to the previously considered case of increased money supply. Deficit finance by borrowing from existing funds is more or less similar in its demand on transaction funds to the case of balanced-budget expansion. However, the insertion of government demand into the loan market will reduce private investment and drive up the rate of interest, and do so more sharply than is likely to occur under tax finance. As a result, more funds will be released into the transaction sphere. The price level will tend to rise more, or to fall less, sharply.

Case c. Let us now examine a model that involves the same system of equations as case b; but we assume no longer that the savings schedule out of a full-employment income must intersect the investment schedule at a feasible rate of interest. There may be no such intersection because the liquidity-preference schedule becomes infinitely elastic at a rate of interest in excess of that required to permit the necessary level of investment;[1] or because the investment and savings schedules become wholly inelastic. In either case, a bidding down of money wages will not help. While the supply of asset money is increased thereby, no increase in investment will result. Real income and employment thus may reach a ceiling short of full employment, while money wages and prices fall toward zero.

In such a system, an increase in money supply will not raise the level of real income or employment, nor will it serve to arrest the chronic decline in price level. Monetary policy will be wholly ineffective, and budget policy will be wholly effective, as they were in the special Keynesian model. The restoration of full employment can be achieved either by expanding the balanced budget or by deficit finance.

Case d. Next, let us combine an otherwise classical system with the Keynesian assumption of money wages that are rigid in the downward direction. For this purpose we shall use equations (17-1) to (17-9) but replace (17-5) with (17-11) and (17-14). This may lead to an unemployment equilibrium. The level of money income, as given by M and V, may be insufficient to finance full-employment income in view of a given floor to the money-wage rate. Here unemployment equilibrium may exist, even though Say's law holds and there is no liquidity preference.

In this case, monetary policy is the hero and fiscal policy is helpless. An increase in money supply raises money income and employment proportionately until full employment is reached. From there on, the classical case applies. An increase in the balanced budget, on the other hand, will be without effect on the level of employment. By lengthening

[1] The level to which the rate of interest would have to fall to permit full employment may again be positive or negative, depending on whether the S and I schedules intersect above or below the zero rate.

the payment structure and reducing V, it may even reduce money income and, hence, real income and employment. Deficit finance through borrowing of existing funds will do no better. Deficit finance via the printing press will be effective, but this effectiveness comes about only because budget policy serves as a vehicle of monetary policy.

Case e. We now combine provision for liquidity preference with the assumption of rigid money wages, thus returning to the system of equations given for the Keynesian model. We fall short of the special Keynesian case in that we assume the shape of the investment, savings, and liquidity-preference schedules to be such that the required amount of investment can be reached if the money supply is sufficiently large.

This is again a system in which unemployment equilibrium may occur. If the money supply is insufficient, the interest rate may be too high to permit the necessary level of investment; and the existence of a floor to money wages limits the extent to which the supply of asset money can be increased by the bidding down of money wages.

In this system, an increase in the money supply will reduce the rate of interest and raise investment. Contrary to the special Keynesian model, or case f, monetary policy will be effective in this system, and so will budget policy. However, note that budget policy without monetary expansion will be less effective than it was in case f. Suppose we consider a policy of balanced-budget expansion. The resulting growth in income leads to a drain of funds from the asset to the transaction sphere, which in turn gives rise to an increase in the rate of interest and a decline in investment. This investment check provides an offset to the increase in income, which otherwise tends to result from expansion of the balanced budget. The increase in income, resulting from expansion in the balanced budget, may thus fall short of the 1:1 ratio achieved under certain conditions in the Keynesian model.

The check to investment that impairs the effectiveness of expansion in the balanced budget operates even more sharply in the case of deficit finance with borrowing from the public. Here, the rate of interest is driven up not only by a resulting reduction in the supply of asset money but also by an increase in the supply of public debt. Either check to investment is inoperative in the Keynesian model, or case f, provided that the supply of asset money is sufficiently large so that the liquidity-preference function is infinitely elastic to the left as well as to the right of the existing supply of asset money.[1]

Wealth Effects on Consumption Allowed for

In the preceding set of cases, we have disregarded certain effects on consumption that may result from changes in the real value of balances

[1] The same result is obtained if the I or S schedules are wholly inelastic.

and their bearing upon the net worth of the consumer. To allow for this consideration, which has come to be known as the Pigou effect, we must rewrite equation (17-1) so as to make saving a direct function of i and Y and an inverse function of net worth. The value of net worth, like that of Y, is defined in real terms.[1]

Case a. The classical system provided for full-employment equilibrium in the absence of a wealth effect, and continues to do so in the presence of a wealth effect. The level of employment and the division of the product are still determined by the real side of the system, the only difference being that the level of saving now comes to be affected by the capital stock. As before, changes in money supply affect the price level and nothing else. Since changes in money supply are balanced by proportional changes in price level, the real value of balances remains unchanged.[2] An expansion in the balanced budget may change the payment structure and, hence, the price level. As a result, the real value of balances may change, and there may be a change in the rate of saving. Deficit finance out of new money again raises the price level. If the deficit is financed by borrowing from the public, private saving may change in response to a resulting change in the rate of interest; and it may change in response to a wealth effect, provided that the public looks upon increased holding of debt as an increase in net worth.

Case b. The classical system with liquidity preference was shown to provide for full employment in the absence of a wealth effect, and continues to do so with a wealth effect. However, we have noted that an increase in money supply will lead to a more than proportionate increase in price level. As a result, the real value of balances declines. In view of the wealth effect, this leads to an increase in saving and a change in the composition of the product that did not occur in the absence of the wealth effect. Similar consequences may result from changes in price level induced by expansion in the balanced budget or by deficit finance with borrowing from existing funds.

Case c. An unemployment equilibrium was shown to be possible even though wages are flexible, provided that there is no wealth effect. The bidding down of money wages and the resulting fall in price level and release of transaction money will be ineffective in raising real income if the rate of interest cannot fall below a certain level, or investment will not rise in response to a decline in interest. Once the wealth effect is allowed for,

[1] Changes in the stock of real capital that result from investment are disregarded for the time being but will be introduced in our later discussion of growth. (See pp. 483 and 550.)

[2] The relationship of money supply to the wealth effect is interpreted in such a way that consumers will consider the *entire* money supply, whether transaction money or asset money, as part of their net worth. If asset money only were included, allowance for the wealth effect would not be permissible in cases *a* and *d*.

the bidding down of money wages results in an increased value of real balances. This raises consumption out of a given income and, hence, pushes up income until full employment is reached.[1]

Given an initial state of unemployment, full employment may now be achieved without the disrupting concomitant of a declining price level. This might be accomplished by increasing the money supply at constant prices, as an alternative approach to raising the real value of balances; or it might be accomplished by budget expansion. Allowance for the wealth effect thus changes the model in two respects: It transforms it into a system that equilibrates at full employment, and it lends potency to the monetary approach in removing temporary unemployment.

Case d. Here the downward rigidity of money wages results in a system in which unemployment equilibrium can prevail even though all income is spent. This situation may persist after a wealth effect on consumption is allowed for. Since money wages cannot be bid below a certain level, the wealth effect does not assure that full employment is achieved automatically. An increase in money supply again serves to restore full employment, but it now has additional bearing on the division of the product between consumption and capital formation. Budget expansion without money creation remains ineffective as a cure for unemployment.

Case e. This, similarly, was a system in which unemployment equilibrium may result, and it remains such after the wealth effect is allowed for. An increase in money supply, which was effective in the absence of the wealth effect continues to be so after a wealth effect is allowed for. Balanced budget expansion is reduced in effectiveness because the failure to increase the money supply as income rises results in a downward shift in the consumption function relative to income. This consumption check is now added to the investment check noted in our prior discussion of this case. Deficit finance out of borrowing from existing funds was shown to involve a greater check to investment than balanced budget expansion. At the same time, such finance may be more favorable in its repercussion on consumption via the wealth effect. Again, this depends on whether or not an increase in public debt is considered an increment to net worth by its holders, similar to an increase in money supply. The effectiveness of deficit finance out of new money, finally, is increased by the wealth effect.

Case f. The extreme Keynesian case remains one in which underemployment equilibrium may occur, even though the wealth effect is allowed for. However, the wealth effect transforms this model from one in which monetary policy is impotent to one in which monetary policy can

---

[1] We shall overlook, for the time being, the complicating factor of cuts in investment in anticipation of further declines in price level.

serve to restore full employment. The effectiveness of monetary policy now operates entirely via stimulation to consumption rather than investment; but it can do the job. The effectiveness of balanced budget expansion is less than it would be in the absence of a wealth effect. The consumption check resulting from the wealth effect is the same as in case e, although the investment check is now absent.

Conclusions

It is evident from the preceding discussion that the effectiveness of various stabilization policies in maintaining full employment and price-level stability depends upon the nature of the underlying systems of income determination.

Let us look once again at systems without wealth effect on consumption and ask how the responsibility for a possible unemployment equilibrium may be allocated between liquidity preference and downward rigidity in money wages. The existence of liquidity preference is no cause for unemployment, provided that the liquidity schedule is less than infinitely elastic over the relevant range. This is shown by case b, which is one of full-employment equilibrium. The existence of liquidity preference may be a cause for unemployment if the shape of the schedule is such that it sets a floor to the rate of interest; and liquidity preference may cause unemployment equilibrium even though money wages are flexible. This is shown by case c.

The existence of downward rigidity in money wages may be a cause for unemployment equilibrium even though there is no liquidity preference. This is shown by case d. Or it may explain unemployment equilibrium even though the liquidity preference is such that it sets no floor to the rate of interest. This is shown by case e. Finally, we may have a situation where there exist both an interest floor and a floor to money wages. In this situation, shown by case f, either factor may be responsible for the effective limit to employment.

We have encountered four possible cases of unemployment equilibrium. Among these, case d can be remedied only by monetary policy. Since money wages cannot be cut, output must be increased by raising money expenditures. Since the propensity to spend in the private sector is unity, this can be done only by increasing the money supply. Unemployment in cases c and f can be remedied only by budget policy. Since liquidity preference is infinitely elastic, an increase in money supply is of no avail. Case e, finally, lends itself to both approaches.

Turning to systems with wealth effect on consumption, downward flexibility of wages assures full-employment equilibrium, even though liquidity preference may be infinitely elastic. Thus, case c becomes one in which full-employment equilibrium is established automatically. In systems where there is a floor to money wages, introduction of the wealth effect does not assure automatic restoration of full-employment equilibrium. Thus, unemployment equilibrium may continue to prevail in cases d, e, and f. However, monetary policy becomes an effective remedy in case f as well as in cases d and e. The effectiveness of budgetary policy without money expansion is reduced somewhat, depending on the applicability of the wealth effect to debt creation.

C. CHANGES IN PRICE LEVEL AND EMPLOYMENT

The major contribution of Keynesian analysis consists in pointing to the crucial role of effective demand and in explaining why effective demand is a fickle thing. Contrary to the assumptions of the classical model, Keynesian analysis shows that there is no simple relation between money supply and total demand. Money may be held or spent, with the result that investment is not equated automatically with savings at a full-employment income. The unwillingness of income recipients to consume, and the unwillingness of savers to invest, may at one time result in a level of investment insufficient to maintain employment; just as the eagerness of these two groups to draw on balances and to spend more than is received may at other times result in inflation. While much remains to be done to improve the particular theories of how consumer and investment expenditures are determined, Keynes's attempt to go behind the global-velocity concept and to derive explicit theories about consumer and investment behavior was a great step forward.

But rarely is a gain made without some loss. While the $C + I$ side of the basic Keynesian identity of $C + I = Y$ proved far superior as a tool of analysis to the VM side of the traditional equation of exchange $VM = OP$, the same cannot be said for the replacement of OP by Y. Rather, this detracted attention from the important fact that changes in expenditures may result in changes in price level as well as output. Keynes, of course, was quite aware of the problems of price inflation, which are treated at some length in *The General Theory*, as well as in the *Treatise*. However, the subsequent discussion in terms of the Keynesian model, and much of the fiscal theory based thereon, did neglect the price-level aspect and thus transformed the model into a special case of depression economics. The developments of the war and postwar periods have made it abundantly clear that the contingency of price-level change cannot be overlooked in a *general* theory of compensatory finance. The concern is with avoiding inflation as well as unemployment.

Rising Prices below Full Employment

Two aspects of the inflation problem may be distinguished: One is the proposition that resources become increasingly scarce and that bottlenecks appear as full employment is approached. Consequently, raising money expenditure may not be the proper way to cut unemployment. The other is the proposition that the political behavior of the public and the price policy of monopolistic groups is such as to necessitate inflation.

Let us consider the first aspect. Arguments in compensatory finance frequently proceed as if the supply schedule of total output is infinitely elastic (with respect to aggregate money expenditure) up to the point of full employment, and wholly inelastic from there on. Such, of course, is not the case. As Keynes noted, there is reason to expect that some price increase will come about at an earlier point.[1] At the same time, there is evidence, both theoretical and empirical, that an increase in expenditures will be reflected in considerable part in increased employment and output, if there is still substantial unemployment.

To begin with, note that a period of severe unemployment will be accompanied by substantial excess capacity in plant and equipment.[2] Business firms operate within the range of declining, or at least constant marginal, cost. As a result, additional labor input and increased employment become possible even in the short run without rising costs. As a higher level of capacity utilization is approached, costs and prices rise. This pressure on cost depends upon the rate at which the higher level of employment is achieved. If sufficiently gradual, additional capacity can be created and take care of the additional labor input. If expenditures increase at a rapid rate, bottlenecks will begin to develop at an earlier point.

Next, we may note that a period of severe unemployment is one where (by definition) additional workers are available at prevailing real wages. The prevailing level of employment is not determined as a point on the classical labor-supply schedule. More workers would be willing to work at the going real wage, and employment is rationed by some method other than prices, such as union membership. As the level of expenditures and employment is increased, employment at the prevailing real wage may be increased until a point on the classical supply schedule is reached. Only thereafter does an increase in the supply of labor require an increase in the real-wage rate. To the extent that increased output merits an increase in real wages due to lower capital cost, a further upward movement along the classical labor-supply schedule becomes possible without rising prices.

All this suggests that an increase in the level of money expenditures—whether implemented by fiscal or monetary measures—may secure full employment with only a modicum of price increase, provided that the movement is sufficiently slow to permit the required adjustment in

---

[1] See J. M. Keynes, *The General Theory of Employment, Interest, and Money*, Harcourt, Brace and Company, Inc., New York, 1936, chap. 21.

[2] See Alvin H. Hansen, *Monetary Theory and Fiscal Policy*, McGraw-Hill Book Company, Inc., New York, 1949, chap. 7.

capacity.   At the same time, the disadvantage of some price rise cannot be avoided altogether and must be weighed against the cost of continued unemployment.   In any case, these difficulties are not peculiar to any particular type of stabilization policy.   If money wages are rigid in a downward direction, full employment can be approached only by raising the level of money expenditure.   If this rigidity does not exist, conditions may be such that real demand can be increased by permitting prices to fall; but this again involves a change in price level.

In the severe depression of the thirties, concentration on a system with more or less constant money wages helped to focus attention on the crucial need for raising the level of money expenditure.   In the full-employment setting of the postwar years, this assumption would not do. While there was room for some debate whether a decline in the level of expenditures reduces prices or employment, it became evident that an increase in money expenditures must raise the level of prices.   The function of stabilization policy became one of maintaining the prevailing level of aggregate expenditures or, more correctly, of providing for an increase therein commensurate with the real growth of output, but not more.

An analysis of the measures required to accomplish this must still be conducted in a system where the price level is held constant.   Just as unemployment must be avoided by closing the deflationary gap, so must price increase be avoided by closing the inflationary gap.   For this purpose, an equilibrium system of income determination may still be applied. This is not true if open inflation is permitted to occur.   We are then confronted with a state of disequilibrium.   The entire system must be formulated in dynamic terms, and the effects of changes in price level upon expenditure behavior must be allowed for.

The preceding discussion applies to the problem of unemployment in a developed economy.   Underemployment in low-income countries is a different story.   While unemployment in developed countries reflects inadequate demand, underemployment in low-income countries typically reflects inadequate resources (capital and otherwise) with which to combine the ample labor supply.   The basic problem here is one of low productivity, not of unemployment.   The remedy, therefore, must be in capital formation and in more productive employment.   Budget policy has an important contribution to make to these objectives, but increasing the level of expenditures in money terms is not the proper approach.

Inflation by Monopolistic Groups

We shall now turn to the second aspect of the inflation problem.   One of the more fashionable propositions of postwar economics has been that full employment and price-level stability are incompatible objectives.   The trouble lies with the political behavior of pressure groups under conditions of high employment.

As far as the economics of the matter are concerned, the point is simple. Assume a given level of output, prices, and hence expenditures. Now, let labor unions demand an increase in money wages not based on an increase in productivity. If such an increase in the wage share can be financed by a reduction in other shares—be it interest, monopoly profits, or other rent incomes—the result will be merely a redistribution of factor shares.

But suppose that this cannot be done and that prices are raised accordingly. The government, in response to such a situation, is caught in a true dilemma. If fiscal policy is such as to maintain the level of expenditures unchanged, prices rise and employment must decline. These results will occur since the same expenditure total will purchase fewer units of output at the higher level of prices. Alternatively, the government may choose to raise the level of expenditures so as to maintain employment at higher prices. Assuming an increasing supply schedule of total output, there is the further possibility of reducing the level of expenditures so as to maintain the level of prices while cutting employment even further.[1]

To make matters worse, if employment is maintained, those initially responsible for demanding increased wages or prices will be assured that whatever they demand, there will be no penalty of unemployment or losses. Thus there is no reason why the same performance might not be repeated. One round of inflation would follow the other, unless the government invoked the threat of permitting unemployment.

Similar considerations apply if the initial disturbance results from a demand for increased profits rather than wages, or if a markup is applied to wage gains that are justified by increases in productivity. If such is the pattern of business and union leadership, the objectives of full employment and price-level stability are indeed incompatible. Whatever the techniques of general restriction—fiscal or monetary—it will not be possible to accomplish both objectives at once. Public policy must then choose between price-level stability and such punishment (unemployment and low profits) as is required to secure more disciplined behavior on the part of pressure groups. As an alternative, direct controls over wages and/or prices may be applied.

There is no denying that one may construct a theoretical system where price-level stability and full employment become totally incompatible objectives. The question is whether such a system reflects a realistic view of the modern economy. The postwar experience of the United States,

---

[1] See Melvin Reder, "The Theoretical Problems of a National Wage-price Policy," *Canadian Journal of Economics and Political Science*, vol. 14, no. 1, pp. 46–61, February, 1948.

while not altogether comforting, hardly supports such an extreme view. Chances are that this latest breakdown theory of capitalism will fare no better than its predecessors.   The solution here, as with earlier prophecies of doom, whether Marxist or Schumpeterian, may be found in the responses of a flexible social structure and in a public policy that adjusts itself to the needs of changing situations.

A Note on Money in the Classical System

Let us return briefly to the proposition that a classical model which separates the real from the monetary part of the system is internally inconsistent.[1]   The issue here is not whether such a system is realistic (obviously, it is not!) but only whether it is inconsistent.   This accusation I feel is unwarranted.[2]

In support of the thesis of inconsistency it has been argued that the acquisition of money, no less than the acquisition of goods, is a utility. The holding of money enters into the budget equation and, therefore, is said to be related to the determination of relative prices.   Now, a clear distinction must be drawn between the proposition that the services of money are useful to society (that they satisfy a social want) and the proposition that money as such appears in the preference schedule of individuals.   The social usefulness of money consists in the fact that it permits a more efficient system of marketing as is available in a barter economy and, hence, permits more extensive division of labor.   This is obvious; but it does not follow that the individual demands money as an alternative to oranges and apples.   His real income is higher and permits him to purchase more oranges and apples because he lives in an economy with an efficient payment system.   The existence of money is useful in the same sense as the existence of sunshine or scientific knowledge.

Suppose, then, that we have a money economy in which relative prices of goods are determined by the real part of the system, even though they may be expressed by using money as a numeraire.   Since we assume that people have no demand for money as such, all money is transaction money.   But how will velocity and hence the price level be determined? Velocity may be determined by technical factors such as train schedules and payment habits, which make for various degrees of overlap in the

---

[1] See Don Patinkin, *The Theory of Money and Prices*, especially chap. 7.   Also, note the extensive literature references given by Patinkin.   What seems to me an unjustified criticism of the simple classical model should not detract from the merit of this study in developing the real balance system based on the precautionary motif.

[2] For a similar criticism see Stefan Valivanis, "A Denial of Patinkin's Contradiction," *Kyklos*, vol. 8, no. 4, pp. 351–368, 1955.   The tragic death of this most brilliant of our young economists has been an irreparable loss to the profession.

payment system.[1]   If people are paid in location X and buy in location Y, velocity will be greater or smaller, depending on whether X is one block or ten blocks away from Y; or velocity may be greater or smaller depending on whether stores are open all night.   Thus, the price level may be explained without a demand for money based on a utility calculus.   At the same time, relative prices are determined in the real part of the system and are independent of any demand for money as such.   Such a system is unrealistic and unattractive to the monetary theorist, as it renders monetary theory a trivial matter.   However, the system is not inconsistent.

Moving now to a more realistic system, various steps may be taken. The first is to introduce cost of investment and to argue that balances will be held if the intended postponement of consumption is so short that investment is unprofitable in view of given costs and yields.[2]   This complicates matters a bit but does not go far in widening the scope of monetary theory.   Next, we may assume that future payment requirements are uncertain.   With this, the decision whether to invest or not, in view of given investment costs and yields, becomes more interesting; and a demand for money as such enters the preference pattern of the individual consumer.   A link is established between the demand for money and relative prices, but we do not arrive at the crux of monetary theory until we introduce a speculative demand for money.

The need to hold money for transaction purposes, or the related need to hold money for precautionary purposes, establishes a "demand" for money in real terms.[3]   The speculative demand for money, in so far as the choice between money and debt is concerned, establishes a demand in money terms, independent of prevailing or expected price level.   Thus, the liquidity-preference schedule in the Keynesian model is written in money terms.   There may exist, however, a further speculative demand for money and claims, as against goods—a demand that depends upon price-level expectations.   In this case, the real value of balances and changes therein enter the speculative demand.

[1] See Howard S. Ellis, "Some Fundamentals in the Theory of Velocity," *Quarterly Journal of Economics*, vol. 52, no. 3, pp. 431–472, May, 1938, reprinted in Friedrich A. Lutz and Lloyd W. Mints (eds.), *Readings in Monetary Theory*, American Economic Association, Richard D. Irwin, Inc., Homewood, Ill., 1951, pp. 89–128.

[2] See J. R. Hicks, "A Suggestion for Simplifying the Theory of Money," *Economica*, vol. 2, no. 5, pp. 1–19, 1935, reprinted in Lutz and Mints, *op. cit.*, pp. 13–32.

[3] The term *demand* appears in quotes above because its use is somewhat confusing vis-à-vis transaction money, where the individual's demand has no underpinning in utility theory.

CHAPTER 18

Compensatory finance: consumption aspects

We now turn to a closer analysis of compensatory budget policies. In the present chapter, we deal with leverage effects of budget policy, which operate through the consumption-income relationship in the private sector. Private investment is assumed to remain fixed. In the following chapter, effects on investment will be taken into account; thereafter some problems of fiscal dynamics and growth are considered. Finally, changes in the structure of claims that result from budget policy, along with their effects on consumption and investment, will be introduced.

A. ALTERNATIVE BUDGET ADJUSTMENTS TO RAISE EMPLOYMENT

Let us first consider the role of budget policy under conditions of unemployment. The price level is assumed to be fixed. Money wages are rigid in the downward direction, and any increase in money expenditures is assumed to be reflected in increased output. Using a truncated form of the Keynesian model, we have a very simple system consisting of two equations. To suit the reader's preference, this system and the following discussion are given in both general and linear form.

	General form	*Linear form*	
	$Y = C + I$	$Y = C + I$	(18-1)
	$C = C(Y)$	$C = a + cY$	(18-2)

With $I = \bar{I}$ given, we can determine C and Y from equations (18-1) and (18-2). Since the price level is fixed, Y, C, and I may be expressed either in real or money terms. The system may be solved for Y which gives us the familiar multiplier equation

$$Y = \cfrac{1}{1 - \cfrac{C(Y)}{Y}} I \quad \text{or} \quad Y = \frac{1}{1 - c}(a + I) \qquad (18\text{-}3)$$

This is the very simple system which underlies most of the conventional theory of compensatory finance and which we shall use to begin with.[1] For the time being we assume that all taxpayers have the same marginal propensity to consume.

Budget Adjustments with Lump-sum Tax

We shall now introduce the budget into the picture and assume that tax yield T_l is obtained through a lump-sum or head tax. Tax yield, therefore, is quite independent of income. Our simple system of income determination now becomes

General form	*Linear form*	
$Y = C + I + G$	$Y = C + I + G$	(18-4)
$C = C(Y - T_l)$	$C = a + c(Y - T_l)$	(18-5)

Given the consumption function, $I = \bar{I}$ and the budget magnitudes $T_l = \bar{T}_l$ and $G = \bar{G}$, we can solve for C and Y. Note that c, as defined in equation (18-5), is the marginal propensity to consume out of income after tax. Substituting and solving for Y, we obtain our new multiplier

---

[1] From a large literature on the subject, see Alvin H. Hansen, *Fiscal Policy and Business Cycles*, W. W. Norton & Company, Inc., New York, 1941, part III, and *Business Cycles and National Income*, New York, W. W. Norton & Company, Inc., New York, 1951, chap. 12; also see N. Kaldor, appendix C in W. H. Beveridge, *Full Employment in a Free Society*, W. W. Norton & Company, Inc., New York, 1945, pp. 344–401; A. G. Hart, "Model Building and Fiscal Policy," *American Economic Review*, vol. 35, no. 4, pp. 531–558, September, 1945; Trygve Haavelmo, "Multiplier Effects of a Balanced Budget," *Econometrica*, vol. 13, no. 4, pp. 311–318, 1945; both Hart and Haavelmo are reprinted in *Readings in Fiscal Policy*, American Economic Association, Richard D. Irwin, Inc., Homewood, Ill., 1955; Paul A. Samuelson, "The Simple Mathematics of Income Determination," pp. 133–158, in *Income, Employment and Public Policy: Essays in Honor of Alvin H. Hansen*, W. W. Norton & Company, Inc., New York, 1948; Erich Schneider, *Einführung in die Wirtschaftstheorie*, 3. Auflage, J. C. B. Mohr (Paul Siebeck), Tübingen, Germany, 1955, dritter Teil, pp. 250–276; Ralph Turvey, "Some Notes on Multiplier Theory," *American Economic Review*, vol. 52, no. 3, pp. 275–295, June, 1953; W. J. Baumol and M. H. Preston, "More on the Multiplier Effects of a Balanced Budget," *American Economic Review*, vol. 45, p. 140, March, 1955; and William A. Salant, "Taxes, Income Determination and the Balanced Budget Theorem," *Review of Economics and Statistics*, vol. 39, no. 2, pp. 153–161, May, 1957. See also the extensive bibliography given in *Readings in Fiscal Policy*.

equation

$$Y = \frac{1}{1 - \dfrac{C(Y - T_l)}{Y}}(I + G) \qquad \text{or} \qquad Y = \frac{1}{1 - c}(a - cT_l + I + G) \quad (18\text{-}6)$$

which is the basis for the following analysis.

Suppose, now, that income is to be raised by a budget adjustment. This may be accomplished in a number of ways. We may raise $\bar{G}$ while holding $\bar{T}_l$ constant, or reduce $\bar{T}_l$ while holding $\bar{G}$ constant, or combine these two adjustments in varying degrees. Alternatively, we may raise both $\bar{G}$ and $\bar{T}_l$, and expansionary results may even be achieved by combining appropriate reduction in $\bar{G}$ and $\bar{T}_l$. The results of the more important policies are as follows:

TABLE 18-1. BUDGET ADJUSTMENTS WITH LUMP-SUM TAX

Type of adjustment	Change in income	
	General form	Linear form
Change in G with T_l constant.....	$\dfrac{dY}{dG} = \dfrac{1}{1 - C'(Y - T_l)}$	$\Delta Y = \dfrac{1}{1 - c}\,\Delta G$ (18-7)
Change in T_l with G constant.....	$\dfrac{dY}{dT_l} = -\dfrac{C'(Y - T_l)}{1 - C'(Y - T_l)}$	$\Delta Y = -\dfrac{1}{1 - c}\,c\,\Delta T_l$ (18-8)
Equal changes in G and T.......	$\dfrac{dY}{dB} = 1$	$\Delta Y = \dfrac{1}{1 - c}(\Delta G - c\,\Delta T_l) = \Delta B$ (18-9)

As shown in equation (18-7), an increase in goods and service expenditures G raises income by an amount equal to ΔG times the multiplier. If the marginal propensity to consume is constant, this multiplier is independent of the lump-sum tax. As shown in equation (18-8), a reduction in the yield of the lump-sum tax by a given amount raises income with $\Delta Y \gtrless |\Delta T|$, depending on whether $c \gtrless \frac{1}{2}$. However, the gain in income per dollar of reduction in yield will be always less than that per dollar of increase in public expenditures on goods and services. This is the case because part of the gain in disposable income due to the reduction of tax is saved. Thus, the multiplicand is smaller. The same holds for a comparison between an increase in goods and service expenditures and an equal increase in transfer payments, which may be treated simply as a negative tax.   The results of a combined increase in G and reduction in T_t are obtained by adding equations (18-7) and (18-8), thus aggregating the expansionary effects of both measures.

The same principle of adding equations (18-7) and (18-8) holds where the increase in expenditures is accompanied by an increase in yield, but here the two adjustments work against each other.   Using the linear expression, we have $\Delta Y \gtreqless 0$ depending on whether $\Delta G / \Delta T_t \gtreqless c$.   Since $c < 1$, the net result will always be expansionary, if $\Delta G > \Delta T_t$, so that a deficit results.   A case of special interest is that of balanced budget expansion, where $\Delta G = \Delta T_t$.   As shown in equation (18-9), we obtain a 1:1 relationship between expansion in income and expansion in budget or ΔB, where $\Delta B = \Delta G = \Delta T_t$.   This is the case independent of the value of c; it constitutes the famous balanced-budget theorem.[1]   As our discussion proceeds, we shall find many reasons why this theorem in its 1:1 version is only a very special case.[2]   However, the result of the simple case is readily explained, and various verbal explanations have been offered. The increase in the balanced budget redistributes income towards the government.   The government's marginal propensity to spend equals 1, while that of the private sector equals $c < 1$.   Thus there results an initial gain in spending of $(1 - c)\, \Delta G$.   Multiplying this by the multiplier $1/(1 - c)$, we obtain a gain of ΔG.   Or, we may argue that the gain from the respending of private receipts from government equals the loss of reduced spending by taxpayers, thus leaving the increase in government spending as a net gain.   By now this seems sensible enough; but the initial furor over the theorem is understandable, if one recalls the pre-occupation of earlier thinking on compensatory finance with the role of public deficit as an offset to private saving.

Finally, there is the possibility that a reduction in tax yield may be accompanied by a reduction in government expenditures.   We now find that $\Delta Y \gtreqless 0$, depending on whether $|\Delta G| / |\Delta T_t| \lesseqgtr c$.   The introduction of a deficit combined with a reduction in expenditures will be expansionary only if $|\Delta G| < c|\Delta T_t|$.*   This differs from the introduction of a deficit with an increase in G, which always leads to an expansion of income.

It follows from all this that the desired increase in income may be secured by a wide variety of budget policies.   On the one extreme, we may increase expenditures and taxes by an equal amount.   This leads to a large increase in public expenditures and a small (zero) deficit.   On the

[1] See the preceding footnote for literature references.

[2] The underlying assumptions are (1) that all taxpayers' marginal propensities to consume are alike (see p. 439); (2) that the price level remains unchanged (see p. 452); (3) that investment is fixed (see p. 465); and (4) that growth is disregarded (see p. 486). Reconsideration of each assumption leads to a change in the theorem.

* See Schneider, *op. cit.*, p. 262.

other extreme, we may reduce taxes or raise transfer payments. This leads to a large increase in deficit and a small (zero) increase in public expenditures. Assuming a constant marginal propensity to consume of $\frac{2}{3}$, an increase of goods and service expenditures by \$2 may be traded for a decrease in tax yield by \$3, or an increase in the balanced budget by \$6 if income is to be raised by \$6.

These approaches are shown diagrammatically in Figure 18-1.* Let schedule LM be the consumption function before the budget is introduced. Since investment is held fixed for the time being, we might think of investment as being included in the intercept of the consumption function. Prebudget income equals OP. Now, let government expenditures of LB

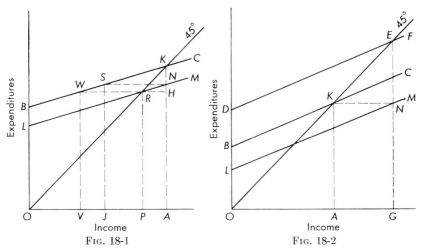

FIG. 18-1   FIG. 18-2

FIGS. 18-1 and 18-2. Budget adjustments with lump-sum tax.

be introduced. The total spendings function shifts upward to BC, and income rises from OP to OA. The increase in income $PA = RH$ equals the increase in government expenditures NK plus the increase in consumption HN. The larger the slope of LM, the greater the increase in consumption and hence the total increase in income. This is the multiplier relationship noted in equation (18-7).

Figure 18-1 may also be used to demonstrate the introduction of a

* As samples of an extensive literature along these lines, see Alvin H. Hansen, "Three Methods of Expansion through Fiscal Policy," *American Economic Review*, vol. 25, no. 3, pp. 382–387, June, 1945; Robert L. Bishop, "Alternative Expansionist Fiscal Policies," in *Income, Employment and Public Policy: Essays in Honor of Alvin H. Hansen*, pp. 329ff.

For an elementary introduction to this apparatus and to income theory in general, see Paul A. Samuelson, *Economics: An Introductory Analysis*, 4th ed., McGraw-Hill Book Company, Inc., New York, 1958, chaps. 11, 12, and 18.

lump-sum tax. Let BC be the consumption function before tax, and let a tax equal to SN be introduced. According to equation (18-8), this results in a parallel downward shift in the consumption function.[1] The tax is measured as the horizontal distance between the consumption function before imposition of the tax, or BC, and the consumption function after the tax is imposed, or LM. Note that this new function again relates consumption to total (not disposable!) income. Income drops to OP, disposable income equals OV, and consumption is $VW = PR = OP$. The decline in income, or PA, falls short of the gain in yield, or $SN = JA$.

Finally, Figure 18-1 may be used to explore the effects of a reduction in tax, in which case OP is the initial and OA the final income. The gain in income, or PA, now falls short of the loss of yield, or JA. However, the ratio of gain in income to loss of yield, or PA/JA, is less than the preceding ratio of gain in income to increase in public expenditures, or PA/NK.

In Figure 18-2 we show the case of balanced-budget expansion. BC is again the consumption function before a tax is imposed, with income at OA. A tax of KN is imposed, and the consumption function shifts to LM. We now add public expenditures of EN equal to the tax yield NK. We thus obtain the total expenditure line DF, and income rises to OG. Private consumption is unchanged at $GN = AK$. The increase in income AG equals the tax yield KN, which equals the increase in public expenditures EN. Balanced-budget expansion, as shown in equation (18-9), makes for a $1:1$ expansion in income.

Budget Adjustments with Income Tax

Let us now consider a system that employs an income tax in place of a lump-sum tax. Tax yield T_y now becomes a function of income and tax rate t, with $T_y = tY$. Equation (18-4) remains unchanged, but (18-5) and (18-6) are rewritten as follows:

General form	*Linear form*	
$C = C[(1 - t)Y]$	$C = a + c(1 - t)Y$	(18-10)
$Y = \dfrac{1}{1 - \dfrac{C[(1 - t)Y]}{Y}}(I + G)$	$Y = \dfrac{1}{1 - c(1 - t)}(a + I + G)$	(18-11)

The results of alternative budget adjustments with income tax are given by the following set of equations:

[1] Whereas the function prior to tax is $C = a + cY$, after tax it becomes

$$C = a + c(Y - T_l),$$

or $C = (a - cT_l) + cY$. The intercept is reduced by cT_l, while the slope remains unchanged.

TABLE 18-2. BUDGET ADJUSTMENTS WITH INCOME TAX

Type of adjustment	Change in income	
	General form	Linear form
Change in G with T_y constant....	$\dfrac{dY}{dG} = \dfrac{1}{1 - C'(Y - T_y)}$	$\Delta Y = \dfrac{1}{1 - c}\,\Delta G \qquad (18\text{-}12)$
Change in G with t constant......	$\dfrac{dY}{dG} = \dfrac{1}{1 - C'[(1 - t)Y](1 - t)}$	$\Delta Y = \dfrac{1}{1 - c(1 - t)}\,\Delta G$ $(18\text{-}13)$
Change in T_y with G constant.....	$\dfrac{dY}{dT_y} = -\dfrac{C'(Y - T_y)}{1 - C'(Y - T_y)}$	$\Delta Y = -\dfrac{1}{1 - c}\,c\,\Delta T_y \;\;(18\text{-}14)$
Change in t with G constant.......	$\dfrac{dY}{dt} = -\dfrac{C'[(1 - t)Y]Y}{1 - C'[(1 - t)Y](1 - t)}$	$\Delta Y = -\dfrac{cY_0}{1 - c(1 - t_1)}\,\Delta t$ $(18\text{-}15)$
Equal changes in G and T_y.......	$\dfrac{dY}{dB} = 1$	$\Delta Y = \Delta B \qquad (18\text{-}16)$

Let us begin again with an increase in G while holding income tax yield T_y constant. The result of equation (18-12) repeats that of equation (18-7). Since income tax yield is held constant, its nature at the margin is similar to that of a head or lump-sum tax. However, the assumption of a constant T_y now implies a reduction in t. As income rises, the tax base expands, and t must be reduced to keep T_y from rising. The higher the initial tax rate and the greater the percentage increase in income, the larger the required decrease in tax rate.[1]

Next, we shall examine a change in goods and service expenditures while holding tax rate t constant. The resulting increase in income, shown in equation (18-13), is less than it is with constant tax yield. Application of the same tax rate t to a larger income base results in an increase in T_y, and this acts as an offset to the expansionary effects of the increases in expenditures. An income tax reduces the marginal propensity to consume from income before tax and hence lowers the multiplier. This is a case of perverse built-in flexibility, to which we shall return later on.[2]

The next adjustment, shown in equation (18-14) involves a reduction in tax yield while holding public expenditures constant. As in the case of the lump-sum tax, such reduction is less effective per dollar than an

[1] For the linear case we have $t_1 Y_1 - t_0 Y_0 = 0$, hence $\Delta t = -t_0(\Delta Y/Y_1)$.
[2] See p. 443.

increase in expenditures. In order to accomplish the desired change in tax yield, a reduction in tax rate is required.[1]

Alternatively, we may think of the adjustment in terms of a change in tax rate as shown in equation (18-15). The subscripts 0 and 1 for the linear formulation reflect values applicable before and after the change, respectively. The rate of increase in income, or $\Delta Y/Y$, will be greater, the larger the decrease in tax rate and the lower the initial rate of tax. In equation (18-16) we return to the balanced budget change where $\Delta B = \Delta G = \Delta T$. The same result is obtained as is obtained under the head or lump-sum tax, but an increase in tax rate is now required.

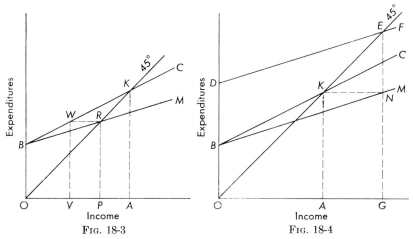

FIGS. 18-3 and 18-4. Budget adjustments with income tax.

A diagrammatic illustration of budget changes with an income tax is given in Figure 18-3. Let BC be the consumption function before tax. Now let an income tax at rate t be imposed. As a result, the consumption function changes from $C = a + cY$ to $C = a + c(1 - t)Y$. The intercept is unchanged but the slope is reduced. If we assume a tax at rate VP/OP, the consumption function pivots down from BC to BM. A

---

[1] If the desired increase in income is such that the required change in yield equals $\Delta \bar{T}_y$, the corresponding required change in tax rate is obtained by equating

$$- \frac{c}{1 - c} \Delta \bar{T}_y = - \frac{cY_0}{1 - c(1 - t_1)} \Delta t$$

so that

$$\Delta t = \frac{1 - c(1 - t_1)}{(1 - c)Y_0} \Delta \bar{T}_y$$

consumer with an income before tax of OP pays VP in tax and has a disposable income of OV. His consumption equals $VW = PR = OP$, which is the new level of income.

In Figure 18-4 we repeat a policy of balanced-budget expansion. BC is the consumption function before tax. An income tax of $t = AG/OG$ is imposed, and the consumption function pivots to BM. We now add public expenditures that will be matched at the new equilibrium by the tax yield. The required increase in expenditures is given by $EN = KN$. We thus obtain the total expenditure line DF. Income rises to OG. Private consumption is unchanged at $AK = GN$. The increase in income AG equals tax yield KN, which equals the increase in public expenditures $BD = NE$.

Income Leverage and Budgetary Balance

Let us now consider how various expansionary policies (other than that of the balanced budget change) will affect the level of surplus or deficit in a budget with income tax.[1]

A policy of raising goods and service expenditures G while holding t constant is shown in equation (18-13). Defining the surplus S as

$$S = tY - G \tag{18-17}$$

and substituting

$$Y = \frac{1}{1 - c(1 - t)} (a + I + G)$$

we obtain

$$S = \frac{t}{1 - c(1 - t)} (a + I + G) - G \tag{18-18}$$

so that

$$\frac{dS}{dG} = \frac{t}{1 - c(1 - t)} - 1 \tag{18-19}$$

Thus an increase in G while raising income will raise, leave unchanged, or lower the surplus, depending on whether $t/[1 - c(1 - t)] \gtreqless 1$ or $c \gtreqless 1$. If $c < 1$, as is usually assumed, we find that the surplus declines with the increase in G. However, we may have $c > 1$ in a stable system, provided that $c(1 - t) < 1$. In this case, an expansionary policy of increasing G will raise the surplus (or reduce the deficit).

Next, consider a policy of reducing t while holding G constant. We

[1] See Erich Schneider, op. cit., p. 270; Assar Lindbäck, Statsbudgetens verkningar på konjunkturutveklingen, Statens Offentliga Utredningar 48, Stockholm Nordiska Bokhandeln, Stockholm, 1956, pp. 65–71; and Bent Hansen, Finanspolitikens ekonomiska teori, Almqvist & Wiksell, Uppsala, Sweden, 1955, pp. 93–95.

now have $T = tY$ and, substituting as before for Y, we obtain

$$T = \frac{t}{1 - c(1 - t)} (a + I + G) \tag{18-20}$$

so that

$$\frac{dT}{dt} = \frac{(1 - c)(a + I + G)}{[1 - (1 - t)c]^2} \tag{18-21}$$

Thus, a decrease in t will raise, leave unchanged, or lower T (and hence the surplus) depending on whether $1 - c \lessgtr 0$ or $c \gtrless 1$.

Finally, let us compare the levels of surplus that prevail while a given level of income is sustained by alternative budget policies. Here it may be shown that a policy of raising G, combined with a corresponding increase in t so as to leave Y unchanged, will raise, leave unchanged, or reduce the surplus, depending on whether $c \lessgtr 1$.*

In short, it is only if $c < 1$ that we can apply the traditional assumptions of fiscal policy according to which expansionary budget measures (short of the balanced-budget case) raise the deficit, and according to which (if income is to remain constant) an increase in government expenditures requires an increase in surplus. For the case of $c > 1$ but $c(1 - t) < 1$, we have the reverse relation between the direction of change in surplus or deficit and the direction of leverage effects.[1] While $c > 1$ is not a plausible assumption in the framework of comparative statics, it may apply for a limited period in a dynamic system, thus leading S to rise with an increase in G or a fall in t.

Differences in Propensity to Consume Allowed For

We have assumed so far that all consumers have the same marginal propensity to consume, so that it is not significant which ones pay the tax.

---

* The initial level of income is given by

$$Y = c(1 - t)Y + G$$

Writing as before
we obtain

$$S = tY - G$$
$$dS = t\,dY + Y\,dt - dG$$

Since $dY = 0$, by substituting for $Y\,dt$, we have

$$dS = \frac{dG}{c} - dG$$

or

$$\frac{dS}{dG} = \frac{1}{c} - 1$$

[1] In a budget with a lump-sum tax, we must have $c < 1$, if the system is to be stable. An increase in G or a reduction in T will reduce the surplus (or increase the deficit) by the amount of change in G or T. Since the change in T must exceed the change in G to obtain the same leverage effect, the change in T will involve a larger reduction in surplus or increase in deficit.

Let us now allow for the possibility that marginal propensities to consume differ among various taxpayers. However, we assume throughout that $c < 1$.

We shall divide consumers into two groups, X and Z, and assume that their marginal propensities to consume differ. The consumption function before introduction of a tax is

$$C = a_x + c_x \alpha Y + a_z + c_z(1 - \alpha)Y \qquad (18\text{-}22)$$

where α is the fraction of income accruing to X, and $1 - \alpha$ the fraction accruing to Z. To simplify, we use the linear form.[1] Let us now reconsider the various budget policies in this setting.

The increase in income in response to an increase in public expenditures with tax payments by X and Z constant is now defined by

$$\Delta Y = \frac{1}{1 - c_x \alpha - c_z(1 - \alpha)} \Delta G \qquad (18\text{-}23)$$

The increase in income secured by raising expenditures with tax yield constant now depends upon a multiplier involving the weighted average of the two propensities to consume. If we have an income tax, the assumption of constant tax yield again requires a reduction in tax rates. We assume this reduction to be such that the rates applicable to X and Z are cut by the same fraction.

The increase in income in response to an increase in budget expenditures with income tax rates applicable to X and Z constant is now given by

$$\Delta Y = \frac{1}{1 - c_x \alpha(1 - t_x) - c_z(1 - \alpha)(1 - t_z)} \Delta G \qquad (18\text{-}24)$$

where t_x and t_z are the rates of tax applicable to the incomes of X and Z respectively.

The balanced-budget theorem must also be adjusted in this setting. The proposition that income increases by an amount equal to the increase in public expenditures still holds for the case of a general proportional income tax, because here the average taxpayer's marginal propensity to consume equals that of the average income recipient.[2] The general proposition ceases to apply for the case of differential tax rates. Let us

---

[1] The formulation of equation (18-22) is more explicit and avoids the somewhat ambiguous distinction between the taxpayer's and average income recipient's propensity to consume, used in my earlier paper, "Alternative Budget Policies for Full Employment," *American Economic Review*, vol. 35, no. 3, pp. 387–399, June, 1945, reprinted in *Readings in Fiscal Policy*, pp. 291–307.

[2] Moreover, we assume that the income from public expenditures accrues to income recipients whose marginal propensity to consume equals that of the average income recipient.

suppose that the entire tax yield is derived from X. We now obtain

$$\Delta Y = \frac{1 - c_x}{1 - c_x\alpha - c_z(1 - \alpha)} \Delta G \qquad (18\text{-}25)$$

where α is again the share of income going to X, while c_x and c_z are the marginal propensities of consumers in groups X and Z respectively. If $c_x = c_z$, the multiplier equals 1, and we are returned to our earlier case. If $c_x > c_z$, we have $\Delta Y < \Delta G$, and if $c_x < c_z$ we have $\Delta Y > \Delta G$. The $1:1$ version of the balanced-budget theorem is merely a special case where the marginal propensities to consume of taxpayers and nontaxpayers are alike. Other exceptions will be noted as we go along.

Where propensities to consumer differ, the choice among various stabilization policies involves the further decision of whom to tax. A given increase in tax yield equal to $\Delta \bar{T}$ leads to different reductions in aggregate demand (or a given decrease in yield leads to a different increase in demand) depending on who pays the additional tax or who is relieved of an old tax. Let the fraction of tax yield derived from X equal β, so that Z pays a fraction equal to $(1 - \beta)$. It is convenient to think of the problem in terms of a lump-sum tax, although with α constant, the argument may be translated readily into an income tax. The relationship between change in income and change in tax yield is as follows:

$$\Delta Y = - \frac{(c_x - c_z)\beta + c_z}{1 - c_x\alpha - c_z(1 - \alpha)} \Delta T \qquad (18\text{-}26)$$

If $c_x = c_z$, this reduces to our earlier formulation of equation (18-8). For any given value of α, the higher both c_x and c_z are, the larger ΔY will be. Moreover, $|\Delta Y|$ will vary directly with β if $c_x > c_z$, and inversely if $c_x < c_z$.

Finally, we may ask what change in income may be obtained if we reallocate a given tax yield $\bar{T}$ between groups X and Z. Let us suppose again that the fraction contributed by X is equal to β. We then obtain the following relationship between change in income and change in the share assumed by X:

$$\Delta Y = \frac{(c_z - c_x)\bar{T}}{1 - c_x\alpha - c_z(1 - \alpha)} \Delta\beta \qquad (18\text{-}27)$$

If $c_z = c_x$, we have $\Delta Y = 0$. The distribution of the tax bill makes no difference. Since the weighted average of the marginal propensities to consume, or $0 < c_x\alpha + c_z(1 - \alpha) < 1$, we know that the denominator is positive. If $c_z > c_x$, the numerator is positive and ΔY rises with an increase in β, the fraction of the tax borne by consumers with the lower marginal propensity. If $c_z < c_x$, the numerator is negative and income falls with a rise in β.

The quantitative importance of variations in β has been dealt with in connection with our earlier discussion of consumption effects.[1]   Since the marginal propensity to consume tends to fall when moving up the income scale, substitution of a progressive for a regressive tax in the depression will raise income in terms of the above model; and more will be gained under conditions of deflation if a given reduction in yield is made by way of tax relief to taxpayers with low incomes.   At the same time, we have seen that differences in the marginal propensity to consume are not so sharp as frequently assumed, so that the quantitative importance of such adjustments is limited.[2]

Nevertheless, the consumption effects of income taxes may differ greatly, depending on whether they are imposed on personal or business income.   This is most evident in the comparison of a personal and a corporation income tax.   Assuming that the corporation income tax is not shifted, a change in corporation income tax may be reflected in either a change in retained earnings or a change in dividends.   Where retained earnings are affected, personal income and hence consumption will be unchanged.   Since a change in corporation tax tends to be reflected in considerable part in a change in retained earnings, substitution of a corporation tax for a personal income tax raises consumption and vice versa.   The distinction between a tax on personal income and a tax on business income is less sharp if the tax is on the profits of an unincorporated firm, where there is a closer fusion between business and personal income; but the same general principle tends to apply.   However, note that we are dealing here with changes in consumer demand only; it remains to be seen whether effects on investment expenditures move in the opposite direction.[3]

Illustration of Alternative Policies

Let us suppose that income is to be raised by a given amount $\Delta \bar{Y}$ and compare the levels of public expenditures on goods and services, tax yield, and deficit that result from the various approaches.   For this purpose, we combine equations (18-23) and (18-26) so that

$$\Delta \bar{Y} = \frac{1}{1 - c_x \alpha - c_z (1 - \alpha)} \Delta G - \frac{(c_x - c_z)\beta + c_z}{1 - c_x \alpha - c_z (1 - \alpha)} \Delta T \quad (18\text{-}28)$$

In place of ΔT we may write $\Delta T = \Delta G - \Delta D$, where ΔD is the deficit. Let us now suppose that income is to be raised by \$100.   The values of α, c_x, c_z, and β are as shown for cases I and II of Table 18-3; the deficits are as specified for policies 1 to 6.   Equation (18-28) then permits us to compute the resulting values of ΔG and ΔT.

[1] See p. 268.
[2] See p. 270.
[3] See p. 465.

TABLE 18-3. NUMERICAL ILLUSTRATION OF ALTERNATIVE BUDGET POLICIES*

Budget policies	Case I $\Delta Y = \$100$ $\alpha = \frac{1}{2}$ $c_x = 0.8$ $c_z = 0.2$			Case II $\Delta Y = \$100$ $\alpha = \frac{1}{2}$ $c_x = 0.8$ $c_z = 0.6$		
	$\beta = 1$	$\beta = \frac{1}{2}$	$\beta = 0$	$\beta = 1$	$\beta = \frac{1}{2}$	$\beta = 0$
1. $\Delta D = 0$						
ΔG	$250	$100	$62	$150	$100	$75
ΔT	250	100	62	150	100	75
2. $\Delta D = 10$						
ΔG	210	90	60	109	77	60
ΔT	200	80	50	99	67	50
3. $\Delta D = 20$						
ΔG	170	80	57	75	53	45
ΔT	150	60	37	55	33	25
4. $\Delta D = \Delta G$						
ΔG	50	50	50	30	30	30
ΔT	0	0	0	0	0	0
5. $\Delta D = 60$						
ΔG	10	40	47	−90	−40	−15
ΔT	−50	−20	−13	−150	−100	−75
6. $\Delta D = -\Delta T$						
ΔG	0	0	0	0	0	0
ΔT	−62	−100	−250	−37	−43	−50

*α = share of income received by consumer group X
c_x = marginal propensity to consume of group X
c_z = marginal propensity to consume of group Z
Y = income
D = deficit
T = tax yield
G = government goods and service expenditures
β = share of tax yield paid by group X

Consider first the results for case I, which involves substantial differences in the marginal propensities to consume of various taxpayers. Policies 1, 2, and 3 are such that $\Delta D < \Delta G$. Thus ΔT is positive, and the required ΔG falls with β. The drain per dollar of ΔT is less severe if a larger part of the tax bill is placed on people with a relatively low propensity to consume. This is most important for the balanced budget, or policy 1, but it also holds for partial-deficit finance, or policies 2 and 3. The latter reflect the kind of situation that results if the tax rate t is held constant. In policy 4 the entire increase in expenditures is deficit-financed. Since $\Delta T = 0$, the value of β does not matter. In policy 5,

$\Delta D > \Delta G$. The increase in expenditures is supplemented by tax reduction or, after T reaches zero, by an increase in transfer payments. The required value of ΔG now falls as β rises, since the potency of tax reduction is great if β is high. In policy 6 we show the limiting case where $\Delta G = 0$ and the entire adjustment is in tax reduction. Again, the required tax reduction rises as β falls. A tax system that bears heavily on people with high propensities to consume acts as a relatively heavy break to expansion, if the expansionary policy involves an increase in yield; by the same token, such a system expedites expansion if the policy involves a reduction in yield.

For any given value of β, the required value of ΔG falls as ΔD rises. This may be seen by moving down any one column. It illustrates the previously noted alternative in expansionary policy between a large budget with a small deficit and a small budget with a large deficit. For the balanced-budget case of policy 1, the required increase in expenditures equals the increase in income (the traditional case of the balanced-budget theorem) for β equaling $\frac{1}{2}$. Here, the 1:1 relation comes about because with α equaling $\frac{1}{2}$, the marginal propensity of taxpayers will be the same as it is for consumers in general. For $\beta > \frac{1}{2}$ the ratio of $\Delta G/\Delta Y > 1$, as the marginal propensity of taxpayers, lies above the average; and the opposite holds for $\beta < \frac{1}{2}$.

In case II, similar results are obtained for a setting where the marginal propensities to consume of X and Z are more nearly alike, and where the marginal propensity to consume of the average income recipient is higher. Deficit finance is more potent, and smaller budgets will do in most cases.[1] Policy 5 now requires a reduction in expenditures, since the assumed deficit exceeds that required for policy 6.

This survey of alternative approaches to providing for a given leverage leaves open the final question of just which solution should be chosen. This choice is not only a matter of stabilization policy; other factors enter and will be explored more fully later on.[2] Let us suppose now that the prevailing level of public expenditures on goods and services is the correct one, measured against the base of a full-employment level of income; and let us assume that distributional considerations require a value of $\beta = 1$. In this case, the only solution in line with a rational budget policy is that of reducing tax yield by \$62 (reference is to case I) and incurring a deficit of that amount. If a given increase in expenditures is desired for Allocation Branch reasons, a corresponding solution can be found. Given the values of ΔY, ΔG, β, and the other relationships involved in our system, ΔD and ΔT may be determined accordingly.

[1] For policy 1 with $\beta = 0$ the required expenditure is higher in case II than in case I, owing to the higher value of c_z.

[2] See p. 517.

Differences in Types of Public Expenditures

Finally, let us consider differences in the consumption leverage of various types of public expenditures. As usual, a distinction must be drawn between goods and service expenditures and transfer payments, and the particular characteristics of each type or expenditure must be allowed for.

Transfer Payments. Changes in transfer payments pose the same problems as changes in tax yield. With a reversal in sign, equation (18-8) may be applied to the case of a lump-sum transfer, and (18-15) to that of an income transfer. It follows that the increase in income secured by a given increase in transfer payments falls short of that secured by a similar increase in goods and service expenditures, unless transfer recipients respend the entire receipt. The initial leakage, which results in a smaller multiplicand, will differ for various types of transfers. In the case of interest payments, the initial leakage may be high. In the case of dole payments, the recipient's marginal propensity to consume may come close to unity. If it equals unity, the resulting increase in income will be the same as for a corresponding increase in goods and service expenditures of government. In the one case, the expansion is entirely in private demand, while in the other, it includes private and public demand. If the marginal propensities to consume of transfer recipients and of tax-payers is the same, an equal increase in transfer payments and tax yield cancels. The leverage of balanced budget expansion is zero in this case.

Goods and Service Expenditures. In dealing with the multiplier effects of goods and service expenditures, it is usually assumed that the marginal propensity to consume of the initial income recipients will be the same, independent of the particular goods and services purchased. As a general rule, this seems reasonable, but special circumstances may arise where such is not the case. For instance, consider work relief. Here the government makes goods and service expenditures, yet the previously unemployed who are hired on such projects may respend the full amount just as would dole recipients. This being the case, we have $\Delta Y = [1 + (1/1 - c)]\Delta G$. The resulting increase in income exceeds that which is normally obtained from goods and service expenditures or from dole payments that are respent in full. Thus, allowances for different initial rates of private spending may be attached not only to reductions in tax yield or to an increase in transfers but also, in certain cases, to goods and service expenditures.[1]

[1] We are not concerned as yet with leakages through changes in inventory or through other effects on capital formation, since investment is assumed to remain fixed. Changes in investment are examined in the following chapter. For an analysis of the effects of expenditures on public works during the thirties, see John Kenneth Galbraith, *The Economic Effects of the Federal Public Works Expenditures, 1933–38*, U.S. National Resources Planning Board, 1940.

B. ALTERNATIVE BUDGET ADJUSTMENTS TO CHECK INFLATION

The preceding discussion dealt with policies directed at securing an increase in employment and income. This is the context in which the theory of compensatory finance was conceived and developed. Let us now turn to a full-employment economy, where restrictive measures may be needed to prevent inflation. Here a decrease in expenditures, an increase in taxes, or a balanced decrease in taxes and expenditures furnish a corresponding set of alternative approaches. The large budget versus the large deficit alternative of expansionary policy is matched by a small budget versus a large surplus alternative of restrictive policy. In this general sense, the problems of expansion and restriction are the same, but certain differences may be noted.[1]

In the preceding discussion of depression policy, we departed from a position of unemployment and then examined adjustments designed to secure a given increase in income. Instead, we could have departed from a position of *full* employment and considered adjustments needed to offset a potential decline in income. Thus for inflation control, we can examine the necessary steps to arrest an inflation in process; or inquire what must be done to forestall inflation and to maintain a stable price level. Let us take the latter view and consider what offsetting adjustments in the budget are needed to hold total expenditures constant while certain increases in demand occur.[2]

Increase in Autonomous Expenditures

Let us consider an economy at a full-employment equilibrium. Now suppose there occurs an increase in autonomous expenditures equal to $\Delta \bar{A}$, whether in investment or in the constant term of the consumption function. If tax yield and public expenditures remain unchanged, income rises as shown by equation (18-7) of Table 1, where A is substituted for G. In a system with income tax, the increase will be as shown in equation (18-13). If we wish income to remain unchanged, we must match $\Delta \bar{A}$ by an offsetting adjustment in the budget so that the net change in income cancels out.

Alternative adjustments for the case of lump-sum tax are shown in Table 18-4.* Assuming the value of $\Delta \bar{A}$ to be negative, the same formula-

---

[1] Our concern at this point is only with differences relating to consumption leverage. Other differences are considered later on. (See p. 467.)

[2] See Lawrence S. Ritter, "Alternative Anti-inflationary Fiscal Policies," *Review of Economic Studies*, ser. 3, vol. 18, no. 47, pp. 129–139, 1950–1951.

* From eq. (18-7) we have $\Delta Y = [1/(1 - c)](\Delta \bar{A} + \Delta G)$. Setting $\Delta Y = 0$, we obtain $\Delta G = -\Delta \bar{A}$. From eqs. (18-7) and (18-8) we have $\Delta Y = [1/(1 - c)] (\Delta \bar{A} - c \Delta T)$. Setting $\Delta Y = 0$, we obtain $\Delta T = \dfrac{1}{c} \Delta \bar{A}$. From eq. (18-9) we have $\Delta Y = [1/(1 - c)] \Delta \bar{A} + \Delta B$. Setting $\Delta Y = 0$, we obtain $\Delta B = -[1/(1 - c)] \Delta A$.

TABLE 18-4. BUDGET ADJUSTMENTS TO OFFSET AUTONOMOUS INCREASE IN
PRIVATE EXPENDITURES

Type of adjustment	Change in income	
	General form	Linear form
Decrease in G with T constant...	$\dfrac{dG}{dA} = -1$	$\Delta G = -\Delta \bar{A}$ (18-29)
Increase in T with G constant...	$\dfrac{dT}{dA} = \dfrac{1}{C'(Y-T)}$	$\Delta T = \dfrac{1}{c}\Delta \bar{A}$ (18-30)
Equal reductions in G and T....	$\dfrac{dB}{dA} = -\dfrac{1}{1-C'(Y-T)}$	$\Delta B = -\dfrac{1}{1-c}\Delta \bar{A}$ (18-31)

tions serve to describe the required adjustments for preventing a decline in income from the full-employment level.

As shown in equation (18-29), $\Delta\bar{A}$ may be offset by an equal decrease in the government's goods and service expenditures with tax yield constant. Since income remains constant, this now implies a constant rate of income tax. Next, $\Delta\bar{A}$ may be offset by an increase in tax yield with government expenditures constant. As shown in equation (18-30), ΔT must exceed $\Delta\bar{A}$. The lower the marginal propensity to consume, the greater the excess. Since $\bar{Y}$ is held constant, the required adjustment in tax rate is obtained readily by substituting $\Delta t\bar{Y}$ for ΔT. Where the initial increase in demand is in government expenditures, the budget must be more than balanced at the margin if an increase in Y is to be avoided. Finally, $\Delta\bar{A}$ may be offset by a balanced-budget contraction as shown by equation (18-31). The decrease in government expenditures and tax yield must equal $\Delta\bar{A}$ times the multiplier. The larger the marginal propensity to consume, the greater the required reduction. A high value of c increases the magnitude of the inflationary gap that is to be checked, but it does not affect the income change per dollar of contraction in the balanced budget. The required reduction in the marginally balanced budget according to equation (18-31) will exceed the required increase in tax yield according to equation (18-30), if $c > \frac{1}{2}$; it will fall short thereof if $c < \frac{1}{2}$.

Increase in Marginal Propensity to Consume

Suppose, now, that the disturbance arises not from an upward shift in autonomous expenditures, but from an increase in the marginal propensity to consume. Using the linear case, Table 18-5 shows the budget adjustments that may be applied to offset an increase in the marginal

TABLE 18-5. BUDGET ADJUSTMENTS TO OFFSET INCREASE IN
MARGINAL PROPENSITY TO CONSUME

Type of adjustment	Change in income (linear form)	
Decrease in G with T constant......	$\Delta G = -\Delta c(Y - T)$	(18-32)
Increase in T with G constant........	$\Delta T = \dfrac{\Delta c(Y - T_0)}{c_1}$	(18-33)
Equal reduction in G and T..........	$\Delta B = -\dfrac{\Delta c(Y - T_0)}{1 - c_1}$	(18-34)

propensity to consume. Subscripts 0 and 1 refer to the position prior to and after the change in c, respectively. The required cut in goods and service expenditures, as shown in equation (18-32), will be greater, the higher the initial level of disposable income. The required increase in tax yield, as shown by equation (18-33), will be greater, the higher the initial level of disposable income and the lower the level of (as distinct from the increase in) the marginal propensity to consume. The required reduction in the balanced budget, as shown in equation (18-34), where $\Delta B = \Delta G = \Delta T$, will be larger, the higher the initial level of disposable income and the larger the absolute level of the marginal propensity to consume.

C. THE ROLE OF MONEY ILLUSION

Thus far we have focused on inflation that is checked from the outset, with price-level stability maintained. In such a case, problems of money illusion do not arise. But if the price level is permitted to change, considerations of money illusion enter as a complicating factor.

Effectiveness of Restriction by Consumption Tax

In popular discussion, it is frequently held that consumption taxes cannot be used to check inflation. On the contrary, they are said to raise prices and are hence inflationary. This is a fallacy, even if we grant that an increase in consumption taxes is added to cost and raises the price level. This rise in price level is a once-and-for-all increase, to be distinguished from the continuous increase that results if the inflationary gap is not closed. Nevertheless, a difference remains: A potential inflationary gap may be closed by an increase in income tax while holding the price level constant; it may be closed by an increase in consumption taxes only while permitting some rise in price level, reflecting the increase in cost due to tax.[1]

Let us now compare the amounts of increase in income tax and in consumption tax that are required to secure the same restrictive effect. The amounts will differ for various reasons. A first cause of difference may be that the two taxes are paid by taxpayers with different marginal propensities to consume. If the comparison is between a general sales tax and a progressive income tax, the change in consumption per dollar of change in yield will be greater under the sales tax. This is the aspect of qualitative tax policy that we have considered in Table 18-3.

A further difference may result from the substitution effect of the consumption tax, which effect is adverse to consumption. Though hardly of great significance for a permanent tax, this effect may be exceedingly important if the taxpayer has reason to assume that the change in tax rate is temporary. As noted before, this is of primary importance for war finance.[2]

On both these grounds, adjustments in a broadly based consumption tax tend to be more potent per dollar of change in yield than adjustments in the personal income tax. It remains to consider a third difference that arises if money illusion is present. For this purpose, let us assume that the marginal propensity to consume is constant and alike for all taxpayers, and that the substitution effect of a general consumption tax is insignificant.

We then compare the amounts by which an income tax and a general consumption tax must be raised respectively in order to secure the same restrictive effects; and we assume—which is crucial to the argument—that the additional consumption taxes are reflected in higher prices, while the increase in the income tax leaves the price level unchanged.

If the increase in income tax yield equals ΔT_y, the initial change in consumption equals $-c\,\Delta T_y$. If consumption is to be reduced by $\Delta \bar{C}$, the required increase in income tax yield equals $\Delta T = -(1/c)\,\Delta \bar{C}$. Since the change in the income tax leaves the price level unaffected, no problem of money illusion arises.

Now consider an increase in consumption tax. As a result, the price level rises while money income remains unchanged. If we assume that

---

[1] This increase in price level cannot be avoided by raising consumption taxes further. It would only add to the increase in price level and, assuming money wages to be rigid in the downward direction, would make for a reduction in real income.

The case is complicated if wages are determined by an escalator clause, but the general conclusion still holds. For an evaluation of the anti-inflationary effectiveness of various taxes, see Richard Goode, "Anti-inflationary Implications of Alternative Forms of Taxation," *American Economic Review*, vol. 42, no. 2, pp. 147–161, May, 1952; and the comments by Carl Shoup, same issue, pp. 161–165.

[2] See p. 263.

the consumer operates under a money illusion, he disregards this change in price level and continues to spend the same amount. Since the sales tax constitutes a diversion of consumer expenditure, consumer expenditures in real terms are now decreased by the amount of tax. In other words, the required increase in consumption tax equals $\Delta T_c = -\Delta \bar{C}$. The required increase falls short of that needed under the income tax. The consumption tax is more efficient per dollar of increased yield than is the income tax.

Let us compare the two taxes if there is no money illusion. Since we have assumed that the income tax leaves the price level unchanged, the required increase in income tax yield is the same with or without money illusion. Also, it is easy to see that the increase in consumption tax becomes less efficient per dollar if we remove the money illusion. Without money illusion, the consumer is aware that the real value of a given money income has fallen as prices have risen. He will adjust himself to this change, and the consumption function in money terms will shift upward. He will raise his expenditures out of a given money income, thus resisting the government's move to cut his consumption.

Granted that removal of money illusion renders the increase in consumption tax less effective, how does this truncated effectiveness compare with the effectiveness of a rise in income tax? The answer is not self-evident, but it may be shown that the efficiency of the increase in consumption tax remains greater per dollar of yield, even if there is no money illusion.[1] This result comes about since the consumer's endeavor to resist the government's restrictive objective can never be wholly effective.

[1] See E. Cary Brown, "Analysis of Consumption Taxes in Terms of the Theory of Income Determination," *American Economic Review*, March, 1950, vol. 40, no. 1, pp. 74–89, March, 1950; and Assar Lindbäck, *Statsbudgetens verkningar på konjunkturutvecklingen*, Statens Offentliga Utredningar 48, Stockholm Nordiska Bokhandeln, Stockholm, 1956, chap. 2, appendix, pp. 32–37.

Brown's proof is as follows: Let I = investment, C = consumption expenditures net of excises, Y_0 = net national product at factor cost, G = government goods and service expenditures, t_y = income tax rate, and t_c = consumption-tax rate. Assuming Y_0 to be full-employment income at the given price level, we solve for the equilibrium level of tax yield under various taxes and assumptions regarding money illusion.

Money Illusion: Income Tax. We have the following two equations:

$$C = a + (1 - t_y)cY_0 \tag{1}$$
$$Y_0 = C + I + G \tag{2}$$

Substituting C as defined in eq. (1) into eq. (2) and solving for the equilibrium yield of tax, we obtain

$$t_y Y_0 = \frac{a + cY_0 + I + G - Y_0}{c} \tag{3}$$

The reduction in consumption due to tax or $ct_y Y_0$ must equal the inflationary gap as it

Such is the case because any attempted increase in consumption, undertaken to adjust to the increased price level, brings with it an increase in tax liability.

---

would be in the absence of taxation. The tax yield must be larger than the inflationary gap because it is reflected only partially in reduced consumption.

Money Illusion: Consumption Tax. We now have the following equations:

$$C + t_c C = a + c Y_0 \qquad (4)$$
$$Y_0 = C + I + G \qquad (5)$$

Substituting as before and solving for the equilibrium yield of tax, we obtain

$$t_c C = a + c Y_0 + I + G - Y_0 \qquad (6)$$

The required tax yield is just equal to the inflationary gap in the absence of tax. The required yield is less than under the income tax with money illusion.

No Money Illusion: Income Tax. The case is similar to income tax with a money illusion since the income tax does not give rise to price-level change.

No Money Illusion: Consumption Tax. In this case, we have

$$C(1 + t_c) = a(1 + t_c) + c Y_0 \qquad (7)$$

as the tax results in a parallel upward shift of the consumption function, and

$$Y_0 = C + I + G \qquad (8)$$

Substituting as before, we now obtain

$$t_c C = \frac{c Y_0 (Y_0 - I - G)}{Y_0 - a - I - G} + I + G - Y_0 \qquad (9)$$

as the required consumption-tax yield. $t_c C$ as defined by eq. (9) is larger than $t_c C$ as defined by eq. (6).

Comparison of Eqs. (9) and (3). The required yield under the consumption tax will be greater, the same, or smaller, depending on whether

$$\frac{c Y_0 (Y_0 - I - G)}{Y_0 - a - I - G} + I + G - Y_0 - \frac{a + c Y_0 + I + G - Y_0}{c} \gtreqless 0 \qquad (10)$$

This reduces to

$$(1 - c)(I + G - Y_0) + a \gtreqless 0 \qquad (11)$$

so that the excess of the required consumption-tax yield over the required income tax yield varies directly with I, G, and a, and inversely with c. Rewriting eq. (11) in different form, we have

$$\frac{a + c Y_0 + I + G - Y_0}{c} - (I + G) \gtreqless 0 \qquad (12)$$

The first term is the income tax yield. It follows that eq. (12) will be equal to zero if the required income tax yield equals $I + G$. This will hold if saving equals zero, in which case the required yield of the two taxes will be the same. If saving is positive, the required income tax will fall short of $I + G$. The left side of eq. (12) is negative, and the required consumption-tax yield will fall short of the required income tax yield. The opposite will hold for the case of dissaving. Since in most real situations saving is positive, the consumption tax is usually more efficient.

The same considerations also bear on the effectiveness of a reduction in the marginally balanced budget as an anti-inflation device. Suppose conditions are such that a reduction in public expenditures matched by an equal reduction in income tax yield reduces income by an equal amount. Disposable income and consumer expenditures remain unchanged, while government expenditures are reduced. Now, let the same reduction in public expenditures be matched by a reduction in consumption taxes. The cut in public expenditures reduces disposable income in money terms. The reduction in consumption taxes is assumed to be reflected in reduced prices. If consumers are subject to a money illusion, they will not be aware of this and spend a larger fraction of their (reduced) money income. If they are not subject to a money illusion, they will find their real income unchanged and will continue to spend the same fraction. Thus, the restrictive effectiveness of the budget contraction will be less if there is a money illusion. While the presence of money illusion increases the restrictive effectiveness of raising the yield of the consumption tax, it reduces the effectiveness of a marginally balanced reduction in the budget if a cut in consumption taxes is involved.

Again, there remains the question whether, in the absence of a money illusion, a reduction in the marginally balanced budget will be more effective if it involves a cut in income tax or a cut in consumption taxes. The same argument which demonstrates that a cut in consumption tax remains more expansionary, even in the absence of a money illusion, also shows that budget contraction will be more restrictive if the reduction is in the yield of income tax.

A parallel argument applies to the case of tax reduction undertaken to secure an increase in the level of income. Assuming the reduction in the consumption tax to be reflected in reduced prices, the resulting increase in consumer expenditures in real terms will equal the full reduction in yield if consumers are subject to a money illusion. While it will be less effective if there is no money illusion, the reduction in consumption tax remains more effective than an equal-yield reduction in income tax.

Similarly, it may be shown that an expansionary policy of increasing a marginally balanced budget with consumption taxes will be less effective if there is a money illusion than if there is none. While the presence of a money illusion increases the effectiveness of a reduction in the yield of consumption taxes, it reduces the effectiveness of balanced budget expansion involving increased yield from consumption taxes. Similarly, balanced budget expansion in the absence of a money illusion is again more effective if the additional yield is derived from an income tax.

The crucial assumption underlying the preceding argument is that introduction of a consumption tax is reflected in increased prices, while its removal is reflected in reduced prices. To the extent that the assumption applies, we have here an important exception to the earlier proposition that our concern need only be with changes in relative prices.[1]   Given the downward rigidity of wages and other costs, considerations of money illusion may be more relevant to an increase in tax yield than to a decrease. However, the assumption of rising prices also requires that the finance can be made available without check to investment.

Expansion of Balanced Budget at Full Employment

The problem of money illusion is encountered whenever the price level changes, whether owing to changes in consumption tax or other reasons. Expansion in the balanced budget under conditions of unemployment raises the level of employment as well as money income.   Thus, the problem of price level is of secondary importance.   Under conditions of full employment, an expansion in the balanced budget cannot but raise prices.   This will be true whether the increase in expenditures is matched by an increase in income or in consumption taxes.[2]

Let us assume a position of full-employment equilibrium and suppose that the government increases goods and service expenditures and income tax yield by equal amounts.   In the absence of a money illusion, the resulting increase in total money income will exceed the increase in expenditures.   The expansionary (inflationary) effect of the balanced budget expansion is in excess of the 1:1 ratio applicable in the case of unemployment.   The increase in price level calls forth an upward shift in the consumption function in money terms, so that the decline in consumer expenditures is less than it would be otherwise.   Provided that consumers have no money illusion, the budget must be overbalanced in order to hold the inflationary effect on a 1:1 basis.   We now have a situation where the 1:1 theorem holds only if there *is* a money illusion.

At the same time no change in price level occurs, and the problem of money illusion does not arise if tax rates are increased sufficiently so as to maintain the aggregate level of money expenditures unchanged.[3]   The increase in income tax yield required to nullify the expansionary effects of a given increase in government expenditures is the same under conditions of unemployment or full employment; but the rise in money income induced by a balanced budget expansion is greater under conditions of full employment.

---

[1] See p. 370.

[2] See Franz Gehrels, "Inflationary Effects of a Balanced Budget under Full Employment," *American Economic Review*, vol. 39, no. 6, pp. 1276–1278, December, 1949.

[3] Gehrels, *ibid.*, p. 1278, argues that it is necessary, under conditions of full employment, to increase income tax yield by over twice the increase in public expenditures. This seems to overlook the fact that there will be no shift in the consumption function if the money expenditures (and hence prices) are held stable.

Open Inflation

In the preceding pages, we have dealt with budget adjustments of such a nature that the potential inflationary gap is closed completely. Hence, the price level remains unchanged or, in the case of the consumption tax, the increase is limited by the amount of tax. Suppose, now, that aggregate expenditures are permitted to increase continuously, since the government fails to close the inflationary gap at the outset.

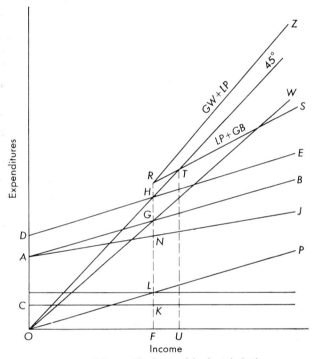

Fig. 18-5. Money illusion and budget inflation.

Consider a case of full-employment equilibrium where the government absorbs a certain share of total output. This is shown in Figure 18-5.* The consumption function is given by AB, after allowing for whatever tax applies. Government expenditures equal OC, and the total-expenditure line DE is obtained by adding OC and AB. Income equals OF, which reflects full-employment output at prevailing prices. Consumption at the initial equilibrium equals FG, and government outlays are $GH = OC$.

* See Arthur Smithies, "The Behavior of Money National Income under Inflationary Conditions," *Quarterly Journal of Economics*, vol. 57, no. 1, pp. 113–129, November, 1942, reprinted in *Readings in Fiscal Policy*, American Economic Association, Richard D. Irwin, Inc., Homewood, Ill., 1955, pp. 122–136.

Private investment is assumed to be fixed and may be disregarded. Now, the government wishes to increase its share in income OF or expenditure FH from FK/FH to FL/FH. This could be the case, for instance, in the transition to a war economy. The increase can be obtained without raising total money income by increasing the rate of income tax so as to lower the consumption function from AB to AJ where $GN = KL$. In this case, the total-expenditure line and equilibrium are unchanged. Government expenditures henceforth are $FL = NH$, and consumption is cut to FN. Prices remain stable, and the problem of money illusion does not arise.

For political or incentive reasons, this may not be a possible policy. Suppose instead that the tax rate is to remain unchanged. In this case, total expenditures will increase and prices will rise. Since OF is the full-employment income, the entire expansion in income beyond OF, or in expenditures beyond FH, will be reflected in a price rise. If the government is to retain a share in real income equal to FL/FH, public expenditures must move along LP as money income increases and prices rise. The final outcome differs, depending on whether or not consumers are subject to a money illusion.

If consumers are subject to a money illusion, their consumption function remains unchanged in money terms at AB. Consumer expenditures move up along GB as income rises. The total-expenditure line now equals RS, obtained by adding LP and GB. As money income expands, the average propensity to save rises. At T it has reached a level equal to the fraction of the product that the government wishes to absorb. The government, which has no money illusion, beats the consumers who do. After the new equilibrium is established at income OU, the price level will have risen by FU/OU. A new equilibrium of money income, such as OU, will result if the fraction of full-employment output that the government wishes to absorb, or LF/HF, does not exceed the marginal propensity to save out of full-employment income.

If consumers have no money illusion, they will fight back by adjusting their consumption function in money terms. Since real income remains unchanged, they will maintain their average propensity to consume unchanged. As money income rises, consumer expenditures now move out along GW. Adding LP to GW, we obtain the total expenditure line RZ. The slope of this line exceeds unity. Money income expands, and prices rise at an increasing rate. Such, at least, will be the case unless certain built-in stabilizers move into action. These may be fiscal in nature as the effective tax rate rises with income or as support payments fall.[1] Or, they may originate in the private sector. Thus, earnings received by individuals with a high marginal propensity to consume (such as wage earners) may lag behind earnings of others with a lower propen-

[1] See p. 505.

sity to consume (such as profits recipients).[1]   At the same time, there may be factors of built-in instability, especially if induced effects of price-level anticipations upon profits are allowed for.   In the extreme case, this takes the form of *Sachflucht* and leads to the sharp rise in velocity that is typical of hyperinflation.

Money illusion of consumers thus facilitates stabilization, and there are other factors that may lead to a tapering off of the inflation process after an initial shock has occurred.   However, there is no need for fiscal policy to rely on these forces.   A potential inflationary gap may be closed at the outset by an appropriate upward adjustment in tax rates, thus holding private expenditures to the full-employment level.   This at least, may be done in so far as the mechanics of fiscal policy are concerned, but it remains to be seen whether the required tax restrictions are always compatible with incentive considerations.

---

[1] For a dynamic model of this sort, see Arthur Smithies, *op. cit.*, pp. 130–135.   In Smithies's discussion, as in that of the present chapter, investment is held fixed.   In a more realistic model, effects of price-level changes upon investment must be allowed for, and the comparison must be between the marginal propensity to spend (rather than to consume) of various taxpayers.   This may greatly change the results, as shown on text p. 464.

CHAPTER 19

Compensatory finance: investment aspects

In the preceding chapter, we have examined the leverage effects of budgetary adjustments under the assumption that private investment remains unchanged. We shall now introduce effects upon investment into the picture, retaining for the time being the preceding framework of comparative statics. For purposes of this chapter we shall consider investment as a component of aggregate expenditures only. The relationship of investment to capacity and growth will be taken up in the next chapter.

A. PROFITABILITY EFFECTS

Let us proceed on the assumption that investment is a function of profit expectations and the rate of interest. An alternative approach, according to which investment is considered a function of disposable income, will be examined later. We shall find that the two approaches lead to quite different results regarding the effects of tax policy on the level of investment.

Role of Transaction Drain

Assuming all taxes to be in the form of an income tax, and disregarding public debt transactions, we have a simple system of income determination given by the following equations:

	General form	Linear form	
	$Y = C + I + G$	$Y = C + I + G$	(19-1)
	$C = C[(1 - t)Y + R]$	$C = a + c[(1 - t)Y + R]$	(19-2)
	$I = I(i)$	$I = d - ei$	(19-3)
	$i = L(M_a)$	$M_a = f - hi$	(19-4)
	$M_a = \bar{M} - M_t$	$M_a = \bar{M} - M_t$	(19-5)
	$M_t = k(Y + R)$	$M_t = k(Y + R)$	(19-6)

where G and R are goods and service expenditures and transfers of government; t is the income tax rate, and M is the total money supply, all of which are given. M_t is transaction money, and M_a is asset money.

Now, let G be changed while holding t, R, and M constant. The resulting change in income is given by

$$\text{General form } \frac{dY}{dG} = \frac{1}{1 - C'[(1 - t)Y](1 - t) + I'(i) \cdot L'(M_a) \cdot k}$$

$$\text{Linear form } \Delta Y = \frac{1}{1 - (1 - t)c + ek/h} \Delta G$$

(19-7)

Comparison with equation (18-13) shows that the size of the multiplier is reduced.[1] The increase in income requires increased transaction funds, and the resulting transaction drain reduces the supply of asset money. This in turn raises the rate of interest, as shown by equation (19-4), and the increase in interest reduces investment, as shown by equation (19-3). The increase in income that results from an increase in government expenditures will be small if k is large, since this means a low velocity of transaction money and hence a heavy transaction drain.   Similarly, the resulting increase in income will be small if the liquidity-preference schedule is inelastic [in which case $L'(M_a)$ is large and h is small] and if the investment schedule is elastic [in which case both $I'(i)$ and e are large]. As ek/h or $I'(i) \cdot L'(M_a) \cdot k$ become large, the increase in Y secured by a given increase in G declines, and in the limiting case it may reach zero. The check exerted by the transaction drain cannot by its very nature result in a net contraction of income.

The role of transaction drain is likely to be of minor importance in checking an expansionary policy under conditions of depression, since in a depression the liquidity schedule tends to be highly elastic.   However, transaction drain is a factor that must be allowed for when considering the fiscal and monetary policies for a growing economy; and it may act as a significant brake to inflation.   We shall return to this later on, in a somewhat different framework.   The simplifying assumption of a constant M must be replaced by a more consistent setting in which the effects of deficit or surplus policy upon the money supply and the general structure of claims are allowed for.[2]

Effects on L and I Functions: First Approximation

In the simple system of income determination given in equations (19-1) to (19-6), we have assumed that the existence of an income tax enters into the consumption function but not into the investment and liquidity-preference functions.   This assumption must now be reconsidered.   In

[1] See p. 435.
[2] See p. 526.

other words, our earlier partial-equilibrium analysis of effects on investment must now be integrated into the general system of income
determination.[1]

We shall begin with a general tax on investment income, and inquire
how such a tax affects profitability and thus the level of investment; and,
in particular, what reformulation, if any, it requires of equations (19-3)
and (19-4).

A highly simplified view of the matter is given in Figures 19-1 and 19-2.
Let OE in Figure 19-1 be the rate of interest determined by the liquidity-
preference schedule LL and the asset money OM_a. Let BA in Figure 19-2
be the investment schedule, so that investment equals OG.

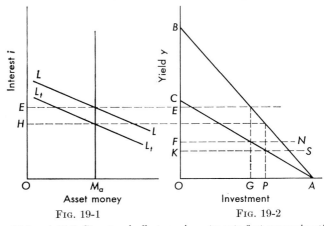

FIG. 19-1   FIG. 19-2

FIGS. 19-1 and 19-2. Structural effects on investment: first approximation.

An income tax is imposed, and budget expenditures are increased by
the gain in yield. To simplify matters, let us disregard possible changes
in the payment structure and assume that lenders are in no way affected by the tax. In this case, the cost of borrowing as defined by
equation (19-4) remains unchanged as well. The interest term in the
investment function, or i in equation (19-3), is replaced by the yield y of
our former analysis[2], and the condition $i = y$ is added. Assuming the tax
law to assure loss offset, investment yield y is cut by the rate of tax.
Thus, if the tax rate is 50 per cent, the net-yield schedule is given by AC.
Introduction of the tax also cuts the net cost of borrowing by 50 per cent
since the cost of borrowing is deducted from taxable income. Thus, the
net cost of borrowing falls from OE to OF. Investment is now determined
by the intersection of the net (after tax) yield schedule AC and the net
cost of borrowing schedule FN. Since both are cut by one-half, investment remains unchanged at OG.

[1] See p. 312.
[2] See p. 318.

If the tax does not provide for full loss offset, yield is reduced by more than the rate of tax, and the AB schedule drops more sharply. The FN schedule remains as before, and investment is reduced.

Effects on L and I Functions: Second Approximation

These results differ from those of our earlier analysis, and are based on too crude an interpretation.[1] We must consider more carefully just how the choices of lenders and investors are affected.

Liquidity Preference and Demand for Real Assets. For purposes of this discussion, let us distinguish between the *lenders*, whose business it is to hold cash or buy debt, and the *investors*, whose business it is to sell debt and purchase real assets with the proceeds.

The lenders operate on the basis of liquidity preference; and the liquidity-preference schedule shows the amount of asset money that they as a group are willing to hold at various rates of interest. The basic idea underlying this schedule is that lenders wish to hold money if they expect the rate of interest to rise and, hence, bond prices to fall; and that they prefer to hold bonds if they expect the rate of interest to fall and, hence, bond prices to rise. Beyond this, two interpretations are possible.

According to one, which we shall refer to as the *certainty hypothesis*, each potential lender feels certain that his particular expectation is correct. He either lends his entire funds or holds them in cash, depending on whether he expects that the rate of interest will fall or rise. If the current rate is relatively low, more investors will expect the rate to rise and prefer to hold cash than will do so if the rate is high. As a result, the liquidity-preference schedule for the group as a whole slopes downward, even though there is no such schedule for the individual investor.

According to another interpretation, which we shall refer to as the *uncertainty hypothesis*, each lender views the interest outlook in probability terms, there being some chance for interest rates to fall and a possibility as well that they may rise. This view is more in line with our earlier theory of investment behavior.

Let us now turn to the investors. To simplify matters, we assume that all investment in real assets involves the same rate of risk r. Schedule A_g in Figure 19-3 is a schedule showing the available supply of such investments at various levels of gross yield. Since investors borrow funds to make real investments, the cost of borrowing must be deducted from this gross yield to obtain the net yield. Let the cost of borrowing, as determined by the liquidity preference of lenders, be equal to EF. Schedule A_n then records the available supply of such investments at various levels of net yield.

The other side of the picture is provided by a schedule showing the

[1] See p. 320.

willingness of investors to borrow and invest at various levels of net yield and risk r. This is shown by the W_{rn} schedule. It may be looked upon as a demand schedule for real investment or as a supply schedule for willingness to take investment risk.

Equilibrium is determined at E, where the two net schedules intersect and real investment equals OC. The gross yield equals CF, the cost of borrowing equals EF, and the investors' net yield equals CE. This interpretation differs somewhat from the usual view of the investment

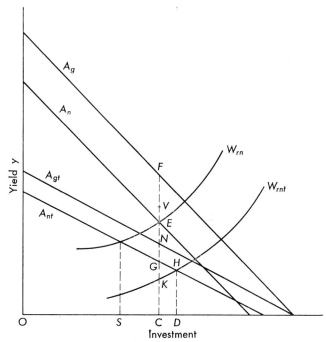

Fig. 19-3. Structural effects on investment: second approximation.

sector in the system of income determination. Whereas the usual I schedule refers to the cost of borrowing as set by the liquidity-preference schedule of the lenders, our A_g schedule refers to this cost plus the reward for risk taking charged by the borrower-investor.

Tax with Loss Offset. Let us now introduce into this system a 50 per cent tax with perfect loss offset. Consider first what happens on the lender's side of the picture. If we proceed on the certainty hypothesis, the tax will leave the cost of borrowing unaffected.[1] Interest income is a pure rent income, and the lender takes what he can get. However, the uncertainty hypothesis is to be preferred. In this case, and assuming full

[1] To simplify matters, we still assume that the supply of asset money is not affected by the introduction of the tax, or that such effects as result are compensated for by monetary measures.

loss offset, we know that the price of risk taking is unaffected.[1]   There is no adverse substitution effect against lending but an income effect in its favor.   At any given market rate or cost of borrowing, the net yield to the lender is reduced by the rate of tax.   As a result of this income effect, lenders attempt to buy more debt.   The liquidity-preference schedule drops; the cost of lending is reduced.[2]   Returning to Figures 19-1 and 19-2, let us suppose that the liquidity-preference schedule drops to L_tL_t. The net cost of borrowing falls to KS, and investment rises to OP.

Taking a more subtle view of the investment side of the picture, we must reconsider the matter in terms of Figure 19-3.   Consider first what happens to the A_g schedule, showing the amount of investments available at various levels of gross yield.   Since perfect loss offset is allowed for, yield is reduced by the rate of tax.   We thus obtain the A_{gt} schedule, showing the gross yield after tax but before deducting the cost of borrowing.   The cost of borrowing has been reduced and now falls short of EF. Let us suppose that it equals VF.   Since the cost of borrowing may be deducted from taxable income, the net cost of borrowing equals 50 per cent thereof.   Schedule A_{nt}, showing the net yield after deducting tax and cost of borrowing, is obtained as a parallel to A_{gt}, so that $GN = \frac{1}{2}VF$.

Finally, we must allow for the fact that private risk as well as the yield of investment is reduced by the rate of tax.   As a result, investors are now confronted with a lower risk proposition.   They are willing to make the same investment at a lower net yield after tax.   Thus, the willingness-to-invest schedule shifts from W_{rn} to the right, to a position such as shown by W_{rnt}.[3]   The two net schedules now intersect at H.   The tax results in an increase in investment from OC to OD.

The result of increased investment remains, though to a lesser degree, if the cost of borrowing is not affected by the tax.[4]   This outcome is in full accord with that of our earlier discussion.

[1] See p. 320.

[2] Note that our two interpretations of liquidity preference are both based on the assumption that there is no utility to the holding of money as such.   (See p. 427.) In other words, money in excess of transaction needs will be held only if this makes for a more profitable investment portfolio (in view of the given outlook and preferences) than would another combination of assets.   The assumption that the holding of money has a utility other than this may underlie Kalecki's conclusion that imposition of a tax raises the cost of borrowing.   See M. Kalecki, "A Theory of Commodity, Income and Capital Taxation," *Economic Journal*, vol. 47, no. 187, pp. 444–450, September, 1937.

[3] The intersection of W_{rnt} with CF must be below G.   Intersection at G would mean that investors hold investment constant even though risk is reduced by the rate of tax and net yield is reduced at a lesser rate.   This would be possible only if income is an inferior good.

[4] In this case, the distance between the A_{gt} and A_{nt} schedules equals one-half EF, and the new A_{nt} schedule intersects CF at K.   As before, the W_{rnt} schedule must intersect CF below K, provided that income is not an inferior good.

Tax without Loss Offset. As before, the results differ if no loss offset is allowed for. If lenders operate under the certainty hypothesis, the cost of borrowing is again unaffected. Since the possibility of loss is excluded, provision for loss offset is irrelevant. If lenders operate under the uncertainty hypothesis, a tax without loss offset carries a substitution effect which is adverse to lending and an income effect which is favorable. On balance, the cost of borrowing may rise, fall, or remain unchanged. If it falls, the decline will be less than under full loss offset.

On the investor's side, the situation differs in two respects from that of the tax with full loss offset. Since the tax leaves private risk unchanged, the W_{rn} schedule remains unchanged. Since yield is reduced by more than the rate of tax, the A_{gt} schedule drops more sharply and its slope is reduced. Whether the cost of borrowing increases or not, the new A_{nt} schedule lies below the schedule with full loss offset. The new level of investment falls short of OS, and the tax reduces investment by more than SC. Again, the result is in line with that of our earlier discussion.

Undoubtedly this model presents much too simple a view of the problem. However, it suggests the kind of system that must be substituted for the liquidity-preference and investment equation of the conventional type, if one wishes to examine profitability effects of taxation upon investment.

B. EFFECTS ON THE SUPPLY OF FUNDS

The discussion of the preceding section has dealt with taxation effects upon the investor's willingness to invest available funds. It is similar in this respect to the traditional monetary analysis in terms of elasticities of the L and I schedules and of changes in money supply. As in the case of monetary analysis, there is another approach—an approach that stresses the availability of funds, more or less independent of their cost.

One is tempted to discard this approach because the budget process—in the confines of the balanced budget, at least—cannot affect the total supply of funds. This is true enough, but it does not eliminate the problem, since the fiscal process may redistribute available funds so as to modify the effective pattern of asset preferences. This aspect is of particular importance where the credit market is imperfect and where potential investors have a strong aversion to incurring debt.[1]

By way of illustration, let us carry this approach to its extreme and replace the liquidity-preference and investment functions of the earlier analysis by an equation showing investment as a function of *available*

[1] See p. 543.

funds, including depreciation charges and retained earnings of business.[1] If this view is taken, the analysis of taxation effects on investment is greatly simplified. Investment is treated as a propensity to spend out of that share of income which flows into depreciation or into retained earnings, just as consumption is treated as a propensity to spend out of that share which is paid out to individuals. Both may be combined into a total *spendings function*.

An approach of this sort, adjusted for time lags, is to be found in econometric models of income determination[2] and in recent growth

[1] Such a model may be illustrated by the following system:

$$Y = C + I + G$$
$$C = C[(W + D)(1 - t_p)]$$
$$I = I[A + P(1 - t_b) - D]$$
$$P = P(Y)$$
$$D = DP(1 - t_b)$$
$$A = A(K)$$
$$Y = P + W + A$$

where G is government expenditures, t_p is the rate of tax on personal income, t_b is the rate of tax on business profits, and K is capital stock, all given. The unknowns to be solved for are income Y, investment I, consumption C, wage income W, dividend income D, profits P, and amortization charges A. In equilibrium, the government deficit or surplus must match the excess of saving or investment in the private sector.

[2] An approach of this sort seems to underly the Klein-Goldberger model. See Lawrence R. Klein and A. S. Goldberger, *An Econometric Model of the United States, 1929–1952*, North-Holland Publishing Company, Amsterdam, 1955. The investment function of the model reads:

$$I = -16.71 + 0.78[(1 - t)P + D]_{-1} - 0.073K_{-1} + 0.14L_{-1}$$

where P is profits, D is depreciation, K is capital stock, L is liquid funds held by business, and the subscript -1 indicates preceding period. Of the items in the equation, the L and D reflect an available-funds approach to investment, while K reflects a profitability approach. P may appear as an index of either profitability or availability of funds. The fact that P is combined with depreciation (which is clearly on the availability side) suggests the latter interpretation. Since K carries little weight, we are left in effect with an availability approach with 0.78 for the propensity to invest out of available funds, compared with only 0.75 for the propensity to consume out of disposable income.

Note also that the empirical profit-investment relationship of the model makes no explicit assumption as to whether the corporation income tax is shifted or not. The identity of profits after tax and profits before tax minus tax, holds in either case. Yet if we wish to predict the effects of a change in profits tax, it would hardly seem possible to do so properly without making a specific assumption as to incidence, i.e., without deciding whether such a tax should be treated as an excise or an income tax. A decision on shifting may not be needed to predict changes in income if the structural relations are held constant, but more refined methods involving greater insight at the micro level are required if the results of structural changes in the tax system are to be predicted.

models.[1] As far as fiscal analysis is concerned, investment is dealt with in terms of an investment function just as consumption is dealt with in the consumption function. Introduction of investment effects merely repeats the procedure applied previously when a distinction was drawn between the propensities to consume of various income recipients in the fixed-investment model.[2] Proceeding along the same line, different propensities to invest may be imputed to savings out of different types of income.

While attractive in its simplicity, this approach hardly provides the basis for an adequate analysis of fiscal effects on investment. Though empirical investment functions of the available-funds type yield an adequate fit, it does not follow that effects on profitability are nonexistent. The very change in available funds may have coincided with changes in profitability and profit expectations, and taxes may have been constant in their effects on profitability.   An investment function that is adequate to predict changes in total income while holding budget parameters constant may not be adequate to trace the results of changes in these parameters.

Empirical aspects aside, effects on investment through changes in availability differ from those through changes in profitability.   Under the availability approach, an increase in tax must reduce investment, provided that the taxpayer's propensity to invest exceeds zero; and the limit to a possible effect on investment expenditure is set by the amount of yield.   The situation is again similar to that found in the preceding discussion on consumption effects.   Under the profitability approach, a tax may increase or reduce investment, and the amount of change in investment may exceed or fall short of the amount in yield.   This is of basic importance for the efficiency of alternative budget adjustments when allowing for investment effects.

C. ALTERNATIVE METHODS RECONSIDERED

Our earlier evaluation of the relative effectiveness of alternative budget policies was based on the assumption that private investment remains unchanged.[3] It remains to consider what modifications are needed if effects on investment are allowed for.

Availability Effects

Suppose first that effects on investment operate through changes in the availability of funds only.   If we assume that the spending patterns of all individuals are the same, the allowance for investment effects becomes

[1] See p. 489.
[2] See p. 438.
[3] See p. 442.

equivalent to assuming a higher propensity to consume.   Provided that the marginal propensity to spend on consumption and investment falls short of 1, all the earlier conclusions (applicable if the marginal propensity to consume falls short of 1) still hold true.

If we allow for differences in spending patterns, the qualitative aspects of tax policy are changed somewhat.   Suppose that the marginal propensities to consume among taxpayers differ, but that the marginal propensity to invest out of saving is the same throughout.   In this case, marginal propensities to spend on consumption plus investment will differ less sharply (in relative terms) than marginal propensities to consume.   Thus, the leverage effect of changes in tax distributions is reduced.   This conclusion holds more strongly so if the marginal propensity to invest out of savings is related inversely to the marginal propensity to consume, as may be the case with regard to risk capital.

Profitability Effects

These are more or less minor qualifications to the reasoning of the preceding chapter, but the picture may change sharply if effects on profitability are allowed for.

For argument's sake, let us suppose that investment I varies inversely with the tax rate t.[1]   Our earlier conclusions regarding the leverage of changes in government expenditures G with constant t remain unaffected. The leverage of an increase in G with constant tax yield T is raised, since the adjustment implies a reduction in t.   The leverage of a reduction in t with constant G is increased as well.   Budget adjustments involving equal direction changes in G and t, on the contrary, are reduced in effectiveness, the change in t now leading to offsetting changes in both I and C.   This includes the case of equal changes in G and T, or balanced-budget adjustments.   Since t is raised, they will have a lesser leverage than in the absence of inverse investment effects.

Indeed, a decline in the balanced budget may now raise the level of income, and budget expansion may reduce it.   Balanced-budget reduction is expansionary if the gain in investment that results from a reduction in tax rate exceeds the associated cut in government expenditure. Balanced-budget expansion is restrictive if the resulting decline in investment exceeds the increase in government expenditures.[2]

A corollary proposition holds that a reduction in t with G constant will increase rather than reduce tax yield.   It applies if the resulting increase in investment raises income by an amount sufficiently great so that the

[1] We assume throughout this discussion that the marginal propensity to consume falls short of 1.   For another set of unorthodox results, obtained with fixed investment, see p. 437 where the marginal propensity to consume is allowed to exceed 1.

[2] To illustrate a setting under which an expansion in the balanced budget may be

gain in yield (equal to the new and lower tax rate times the rise in income) more than offsets the loss in yield (equal to the reduction in tax rate times the initial level of income).[1]

---

restrictive, let us write the following as our system of income determination:

$$Y = C + I + G \tag{1}$$
$$C = A + c(1 - t)Y \tag{2}$$
$$I = D - nDt \tag{3}$$
$$T = G \tag{4}$$
$$T = tY \tag{5}$$

According to eq. (3), investment is related inversely to the tax rate. From this system, we obtain

$$Y = \frac{A + D - nDt}{(1 - c)(1 - t)} \tag{6}$$

and

$$\frac{dY}{dt} = \frac{(1 - c)[A + D(1 - n)]}{[(1 - c)(1 - t)]^2} \tag{7}$$

From eq. (7) we conclude that

$$\frac{dY}{dt} \gtreqless 0 \text{ if } n \gtreqless 1 + \frac{A}{D}$$

Thus, balanced-budget changes are neutral if $n = 1 + A/D$.

In terms of finite differences, bearing in mind that $\Delta T = \Delta t Y_0 + t_1 \Delta Y$, we obtain from eqs. (1) to (5) the expression

$$\Delta Y = \frac{(1 - c)Y_0 - nD}{(1 - c)(1 - t_1)} \Delta t \tag{8}$$

so that $\Delta Y \gtreqless 0$ if $nD \gtreqless (1 - c)Y_0$. As $Y_0 = \frac{A + D(1 - nt_0)}{(1 - c)(1 - t_0)}$, both formulations give the same condition.

There would seem to be no particular reason to assume that $A <$ or $> D$. Either may be the case. If $A = D$, balanced budget expansion is restrictive if $n \geqq 2$, which means that investment becomes zero as the tax rate reaches 50 per cent.

Other investment functions can be devised that give more or less similar results, as, for instance, $I = n - mT = n - mtY$. On the other hand, for an investment function of such a propensity type that $I = n + w(1 - t)Y$, balanced-budget expansion must raise Y, since the investment function merely adds another relationship that is analytically similar to the consumption function.

[1] Using eqs. (1) to (3) as before, and completing the system with

$$G = \bar{G} \tag{9}$$

we obtain

$$Y = \frac{A + G + D - Dnt}{(1 - c + ct)}$$

from which

$$\frac{dY}{dt} = -\frac{(A + G + D)c + Dn(1 - c)}{(1 - c + ct)^2} \tag{10}$$

which is always negative. Tax reduction raises income as it does in a model with a propensity to invest function.

Defining $T = tY$, we obtain

These results, which turn the conventional conclusions of fiscal policy topsy-turvy, cannot come about if investment effects are limited to the availability type. In this case, balanced-budget leverage may become zero as the marginal propensity to spend in the private sector reaches 1; but it cannot become negative. Similarly, a reduction in tax rate cannot increase yield, since restoration of the old yield would annul the cause of increase in income. The unorthodox theorems can hold only if investment is related inversely to the tax rate, and if this relationship is sufficiently strong. While such a condition is unlikely, it is not impossible; it should be kept in mind, if only to demonstrate that the conventional conclusions are based on empirical hypotheses rather than abstract logic. Further qualifications to the conventional doctrine arise when effects on growth are allowed for.

D. CHECKING INFLATION

As in the discussion of consumption aspects, special problems arise in applying fiscal controls to checking inflation. These will now be considered in a preliminary fashion. A fuller treatment of the matter must be postponed till the next chapter, where effects of investment upon capacity and growth are dealt with extensively.

High Taxes as a Cause of Capital Shortage

It has been argued that taxes on investment cannot be used to check inflation because they curtail capacity and hence reduce available supplies. In evaluating this argument, one must distinguish between two cases: one in which the comparison is between no tax and introduction of a tax that reduces investment, and another where the comparison is between a tax which reduces investment and a tax which reduces consumption by the same amount.

Introduction of a tax that reduces investment results in an immediate reduction in expenditures, but in only a gradual loss of potential capacity. Suppose, for instance, that the annual rate of investment is reduced by

$$T = \frac{(A + G + D)t - nDt^2}{(1 - c + ct)} \tag{11}$$

and

$$\frac{dT}{dt} = \frac{(1 - c)(A + G + D - 2nDt) - nDct^2}{(1 - c + ct)^2} \tag{12}$$

so that

$$\frac{dT}{dt} < 0 \quad \text{if} \quad n > \frac{(1 - c)(A + G + D)}{tD[2 - c - c(1 - t)]} \tag{13}$$

In terms of finite differences, we now have

$$\Delta T = -\frac{\Delta t}{D} \frac{(1 - c)(ct_0 Y_0 + \Delta tn)}{(1 - c + ct_1)c} \tag{14}$$

$1 billion. With a multiplier of 2.5, this means an eventual reduction in the annual rate of spending of $2.5 billion. Setting the length of the income-expenditure period equal to four months, a reduction in the annual rate of spending by $2.2 billion is reached within one year. Assuming investment to result in a 20 per cent net return per annum, the potential loss of output within a year will be $200 million, and a level of $2.5 billion will be reached only after 12 years. Thus, the net deflationary effect of the tax will be substantial for a good many years. In the cyclical context, at least, the deflationary effect of reducing investment expenditures will outweigh the inflationary effect from the loss of potential additions to capacity.

By the same token, removal of a tax on investment will have an inflationary effect for a considerable period. Replacement of a tax on investment with a tax on consumption, on the other hand, is deflationary from the outset. While expenditures are unchanged, increased capacity becomes available. However, it must again be kept in mind that this additional capacity is built up slowly, so that the consideration remains of secular rather than of cyclical importance.

High Taxes as a Cause of Spending

While taxes are usually blamed for reducing investment, it has been argued as well that a profits tax cannot be used to check inflation because it encourages business spending.

The argument says, in its crudest form, that a high rate of tax reduces the net cost of labor, plant, or materials because such outlays can be deducted from taxable income. Thus, if the tax rate is 90 per cent, the government "contributes" 90 cents of every dollar that the business spends. This being the case, the tax is said to encourage additional costs to be undertaken.

Suppose that the tax is expected to be permanent. In this case, an increase in tax rate cannot render previously unprofitable investments profitable; or, for that matter, it cannot enable the employer to grant a wage increase that otherwise would have been impossible. If profits before tax are $P_b = S - C$, where S is sales proceeds and C is costs, profits after tax are $P_a = (1 - t)(S - C)$. Now P_a is obviously smaller than P_b, since $1 - t < 1$. The substitution effect is adverse, and investment declines unless the income effect is decisive.

The situation differs where the increase in tax rate is expected to be temporary.[1] In this case, otherwise unprofitable investments may be rendered profitable by an increase in tax, provided that depreciation may be charged in advance of the receipt of profits, and sufficient other

[1] See Dan T. Smith, "Note on Inflationary Consequences of High Taxation," *Review of Economics and Statistics*, vol. 34, no. 3, pp. 243–247, August, 1952.

income (or provision for perfect loss offset) is available against which to charge it. Let us suppose that the entire depreciation may be charged during the period of temporarily high tax rates, with other income sufficient to absorb the depreciation charge; and that the entire profits are expected to accrue during the subsequent period of low tax rates. As before, profits before tax are $P_b = S - C$. Profits after tax now are $P_a = (1 - t_l)S - (1 - t_h)C$, where t_l is the low tax rate of the future and t_h is the high tax rate of the present. Profitability has risen, since $[(1 - t_l)S - (1 - t_h)C]/(S - C) > 1$, provided that $P_b > 0$. If depreciation extends into the low-rate period, and profits accrue in part in the low-rate period, the gain in profitability is less marked, but a gain remains as long as the fraction of profits that accrues during the high-rate period exceeds the fraction of profits that accrues during the low-rate period. This consideration explains the potency of accelerated depreciation in a period of temporarily high tax rates; it also explains how expectation of early tax reduction may induce outlays, such as advertising or labor hoarding, which can be expensed but which are nevertheless in the nature of investment. These factors may interfere with the restrictive effectiveness of profits taxation during a war economy, especially toward the end of a war, when a reduction in tax rates is predicted in the foreseeable future.

Similar inducements can be given to consumer spending. A proprietor may find it worthwhile to incur additional business expenses, for example, convention trips, which add to his consumption but which may be charged against a profits tax. An employee may avoid a personal income tax by receiving wages in kind (such as the services of a company car), which, per dollar of cost to the company, would add more to his net wages than a corresponding cash income. In both cases, the problem is one of faulty definition of taxable income rather than high rates of tax. However, the difficulties of applying a proper income concept increase with the level of rates, since avoidance becomes more worthwhile.

Cost-push Inflation

Notwithstanding these and other difficulties, fiscal controls are well adapted to deal with inflation if the problem is one of checking excessive demand. They are less well adapted to deal with a cost-push type of inflation where equilibrium cannot be restored by curtailing demand. In a setting where powerful sectors of the economy are in a position to administer prices—of labor or products—demands for higher cost payments and/or prices may be the originating factor in the inflation process. Or, adjustments on the supply side may accentuate an inflationary process that began with an impulse on the demand side. This might be the case if wages follow prices, but a percentage markup is made on increased wage costs.[1]   In such situations, the fiscal or monetary authority may be left with the dire choice between validating the rising level of prices by assuring a corresponding growth in demand, thus underwriting inflation, or checking the increase in price level by curtailing aggregate demand, thereby imposing unemployment.

The difficulty in such a situation is not that fiscal or, for that matter, monetary policy is incapable of curtailing demand.   Rather, it is that a restriction in aggregate demand does not solve the dual task of achieving high employment *and* price-level stability.   To meet the problem, other types of control are required.   These may be of a nonfiscal sort, such as some forms of national wage-price policy, or they may involve fiscal devices.   The choice of the appropriate techniques depends upon the nature of the forces that make for rising costs.

Suppose that the major cause is an annual demand by unions for a given percentage increase in money wages, independent of changes in productivity.   In such a case, it may seem appropriate to engage in a fiscal-monetary policy to raise the rate of investment.   The rate should be raised to that level which will validate the demand for wage increases without inflation by creating corresponding gains in labor productivity.   With regard to monetary policy, this would take the form of easy credit for investment and tight consumer credit.   In fiscal policy, it would take the form of productivity-increasing expenditures and of taxes that deter consumption rather than investment.[2]   Presumably, this would limit the use of progressive income and profit taxes and call for heavier taxation of wage income.   As a result, the gain in wage rates that was to be sustained may well be canceled by higher taxes on wage income.   If such taxes are taken into account when formulating wage demands, the policy breaks down.   To avoid such a result, the desired cutback in consumption might be obtained through taxes on luxury consumption or a progressive spendings tax.   Or, the difficulty might be met in part by government expenditures aimed at technological improvements of a labor-saving sort, so as to raise labor productivity with a given level of investment.

While it might be possible, with one or another of these policies, to solve the conflict between full employment and price-level stability by raising the rate of growth, this is not necessarily an efficient solution. The proper rate of growth in the efficient system is determined by the

[1] For such models see James Duesenberry, "The Mechanics of Inflation," pp. 144–149; and Franklin D. Holzman, "Income Determination in Open Inflation," pp. 150–158, both in *Review of Economics and Statistics*, vol. 32, no. 2, May, 1950.

[2] See W. Fellner, "Relative Emphasis in Tax Policy on Encouragement of Consumption or Investment," in *Federal Tax Policy for Economic Growth and Stability*, 80th Cong., 1st Sess., Joint Committee on the Economic Report, pp. 210–217.

more relevant considerations of time preference,[1] and the problem of cost-push inflation may have to be met by more direct approaches.[2]

Suppose, now, that wage demands are not determined independently of profit margins but are aimed at maintaining a given share in the total of wages plus profits, or raising this share. If the focus is on profits *after* tax, a policy of reducing profits taxes would accentuate the difficulty rather than relieve it. In such a case, the solution might point in the opposite direction and call for increased taxation of profits. A still different type of policy, calling for a high marginal tax on profits, is required where cost-push inflation originates with price rather than wage policy, and so forth.

The actual situation involves a mixture of these various cases. The ideal tax policy, designed to cover all contingencies, would be through a tax on wages that applies to wage gains in excess of productivity gains and through a tax on profits that applies to profits from increases in price not justified by increased costs, both taxes being applied at marginal rate of 100 per cent. This, however, is not a feasible solution; it is merely a restatement of the problem in terms of tax policy. It remains to be seen whether, and to what extent, selective tax policy can contribute to the appropriate solution; and to what extent the objective of full employment without inflation must be permitted to determine the desirable rate of growth.

[1] See p. 553.

[2] On the problems of price structure and inflation, see Gardner Ackley, "A Third Approach to Inflation," in *The Relationship of Prices to Economic Stability and Growth*, Joint Economic Committee, 85th Cong., 1958. See also J. K. Galbraith, "Market Structure and Stabilization Policy," *Review of Economics and Statistics*, vol. 34, no. 2, pp. 124–133, May, 1957, especially the proposal that the employer's willingness to grant wage increases should be restrained by a temporary price freeze after wages have been raised. Finally, see Bent Hansen, *The Theory of Inflation*, George Allen & Unwin, Ltd., London, 1951, pp. 177–181, for the use of selective tax policy in closing inflationary gaps in the factor and product markets.

CHAPTER 20

Fiscal dynamics and growth

In the preceding discussion we have examined the effects of compensatory finance in terms of comparative statics; that is to say, we have compared the equilibrium level of income which prevails prior to a change in budget policy with that which is reached after a change has been made and all necessary adjustments have been completed. This approach has the merit of simplicity, but it is subject to serious shortcomings.

Even if we assume that the system is in initial equilibrium and that it tends toward a new equilibrium after a change in budget policy is made, an infinite number of periods must pass until this new equilibrium is reached. We must be concerned not only with the level of the new equilibrium but also with the way in which income moves towards it.

Moreover, the economy may not be at an equilibrium level of income to begin with, but in a process of change over a period of time. Depending upon the nature of the underlying relationships, this change may or may not lead to a new equilibrium level of income. We shall examine how changes in fiscal policy affect the path of change in income over time, and what bearing the change will have on the new equilibrium level of income, if one exists. By comparing the movement of income over time as it proceeds under alternative fiscal policies, we shall measure the effects of fiscal policies in terms of what can be referred to as comparative dynamics.

The essence of a dynamic system of income determination is that the spendings function for consumption and investment as well as the budget function for expenditures and taxes are defined with respect to the time period in which they occur, and that these relationships in time have a decisive influence on the movement of income.[1] As anyone at all

[1] See Ragnar Frisch, "Propagation Problems and Impulse Problems in Dynamic Economics," in *Economic Essays in Honour of Gustav Cassel*, George Allen & Unwin, Ltd., London, 1933, pp. 171–208; and J. R. Hicks, *Contribution to the Theory of the Trade Cycle*, Oxford University Press, New York, 1950.

acquainted with dynamics knows, the resulting generation of income depends in many subtle ways upon the precise time lags that appear in the various spending functions of the system, as well as upon the relative sizes of the various coefficients involved. No attempt will be made here to enter into these complexities of dynamic theory. Rather, we shall limit the discussion to a number of very simple models. In particular, the discussion will be restricted to typical expansionary or contractive processes, without dealing with the problem of turning points and the variety of formulations by which these turning points have been explained. Our objective can only be to provide a brief introduction to the kind of problems that will be encountered in future years when fiscal theory is reformulated in dynamic terms.[1]

A. DYNAMIC MODELS WITH STATIONARY EQUILIBRIUM: INVESTMENT AS A FUNCTION OF LEVEL OF INCOME

We shall begin with various systems in which the capacity-creating effects of investment are still disregarded. This is the type of dynamics that relates to the discussion of cyclical problems. The long-run problems of growth are considered in section C.

System without Budget

First, let us examine a model in which private expenditures on consumption as well as on investment are related to the income of the preceding period. This implies an investment function more or less similar to that previously referred to as a propensity to invest out of income.[2] However, the ratio of current investment to past income may now exceed the propensity to save. It thus differs from the system dealt with earlier, where, by the nature of comparative statics, the propensity to invest could not exceed the propensity to save.

Let us again turn to the familiar equation

$$Y_n = C_n + I_n \qquad (20\text{-}1)$$

showing income in period n equal to expenditures of that period, including consumption and investment. Private expenditures on consumption and investment may be combined, since both are assumed to be a function of the income of the past period and since investment effects on capacity are disregarded for the time being.[3] We may write

$$C_n + I_n = E_n \qquad (20\text{-}2)$$

---

[1] I am indebted to Herbert Geyer, who has contributed greatly to the development of this chapter.

[2] See p. 463.

[3] See p. 483.

where E_n is total private expenditure in period n. Defining E as a function of the income of the past period plus a constant, we have

$$E_n = eY_{n-1} + A \tag{20-3}$$

This is a nonhomogeneous linear difference equation of the first order. The solution of such a system is given by

$$Y_n = Z + r^n K$$

where Z defines the constant particular solution that is the equilibrium level of income, and $r^n K$ defines the difference between the actual income and the equilibrium level, with K to be determined consistently with the initial value of Y.*

The equilibrium level of income in the absence of a budget, or Z_a, is determined by setting $Y_n = Y_{n-1}$ so that

$$Z_a = \frac{1}{1 - e} A \tag{20-4}$$

An economically meaningful equilibrium exists if $Z_a > 0$, which will be the case if $e < 1$. The root of the homogeneous part of the system is given by

$$r_a = e \tag{20-5}$$

The system has no oscillations if $r_a > 0$. This condition is met, since $e > 0$. The system is stable (converges to an equilibrium level) if $r_a < 1$, which is the case only if $e < 1$. Thus the same condition that is required for the existence of an equilibrium income also assures that income converges toward this equilibrium. Depending on whether the initial income is above or below the equilibrium, income will fall or rise toward this level and approach it asymptotically. The system is unstable (does not converge towards an equilibrium level) if $r_a > 1$, which is the case if $e > 1$, that is, the marginal propensity to spend exceeds one. Given a positive initial value, income moves up indefinitely. If $e = 1$, income remains suspended at whatever level it happens to be.

Budget with Fixed Expenditures and Tax Yield

We shall now introduce a budget and begin with the assumption that expenditures as well as taxes are fixed. Noting that the private propensity to spend, or e, refers to income after tax, we now have

$$Y_n = e(Y_{n-1} - T_f) + R + A \tag{20-6}$$

---

* The reader who is not acquainted with difference equations may wish to consult the introduction into the technique of solving such equations and the discussion of their stability conditions, given in W. J. Baumol and Ralph Turvey, *Economic Dynamics*, The Macmillan Company, New York, 1951. Also, see R. G. D. Allen, *Mathematical Economics*, Macmillan & Co., Ltd., London, 1956, chaps. 1–8.

where R is the fixed amount of government expenditures, and T_f is the fixed tax yield. We obtain the equilibrium level of income

$$Z_f = \frac{R - eT_f + A}{1 - e} \tag{20-7}$$

which may be compared with Z_a to determine the change in the equilibrium level due to introduction of the budget. We find that

$$Z_f = \left(\frac{R - eT_f}{A} + 1\right) Z_a \tag{20-8}$$

Thus, $Z_f > Z_a$ if $R/T_f > e$, which must be the case if there is an equilibrium income. The equilibrium level is increased if the ratio of government expenditures to tax yield exceeds the ratio of private expenditures to disposable income. In the balanced-budget case, $Z_f > Z_a$ if $e < 1$, which is precisely the condition for the working of the balanced-budget multiplier.[1]

The root of the system is equal to r_a, the root of the system in the absence of budget activity. A budget where neither taxes nor expenditures are related to income may affect the equilibrium level of the system but not its stability.

Budget with Expenditure and Tax Rates as Parameters

We now introduce a budget in which expenditures as well as taxes depend upon income. Let the government's expenditure function be

$$G_n = gY_{n-1} + R \tag{20-9}$$

where the component R is a lump sum or rock-bottom amount, while the component gY_{n-1} is such that expenditures vary positively with the national income of the last period. In the context of stabilization policy, this is not a sensible assumption, since it involves a perverse type of built-in flexibility.[2] Other assumptions will be considered later, but it is convenient to begin with this formulation.

The tax function of the government is given by the expression

$$T_n = tY_{n-1} \tag{20-10}$$

where t is the average rate of tax, which is assumed to be constant and hence equals the marginal rate. The possible addition of a lump-sum tax that is independent of income will be considered later.

General Case. Let us now consider the general case of a system that may run a deficit or surplus, either at the margin or for the total budget.

---

[1] See p. 432.

[2] Destabilizing expenditure behavior may also be expressed as $G_n = jT_n + R$, where $T_n = tY_{n-1}$. As long as t is fixed, we have $j = g/t$, so that this case need not be dealt with separately.

The definition of income for period n is now given by

$$Y_n = e(Y_{n-1} - tY_{n-1}) + A + gY_{n-1} + R$$
or
$$Y_n = [e(1 - t) + g]Y_{n-1} + A + R \tag{20-11}$$

Proceeding as before, we obtain the equilibrium income for the budget with expenditure and tax parameters:

$$Z_p = \frac{A + R}{1 - e(1 - t) - g} \tag{20-12}$$

As noted before, an equilibrium exists if $Z_p > 0$. This is the case if $1 > e(1 - t) + g$; in other words, if the total (private plus public) propensity to spend out of national income does not exceed unity.

The root of the homogeneous part is given by

$$r_p = e(1 - t) + g \tag{20-13}$$

The system has no oscillation if $r_p > 0$, which must always be the case. It converges to an equilibrium level if $r_p < 1$, which is the case if $1 > e(1 - t) + g$. Again, the condition for existence of an equilibrium also assures that the system converges towards it. The system is unstable if $r_p > 1$, which is the case if $1 < e(1 - t) + g$, that is, if the combined private and public marginal propensity to spend exceeds 1.

We may now compare Z_p and Z_a, to determine how the equilibrium level of income is changed by the introduction of the budget. Assuming $R = 0$, we find that $Z_p > Z_a$ if $1 > e(1 - t) + g$, which is our old condition for the existence of an equilibrium solution. Also, we may state that

$$Z_p = \frac{1 - e}{1 - e(1 - t) - g} Z_a \tag{20-14}$$

so that $Z_p > Z_a$ if $e < g/t$. Since $e < 1$ if an equilibrium exists in the system without budget, the equilibrium level is increased if the budget is marginally balanced or underbalanced within certain limits. An equilibrium ceases to exist if the deficit rate becomes so large that $1 < e(1 - t) + g$. The equilibrium level may also rise if $t > g$, provided that the rate of surplus is small enough.[1]

---

[1] As in the treatment of comparative statics (see p. 435) we may inquire what budget adjustments will serve to secure a given desired increase in the level of equilibrium income. Defining the desired level Z_d as mZ_p, where Z_p is the prevailing level and $m > 1$, we obtain for the alternative approaches

$$\Delta g = \frac{m - 1}{m} [1 - e(1 - t) - g_0]$$

$$\Delta t = \frac{(1 - m)[1 - e(1 - t) - g]}{me}$$

$$\Delta R = (m - 1)(A + R_0)$$

Turning now to a comparison between r_p and r_a, we obtain

$$r_p = \left[(1 - t) + \frac{g}{e} \right] r_a \qquad (20\text{-}15)$$

We find that $r_p > r_a$ if $e < g/t$, and vice versa. If the introduction of the budget raises the equilibrium level of income, it also increases the root of the system and renders it less stable. At any time the actual income will be further from the equilibrium income. If the actual income for any given time is above the equilibrium income, it follows that the level of income will be higher than it would be in the absence of a budget.[1] This somewhat unusual conclusion—that a budget which raises the equilibrium level also reduces stability—reflects the assumption that government expenditures are a positive function of income. As we shall see, the result changes if this assumption is dropped.

Marginally Balanced Budget. We may now consider the case of a marginally balanced budget, so that $g = t$. The equilibrium level of income with the budget in the picture now becomes

$$Z_{pm} = \frac{A + R}{1 - e(1 - g) - g} \qquad (20\text{-}16)$$

An equilibrium income exists if $e(1 - g) + g < 1$, which will be the case if $e < 1$. Since the government's marginal propensity to spend equals 1, the combined public and private marginal propensity to spend falls short of 1 if $e < 1$. The root of the system now equals

$$r_{pm} = e(1 - g) + g \qquad (20\text{-}17)$$

The system can have no oscillation and converges to an equilibrium if $e < 1$. As before, the condition for existence of an equilibrium is the same as that for convergence toward an equilibrium.

Comparing the equilibrium income with and without budget, and assuming $R = 0$, we now find that $Z_a < Z_{pm}$ if $g > 0$. Thus, introduction of the budget raises the equilibrium level, the relation being

$$Z_{pm} = Z_a + gZ_{pm} \qquad (20\text{-}18)$$

the equilibrium level of income being increased by the amount of government expenditures at the new equilibrium level.

Comparing the roots of the system with and without budget, we find

[1] The same conclusion holds if the actual income is below the equilibrium income and rises toward it. In this case, it may be shown that the effect of the increase in the equilibrium level (due to introduction of the budget) will outweigh the effect of the decrease in the root, which makes for a lower income relative to the equilibrium level.

that $r_a < r_{pm}$ if $e < 1$. The relationship between r_{gm} and r_a is given by

$$r_{pm} = \left[1 - g \left(1 - \frac{1}{e} \right) \right] r_a \tag{20-19}$$

Thus, the introduction of the budget again raises the stability of the system. Since the equilibrium level is raised as well, income at any time will be higher than without the budget.

Totally Balanced Budget. Let us now turn to the case of a totally balanced budget. If $R = 0$, the condition for a totally balanced budget is the same as it would be for a marginally balanced budget. If $R > 0$, equation (20-6) becomes

$$Y_n = e(Y_{n-1} - gY_{n-1} - R) + gY_{n-1} + R + A \tag{20-20}$$

and the equilibrium level of income with a totally balanced budget is given by

$$Z_{pt} = \frac{(1 - e)R + A}{1 - e(1 - g) - g} \tag{20-21}$$

The condition for an equilibrium to exist is the same as in the marginally balanced budget. The root of the system, or r_{pt}, is the same as it is for the marginally balanced budget, or r_{mt}.

A comparison of the equilibrium level Z_{pt} with the equilibrium level in the absence of a budget Z_a shows that $Z_a < Z_{pt}$ if $(1 - e)/g > - A/R$. This must always be the case. Since the comparison is between equilibrium levels, $e < 1$. The relationship between the two equilibrium incomes is given by

$$Z_{pt} = \frac{(1 - e)R + A}{(1 - g)A} Z_a \tag{20-22}$$

which may be reconciled readily with equation (20-8) above. Since the root of the system is the same as for the marginally balanced budget, the discussion of equation (20-16) again applies.

Comparison of the equilibrium for the totally and the marginally balanced budgets shows that $Z_{pm} > Z_{pt}$ if $eR/[1 - e(1 - g) - g] > 0$, which must again be the case. The relation between the two equilibriums is given by

$$Z_{pm} = \frac{A + R}{A + (1 - e)R} Z_{pt} \tag{20-23}$$

Budget with Fixed Expenditures and Tax Parameters

The expenditure function of the preceding model divided budget expenditures into two components, including a fixed part and a part that varied directly with income. Such an assumption is reasonable for the treatment of growth problems, and we shall return to it in that connection.[1]   At the same time, this assumption is not in line with a sensible policy of compensatory finance in the cyclical setting.   Let us reconsider the preceding conclusions while holding public expenditures fixed at level R.   At the same time, the tax function is the same as in equation (20-10).

The new equilibrium level, after introduction of the budget Z_{pf}, is obtained from equation (20-12) by setting $g = 0$.   By comparing this expression with Z_a as defined in equation (20-4), we obtain

$$Z_{pf} = \frac{(A + R)(1 - e)}{A[1 - e(1 - t)]} Z_a \qquad (20\text{-}24)$$

It follows that $Z_{pf} \gtreqless Z_a$ if $t \lesseqgtr R(1 - e)/Ae$.   Thus, the equilibrium level of income may be raised or reduced, depending upon the level of t relative to R, A, and e.   In general terms, the introduction of the budget will leave Z unchanged if etZ_a, which is the loss in private expenditures due to taxation at the old equilibrium income, is equal to R, which is the gain through governmental expenditures.   This may be readily reconciled with the previous condition.   A deficit budget, or a budget that lacks an adequate surplus, raises the equilibrium level.

The new root of the system is obtained from equation (20-13) with $g = 0$, so that, for a comparison of the roots,

$$r_{pf} = (1 - t)r_a \qquad (20\text{-}25)$$

Since $0 < t < 1$, introduction of the budget increases the stability of the system which, of course, is the central point of the built-in flexibility proposition.

Pump Priming

All the preceding policy adjustments involved permanent changes in budget policy, whether in terms of g and t or T_f and R.   As such they differ from the type of measure that in the thirties was referred to as pump priming.   According to this view, the problem of antidepression policy is one of moving the economy from dead center.   Once this is accomplished, the initial change in budget parameters may be repealed, but the economy nevertheless continues on its higher course.

Suppose that the economy is at an equilibrium level of income that falls short of full employment.   Changes in budget parameters are made that cause the level of income to rise.   After income reaches or exceeds a certain threshold, or after a certain rate of increase is reached, there occurs an upward shift in the investment or consumption function that now provides the leverage initially secured by the budget adjustment.   Models of this type, which involve nonlinear spendings functions, may

[1] See p. 485.

be feasible, but the nature of the resulting systems becomes very complex and cannot be examined here.

B. DYNAMIC MODELS WITH STATIONARY EQUILIBRIUM: INVESTMENT AS A FUNCTION OF CHANGE IN INCOME

Let us turn to a second type of dynamic system. The capacity-creating effects of investment are still disregarded, but investment is now a function of change in income. Consumption remains a function of past income, as before.

Income Determination in Absence of Budget

We now have the following system:

$$Y_n = C_n + I_n \qquad (20\text{-}26)$$
$$C_n = cY_{n-1} + A \qquad (20\text{-}27)$$
$$I_n = \beta(Y_{n-1} - Y_{n-2}) \qquad (20\text{-}28)$$

so that

$$Y_n = (c + \beta)Y_{n-1} - \beta Y_{n-2} + A \qquad (20\text{-}29)$$

This is a second-order linear nonhomogeneous difference equation, the equilibrium solution for which is given by $z_a = Y_n = Y_{n-1} = Y_{n-2}$; thus

$$z_a = \frac{1}{1 - c} A \qquad (20\text{-}30)$$

The equilibrium level of income is independent of investment, which in equilibrium equals zero. For $0 < c < 1$ an equilibrium exists. This second-order system has two roots, which are determined by

$$r_a{}^2 - (c + \beta)r_a + \beta = 0 \qquad (20\text{-}31)$$

Consistent with initial conditions and z_a, these roots set the course of income over time. Depending upon the size of the roots, we may get various patterns of income movement toward, away from, or around the equilibrium. This may be established without solving for the r's by reference to stability conditions.[1] In the above system, income is stable if both c and β are positive and smaller than unity.

[1] See Paul A. Samuelson, *Foundations of Economic Analysis*, Harvard University Press, Cambridge, Mass., 1947, p. 436, expression 183. If we have for (20-31)

$$r^2 + a_1 r + a_2 = 0$$

each of the following conditions must be met:

$$1 + a_1 + a_2 > 0$$
$$1 - a_2 > 0$$
$$1 - a_1 + a_2 > 0$$

if the system is to be stable, i.e., converge toward equilibrium by some pattern.

Budget with Fixed Expenditures and Tax Yield

We now introduce the budget and again begin with a case where budget expenditures R and tax yield T_f are fixed.

Income in period n now equals

$$Y_n = (c + \beta)Y_{n-1} - \beta Y_{n-2} + A + R - cT_f \qquad (20\text{-}32)$$

The equilibrium solution is now given by

$$z_f = \frac{A + R - cT_f}{1 - c} \qquad (20\text{-}33)$$

and the roots remain unchanged, as determined by equation (20-31). Introduction of the budget does not affect the stability of the system, but the equilibrium income is raised if $R > cT_f$. The relation between the equilibrium levels before and after budget is given by

$$z_f = \left(\frac{R - cT_f}{A} + 1\right) z_a \qquad (20\text{-}34)$$

which is similar to equation (20-8) of the preceding section. If $c < 1$ so that the system is stable, a balanced budget raises the equilibrium level of income, and with stability unchanged income will be higher for any period.

Budget with Expenditure and Tax Rates as Parameters

We now proceed to a system where government expenditures and tax yield are defined as in equations (20-9) and (20-10) preceding. Income in period n now equals[1]

$$Y_n = [c(1 - t) + g + \beta]Y_{n-1} - \beta Y_{n-2} + A + R \qquad (20\text{-}35)$$

The equilibrium solution is given by

$$z_p = \frac{A + R}{1 - c(1 - t) - g} \qquad (20\text{-}36)$$

The system has an equilibrium if $1 > c(1 - t) + g$, that is, if the private propensity to spend on consumption and the propensity to spend by government add to less than 1. By comparison with z_a as defined in

---

[1] It will be noted that this system differs from that in Samuelson's famous initial formulation (see Paul A. Samuelson, "Interactions between the Multiplier Analysis and the Principle of Acceleration," *Review of Economics and Statistics*, vol. 21, pp. 75–78, 1939) in that our accelerator relates to changes in total income, including investment and government expenditures, and not to changes in consumption only.

equation (20-30), we obtain

$$z_p = \frac{(A + R)(1 - c)}{A[1 - c(1 - t) - g]} z_a \tag{20-37}$$

Introduction of the budget may either raise or lower the equilibrium level. The larger are R and g, and the smaller is t, the larger will be the expression on the right side.

The roots of the system are determined by

$$r_p{}^2 - [c(1 - t) + g + \beta]r_p + \beta = 0 \tag{20-38}$$

Applying the stability conditions, we find that for the system to be stable we must have $c(1 - t) + g < 1$ and $\beta < 1$. These two conditions are readily seen. Also, we must have $1 + (1 - t)c + g + 2\beta > 0$, which will be the case for our system. If the first condition is met, but not the second, the system has an equilibrium but is unstable.

Comparison of the first stability condition with and without the budget shows that stability is not affected if $ct = g$. Assuming $c < 1$ and $\beta < 1$ so that the initial system is stable, introduction of the budget may render the system unstable if $g - ct$ is sufficiently large. This again reflects the destabilizing effect of varying government expenditures directly with income. If the system after introduction of the budget is to be stable, we must have $g < 1 - c(1 - t)$. The government's propensity to spend must not exceed the community's propensity to save. Should the initial system be unstable because $c > 1$, introduction of the budget may provide for stability if $ct - g$ is sufficiently large. The second stability condition $\beta < 1$ is not affected. The third stability condition must always be met, given the reaction structure here under consideration, with or without a budget.[1]

Marginally Balanced Budget. The case for the marginally balanced budget may be obtained by setting $g = t$ in equations (20-37) and (20-38). Comparing the equilibrium level of income for a marginally balanced budget z_{pm} with z_a, we find that

$$z_{pm} = \frac{1 + R/A}{1 - g} z_a \tag{20-39}$$

where $z_{pm} > z_a$, since $g < 1$ if an equilibrium exists.

The first stability condition in the absence of a budget was met if $1 > c$.* With the marginally balanced budget, it is met if $1 > c +$

---

[1] The condition is given by

$$1 + c + g + 2\beta - ct > 0$$

Since c, g, β, and t are all positive, the condition must be met.

* The second condition $\beta < 1$ is unaffected. The third is met again with or without budget, but the lower limit is reduced, as may be expected.

$g(1 - c)$. This will always be the case if the system tends toward an equilibrium income. This tendency cannot be destroyed by the introduction of a marginally balanced budget, provided $g < 1$. However, the speed at which equilibrium is approached will be reduced as $c + g(1 - c) > c$, assuming throughout that $c < 1$.

Budget with Fixed Expenditures and Tax Parameters

As before, we may now turn to a more reasonable model, where the level of public expenditures is fixed while tax yield remains a function of income. The new equilibrium level of income z_{pf} is obtained from equation (20-36) by setting $g = 0$, and its relation to the prebudget equilibrium is obtained similarly from (20-37). We find that $z_{pf} \gtreqless z_a$, depending on whether $t \lesseqgtr [(1 - c)R]/cA$.

The equation determining the roots of the system is obtained from (20-38) by setting $g = 0$. For the system to be stable, we must have $c(1 - t) < 1$. Also, we must have $\beta < 1$ and $1 + (1 - t)c + 2\beta > 0$. All conditions are met if the system was stable prior to introduction of the budget. Introduction of the budget now is always stabilizing and causes the system to converge more rapidly toward equilibrium. More will be said about this in our later discussion of built-in flexibility.[1]

C. BUDGET POLICY AND GROWTH

So far, our concern has been with the effects of changes in investment on the level of aggregate demand, and hence on the level of income, employment, and prices. In other words, we have dealt with the short-run Keynesian role of investment as providing offsets to saving. We shall now turn to another aspect of investment that must be considered as well. This is the classical function of investment providing additions to capacity, thereby generating growth in income at full employment. This makes for a basic change in the setting and objectives of a stabilizing fiscal policy. The concept of stabilization previously directed at achieving and maintaining a stationary level of full-employment income at stable prices must be replaced by one of securing a growing level of capacity income at stable prices. Moreover, there is the further problem of choosing between various rates of growth.

As investment occurs, the economy's capacity to produce is expanded. Hence, income must grow if full employment of resources is to be maintained. For this to be the case, expenditures must grow to provide the necessary increase in demand. The rate of growth required to maintain full employment without inflation will be referred to as the required rate of growth.

[1] See pp. 505ff., especially p. 512.

Now it is by no means necessary that the actual rate of growth of expenditures will just match the required rate of growth. Suppose that the level of investment is such that, combined with the other relationships in the system, we obtain a rate of growth in expenditures that exceeds the required rate of growth. We should then be confronted with an inflationary situation. Or, suppose that the expenditure rate of growth falls short of the required rate. In this case, capacity is not utilized fully, and sooner or later labor becomes unemployed and/or prices fall. To avoid either of these contingencies, stabilization policy must aim at maintaining equality between the two rates of growth once an initial level of full employment has been established. Moreover, public policy may aim at raising or lowering the rate at which balanced growth proceeds.

Our first task will be to see how the required rate of growth is determined. Thereafter, we shall make various assumptions regarding investment behavior in the private sector; we shall also consider for each case how the resulting expenditure rate of growth may be equated with the required rate of growth and what policy problems arise in the process.

Determination of Required Rate

Let us begin with the addition to capacity income that results from a given level of investment. We have the increase in capacity income or $Y_n^c - Y_{n-1}^c = \Delta Y_n^c$ determined by

$$\Delta Y_n^c = s(I_{n-1} + \gamma G_{n-1}) \tag{20-40}$$

where s is the ratio of increase in capacity income to increase in capital stock.[1] The coefficient γ is the fraction of government expenditures G that goes into capacity-increasing investment. Such investment may involve public services, for example, programs for health and education, and does not require the creation of physical assets owned by government.

---

[1] The assumption that investment adds to capacity of the following period and the resulting growth rate of eq. (20-47) is similar to that used by Warren L. Smith, "Monetary-Fiscal Policy and Economic Growth," *Quarterly Journal of Economics*, vol. 71, no. 1, pp. 36–55, February, 1957; J. C. Gurley, "Fiscal Policy in a Growing Economy," *Journal of Political Economy*, vol. 61, no. 6, pp. 523–535, December, 1953; and E. Cary Brown, "Fiscal Policy in a Growing Economy: A Further Word," *Journal of Political Economy*, vol. 64, no. 2, pp. 170–172, April, 1956.

The formulation in eq. (20-40) differs from that underlying Domar's basic equation $\Delta I/I = \alpha\sigma$, where investment must be assumed to add to capacity during the period when it is made. See Evsey D. Domar, "Expansion and Employment," *American Economic Review*, vol. 37, no. 1, pp. 34–55, March, 1947, reprinted in Domar's *Essays in the Theory of Economic Growth*, Oxford University Press, New York, 1957, pp. 83–108. For a further discussion of the role of budget policy in growth see Arthur Smithies, "The Control of Inflation," *Review of Economics and Statistics*, vol. 39, no. 3, p. 272, August, 1957.

To simplify matters, we shall assume that the same value of s applies to both public and private investment.[1]

Turning to the demand or expenditure side of the picture, we have

$$Y_n^e = C_n + I_n + G_n \tag{20-41}$$
$$C_n = (1 - \alpha)(1 - t) Y_n^e \tag{20-42}$$
$$G_n = g Y_n^e \tag{20-43}$$

Hence
$$\Delta Y_n^e \equiv \frac{1}{\alpha(1 - t) + t - g} \Delta I_n \tag{20-44}$$

Consumption is now related to current rather than past income. As before, t is the rate of tax, and g is total government expenditure G as a fraction of income. Whereas ΔY_n^c depends upon the *level* of *total* (private and public) investment, ΔY_n^e depends (with fixed levels of g and t) upon the *change* of *private* investment.

Under the balanced conditions of required growth, income change determined from the expenditure side must be equal to income change determined from the capacity side, so that

$$\Delta Y_n^e = \Delta Y_n^c = \Delta Y_n^r \tag{20-45}$$

where Y^r is the required increase in income. Setting (20-44) equal to (20-40), we obtain the equivalent to the Domar equation:

$$\frac{\Delta I}{I_{n-1} + \gamma g Y_{n-1}^r} = s[\alpha(1 - t) + t - g] \tag{20-46}$$

The assumption of constant average values of α, g, and t permits us to rewrite this expression as

$$R^r = \frac{\Delta I_n^r}{I_{n-1}^r} = \frac{\Delta Y_n^r}{Y_{n-1}^r} = s[t + \alpha(1 - t) - g(1 - \gamma)] \tag{20-47}$$

where R^r is the required rate of growth, that is to say, the rate required for full utilization of resources and price-level stability.

We thus find that budget parameters enter into the determination of

---

[1] The reader who wishes to allow for a different value of s for public investment may write $\gamma = wz$, where z is government investment as a fraction of government expenditures, and sw is the income-capital ratio applicable to government investment. This replaces γ with two parameters, w and z.

The need for distinguishing between different values of s for different types of investment may be of particular importance with regard to the time lag with which capital formation results in increased output. Investment by government is frequently of a kind that affects productivity slowly—as, for instance, expenditures for education. In comparison, private investment is typically of a sort that adds to output in a shorter period. In a more complete analysis, such differences in the lags of income responses to various types of investment must be allowed for; but, unfortunately, the mathematics of the problem is complicated greatly if this is done.

the required rate of growth. Budgetary measures may involve changes
in t, g, and γ, and may affect the required rate of growth in various ways.
It follows from (20-47) that

$$\frac{\partial R^r}{\partial t} = +s(1 - \alpha) > 0 \qquad (20\text{-}48)$$

$$\frac{\partial R^r}{\partial g} = -s(1 - \gamma) \begin{array}{l} < 0, \text{ if } \gamma < 1 \\ = 0, \text{ if } \gamma = 1 \end{array} \qquad (20\text{-}49)$$

$$\frac{\partial R^r}{\partial \gamma} = +sg > 0 \qquad (20\text{-}50)$$

In other words, R^r rises if we reduce g and raise t or γ. The decline
in R^r that results from a given increase in g will be related inversely to γ.
If $\gamma = 1$, changes in g have no bearing on R^r. Demand is not affected,
nor is total capacity creation, the only change being in the division of
investment expenditures between the public and private sectors. If
$\gamma < 1$, the level of R^r declines as g rises, resources being transferred from
private investment to public uses that include consumption. An increase
in t raises R^r, as would an increase in α. Less resources are devoted to
consumption, and more can be placed into private investment. An
increase in γ, similarly, raises R^r. Since the government increases its
addition to capacity without raising its addition to demand, an increase
in income and in private investment is called for.

For the case of a balanced budget where $t = g$, equation (20-47)
reduces to

$$R^r = \frac{\Delta Y_n{}^r}{Y_{n-1}^r} = \frac{\Delta I_n}{I_{n-1}} = s[\alpha + (\gamma - \alpha)g] \qquad (20\text{-}51)$$

By the nature of the system, changes in the rate of private investment
provide the equilibrating force. We now have

$$\frac{\partial R^r}{\partial g} = +s(\gamma - \alpha) \begin{cases} > 0 \text{ if } \alpha < \gamma \\ = 0 \text{ if } \gamma = \alpha \\ < 0 \text{ if } \alpha > \gamma \end{cases} \qquad (20\text{-}52)$$

$$\frac{\partial R^r}{\partial \gamma} = +sg > 0 \qquad (20\text{-}53)$$

In other words, an increase in g will raise R^r if $\gamma > \alpha$; it will leave R^r
unchanged if $\gamma = \alpha$, and reduce R^r if $\gamma < \alpha$. This may be expected,
since capacity growth will be faster if the spending is done by whoever
channels a larger fraction of his income into investment. Again we are
confronted with a significant modification in the conventional balanced-
budget theorem. An increase in γ, for the same reason, raises R^r.

In order to evaluate the policy problems that result from these effects
of budget policy on the required rate, we must consider further the rate at

which expenditures actually tend to grow with given budget parameters. Only then can we examine the role of fiscal policy in obtaining balanced growth. The expenditure rate of growth depends on the behavioral relationships that determine consumption and investment. In defining the required rate, a consumption function was introduced, but the increase in investment was taken as given. We must now introduce an investment function. A number of possible situations will be considered, giving rise to different policy problems.

Balanced Growth in the Classical Setting

Let us begin with an economy where, for any set of budget parameters, private expenditures always adjust themselves to provide an expenditure rate of growth identical with the required rate. Since the consumption function is given by equation (20-42), this implies completely flexible investment, with ex ante saving and investment always equal. This may be described as a classical setting, using the term somewhat loosely. In such a case, equation (20-47) describes not only the required rate but also the actual path of balanced growth. Public policy is not concerned with maintaining an equality between the required and the expenditure rates of growth. This equality and, hence, full resource utilization and price-level stability exist automatically.[1]

However, public policy may affect the rate at which balanced growth proceeds. The question of just how high this rate should be set will be considered later.[2] Our present concern is only with the effects of budget policy upon the rate of balanced growth. These effects are as shown in equations (20-48) to (20-50) and need not be repeated. The growth rate may be increased by raising γ and t, and for $\gamma < 1$ by lowering g. If we assume that g and γ are determined by the Allocation Branch, the government may nevertheless secure any desired rate of growth (to the point of zero consumption) by raising t accordingly.

Balanced Growth with a Fixed Rate of Growth in Private Investment

In the preceding case of flexible investment, our only concern was with the effects of changes in budget parameters on the required rate of growth. These effects will remain in the picture throughout the following discussion. However, we must now consider cases where the spendings functions in the private sector are such that the actual expenditure rate R^e may differ from the required rate R^r.

Let us begin with a setting where the rate of increase in private investment $\Delta I^e/I^e_{n-1}$ is fixed exogenously. This is more or less analogous to the

[1] More precisely, if price-level stability is to be maintained, stabilization authorities must provide for an increase in money supply required to transact the growing output at constant prices.

[2] See p. 553.

assumption of a fixed value of I found in static Keynesian models. Otherwise the reaction structure remains as before. For given budget parameters appearing on the right side of equation (20-47), the equation tells us what will be the required value of $\Delta I^r/I^r_{n-1}$. Now suppose that the prevailing equality of both rates threatens to be interrupted. The exogenously given value $\Delta I^e/I^e_{n-1}$ threatens to rise and to exceed the required rate. Assuming full utilization of resources to begin with, this gives us a potentially inflationary situation. It may be prevented by an increase in γ or t, or a decrease in g, and the opposite adjustments may be applied to remedy a situation of potential unemployment.[1] Whatever is done, the budgetary adjustment must be such that the right side of equation (20-47) is made to equal the given new value of $\Delta I_n^e/I^e_{n-1}$.

Returning to the balanced-budget case, a situation of potential inflation may be met by an increase in γ. Also, it may be met by a decrease in g where $\gamma < \alpha$, this being a long-run version of our earlier theorem that an increase in the balanced budget may reduce income; and by an increase in g where $\gamma > \alpha$. If $\gamma = \alpha$, adjustments in budget size will not help. The fixed ratio $\Delta I_n^e/I^e_{n-1}$ is incompatible with given values of s and α, and a divergence from the required rate cannot be prevented. It may remain possible, however, to forestall potential inflation by raising the value of γ and to check potential deflation by reducing it.

As long as the rate of growth of private investment is given, the balanced rate of growth will be the same, whatever particular budget adjustments are used to forestall a potential unbalance. By the same token, it is impossible, in a situation of balanced growth, to change the rate of growth without disturbing the state of balance. There is only one possible rate of required growth in this case, and this is the given rate of growth of private investment. If the values of g and γ are given by considerations of the Allocation Branch, the required value of t is determined by the rest of the system.

---

[1] The following procedure of comparing the revised rate of growth with an explicit expenditure rate of growth follows that introduced by Warren Smith, *op. cit.* A similar formulation is found in Arthur Smithies, *op. cit.*, p. 282.

Note that the policy action must be such that it will prevent a gap from developing between the two rates. If the expenditure rate is permitted to exceed the required rate for only one period, the base amount of income subject to the expenditure rate will exceed that which is subject to the required rate. If both rates are equated thereafter, we are left nevertheless with a rising inflationary gap. Since, for purposes of growth theory, a rather lengthy period may be employed, we can assume that an adjustment is brought about within the same period of potential divergence To avoid the complications that otherwise result, this assumption is made throughout the following discussion of policy adjustments. Moreover, we assume that potential divergences between both rates are such that they may be prevented by small (to be exact, infinitely small) changes in the budget parameters. However, the approach might be adjusted to take account of finite changes.

Balanced Growth with Investment a Function of the Level of Past Income

Both the preceding assumptions are surely unrealistic. We cannot expect that private investment will adjust itself automatically to whatever growth rate is required. Nor will it be fixed independent of other parameters in the system. Rather, investment will vary according to some specific investment function.

Let us now consider the following expenditure system with an investment function:

$$Y_n^e = C_n + I_n + G_n \qquad (20\text{-}54)$$
$$C_n = (1 - \alpha)(Y_n^e - T_n) \qquad (20\text{-}55)$$
$$T_n = Y_n^e \qquad (20\text{-}56)$$
$$G_n = g Y_n^e \qquad (20\text{-}57)$$
$$I_n = b(Y_{n-1}^e - T_{n-1}) \qquad (20\text{-}58)$$

The system is similar to that shown in equations (20-41) to (20-43) except for the addition of an investment function. Expenditures in period n equal

$$Y_n^e = (1 - \alpha)(1 - t)Y_n^e + b(1 - t)Y_{n-1}^e + g Y_n^e \qquad (20\text{-}59)$$

Solving for Y_n^e/Y_{n-1}^e and subtracting 1 from both sides, we obtain the rate of growth of income or expenditure determined from the demand side

$$R^e = \frac{Y_n^e - Y_{n-1}^e}{Y_{n-1}^e} = \frac{(b - \alpha)(1 - t) + g - t}{\alpha(1 - t) + t - g} \qquad (20\text{-}60)$$

for the above system.[1]

The increase in capacity income is again as defined by equation (20-40), and the derivation of the required rate of growth R^r remains unchanged as given in equation (20-47). Introduction of an investment function into the determination of expenditure growth does not enter into the definition of the required rate. This follows from the nature of the required or equilibrium rate, since in equilibrium there must always be an equality between private investment and income not spent on private consumption or by government. While equation (20-58) defines planned investment, plans may not be realized unless the values of R^e and R^r are equal to each other.[2]

A situation where R^e threatens to exceed R^r is one of potential inflation pressure. In order to prevent a deviation of the two rates, we may reduce R^e and/or raise R^r. The direction of the appropriate changes in the

---

[1] Equation (20-60) is similar to eq. (20) of Smith, *op. cit.*, p. 45, except that the rate of interest is here omitted.

[2] If plans are not realized, investment behavior in the next period will hardly conform to eq. (20-58), since investors will want to adjust for inventory changes. This is a serious defect in a simplified analysis of this sort.

governmental parameters can be found by differentiating the expressions for R^r and R^e with respect to t and g. From equation (20-60), we have

$$\frac{\partial R^e}{\partial t} = \frac{b(g-1)}{[\alpha(1-t)+t-g]^2} < 0 \qquad (20\text{-}61)$$

and

$$\frac{\partial R^e}{\partial g} = \frac{b(1-t)}{[\alpha(1-t)+t-g]^2} > 0 \qquad (20\text{-}62)$$

Thus R^e is reduced by an increase in t and a reduction in g. Previously [see equations (20-48) and (20-49)] we noted that R^r may be increased by a reduction in g and an increase in t. By raising t or lowering g, the two rates may thus be moved together, and the potential inflationary gap may be avoided. Thus, balanced growth may be maintained by the appropriate fiscal adjustment.

However, the *level* at which balanced growth is reached depends upon which approach is taken. From equations (20-48) and (20-49) we note that R^r will respond more sharply to a small change in t, if $\gamma > \alpha$; and that it will respond more sharply to a change in g, if $\gamma < \alpha$. From (20-61) and (20-62) we note that R^e will respond more sharply to a small change in t, if $t > g$, and more sharply to a small change in g, if $t < g$. Suppose, now, that $\alpha < \gamma$ and $t < g$. In this case, an increase in t will restore balance (close the inflationary gap) at a higher rate of balanced growth than a decrease in g. The adjustment is made more largely by moving up R^r than by pulling down R^e. The opposite holds if $\alpha > \gamma$ and $t > g$. In this case, balance will be reached at a higher level if the inflationary gap is closed by reducing g. Similarly, a potentially deflationary gap will be closed at a higher level by raising g if $\alpha < \gamma$ and $t < g$; and it will be closed at a higher level by lowering t if $\alpha > \gamma$ and $t > g$.*

A similar observation holds for adjustments in γ. An increase in γ raises R^r. To the extent that the potential inflationary gap may be closed in this fashion, R^r is moved up toward R^e, and balanced growth is restored at a higher level. While this discussion is in terms of a highly simplified model, it shows how preferences regarding the desirable rate of growth enter into the choice of stabilization policies. Further complications enter if a distinction is drawn between various types of potential imbalance.[1]

* No ready conclusions can be drawn for the combinations $\alpha > \gamma$ with $t < g$, and $\alpha < \gamma$ with $t > g$. Here the result depends on the particular values involved.

[1] For a discussion along these lines see Arthur Smithies, *op. cit.*, p. 278. While his formal apparatus is quite similar to the one used here and by Warren L. Smith, Smithies' general discussion provides a more sophisticated framework. He distinguishes between the rate of growth required to secure full utilization of capacity and the rate required to secure full utilization of labor, both of which must be equated with the expenditure rate of growth to secure balanced growth. Different budget adjustments are called for, depending on which rates diverge. For a fuller development of

For the case of a balanced budget, equation (20-60) reduces to

$$R^e = \frac{b - \alpha}{\alpha} \qquad (20\text{-}63)$$

so that the expenditure rate is independent of the level of the balanced budget.[1] Such being the case, a balanced-budget adjustment to close an inflationary gap will operate through its effect on R^r only. As shown in equation (20-52), it will involve an increase in g and t if $\alpha < \gamma$, and a decrease if $\alpha > \gamma$.

---

this approach, a production function must be introduced. See Robert M. Solow, "A Contribution to the Theory of Economic Growth," *Quarterly Journal of Economics*, vol. 70, no. 1, pp. 65–94, February, 1956. Only then can we give a precise meaning to the concepts of full capacity versus full-employment output, labor shortage, and capital shortage.

[1] This is a somewhat puzzling result, as it appears to contradict our traditional notions about the effects of balanced-budget expansion in comparative statics. If there is to be growth with a balanced budget, we must have $b > \alpha$, which suggests that an expansion in g and t should reduce R^e, just as the conventional expansionary effect of an increase in the balanced budget follows from the assumption of $\alpha > 0$, with $b = 0$. However, note that the present formulation is complicated by the introduction of an investment lag, which makes a simple analogy to the static model inapplicable.

Moreover, it should be kept in mind that other expenditure systems might be devised in which R^e is affected by the level of the balanced budget. Consider, for instance, the following system:

$$\begin{aligned}
Y_n^e &= C_n + I_n + G_n \\
C_n &= (1 - \alpha)(Y_{n-1}^e - T_n) \\
T_n &= \tau Y_{n-1}^e \\
G_n &= \epsilon Y_{n-1}^e \\
I_n &= b(Y_{n-1}^e - T_n)
\end{aligned}$$

The expenditure rate of growth now equals

$$R^e = (b - \alpha)(1 - \tau) + \epsilon - \tau$$

with $\qquad \dfrac{\partial R^e}{\partial \tau} = \alpha - b - 1 < 0 \qquad$ and $\qquad \dfrac{\partial R^e}{\partial \epsilon} = 1 > 0$

With a balanced budget we now have

$$R^e = (b - \alpha)(1 - \epsilon) \qquad \text{and} \qquad \frac{\partial R^e}{\partial \epsilon} = \alpha - b < 0$$

since, in order to have growth with a balanced budget, we must have $b > \alpha$. This result is consistent with the basic balanced-budget theorem, according to which a budget increase is expansionary if the private spendings propensities add to less than 1, and is neutral if they equal 1. In the case dealt with in this note, the private propensity exceeds 1, hence the restrictive effects of balanced-budget expansion. However, use of this expenditure system would call for corresponding adjustments in eqs. (20-42) and (20-43) and in the resulting formulation of R^r, which entails a new set of difficulties.

Instead of dealing with the problem of how to close a potential inflationary or deflationary gap, let us now suppose that balanced growth proceeds undisturbed. However, the government wishes to move to a higher or lower level of growth. Again setting aside for later consideration just what rate of balanced growth is desirable, let us turn to the adjustments that may be made in order to affect this rate.[1] Holding γ constant, the combined adjustments in g and t required to change the balanced rate of growth are given by[2]

$$\frac{\partial t}{\partial R} = \frac{s[\alpha(1 - t) + t - g]^2(1 - \gamma) + b(1 - t)}{sb[(1 - \alpha)(1 - t) - (1 - \gamma)(1 - g)]} \qquad (20\text{-}64)$$

and
$$\frac{\partial g}{\partial R} = \frac{s[\alpha(1 - t) + t - g]^2(1 - \alpha) + b(1 - g)}{sb[(1 - \alpha)(1 - t) - (1 - \gamma)(1 - g)]} \qquad (20\text{-}65)$$

The numerator is positive in both cases, and the denominator is the same for both expressions. Therefore, a change in the balanced rate of growth requires both g and t to be changed in the same direction. An increase in the balanced rate of growth requires both g and t to be increased or decreased, depending on whether the common denominator is positive or negative, that is, on whether

$$(1 - \alpha)(1 - t) + (1 - \gamma)g \gtrless 1 - \gamma \qquad (20\text{-}66)$$

That is to say, the required direction of change depends on the size of the total (private plus public) propensity to consume and on the fraction of government expenditures going into consumption. The adjustment will involve a deficit rate (where $g > t$) or a surplus rate (where $t > g$), depending on whether the numerator of equation (20-65) exceeds or falls short of that of (20-64). The adjustment is possible with a marginally balanced budget only in the special case where the two numerators are equal to each other, that is, if $\alpha = \gamma$ and $t = g$.

With a constant γ, as assumed in deriving equations (20-64) and (20-65), a given rate of balanced growth requires a certain level of g and a certain level of t, which are defined by this system. The same rate of growth might be combined with various levels of g and t if γ is introduced as a further policy variable.

[1] See p. 553.
[2] We have two equations:

$$R^r = s[t + \alpha(1 - t) - g(1 - \gamma)]$$

and for $R^r = R^e$

$$s[t + \alpha(1 - t) - g(1 - \gamma)] = \frac{(b - \alpha)(1 - t) + g - t}{\alpha(1 - t) + t - g}$$

in four unknowns, R^r, t, g, and γ. By holding one of these (say γ) constant, changes in R in response to changes in g and t may be determined by differentiating the system. I am indebted to Warren L. Smith for suggesting this approach.

Adjustments in Tax Structure

Further policy dimensions may be added in the form of structural tax adjustments, shifting the burden between income subject to consumption and income subject to investment, along the lines applied in our earlier discussion of comparative statics.[1] For this purpose, the system of equations (20-54) to (20-58) may be refined by distinguishing between various income sources subject to different tax rates and propensities to consume. The system may now read

$$Y_n^e = C_n + I_n + G_n \tag{20-67}$$
$$C_n = (1 - \alpha^L)(Y_n^{eL} - T_n^L) + (1 - \alpha^P)(Y_n^{eP} - T_n^P) \tag{20-68}$$
$$T_n^L = t^L Y_n^{eL} \tag{20-69}$$
$$T_n^P = t^P Y_n^{eP} \tag{20-70}$$
$$Y_n^{eL} = (1 - p) Y_n^e \tag{20-71}$$
$$Y_n^{eP} = p Y_n^e \tag{20-72}$$
$$G_n = g Y_n^e \tag{20-73}$$
$$I_n = b(Y_{n-1}^{eP} - T_{n-1}^P) \tag{20-74}$$

where α^L and α^P are the propensities to save, and t^L and t^P are the tax rates applicable to labor and profit income; p is the fraction of income going to profits, and $1 - p$ is the fraction going to wages. From this we obtain

$$R^e = \frac{Y_n^e - Y_{n-1}^e}{Y_{n-1}^e}$$
$$= \frac{bp - \alpha^L(1 - p) - \alpha^P p - t^L(1 - p)(1 - \alpha^L) - t^P p(b + 1 - \alpha^P) + g}{\alpha^L(1 - p) + \alpha^P p + t^L(1 - p)(1 - \alpha^L) + t^P p(1 - \alpha^P) - g} \tag{20-75}$$

as the expenditure rate of growth. The effects of changes in the governmental parameters are given by

$$\frac{\partial R^e}{\partial t^L} = \frac{-pb(1 - \alpha^L)(1 - t^P)(1 - p)}{[\alpha^L(1-p) + \alpha^P p + t^L(1-p)(1-\alpha^L) + t^P p(1-\alpha^P) - g]^2} < 0 \tag{20-76}$$

$$\frac{\partial R^e}{\partial t^P} = \frac{-pb[(1 - g) - (1 - \alpha^L)(1 - t^L)(1 - p)]}{[\alpha^L(1-p) + \alpha^P p + t^L(1-p)(1-\alpha^L) + t^P p(1-\alpha^P) - g]^2} < 0^* \tag{20-77}$$

$$\frac{\partial R^e}{\partial g} = \frac{pb(1 - t^P)}{[\alpha^L(1-p) + \alpha^P p + t^L(1-p)(1-\alpha^L) + t^P p(1-\alpha^P) - g]^2} > 0 \tag{20-78}$$

[1] See p. 439.

* Provided that $(1 - g) > (1 - \alpha^L)(1 - t^L)(1 - p)$. This condition states that the fraction of output purchased privately must exceed the ratio of consumption by wage earners to total income. Since the coefficients are defined in ex ante terms, we cannot be sure that this condition is always met. It is assumed to be met for purposes of this discussion, and it must be met under conditions of balanced growth.

In order to analyze the effects of policy changes on the equilibrium rate of growth, the required rate of equation (20-47) must be adjusted accordingly. Substituting the new consumption function

$$C_n = (1 - \alpha^L)(1 - t^L)(1 - p)Y_n{}^e + (1 - \alpha^P)(1 - t^P)pY_n{}^e \quad (20\text{-}79)$$

for equation (20-42) into the system of equations (20-40) to (20-45), we obtain

$$R^r = \frac{Y_n{}^r - Y_{n-1}^r}{Y_{n-1}^r}$$
$$= s[t^L(1 - \alpha^L)(1 - p) + \alpha^L(1 - p) + t^P p(1 - \alpha^P) + p\alpha^P - g(1 - \gamma)] \quad (20\text{-}80)$$

The effects of changes in the government parameters upon this required rate are given by

$$\frac{\partial R^r}{\partial t^L} = s(1 - \alpha^L)(1 - p) > 0 \quad\quad\quad (20\text{-}81)$$

$$\frac{\partial R^r}{\partial t^P} = sp(1 - \alpha^P) > 0 \quad\quad\quad (20\text{-}82)$$

$$\frac{\partial R^r}{\partial g} = -s(1 - \gamma) < 0 \quad\quad\quad (20\text{-}83)$$

$$\frac{\partial R^r}{\partial \gamma} = sg > 0 \quad\quad\quad (20\text{-}84)$$

Bringing together these results, we note that R^e moves inversely to t^L and t^P, whereas R^r moves with t^L and t^P. Suppose, now, that we have a potentially inflationary situation where $R^e > R^r$. The expenditure rate may be reduced by raising either tax. The required rate will be raised in either case. Thus the two rates are moved together from both sides. However, the level at which balanced growth is restored depends upon which rate is adjusted.

To illustrate this relationship in its simplest form, let us assume that income is divided equally between profit and wage income, so that $p = 1 - p$; and that the propensity to consume out of disposable wage and profit income is the same, so that $1 - \alpha^L = 1 - \alpha^P$. In this case, it follows from equations (20-81) and (20-82) that R^r rises equally with a small change in yield, whether this rise is due to a rise in t^P or in t^L. However, it also follows from equations (20-76) and (20-77) that the resulting reduction in R^e will be the same in both cases only if

$$(1 - g) = 2[(1 - \alpha^L)(1 - t^L)(1 - p)]$$

If $(1 - g)$ falls short of the expression on the right, the reduction in R^e will be less if the increase is in t^P. Therefore, balanced growth will be restored at a higher level by raising t^P. If $(1 - g)$ exceeds the expression on the right, the increase in t^L has the lesser effect on R^e and serves to restore balanced growth at a higher rate.

If we assume that $p < 1 - p$ with $1 - \alpha^L$ still equal to $1 - \alpha^P$, we find that an increase in t^L will raise R^r more than will an increase in t^P. This tendency will be even more pronounced if we assume $1 - \alpha^L > 1 - \alpha^P$. The preceding general observations again apply to effects on R^e. In a realistic setting, the comparative results of alternative adjustments thus depend on a number of factors, including α^L, α^P, p, g, and the initial level of tax rates t^P and t^L. No ready generalizations can be made, but it is evident that the choice between alternative tax adjustments may have a significant bearing on the level at which balanced growth is restored.

As before, we may consider the possibility of raising or lowering the rate of growth under conditions of balanced growth. An increase in one of the tax rates will raise R^r and lower R^e, while a reduction in the other will lower R^r and raise R^e. Conditions may be such that the net effect of an increase in t^L and a reduction in t^P leads to a higher level of balanced growth while maintaining the same ratio of total tax yield to income, and maintaining the same levels of g and γ. It is more likely, however, that the adjustment in tax structure will have to be accompanied by a change in this ratio, or else in g or γ.

Finally, monetary policy may be introduced into the picture.[1] By adding these additional variables, public policy is given a greater degree of freedom in combining various rates of growth with various budget structures, and in particular with various levels of g and γ. However, there is no reason to assume that it will always be possible to combine any growth objective with any particular level of g determined by the Allocation Branch, and any particular tax structure determined by the Distribution Branch.

System with Accelerator Function

We now turn to the accelerator type of investment function, as we did in our treatment of dynamics. The proper procedure would be to take the accelerator model given in equations (20-35) to (20-38) and to determine the conditions under which such a system can describe a steady rate of growth.[2] Having established the new expenditure rate of growth, the effects of various budgetary changes can again be determined. The

[1] See Warren L. Smith, *op. cit.*

[2] For such conditions, see W. J. Baumol, *Economic Dynamics: An Introduction*, The Macmillan Company, New York, 1951, pp. 196–198. Also see D. Hamberg, *Economic Growth and Stability*, W. W. Norton & Company, Inc., New York, 1956; and Sidney S. Alexander, "The Accelerator as a Generator of Steady Growth," *Quarterly Journal of Economics*, vol. 63, no. 2, p. 174, 1949.

analysis is somewhat more complicated and will not be undertaken here. However, we may expect that increases in g would again raise the expenditure rate of growth, and that increases in t would reduce it.

The difficulties inherent in the second-order system of equations (20-35) to (20-38) may be avoided in a simpler system where investment is a function of $Y_n - Y_{n-1}$. Such a model is given by our earlier equations (20-41) to (20-43) combined with the investment function

$$I_n = \beta(Y_n^e - Y_{n-1}^e) \tag{20-85}$$

We then have

$$Y_n^e = [(1 - \alpha)(1 - t) + g]Y_n^e + I_n \tag{20-86}$$

and the growth rate equals

$$R^e = \frac{g - \alpha(1 - t) - t}{\alpha(1 - t) + t - g - \beta} \tag{20-87}$$

with

$$\frac{\partial R^e}{\partial t} = \frac{\beta(1 - \alpha)}{[\beta - \alpha(1 - t) - t + g]^2} > 0 \tag{20-88}$$

and

$$\frac{\partial R^e}{\partial g} = -\frac{\beta}{[\beta - \alpha(1 - t) - t + g]^2} < 0 \tag{20-89}$$

Thus, an increase in t raises R^e, as does a reduction in g. The changes in R^e are in the same direction as for the required rate, as shown in equations (20-48) and (20-49). However, the effects on R^e and R^r may differ in magnitude. Changes in γ affect R^r but not R^e, and hence may be used to reduce differences in the two rates.

For the balanced-budget case, we have

$$R^e = \frac{\alpha(1 - g)}{\beta - \alpha(1 - g)} \tag{20-90}$$

and

$$\frac{\partial R^e}{\partial g} = -\frac{\alpha\beta}{[\beta - \alpha(1 - g)]^2} < 0 \tag{20-91}$$

An increase in the balanced budget lowers R^e. If $R^e > R^r$, which is defined by equation (20-51), the two rates may be brought together by raising g, which lowers R^e, and raises R^r if $\gamma > \alpha$. If $\gamma < \alpha$, an increase in g will lower both rates and may not work. However, the adjustment may always be secured by raising γ, at least until $\gamma > \alpha$.

Such a system is readily treated, but the results do not seem particularly useful.[1] In this system ex ante saving and investment are treated as

[1] See J. C. Gurley, "Fiscal Policy in a Growing Economy," *Journal of Political Economy*, vol. 61, no. 6, pp. 523–535, December, 1953; and E. Cary Brown, "Fiscal Policy in a Growing Economy: A Further Word," *Journal of Political Economy*, vol. 64, no. 2, pp. 170–172, April, 1956; and Warren L. Smith, "Professor Gurley on Fiscal Policy in a Growing Economy," *Journal of Political Economy*, vol. 62, pp. 440–441,

equal for any period, which results in a positive relationship between the propensity to save and the rate of growth. An increase in g reduces the expenditure rate of growth, while an increase in t raises it. To avoid this unrealistic result, the accelerator type of investment function should make use of a second-order system.

Unemployment, Inflation, and Capital Shortage

The structure of the preceding growth models is such that a potential situation of unemployment can be avoided by raising the expenditure rate of growth. This may not be possible in a system where wage or price rigidities impose obstacles to the full utilization of all factors.

Suppose that real wages are rigid in the downward direction, and that the existing capital stock is insufficient to employ the entire labor force at the prevailing real-wage rate. The remedy is not in a general increase in the expenditure rate of growth. In order to remove unemployment it will be necessary to reduce consumption, increase saving, and thus permit increased investment without inflation.[1] This requires substitution of taxes on consumption for taxes on investment, or a budget surplus that permits additional private investment by credit expansion. As the supply of capital is increased relative to that of labor, a larger labor force can be employed at the given real-wage rate.

This model bears some similarity to the case of underdeveloped countries. Here the basic problem is one of overcoming underemployment by raising real income. This requires an increase in capital, including skills as well as plant and equipment. The increase cannot be accomplished simply by raising the level of aggregate demand. Forced saving through inflation may be used to transfer resources to capital formation, but the resulting choice of investment is inefficient at best, and the allocation of the burden inequitable. The better approach is to transfer resources to capital formation without inflation, and this requires a transfer of demand rather than an addition to total demand. Indeed, it is not surprising that the Keynesian remedy to unemployment is inapplicable. The basic problem is not one of unemployment to begin with; rather it is one of low productivity due to capital shortage and a resulting real-wage rate so low that a high level of leisure is preferred. What appears to be a high level of unemployment is, in fact, a situation of poverty with full employment in the classical sense.

In a developed economy, it is evident that the capital-shortage model

---

October, 1954. In comparing the Gurley-Brown discussion with the present one, note that the former does not distinguish between the required and expenditure rates, thus assuming that growth necessarily proceeds in a balanced fashion.

[1] See William Fellner, *Trends and Cycles in Economic Activity*, Henry Holt and Company, Inc., New York, 1956, pp. 212–215 and 357–367.

does not fit the case of unemployment in the usual type of depression to which we have been accustomed. In such a depression, excess capacity is combined with unemployment, and the remedy must be found in raising the level of total demand. Given substantial excess capacity to begin with, this increase must be primarily in the form of consumer demand. However, unemployment due to capital shortage may develop if money wages are raised ahead of productivity gains and if demand is restricted so as to keep prices from rising. Increased capital formation may then prove helpful to verify a given rate of increase in money wages.[1] Moreover, the issue of capital shortage may arise in dealing with demand inflation, where a sustained excess of potential demand might be met by raising capital formation and hence the required rate of growth.[2]

Secular Stagnation and Inflation

Most of the early discussion of fiscal policy was developed against the background of the stagnation hypothesis. In retrospect, this may be seen as a special case of a growth model.[3] There are two distinct parts to the stagnation problem. The first deals with changes in the rate of growth of capacity, or full-employment, income and the reasons why this rate of growth may be expected to decline. The second part deals with the differential between capacity income and the income that is actually achieved in the absence of compensatory adjustments.

The first proposition, of a declining rate of growth of capacity income, is the heart of classical economics: It is simply an expression of the basic law of diminishing returns. Given the fixed supply of natural resources, the size of population, and the state of technical development, the profitability of investment must decrease as the stock of capital grows. The rate of net accumulation hence decreases, and so does growth. Given these assumptions, the proposition stands.

The crux of the argument, and the downfall of the classical doctrine, lies in the assumption of unchanged technique. To date, technical progress has more than offset the increasing scarcity of natural resources. Together with an increasing labor supply, progress in science has been

---

[1] See p. 470.

[2] See p. 467.

[3] For a general survey of the stagnation thesis, see Benjamin Higgins, "Concepts and Criteria of Secular Stagnation," in *Income, Employment and Public Policy: Essays in Honor of Alvin H. Hansen*, W. W. Norton & Company, Inc., New York, 1948, chap. 4, pp. 82–107. Also see Alvin H. Hansen, *Fiscal Policy and Business Cycles*, W. W. Norton & Company, Inc., New York, 1941, pp. 38–46, reprinted in *Readings in Fiscal Policy*, American Economic Association, Richard D. Irwin, Inc., Homewood, Ill., 1955, pp. 540–557.

sufficient to sustain a rising level of investment and a growing population at a rising standard of living. Evidently there is little reason to expect the rate of growth of full-employment output, total or per capita, to fall off over the foreseeable future. Atomic energy is strong evidence to the contrary.

The second proposition, of a widening gap between potential and actual income, is an element of Keynesian economics. At any one time, demand may exceed full-employment output or fall short of it. Our discussion of the thirties was concerned with the latter case. The deflationary gap between actual and potential income was expected to persist and to widen, and this for a number of reasons. Investment was expected to become inadequate due to a declining rate of population growth, the disappearance of frontiers, a general slowing down of innovations, and the increasingly "capital-saving" nature of innovation. Moreover, the need for a high rate of investment was expected to rise due to a rising average propensity to save and a rising volume of gross savings by business.

These hypotheses fitted the pattern of the thirties, but subsequent developments differed from it. Population trends changed, the consumption function shifted upward, and investment remained at a high level. All this occurred under the protective umbrella of a large defense budget. Indeed, the prophecy of secular deflation turned into one of secular inflation. Chances are that the course of events will disprove the new doctrine no less than the old, but this is not our immediate concern.

Our concern is rather with the implications for fiscal policy that arise from a secular trend toward deflation or inflation. The preceding discussion permits us to distinguish between various types of stagnation and their fiscal implications. Returning to the system of equations (20-47) and (20-60), let us simplify matters by assuming that the values of g and γ are fixed by the Allocation Branch. The value of t must then be adjusted to assure the equilibrium rate of growth. If this leaves us with $t = g$, equilibrium growth at the given level of g requires a balanced budget. If it leaves us with $t < g$, it requires a constant rate of deficit, or ratio of deficit to income; and if it leaves us with $t > g$, a constant rate of surplus is called for.

One may wish to refer to a situation where $t < g$ as one of stagnation. Nevertheless, the deflationary gap, or deficit as per cent of income, is constant. Let us refer to this as a state of stable stagnation. If conditions are such that α rises with income or that the rate of growth of investment declines, t must be reduced to offset these changes. The deflationary gap or the rate of deficit then rises, relative to income. This might be referred to as a case of increasing stagnation. A case of declining α, or rising rate of growth of investment, might be referred to as one of decreasing stagnation. Thus defined, the state of stagnation depends upon the levels of g and γ, as set by the Allocation Branch, and will change with changes in g and γ.[1]

The distinction between conditions of stable and increasing stagnation is of interest in relation to the public debt.[2]   For the case of stable stagnation, public debt will grow at the same rate as income.   The ratio of debt to income will remain at or approach a constant.   The higher the rate of growth, the larger the absolute deficit, but the lower the ratio of debt to income.   With a constant average rate of interest on public debt, the ratio of interest payments to national income also approaches a constant. Thus, there is no need to fear that an ever-rising tax rate is required to finance interest payments.   This possibility arises only in the case of increasing stagnation, where the ratio of deficit to income rises; or in a setting where, for classical reasons, income grows at a decreasing percentage rate.

---

[1] The reader who finds this concept objectionable will note that it results from the simplified assumption of the growth model, in which expenditures of the Allocation Branch are treated as independent of taxes raised by this branch.   In a more refined system, we must assume that such expenditures are paid for by benefit taxes.   The demand for government services then may be looked upon as part of the private spendings function.   (See p. 33.)   With distributional tax-transfer adjustments given by the Distribution Branch, only the level of t_s, or taxes of the Stabilization Branch, remain for purposes of stabilization.   In this case, the state of stagnation depends upon the level and sign of t_s or changes therein, and becomes independent of the government's expenditures on goods and services.

[2] See Evsey D. Domar, "The Burden of Debt and The National Income," *American Economic Review*, vol. 34, no. 4, December, 1944, pp. 798–827.   Reprinted as chap. 2 in E. D. Domar, *Essays in the Theory of Economic Growth*, Oxford University Press, New York, 1957.

CHAPTER 21

Further problems in compensatory finance

Certain further aspects of compensatory finance, including the problems of flexibility and neutrality, remain for consideration.

A. PROBLEMS OF TIMING AND FLEXIBILITY

Since changes in income occur over a time period, the initiation and execution of fiscal policies must be timed properly if destabilizing changes are to be compensated for. In order to secure a flexible policy, it is necessary to minimize the lag between (1) the occurrence of a need for policy adjustments and the recognition of this need; (2) recognition of the need for changes in policy and the implementation of such changes; and (3) introduction of policy changes and their realization in effectively altering the level of income.[1]

Recognition of the Need for Policy Changes

If deviations from equilibrium growth are to be checked at the outset, policy must be planned on the basis of income predictions. Within

[1] See Milton Friedman, "A Monetary and Fiscal Framework for Economic Stability," *American Economic Review*, vol. 38, pp. 245–264, June, 1948, reprinted in Milton Friedman, *Essays in Positive Economics*, University of Chicago Press, Chicago, 1953, and in Friedrich A. Lutz and Lloyd W. Mints (eds.), *Readings in Monetary Theory*, American Economic Association, Richard D. Irwin, Inc., Homewood, Ill., 1951, pp. 369–393. Also see the papers by E. E. Hagen and A. G. Hart and the discussion by Benjamin Higgins, "Problems in Timing and Administering Fiscal Policy in Prosperity and Depression," *American Economic Review*, vol. 38, no. 2, pp. 416–451, May, 1948.

certain limits this may be done—and, in fact, is done, as in estimating prospective tax yields, financing requirements, or agricultural markets. Moreover, progress is made in developing forecasting methods, and valuable information on expenditure plans is becoming available from survey techniques. Nevertheless, the possibility of preventive action remains limited as yet. The problem of stabilization is still primarily one of remedial adjustments aimed at preventing further destabilization and restoring an equilibrium.

For remedial adjustments to be possible, the change in the underlying factors must be sufficiently slow and the possibility of policy adjustment sufficiently fast, so that one remedy becomes effective before a new one is called for. Thus, situations might be constructed where no effective stabilization policy is possible and where attempts at a stabilizing policy are as likely to accent as to reduce deviation from equilibrium income.[1] This is not the typical case. Economic fluctuations tend to be such that a movement, once started, continues for some time, thus permitting compensatory action before a reversal of policy is required. However, flexibility in adjusting budget parameters is important, and preference must be given to policies which may be changed promptly and for which changes will become effective in a short period.

Speed of Policy Initiation

After fiscal authorities have recognized the need for action, some policies may be changed more promptly than others. The adaptability to change depends on political as well as technical considerations. The authority to change tax rates is vested in Congress and not in the executive branch of the government. While it may be possible to secure expeditious action by Congress when the need is for reduction in tax rates, it may not be possible when an increase is needed. In order to secure the necessary flexibility, authority to change tax rates within a prescribed pattern might be delegated to the executive branch or to a joint executive-legislative group; and Congress could lay down general rules as to when such rate changes should be undertaken. In this way, greater flexibility might be secured without damage to the sound principle that final responsibility for tax policy should rest with the legislature.[2]

The executive branch has somewhat greater freedom in the timing of

---

[1] The broad problem of forecasting cannot be examined here. For a general discussion see Robert A. Gordon, *Business Fluctuations*, Harper & Brothers, New York, 1952, chap. 15, pp. 449–483. For a pessimistic view, see Milton Friedman, "The Effects of a Full-employment Policy on Economic Stability," *Essays in Positive Economics*, pp. 117–133.

[2] See the British *White Paper on Employment Policy*, Cmd. 6527, May, 1944, where a countercyclical variation of social insurance contributions is proposed; and the discussion in W. H. Beveridge, *Full Employment in a Free Society*, W. W. Norton & Company, Inc., New York, 1945, pp. 263–264.

capital expenditures, especially where appropriations are made for a particular project rather than for a time period; and the delegation of authority to the executive branch in matters of expenditure timing is less controversial. Thus the determination of expenditures is more flexible in so far as political considerations are concerned.

However, tax policy has the advantage on technical grounds. After a change in tax rates has been decided upon, it may be put into effect within a relatively short period. In the case of the income tax, rates or exemptions may be adjusted without calling for any change in the basic definition of taxable income; and tax payments will be affected promptly through source withholding. In the case of the corporation tax, prompt effectiveness results, since the taxpayer is usually on an accrual basis, especially where tax reserves are invested in government securities. Similar flexibility of adjustment applies to a general sales tax, but less so to a complex system of differential excises.

This ready adjustability does not exist in the case of expenditure programs. Even if planned well in advance, public works cannot be put into operation at a moment's notice.[1] Contracts must be placed and many details must be decided upon before the work can be started. Once started, a public-works program cannot be terminated at will. Projects in process may have to be completed to avoid deterioration, even though compensatory needs may have changed.

Time Lag in Effectiveness of Policy

Finally, let us consider the time required for a change in policy to become effective. The nature of this problem may be illustrated by reference to the simple multiplier process set into motion by a change in government expenditures. Considering the multiplier process over a very long period, we have

$$Y_n - Y_0 = \Delta G + c \, \Delta G + c^2 \, \Delta G \, \cdots \, + c^n \, \Delta G = \frac{1}{1-c} \Delta G \quad (21\text{-}1)$$

where $n = \infty$. Considering the resulting change in income for x periods, where $x < \infty$, we have

$$Y_x - Y_0 = \Delta G + c \, \Delta G + c^2 \, \Delta G \, \cdots \, + c^x \, \Delta G = \frac{1-c^{x+1}}{1-c} \Delta G \quad (21\text{-}2)$$

Now, let F_x be the ratio of the increase in income by period x to the increase in income by period n. We then have

$$F_x = \frac{Y_x - Y_0}{Y_n - Y_0} = 1 - c^{x+1} \quad (21\text{-}3)$$

[1] See J. M. Clark, *Economics of Planning Public Works*, National Resources Committee, Washington, 1935. Also see Benjamin Higgins, "The United States Public Works Reserve," *International Labor Review*, 1944, part III, pp. 581–607, and literature there given.

Thus, the fraction of the total increase in income that is accomplished in any given period will be smaller if c is large. A possible set of results for $\Delta G = 100$ is shown in Table 21-1.

TABLE 21-1. INCREASE IN INCOME REACHED AFTER GIVEN NUMBER OF PERIODS
($\Delta G = 100$; figures rounded)

Number of periods	Absolute increase			Per cent of total increase*		
	Values of c			Values of c		
	0.8	0.6	0.5	0.8	0 6	0.5
0	100	100	100	20	40	50
1	180	160	150	36	64	75
3	295	217	188	59	87	94
5	380	238	196	74	95	98
7	416	246	198	83	98	99
∞	500	250	200	100	100	100

* Equals $100(1 - c^{x+1})$.

The information in Table 21-1 is of some interest, but has no operational meaning unless we can translate into calendar terms the concept of a period. In a simple situation, where no inventory fluctuations occur, the sequence of equation (21-1) involves the time elapsed between earning by the consumer and his spending (the Robertson lag), and between consumer spending and the receipt of income from production undertaken to meet consumer spending (the Lundberg lag). This involves not only the payment habits of the producer but also the period involved in production.[1] Moreover, the picture is complicated because different stages of production introduce further lags between income receipt and spending. Finally, production may be initiated before or after demand is realized, thus resulting in inventory changes.[2] For these and other reasons, it is exceedingly difficult to translate the period concept into calendar terms. The length of the period may vary widely over the cycle and depend upon the particular sectors of the economy in which the change occurs. By the same token, there is no simple link (although there is a distant relation-

[1] See Lloyd A. Metzler, "Three Lags in the Circular Flow of Income," pp. 11–32, in *Income, Employment and Public Policy: Essays in Honor of Alvin H. Hansen*, W. W. Norton & Company, New York, 1948.

[2] J. W. Angell, "The Components of the Circular Velocity of Money," *Quarterly Journal of Economics*, vol. 51, pp 224–273, February, 1937; F. Machlup, "Period Analysis and Multiplier Theory," in *Readings in Business Cycle Theory*, American Economic Association, Richard D. Irwin, Inc., Homewood, Ill., 1949, pp. 203–234; Richard M. Goodwin, "The Multiplier," in Seymour Harris (ed.), *The New Economics*, Alfred A. Knopf, Inc., New York, 1947, pp. 482–499; and Gardner Ackley, "The Multiplier Time Period," *American Economic Review*, vol. 41, no. 3, pp. 350–368, June, 1951.

ship) between the concepts of the multiplier time period and income velocity.[1]

A more constructive approach to this problem is taken in econometric models that work with lags based on observed time series, such as annual data. A dynamic model of this sort may be used to trace the effects of changes in fiscal policy over time, and to measure what change has been accomplished after any given number of years.[2]

Dynamic models of the type considered in the preceding chapter are based on the assumption that the period involved in the multiplier process is of the same length as the period involved in the budgetary and investment processes, and that the lags are stable. This assumption is necessary in order to avoid very complicated models, but actual policy must allow for differences in lags, especially in the first period. Thus, responding may be quicker or slower, depending on whose disposable income is increased; and this may differ depending on whether government expenditures are increased or taxes are reduced. Goods and service expenditures of government may be directed at items supplied out of inventories or currently produced, and the resulting change of income over time will differ accordingly.[3]

Determinants of Built-in Flexibility

Compensatory effects of the budget may result from changes in the basic tax and expenditure parameters, undertaken to compensate for disturbances that originate in the private sector. Or, such disturbances

---

[1] Assuming that inventory remains constant, the income velocity of transaction money may be said to equal $12/m$, where m is the multiplier time period, or income-propagation period. This period has been estimated at four months. See Machlup, op. cit.

While there exists this conceptual relationship between income velocity and the multiplier time period, it does not follow that income velocity offers a statistical method of estimating the multiplier time period. The relationship applies only to the income velocity of transaction money and not to that of the total money supply; and the amount of transaction money is not known. The estimate of four months, or an income velocity of three, is based on the rather crude assumption that demand deposits plus currency outside banks equals transaction money. Moreover, inventory fluctuations do occur, so that the actual time period may differ from the income-propagation period under conditions of constant inventory. Nevertheless, some of the factors that bear on income velocity also enter into the determination of the multiplier time period.

This relationship between income velocity and the multiplier time period does not imply a relationship between the level of income velocity for a finite period and the size of the multiplier over infinity. If the money supply and investment are given while the consumption function shifts, income velocity for any given period varies with the size of the multiplier, but this is a purely definitional relationship.

[2] For a beginning along these lines see, Arthur Goldberger, 'Properties of an Econometric Model of the United States,'' unpublished doctoral dissertation, University of Michigan, Ann Arbor, Mich., 1958.

See p. 444.

may give rise to automatic changes in public expenditures or tax yield—changes resulting while tax and expenditure parameters are held constant. Certain public expenditures, such as unemployment benefits or price-support payments, are geared to move in a countercyclical fashion. Similarly, tax yields obtained from given statutory rates rise and fall with changes in the level of income and, hence, in the tax base. Thus, a decline in income automatically leads to a reduction in surplus or an increase in deficit; and an increase in income automatically leads to a reduction in deficit or an increase in surplus. As a result, fluctuations in the level of national income are lessened.

Such automatic changes (with tax and expenditure parameters constant) are referred to as built-in flexibility.[1] The existence of built-in flexibility is particularly valuable where policy initiation is rigid or where frequent changes in tax or expenditure parameters are held undesirable for other reasons. What are the factors that determine the magnitude of this automatic effect? Let us assume first that government expenditures remain unchanged, and concentrate on changes in tax yield that result while statutory rates of tax (the tax formulas) are held constant. The response of changes in tax yield T to changes in the level of national income Y may be expressed in the form of an arc elasticity

$$E_T = \frac{\Delta T/T_0}{\Delta Y/Y_0} \tag{21-4}$$

where T_0 and Y_0 are the initial levels of yield and income. E_T measures the percentage change in yield that results with a given percentage change in income. The value of E_T thus defined depends upon the initial level of tax rates, the progressivity of the rate structure, and the responsiveness of the tax base to changes in total income.

Let us consider these two factors separately. If the statutory-rate structure is progressive, the ratio t of tax yield T to tax base B rises as the tax base increases. The ratio t is the average statutory rate of tax. Ratio t depends on the statutory-rate formula, such as a progressive schedule of income tax rates, and upon the size and structure of the tax base B. Depending on the type of tax, the tax base, or B, equals taxable income, wages, gross receipts, assessed property value, and so forth. In elasticity form, we have

$$E_t = \frac{\Delta t/t_0}{\Delta B/B_0} \tag{21-5}$$

---

[1] See R. A. Musgrave and M. H. Miller, "Built-in Flexibility," *American Economic Review*, vol. 38, no. 1, pp. 122–128, March, 1948, reprinted in *Readings in Fiscal Policy*, American Economic Association, Richard D. Irwin, Inc., Homewood, Ill., 1955, pp. 291–307; E. Cary Brown, "The Static Theory of Automatic Fiscal Stabilization," *Journal of Political Economy*, vol. 63, no. 5, pp. 427–440, October, 1955; William Vickrey, "Some Limits to the Income Elasticity of Income Tax Yield, *Review of Economics and Statistics*, vol. 31, pp. 140–145, May, 1949.

where E_t is the elasticity of the average statutory tax rate t with respect to changes in tax base B. The value of E_t exceeds 1 for a progressive income tax, and equals 1 for all flat-rate taxes, whether on income, sales, or property.[1]

Turning now to the tax base B, we have the elasticity formula

$$E_b = \frac{\Delta B/B_0}{\Delta Y/Y_0} \qquad (21\text{-}6)$$

where E_b is the elasticity of the tax base with regard to changes in total income. The value of E_b does not depend upon the progressivity of statutory rates but merely relates to the responsiveness of the tax base to changes in income. Let us assume that cyclical fluctuations in profits exceed those of total income, while fluctuations in wage income fall short thereof. The value of E_b in this case exceeds 1 for a tax on profits and falls short of 1 for a tax on wages.

The value of E_T, or the elasticity of yield with respect to income, may now be expressed in terms of E_t and E_b. Combining equations (21-4) to (21-6), we obtain

$$E_T = \left(1 + E_t \frac{B_1}{B_0}\right) E_b \qquad (21\text{-}7)$$

as the new expression for E_T.* The elasticity of tax *yield* E_T varies

---

[1] The value of E_t for a flat-rate income tax with exemptions exceeds 1 if B is defined properly as income before exemptions. In other words, exemptions are simply a zero-rate bracket, and a flat-rate income tax with exemptions is progressive.

* From eq. (21-4) we have

$$E_T = \frac{\Delta T}{T_0} \frac{Y_0}{\Delta Y} \qquad (1)$$

which may be written as

$$E_T = \frac{t_0 \Delta B + \Delta t\, B_1}{t_0 B_0} \frac{Y_0}{\Delta Y} \qquad (2)$$

or as

$$E_T = \frac{\Delta B + (\Delta t/t_0) B_1}{t_0 B_0} \frac{Y_0}{\Delta Y} \qquad (3)$$

From eq. (21-5) we have

$$\frac{\Delta t}{t_0} = E_t \frac{\Delta B}{B_0} \qquad (4)$$

and from eq. (21-6) we have

$$\frac{Y_0}{\Delta Y} = \frac{E_b B_0}{\Delta B} \qquad (5)$$

Substituting eqs. (4) and (5) into (2), we obtain eq. (21-7) above.

Alternatively, we may write eq. (2) as

$$E_T = \frac{\Delta t B_0 + t_1 \Delta B}{t_0 B_0} \frac{Y_0}{\Delta Y} \qquad (6)$$

which, after similar substitutions, gives us an alternative form of eq. (21-7):

$$E_T = E_b \left(E_t + \frac{t_1}{t_0}\right) \qquad (7)$$

directly with the elasticities of tax rate E_t and yield base E_b, and (E_t being greater than unity) with B_1/B_0. For any given value of E_b, the ratio B_1/B_0 reflects the rate of increase in income.[1]

A Measure of Built-in Flexibility

Let us suppose, now, that there occurs a change in private investment leading to a change in income equal to

$$\Delta Y = c(\Delta Y - \Delta T) + \Delta I \qquad (21\text{-}8)$$

where c is the marginal propensity to consume, ΔI is the postulated change in investment, and ΔT is the change in tax yield, either given independently or as a function of income Y. Solving equation (21-4) for the change in tax yield ΔT and substituting into (21-8), we obtain

$$\Delta Y = \frac{1}{1 - c[1 - E_T(T_0/Y_0)]} \Delta I \qquad (21\text{-}9)$$

where use is made of the combined elasticity concept E_T. We note that the larger E_T and T_0/Y_0 are, the smaller the resulting change in income will be. The initial level of yield relative to total income, or T_0/Y_0, reflects both t_0, the ratio of yield to tax base, and B_0/Y_0, the ratio of tax base to income. The expression for E_b and E_t, given in equation (21-7), may be substituted into equation (21-9) in order to separate the roles of rate and base elasticity.[2]

As a convenient measure for the compensatory effectiveness of built-in flexibility, we may write

$$\gamma = 1 - \frac{\Delta Y}{\Delta Y_a} \qquad (21\text{-}10)$$

where ΔY is the change in income in the particular system under discussion, with its specific value for E_T and T_0/Y_0; and ΔY_a is the change in

---

[1] As an alternative formulation of the same approach, we may define changes in yield with small changes in income as a function of changes in tax base and of changes in the average statutory rate.   Given

$$T = tB \qquad (1)$$
$$t = t(B) \qquad (2)$$
$$B = B(Y) \qquad (3)$$

hence $T = t[B(Y)] \cdot B(Y)$

and $$\frac{dT}{dY} = t[B(Y)] \cdot B'(Y) + B(Y) \cdot t'[B(Y)] \cdot B'(Y) \qquad (4)$$

where the change in yield equals the sum of the average statutory rate times the change in base, plus the tax base times the change in the statutory rate.

[2] Equation (21-8) may be expressed alternatively as

$$\Delta Y = c(\Delta Y - t_{em} \Delta Y) + \Delta I \qquad (21\text{-}8a)$$

where t_{em} is the effective *marginal* rate of tax.   Note that t_{em} is the ratio of increase in income in a system where yield does not vary with income so that E_T is equal to zero. Thus $\Delta Y/\Delta Y_a$ is the ratio of actual change in income to what the change in income would be without built-in flexibility; and γ, which is 1 minus this ratio, measures the fraction of the change in income that is prevented because of the existence of built-in flexibility. If $\gamma = 0$, there is no built-in flexibility; if $\gamma = 1$, built-in flexibility is perfect; that is, total income remains unchanged.

Substituting $[1/(1 - c)]\Delta I$ for ΔY_a and the expression of equation (21-9) for ΔY, we obtain

$$\gamma = \frac{cE_T(T_0/Y_0)}{1 - c[1 - E_T(T_0/Y_0)]} \qquad (21\text{-}11)$$

which defines the coefficient of effectiveness of built-in flexibility in terms of c, E_T, and T_0/Y_0.* The value of γ for any given value of c varies directly with E_T and T_0/Y_0, or $\Delta T/\Delta Y$. It is evident that T_0/Y_0 must be less than 1; but E_T is not subject to this limitation. As the product $(T_0/Y_0)E_T$ increases, so does γ. When $(T_0/Y_0)E_T$ reaches unity, γ becomes equal to c; at the same time, ΔY becomes equal to ΔI, as follows from equation (21-9). For all practical purposes, this may be considered the upper limit of effectiveness of built-in flexibility. The effective marginal rate of tax, or $\Delta T/\Delta Y$, hardly rises above 100 per cent.[1] And even if it does, γ can never reach unity as long as $c < 1$. This is seen readily from equation (21-11). If $c < 1$, the effectiveness of built-in flexibility can never be such as to hold income entirely stable.

---

yield to the entire increase in income, not only to the increase in tax base. It allows for changes in the ratio of tax base to income as well as for changes in the statutory rate, and must not be confused with the *statutory* marginal rate, which is the ratio of increase in yield to tax base. Solving for ΔY, we obtain

$$\Delta Y = \frac{1}{1 - c(1 - t_{em})}\Delta I \qquad (21\text{-}9a)$$

which, of course, is the same as eq. (21-9), since $t_{em} = \Delta T/\Delta Y = E_T(T_0/Y_0)$ The formulation of eq. (21-9) seems more useful since it permits us to explain the effective marginal rate in terms of the two elasticities of statutory rate and tax base, which are the direct policy parameters. Moreover, it explicitly introduces the initial ratio of yield to income, which is a given fact for tax policy.

* Since $E_T(T_0/Y_0) = \Delta T/\Delta Y$, eq. (21-11) may be written also as

$$\gamma = \frac{c(\Delta T/\Delta Y)}{1 - c[1 - (\Delta T/\Delta Y)]}$$

and the same conclusions apply.

[1] It is possible for the effective marginal rate $\Delta T/\Delta Y = (T_0/Y_0)E_T$ to exceed 1 even though the statutory marginal rate s is less than 1. We may write

$$\Delta T = s(b_0 Y_1 - b_1 Y_0)$$

where s is the statutory marginal rate of tax applicable to taxable income (say,

The preceding analysis may be expanded to allow for changes on the expenditure side as well as the tax side of the budget. Transfer payments such as unemployment benefits or relief may be introduced easily and may be treated as negative taxes. Price-support payments, similarly, are related inversely to income. Other goods and service expenditures, such as capital outlays of state and local governments, may vary directly with changes in the level of income, and so forth. All these elements of built-in flexibility may be allowed for, but the essential principle remains the same.

Quantitative Appraisal

Turning briefly to the magnitude of γ in the current setting of the United States, let us begin again with the tax phase of built-in flexibility. Following equation (21-11), the two variables to be considered are the initial ratio of yield to total income T_0/Y_0 (or the weight of the budget in the economy) and the elasticity of tax yield E_T with regard to total income reflecting in turn the elasticity of statutory tax rates and the elasticity of the tax base. In order to estimate the value of E_T for the tax structure as a whole, E_T must be computed as the weighted average of the elasticities applicable to the various taxes that compose it. These in turn differ considerably, the major source of variation being in the E_b rather than the E_t determinant of E_T. In fact, E_t is positive only in the case of the progressive income tax; and even then the coefficient is but slightly above zero, except for the rather unusual case where very large changes in income are considered. For all practical purposes, differences in the yield elasticity of various taxes may be traced to differences in E_b. Here the tax on corporation profits leads as the most elastic, followed by taxes on luxury consumption, upper-bracket income taxes (where the profit component is heavy), and trailed at the other end of the scale by the payroll tax, excises on mass-consumption goods, and the poll tax, in declining order. The elasticity of the property tax poses a special problem, as it greatly depends upon the frequency with which property values are reassessed. Given present methods of administration, the value of E_b in the property tax is very low, although frequent revision of assessment would render the elasticity much higher and might move it close to that of the profits tax.

---

profits), while b_0 and b_1 are the initial and final shares of tax base in total income. Now $\Delta T/\Delta Y > 1$ if

$$s > \frac{Y_2 - Y_0}{b_1 Y_1 - b_0 Y_0}$$

In the case of $s = 1$, this will be true if the change in taxable income (say, profits) exceeds the change in total income, thus involving an absolute decline in another income share (say, wages). If $s > 1$, the excess of change in taxable income over change in total income must be correspondingly larger.

For the federal tax structure of the mid-fifties, the value of E_T may approach 1.5, although the result in any particular case will depend upon the nature and amplitude of the fluctuation under consideration. The value of E_T is lower if state and local taxes are included. With an E_T of approximately 1.4, the value of γ depends upon the level of t_0. At current budget levels, t_0 is about 0.25. We thus obtain $t_0 E_T = 0.35$. Using a value of $c = 0.6$, which would allow for corporate as well as private saving, we arrive at a value of γ of about one-third. To this must be added adjustments on the expenditure side of the budget, which may be expected to raise the value of γ for the budget as a whole to perhaps as much as 0.40. Based on an optimistic estimate, built-in flexibility of the budget may be expected to avoid up to 40 per cent of the fluctuations in income that would occur in its absence.[1]

At the same time, note that the level of γ depends greatly upon the level of initial tax rates, or t_0. If t_0 is assumed to be 0.20 instead of 0.25, the value of γ for tax adjustments is reduced to below 30 per cent; if t_0 rises to 0.30, the value of γ, excluding fluctuations in expenditures, is increased to nearly 40 per cent. Establishment of a more peaceful world would result undoubtedly in a considerable reduction in t_0 and hence in γ. Some offset might be provided through qualitative changes in the tax structure aimed at raising E_T, such as increased progression in the income tax and heavier reliance on profits taxes. However, the possibility of such adjustments is limited, and they may interfere with other considerations of budget policy. We are left with the conclusion that the blessings of built-in flexibility greatly depend on the existence of a large budget.[2] Indeed, a large budget would be a stabilizing factor even if expenditures and tax yield remained unchanged over the cycle. Such a budget would not serve to offset fluctuations in the private sector, but it would provide a

[1] For a quantitative appraisal of built-in flexibility, see Arthur Goldberger, *op. cit.*, and David Lusher, "The Stabilizing Effectiveness of Budget Flexibility," in *Policies to Combat Depression*, National Bureau of Economic Research, Inc., New York, 1956, pp. 77–90. In the same volume, also see the contributions by Richard Goode, "The Corporation Income Tax in a Depression," pp. 149–170; and by J. A. Pechman, "Yield of the Individual Income Tax during a Recession," pp. 123–145; also see Melvin White, *Personal Income Tax Reduction in a Business Contraction*, Columbia University Press, New York, 1951; and E. Cary Brown, "Fiscal Policies in the Thirties: A Reappraisal," *American Economic Review*, vol. 46, no. 5, pp. 857–879, December, 1957, where the inadequacy of compensatory measures during the thirties is demonstrated.

[2] The above magnitudes for γ do not allow for such effects on private expenditures as may result from changes in the holding of liquid assets associated with current changes in surplus or deficit. If deficit and surplus are reflected in changes in the money supply, the effectiveness of built-in flexibility may be increased considerably under certain conditions. See Milton Friedman, "A Monetary and Fiscal Framework for Economic Stability," *American Economic Review*, vol. 38, pp. 245–264, June, 1948. If debt finance is used, the opposite may be the case. (See p. 545.)

stable core of expenditures on goods and services. The larger this stable core relative to total income, the less fluctuation there will be on an over-all basis.

Formula Flexibility

While the power of built-in flexibility in the narrow sense of the term is limited, a much higher degree of potency may be secured by reliance on so-called formula flexibility.

Formula flexibility refers to an arrangement whereby changes in tax rates and/or expenditure levels are legislated in advance, to go into effect if and when specified changes in income occur. For instance, it might be legislated that income tax rates be reduced or public expenditures raised by x per cent if income falls by y per cent. Or, the change in tax rate may be related to changes in other strategic variables such as employment. In this way, the countercyclical movement of tax yield and expenditures may be increased. Indeed, there is no difference in principle between this type of built-in flexibility and that which results from changes in the effective rate of tax due to automatic changes in the ratio of tax base to national income. If the formula flexibility thus provided for is tailored properly to the structural relationships of the dynamic system to be stabilized, the remaining degree of instability might be reduced to narrow limits. Whether or not this can be done depends upon the structure of the instability that is to be dealt with.[1]

Let us consider a simple pattern of instability that may be brought close to stability by the help of formula flexibility. For this purpose, we return to a system of income determination similar to that given in equation (20-35).* In this system, instability results from an accelerator type of investment function. If the instability is to be removed, some adjustment must be made in budget parameters that will counteract the accelerator. This may be done by introducing a tax that applies to changes in income, or an expenditure formula that links public expenditures inversely to changes in income. Thus a decelerator may be built into the budget parameters, which counteracts the investment accelerator.

Our system, then, consists of the following equations:

$$Y_n = C_n + I_n + G_n \tag{21-12}$$
$$C_n = c(Y_{n-1} - T_n) + A \tag{21-13}$$
$$I_n = \beta(Y_{n-1} - Y_{n-2}) \tag{21-14}$$
$$T_n = tY_{n-1} + \tau(Y_{n-1} - Y_{n-2}) \tag{21-15}$$
$$G_n = R - \delta(Y_{n-1} - Y_{n-2}) \tag{21-16}$$

---

[1] See the proposal in the British *White Paper on Employment Policy*, Cmd. 6527, May, 1944.

* See p. 481.

The symbols are the same as before, with the addition of τ, which is the tax rate applicable to the change in income, and δ, which is the change in expenditures in inverse relation to income. The time pattern of the government deceleration is set to coincide with that of the investment accelerator. We obtain

$$Y_n = [c(1 - t) + \beta - c\tau - \delta]Y_{n-1} - [\beta - c\tau - \delta]Y_{n-2} + A + R$$
(21-17)

and the equilibrium level

$$Z = \frac{A + R}{1 - c(1 - t)}$$
(21-18)

We may now take this system, which is similar in behavior to the Hicksian elementary case[1] and, following Samuelson, show diagrammatically the boundaries yielding different qualitative patterns of behavior of national income.[2] The result is shown in Figure 21-1.*

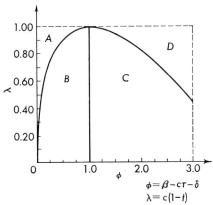

FIG. 21-1. Stability regions, with accelerator depending on income.

Along the ordinate we measure $\lambda = c(1 - t)$, which is the propensity to consume out of income before tax; and on the abscissa we measure $\phi = \beta - c\tau - \delta$, which is the net accelerator. Each of the four regions, marked A, B, C, and D, represent different qualitative behavior patterns

[1] See J. R. Hicks, *Contribution to the Theory of the Trade Cycle*, Oxford University Press, 1950, pp. 65ff.

[2] See Paul A. Samuelson, "Interactions between the Multiplier Analysis and the Principle of Acceleration," *Review of Economic Statistics* vol. 21, no. 2, pp. 75-78, May, 1939, reprinted in *Readings in Business Cycle Theory*, American Economic Association, Richard D. Irwin, Inc., Homewood, Ill., 1949.

* This figure is constructed by reference to the stability conditions for such a system given in Hicks, *op. cit.*, p. 185. In region A, where the roots are real, we have case 1; in region B, with complex roots and a modulus <1, we have case 2; in region C, with complex roots and a modulus >1, we have case 3; and in region D, with real roots, we have case 4.

of national income.   Region A represents those combinations of λ and ϕ
that lead to a steady convergence of income to equilibrium, whether from
above or below.   Region B represents combinations of λ and ϕ, which lead
to convergence to equilibrium by dampening cycles.   Region C represents
combinations leading to explosive fluctuations, while region D represents
steady divergence away from equilibrium.   Combinations falling on the
dividing line between B and C, where $\phi = 1$, involve a cyclical movement
of constant amplitude around the equilibrium level.

Let us begin with a situation where t, τ, and δ are equal to zero.   Then ϕ
and λ are determined by β and c alone.   If the combination lies in region
C, we have explosive oscillations.   Suppose, now, that the prevailing
equilibrium level Z is to be retained; we may then reduce ϕ by raising τ

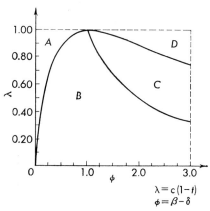

FIG. 21-2. Stability regions, with accelerator depending on consumption.

and/or δ, thus moving our point in the diagram horizontally to the left.
As the dividing line between B and C is reached, the fluctuation becomes
one of constant amplitude.   As ϕ is reduced further, we enter region B; the
fluctuation is lessened and converges to the equilibrium.   Further movement toward the left within B speeds up the process of convergence.   If
we wish to raise the equilibrium level as well as reduce instability, we must
also reduce t.   A change in t without a change in ϕ, however, still leaves
the system explosive.

The type of adjustment in budget parameters required to secure stability depends altogether on the structure of the system.   Thus the
adjustments called for in the preceding system may be compared with
those applicable in Samuelson's system, where the accelerator relates to
changes in consumption rather than in total income.[1]   The resulting
diagram of boundaries is shown in Figure 21-2, where areas A, B, C, and D

[1] Paul A. Samuelson, "Interactions between the Multiplier Analysis and the Principle of Acceleration," *Review of Economics and Statistics*, vol. 21, p. 76, 1939.

are subject to the same behavior as before.[1] Suppose again that we are in region C. Movement into region B may now be accomplished by an increase in t. This was not possible in the preceding case. If the resulting decline in the equilibrium level is to be avoided, the movement into region B may again be accomplished by a decelerator effect. Attached to the expenditure side of the budget, the inverse relationship must now be between expenditures and changes in consumption, rather than changes in total income. The formulation of the decelerator in the budget must follow that of the accelerator in the private sector. The introduction of a decelerator device on the tax side is more complex in this case.

So far we have considered simple systems that assume a constant reaction structure. The problem becomes much more complicated if we consider nonlinear systems, such as the Hicks cycle scheme, where the accelerator works in the upswing but not in the downswing.[2] The stabilization formula would thus have to differ for the two phases of the cycle. The decelerator-type formula as previously described would work in the upswing; but if left for the downswing, it might develop destabilizing effects. Therefore, it must be dropped at the upper turning point and be replaced by a new policy, such as an increase in R, the fixed component of government expenditures. Conceivably a built-in formula might be devised at the outset so as to provide for this substitution; and even more complicated combinations might be enacted to take care of more complicated behavior patterns. This, however, leads the concept of formula flexibility ad absurdum. In a complex world, the task of devising a once-and-for-all formula is vastly more complicated than that of changing formulas (that is, undertaking discretionary action) as conditions change.

Rules versus Discretion

The limitation of built-in flexibility, therefore, is not given by the insufficient potency of the orthodox type of flexibility. Use of formula

---

[1] The diagram is the same as that given by Samuelson, except that the ordinate here refers to $\lambda = c(1 - t)$ rather than to c, and that the abcissa refers to $\phi = \beta - \delta$ rather than to β alone. The regions remain unchanged, since the introduction of t is equivalent to a variation in c, and the expenditure decelerator is designed to be equivalent to an inverse change in β. The five basic equations are:

$$Y_n = C_n + I_n + G_n$$
$$C_n = c(Y_{n-1} - T_n) + A$$
$$I_n = \beta(C_n - C_{n-1})$$
$$T_n = tY_{n-1}$$
$$G_n = R - \delta(C_n - C_{n-1})$$

which leads us to

$$Y_n = \lambda(1 + \phi)Y_{n-1} - \lambda\phi Y_{n-2} + A + R$$

with
$$\lambda = c(1 - t) \quad \text{and} \quad \phi = \beta - \delta$$

[2] See Hicks, *op. cit.*, pp. 45ff. and 101ff.

flexibility readily overcomes this obstacle. The limitation arises because the economic system is too complex to permit the design of a formula that will work adequately in all situations. In other words, there is no perpetually applicable type of remedial adjustment which, if made only once, will transform the economy into a state of permanent bliss, where henceforth the invisible hand will maintain the social order to perfection.

Depending upon one's views, this may be a pleasant or an unpleasant finding. Much of the interest in built-in flexibility, expressed in recent years, is not just a matter of technical economics. Broader issues of social philosophy are involved. To some, the problem is one of rules versus authority, where reliance on built-in flexibility is identified with rules and lawful government, while discretionary action is linked to human frailty and arbitrariness.[1] To others, discretionary action is nothing to be feared; indeed, it offers the challenge of freedom derived from a positive guidance of human, including social affairs.[2] Such differences in philosophy are of great importance, even though they cannot be captured in neat functions. Yet no good purpose is served, as a matter of practical policy, by a contrast in extremes. All reasonable men are for government by rules, if this is interpreted to mean that government should be lawful. At the same time, it is at the very heart of the common law conception that laws must be adjusted to meet changing conditions, and that discretion is required in their application.

The need for adaptability is of special importance in the field of stabilization policy, where governmental responsibility is confronted with ever-changing conditions. These conditions may be met in part by automatic reactions of the fiscal structure. If proper in scope and quality, such responses are all to the good, but they do not solve the entire problem. More or less frequent adjustments, monetary or fiscal, to changing conditions are required. Whether these adjustments are referred to as frequent changes in rules or as discretionary action is essentially a matter of

---

[1] See essays by Henry C. Simons, collected in *Economic Policy for a Free Society*, University of Chicago Press, Chicago, 1948; and Milton Friedman, *op. cit.*, and *Essays in Positive Economics*, University of Chicago Press, Chicago, 1953.

[2] See Don Juan's eloquent dialogue with the devil in G. B. Shaw's "Man and Superman," *Nine Plays*, Dodd, Mead & Company, Inc., New York, 1945, p. 646, quoted with permission of the Public Trustee and the Society of Authors, London:

THE DEVIL: What is the use of knowing?

DON JUAN: Why, to be able to choose the line of greatest advantage instead of yielding in the direction of the least resistance. Does a ship sail to its destination no better than a log drifts nowhither? The philosopher is Nature's pilot. And there you have our difference: to be in hell is to drift: to be in heaven is to steer.

THE DEVIL: On the rocks, most likely.

DON JUAN: Pooh! which ship goes oftenest on the rocks or to the bottom? the drifting ship or the ship with a pilot on board?

semantics; whatever term is used, the task at hand is too complex to permit a once-and-for-all solution.

B. NEUTRALITY OF STABILIZATION POLICY

The stabilization function of budget policy is but one among other functions. It must be carried out so as not to disturb these other functions and to avoid accidental interference with the private sector of the economy. In this sense, stabilization policy should be neutral. Some implications of this principle are here considered for the relatively short-run setting of cyclical stabilization. Similar problems, which arise in determining an optimal rate of growth, are examined later.[1]

Countercyclical Adjustments of Public Services

From the preceding discussion, two conclusions may be drawn. One is that, per dollar of deficit or surplus, changes in goods and service expenditures of government are the most potent means of raising or lowering the level of aggregate demand.[2] Such at least is the case if incentive effects on private investment are disregarded.[3] The other conclusion is that the level of goods and service expenditures provided for by the Allocation Branch should be determined against the background of a full-employment level of resource utilization.[4] Assuming that the proper level of public services prevails to begin with, no use should be made of changes in the level of public expenditures on goods and services as a means of stabilizing aggregate demand. Reliance should be placed on tax and transfer adjustments in the budget of the Stabilization Branch, even though they are less efficient, per dollar of change in deficit or surplus.

Thus ditch-digging expenditures have no place in an efficient anti-depression policy, and it is wasteful to cut essential public expenditures to check inflation. Outlays on ditch-digging expenditures will be better in a depression than a do-nothing policy; demand is created in the process, which gives rise to further and useful production. At the same time, it is better to obtain useful production in the first place—production of a type that can be secured by transfer payments which increase private demand. Precisely the same argument calls for increased taxes (leading to the reduction of less important private outlays) in the case of anti-inflation policy, rather than for a reduction in public services that are still considered essential.

This suggests that efficient stabilization policy as a general rule avoids

[1] See p. 553.
[2] See p. 432.
[3] See p. 465.
[4] See p. 38.

anticyclical changes in the level of public services.   To this, certain qualifi-cations must be considered.   The preceding argument has been based on the assumption that the proper level of public services prevails to begin with.   If the initial level is deficient, a period of depression is a good time in which to catch up; and if the initial level is excessive, a period of infla-tion is a good time in which to cut back.   Next, it might be argued that the proper level of public services need not be achieved for any short-time period.   Variation of public works over the cycle need not distort the level of public expenditures for the period of the cycle as a whole, provided, of course, that the cycle can be predicted so that expenditures can be timed so as to fit the long-run program.   Moreover, the impact of a depression may differ markedly on a regional basis, super-imposing the structural problems of declining areas over the more general problems of lessened demand for the economy as a whole.   In such cases, a regional, rather than a nationwide, remedy may be needed.   This cannot be given readily in the form of tax relief, as regional tax relief would be inequitable and relatively ineffective.   Relief payments can be concentrated in depressed regions, but the dole approach may be held undesirable as a matter of social policy.   In this case, work relief—or, better, public works—are called for.   Broader considerations of social policy may override the purely allocational considerations.   Finally, public works may be desir-able since they can be designed to utilize existing capital equipment and to avoid the cost of temporary dislocations.[1]   Resource allocation may be more efficient on balance if existing rigidities are taken into consideration.

These considerations introduce important exceptions to the rule, but they do not invalidate the basic principle.   In the absence of such special considerations, reliance on tax and transfer adjustments is called for—unless it can be shown that consumer demand for the satisfaction of social wants varies over the cycle.   If the cycle were permitted to run its course, with resulting changes in the level of income and employment, the demand for public services would fluctuate with private demand, assum-ing income elasticity of demand for public services exceeds zero.   This would call for fluctuations in the expenditures of the Allocation Branch so as to accentuate the cycle.   But such fluctuations will not occur if income is stabilized.   However, even though cyclical fluctuations in aggregate demand are eliminated, the cycle survives in the form of fluctuations in the structure of demand.

Suppose that private investment drops and that the Stabilization Branch undertakes tax reductions or transfer payments sufficient to restore a full-employment level of income.   Will not consumers wish to

---

[1] See Alvin H. Hansen, *Economic Policy and Full Employment*, McGraw-Hill Book Company, Inc., New York, 1947, p. 212.

purchase additional public, as well as private, services? As private investment declines, resources are released which must now be employed otherwise. If we look upon private investment as a provision for future private consumption, the drop in private investment means that provision for future private consumption must be reduced. This does not reflect a change in consumer tastes adverse to future consumption, as would a decline in investment in the classical system, but rather a rigidity (for example, the liquidity trap) in the permissible level of investment. Consumers are compelled to devote less resources to future private consumption; hence, they must devote more to other uses. These resources may be used for current private consumption and/or the satisfaction of social wants. The satisfaction of social wants that are complementary to future private consumption will be reduced, while the satisfaction of social wants that are independent of, or rival to, future private consumption will be increased. On balance, it is reasonable to expect that the demand for the satisfaction of social wants will be increased along with the demand for the satisfaction of current private consumption. Thus the resources released from private investment will not be directed entirely toward increased satisfaction of current private wants. They will be directed in part toward the increased satisfaction of social wants.

On the basis of this reasoning, some degree of countercyclical variation in the level of public services is required in the efficient budget system.[1] Some increase in public services during the depression does not constitute make-work expenditure but is called for as a matter of efficient allocation. To be sure, the resulting allocation will not be so efficient as it would be if private investment had remained flexible and if provision for future private consumption had not been limited. In other words, stabilization policy does not fully restore the innocence of the classical system. At the same time, allocation will be more efficient—given the rigidity in private investment—than it would be if full employment were restored while holding fixed the level of public services or of private consumption.

Such a conclusion is in line with our earlier system of tax and expenditure determination for the Allocation Branch, where the demand for public services was determined on the basis of a disposable income defined to

[1] This conclusion was reached, though by different reasoning, by Paul A. Samuelson, "Principles and Rules in Modern Fiscal Policy: A Neo-classical Reformulation," in *Money, Trade, and Economic Growth: In Honor of John Henry Williams*, The Macmillan Company, New York, 1951, p. 160. Samuelson holds that the supply of public services should increase with a decline in private investment if the *income elasticity* of demand for public services exceeds zero. It seems to me that the problem is not one of income elasticity. The introduction of a ceiling to private investment does not constitute an increase but rather a decline in real income. The issue, rather, is one of rivalry and complementarity of public services to future private consumption.

include transfer payments from the Stabilization Branch.[1] This points to a further problem in efficiency. In order to secure a level of demand that is adequate to maintain full employment, the disposable income of consumers must be raised above the level of factor earnings. Consumers will act as if this higher level of disposable income was, in fact, real income. Only if they proceed on the basis of this income illusion can they be induced to increase their outlays. At the same time, the income elasticity of demand for various private services will differ with the level of income that consumers think they receive. Since consumers determine their demand on the basis of their swollen disposable income, the resulting allocation—including allocation between different private wants—will diverge from that which would prevail if full employment could be secured while holding disposable income equal to earnings. Thus the resulting allocation falls short of an efficient solution in a more general way, extending beyond the case of future private wants. Compensatory finance restores full employment, but, we repeat, it does not return us to the innocence of the classical system.[2]

Light versus Heavy Taxes

Turning now to the structural aspects of cyclical tax policy, we recall our earlier finding that changes in tax yield will be more or less efficient per dollar of yield, depending on whether the tax (which is imposed or removed) bears heavily or lightly on the level of private expenditure.[3] Let us define *heavy taxes* as taxes which, per dollar of yield, result in a relatively heavy reduction in the expenditures of the taxpayer; and *light taxes* as those which result in a relatively light reduction. In a situation where a given compensatory effect is called for, should the adjustment be in heavy or in light taxes?[4]

Frequently this choice is made on the basis of certain secondary objectives. Suppose the secondary objective is to hold the level of tax rates at a minimum, for incentive or other reasons. In this case, heavy taxes will be good taxes. When taxes need to be increased, the addition should be in heavy taxes.[5] When they must be cut, the reduction should be in light taxes. Next, suppose that the secondary objective is to minimize public debt. In this case, the opposite holds: Light taxes will be good taxes. If taxes are to be increased, the addition should be in light taxes, since this

---

[1] See p. 33, eqs. (2-2) and (2-3).

[2] See p. 554. For a more optimistic view, see J. M. Keynes, *The General Theory of Employment, Interest, and Money*, Harcourt, Brace and Company, Inc., New York, 1936, pp. 11–32.

[3] See p. 440.

[4] For a similar approach see Kjeld Philip, *Skattepolitik*, Gyldendal, Copenhagen, 1955.

[5] The same principles apply to changes in yield that result from built-in flexibility.

permits a higher over-all level of taxation and a bigger surplus. If taxes are to be reduced, the cut should be in heavy taxes, since this curtails the necessary reduction. Finally, suppose that the secondary objective is to minimize fluctuations in the average level of tax rates. In this case, all changes (up *or* down) should be in heavy taxes. Such changes are more effective per dollar of change, and hence smaller adjustments will suffice.

Assuming investment to remain unaffected by taxation, heavy taxes tend to be regressive, and light taxes tend to be progressive. Thus, the first objective favors regression, the second favors progression, and the third favors progression in the depression and regression in the boom. These conclusions may be modified or changed if effects on investment are introduced. If such effects operate via the supply of funds, differences between the various approaches will be reduced; if effects on investment operate through changes in profitability, the rating of various taxes may be changed, and progressive taxes may become heavier than regressive taxes. While it is reasonable to assume that regressive taxes will be heavier than progressive taxes during the depression, no such simple conclusion can be drawn for the period of inflation. Moreover, conclusions may differ, depending on whether we consider the cyclical picture only or whether long-run effects on growth are allowed for.

Among these various secondary objectives, most consideration has been given to minimizing public debt. The popular case against consumer taxes in the depression was based on the proposition that such taxes are more deflationary. By appealing to the fear of public debt, the argument gave convenient support to distributional objectives, but the logic is of a rather precarious sort: What seems a good case for progression in the depression may turn into a corresponding case for regression in a subsequent inflation.[1]

This entire approach to tax policy becomes untenable once the problem of stabilization policy is viewed in the context of the total budget, satisfying the requirements of the Allocation and Distribution, as well as of the Stabilization Branch. Here the degree or kind of distributional adjustment is determined independently of the requirements of the Stabilization Branch. It enters as a factor in determining the required scope of stabilization policy, but the implementation of this policy remains neutral with regard to distribution. The progressivity of the tax structure in the *net* budget may vary over the cycle, but this does not reflect a change in the budget of the Distribution Branch. Rather, it reflects a change in the weight of the distributional adjustment in the total budget.[2] Distributional adjustments do not enter into an efficient stabilization policy, since full employment and price-level stability may be achieved without impair-

[1] See p. 39.

[2] Change in progressivity is interpreted to mean that the ratio between effective

ing the "proper" state of distribution. Again, circumstances may arise that require exceptions to the rule, but this does not destroy its importance as a principle of efficient budget planning.

Taxation and Fiscal Discipline

At the normative level, no conflict exists between the allocation and stabilization functions of budget policy. The allocation budget is planned to meet individual preferences on the basis of a full-employment income. Subject to certain exceptions, the allocation budget is balanced, independent of whether the budget of the Stabilization Branch and hence the net budget requires a deficit or a surplus.[1] However, a conflict may arise in the course of fiscal politics, where the two objectives are not distinguished properly, and excessive attention is focused on the net budget.

Under conditions where stabilization policy requires a deficit, people may feel that an extension of public services is virtually costless, and this may lead to an overexpansion of public services. The function of taxes as an index of opportunity cost is impaired. Assuming that stabilization policy requires a surplus, people may feel that public services are more costly than they really are, and the supply of public services will be deficient. Again a distortion results. It is the discipline function of taxation to avoid the illusion of either the under- or overpricing of public services.

It may be asked whether there is any rule for budget policy that permits the use of fiscal policy as a stabilizing device and, at the same time, assures that the level of public services will not be distorted (in one or the other direction) by a cost illusion. The traditional rule—that the budget should be balanced at all times—meets the discipline objective. An increase in expenditures by $1 always requires additional taxes of $1; and a reduction in expenditures by $1 always permits a corresponding tax cut.[2]

---

rates of tax at various levels of income is increased or reduced. This is the previously noted concept of liability progression. (See p. 121.)

Suppose that individual A receives earnings of $100 and individual B receives earnings of $50. Let the Distribution Branch impose a tax of $10 on A and make transfers of $10 to B. This leaves A with $90 and B with $60. Now suppose that each spends 30 per cent thereof for Allocation Branch purposes. Thus, A pays $27 and B pays $18. As a result, A's net taxes equal $37, and B's net taxes equal $8. Now suppose that $30 must be collected in additional taxes for stabilization purposes. This will be divided between A and B in the ratio of 90:60, leaving A with a net tax bill of $55 and B with a net tax bill of $20. The initial ratio of 37:8 equals 4.6, while that of 55:20 equals 2.75. Since the ratio is reduced, the degree of progression in the net budget is reduced. This result reflects the fact that the weight of the Distribution Branch in the total budget picture is reduced.

[1] See p. 558 for a discussion of these exceptions.

[2] The logic of such a system requires lump sum taxes, or taxes with zero built-in flexibility, with yield adjusted at all times to match the level of public expenditures.

At the same time, such a policy requires a reduction in public expenditures and/or an increase in tax rates when the level of income declines, and vice versa when the level of income rises. It results in perverse formula flexibility and accentuates fiscal instability.

Various alternatives have been proposed. Thus, it has been suggested that deficits incurred in the depression should be carried forward into subsequent budgets and made good in prosperity years. The budget is to be balanced over the cycle, while permitting whatever deficits are needed in the depression.[1] This policy leaves full freedom for compensatory action but may not satisfy the discipline objective. Deficits incurred in the depression will be paid off in the subsequent inflation only in the case of a perfectly symmetrical cycle, moving around a full-employment level of income. If there is a bias in the deflationary or inflationary direction, public services will be permanently under- or overpriced. Moreover, the same imperfections that lead to inefficient policy in the first place may also invalidate the rule in the inflation phase of the cycle, when increased tax rates are needed.

As a second possibility, it has been suggested that expenditure programs should be held constant over the cycle and that tax rates should be set so as to balance the budget at a full-employment level of income. This permits such countercyclical swings in deficit and surplus as result from the automatic working of built-in flexibility in the tax and expenditure structure. At the same time, any new expenditure program calls for an increase in tax rates sufficient to produce an equal gain in yield at a full-employment level of income.[2] Under this plan new public services are still somewhat underpriced in the depression and overpriced in the boom, but the differential with true cost is much less than under outright deficit or surplus finance. This approach, therefore, is rather satisfactory with

[1] See Gunnar Myrdal, "Fiscal Policies in the Business Cycle," *American Economic Review*, vol. 29, no. 1, pp. 183–193, March, 1939. For a similar approach, see "Federal Expenditures and Revenue Policy for Economic Stability," National Planning Association, Conference of University Economists, reprinted in *Readings in Fiscal Policy*, American Economic Association, Richard D. Irwin, Inc., Homewood, Ill., 1955, especially p. 400.

[2] See *Taxes and the Budget: A Program for Prosperity in a Free Economy*, Committee for Economic Development, Research and Policy Committee, New York, 1947; reprinted in *Readings in Fiscal Policy*, pp. 361–370. The "stabilizing budget policy," as proposed by the C. E. D., provides for a surplus at a high level of employment rather than for a balanced budget. On stabilization grounds the surplus target is preferable, *if* we assume secular pressure toward inflation. See also Walter W. Heller, "CED'S Stabilizing Budget Policy after Ten Years," *American Economic Review*, vol. 47, no. 5, pp. 634–651, September, 1957; and Arthur Smithies, "Federal Budgeting and Fiscal Policies," in Howard S. Ellis (ed.), *Survey of Contemporary Economics*, American Economic Association, Richard D. Irwin, Inc., Homewood, Ill., 1948, chap. 5, pp. 174–209.

regard to the discipline objective; but it is less satisfactory as a stabilization device. Not only is the stabilizing effectiveness of built-in flexibility inadequate to deal with the entire task of cyclical stabilization, but it is by no means certain that the rule (of setting tax rates to equate yield and expenditures at a full-employment income) leads to stability at, or dampened fluctuations around, a full-employment income.

Setting tax rates so as to balance the budget at a full-employment income does not assure us that a full-employment income is maintained, or that it is reached on the average. Suppose that the economy is in a secular depression. In this case, the rule will leave us with a budget that raises the level of income and lowers fluctuations; but it will not restore full employment, and fluctuations will still be around a depressed level. If there exists a secular tendency toward inflation, such a policy will not restore price-level stability. It may serve to dampen cyclical fluctuations without establishing the proper level of income around which the cyclical fluctuation occurs. Matters are improved if we amend the rule and set tax rates so as to leave whatever deficit or surplus is required on the average so as to secure a full-employment income. But even if this is done, there remains the question whether cyclical fluctuations will be lowered sufficiently if exclusive reliance is placed on built-in flexibility.

What matters, from the point of view of the discipline function, is that the budget should be balanced at the margin. This suggests a further possibility, which is to permit a deficit or surplus for the total budget but to require a marginal balance. Such a rule would score fully as far as an efficient appraisal of the desired level of public services is concerned; but how would it do on stabilization grounds?

Consider a situation of *secular* inflation or deflation. Suppose deflation prevails and full employment has been restored by providing for the level of deficit that is needed with a given level of public services. Now the public desires to raise or lower the level of public services. If demand is to be held constant, the required increase or decrease in tax yield must exceed the change in public expenditures.[1] Thus, public services are overpriced to some extent. This may be avoided if the budget is strictly balanced at the margin, but here stabilization policy falls short of its objective. The defects of the marginally balanced budget may not be too serious for the secular case, but the rule fails the compensatory test in a cyclical setting. In its effect on fluctuations, the marginally balanced budget will do no better than the totally balanced budget. The marginally balanced budget remains superior only in that it may adjust the level around which the cyclical fluctuations occur.

Which, if any, of these rules should be adopted depends upon the relative weights to be assigned to the discipline and the stabilization objectives.

[1] See p. 432.

This in turn depends upon the potential pressures making for inefficiency in the determination of public expenditures, and upon the potential instability of the level of income. Among the rules here considered, the compromise offered by the cyclically balanced budget is perhaps best, but it leaves us with an excessively severe limitation on the scope of stabilization policy. The more satisfying solution is to educate the voters so that proper expenditure determination can be combined with freedom of action in stabilization policy.

CHAPTER 22

Liquidity aspects of fiscal policy

In the preceding discussion of deficit and surplus finance we have disregarded resulting changes in the claim structure of the economy. Such changes are an inevitable by-product of unbalanced budgets, and their effects upon the level of economic activity must now be allowed for.

A. FISCAL OPERATIONS AND CHANGES IN THE STRUCTURE OF CLAIMS

Whenever the government incurs a deficit, claims are issued in an amount equal to the excess of expenditures over receipts. The new claims may be in the form of money, obtained through the creation of bank credit or the issue of government money; or they may be in the form of public debt. Similarly, a surplus results in the destruction of claims, whether through withholding of tax receipts and a resulting decrease in the money supply, or through the use of surplus receipts for debt retirement and a resulting reduction in public debt.

Effects of Budget Policies on the Structure of Claims

The effects of budget policy upon the structure of claims may be studied most conveniently in an economy without fractional-reserve banking, that is, with a so-called 100 per cent reserve system.[1] While rather heroic as an actual design for policy, such a system is convenient as an expository device. All money, in this case, is government or reserve money. The money supply is increased when the government draws on newly created money to finance expenditures or debt repayment; the supply is decreased when the government withdraws money through taxation or borrowing and withholds the proceeds.

[1] See note 2, p. 531.

In this system, the government may change the liquidity structure of the economy by effecting changes in the supply of money, debt, or both.[1] The results of various possible policies are arranged in Table 22-1. Of the nine policies listed, only policy 1 leaves the liquidity structure unchanged. Policies 2, 3, and 4 increase the supply of debt or money or both. Policies 5, 6, and 7 reduce the supply of debt or money or both. Policies 8 and 9 involve exchanges between money and debt.

TABLE 22-1. EFFECTS OF BUDGET POLICIES ON THE STRUCTURE OF CLAIMS

Change in supply of debt	Change in supply of money		
	+	0	−
+	4 Deficit financed by mix of debt and money	2 Deficit financed by debt	9 Money retirement financed by borrowing
0	3 Deficit financed by new money	1 Equal changes in expenditures and tax yield	6 Money retirement financed by current surplus
−	8 Debt retirement financed by new money	5 Debt retirement financed by current surplus	7 Current surplus used to retire mix of money and debt

This, to be sure, is not a complete catalogue of policies.[2] Once different types of public debt are allowed for, there is the additional possibility of policy 10, involving exchanges between such debts. Allowance for government lending introduces a whole new set of transactions, including the granting of loans financed out of tax proceeds (policy 11), borrowing (policy 12), or new money (policy 13); and the recall of loans with proceeds being disbursed as expenditures (policy 14), in repayment of debt (policy 15), or held in balances (policy 16).* In addition, a similar set of

[1] The term *changes in the supply of debt*, as explained later, refers to changes in coupon bill or maturity value rather than to changes in the market value of the total debt outstanding. (See p. 544.)

[2] See A. P. Lerner, *The Economics of Control*, The Macmillan Company, New York, 1944, p. 312.

* Considering public loans as negative debts, policy 11 may be considered similar to 5, policy 13 similar to 8, policy 14 similar to 2, policy 16 similar to 9, with policies 12 and 15 being offsets to each other. However, these similarities relate to resulting changes in the aggregate of net claims only. Beyond this the various policies may differ, since they may result in quite different distributions of available funds.

transactions (17 to 21) arises in the purchase or sale of assets. All these form part of the arsenal of possible fiscal operations, but for purposes of this discussion, our primary concern will be with the nine alternatives shown in Table 22-1.

Distinctions between Fiscal and Liquidity Policies

The scheme of Table 22-1 permits us to draw a distinction between various types of policies based on their economic characteristics rather than on the government agencies in which they originate.

First Distinction. Let us define pure fiscal policy as measures which involve tax and/or expenditure action, but which leave the structure of claims unchanged; and pure liquidity policy as measures which involve changes in the structure of claims, but which involve no tax and/or expenditure action. Also, let us distinguish between changes in the structure of claims involving changes in the supply of money only, these being referred to as pure monetary policy; and others involving changes in debt only, these being referred to as pure debt policy. We then obtain the following classification of policies:

TABLE 22-2. FISCAL AND LIQUIDITY POLICIES

	Policy number as per Table 22-1
Pure fiscal policy	1
Pure liquidity policy:	
Pure monetary policy	22
Pure debt policy	10, 12, 15
Mixed monetary and debt policy	8, 9, 13, 16
Mixed fiscal and liquidity policy:	
Fiscal and pure monetary policy	3, 6
Fiscal and pure debt policy	2, 5, 11, 14
Fiscal and mixed liquidity policy	4, 7

The only policy of a purely fiscal sort is the balanced-budget transaction,[1] while there are a variety of policies of the purely liquidity type. Policy 22, or pure monetary policy, has not been mentioned so far because there can be no such policy in a 100 per cent reserve system. If a fractional-reserve system is allowed for, policy 22 may be considered a change in reserve requirements or the multiple effect of changes in reserve money, whether due to open-market or budget operations.

Second Distinction. Taking a somewhat different approach, we may distinguish between the causal relationships upon which the effects of any one policy are based. Suppose, first, that private investment remains

[1] Even here, changes in the asset structure come about indirectly as the demand for transaction money (and hence the supply of available asset money) changes with resulting changes in the level of income. If this is allowed for, it appears that a "purely fiscal" policy does not exist.

unchanged, so that only effects on consumption must be considered.   The major leverage effects of various policies may then be divided between (1) those which result from the dependence of consumption on disposable income and (2) those which result from the dependence of consumption on the level of wealth or on the ratio of wealth to income.   The first group of policy effects may be referred to as *income effects;* the second as *wealth effects.*   In addition, substitution effects may result from savings or spendings incentives provided by particular tax or expenditure policies. Income and wealth effects are interdependent, and adjustments to any one change in policy will involve both types of effects.   This is evident for the cases of deficit or surplus finance, which involve both effects from the outset.   A pure fiscal measure, which is a balanced change in expenditures and taxes, begins with an income effect only, as the claims structure remains unchanged.   However, the wealth effect may enter the subsequent adjustment as the level of wealth is changed relative to that of income.   Similarly, a pure liquidity measure, such as substitution of money for debt, begins with a wealth effect only, but changes in expenditures induced thereby are subject to the multiplier action of the income effect.   Thus, it is not possible to say that certain policies will only have income effects while others will only have wealth effects.   The initial effect may be one or the other, but both effects swing into action as the adjustment proceeds.

A corresponding distinction might be drawn for fiscal effects on investment.   Changes in investment may result as a function of initial changes in income, whether through a propensity to invest or through an accelerator type of investment function; these are income effects more or less similar to the income effects on consumption.   Or, changes in investment may result from changes in the level or structure of claims, and such changes in investment may be said to represent *claim effects.*   Profitability effects of taxation represent a further type of substitution effect. Since the factors that underlie the claim effect on investment differ fundamentally from those which underlie the wealth effect on consumption, different terms are used for the two effects; however, both result from deficit or surplus finance.

Preliminary Conclusions

We may now reconsider our earlier discussion of deficit and surplus finance.   Account must be taken of the fact that deficit finance involves the addition of claims and that resulting changes in the structure of claims differ depending on what claims (money or debt) are added or withdrawn.

In order to determine the implications of these changes, we shall have to consider their effects upon the level of consumption and investment expenditure. This will be done in some detail in the following pages. Now some preliminary policy conclusions may be stated. These are based on the following hypotheses: (1) that the ratio of consumption to income will increase with the supply of money or, with some qualification, the supply of public debt; and (2) that the level of investment will rise with an increase in the supply of money and fall with an increase in the supply of debt.

With this in mind, let us reconsider the effectiveness of various policies aimed at raising the level of income. Policy 1 is clearly expansionary, as are policies 3 and 8. For a given increase in public expenditures, policy 3 is clearly more expansionary than 1. This is the case not only because the initial income effects are greater under policy 3 but also because there will be an expansionary wealth effect on consumption which is not present under 1. Policy 2 is likely to be expansionary on balance, although the claims effect on investment is restrictive. For a given size of deficit, policy 3 is clearly more expansionary than policy 2. This is evident if we think of policy 2 as a composite of 3 and 9. Since policy 9 is restrictive, policy 2 must be less expansionary than policy 3.

Budget contraction by policy 1 is clearly restrictive, as are policies 6 and 9. For a given decrease in public expenditures, policy 6 is clearly more restrictive than policy 1. Policy 5 is likely to be restrictive on balance, although it implies an expansionary claim effect on investment. For a given surplus policy, however, policy 6 is clearly more restrictive than policy 5. Again, 5 may be thought of as a composite of policies 6 and 8, where 8 is expansionary.

It follows that debt retirement (policy 8) is inherently an expansionary measure that should be undertaken in the depression, while borrowing (policy 9) is inherently a restrictive measure that should be undertaken in the boom. This is not to say that deficit finance out of borrowing (policy 2) will not be expansionary on balance, or that debt retirement out of current surplus (policy 5) will not be restrictive on balance. For expansionary policy, a combination of policies 9 and 3, as implied in policy 2, is less effective than reliance on 3 alone, but the most effective combination is 3 and 8. For restrictive policy, a combination of policies 6 and 8, as implied in policy 5, is less effective than reliance on 6 alone, but the most effective combination is 6 and 9.

The role of wealth and claim effects is of particular importance for the secular aspects of stabilization policy. Changes in the structure of claims that result from current policies of deficit or surplus persist in the future, even after the current deficit or surplus is discontinued. Such changes take time to accumulate, and the resulting wealth effect gains in strength as the adjustment proceeds. Over time, it may become an important factor in determining the required rate of deficit or surplus.

Fractional-reserve Banking

The simplifying assumption of 100 per cent reserve money makes it possible to distinguish neatly between tax finance, new-money finance, and debt finance. Allowing for fractional-reserve banking, a wider variety of cases must be distinguished.

A first possibility is again tax finance. A second possibility is issuance of government money or borrowing from the central bank. Since the central bank is an instrument of public policy no less than the Treasury, both types of finance amount to the same thing, and may be referred to as reserve-money finance.[1] A third possibility is borrowing from the commercial banks, or bank-credit finance; and a fourth possibility is borrowing from the nonbank public. Fractional reserves complicate the problem, but the essential principle remains unchanged.

Reserve-money finance, whether in payment for current government expenditures or for debt retirement, increases the reserve money available to the commercial banks. As a result, bankers as a group *may* lend a multiple of this amount to the nonbank public, thus increasing the money supply in the hands of the nonbank public by a multiple of the increase in reserve money. Transactions reducing the supply of reserve money may—and if the system is loaned up, will—induce bankers to curtail the money supply to the nonbank public by a multiple of the reserve money. Transactions involving changes in the supply of reserve money will, therefore, tend to be more potent per dollar of change than are transactions changing the money supply in a 100 per cent reserve system.[2]

Finance by bank credit does not involve the potential of multiple expansion as does finance by reserve money. At best, the former will

[1] Borrowing from the central bank and printing-press finance are identical in that both increase the supply of reserve money. At the same time, actual policy decisions may differ, depending on what governmental agency, e.g., Treasury or Federal Reserve System, is charged with the responsibility of increasing the supply of reserve money.

[2] The picture is complicated slightly by changes in the currency holdings of the nonbank public. However, we may assume, for purposes of this argument, that the ratio of currency to deposit holdings is constant. Let R be required reserves to be held in government money, F government money in the form of currency, M total money (cash plus deposits) held by the nonbank public, r the reserve ratio of banks, b the fraction of its money holdings that the nonbank public holds in currency, and D deposits. We then have these conditions for the loaned-up banking system:

$$M = bM + D$$
$$F = bM + R$$
$$R = rD$$

from which we obtain

$$M = \frac{1}{r + b(1 - r)} F$$

as the money supply that the loaned-up system furnishes to the nonbank public.

increase the money supply in the hands of the nonbank public on a 1:1 basis, and thus equal the case of finance by new money in the 100 per cent system. Such expansion in the money supply results only if there is slack in the banking system, as is typically the case under conditions of depression. In the boom, when the banking system is loaned up, bank-credit finance does not increase the money supply, since government borrowing from the banks is offset by a corresponding reduction in bank holdings of private debt. Similarly, retirement of public debt held by banks will not reduce the money supply to the nonbank public if, as is usually the case in the boom, the banks fill the slack by the acquisition of private debt.

From a formal point of view, there is little difference between what is generally referred to as central-bank and debt-management policies. Open-market operations by the central bank are quite similar in nature to refunding operations by the Treasury. The only difference is that the latter usually involve exchanges between types of debt, while the former involve exchanges between debt and money. Similarly, discount operations by the central bank may be likened to lending operations by the Treasury. Changes in reserve requirements are in a different category, since they involve compulsion rather than exchange transactions. They constitute changes in the requirement for compulsory holdings of certain types of government obligations (reserve money) imposed on certain types of investors (commercial banks). Similar requirements could be applied to the holding of other obligations (bonds) by other investors such as insurance companies.[1]

Allowance for fractional-reserve banking reinforces the need for considering debt and monetary policy in conjunction with each other. To this, fractional-reserve banking adds one important factor: The liquidity preference or preferred-asset ratio of the banker occupies a strategic position in the picture. The weight to be attributed to bankers' preferences must not be measured by the reserve money that they can release or collect but by the multiple changes in the money supply to the nonbank public that result from such action. Because of this an economy on a fractional-reserve basis may be said to be as volatile, especially in the downward direction, as the liquidity preference of its bankers. The risk of destabilizing changes in the liquidity preference of bankers is the prime argument in favor of 100 per cent reserve money.[2] While the role of fractional-reserve banking qualifies our conclusions, it does not change

---

[1] See p. 587.

[2] Transition difficulties aside, the principle of the 100 per cent plan is rather tempting. The case for fractional-reserve banking can hardly be made on the grounds that fluctuations in bank credit that come about under fractional reserves are "on balance" stabilizing rather than destabilizing. This, in effect, would be to argue that the commercial-loan theory is more or less correct, which is a dubious proposition. A better argument for fractional reserves is that the slack they supply aids in securing

the principle. To simplify matters, the following discussion proceeds on the assumption of a 100 per cent reserve system.

B. WEALTH EFFECTS ON CONSUMPTION

We shall begin with possible effects of changes in the level or structure of claims upon the level of consumption. Effects on investment and considerations of growth are disregarded for the time being.

Consumption as a Function of Income and Wealth

In the preceding chapters, consumption has been treated as a function of disposable income only. We now consider the further proposition that the propensity to save or consume out of any given level of income depends upon the wealth of consumers. Since provision for future reserves is a major motivation for saving, consumers find less reason to save if they already dispose over large reserves. This consideration, which underlies the so-called Pigou effect, may now be introduced into our consumption function.[1] While statistical evidence is incomplete, the underlying proposition seems reasonable in terms of target saving.[2]

---

a proper allocation of credit. Though this point carries more weight, it has been treated rather lightly by the proponents of the 100 per cent plan.

Out of a prolific literature on this subject, see, for example, the contributions by Henry C. Simons and A. G. Hart in Friedrich A. Lutz and Lloyd W. Mints (eds.), *Readings in Monetary Theory*, American Economic Association, Richard D. Irwin, Inc., Homewood, Ill., 1951.

[1] Listing various applications of this principle, Gardner Ackley distinguishes between the Pigou effect, the Lerner effect, and the Keynes effect. See Gardner Ackley, "The Wealth-Saving Relationship," *Journal of Political Economy*, vol. 59, no. 2, pp. 154–161, April, 1951.

The Pigou effect is the increase in consumption out of a given real income that results as the price level declines and the real value of money balances rises. Its significance is to show (see p. 420) that, disregarding dynamic factors, an under-employment equilibrium is incompatible with flexible wages. See A. C. Pigou, *Employment and Equilibrium*, 2d ed., Macmillan & Co., Ltd., London, 1949, chap. 9.

The Lerner effect is the upward shift in the consumption function that occurs as the level of claims (money or public debt) is increased in the course of deficit finance, thus leading to an equilibrium level of public debt at which full employment prevails without a further deficit. The Lerner effect is of primary interest in our context. See A. P. Lerner, "The Burden of the National Debt," in *Income, Employment and Public Policy: Essays in Honor of Alvin H. Hansen*, W. W. Norton & Company, Inc., New York, 1948, pp. 264ff.

The Keynes effect is the change in consumption that results from the growth in real assets as investment proceeds. Provided that the capital-output ratio is constant, assets grow at the same rate as income, so that the Keynes effect is neutralized. However, Ackley notes that the effect may explain consumption behavior in periods of departure from equilibrium growth.

[2] See p. 264. Verification of this hypothesis by consumer-budget data is difficult since, among spending units with a given income, some are temperamentally inclined

Let us suppose that consumption is related directly to the absolute level of net worth. The consumption function may then be written as

$$C = a + cY + wN \tag{22-1}$$

or

$$\frac{C}{Y} = \frac{a}{Y} + c + w\,\frac{N}{Y} \tag{22-2}$$

where N is the net worth of the consumer. To simplify matters, let us suppose that $a = 0$. We then obtain the consumption surface $ADPL$ of Figure 22-1. On the horizontal axis, we measure Y; on the vertical axis we measure C/Y; and on the third axis, we measure N/Y. If $N/Y = 0$, the propensity to consume is $OA = c$, independent of the value of Y. The line AD thus pictures a consumption-income relationship of the usual type, without wealth effects. Now suppose that $Y = OE$. As N is increased, N/Y rises and we move up FG, thus obtaining a rising value of C/Y. At point H, where $Y = OE$ and $N/Y = OR$, we have $C/Y = OS$, including the income component OA and the wealth component $KL = AS$. The ratio C/Y rises as N is increased while Y remains constant, and it remains constant as Y is increased while N/Y remains constant, N being increased at the same percentage rate as Y.*

---

to save while others are not. The former will have relatively high ratios of net worth to income, while the latter will have low ratios. Thus we may find, in a cross section of spending units, a positive correlation between high rates of saving and high ratios of net worth to income. Nevertheless, for any one consumer, the rate of saving may usually be related negatively to the ratio of net worth to income.

Further complications arise from fluctuations in income. Empirical evidence shows that the significance of a high ratio of net worth to income differs, depending on whether we deal with spending units whose income is rising or falling. In the case of falling incomes, a high ratio appears to be associated with low rates of saving, or high rates of dissaving, whereas the opposite relationship appears to hold for units with rising income. See Lawrence R. Klein, "Estimating Patterns of Saving Behavior from Sample Survey Data," *Econometrica*, October, 1951.

Finally, note that the very concept of what consumers consider an adequate wealth position is relative. The aspiration level may change in the process of accumulation —a development similar in principles to the factors underlying an upward shift in the consumption function as income rises. See George Katona, *Psychological Analysis of Economic Behavior*, McGraw-Hill Book Company, Inc., New York, 1951, p.106.

* The reader may feel that this is too simple a formulation and that the wealth effect should be dependent upon assets held relative to income. Let us assume that the desired net worth equals a multiple of income kY, and that consumption in each year is reduced by a fraction p of the amount by which net worth falls short of this goal. We then have

$$C = cY - p(kY - N) \tag{22-1a}$$

and

$$\frac{C}{Y} = c - pk + p\,\frac{N}{Y} \tag{22-2a}$$

As before, C/Y remains constant if N and Y grow at the same percentage rate. I am indebted to Sidney Alexander for suggesting this formulation.

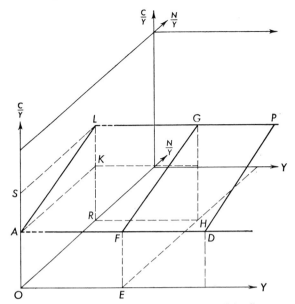

FIG. 22-1. Consumption surface with wealth effect.

New-money Finance

Let us now reexamine the impact of fiscal policies on consumption, with due allowance for the wealth effect. To begin with, we shall disregard public debt. We assume that all deficits are financed by new money and that all surplus results in a reduction in the money supply. In other words, we shall consider policies 3 and 6 of Table 22-1. Real capital assets, created by investment, are disregarded for the time being, so that the net worth of consumers equals the money stock M, and a surplus or deficit in the budget is reflected in a corresponding increase or decrease in net worth.[1]

As the budget is introduced, the consumption function of equation (22-1) becomes

$$C = a + c(Y - T) + wM \qquad (22\text{-}3)$$

where T is lump-sum tax yield, and the net worth of consumers is assumed to consist of the money supply M. We now set $T = G$, since a balanced budget and hence a constant level of M are necessary conditions of

---

[1] Considering the community as a whole, it is obvious that national wealth in real terms is not affected by the issuance of money. Nevertheless, an increase in the holding of money by any one individual expands that individual's net worth just as much as an increase in his real wealth does; and this is what determines his expenditure behavior. The same applies to all consumers as a group. Of course, if expenditures should increase so as to raise prices and money incomes as a result, the wealth effect on consumption would play itself out.

static equilibrium with wealth effect. Substituting into

$$Y = C + I + G \tag{22-4}$$

we obtain

$$Y = \frac{1}{1 - c} (w\bar{M} + I + a) + G \tag{22-5}$$

as the equilibrium level of income, corresponding to a given value of $M = \bar{M}$. The larger are w and M, the higher will be the level of Y for any given values of G, c, and I. Solving for M, we obtain the equilibrium level of M corresponding to the given full-employment level of income $Y = \bar{Y}$, as

$$M = \frac{1}{w} [(1 - c)(\bar{Y} - G) - I - a] \tag{22-6}$$

The smaller are G, c, and w, the larger is the equilibrium level of money supply for any given level of Y.*

Suppose, now, that the level of income is to be raised by $\Delta\bar{Y}$, with I, G, and T constant. We then have the required change in M given by

$$\Delta M = \frac{1 - c}{w} \Delta\bar{Y} \tag{22-7}$$

The required increase in money supply, or ΔM, will be smaller for any given ΔY, the larger c and w are.

Equation (22-7) shows the equilibrium solution for a given change in Y. In the process of adjustment a deficit must be incurred, to be financed by an increase in money supply, and a policy of deficit must be continued until the required increase in money supply is built up. Let us begin with a balanced budget and suppose that the adjustment is secured by increasing G with T constant. If the required increase in Y is to be obtained in the first round, the initial increase in G must be $\Delta G = \Delta Y$, as would be the case in the absence of a wealth effect. In the second round, government expenditures must be cut back. This cutback must be sharper than it would be in the absence of a wealth effect, when ΔG is reduced to $(1 - c) \Delta Y$. Not only is part of the slack taken up by the multiplier effect of the initial injection, but an amount of new money equal to the deficit of the first period has been added to the net worth of consumers, thus leading to an increase in consumption out of a given disposable income. In the absence of a wealth effect, ΔG remains at $(1 - c) \Delta Y$ for all successive periods if the initial increase in income is to be maintained; but further reductions of ΔG in each successive period are called for if a

* Note the similarity between this formulation and A. P. Lerner's concept of equilibrium level of public debt. See note 1, p. 533, and the discussion of debt finance on p. 538.

wealth effect applies. As M increases with each successive deficit, consumption out of the full-employment income rises. When the equilibrium level of M is reached, no further deficit is required, as planned saving has fallen to the level of investment.

But all this is a gradual process. It takes time to inject the necessary volume of claims into the system. This cannot be done all at once without overshooting the mark, since the increase in public expenditures needed to introduce claims creates an income effect that must be held within proper limits.[1] Because of this, the operation of the wealth effect comes about slowly. It is hardly a major factor in the short-term context of cyclical adjustments; at the same time, it may be of great importance in appraising the efficacy of fiscal policy in the long run.

Debt Finance

Let us now turn to the more conventional case of debt finance, including deficits financed by borrowing, or policy 2 of Table 22-1, and debt retirement financed out of surplus, or policy 5. To avoid the complicating factor of borrowing from commercial banks, the earlier assumption of a 100 per cent reserve system is retained. Also, let us simplify matters by assuming that all bonds are in the form of consols.[2] Now we may ask how the results of consol finance compare with those of new-money finance.

Let us look again at the case of deficit. The issuance of bonds, as will be shown presently, tends to drive up the rate of interest.[3] This may affect the rate of saving out of a given level of income. Depending upon the motivation involved, saving may either rise or fall. The motivation of target saving, implicit in the wealth effect, points toward a decline in saving, but the more usual assumption is that the rate of saving will rise.[4] Postponement of consumption is considered a disutility but becomes more profitable as interest increases. Thus funds that otherwise would have gone into consumption are diverted into the purchase of government

---

[1] The question arises whether an increase in the money stock cannot be secured without an income effect. Obviously, this is not possible by way of fiscal policy. Nor can the result be obtained readily by monetary policy with fractional-reserve banking, since, for the group on a whole, the increase in credit to the nonbank public will be offset by increased indebtedness of the public to the banks. However, distributional changes may result that alter the potency of the wealth effect.

[2] The use of finite maturities complicates matters but does not change the principle of the argument. See p. 545. Changes in private debt are disregarded because they do not affect the *net* claim position of the private sector.

[3] The reader may wish to pass over the following discussion and return to it after considering effects on investment described in the following section. Since we assume a setting of unemployment, changes in price level are disregarded for the time being.

[4] See p. 260.

bonds. To the extent that this occurs, the initial results of loan finance are similar to those of finance by consumption taxes.[1] However, this is not likely to be the typical situation. For purposes of this discussion, let us assume that the rate of saving is not affected by a change in the rate of interest, at least not along these lines.

The question remains whether the issuance of bonds will have the same wealth effect as the issuance of money. At first sight, the answer would seem to be yes: If people's net worth is increased by the holding of additional money, it will be increased also by the holding of additional bonds. But this is too simple a view. The difficulty lies in defining what is meant by additional bonds. As the Treasury proceeds to borrow, it must issue new obligations and raise its coupon bill. But this does not mean that the market value of total consols outstanding must increase accordingly. If the issuance of new obligations drives up the rate of interest, an increasing volume of coupon payments is capitalized at a rising rate of interest. This counteracts a possible increase in the market value of total consols outstanding.

At one extreme, investors insist on holding money and debt in a fixed ratio. In this case, the market value of the total debt remains constant, and the entire adjustment is in the rate of interest. The net worth of bondholders as a group is not affected, gains from the acquisition of new bonds being offset by capital losses suffered from the holding of old bonds. Some will gain while others will lose; but for the group as a whole there will be no change in net worth; defined as current market value of claims held. There will be no wealth effect, although the finance of interest charges, operating as a system of redistribution, may have significant income effects.[2]

At the other extreme, investors are indifferent as between the holding of consols and money. In this case, the issuance of bonds leaves the rate of interest unchanged, and the market value of total debt rises with the issuance of new consols. In this setting, the wealth effect is fully operative.[3] The situation is the same as for new-money finance. We arrive at

[1] See p. 263.

[2] Bondholders as a group come to claim a larger coupon income as the deficit continues. If interest charges are tax-financed, this gain will be offset by the increased tax commitments on the part of the taxpayers. If taxpayers' propensity to consume exceeds that of interest recipients, the required rate of deficit is increased.

If interest charges are loan-financed, such an offset does not arise. Provided that part of the interest income is spent on consumption, the rising level of coupon income raises consumption at any given level of employment or earned income. Assuming investment to remain fixed, an equilibrium level of interest payments by deficit finance is reached where the desired level of income is sustained, while other government expenditures are tax-financed.

[3] This conclusion is based on the assumption that taxpayers who must finance future interest charges do not capitalize this liability and find their net worth reduced accordingly.

an equilibrium level of debt similar to the previously determined equilibrium level of money, with interest payments being fully tax-financed.[1]

Actual conditions fall between these extremes. Changes in the supply of debt may be offset in part by changes in the rate of interest, but hardly in their entirety. Issuance of debt will lead to some increase in the market value of total debt. Debt finance will carry some wealth effect, though less than new-money finance, and with a correspondingly higher equilibrium level of claims. Under conditions of potentially severe depression or stagnation, the response of interest rates to an increase in the supply of debt will tend to be slight.[2] An increase in the supply of debt will be accompanied by a more or less corresponding increase in the market value of total debt outstanding. The wealth effect of loan finance, therefore, will be more or less similar to that of new-money finance, especially if government obligations are in finite and fairly short-term maturities, and not in the form of consols.

Similar considerations apply to surplus finance. Surplus finance to retire debt has an asset effect only if the resulting decline in the rate of interest does not suffice to prevent a decline in the total market value of the outstanding debt. Under conditions of brisk business, when restrictive action is required, changes in the supply of debt are likely to meet an active response in the rate of interest. The wealth effect on consumption will be less pronounced than in the case of depression policy.

Mixed Money and Debt Finance

In the case of mixed money and debt finance, the wealth effect of money finance may be boosted by the existence of outstanding debt. If the issuance of money reduces the rate of interest, the market value of outstanding consols is increased, and the wealth effect of money creation is accentuated. A corresponding argument applies to debt retirement through surplus finance.

Let us now consider refunding operations. Such operations involve exchanges between money and debt, and may be pursued quite independently of the state of budgetary balance or fiscal transactions. Suppose, first, that money is injected into the budget to retire outstanding debt, as described in policy 8 of Table 22-1. If the rate of interest remains unchanged, net worth remains unchanged as well, and there will be no wealth effect. If the rate of interest declines so as to prevent a fall in the market value of total bonds, net worth will increase by the amount of

---

[1] The equilibrium level of debt will be higher or lower, depending on the consumption effects of distributional changes inherent in the tax-interest circuit.

[2] See p. 536. The above seems a somewhat paradoxical conclusion. It is usually argued that liquidity preference is elastic in the depression because investors wish to hold money. If so, will not an increase in public debt force a relatively sharp rise in the rate of interest? For an explanation, see p. 546.

money injected. The expansionary wealth effect will be at a maximum. Actual situations, however, fall between these extremes. The wealth effect of refunding operations will tend to be relatively ineffective under conditions of depression. Since the resulting decline in the rate of interest will be slight, net worth will rise but little. The same characteristics of the depression setting which suggest that debt finance of current deficit carries a wealth effect also suggest that substitution of money for debt will be ineffective.[1]

The sale of debt to reduce the supply of money, or policy 9 of Table 22-1, presents the reverse situation. The restrictive wealth effect will be at its maximum if the rate of interest rises so as to prevent an increase in the market value of total bonds. Since the rate of interest may be expected to respond markedly under conditions of brisk business, the wealth effect of refunding operations will be relatively effective. This is true for the very same reason that debt retirement out of current surplus will be relatively ineffective.

C. CLAIMS EFFECTS ON INVESTMENT

We shall now turn to the effects of changes in the level or structure of claims on private investment. To begin with, the expenditure side of investment only is allowed for. Effects on capacity and growth will be introduced later on.

New-money Finance

Let us assume that the level of income is to be raised, and that a deficit is incurred for the purpose. As the deficit is incurred, the money supply is increased in each period. Assuming that liquidity preference is not infinitely elastic, lenders will provide investable funds at a lower rate of interest. Provided that the investment schedule is elastic, a higher volume of investment becomes profitable, and private investment increases. A lesser deficit and an addition to money supply is required in each subsequent period. If the rate of interest continues to fall and private investment continues to rise, we eventually reach a point where no further deficit is needed to maintain the higher level of income. The investment effect of the resulting increase in money supply renders the need for further deficits self-terminating; and precisely the same argument applies to the opposite case of restrictive action through surplus finance and reduction in money supply. In either case, there results an equilibrium level of money supply.

The factors determining this equilibrium level may be defined conven-

---

[1] The reader will bear in mind that effects on investment are disregarded for the time being.

iently with the help of a simple system of income determination similar to the system used in our earlier discussion of investment effects.[1]

General form	Linear form	
$Y = C + I + G$	$Y = C + I + G$	(22-8)
$C = C(Y - T)$	$C = a + c(Y - T)$	(22-9)
$T = G$	$T = G$	(22-10)
$I = I(i)$	$I = d - ei$	(22-11)
$i = L(M_a)$	$M_a = f - hi$	(22-12)
$M_a = M - M_t$	$M_a = M - M_t$	(22-13)
$M_t = \dfrac{1}{V}\, Y$	$M_t = \dfrac{1}{V}\, Y$	(22-14)

Equations (22-8) and (22-9) are self-explanatory; the wealth effect on consumption is now disregarded. Equation (22-10) shows a balanced budget, goods and service expenditures G being equal to tax yield T. Since growth is disregarded for the time being, equality of G and T is again a necessary condition of equilibrium, once claim effects are allowed for.[2] Equation (22-11) is the usual investment schedule, and (22-12) is the liquidity-preference schedule. The liquidity-preference schedule refers to the holding of M_a, or money held as an asset in investment portfolios. It excludes M_t, or transaction money. The relationship of M_a to the total money supply is given by equations (22-13) and (22-14), where the velocity of transaction money V is constant.

Assuming full-employment income to be given at $\bar{Y}$, and the level of government expenditures at $\bar{G}$, we may solve the above system for M, thus obtaining the equilibrium level of money supply. We now have

$$M = f + \frac{1}{V}\, \bar{Y} - \frac{h}{e}\,[a + d - (1 - c)(\bar{Y} - \bar{G})] \qquad (22\text{-}15)$$

in the linear form corresponding to equation (22-6). It follows that the larger f and e are, and the smaller a, d, c, h, and V, the higher will be the equilibrium level of claims. The corresponding expression for the general form is given by

$$M = C(Y - G) + I\left[L\left(M - \frac{1}{V}\, Y\right)\right] + G \qquad (22\text{-}16)$$

As in the preceding discussion of the wealth effect, we may again determine the increase in M required to secure a given increase in Y. Setting

[1] See p. 535.
[2] This is true provided the shape of the L and I schedules leads to a change in Y with a change in M.

ΔG and ΔT equal to zero, and solving for ΔM, we obtain

$$\Delta M = \left(\frac{h(1 - c)}{e} + \frac{1}{V} \right) \Delta Y \qquad (22\text{-}17)$$

in the linear form corresponding to equation (22-7), and

$$\frac{dM}{dY} = \frac{L'(M_a)[1 - C'(Y - g)]}{I'(i)} + \frac{1}{V} \qquad (22\text{-}18)$$

in the general form. We thus determine the change in M required to maintain a given increase in income after the budget is balanced and returned to its initial level.

As before, we note that the required change in money supply cannot be accomplished at once, but must be provided for gradually. Policies of deficit or surplus carry an immediate income effect that must be held within proper limits. Monetary policy will be more efficient, the smaller the eventual change in money supply required to hold income at the desired level without further deficit or surplus. According to equation (22-17), monetary policy will be more efficient under the following conditions:[1]

1. The larger c is, or the greater the multiplier effect of a given increase in investment

2. The smaller h is, or the less elastic the liquidity-preference schedule

3. The larger e is, or the more elastic the investment schedule

4. The larger V is, or the less the drain from asset into transaction money for any given increase in Y

Under conditions of depression, when expansionary action is required, the investment schedule tends to be inelastic and liquidity preference tends to be elastic. In other words, e tends to be small and h tends to be large. A relatively large change in money supply is required to achieve a given increase in investment. In the absence of a wealth effect on consumption, the self-terminating nature of deficit finance is effective only over a very long period, or not at all. In the extreme case, h reaches infinity, and the rate of interest cannot decline below a certain floor level. This is one of the conditions of the special Keynesian case of unemployment equilibrium.[2] In such a setting, an increase in the money supply will not raise investment. Barring a possible wealth effect on consumption, there is no self-terminating force in deficit finance. The current income effect of the deficit is the only leverage factor. While this is one extreme situation, it reflects the familiar observation that

[1] For a diagrammatic discussion of these familiar propositions, see Alvin H. Hansen, *Monetary Theory and Fiscal Policy*, chap. 12.

[2] See p. 413.

monetary policy, or changes in the money stock, are more or less ineffective under conditions of severe depression.

Under conditions of boom when restrictive fiscal action is required, the investment schedule tends to be relatively elastic, and the liquidity-preference schedule tends to be relatively inelastic. In other words, e tends to be large and h tends to be small. Under such conditions, a relatively small reduction in M will secure a relatively large reduction in investment. In the extreme case, where h is zero, investors wish to hold no asset money, or a fixed amount of asset money. All changes in money supply take the form of changes in transaction money, and ΔY equals ΔMV. Changes in the level of income can be secured only by change in the money supply. The monetary results of surplus or deficit operations, far from being a by-product, become the heart of the matter. While this is another extreme situation, it indicates that monetary restriction can be most effective under conditions of boom. The question in this case is not whether monetary policy can be effective in applying restriction, but rather, what combination of fiscal and monetary restriction should be applied. Normally, the problem is not one of overcoming a severe depression or fighting a severe inflation but of dealing with lesser fluctuations. Under such conditions, changes in money supply affect investment to some degree and constitute a more or less significant, though not the sole, element of policy adjustment.

Debt Finance

We shall now allow for debt finance of current deficit, debt retirement out of tax receipts, and exchanges between debt and money. To simplify matters, we shall retain the assumption that all debt is in the form of consols, that is, debt obligations without fixed maturity date.

Debt transactions differ from tax or new-money finance in that they involve a voluntary exchange. If the government wishes to place new debt or to retire outstanding debt, it must do so on terms that are acceptable to the investor. In other words, it must meet the evaluation that the market places upon such debt. Let us begin with an individual investor who decides how to hold his assets.[1] He will choose that combination of assets which seems best in view of his market appraisal and his preferences between gain and safety. Let us suppose that this investment choice is between cash, government bonds, and equity investment, that is, corporate shares or goods. What then determines his choice between these particular categories of assets?

First, there is the choice between the holding of money and of consols. The former has the advantage of enabling the investor to benefit from a possible rise in the rate of interest. The latter has the advantage of

[1] See p. 313.

providing an interest income at a yield determined by the purchase price and the coupon rates; also, it insures the holder that he will not suffer from a possible fall in interest rates. The investor will hold money only to the extent that these prospects, together with his attitude toward gain and risk, make it desirable to forego the income obtained from the holding of bonds.

Next, there is the choice between the holding of money and bonds and the holding of equity assets. This choice depends on expectations of changes in price level rather than in interest. If the price level is expected to rise, the holding of equity assets will tend to be preferable to the holding of cash or consols, and vice versa if the price level is expected to fall.

Let us disregard equity assets for the time being and consider the choice between money and debt. We may now reconstruct equation (22-12) to allow for the holding of consols as well as money. In other words, we replace the liquidity-preference schedule by a surface, relating the amount of asset money, consols outstanding, and the rate of interest. Just as investors are willing to absorb an increased supply of money only at a reduced rate of interest, so they are willing to absorb an increased supply of consols only at an increased rate of interest.

This relationship may take a variety of forms, illustrated by the simplest hypothesis that investors as a group wish to hold a given fraction of their total claims, consisting of money and public debt, in the form of debt.[1] Let the supply of asset money equal M_a and the fraction of the claims that people wish to hold in debt D be given by β.* We obtain

$$\beta = \frac{D}{M_a + D} \qquad \text{or} \qquad D = \frac{\beta}{1 - \beta} M_a \qquad (22\text{-}19)$$

where D is the market value of government bonds outstanding. The market value of bonds outstanding depends on β and M_a; and any change in M_a with β constant must result in an equal percentage change in D. For the case of consols, we also know that

$$D = \frac{U}{i} \qquad (22\text{-}20)$$

where U is the coupon bill and i is the market rate of interest. Substi-

---

[1] See Kenneth Boulding, "A Liquidity Preference Theory of Market Price," *Economica*, vol. 11, pp. 55–63, May, 1944, reprinted in *Readings in Price Theory*, American Economic Association, Richard D. Irwin, Inc., Homewood, Ill., 1952. Also see my "Money, Liquidity and the Valuation of Assets," in *Money, Trade and Economic Growth: In Honor of John Henry Williams*, The Macmillan Company, New York, 1951, pp. 216–242.

* The value of β for individual investors differs, so that the β in eq. (22-19) should be considered an average value, weighted according to the distribution of asset holdings.

tuting U/i for D in equation (22-19) we have the basic equation

$$i = \frac{U}{M_a} \frac{(1 - \beta)}{\beta} \tag{22-21}$$

which defines the general relationship between asset preference, money supply, the coupon bill, and the rate of interest.[1]

An increase in U with M_a unchanged raises the rate of interest, investors being willing to absorb the increase in U only at a higher rate of interest. An increase in M_a without an increase in U leads to the opposite adjustment. The elasticity of i in terms of M_a is unity, any given percentage change in M_a being reflected in an equal but inverse percentage change of i. Similarly, the elasticity of i in terms of U is unity, but the change is now in the same direction. If U and M_a increase at the same rate, i remains unchanged, provided β remains constant.

The resulting asset preference is plotted in Figure 22-2, with M_a measured along the horizontal axis, i along the vertical axis, and U along the third axis. Moving down curves such as AC or DJ, we observe the decline in i as M_a is increased while holding U constant. Moving up lines such as FD, GH or KJ, we observe the rise in i as U is increased while M_a is held constant. Points such as B and J involve equal ratios of M_a/U and, hence, equal values of i. It will be noted that the surface forms a rectangular hyperbola when moving parallel to the M_a axis, but a rising straight line when moving from lower to higher values of U. While this is by no means the only possible pattern, it is a convenient one for purposes of this discussion.

Let us now substitute equation (22-21) for (22-12) in our initial system, given by equations (22-8) to (22-14). Proceeding as before, we obtain

$$\Delta \frac{U}{M_a} = - \frac{(1 - c)\beta}{(1 - \beta)e} \Delta Y \tag{22-22}$$

in the linear form, corresponding to equation (22-17) for the case of new-money finance. As before, $M_a = M - \frac{1}{V} Y$. The required change of policy is now defined in terms of the ratio U/M_a, and not the level of M_a as such. In other words, the concept of an equilibrium *level* of claims is replaced by that of an equilibrium *structure* of claims. The reduction in U/M_a required to accomplish a given increase in Y will now be smaller; that is, a policy of changing the structure of claims will be more effective, the smaller β is and the larger V, c, and e are.

It may be readily seen that the larger V, c, and e are, the more potent a change in the structure of claims will be. If V is large, the increased

---

[1] If debt with finite maturity is considered, the relationship expressed in (22-20) becomes more complicated, but the principle is unchanged.

demand for transaction money will have a small dampening effect. If c is large, the multiplier will be large, and any given change in investment will lead to a large change in income. If e is large, the investment schedule will be elastic, and a small change in i will lead to a large change in I.

So far all is clear, but an explanation is required of why a small value of β increases the effectiveness of a change in the claim structure. A small value of β simply means that people dislike to hold bonds, so that i will be

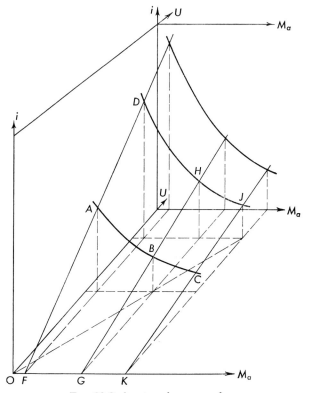

FIG. 22-2. Asset preference surface.

high for any given value of M_a/U. This follows from equation (22-21), according to which the elasticity of i in terms of M_a or U is always unity. The absolute reduction in i and hence the rise in Y, which results from a given increase in M_a or decrease in U, will thus be large if β is small. A large value of β, on the contrary, means that i is low, so that a given increase in M_a or decrease in U results in a large absolute fall in the value of i.

Turning to the cylical aspect of the matter, we may expect the liquidity-preference schedule to drop as the economy moves into a depression. The level of interest that is considered normal is adjusted downward.

Capital gains are to be made in the purchase of bonds. Thus the price of bonds is bid up, and i is reduced. A further decline in i results as the supply of asset money increases, owing to a decline in income and a resulting drain of money from the transaction sphere.[1] In terms of our analysis, we find that β increases, thus reducing i; and a further decline in i results from the concurrent rise in M_a.

This is illustrated in the liquidity-preference schedules of Figure 22-3, which may be thought of as a vertical plane cut out of Figure 22-2 so as to slice the surface parallel to the horizontal axis. Let l_1l_1 represent the relationship between i and M_a for a given value of U and β. As the economy moves into a depression, β rises and the schedule drops to l_2l_2. The supply of asset money concurrently increases from OC to OD,

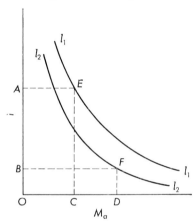

FIG. 22-3. Relation of M_a and i for given value of U.

so that the rate of interest falls from OA to OB. Monetary policy becomes less potent because the slope of l_2l_2 at F is less than the slope of l_1l_1 at E. This is the case not only because M_a has been increased but also because the entire schedule has dropped. The proposition that liquidity preference is highly elastic in the depression must not be identified with the statement that investors are anxious to hold money. In part, the increase in elasticity has come about precisely because investors wish to hold less money and more debt, thus pushing the liquidity-preference schedule downward.

This, to be sure, is an overly simplified view. For a more complete analysis, a broader choice of assets must be considered. Investors may wish (1) to substitute claims (money or debt) for goods as they expect the price level to fall; (2) to substitute public debt for private debt as they

---

[1] In the fractional-reserve system, the money supply held by the nonbank public tends to decline in the depression, but excess reserves of banks increase. Excess reserves become the strategic component of asset money. (See p. 531.)

expect the default risk of private debt to rise; (3) to substitute debt for money as they expect the rate of interest to fall; and (4) to substitute money for debt in order to meet contingencies in an imperfect credit market. Among these forces, (1), (2), and (3) make for a decline in the yield of public debt, while only (4) makes for an increase. The yield on private debt is forced up by (2), thus making for a widening rate spread between rates on public and private debt. Thus, a substitution of public debt for money may accompany a desire for increased holding of cash (relative to private debt).

Equation (22-22) allows for motivation (3) only. Nevertheless, it helps to explain why changes in the liquidity structure are relatively ineffective during periods of depression. Since i is low (owing to the rise in β and the increase in M_a during the downswing), any given increase in M or decrease in U will result in only a slight absolute fall in i. For the same reason, an increase in U will do little to raise i. All this applies to the case of consols. If debt of finite maturity is introduced, a greater change in the value of debt is needed to secure a given change in i, thus reducing the effectiveness of liquidity policy with a given value of β.

D. CONSUMPTION AND INVESTMENT EFFECTS COMBINED

We may now combine the consumption aspects considered in section B with the investment aspects considered in section C.

New-money Finance

Let us begin with a system where there is no debt, so that the deficit or surplus must be reflected in changes in the money supply.[1] The expansionary income effects of deficit finance are now augmented by the expansionary wealth effects of the increased money supply on both consumption and investment.[2] The same symmetry applies to the restrictive effects of surplus finance. Returning to Table 22-1, policies

---

[1] The combined asset effects on consumption and investment for a system without debt are obtained by substituting eq. (22-3) for (22-9) in the system of eqs. (22-8) to (22-14). For the linear case, we then obtain

$$\Delta Y = c \, \Delta Y + w \, \Delta M - e \, \frac{(1/V) \, \Delta Y - \Delta M}{h}$$

which reduces to

$$\Delta M = \frac{(1 + e/vh - c) \, \Delta Y}{w + e/h}$$

thus combining eq. (22-7), which allows for consumption effects only, with eq. (22-17) which allows for investment effects only.

[2] Note that the effects of changes in money supply on investment have been related to changes in M_a, while those on consumption are related to changes in M.

3 and 6 are clearly more potent, per dollar change in public expenditures, than is policy 1.

Debt Finance

Turning now to a system in which debt is allowed for, consider deficit finance out of new money, or policy 3 of Table 22-1.* The expansionary income effect is again supported by an expansionary investment effect, provided that the rate of interest falls and investment responds to it. The fall in the rate of interest increases the value of outstanding debt and thus boosts the expansionary wealth effect on consumption beyond what it would be in the absence of debt. Even if the rate of interest does not respond, a favorable wealth effect on consumption remains, similar to that observed in the absence of debt. The same principles apply to the restrictive effects of retirement of money by budget surplus, or policy 6. Policies 3 and 6 are both rendered more potent by the presence of debt.[1]

Turning now to deficit finance by debt, or policy 2, the expansionary income effect may be supported by an expansionary wealth effect on consumption. This will be the case only if D and hence D/M increases, which requires that the rate of interest be relatively unresponsive. In this case, restrictive effects on investment will be relatively slight. At the other end of the scale, we may find that the rate of interest responds sharply, in which case expansionary wealth effects on consumption will be slight or absent, while restrictive investment effects may be severe. Under conditions of depression, when deficit finance is required, the former condition is more likely to apply. In this setting, the effects of policies 2 and 3 may differ but little.

A corresponding argument applies to surplus finance where the surplus is used to retire debt, or policy 5. If the rate of interest falls so that D remains unchanged, there will be no wealth effect on consumption, but the restrictive income effect of surplus finance will be counteracted by an expansionary effect on investment. If the rate of interest does not fall,

* Even a change in the balanced budget, or policy 1, is affected by the allowance for debt. The drain on asset money (in the case of budget expansion) now tends to result in a detrimental investment effect; and the rise in Y relative to a constant M tends to result in a depressing effect on consumption. This will be the case the more so if D declines owing to a rising i and a constant U. (See p. 528, note 1.)

[1] The combined asset effects on consumption and investment for a system with debt are obtained by substituting eq. (22-3) for (22-9), and eq. (22-21) for (22-11), in the system of eqs. (22-8) to (22-14). We now obtain

$$\Delta M = \left\{ 1 - c + \frac{eU(1 - \beta)}{V\beta[M_0 - (1/v)Y_0]^2} \right\} \left\{ w + \frac{eU(1 - \beta)}{[M - (1/v)Y_0]^2} \right\}^{-1} \Delta Y$$

where M_0 and Y_0 are the initial levels of income and money supply. They must be allowed for in this case because the consumption effects of changes in U/M are not linear.

there will be no investment effect, but D will decline, and there will be a restrictive wealth effect on consumption. In the boom, when surplus finance is needed, the expansionary investment effect may well be important, and policy 5 will be substantially less potent than a withholding of the surplus, or policy 6.

There remains the case of pure liquidity policy, or exchanges between money and debt. Substitution of money for debt, or policy 8, results in a decline in i if β is constant. This has an expansionary effect on investment as well as on consumption. Substitution of debt for money, or policy 9, has a restrictive effect on both counts. Again, there is reason to expect that the impact of pure liquidity policies, particularly on investment, will be greater in the boom than in the depression.

E. LIQUIDITY STRUCTURE AND GROWTH

It now remains to reintroduce the effects of investment on capacity and to reconsider changes in the structure of claims in a growing economy.

Claim Effects in the Growth Model: Effects on Required Rate

Let us return to a growth model of the type represented by the required-rate system of equations (20-41) to (20-45), and the expenditure-rate system of equations (20-54) to (20-58).* In these systems, no allowance was made for changes in the structure and the level of claims that result from deficit or surplus finance. These changes must now be examined.[1]

Effects on the required rate of growth involve effects on the level of consumption only. Following equation (22-2) we assume that the ratio of consumption to disposable income is related positively to the ratio of claims to income. A balanced-budget policy, where $g = t$, now implies a rising rate of growth, since the ratio of consumption to income falls as the ratio of claims (money plus government debt) to income declines.[2] The system approaches a situation where the propensity to consume equals $(1 - t)c$, and private investment becomes a constant fraction of income.

A deficit budget is required if growth is to proceed at a constant rate from the outset.[3] Beginning with a given excess of g over t, the growth

* See pp. 485 and 489.

[1] See Gardner Ackley, "The Wealth-Saving Relationship," *Journal of Political Economy*, vol. 59, no. 2, pp. 154–161, April, 1951, for a general discussion of the relationship between assets and growth. Also, see Franz Gehrels, "Government Debt as a Generator of Economic Growth," *Review of Economics and Statistics*, vol. 39, no. 2, p. 183, May, 1957.

[2] We assume that s, and hence the ratio of capital stock to income, remains constant, so that a decrease in the ratio of claims to income will not be offset by an increase in the ratio of equity assets to income.

[3] Alternatively, the increase in claims may be supplied through banking policy, e.g., easing of reserve requirements.

rate in subsequent periods will fall if income grows at a slower rate than the stock of claims, since the excess implies a rising ratio of claims to income and hence an increasing propensity to consume. The rate of growth may rise asymptotically and approach a constant. For balanced growth to proceed at a constant rate, the rate of deficit must be such that income and the stock of claims grow at the same rate.

In the absence of claim effects, we concluded that the required rate rises with an increase in t and γ and a decrease in g.* The same holds in the present case. Indeed, it is evident that changes in t and g exert a more potent effect on the required rate once claim effects are allowed for. An increase in t again reduces consumption by reducing disposable income. In addition to this, an increase in t reduces the claim to income ratio for future periods, thereby lowering the propensity to consume out of a given disposable income. The same holds for a decrease in g.† The bearing of claim effects on the potency of changes in γ is more complex. As γ is increased, the level of income grows more rapidly, but so does the level of claims if $g > t$. Growth of income will be speeded up or retarded by claim effects, depending on whether the ratio of claims to income rises or falls.

---

* See p. 486.

† The reader who wishes to approach these problems in a formal fashion may introduce claim factors into eqs. (20-41) to (20-45). The adjusted system may be written as follows:

$$Y_n{}^r = C_n + I_n + G_n$$
$$C_n = (1 - \alpha)(1 - t)Y_n + w(O_n + A_n)$$
$$G_n = gY_n{}^r$$
$$A_n = \frac{1}{s} Y_n{}^r$$
$$O_n = \bar{O} + (g - t) \sum_{N=0}^{N=n-1} Y_N{}^r$$
$$Y_n{}^r = Y_{n-1}^r + sI_{n-1}$$

where $\bar{O}$ is the initial stock of government obligations, O_n the stock at period n, and A the stock of capital. To simplify, we set γ equal to zero so that all government expenditures are for consumption. From this system we obtain

$$y_n{}^r = [s\alpha(I - t) + s(t - g) + 1 - w]Y_{n-1} - sw \left[(g - t) \sum_{N=0}^{N=n-1} Y_N{}^r - \bar{O} \right]$$

This formulation may be used to compute the value of Y^r for successive periods, assuming given values of $\bar{O}$, s, α, t, g, and w. However, new initial values for the difference equation apply for each successive period, since the stock of obligation changes. A general solution for the growth rate over time is not readily obtainable.

Claim Effects in the Growth Model: Effects on Expenditure Rate

When introducing claim effects into the expenditure rate, effects on investment as well as consumption must be allowed for; and effects on investment differ, depending on the type of claims that are issued.

New-money Finance. Proceeding as before, we begin with a system where all government claims are in the form of money. An increase in claims will be expansionary with regard to consumption as well as investment. As distinct from the case of the required rate, we now find that the expenditure rate of growth declines unless there is a deficit that expands the level of claims at the same rate as the level of income.[1] Similar to the case of the required rate, allowance for claim effects renders changes in g and t more potent in their effects upon the expenditure rate. This applies to resulting effects on consumption as well as investment.

As in the absence of claim effects, an increase in t or a reduction in g raises the required rate and reduces the expenditure rate. Since the adjustment is now more efficient, a smaller change in g or t will suffice to close any given potential gap between the required rate and the expenditure rate.

Debt Finance. Let us now move to the other extreme and assume that all government obligations take the form of long-term debt. In this case, an increase in government obligations raises consumption but reduces investment. The net effect on the expenditure rate may be in either direction. If expansionary, the general argument is the same as it was with money finance. If restrictive, we now find that allowance for claim effects reduces the potency of changes in g and t in their effect on the expenditure rate. Conceivably, the restrictive effects of debt issue may become so strong that the expenditure rate now moves inversely to changes in g, and directly with changes in t. In this case, a decrease in g or an increase in t will raise both the required rate and the expenditure rate. These raises may render it impossible to close, by fiscal adjustment, a potential gap between the two rates, depending on the relative degrees of change in them.

Mixed Money and Debt Finance. The more realistic policy is one in which government obligations include money as well as debt. The outcome combines the results of the two preceding cases, depending on what part of the obligations is in money and what part is in debt.[2]

In addition, we now have the possibility of varying the money-debt ratio, thereby reintroducing liquidity policy into the picture. If we

---

[1] Or unless this expansion is provided for through banking policy.

[2] Introducing claim effects into eqs. (20-54) to (20-58), we may now write

assume that the consumption effect is the same for both types of claims,[1] changes in the mix of claims will have no effect on the required rate. However, substitution of debt for money will reduce the expenditure rate, and substitution of money for debt will raise it.   This holds, whether the change in mix applies to the entire stock of obligations, or whether it is limited to the increment (deficit) or decrement (surplus) of claims.   Thus, liquidity policy enters as a further policy tool for securing balanced growth.

The Efficient Rate of Growth

Having examined the effects of fiscal policies upon the rate of growth, let us return to the normative problems of what rate of growth is to be aimed at, and which policy tools should be used to secure it.

We may safely assume that balanced growth is desirable, that is, that inflation, unemployment, and excess capacity are to be avoided.   However, various rates of balanced growth are possible, and a choice must be made among them.   In the setting of the classical system, it can be argued

$$Y^e = C_n + I_n + G_n$$
$$C_n = (1 - \alpha)(1 - t)Y_n{}^e + w(O_n + A_n)$$
$$G_n = gY^e$$
$$A_n = \frac{1}{j} Y_n{}^e$$
$$O_n = \bar{O} + (g - t) \sum_{N=0}^{N=n-1} Y_N{}^e$$
$$D_n = dO_n$$
$$M_n = O_n - D_n$$
$$I_n = b(1 - t)Y_{n-1}^e + uM - qD_n$$

where D is government debt, M is money, and d is the fraction of total government obligations D held in the form of debt.   The coefficient j corresponds to s in the required-rate system, and both will be equal in equilibrium.   From this system we obtain

$$Y_n{}^e = \frac{b(1 - b)}{t - g + (1 - t) - w/j} Y_{n-1}^e$$
$$+ \frac{[w + u(1 - d) - qd]\left[\bar{O} + (g - t) \sum_{N=0}^{N=n-1} Y_N{}^e\right]}{t - g + \alpha(1 - t) - w/j}$$

As for the required rate system given in p. 551, note †, this approach may be applied to compute the level of income for successive periods.   As noted before, new initial values for the difference equation result for each period, and a general solution is not readily feasible.

[1] As shown on p. 538, this is a dubious assumption.

that the optimal rate of growth is determined by market choice, and in accordance with consumer preference as reflected in the supply of saving at any given rate of interest or efficiency of investment. If this argument is granted for a system without budget, it may be extended also to a system with a budget. The budget of the Distribution Branch is again used to establish the proper state of distribution, which in turn will affect the supply of saving and the resulting rate of growth. At the same time, the supply of saving continues to be determined by consumer choice. While distribution policy affects all aspects of allocation, the resource use that results still reflects consumer choice based on the desired state of distribution. The budget of the Allocation Branch is again balanced on a pay-as-you-use basis,[1] and its taxes are allocated (in our ideal system, at least) according to consumer preferences. Goods and services provided by the Allocation Branch may meet social wants of a current sort, or they may satisfy future social wants. The requirement that such services reflect consumer preferences is equally applicable (or subject to equal objections) in both cases.[2] Thus, we may conclude that the rate of growth in the classical system is determined in accordance with consumer preferences, even though a budget is allowed for.

There is no such simple answer once we step outside the bounds of the classical system and consider a possible divergence between the required and the expenditure rates of growth. Let us suppose, first, that all government obligations are in the form of money, and assume that the expenditure rate falls short of the required rate. Various adjustments may be made in budget parameters to secure balanced growth; and depending on which adjustment is chosen, balanced growth will be reached at a higher or lower rate.[3] In choosing the proper adjustment, two criteria may be applied. One is that public policy should attempt to honor the required rate, since this is the rate that would prevail if investment in the private sector were always adjusted to match intended saving. Depending on the circumstances of the case, an increase in g rather than a reduction in t might be required. Another criteria is that the proper values of g and γ should be determined by considerations of the Allocation Branch, so that all stabilizing adjustments must be in t. Thus it appears that it may not be possible to satisfy both criteria at the same time.

If liquidity policy is added to the picture, a gap between required and expenditure rates may be closed by adjustments in the liquidity structure; and changes in this structure may serve to raise or lower the rate at which balanced growth proceeds. Stabilization policy gains an additional degree of freedom. The proper level of g may be maintained, and the

[1] See pp. 16 and 558.
[2] See p. 86.
[3] See p. 490.

dilemma of the preceding paragraph may be avoided. However, it now becomes doubtful whether the required rate should be honored. The level of saving, and hence the required rate of growth, now depend upon the prevailing level and structure of claims, both of which are the result of public policy decision rather than consumer choice. The concept of a market-determined rate of growth breaks down in the compensatory system, and it becomes exceedingly difficult to establish a clear-cut standard of what constitutes an efficient rate of growth. This rate must be determined through the political process, as the satisfaction of social wants in the classical system is determined. However, the latter poses a simpler problem. The verification of social wants through the political process is more or less analogous to the verification of private wants in the market, both being based on the preferences of individual consumers, weighed by the given distribution of income.[1] Determination of the proper rate of growth in the compensatory system involves the additional policy parameter of setting the prevailing liquidity structure and thereby affecting the level of planned saving for any given level and distribution of income. While stabilization policy can take care of instability, it does not return the system to the automatic purity of the classical model.

[1] See pp. 9 and 86.

CHAPTER 23

Classical theory of public debt

Before proceeding with the discussion of debt policy as a stabilization device, let us pause to examine what may be called the classical aspects of debt theory, that is, the use of debt policy to serve objectives of the Allocation and the Distribution Branches. This is *the* problem of debt policy in a system where no stabilization is required. In a more realistic setting, allocation and distribution objectives cannot be divorced from the stabilization function. Indeed, they may prove incompatible with the latter. We shall consider internal debt first, leaving external debt for later examination.

A. INTERNAL DEBT IN THE CLASSICAL SYSTEM

In the classical system all private income is spent on either consumption or investment. Full employment is secured automatically. Price-level stability is maintained if the money supply is held stable or is increased at the same rate at which real income grows. In this setting there is no need for compensatory finance. Loan finance is as effective as tax finance in reducing aggregate demand, and debt retirement is as effective as goods and service expenditures of government in expanding demand. What role, then, can be assigned to public debt policy in such a system?[1]

The choice between tax and loan finance remains important because it determines the way in which the resource withdrawal from the private sector will be divided between consumption and capital formation. Let us define the classical system as one in which saving is a function of dis-

---

[1] For a somewhat similar discussion see James M. Buchanan, *Public Principles of Public Debt*, Richard D. Irwin, Inc., Homewood, Ill., 1958. Buchanan's volume became available after compilation of this manuscript and is not dealt with here.

posable income as well as of interest. If the savings schedule is wholly inelastic to interest while the investment schedule is elastic, the entire resource withdrawal under loan finance will be from private capital formation. Private savings will be absorbed in part by public borrowing. Private investment will fall and the interest rate will rise, but saving and hence consumption will remain unchanged. Tax finance will result in a withdrawal from both private capital formation and consumption, depending on the taxpayers' marginal propensity to consume.[1]

If the savings schedule is interest-elastic while the investment schedule is wholly inelastic, the entire resource withdrawal for loan finance will be from private consumption. The rate of interest will rise until saving increases by the amount of public borrowing. Tax finance must give the same result since investment remains unchanged. If both the saving and investment schedules are interest elastic, the resource withdrawal will be spread between consumption and capital formation for both types of finance. The more interest elastic saving is, and the less elastic investment is, the smaller the share contributed by capital formation will be. However, the share contributed by consumption will be larger in the case of tax finance than in the case of loan finance.

The result depends, moreover, on the type of expenditures the government makes. If the government spends for investment, resource withdrawal will be more from private capital formation, provided that government investment enters into the same total investment schedule as does private investment. Government investment will then drive down the rate of interest and lower saving. However, government investment may raise the share contributed by private investment, if the public investment does not draw on the same investment outlets but raises the efficiency of private investment.[2]

The choice between loan finance and tax finance thus involves a choice between a resource withdrawal largely from private capital formation and one largely from private consumption. A fiscal policy designed to accentuate growth relies on tax finance, while a policy designed to support present consumption relies on loan finance. If regulation of the rate of growth is considered a function of budget policy, such regulation is the

---

[1] For convenience we shall assume a lump-sum tax, so that substitution effects need not be considered.

[2] The same general principles apply, but the details differ, for a primitive classical system in which saving is a function of the rate of interest only. If government expenditures are for consumption, resource withdrawal through taxation must always come out of private consumption. Since the rate of interest is not changed by the imposition of the tax, private saving remains unchanged, as does private investment. The results for borrowing depend again on the elasticities of the investment and saving schedules: and as before, the results may differ if government expenditures are for investment.

crucial consideration in the choice between loan and tax finance. However, this is not the case in the classical system. Here the rate of growth may be determined by consumer preference between present and future consumption, and by the return on capital that is obtained in the market.[1] The government's choice between loan and tax finance is to be made as a part of this process; the purpose is not to interfere with the market-determined rate of growth, but to align the choice between present and future satisfaction of social wants, with the choice between present and future satisfaction of private wants.

Our argument has been that the budget of the Allocation Branch should be balanced, since the opportunity cost of resource withdrawal must be allocated to the individuals whose wants are satisfied; but we have also noted that annual balance was not necessary, since the cost of durable goods or of lasting services should be allocated over their useful life.[2] We must now consider more carefully just when loan finance is called for in the budget of the Allocation Branch.

Pay-as-you-use Finance

Let us suppose that people want to provide for the satisfaction of certain social wants involving initial capital expenditures. The facilities may be durable consumer goods such as playgrounds, capital goods such as highways, or productivity-increasing services such as investment in education. In these cases, present expenditures will provide for future benefits. Where the initial outlay is large, taxpayers may not wish to assume the entire cost at once and may prefer to pay over the years as the services of the new facility are enjoyed. This reflects the same motivation underlying the purchase of a house on a mortgage or of an automobile on an installment basis. The option of pay-as-you-use finance increases the flexibility of consumer budgeting and adds to the efficiency of private finance. Precisely the same results occur in public finance. The question is only how the principle can be implemented at the public level.

Matters are simple enough if we assume that there is a continuous stream of capital outlays. In such a case, tax finance of new projects becomes equivalent to pay-as-you-use finance of old projects. This solution is not open if we consider the financing of a single and discontinuous project. Here we are confronted with the inevitable fact that provision of a durable facility requires the full resource input in the *initial* period. Resources must be withdrawn from other uses, thus giving rise to a current opportunity cost that the community must assume at once. There is no escape from this, whatever the sources of internal finance. The government's internal borrowing, unlike external borrowing, does not increase

---

[1] See p. 553.

[2] See p. 16.

the supply of resources available to the group as a whole. It cannot obviate the need for releasing resources from other uses.

However, it makes a difference whether this release is from present consumption or from capital formation. The immediate burden of a heavy public outlay in terms of current consumption is cushioned if the resources are withdrawn from private capital formation. This is accomplished by the use of loan finance. In a perfect system, with rational taxpayer behavior and a pure credit market, it will be equally advantageous for the government to use tax or loan finance. If the taxpayer wishes to spread his burden, he may secure a tax or consumer loan and thus obtain command over resources that otherwise would have gone into capital formation. The outcome will be similar to that of public loan finance, the only difference being that private rather than public debt is issued. In the real world, where credit facilities are not available on equal terms to all taxpayers, this equality does not apply. Public loan finance may then be thought of as a means of enabling individual taxpayers to secure tax credit at equal terms. By placing payment on a pay-as-you-use basis, loan finance remains a significant instrument of policy, even though it does not increase the total availability of resources.[1] By the nature of the pay-as-you-use principle public debt issued for such purposes should be repaid as the benefits from the initial expenditure are being exhausted. The principle is the same as for consumer credit on the private level.

Proceeding on this basis, we may draw up a budget statement that divides the budget accounts into a current and a capital part.[2] This is illustrated in Table 23-1. The current budget should be tax-financed. On the expenditure side, we include expenditures to provide goods and services, the benefits from which accrue currently. Also we include an

[1] This fact seems to be overlooked by A. C. Pigou, *A Study in Public Finance*, 3d ed., Macmillan & Co., Ltd., London, 1951, p. 38, who argues that there can be no transfer of costs by internal borrowing because the resource use must occur at once. However, in his *Political Economy of War*, 2d ed., Macmillan & Co., Ltd., London, 1940, chap. 7, Pigou notes that in the case of war finance the future is burdened if the "real war fund" is drawn from capital formation. This, precisely, is the central point of our argument.

[2] Out of a considerable literature on capital budgets, see Erik Lindahl, *Studies in the Theory of Money and Capital*, Rinehart & Company, Inc., New York, 1939, pp. 367–384; Gunnar Myrdal, "Fiscal Policy in the Business Cycle," *American Economic Review*, vol. 29, Supplement, no. 1, pp. 183–193, March, 1939; Benjamin Higgins and R. A. Musgrave, "Deficit Finance: The Case Examined," *Public Policy*, Harvard University Press, Cambridge, Mass., 1941, vol. II, pp. 193–203; *Budgetary Structure and Classification of Government Accounts*, United Nations, Department of Public Information, New York, 1951; J. R. Hicks, *The Problem of Budgetary Reform*, Oxford University Press, New York, 1948; J. A. Maxwell, "The Capital Budget," *Quarterly Journal of Economics*, vol. 57, pp. 450–465, 1942–1943; Richard Goode and Eugene A. Birnbaum, "Government Capital Budgets," *International Monetary Fund Staff Papers*, vol. 5, pp. 23–46, February, 1956.

allowance for the current use of benefits purchased in past periods. This includes amortization charges against government assets, as well as against private assets created by past public services. Moreover, we include interest on funds borrowed for this purpose, thus allowing for the cost of placing payment on a pay-as-you-use basis.

TABLE 23-1. BUDGET FOR PAY-AS-YOU-USE FINANCE
(In dollars)

Current budget			
Taxes	83	Expenditures for current benefits...	75
Deficit	17	Interest	5
		Amortization	20
		Surplus	0
Total	100	Total	100

Capital budget			
Amortization	20	Expenditures for future benefits:	
Sale of assets	3	Resulting in acquisition of assets	18
Net borrowing	24	Not resulting in acquisition of assets	12
Net increase in provision for future benefits	0	Net decrease in provision for future benefits	17
Total	47	Total	47

The capital budget is to be loan-financed. On the expenditure side we include the cost of providing for goods and services, the benefits from which will accrue in the future. These expenditures may result in the acquisition of assets by government, such as buildings or highways; or they may create private assets, such as educational training. Either outlay provides for future benefits and is included. On the revenue side of the capital budget, we record charges against the provision for future benefits. These include amortization charges as recorded in the current budget, the sale of assets held by government, and proceeds from the sale of government debt. The last two items both absorb funds that otherwise would have been channeled into private investment.

The state of balance in the budget, as recorded in Table 23-1, is not in accord with pay-as-you-use finance. Tax receipts in the current budget fall short of the provision for current benefits. This deficit in the current budget reappears as a net decrease in the provision for future benefits in the capital budget. Unless justified by certain other considerations, a deficit or surplus in the current budget is not compatible with efficient budgeting.[1]

---

[1] Notwithstanding this lack of balance in the provision for future benefits, note that total cash outgo, or payments to the public, equals total cash inflow (including proceeds from borrowing) from the public. This will hold if total payments are to remain unchanged, since we are dealing with a classical system.

Now it is important to note that the deficit in the current budget, or the decrease in the provision for future benefits in the capital budget, does *not* equal the change in the net worth of the government. Using the same figures as before, a budget statement designed to equate deficit with reduction in the government's net worth would look as follows:

TABLE 23-2. BUDGET FOR NET-WORTH APPROACH
(In dollars)

Current budget			
Taxes	83	Expenditures not resulting in acqui-	
Deficit	29	sition of assets	87
		Interest	5
		Amortization	20
Total	112	Total	112

Capital budget			
Amortization	20	Expenditures resulting in acquisi-	
Sale of assets	3	tion of assets	18
Net borrowing	24	Decrease in net worth	29
Increase in net worth	0		
Total	47	Total	47

Table 23-2 differs from Table 23-1 in that expenditures which provide for future benefits without involving the acquisition of assets are now recorded in the current budget. As a result, the balance shows the change in the government's net worth, defined as assets minus liabilities.[1]

This formulation of the capital budget implies the proposition that a sound budget policy is one that does not permit net worth to fall; and that changes in net worth are the significant factor in determining the proper state of budgetary balance. This proposition is based on an analogy to the finances of the private firm, an analogy that is applicable only for the

[1] This seems to be the approach followed in the budget system recommended by the United Nations, *Budgetary Structure and Classification of Government Accounts*, p. 15, where capital expenditures are defined as the purchase of assets with a long life expectancy. At the same time, the UN statement holds (p. 14) that "there is neither a conceptual nor an institutional link between the capital account and borrowing for purposes of asset acquisition." If this is the case, there is no reason for separating the balance of the current budget from the balance for the total budget. The determination of capital costs involved in particular expenditure projects and the administration of government assets may be accomplished without an over-all division of the budget into a current and a capital budget, and without singling out the state of balance in the current budget. If the division *is* made, its usefulness must derive from the policy significance of the concept of surplus or deficit used in the current budget. This is the crucial point in interpreting any budget statement. See my "The Nature of Budgetary Balance and the Case for the Capital Budget," *American Economic Review*, vol. 29, no. 2, pp. 260–271, June, 1939.

special case of public enterprises but not for the general type of budgetary activity.   In order to be solvent, a private corporation must have assets that will match its debt.   If assets increase, debt can be increased, but not otherwise.   Applying this reasoning to the government, one is tempted to conclude that borrowing in the capital budget is sound, while borrowing in the current budget is unsound.   This is a fallacy that over-looks the essentially different nature of government and business firms.

The purpose of business finance is to increase net worth, but this is not the case for government finance.   Assets held by the firm are the collateral against the firm's debt, but no such reasoning applies to government assets.   The solvency of government depends on the productive powers of the economy and on the taxable capacity that they comprise. Government-held assets have little, if anything, to do with the matter. While the net-worth approach might serve to sell businessmen on the idea of unbalanced budgets, this is a point in fiscal politics rather than economics.[1]

As far as the economics of the matter are concerned, focus on the acquisition of assets as a criterion of budget planning only serves to disturb the proper allocation of budgetary resources.   It encourages the cement-and-steel concept of economic development and reinforces the ancient prejudice in favor of expenditures on hardware as distinct from services, a prejudice dating back to the physiocrats and Adam Smith's misleading use of the terms *productive* and *unproductive*.   The resulting damage to budget planning is especially serious in underdeveloped economies, where basic services are of primary importance, but the damage is by no means limited to such places.   It is only too frequent, in United States municipal finances, that elaborate school structures can be built on debt issue, while no adequate funds for teachers' salaries can be secured, since tax finance is required.

Notwithstanding a superficial similarity between the pay-as-you-use approach and the net-worth approach, the underlying philosophies are totally different.   The former approach presents a legitimate, if some-what subtle, argument for loan finance in the provision of future benefits. The latter is based on a falacious analogy, and distorts fiscal planning. Since it is difficult in practice to separate the two approaches, great care must be taken if the pay-as-you-use approach is to be formalized in a double budget system.

Intergeneration Equity

The general principle of pay-as-you-use finance gains in importance if we allow for the fact that facilities provided for by government will be

[1] Such implications may be found in many places—for instance, in the previously noted paper by Myrdal.

used frequently by several generations of taxpayers. This is particularly true in municipal finance, where the composition of the resident group is subject to more or less frequent change. Here the principle of pay-as-you-use finance follows directly from that of benefit taxation, and loan finance is required to distribute costs among the various generations.

To illustrate the point, consider a project whose services become available in equal installments over three periods. Also, suppose that the life (or residency) span of each generation covers three periods, and that the population is stable. Finally, assume that loans advanced by any one generation must be repaid within its life span. In each period the benefits accrue to three generations, including generations 1, 2, 3 in the first period; 2, 3, 4 in the second; and 3, 4, 5 in the third period. To contribute their proper share, generations 1 and 5 should each pay $\frac{1}{9}$ of the cost; generations 2 and 4 should each pay $\frac{2}{9}$; and generation 3 should pay $\frac{3}{9}$. Let us now suppose that the total cost is $100, and that it is to be allocated accordingly. To simplify matters, we will disregard the allocation of interest cost.[1]

The entire outlay of $100 must be raised and spent in the first period. Of this, $33.3 is obtained by taxation, divided equally between generations 1, 2, and 3. The remainder is obtained by loans from generations 2 and 3. There can be no loans from generation 1 owing to our rule that each generation must be repaid during its life span. In the second period, tax revenue is again $33.3, contributed now by generations 2, 3, and 4; the debt held by generation 2 is retired in full, and loans of $16.6 are advanced by generation 4 to retire part of the debt held by generation 3. In the third period, the tax revenue of $33.3 is contributed by generations 3, 4, and 5. It is used to retire the remainder of the debt held by generations 3 and 4. In retrospect, the total cost has been divided between the five generations in accordance with benefits received. Loan finance in this case not only provided credit to taxpayers but resulted in a bona fide division of the cost between generations—a result impossible to secure through tax finance.[2]

Concerning the change in resource allocation in the private sector, let

---

[1] The interest will be divided between the generations in proportion to their share in the postponement of payment, so that $\frac{1}{4}$ is contributed by generations 2 and 4 each, while 3 pays $\frac{1}{2}$.

[2] Note that this financing pattern does not involve tax discrimination between generations. The tax in any one period applies alike to the members of all generations living. While the schedule of debt transactions in each period involves a distinction between generations, our scheme does not necessitate the use of bonds that are non-transferable among generations. Rather, the government can borrow and retire debt independent of the particular holder. The general pattern of Table 23-2 comes about on its own accord, provided that each generation consumes its assets while still present.

TABLE 23-3. INTERGENERATION EQUITY THROUGH LOAN FINANCE
(In dollars; figures rounded)

Period	Source of funds*	Payments for each generation					Total payments in period
		1	2	3	4	5	
1	Taxes............	11.1	11.1	11.1	†	†	33.3
	Loans............	.....	33.3	33.3	†	†	66.7
	Repayments.....	.....	......	......	†	†	
	ΔC............	−8.3	−8.3	−8.3	†	†	−25.0
	ΔI............	−2.8	−36.1	−36.1	†	†	−75.0
2	Taxes............	†	11.1	11.1	11.1	†	33.3
	Loans............	†	......	......	16.6	†	16.6
	Repayments.....	†	33.3	16.6	......	†	49.9
	ΔC............	†	−8.3	−8.3	−8.3	†	−25.0
	ΔI............	†	30.5	13.8	−19.4	†	25.0
3	Taxes............	†	†	11.1	11.1	11.1	33.3
	Loans............	†	†				
	Repayments.....	†	†	16.6	16.6	.....	33.3
	ΔC............	†	†	−8.3	−8.3	−8.3	−25.0
	ΔI............	†	†	13.8	13.8	−2.8	25.0
1–3	Taxes............	11.1	22.2	33.3	22.2	11.1	100.0
	Loans............	.....	33.3	33.3	16.6	.....	83.2
	Repayments.....	.....	33.3	33.3	16.6	.....	83.2
	ΔC............	−8.3	−16.7	−25.0	−16.7	−8.3	−75.0
	ΔI............	−2.8	−5.5	−8.4	−5.5	−2.8	−25.0

* ΔC indicates change in consumption.
ΔI indicates change in investment.
† Unborn or deceased.

us assume that 75 per cent of tax receipts comes from consumption, and 25 per cent from saving. Since we are dealing with a system in which planned saving is matched by investment, the latter fraction is reflected in reduced capital formation in the private sector. Moreover, we assume that saving is inelastic to interest, so that the full amount of government borrowing is withdrawn from private capital formation. Repayment of government debt is reflected similarly in increased capital formation in the private sector. As shown in the last column of Table 23-3, we find private consumption reduced by $25 for each period, thus reflecting the principle of pay-as-you-use finance. Private capital formation is reduced by $75 in the first period and increased by $25 for each of the following periods. The net reduction in private capital formation for all periods as a whole equals $25. Thus the total cost is divided between consumption and capital formation in accordance with the marginal propensity to consume. This is true since we assume that saving is not elastic to interest. If interest elasticity is allowed for, the insertion of government demand in the loan market, by driving up the rate of interest, may lead to an increase in the rate of saving, with a corresponding transfer of part of the cost to private consumption.

Old-age Insurance

As far as the structure of the capital budget is concerned, the considerations of intergeneration equity lead to the same principles as those which underlie Table 23-1 and need not be repeated. However, one case of intergeneration equity, which has received special attention since the thirties, should be noted. This is the financing of a system of old-age insurance in which insurance benefits and contributions are on a strictly contributory and quid pro quo basis.

In such a plan, those who are aged when the system is introduced should receive no benefits since they have not contributed in the past; those who are middle-aged at the time of introduction should receive some benefits when they retire, since they have contributed for part of their working lives; but the full benefits should become available only to those who are at the beginning of their working lives when the plan is introduced. This requires contributions in excess of benefit payments for the early years, until a situation is reached where everyone has contributed over his entire working life. At that time, receipts from current taxes and interest in the reserve account will come into balance with benefit payments, and the system will be on a pay-as-you-go basis. The difficulty lies with the earlier period in which receipts are in excess of payments.[1]

These excess receipts may be hoarded, used to store goods, or invested. The first procedure would not accomplish the desired objective but would merely give rise to the inequities of price-level change. The second procedure would meet the requirement that those of working age should contribute while the aged should receive no benefits; nevertheless, it would be an absurd solution. Quite apart from storage cost and deterioration, the goods thus set aside would be lost to the community forever. Putting it differently, such a plan would fail to realize the earnings that might be derived by investing the resources set aside. The third and proper solution, therefore, is to return the initial surplus to the capital

[1] On the general problem of financing old-age insurance, see A. W. Willcox, "The Old-age Reserve Account: A Problem in Government Finance," *Quarterly Journal of Economics*, vol. 51, no. 3, p. 460, May, 1937; Seymour Harris, *Economics of Social Security*, McGraw-Hill Book Company, Inc., New York, 1941, chap. 9, pp. 199–227; Alan T. Peacock, *The Economics of National Insurance*, W. Hodge, London, 1952; and Ida C. Merriam, *Social Security Financing*, Federal Security Agency, Bureau Report no. 17, Washington, 1952, chap. 2, pp. 32–52.

market and to credit a reserve account or trust fund with the assets thus purchased.

As a result, resources are transferred from consumption to capital formation in the initial period; future income of the reserve fund will be supplemented by a corresponding capital income on this initial investment. Those of working age when the plan is introduced can be called upon to contribute the full amount of their future benefit, adjusted to an actuarial basis and discounted to its present value in the initial period. As the system matures, the contributions of those of working age, together with the capital income of the reserve account, will pay the benefits of the aged. At this point, a pay-as-you-go basis is achieved. The rate of tax required to finance the matured system will henceforth be less than it would be if a pay-as-you-go plan had been followed from the beginning. This is true because the income of the system is supplemented by the earnings obtained from the reserve. Throughout, the principle of intergeneration equity is complied with.

The principle remains the same whether the surplus of the initial period is returned to the capital market through government lending or whether it is used to retire government debt held by the public. In the latter case, government debt is shifted from the public to the reserve fund or trust account. According to the assumption of the classical system, funds made available through either channel flow into private investment. Thus, the effect of debt retirement on capital formation is the same as it would be if direct investments were made by the government. In the one case, the reserve fund receives income from private assets; in the other, it receives interest on public debt. Assuming the yield on government and on comparable private securities to be similar, the combined tax rate (that is, the rate for retirement contributions plus the rate of tax required to finance interest on public debt) will be the same in both cases. The taxes needed to finance interest payments to the reserve fund would have been needed otherwise to finance interest payments on public debt held outside the reserve fund.

Similarly, the principle remains the same if the surplus from the insurance operation is used to finance expenditures that otherwise would have been financed by borrowing. In the efficient system, it makes no difference whether new debt is issued to the reserve fund rather than to the public, or whether outstanding debt is transferred from the public to the reserve fund. However, the result differs if, as a matter of fiscal politics, the additional receipt *causes* an increase in public expenditures that otherwise would not have occurred.

These considerations apply to an insurance scheme that is on a strictly contributory basis. If the present aged are to receive benefit payments when the plan is introduced, a contribution from the general budget is required.   If the coverage of the scheme by occupations is comprehensive, the resulting transfer is between generations only; if the coverage is limited, a wider set of transfers is involved.   Where the relationship between tax and benefit formulas is such as to involve redistribution between income groups, as is the case with the United States system, the application of the contributory principle is limited to begin with, and objections to the initial inclusion of the aged are reduced accordingly.

Loan Finance to Adjust Distribution

So far we have been concerned with the use of loan finance in the budget of the Allocation Branch.   We shall now turn to an application in the context of the Distribution Branch.   Under conditions of war economy, it may be necessary for reasons of economic policy to secure a sharp reduction in consumption.   This may render it necessary to obtain a larger share of total proceeds from the lower-income groups than seems desirable on grounds of distributional considerations.   If so, wartime withdrawals may be arranged so as to provide for a subsequent adjustment after the war.   Wartime withdrawals from the lower-income groups may take the form of refundable taxes or forced loans, to be repaid subsequently by transfers from the upper-income groups.[1]   Thus loan finance may serve as a means of intertemporal redistribution between income brackets, as well as a means of intertemporal shifts between generations.

Loan Finance to Reduce Tax Friction

Let us now turn to still another function of loan finance–minimizing fluctuations in the level of tax rates due to fluctuations in the level of public expenditures.   The avoidance of fluctuations in tax rates may be desirable because changes in rates introduce an element of uncertainty that is disruptive.   More important, intermittant loan finance may be desirable where frictional effects of taxation become an increasingly serious problem as the level of taxation (the ratio of tax yield to income) rises.   If we assume that friction rises at an increasing rate with the level of taxation, friction may be reduced over the years if a fairly stable rate of taxation can be maintained.   This requires the use of loan finance.

At the level of state and local finance, the case of nonrecurrent, extraordinary expenditures largely coincides with that of lumpy outlays on durable goods.   The objective of using loan finance so as to reduce tax friction thus supplements the objective of achieving intergeneration equity.   At the level of national government, the most important case of extraordinary expenditure needs is that of war finance.   Not only is this the most striking case of temporarily high expenditure needs, but also

[1] See the previous reference (p. 250) to Keynes's scheme for war finance.

the emergency setting of war economy accentuates the need for avoiding detrimental incentive effects. Effects on work incentives in particular tend to be less detrimental in response to loan finance than in response to taxation.[1]

Loan finance, unless wholly compulsory, is more flexible in its adaptation to the capacities of the individual contributors than is tax finance. Moreover, there is an asymmetry in the accounting rules of lenders and taxpayers; lenders find their net worth unchanged after making a loan, while taxpayers fail to reduce their net worth by the present value of the future burden of debt service. Considerable reliance on borrowing is thus a proper and inevitable instrument of war finance. Moreover, loan finance serves to reduce private capital formation, whereas taxes fall more heavily on consumption. Thus there occurs some degree of burden transfer to future generations, even though the resource input for war production cannot be postponed. However, this consideration is of secondary importance, since the war economy is usually one in which direct controls of private investment are required, and the logic of the classical system is suspended.

Considerations such as these lend some validity to the argument for dividing the budget into an "ordinary" and an "extraordinary" part, and for requiring tax finance of the former only. However, the validity is limited indeed. By the logic of the case, the extraordinary budget must be balanced over a longer period, matching a surplus when expenditures are unusually low with a deficit when they are unusually high. Since it is difficult to determine what is usual or unusual, the institution of the extraordinary budget is open to abuse; and where such budgets have been used, the result has generally been detrimental. The rule that ordinary expenditures must be tax-financed leads, in times of stringency, to curtailment of precisely those expenditures that are most basic to governmental functions, as well as to overexpansion of outlays that may claim classification as extraordinary.

Indeed, it may well be argued that the entire concept of the extraordinary budget involves an inherent fallacy. If it is the objective to stabilize the level of tax rates, it does not follow that ordinary outlays should be tax-financed while extraordinary outlays should be loan-financed, but rather that a fraction of *total* financing should be loan-financed when *total* expenditures are unusually high, and that there should be debt retirement when they are unusually low. Thus the logic of the argument points to the planning of total annual budgets in the context of, say, a ten-year budget rather than to a division of annual budgets into an ordinary and an extraordinary part. This bears some

[1] See p. 250.

similarity to the proposal, made in the context of the compensatory setting, that the budget should be balanced over the cycle.[1]

Loan Finance of Self-liquidating Projects

Let us now consider the use of loan finance for self-liquidating projects. Self-liquidating projects may be defined narrowly as investments in public enterprises that provide a fee or sales income sufficient to service the debt incurred in their financing; or they may be defined broadly as expenditure projects that increase future income and the tax base. Such projects permit servicing (interest and amortization) of the debt incurred in their financing without requiring an increase in the future level of tax rates.

Public Enterprise. Self-liquidating investments of the narrower type are a special case where an analogy to business finance is appropriate. Public enterprises may be considered part of the private rather than public sector of the economy. The initial outlay cannot be financed by the advance collection of fees. As in private investment, the required capital is obtained properly on a loan basis and must be amortized out of subsequent sales proceeds. This procedure is in compliance with pay-as-you-use finance as well as intergeneration equity. Thus there is good reason for separating the accounts of public enterprises from the general budget. However, a link is provided by enterprise losses that appear as a subsidy on the expenditure side of the current sector of the general budget, and by enterprise profits that appear on the revenue side as an excise tax.[2] Notwithstanding the separation of basic accounts, the enterprise and general budgets may be combined subsequently in an over-all budget, which in turn may be divided into a current and a capital account.

Reproductive Expenditures. Self-liquidating investments of the broader type do not permit this analogy to business finance. Nevertheless, they provide for future benefits; thus the arguments for pay-as-you-use finance and intergeneration equity apply. Moreover, taxable income is increased in the future so that the debt may be retired without an increase in tax rates, or with a lesser increase than would be needed for immediate tax finance. Thus, loan finance of outlays that raise the future level of taxable income is sustained on grounds of tax friction as well as considerations of intergeneration equity. Expenditures for resource development offer a good illustration. The loan finance of outlays that provide for future benefits but do not raise the level of future taxable income involves justification by intergeneration equity only—as, for instance, in the construction of playgrounds. While the benefits thus

---

[1] See p. 523.

[2] For a general discussion of the relationship between enterprise accounts and general budget, see J. R. Hicks, *The Problem of Budgetary Reform*, Oxford University Press, New York, 1948.

provided for increase future real income, this income is not imputed to the tax base.

The Capital-formation Approach

A final view of the capital budget is focused on the contribution of budget policy to total capital formation, public or private, in the economy. For this purpose, the balance of the current budget must be defined to show the net addition (surplus) or reduction (deficit) in capital formation that results.

We shall now record, on the receipt side of the current budget, all receipts drawn from private consumption. This will include varying shares of different taxes, depending on the taxpayers' marginal propensity to consume and on possible substitution effects. In the case of death duties, no revenue is counted, whereas for a spendings tax, a multiple of the yield is entered. On the expenditure side of the current budget we must include public outlays that provide for current services in the nature of consumption. Also, we include amortization of government assets and private-consumption expenditures out of public transfer payments.

On the receipt side of the capital budget we record the surplus from the current budget, amortization charges, and receipts from funds that otherwise would have been channeled into capital formation in the private sector.[1] This includes varying shares of taxes, profits, or borrowing, depending on their origin. On the expenditure side we record government outlays on capital formation whether or not they result in the acquisition of assets, as well as private capital formation out of public transfers. Capital formation in this sense includes provision for durable consumer goods as well as for capital goods that are means of production. However, a division should be made between the two, since only the latter are investments as the term is used in measuring the effects of budget activity upon economic growth.[2]

The existence of a deficit or surplus under the capital-formation approach is of great importance to the fiscal planning of underdeveloped countries, where the contribution to economic growth may be the very focus of budget policy. Indeed, it may well be the most important concept of budgetary balance, next to the totally different concept of net contribution to aggregate demand that arises in the compensatory system. If it can be assumed that tax finance comes largely from consumption, whereas loan finance (drawn from the nonbank public) comes

---

[1] A partial allowance for this point of view is reflected in the United Nations' (*Budgetary Structure and Classification of Government Accounts*, United Nations, Department of Public Information, New York, 1951, p. 41) receipts from death duties in the capital account.

[2] See p. 484.

largely from private capital formation, the requirement of tax finance for current expenditures implies that budget policy should not retard total capital formation.

B. INTERNAL DEBT IN THE COMPENSATORY SYSTEM

We must now inquire how the preceding arguments for debt finance stand up in the more realistic context of a system where liquidity preference exists and where there is no necessary equality between saving and investment at a full-employment income. While the choice between tax and loan finance did not affect the level of aggregate demand in the preceding system, substitution of tax for loan finance now reduces the level of demand. Therefore we must examine how the foregoing argument can be reconciled with the requirements of compensatory finance.[1]

Fixed-investment Model

Let us begin with the extreme case of an economy where saving is inelastic to interest and the level of private investment is fixed. In such a system the proper level of aggregate expenditure must be maintained by stabilization policy.

Since private investment is fixed, any increase in public expenditures must be offset by a corresponding decrease in private expenditures on consumption. If we assume that public borrowing leaves private consumption unchanged, loan finance raises aggregate demand by the same amount as does finance out of new money. Given an initial situation where the budget is adjusted to provide for the proper level of private demand, *any* increase in public expenditure must be accompanied by increased taxation so that $\Delta T = \Delta G/c$, where c is the taxpayers' marginal propensity to consume. This rule applies whether such expenditures are for current services or for capital outlays.

Pay-as-you-use Finance. It follows that borrowing cannot be used as a means of pay-as-you-use finance. Any increase in public goods and service expenditures, whether for current services or durable goods, now requires that there be a corresponding adjustment in taxation. If loan finance is used in the first period, as shown in Table 23-3, prices will rise, and the entire burden falls on generations 1, 2, and 3. If tax proceeds are

---

[1] For a discussion of this problem, see Arthur Smithies, "Federal Budgeting and Fiscal Policies," in Howard S. Ellis (ed.), *Survey of Contemporary Economics*, American Economic Association, Richard D. Irwin, Inc., Homewood, Ill., 1948, pp. 174–210, whose argument is based on the implicit assumption of a fixed-investment model; and Paul A. Samuelson, "Principles and Rules in Modern Fiscal Policy: A Neo-classical Reformation," in *Money, Trade, and Economic Growth: In Honor of John Henry Williams*, The Macmillan Company, New York, 1951, pp. 170ff., who argues that—for the long run, at least, the classical model is more or less applicable.

used in the second period to retire debt, this transaction will cause a reduction in employment and real income rather than secure a transfer out of full-employment income.

By the very nature of the present model, current expenditures of government must come out of a reduction of current consumption in the private sector. Pay-as-you-use finance for the group as a whole is impossible. The rationale of capital budgeting, as shown in Tables 23-1 and 23-3, is inapplicable. There is no logical link, in this case, between the appropriateness of (1) tax or loan finance and (2) the distinction between public expenditures for current benefits and public expenditures for future benefits. There remains a justification for loan finance of public expenditures that raise future taxable income—a justification based on the proposition that it is desirable to avoid temporary changes in tax rate.

Intergeneration Equity. While pay-as-you-use finance is impossible, intergeneration equity may still be applied. To be sure, it cannot be achieved in the present setting through loan finance, but it may be accomplished through a tax-transfer scheme. Let us return to the case of Table 23-3 and the task of allocating the cost of $100 between our five generations; as before, generations 1 and 5, must bear $\frac{1}{9}$ of the cost, while generations 2 and 4 contribute $\frac{2}{9}$, and generation 3 contributes $\frac{3}{9}$. We now obtain the picture of Table 23-4.

In order to reduce consumption by $100 in the first period, and assuming the marginal propensity to consume at $\frac{3}{4}$, $133.3 must be paid in taxes. In all subsequent periods tax payments and transfers must cancel so as to maintain total consumption unchanged. For the three periods as a whole, the reduction of consumption of $100 is divided between the five generations in the required proportions, as is the net-tax bill of $133.3. While intergeneration equity cannot be secured through loan finance, it can be secured through a tax and transfer scheme. However, this is subject to the condition that consumers respond to refundable taxes as if they were outright taxes, and to the refund as if it were an addition to income. If such taxes and refunds are considered loans, without effect on current consumption, intergeneration equity does not work.

Old-age Insurance. Similar difficulties arise in the financing of old-age security. Lending out the surplus or retirement of public debt in the initial period will not raise the level of private investment. Whatever is done with the surplus, an excess of receipts over payments reduces aggregate demand and necessitates expansionary fiscal measures somewhere else. Such measures may take the form of reduced taxation or increased expenditures. In both cases the decrease in publicly held debt owing to reserve finance must be offset fully, or nearly so, by new borrowing needed to finance an additional deficit in the general budget.

TABLE 23-4. INTERGENERATION EQUITY THROUGH TAX-TRANSFER PLAN
(In dollars; figures rounded)

Period	Source of funds*	Payments for each generation					Total payments in period
		1	2	3	4	5	
1	Taxes........	14.8	59.2	59.2	†	†	133.3
	Transfers....	......	......	......	†	†	
	ΔC........	−11.1	−44.4	−44.4	†	†	−100.0
2	Taxes........	†	......	......	29.6	†	33.4
	Transfers....	†	29.6	......	......	†	33.4
	ΔC........	†	22.2	......	−22.2	†	
3	Taxes........	†	†	......	......	14.8	14.8
	Transfers....	†	†	14.8	......	......	14.8
	ΔC........	†	†	11.1	......	−11.1	
1–3	Taxes........	14.8	59.2	59.2	29.6	14.8	177.6
	Transfers....	......	29.6	14.8	......	......	44.4
	Net Tax.....	14.8	29.6	44.4	29.6	14.8	133.2
	ΔC........	−11.1	−22.2	−33.3	−22.2	−11.1	100.0

* ΔC indicates change in consumption.
† Unborn or deceased.

Whether publicly held debt is reduced or increased on balance depends on the extent to which private demand is reduced per dollar of insurance contribution, and the extent to which it is increased per dollar of tax reduction or additional public expenditure.

Suppose that the offsetting measure in the initial period is through tax reduction. The resulting benefits will accrue either to the very people who pay the contribution, in which case the transaction cancels or to others, in which case there is a spurious redistribution no less objectionable than a payment of old-age benefits to noncontributors in the initial period.

Suppose, now, that the government offsets the deflationary effect of the initial surplus by increasing goods and service expenditures. In other words, the surplus receipts of the reserve account are used to finance additional expenditures. If such expenditures are for purposes of current consumption, no contribution is made to the solution of our problem.[1] However, something might be accomplished through public capital forma-

---

[1] To the extent that the aged in the initial period are benefited, we may as well start out on a pay-as-you-go basis. To the extent that the benefits accrue to the contributors in the initial period, no resources are surrendered, and the transaction cancels.

tion.   If contributors are called upon to finance public investments in the initial period, the benefits from such investments can be enjoyed by those of working age in the subsequent period.   This second group might then be called upon to pay for such services by sustaining the retirement benefits of the aged, who, as contributors in the preceding period, provided for the second group's benefits.   However, such an approach is workable only within the limits set by the existence of a legitimate demand for durable public goods in the initial period.

Mixed System

In the more realistic intermediary case, changes in the supply of funds have some bearing on the level of investment, with varying degrees of effectiveness, depending on economic conditions at any particular time.

In such a setting, the classical principles of loan finance may be applied, but with qualifications.   While loan finance will affect the level of expenditure, it will not do so on a 1:1 basis.   Returning to Table 23-1, the level of debt transactions must now be higher than it was in the classical model.   In other words, loan finance of additional public expenditures must be supplemented by restrictive liquidity measures so as to obtain the proper release of resources from private capital formation.

In the case of social-security finance, we now find that the net effect of retiring public debt out of tax surplus in the initial period will not be so deflationary as in the fixed-investment model.   Some of the funds paid out in redemption of public debt will be channeled into private investment, but the net effect is likely to remain deflationary.   Some adjustment must be made to offset this.   Policy may move from more to less deflationary types of taxes, thus raising private consumption.   Where this interferes with the objectives of the Distribution Branch, a gain in the equity of allocating retirement cost is traded against a loss in equity in the remainder of the tax structure.   The offset, therefore, must be provided by an expansionary liquidity policy, that is, a substitution of money for debt in the initial period, thus raising private investment.   On balance, reserve finance involves a change in the mix of stabilization policy toward sharper tax and slighter liquidity restriction, thus providing for a consequent shift of resources from private consumption to capital formation.   Reserve finance will be effective only to the extent that this shift can be accomplished.[1]

---

[1] As a practical matter, the choice between the pay-as-you-go and the reserve approach to old-age security might be determined by considerations of fiscal politics rather than fiscal theory.   Thus it can be argued for the reserve approach that the contractual framework of the reserve system protects it against political raids; but it can be argued against the reserve approach that additional tax receipts tend to encourage nonessential additions to expenditures, and that a surplus in the reserve plan makes it more difficult to obtain adequate deficits when needed.

We conclude that the principles of intergeneration equity and reserve finance, while largely inoperative in the fixed-investment model, are not without basis in the mixed system. At the same time, the case is not so clear-cut as in the classical system. For the case of central finance, which must carry the responsibility of stabilization policy, it may be the better part of wisdom to conclude that there should be no association between types of expenditure and the choice between internal loan or tax finance. The capital-budget approach is more generally applicable to the case of local finance, where there is no immediate concern with stabilization policy. Moreover, local borrowing usually involves a draft on external resources.

C. EXTERNAL DEBT

We now turn to the case of external borrowing—either external borrowing by local government or foreign borrowing by national government. The crucial difference between internal and external finance is that the latter permits an import of real resources, thereby enabling the government to provide additional facilities without an immediate reduction in other uses of resources, whether for consumption or capital formation. That is, the realization of opportunity cost is postponed until later, when the debt is serviced and repaid, thus giving rise to an outflow of resources at that time.

Local Finance

All this is of particular importance for borrowing by local governments, because such borrowing is largely in the nature of external borrowing.

Pay-as-you-use finance may now be supplemented by external borrowing, as durable facilities may be provided for without a reduction in other types of domestic capital formation. We have, in this case, a perfect analogy between the individual consumer who increases the volume of immediately available resources through the use of installment credit, and the group that borrows from abroad to provide for capital investment in durable consumer goods. Similarly, intergeneration equity in the provision of durable goods may be implemented by initial finance through external borrowing and by amortization of the debt in line with the accretion of benefits to subsequent generations.

External borrowing, in terms of this reasoning, requires that the capital be obtained from abroad but not that the public facility as such be imported from abroad.[1] If, for example, the internal public expenditure is the local purchase of bricks for a school building, the import results from

---

[1] Capital may be obtained from abroad by selling debt abroad or by selling debt at home to lenders who withdraw the necessary funds from abroad.

the brick producer's expenditures on externally supplied goods and services, or on internally produced goods and services that otherwise would have been exported.

National Finance

Foreign borrowing by national government accomplishes the same import of resources as does external borrowing by local government. Where national government can draw on foreign borrowing, the logic of the capital budget applies with regard to both pay-as-you-use finance and provision for intergeneration equity. This holds even if the domestic setting is more or less similar to that of our fixed-investment model.

However, national borrowing abroad poses a transfer problem in foreign exchange—a problem that does not arise in the case of external borrowing by local government.[1] Borrowing from abroad, especially if put to unproductive use, not only may result in a burdensome drain of resources in subsequent periods when the debt must be serviced, but may also give rise to difficulties in the balance of payment. At the same time, foreign borrowing, if used to secure economic growth, will create the export capacity necessary to service the debt at a future date.[2] The role of foreign borrowing or other forms of capital import is vital in the early stages of economic development. It permits capital formation without reduction in the current level of consumption, which may be close to subsistence standards. It also provides the foreign exchange needed to secure capital equipment that cannot be secured at home. The extent to which budget transactions ease or curtail the scarce supply of foreign exchange thus constitutes another important type of budgetary balance.

Conclusion on Concepts of Balance

In concluding this discussion, it must be emphasized that there is no single type of budgetary management or concept of budgetary balance that serves all purposes of fiscal planning. There are many useful concepts that may be used side by side; there are other concepts that are misleading and should be discarded.

Among the useful concepts, we have noted those associated with pay-as-you-use finance and total capital formation in the economy. Further considerations involve the avoidance of unnecessary changes in tax rates, the finance of self-liquidating expenditures, and the supply of foreign exchange. In the compensatory system, there is the additional concept

---

[1] At the same time, interregional capital movements may result in transfer burdens and gains in the sense of changes in employment or terms of trade associated with resulting changes in the allocation of resources.

[2] See Evsey D. Domar, "Foreign Investment and Balance of Payments," *American Economic Review*, vol. 40, pp. 805–826, December, 1950.

of balance that measures the budget's net contribution to the income scheme—a concept dealt with in preceding chapters, which need not be recalled here. There are other applied concepts, such as a balance that measures financing requirements for purposes of debt management.

Whatever the specific purpose of the concept of balance, the crux of the problem is always the policy meaning of the concept to be used. This must be defined first, and from the definition the detailed grouping of various revenue and expenditure items must be derived.

D. THE BURDEN OF DEBT

The preceding discussion throws some light on the frequently used concept of burden of debt. Assuming that a debt has been incurred in the past, let us consider whether, and in what sense, the existence of such a debt involves a burden.

Wasteful Use of Foreign Loans

The existence of external debt involves a burden for the group as a whole, since resources must be surrendered in servicing it. Taxpayers as a group would be better off if the debt was forgiven. At the same time, the present generation might be better off after allowance for debt service than it would have been without past borrowing. Past investments of the resources thus gained may more than pay for the debt service. By the same token, the present generation will be worse off if past imports have been used for consumption. This is but the counterpart of our earlier conclusion that outside borrowing is a means of transferring resources between generations.

The argument applies to the outside debt of local governments and to the foreign debt of national governments. It does not apply in this form to internally held public debt. The collection of taxes to finance amortization or interest charges on domestically held debt does not reduce the availability of resources for the group as a whole. Yet it does not follow that domestic debt is irrelevant just because its service involves a mere transfer within the group.

Interest as Social Cost

Let us return to a classical model where loan finance curtails the scarce supply of savings available for private capital formation. Here interest on public debt may be considered the opportunity cost of previous earnings from private investment. Debt retirement in turn increases the supply of funds available to private capital formation, provided that the funds are obtained from taxes that reduce consumption.

In this setting, the existence of public debt implies a burden in that

current national income would have been higher if past outlays of government had been tax- rather than loan-financed. The principle is similar to
that observed previously in the use of domestic borrowing to implement
pay-as-you-use finance. At the same time, it does not follow that current
income would be higher had past loan-financed expenditures not been
made. Current income would be higher only if public borrowing served
to finance past consumption, of if public investment was less productive
than private investment would have been.

These considerations do not apply in the fixed-investment model, where
public borrowing does not affect the level of private capital formation.
Here debt service is a distributional phenomenon, which does not involve
a draft on scarce resources. Public debt in this case does not involve an
opportunity cost of previous private investment.

In the mixed model, the significance of public debt is more difficult to
interpret. Loan finance, as distinct from tax finance, may raise the rate
of interest and impair private investment. But the change in private
investment may be a mere fraction of the debt issued. Moreover, the
issuance of debt may be matched by an offsetting increase in money
supply so that the rate of interest remains unchanged.[1] Thus interest
payments on public debt become a price paid for choosing one particular
type of stabilization policy, and cease to be an index of the opportunity
cost incurred in reduced private investment. At the same time, the
choice between tax finance and loan finance retains some bearing on the
level of private investment, and the argument of the classical model
remains applicable to some degree.

Tax Friction

Setting aside, for the moment, the type of cost dealt with in the preceding section, the transfer process of debt service may be burdensome in
another sense: It may cause dislocations in the functioning of the private
sector; or, to put it differently, the transfer process of debt service may
pre-empt taxable capacity, thus forcing budgetary retrenchment along
other lines. This may be readily seen if we visualize a situation where,
say, 90 per cent of taxable income (including national income and interest
payments) is absorbed in taxes needed to finance interest charges; such
taxes may be a multiple of national income. As shown in the discussion
of growth, it is most unlikely that a situation of this type would arise
under peacetime conditions, since an extreme degree of stagnation
would be required.[2] Nevertheless, the problem may arise as the result of
war finance.

---

[1] See p. 527.
[2] See p. 500.

At first sight one might be inclined to argue that tax finance of interest charges creates no problem of tax burden, since any increase in the interest bill also leads to an increase in taxable income and, hence, in the tax base. This proposition implies that tax friction remains unchanged when equal absolute amounts are added to the tax bill and the tax base. The situation differs if we accept the more reasonable hypothesis that tax friction depends on the level of tax *rates*. While the inclusion of interest payments in the tax base lessens the increase in the required level of tax rate, the required rate nevertheless rises as interest payments are increased relative to national income. Thus increased tax friction may result.

TABLE 23-5. INTEREST FINANCE AND TAX BURDEN

Budget items	Economy		
	A	B	C
1. Private expenditures..................................	$70	$100	$100
2. Government goods and service expenditures.............	30		
3. Total expenditures or income.........................	100	100	100
4. Government transfers.................................	...	30	43
5. Taxable income (line 3 + line 4).....................	100	130	143
6. Taxes...	30	30	43
7. Disposable income (line 3 + line 4 − line 6 = line 1)......	70	100	100
8. Tax rate (line 6:line 5) in per cent....................	30	23	30

Let us now consider whether the problem of tax friction is less serious if taxes are used to finance interest payments than if taxes are used to finance goods and service expenditures. Compare economies A and B of Table 23-5. Both have a national income of $100 and government expenditures of $30. In economy A these expenditures are on goods and services, and in economy B they are on interest. Assuming a classical economy where all income is spent, stability of price level requires that the budget be balanced in both cases. In economy A, this involves a tax rate of 30 per cent. In economy B the tax base is larger because interest income is added to earnings; the tax rate is 23 per cent. A comparison between economies A and B suggests that the burden of tax friction is lighter in economy B. This is the case not because the private use of resources is larger in economy B, but because the tax rate is lower. Our conclusion is contingent on the condition that interest payments are taxable; if they are not, the result will be the same in both cases. Putting it differently, the tax rate required with a given level of budget expenditures will be less if these expenditures consist of transfer payments than if they consist of goods and service expenditures. This rule, shown here to hold for the classical system, applies a fortiori in a compensatory setting.[1]

Alternatively, we may compare two economies where the required tax rates are the same. In economy C, government expenditures are again on interest and exceed those of economy A by an amount such as to leave the required rates of tax the same. If tax friction is a function of the rate of tax paid on earned income, the degree of tax friction will be the same in both situations. This is the case even though the ratio of earned income to taxable income is higher in economy A than in economy C.

The friction aspect of debt burden may be avoided if the debt service itself is loan-financed.[2] In the classical system, loan finance of interest payments involves a further draft on the supply of saving and a corresponding transfer of resources from private investment to consumption. Thus the avoidance of friction is accomplished at a cost only. In the fixed-investment model, interest payments may be financed by borrowing of existing funds or by the creation of new money. As an offset, a somewhat higher level of taxation will be called for to maintain the proper level of aggregate demand. Depending on who receives the interest and who pays the additional taxes, a redistribution of income may result, and a rentier class may come into existence, the disadvantages of which must be measured against the gain of reduced tax friction.

---

[1] We must consider the additional fact that goods and service expenditures are fully spent, while transfer payments are not fully respent. Because of this the required level of tax rate in the transfer case is reduced further.

Beginning with a full-employment income Y and a constant average propensity to consume c, compare the tax rate t_g required to offset the level of goods and service expenditures G, with the tax rate t_u required to offset the level of the interest payments U. Holding private investment I constant, we have

$$t_g = \frac{G(1 - c)}{Ic} \quad \text{and} \quad t_u = \frac{U(1 - c)}{I}$$

If $U = G$, we obtain $t_u = ct_g$; hence $t_u < t_g$ for $c < 1$.

[2] See A. P. Lerner, "The Burden of the National Debt," in *Income, Employment and Public Policy: Essays in Honor of Alvin H. Hansen*, W. W. Norton & Company, Inc., New York, 1948, pp. 255–275.

CHAPTER 24

Compensatory aspects of debt policy

We shall now resume our earlier discussion of debt as an instrument of stabilization policy. Deficit or surplus finance, as noted in Chapter 22, involves changes in the level and possibly also in the structure of claims. These changes in claims may affect the level and structure of private expenditures. The expansionary or restrictive effects of a deficit or surplus, therefore, depend on how the deficit is financed and to what uses the surplus is put. Quite apart from the state of deficit or surplus, exchanges between different types of claims—money and various forms of debt—may be used to increase or reduce liquidity and thus affect the level and structure of private expenditures. Stabilization policy thus involves a choice between fiscal and liquidity measures and among various types of measures under each of these categories. In view of these manifold possibilities, what can be said about the "proper" mix of stabilization policy?

In part, this mix is decided upon by considerations of administrative feasibility and by the promptness with which various policies may be adjusted. But this is not all. Various types of stabilization measures, while equally successful in maintaining full employment and price-level stability, may differ significantly in other respects: Incidence or distributional effects, as well as effects upon the rate of growth and other aspects of resource allocation may differ in various stabilization measures. Such differences must be accounted for in choosing the proper mix of stabilization policy.

A. THE PURCHASE OF ILLIQUIDITY

To begin with, let us assume that taxes are to be adjusted so as to provide a given state of budgetary balance; and that a given degree of restriction or expansion in the level of private expenditures is to be accomplished by liquidity policy, a term used here to include monetary as well as debt policy. In Chapter 22 this problem was considered on the assumption that there is a choice between money and consols only. We must now allow for a further choice between different types of public debt. While maintaining a given level of private expenditures or securing a given change, the mix of claims might be made to include more money and less liquid debt, less money and more liquid debt, a larger and less liquid debt, a smaller and more liquid debt, and so forth.

Our immediate problem is to determine what mixture of claims or what changes in that mixture offer the most desirable solution. The appropriate mix of reliance on fiscal and liquidity restriction will be taken up later. All this falls within the enlarged scope of the Stabilization Branch, defined now to include monetary and debt operations, as well as proportional transfers and tax withdrawals.

Criteria of Policy

The government is never forced to borrow in the market or to maintain and service outstanding debt. There is always the option of monetizing the debt, that is, of printing money and purchasing the outstanding obligations. Whether this is done outright or through the open-market operations of the central bank need not concern us now. For purposes of this discussion, both central bank and Treasury are considered integral parts of one and the same public policy. If it is decided not to monetize the debt, there should be a good reason, since the servicing of the debt involves a cost to the government. This cost must be looked upon as the price paid for persuading people not to spend on consumption or private investment but to tie up their funds in the purchase of public assets. This purchase of nonspending, or illiquidity, serves to avoid the inflationary increase in private expenditures that could result if the debt were turned into money. It is this purchase of nonspending, or illiquidity, that is the crux of debt policy.[1]

The principles of purchase policy, which require that the government obtain its materials and services as cheaply as possible, also apply in the present case.[2] An efficient liquidity policy, which term is used to cover monetary as well as debt policy, is one that secures the desired degree of nonspending, or illiquidity, at the least cost. A policy that does not

[1] For a similar emphasis, see Earl R. Rolph, "Principles of Debt Management," *American Economic Review*, vol. 47, no. 3, pp. 302–320, June, 1957; and Jacob Cohen, "A Theoretical Framework for Treasury Debt Management," *American Economic Review*, vol. 45, no. 3, pp. 320–344, June, 1955, and "On the Theory and Measurement of Treasury Interest Saving," *Southern Economic Journal*, vol. 17, no. 3, pp. 257–269, January, 1951.

[2] See p. 46.

meet this requirement is inefficient. Such a policy contains elements of subsidy that are not within the legitimate scope of action for the Stabilization Branch.

The least-cost principle implies no a priori case against liquidity restriction simply because the latter involves a budgetary cost. The distributional effects of debt service enter the picture as one of the factors that determine the incidence of liquidity restriction; and this incidence must be compared with that of alternative methods of restriction when determining the proper mix of stabilization policy. Provided that this consideration is allowed for, increased interest cost is no objection to liquidity restriction.

Nor does the principle of least cost establish a case in favor of such types of debt as can be placed most cheaply per dollar of debt. Given a rising pattern of yield, it will be more expensive for the Treasury to borrow $100 million on a long- than on a short-term basis. This does not mean that borrowing short is the more efficient solution. It may be that the degree of illiquidity, or reduction in private spending, secured by selling $100 million in long-term debt so much exceeds that obtained by borrowing an equal amount in short-term debt that a given outlay in interest cost for long-term debt will secure more illiquidity; such an outlay, however, will involve a smaller total debt than it would for short-term debt. Or, it may pay to place nonmarketable debt at a higher yield than marketable issues, and so forth. More likely than not, the answer lies in a mix of various types of obligations.

Determination of the most efficient mix of public debt thus involves two steps: First, there is the appraisal of market preferences, or the cost at which various types of obligations may be placed. Second, there is the more difficult task of appraising the relative degrees of illiquidity, or nonspending, that are secured by borrowing a given amount through the sale of various types of obligations. Only if both factors are considered can we determine which mix provides the most efficient policy. The problem is similar to that of determining the labor cost of various types of labor as a function of their marginal productivities and wage rates.

The principle of securing the desired degree of illiquidity, or nonspending, at minimum cost is a simple and sensible point of departure for the theory of debt management. At the same time, it must not be permitted to blur the complexities of the problem.

Types of Debt Instruments

In purchasing illiquidity, the government may enter into a wide variety of debt contracts. These may differ with regard to maturity, marketability, and many other features.

Maturity. Most important, perhaps, is the choice between obligations of differing maturity. Classifying claims accordingly, we obtain a spectrum ranging from claims of zero maturity over claims of finite maturity including short- and long-term obligations, to obligations of infinite maturity or consols.   Claims of zero maturity include money, but they also include savings bonds payable at a specified price on demand. Even in the case of finite maturities, the Treasury need not fix a single date at which the debt must mature.   The contract may be drawn so as to fix the maximum maturity date, while an option to terminate earlier is left either to the Treasury, as in the use of call dates, or to the lender, as in the case of Series E savings bonds.   Alternatively, the maturity for particular bonds may be determined each year on a lottery basis, as is done widely in South America; or the debt contract may entitle the lender to refund on a later date (either at maturity or before) into specified issues to be made available at that time.

On some occasions, the Treasury may have to pay more for placing short issues and, at other times, more for placing long ones, the latter being perhaps the more normal state of affairs.   The problem, then, is to determine in which case more liquidity is surrendered by the investor per dollar of coupon payment.   This determination of the proper maturity mix, in the classical terms of funded versus floating debt, has traditionally been the central problem of debt management.

Marketability.   Variations in the degree of marketability provide a second dimension of debt policy.   In the case of marketable issues, the Treasury contract is with the bearer, whoever he may be, the identity of the individual investor being of no importance.   In the case of non-marketable issues, such as savings bonds carried over from the war, the contract is with a particular investor who must hold the obligation until the Treasury redeems it.   To the investor nonmarketability is a disadvantage that must be compensated for by higher returns or, as in the case of savings bonds, by granting him an option to terminate the contract at an earlier date.   From the Treasury's point of view, such concessions must again be weighed against the advantages secured by the use of non-negotiable instruments.

Finally, the Treasury may issue restricted debt, that is, debt of limited marketability.   Here the Treasury differentiates between groups of lenders by making certain debt contracts available to particular groups only.   This excludes sales to ineligible investors but may permit marketability among eligible investors.   An illustration is given by the wartime practice of rendering long-term bonds ineligible for bank holding until they drop to a certain maturity.   Under other conditions, it may be desirable to limit certain issues to banks and to render the issues ineligible for nonbank investors.[1]

---

[1] This may serve to avoid activation of idle balances, which results as commercial banks sell their holdings of government debt to the public and, in turn, expand loans

From the eligible lender's point of view, restriction is a disadvantage since the range of marketability is limited.   To the extent that he is given favorable treatment, restriction will be to his advantage.   From the Treasury's point of view, however, restriction makes it possible to act as a discriminating monopolist by bottling up the market and charging in each sector what the traffic will bear.   By the same token, restriction may serve to implement subsidy objectives through debt policy.

A distinction in principle may be drawn between considerations of maturity and marketability on the one side, and a policy of restriction on the other.   The choice among maturities and between the use of marketable or nonmarketable issues may be thought of as analogous to product differentiation.   Confronted with given lenders' preferences and attitudes, the Treasury will supply the issues that are most efficient, that is, issues that purchase illiquidity at the least cost.   The use of restriction, on the other hand, introduces a policy similar to that of price discrimination by a monopolist.   This raises the nice question of whether the rules of the game, or the concept of efficient policy, should be defined so as to permit or exclude discriminatory pricing.   Moreover, restriction on marketability and eligibility may be applied if it is desired to subsidize particular groups of investors, thus combining policies of the Distribution Branch with those of the Stabilization Branch.

To clarify matters, let us distinguish between four types of debt policy:

1. The Treasury does not use restricted debt and selects its debt instruments in such a way as to minimize cost in view of prevailing lender preferences.

2. The Treasury does not use restricted debt and selects its debt instruments in such a way as to exceed minimum cost.

3. The Treasury uses restricted debt and selects its debt instruments and policies of restriction so as to minimize cost.

4. The Treasury uses restricted debt and fails to minimize cost.

Now it is evident that policy 3 will purchase a desired degree of illiquidity at a lower cost than policy 1, but it does not follow that a distributionally neutral policy should be defined in terms of policy 3.   This is a normative matter.   In the last resort, it depends on how the proper state of distribution is to be defined.   If such a state implies a competitive pricing system, and the policies of the Distribution Branch are adjusted accordingly, a neutral solution should be defined in terms of policy 1; but

_____

by purchasing private debt. The shift of public debt from the nonbank public to the banks, while inflationary in a system with excess reserves, may well be deflationary in a loaned-up system; and vice versa for a shift of debt from banks to the nonbank public. See, in this connection, Lawrence H. Seltzer, "The Problem of Our Excessive Banking Reserves," *Journal of the American Statistical Association*, vol. 35, pp. 24–36, 1940.

if the proper state of distribution implies an imperfect system, policy 3 may be the neutral solution. In the normative model, then, the question of whether efficient policy should permit discriminatory pricing can be answered only in relation to the definition of proper distribution as seen by the Distribution Branch.[1]

In any case, policies 2 and 4 are not distributionally neutral. The principle of tailoring the debt to the preferences of the market is not only compatible with a neutral solution but also part and parcel of policy 1. Overextension of one or another type of debt, while advantageous to certain lender groups, is a different matter; it increases cost and is not distributionally neutral. As shown in policy 2, overextension may occur without restriction. Restriction, however, increases the possibilities of favoring or subsidizing one or another group of lenders. If debt policy is to be redistributional by design, policy 4 will be more effective in securing such subsidy or penalty objectives than will policy 2.

Compulsion. Note that all these debt instruments, whatever the degree of marketability or restriction, involve purely voluntary contracts between lender and borrower. It is only in this setting that the least-cost principle can be applied. An entirely different situation arises when lending is placed on a compulsory basis. This may take the form of outright lending requirements or of refundable taxes that are similar in principle to forced loans. Since such loans are compulsory, they may be non-interest-bearing, and the maturity date may be left at the Treasury's discretion. This type of compulsory lending has been discussed at length in connection with war finance, though in most countries it has been applied but sparingly.

A quite different application of the principle of compulsory lending appears in the use of reserve requirements for commercial banks. Provided that bankers adhere to a self-imposed margin of liquidity, the use of compulsory reserve requirements is not an essential tool of credit control. Credit control may be exerted through open-market and discount operations, thus involving voluntary debt transactions only. This, indeed, is the usual practice in countries where the supply of commercial credit originates from a small number of large banks that are readily subject to moral suasion. In countries such as the United States, where the supply of credit is distributed over a large number of banks, the use of compulsory reserve requirements is a convenient device to insure a minimum state of illiquidity at all commercial banks. Moreover, changes in the required reserve ratio (or compulsory lending ratio) afford an additional tool of monetary control.

Member banks must hold cash deposits at the central bank in adherence

[1] See pp. 19 and 78.

to reserve requirements. Thus member banks usually hold compulsory and non-interest-bearing loans. However, there is no inherent necessity for cash deposits. Central banks could pay interest on reserve deposits, so that the earning position of commercial banks would be rendered more or less independent of the level of reserves.[1] Or, the requirement for cash reserves could be supplemented by a requirement to hold certain types of government debt.

The tradition has been to apply reserve requirements to commercial banks only, while excluding other lenders. As the position of institutional investors gains in importance in the capital market, the question arises whether similar requirements should not be applied as well to institutional lenders of the nonbank type. If so, a system of security reserves may be more appropriate than one of cash reserves.

Differences between Lenders

In purchasing illiquidity, or nonspending, the Treasury does not deal with a homogeneous body of lenders or with a homogeneous mass of private debt which is to be displaced by public debt. Different groups of lenders have distinct preferences for various types of debt, public and private; and by issuing debt that appeals to one or another group, the Treasury may influence the particular type of private debt for a restricted market, as well as the particular type of private expenditure that is to be cut back.

Let us consider the simple proposition that government long-term debt is a substitute, from the lender's point of view, for private long-term debt; and that government short-term debt is a substitute for private short-term debt. If the government sells additional debt in long maturities, this will primarily tighten the terms at which private debt of long maturities may be placed; if the government issues short maturities, this will primarily tighten the private market for short term debt. A lengthening of the structure of public debt will tend to raise long-term rates relative to short-term rates and ease the market for short-term private debt relative to that for long-term private debt. This in turn will affect the availability of funds to borrowers who wish to borrow short, relative to those who wish to borrow long. As a result, it will affect the flow of expenditures between investments that depend upon short and long financing. While long-term investments may be financed by short-term funds, and vice

---

[1] This in turn raises the question of what constitutes adequate bank earnings—a difficult question to answer, since the appropriate level of bank capital itself is a matter of policy rather than technological considerations. Another basic question is also suggested: whether it is desirable for the government to subsidize banking services through interest payments on bank-held debt (as it subsidizes the building of public roads), or whether the users of banking services should pay a larger share of the cost.

versa, the type of public debt nevertheless affects the flow of private investment expenditures.

In a 100 per cent reserve system, more or less the same reasoning applies to exchanges between money and debt as applies to exchanges between long- and short-term debt. Substitution of short-term public debt for money tends to curtail the market for private short-term debt, whereas substitution of long-term public debt tends to curtail the market for private long-term debt.

In a fractional-reserve system, the results depend on whether or not the system is fully loaned up. If it is loaned up, an exchange of debt for money may result in a multiple curtailment of funds available to purchase private debt. This will be the case whether the additional public debt is short or long, and whether it is purchased by bank or nonbank investors. Shifts of public debt from the nonbank to the bank sector involve a reduction in the demand for private debt by the banking system, and an increase in the demand for private debt by nonbank investors. This leaves the money supply in the hands of the nonbank public unchanged, although the rate of money turnover may be affected. If there is slack in the system, an exchange of public debt for money may have little effect on funds available for private investment. A shift in the holding of public debt between the bank and nonbank sector may now change the money supply available to the nonbank public, since bank holding of private debt may remain unchanged.

Similar considerations bear on the choice between marketable and non-marketable securities and among other technical features of debt issues that appeal in varying degrees to various types of lenders. The lenders' particular preferences differ with their business or personal positions and depend upon the constraints that the liability side of their balance sheets places upon them. Commercial banks, the liabilities of which are short-term debts, will be cautious regarding long-term investment. Insurance companies, whose commitments are in long-term contracts, will be inclined to match these with correspondingly long-term investments. Small savers will be interested in obligations that may be liquidated readily in case of personal needs, and so forth.

In view of all this, it is evident that the simple requirement of minimum cost omits an important part of the problem. If all private debt were of the same type, the choice of public debt would not affect the type of private borrowing that is curtailed; and if there were only one type of private investment, there would be no qualitative effect on the reduction in expenditures by the lender. In this case, we could simply proceed along the earlier lines of determining the structure of public debt that secures the desired reduction of private expenditures at the least cost. Matters are complicated considerably once we allow for the fact that the private-debt obligations that are displaced, and the expenditures to which these obligations may give rise, are not homogeneous. In view of this lack of homogeneity, the pattern that results if a given aggregate reduction in private expenditures is obtained at minimum cost may not be the optimal one; a different pattern may be more desirable, even though a higher cost is involved.

Let us assume that the capital market is perfect, and complies with all the conditions of pure competition, perfect market knowledge, and mobility. Thus at any one time, we have a level and distribution of private investment expenditures that reflect not only the usual parameters of consumer preference and cost but also the portfolio preferences of investors and the distribution of net worth among them. As additional government debt is issued, private debt is displaced. Now let a given reduction in private expenditure be produced by the sale of public debt. By choosing the debt obligations that secure this objective at minimum cost, we assure a cutback in those private expenditures for which the market is least willing to pay. The market test, in this case, reflects not only consumer preferences for the goods to be produced by alternative investments but also lender preferences for the kind of obligations involved in financing them. Resource allocation is conditioned by investor sovereignty as well as consumer sovereignty.

The assumptions that underlie this reasoning are not very realistic, as we have stated. Indeed, they may be inconsistent with the very essence of our problem. If the market is perfect in all respects, no uncertainty prevails. If no uncertainty prevails, lenders will be indifferent as between short and long obligations, since yields will converge to the same level. Investments that require the tying up of capital for a long period may then be financed by short-term debt obligations and vice versa. Moreover, in the absence of uncertainty, other types of risk may be transformed into insurance costs, thus resulting in an all-round equalization of net yields. In such a setting, the cost to the government would be the same whatever type of debt is issued.

Such is not the case in the real world. Uncertainty is an important factor, and various types of rigidities prevail in the capital and money markets. A policy that determines the mix of government obligations by the least-cost rule may be said to be distributionally neutral; yet it is likely to involve elements of arbitrariness in its effects on allocation, which may justify or require deviation from the rule.

Continuity of Debt Policy

A final complication arises from the peculiarly continuous nature of debt policy. This is most obvious in a setting where we assume that the Treasury cannot engage in exchanges between types of debt prior to maturity. Here any debt once issued will remain a part of the debt structure until it matures. Hence the composition of the public debt at any one time will reflect the decisions of debt policy over the past period in which the debt was issued. Only to the extent that debt matures is there flexibility of adjustment. Otherwise the outstanding structure of the public debt is a given factor in the economic picture. Such being the case, the planning perspective for debt policy must be as long as the longest maturity. Since the ideal structure of the debt will differ with changing economic conditions, it must be designed to meet the requirements of the situation most of the time. Above all, it must be designed so as to contribute to the built-in stability of the system.

The problem of continuity remains, though to a modified degree, if we assume that the Treasury is free to issue new debt at any time, and to use the proceeds to repurchase old debt prior to maturity. In this case, the managers of debt policy are free to adjust the composition of the debt structure whenever they please. However, they must do so at terms that are acceptable to the market.[1] As a result, the yield at which a security is issued defines the cost that must be carried by the Treasury over the entire life span of the security, up to its contractual maturity. This will hold true even though the borrowing rates may drop in the meantime and the Treasury decides to refund the debt prior to maturity. While the Treasury may now borrow at a lower rate, it must borrow more in order to repurchase the older issue at its increased market price. The planning perspective of debt management must still be as long as the longest maturity under consideration. Indeed, it may be argued that the planning perspective must extend to infinity in order to determine what should be the maximum maturity.

These considerations indicate the crucial importance of continuity in debt management. While all types of stabilization policy are continuous in the sense that today's action bears upon tomorrow's setting, debt policy is also continuous in the sense that current action involves a long-term commitment. Debt policy deals with stocks, whereas fiscal policy deals with flows. Again this greatly complicates the simplified picture presented in our initial discussion of debt policy.

B. THE TERM STRUCTURE OF RATES

For a closer examination of the problem of maturity, we shall assume that all debt is marketable, unrestricted, and voluntary. The first step

---

[1] Of course, the government may always ease credit to obtain whatever level of rates is desired for purposes of refunding. This possibility is excluded here because we assume the policy to be one of maintaining the given degree of illiquidity.

is to consider the factors that determine the relative cost of placing short- and long-term debt.

Rate Structure with Certainty and Uniform Market Outlook

The academic theory of rate structure rests on the proposition that long-term rates should be viewed as the average of future short-term rates. This proposition dates back to Irving Fisher, and was refined later by J. R. Hicks.[1]   If short rates are expected to rise, a lender will not commit himself to long terms unless the yield is sufficient to compensate him for foregoing the opportunity of a series of short-term investments at rising rates.[2]   Thus, if short rates are expected to rise, long rates must be above short rates; and vice versa if short rates are expected to fall.[3]   By the same token, all rates will be the same if short rates are expected to remain stable.

Let us assume that there is no uncertainty about the level of future short-term rates and that all investors know precisely what these rates are going to be.   Thus there exists a uniform and certain market outlook. Now let the expected level of short rates be as shown in Figure 24-1, so that yields on one-year obligations will equal 1 per cent for the first year, 3 per cent for the second year, 4 per cent for the third year, 4.5 per cent for the fourth year, and 5 per cent thereafter.   On this basis, we obtain the patterns of yields or rate structures shown in Figure 24-2.   The pattern, as it appears at the outset of year 1, is shown in the year-1 curve.   An

[1] Irving Fisher, *The Theory of Interest*, The Macmillan Company, New York, 1930, p. 210; J. R. Hicks, *Value and Capital*, Oxford University Press, London, Clarendon Press, 1939, p. 144; and Friedrich A. Lutz, "The Structure of Interest Rates," *Quarterly Journal of Economics*, vol. 55, pp. 36–63, 1940–1941, reprinted in *Readings in the Theory of Income Distribution*, American Economic Association, Richard D. Irwin, Inc., Homewood, Ill., 1946, pp. 499–529.

[2] If we specify that interest is paid at the end of the debt contract, the same capital sum must be arrived at by a series of short contracts and by one long contract.   Thus

$$(1 + R_n)^n = (1 + r_1)(1 + r_2) \cdots (1 + r_n)$$

where R_n is the long rate for an investment of n periods, and $r_1, r_2, \cdots, r_n$ are the expected short rates for the respective periods.   Disregarding compound interest, we have $nR_n = r_1 + r_2 + \cdots r_n$.   See J. R. Hicks, *op. cit.*, p. 145.

Assuming that interest on long debt is paid at the same intervals as interest on short debt, and using compounding, we have

$$R_n = \frac{(1 + r_1)(1 + r_2) \cdots (1 + r_n) - 1}{(1 + r_2)(1 + r_3) \cdots (1 + r_n) + (1 + r_3) \cdots (1 + r_n) + \cdots + (1 + r_n) + 1}$$

See Lutz, *op. cit.*, p. 500.

[3] It may be noted that Fisher, *op. cit.*, p. 210, considers the current short rate a function of the prospect for long rates, rather than the other way around.   Formally, the case may be put either way.   What matters is that the rate structure is interdependent in the indicated fashion.

investor will purchase a one-year obligation at terms that offer a yield of
1 per cent, a two-year obligation at 1.98 per cent, a three-year obligation
at 2.63 per cent, a four-year obligation at 3.07 per cent, a five-year obligation at 3.42 per cent, and a consol at 5 per cent. The demanded yield in

TERM STRUCTURE OF RATES WITH CERTAIN AND
UNIFORM OUTLOOK

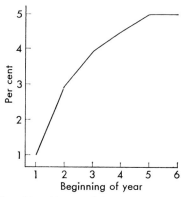

FIG. 24-1. Expected level of one-year
yields.

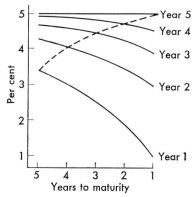

FIG. 24-2. Resulting pattern of rates.

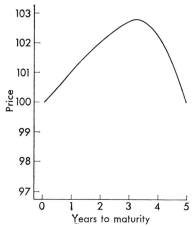

FIG. 24-3. Issue price for bonds of various maturities.

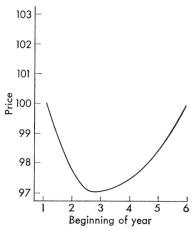

FIG. 24-4. Expected market price of
five-year bond.

each case is equal to the average of future short-term rates for the same
period.[1] The corresponding pattern of yields for the beginning of year 2
is shown in the year-2 curve of Figure 24-2. This pattern is somewhat
higher, since the 1 per cent rate is dropped at the beginning of the period,
and a second 5 per cent rate is added at the end. The corresponding

[1] The yields are obtained by applying the final formula given on p. 591, note 2.

pattern of yields for the beginning of the fifth year is a horizontal line at 5 per cent. The diagonal line shows the yields that a five-year bond, purchased at the beginning of year 1, is expected to carry for the remainder of its life period at the beginning of each successive year.

In Figure 24-3 we see the price at which obligations of various maturities can be issued at the outset of the first year, it being assumed that all carry a coupon (annual payment) of $3.42 and pay $100 at maturity. The bond sells at par if issued for a five-year term, and above par if issued for a shorter term. This follows because according to Figure 24-1, yields rise with the length of the term; and because with a fixed coupon payment, the yield falls as the issue price rises. The issue prices shown in Figure 24-3 for bonds of various maturities provide the yields stipulated for the respective maturities in the year-1 curve of Figure 24-2.* As will be seen from Figure 24-3, the premium rises with the maturity up to a certain point and then falls back toward zero.

Figure 24-4 shows the market prices at which a five-year bond issued at the outset of year 1, paying $100 at maturity and carrying an annual coupon of $3.42, is expected to sell over the next five years. At the beginning of year 1, such a bond can be issued at par. At the beginning of the second year, the remaining maturity has been reduced to four years. But the yield expected on a four-year maturity is now 4.09 per cent, as shown in Figure 24-2. The bond, therefore, goes to a discount and sells for $97.57.† At the beginning of the third year, the remaining maturity has declined to three years, but the expected yield for a three-year bond is now 4.48 per cent. Thus, the price declines further. The required yield continues to rise thereafter, but the price of the bond turns up in anticipation of the approaching redemption payment at $100. The curve of Figure 24-4 thus records the price of the bond that at each point of time provides the yield set by the effective pattern of rates as shown in the diagonal line of Figure 24-2.

In a perfect market of this sort, arbitrage will operate to establish a term structure of rates (or relative prices of bonds) that will be in accord with the future level of short-term rates. By the same token, there will be a tendency to equalize rates only if future short rates are taken to be constant. Given such a perfect market, the cost of borrowing over any specified period will be the same to the Treasury, whatever combination of maturities it chooses. The present value of the total coupon bill (payable

---

* The premium K on a bond maturing in n years, carrying a coupon of g and a yield of i, is equal to

$$K = (g - i)a_n$$

where $a_n = [1 - (1 + i)^{-n}]/i$. See Rietz et al., *Mathematics of Finance*, rev. ed., Henry Holt and Company, Inc., New York, 1937, p. 97 and tables on p. 317.

† Computation is based on the same formula used for Fig. 24-3.

over five years) for borrowing \$100 over a five-year period will be the same for each maturity mix. Similarly, the lender will be indifferent as between loan contracts of varying maturities. Since the outlook is certain, he knows that issues of varying maturities will be traded against each other at any given time at predetermined rates of exchange. Differences in maturity, therefore, are nothing but a formality. There is no problem of debt management in the perfect market. The so-called pure theory of rate structure fully explains the rate structure only under conditions where, for purposes of debt policy, it is a trivial matter.

Rate Structure with Certainty and Diverse Market Outlook

Let us retain the assumption of certainty and allow for the possibility that lenders and borrowers differ in their appraisals of the outlook, though each is subjectively certain of his view.[1] This is not a very sensible set of assumptions, since those who prove wrong will learn that the outlook is uncertain; however, it is a useful step in developing the argument.

The investor's decision to borrow or to lend short or long now involves an appraisal not only of the future outlook for short rates but also of the appropriateness of present long rates in the light of his subjective evaluation of future short rates. Thus, one lender may expect that future short rates will rise, but rise less than the consensus of the market expects. He feels that the price of long terms is undervalued (their yield is set too high) and hence finds it profitable to hold long terms. Another lender may expect a sharper rise in short rates than does the consensus. He will feel that long terms are overvalued and will lend short. Borrowers will be in the opposite position. A borrower who anticipates a lesser rise in long terms than does the consensus will prefer to borrow short, and one who expects a sharper rise will borrow long.[2]

Lenders and borrowers in this case will not be indifferent as between long and short terms. Their preferences will depend on the difference between their own views of the market outlook and that of the consensus. The market, accordingly, will reflect subjective expectations on the part of various lenders and investors, weighed by their respective shares in the market. If the pattern of rates is rising (long rates are above short rates), the consensus will be one of rising short rates, but the particular rate spread will be a reflection of a diverse set of subjective opinions as to the degree of increase in short rates.

Rate Structure with Uncertainty

The nature of the preceding approach requires that the time span over which expectations on short-term rates extend must be sufficiently long to

---

[1] See Lutz, *op. cit.*, p. 512.

[2] For a diagrammatic presentation, see *ibid.*, p. 517.

cover the longest maturity under consideration.[1] This period is usually too long and the problem too complex to permit a high degree of certainty. Borrowers or lenders will be able, at best, to think in terms of a probable set of short rates over future years; and they will be aware that uncertainty attaches to what they consider the most probable set of rates.

Suppose that a borrower obtains funds on long term and then finds that the general level of rates drops. As a result, he loses the advantage he would have gained from the decline in rates if he had initially borrowed short. This loss is irreparable for the period of his commitment. It cannot be recouped by borrowing new funds at the reduced rate and using the proceeds to pay off the old debt. If the debt is retired prior to maturity, it will have to be purchased at a premium so that a correspondingly larger amount of new debt must be incurred. Nothing is gained, and the benefits of lower rates are lost until the maturity date is reached. Thus it would have been a good precaution to borrow short. But precisely the opposite holds if the pattern of rates should rise. Depending on the borrower's expectations regarding future changes in the level of rates, he will arrive at what seems to him the best mix of waiting, borrowing short, and borrowing long. The same principles apply to the lender's side of the market. Lenders who have loaned on long term lose if rates rise and gain if rates fall. The optimal choice between staying in cash, lending short, and lending long again depends on the lenders expectations regarding future changes in the level of rates.

Depending on the state of expectations and the resulting pattern of demand for, and supply of, short- and long-term debt, the resulting term structure of rates may be a rising or falling one. Is there any reason to expect that "normally" long rates will exceed short rates, or vice versa?

Borrowers may prefer to borrow long, since this saves the cost of reborrowing at frequent intervals. Other things being equal, they will be willing to pay more for a long contract. By the same token, lenders will prefer to avoid the cost of frequent relending. Other things being equal, lenders will be willing to take a smaller return for a long loan. These two forces may cancel, or the net effect may be in either direction. In any case, most financial transactions are carried out in large volume, and the cost factor is subject to heavy economies of scale. Thus the cost of contracting is hardly of major importance and shall now be disregarded.

---

[1] At the same time, the theory does *not* imply that long-term bonds are purchased with the intention of holding such issues to maturity. Whatever the intention of any particular investor who purchases long terms, he must consider the price at which it will be possible to sell long-term issues prior to maturity; and with this, he must consider the future outlook for short-term rates over the entire period of the long-term issue.

A more interesting consideration arises from certain differences in the market behavior of short- and long-term securities. From the very nature of these securities, it follows that equal percentage changes in yield to maturity will involve greater percentage changes in the price of long-term securities. Following de Scitovszky, we may apply the concept of elasticity of expectation to the way in which expected changes in yield are related to past changes.[1] We obtain the following pattern:

TABLE 24-1. EXPECTED CHANGES IN BOND YIELDS AND PRICES FOR SHORT-
AND LONG-TERM DEBT

Elasticity of expectations E	Percentage fluctuations	
	Yields	Security prices
$E > 1$	Greater for long term	Greater for long term
$E = 1$	Equal	Greater for long term
$0 < E < 1$	Greater for short term	Greater for long term
$E = 0$	Greater for short term	Equal
$E = <0$	Greater for short term	Greater for short term

The typical behavior of security markets has been to record wider fluctuations in the rates of short- than of long-term securities, combined with wider fluctuations in the prices of long- than of short-term issues. This is compatible with the hypothesis that the elasticity of expectation has usually been between zero and one. A rise in rates tends to create an expectation that there will be some reverse adjustment in the future, but that the level of rates will remain somewhat above that which had prevailed prior to the change.

Given this market pattern, the lender who commits his funds over a long period faces the prospect of larger fluctuations in the market value of his investment. Suppose that a private investor has purchased long-term government obligations and that the rate of interest rises thereafter. The market value of his obligation declines accordingly, and the decline in value is greater than it would have been, had he invested short. The investor will regret having tied up his funds in long terms. But by the same token he will be pleased to have lent long if it should turn out that rates fall. All this the investor must have accounted for when initially

[1] See J. R. Hicks, op. cit., p. 205; and Tibor de Scitovszky, "A Study of Interest and Capital," Economica, New Ser., vol. 7, no. 27, pp. 293–317, August, 1940.

The elasticity of expectations is defined in these studies as the ratio of percentage change in expected future yields to percentage change in present yields. If the elasticity is unity, both change at the same rate; if it is less than unity, future yields are expected to rise less; and if it is zero, future expected yields remain unchanged. With an elasticity greater than unity, future expected yields rise more than present yields, and with an elasticity of less than zero, they decline.

assessing the market outlook. So far we see no reason why he should have an intrinsic preference for either short- or long-term debt.

This indeed is all that can be said, provided that we assume a credit market that is perfect—in the sense that any one investor is always in a position to borrow at the going market rate, even at short notice. Suppose that an investor who has purchased long terms finds that he must meet his liabilities on short notice. If the market value of his long terms has fallen, he may be forced to liquidate at a loss, and it may even be necessary to borrow additional funds to meet the demands of his creditors. This is unfortunate, but again the problem is merely one of suffering the penalty for having made a mistaken investment decision, a penalty that will be offset by the possibility of greater gains if rates decline. There is still no reason why the lender should have an intrinsic preference for either long or short debt.

This, however, is not a realistic picture. While the investor will have little difficulty in selling his holding of government debt in a more or less perfect market, he may not always be in a position to borrow at the going market rate so as to meet additional requirements. There are two reasons for this: First, the market may be imperfect in the sense that the time pressure of having to find additional funds at short notice may force the borrower to offer a higher return. Secondly, and more important, the cost at which the investor can borrow will tend to rise with the decline in the market value of his assets. He has become a poorer credit risk, and is confronted again with the linkage of risks.[1] This principle, at last, supplies us with a reason why the investor, other things being equal, will prefer to lend short. The private borrower, for the same reasons, will prefer to borrow long. In a situation where the expectation is for short rates to remain unchanged—or, in Hicksian terms, where the elasticity of expectation is unity—there is reason to suppose that the long rate will lie somewhat above the short rate. While the government may not share the considerations of the private borrower, it must nevertheless overcome the loss aversion of the private lender, and be prepared to pay a higher yield for the sale of long-term debt.[2]

This conclusion is reinforced if we allow for the additional consideration that uncertainty as to the underlying market appraisal increases with the length of the commitment. In absence of market imperfections, this uncertainty would extend to possible gains as well as losses, and would

---

[1] This applies in particular to the investor who uses equity capital only. If debt appears on the liability side of his balance sheet, and if we assume the lender to adhere consistently to evaluation by market price, the decline in the market value of assets may be offset more or less, or even outweighed by a decline in the value of liabilities. What counts is the ratio of *net* holdings of claims to net worth prior to the change in yields.

[2] For a somewhat similar discussion, see J. R. Hicks, *op. cit.*, chap. 13.

provide no reason why one or the other yield should be higher. Given the imperfections noted in the preceding paragraph and the resulting loss aversion, a positive relationship between uncertainty and length of commitment adds to the increment in yield on long-term debt.

Institutional Factors

The academic theory of rate structure, based upon expectations of change in the level of rates, offers a useful framework, but one that must be supplemented by a set of more institutional considerations. The preference between short and long commitments is not wholly a matter of expectation. It depends as well upon the needs and obligations of particular lenders or borrowers, and these needs and obligations depend upon market conditions.

In the cyclical setting we observe qualitative as well as quantitative changes in the demand for funds (or the supply of private debts) that have important bearing on the rate structure. Long-term investments may be financed by short-term credit and vice versa, but this is not the typical case. For reasons inherent in the structure of the capital market and the nature of the particular activities involved, various transactions are usually financed by debts of certain maturities. Thus, the demand for inventory accumulation most often leads to the supply of short-term debt; demand for plant expansion and construction typically leads to the supply of long-term debt; installment purchases of consumer goods usually involve intermediate term credit; stock-exchange speculation most frequently requires short credit, and so forth. As the weight of these transactions changes over the cycle, so does the supply of various types of private debts. Unless offset by compensatory changes in the supply of public debt, these changes in market conditions will give rise to corresponding changes in the term structure of rates.[1]

The tendency for the short rate to rise relative to the long rate in the upswing is consistent with the hypothesis that investors expect the boom to end and the level of rates to fall. Yet an alternative or supplementary explanation may be found in an increased demand for short-term credit, based on inventory speculation and expectation of a temporary rise in prices.

If a longer view is taken, certain structural changes in the composition of the market must be accounted for. The great rise of institutional investment—in the form of life insurance companies, investment trusts, and, more recently, pension funds—cannot but have a profound effect on the pattern of demand for various types of debt. The increasing impor-

---

[1] For an analysis of rate structure along these lines see John M. Culbertson, "The Term Structure of Interest Rates," *Quarterly Journal of Economics*, vol. 71, no. 4, pp. 485–517, November, 1957.

tance of internal financing in lieu of bank borrowing by large corporations affects the pattern of supply of private debt, and the supply of public debt itself competes for various types of private funds. All these factors must be accounted for when explaining historical changes in the term structure of rates. Expectations regarding the future level of rates are a factor in the picture, but they are by no means the only one.

C. THE OPTIMAL MATURITY STRUCTURE

We now return to the policy question of how to determine the optimal maturity mix. We shall retain the earlier assumption that all debt is fully marketable and voluntary.

The Classical Case for Funding

The classical prescription for debt management has been that sound debt policy requires funding in more or less long-term issues.[1] Short-term or floating debt is said to leave the government at the mercy of impatient lenders; moreover, it is likely to be absorbed by banks and hence is inflationary. For these reasons, legitimate borrowing in peacetime should be long-term; and war debt, if not issued long in the first place, should be converted in the postwar period. A funded debt is said to have the additional advantage of making for simplicity and certainty in the debt structure, and may be linked with an orderly plan for debt retirement.

The major argument for long-term debt thus was the protection it afforded the Treasury against sudden insistence by lenders that the debt be paid off, leaving the Treasury tottering on the verge of bankruptcy, save for the grace of its creditors. This may have been a realistic and sensible approach at a time when the government did not dispose over the central bank authority, when the supply of funds was derived largely from a small group of financial houses, and when government debt in general was considered a rather marginal investment. By the same token, these considerations do not apply in the modern setting of the Western economy where the government has the monetary authority, and public debt has become a broadly placed, continuous, and integral factor in the financial structure of the country.

In a perfect market, at least, this change in financial structure renders the problem of refunding of nominal importance. The fact that this or

---

[1] See David Ricardo, "Essay on the Funding System," *Works and Correspondence*, vol. IV (1951), ed. P. Sraffa, Cambridge University Press, New York, 1951–1955. Also, see C. F. Bastable, *Public Finance*, 3d ed., The Macmillan Company, New York, 1928; and *Public Debts*, H. C. Adams, D. Appleton & Company, Inc., New York, 1892, part II, chap. 2.

that bond matures has no bearing on the basic willingness of investors to hold public debt of various kinds. The problem of refunding becomes a formality, indistinguishable from the ever-present task of trading debts (whether matured or not) so as to maintain an optimal debt structure.

Under more realistic conditions, refunding at maturity continues to be important. Since it is not customary to undertake changes in debt structure except at maturity, the more frequent maturity of short debt gives greater freedom to revise the debt structure. This is an advantage of shorter issues.[1]

It cannot be overlooked that the refunding of maturing debt in an imperfect market raises marketing problems. As in all aspects of liquidity control, such difficulties may become acute under conditions of inflation, when stabilization policy calls for rising yields and falling bond prices. In such a market, investors may want to hold out for better terms, particularly because an exchange of investments at maturity will not realize any losses. The Treasury, having to refund at maturity, may find itself cornered by large lenders or groups of lenders who hold out. Thus there may develop an imperfect market situation, rendering it difficult to determine the proper terms at which bonds should be issued. If the debt is short, it will mature more frequently, and this problem has to be faced at briefer intervals. At the same time, the problem will be less serious if and when it does arise.

On balance, these considerations furnish us with no prima facie case for or against funding. We must return to the basic question of which is the more efficient way to secure the desired degree of illiquidity, or nonspending.

Effects of Changes in Debt Structure on the Level of Investment

Let us consider effects of changes in debt structure on the level of private investment. Effects of a given debt structure on the stability of investment will be left for later examination.

---

[1] Present arrangements in the United States set a twofold limitation to the freedom of debt management. Dealings in debt prior to maturity are limited to exchanges between debt and money in the course of open-market operations, and the Federal reserve bank can only sell such debt as it has in its portfolio. The Treasury does not engage in such transactions and, in fact, cannot purchase its debt above par. Neither restriction seems sensible.

As a first step toward greater flexibility, debt purchased by the Federal Reserve System may be converted into a general and non-interest-bearing obligation, with the Federal Reserve System authorized to exchange this against specific types of debt as needed, when open-market sales are made. As a second step, the concept of open-market operations may be extended to exchanges between types of debt as well as debt and money. Whether such exchanges should be made by the Federal Reserve System or the Treasury, or by a joint authority in charge of liquidity policy, need not be considered here.

A given degree of restriction may be obtained through various combinations of public debt differing in composition and total amount. The problem, then, is to find that combination which secures the desired degree of restriction at least cost. While additional considerations enter, this at least provides a starting point for discussion.

It is tempting to approach this problem in terms of a simple isocost and isoexpenditure diagram. The terms at which investors are willing to hold various combinations of long and short debt are reflected in the isocost, or CC, curves of Figure 24-5. Each point on C_1C_1 shows combinations of long and short debt that investors are willing to hold for a given return or

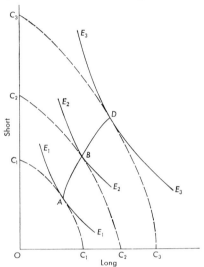

FIG. 24-5. Optimal debt structure.

interest bill; C_2C_2 shows the combinations acceptable at a higher interest bill, and so forth.

In constructing the CC curves it is evident that each curve must slope down from the left to the right. This follows because the holding of either short or long debt involves a disutility or surrender of liquidity, and a loss of earnings from alternative investments that must be rewarded. Since the interest bill is held constant, investors will accept increased holdings of short-term debt only if their holdings of long-term debt are reduced. Moreover, we may expect the slope of the CC curves to fall short of -1. Moving down any one CC curve, it is reasonable to assume that investors will insist on surrendering a larger amount of short debt than is added in long debt—if we assume that lending long involves a higher degree of risk and illiquidity and, hence, demands a higher return. Barring expectations of declining short-term rates, this is in line with our earlier conclusion. Since the total debt is reduced while the average maturity is lengthened, the substitution of long- for short-term debt through open-market operations involves an increase in the money supply.[1] Finally, we may assume that the slope of any one CC curve steepens when moving down from the left to the right. For reasons similar to those underlying Hart's linkage of risk, successive additions to cash result in declining gains in liquidity, while successive additions to long terms result in increasing reductions in liquidity.[2] Therefore, we may expect the CC curves to be concave to the origin.

Consider the shape of the corresponding set of EE, or isoexpenditure, curves. The points on any one isoexpenditure curve show combinations of debt that impose the same degree of restriction upon private investment expenditures, with expenditures becoming higher as we move out toward successive EE curves. The addition of long-term debt, while leaving short-term debt unchanged, is restrictive. Short-term debt, therefore, must be reduced if expenditures are to remain constant. Any one EE curve must slope down from the left to the right. If we assume that long-term debt is more restrictive than short-term debt, the slopes must again fall short of -1, and lengthening of the average debt maturity again involves an increasing money supply. Finally, it is reasonable to assume that the restrictive effect of substituting long terms becomes increasingly severe as we move down any one EE curve; while the expansionary effect of reducing the holding of short terms and of increasing the money supply declines. The EE curves as well appear to be concave to the origin.

We are thus deprived of the neat set of tangency solutions that would result if either set of curves were straight or convex to the origin.[3]   A

---

[1] Alternatively, we may draw the CC curves on the assumption that the money supply is held constant, whether through fiscal adjustments or through changes in reserve requirements. In the former case, income effects must be allowed for, at least in the short run. In the latter case, it is evident that an increase in reserve requirements reduces the cost of securing illiquidity. An increase in reserve requirements may be likened to a compulsory and non-interest-bearing loan.

[2] See A. G. Hart, *Money, Debt and Economic Activity*, New York, Prentice-Hall, Inc., Englewood Cliffs, N.J., 1948, pp. 198ff.

[3] Such a solution is obtained by Earl R. Rolph, "Principles of Debt Management," *American Economic Review*, vol. 47, no. 3, pp. 302–320, June, 1957, who draws the CC curves concave to the origin, but draws the EE curves convex to the origin. The shape of the CC curves is explained simply by pointing to the rise in long yields relative to short yields, which results as the debt is lengthened. (See Rolph, p. 315.) In deriving the shape of the EE curves, Rolph argues correctly that a shortening in debt while moving along the same EE curve requires an increase in total debt and hence a corresponding reduction in money supply. This renders short debt an increasingly poor substitute for money. From this correct premise Rolph then concludes on p. 313, note 20, that increasing amounts of short debt must be added for subsequent reductions in long debt. As I see it, the opposite conclusion holds. If short debt becomes a poorer substitute for money, it becomes more like long debt; and if short debt becomes more like long debt, decreasing amounts of short debt may be substituted to replace long debt.

tangency solution may still be obtained if the one set of curves is consistently more concave than the other, but this may not be the case. There may be no single set of best solutions; or the solution may become one of borrowing all in long-term debt or all in short-term debt.   The neat result, typically applicable in a system involving indifference curves and a production-transformation schedule (subject to decreasing returns) may not apply in this case, where both the CC and EE curves relate to the same investment behavior and depend upon the same set of expectations and opportunities for private investment, rather than on quite distinct sets of conditions such as technology and taste.   Indeed, one may ask whether the two sets of curves will not be the same.[1]

The case becomes more determinate if we introduce the possibility that the isoexpenditure curves, as seen by the Treasury, include additional considerations not reflected in the preferences of the private investors—considerations that reduce the attractiveness of long-term debt from the Treasury's point of view.   A lengthening of the debt structure may complicate the task of maintaining an orderly market, and lending long may be disadvantageous if the long-run prospect is for declining rates. On the other hand, a lengthening of the debt structure may increase the effectiveness of debt as a built-in stabilizer, which increases the attractiveness of long-term debt from the Treasury's point of view.   On balance, these considerations *may* render the isoexpenditure curves (now more precisely referred to as isostabilization curves) convex to the origin, as shown by the CC lines within Figure 24-5.   In this case, the optimum combinations for various levels of expenditures would fall on a contract curve such as AD, the proper point on this curve being determined by the desired mix of restriction by liquidity control and by other policies. However, there is no assurance that this neat solution applies.

Effects of Given Debt Structure on the Variability of Investment

We now turn to the effects of a given debt structure upon possible changes in the level of private investment, or the contribution of debt structure to the built-in stability of the economy.

---

[1] If investors hold public-debt combinations X and Y for the same return, they must find themselves in equally satisfactory positions with regard not only to public debt but to their entire portfolios.   If combination X should permit a superior position regarding private investment than combination Y, investors would be willing to hold X at a lower return.   Thus, their portfolio position net of government debt must be equally attractive in both cases.   If this means that the same volume of private assets is held, isoexpenditure lines are the same as isocost lines, and all combinations on any one line are equally effective.   Such need not be the case, since the risk-income relationship among various private assets may differ; but it is not an unreasonable assumption to make.

Locked-in Effect. It is argued frequently that long-term debt is sticky and more likely to remain with private investors than is short-term debt. Holders of long-term obligations are considered less likely to sell their obligations at a time of high activity and rising interest rates than are holders of short-term debt. Because of this, long-term debt is said to be a more effective means of securing nonspending. The underlying argument appears simple enough: As interest rates rise, the price of long terms tends to fall more sharply than the price of short terms.[1] Investors, therefore, are confronted with a larger realized loss when selling long terms. In order to avoid such a loss, they will not sell.

This argument may be interpreted at various levels. If an investor suffers a decline in the value of his capital assets, it is indicative of a preceding error in investment policy. Realization of the loss implies an explicit recognition of this error, which is unpleasant. Thus the investor may refuse to realize the loss, even though it would be rational to do so. Moreover, realization of losses may adversely affect his credit standing, provided that lenders appraise (if irrationally) their assets by maturity rather than market value. Where such is the case, realization of losses is to be avoided. The investor who holds long-term government securities is "locked in," and cannot switch to other assets.[2]

Let us now set aside these considerations and assume rational behavior by all concerned. Thus it is evident that an investor has suffered a loss, once the market value of his securities has fallen. Whether this loss is realized or not has no bearing on its actual existence. The only consideration that determines whether to sell or not is the future profitability of retaining present holdings compared with switching to other assets. Such changes in the market value of present holdings as may have occurred in the past are relevant only in so far as they create expectations regarding future changes in prices and yields.

The rational investor considers himself disposing over a given value of assets, including cash and the *market* value of his securities, and decides which is the most profitable portfolio combination in view of the expected yields to be derived from the purchase of various securities. Retention of past holdings is similar in principle to the sale and repurchase of these holdings. Subject to possible income effects, losses incurred in the past are irrelevant. Investor X, who has suffered a decline in the value of his

---

[1] See p. 596.

[2] We have argued earlier (p. 597) that the lender may prefer investment in short terms in order to avoid depressing effects on his credit standing, which may result from a sharp decline in the market value of his holdings of long terms. The assumption then was that lenders evaluate assets of borrowers at market value. The present consideration, relating to the locked-in effect, is based on the assumption that lenders evaluate by maturity value. The two points are thus inconsistent, and the latter is offered only in an attempt to explain what might be meant by the locked-in effect.

government bonds, is in the same position as investor Z, who held cash and remained unaffected. Both are concerned with the question of how the past rise in yields will affect the future behavior of the market.

Let us suppose that prior to the change, government consols sold at $100 and carried a coupon of $5 or 5 per cent. Private consols sold at $100 and carried a coupon rate of $7 or 7 per cent. The absolute difference of 2 per cent is the premium required by investors to compensate for the default risk and lesser marketability of private issues. Now let the price of government consols drop to $50. Subsequent developments depend upon the elasticity of expectations.

Suppose, now, that this elasticity is zero. More specifically, let us assume that investors expect the yield of consols to return to 5 per cent after one year. Investment of $50 in government consols will thus be rewarded with a capital gain of $50 and a coupon payment of $5. The yield is $55 \times 100/50 = 110$ per cent.[1] If an investment in private debt is to be equally attractive, the yield must be 112 per cent. A decline in the price of private debt to $50 would increase the yield to $57 \times 100/50 = 114$ per cent, which is too high. The proper result is obtained if the price falls to $50.47. In this case, the expected capital gain is $49.53, and adding the coupon payment of $7, the yield equals $56.53 \times 100/50.47 = 112$ per cent. These are the terms at which the investor is indifferent between purchasing government or private debt.

Turning now to the borrower's side of the market, we note that the government can sell consols at a par value of $100 by offering a coupon rate of $10 or 10%. Private borrowers who wish to obtain $100 must offer $7 \times 100/50.47 = \$13.9$. Thus private borrowers, in order to compete with the government, must be willing to accept an increase in the cost of borrowing of 6.9 percentage points, compared to only 5 percentage points for the government. To simplify computation, these comparisons are between government and private consols. As various maturities are considered, we find that the longer the maturity of the debt, the greater the differential in the required additions to the yields of public and private debts.[2]

A similar argument applies, and the conclusion is strengthened, if we assume that the premium on private debt that the lender demands is

---

[1] If y is the yield, p the market price, and c the coupon payment, we have

$$y = \frac{(100 - p + c)100}{p}$$

[2] The basic argument of this paragraph is drawn from Warren L. Smith, "On the Effectiveness of Monetary Policy," *American Economic Review*, vol. 46, no. 4, September, 1956. However, the principle is here stated in more general terms, independent of whether any particular investor has suffered a loss in the past.

defined as a fraction of the yield on government debt. Realizing the same initial yields of 5 and 7 per cent, let us suppose that the required yield on private debt equals $\frac{7}{5}$ of the yield on government debt. As the yield on government debt rises to 110 per cent, yield on private debt must rise to 154 per cent. To accomplish this, the value of private bonds must fall to \$42.10, where $(57.9 + 7)/42.1 = \$1.54$. Private business must now offer $(7 \times 100)/42.1 = \$16.7$ to sell \$100 worth of consols. The private borrower must accept an increase in the cost of borrowing of 9.7 percentage points, against 5 percentage points for the government. Again, the longer the maturity of the debt, the greater this differential.

This conclusion is significant, but it hardly supports the thesis that the private lender is locked in by capital losses. Rather, it suggests that if the government accepts a given increase in its cost of borrowing long, an even greater increase results in the cost of borrowing long on the part of private investors. Since this differential is greater if the government borrows long than if it borrows short, the argument speaks in favor of borrowing long.

Note, however, that the conclusion arrived at here depends on the assumption that investors expect yields to return to the old level. If we assume the elasticity of expectations to be unity, so that rates are expected to remain at the higher level, the argument does not apply. In this case, a decline in the price of government consols to \$50 raises yield to 10 per cent, and no more. Returning to the assumption of an absolute differential of two percentage points, the corresponding yield on private debt must rise to 12 per cent, which is accomplished by a decline in price to \$58.3. The cost of borrowing increases by 2 per cent for the government as well as for private borrowers. If the yields on government and private debt stand in a fixed ratio to each other, we now find that the cost of borrowing for government and for private borrowers rises at the same percentage rate.

The Orderly Market. The preceding argument suggests that, other things being equal, it will be advantageous from the Treasury's point of view to place long-term debt. But this is only a part of the picture. We now turn to another aspect of the problem that points in the opposite direction.

The hesitancy of bond holders to liquidate bonds at a loss, which underlies the locked-in argument, rests on the assumption that the rise in yields and decline in prices is temporary. The present consideration, which underlies the problem of maintaining an orderly market, refers to a situation where the elasticity of yield expectations exceeds 1 and investors expect a continued decline in the market. As bond prices fall moderately and gradually, the expectation may be for return to a more or less normal level. When the decline continues, and especially if it proceeds at an increasing rate, the investor's attitude may change.   The hope for future capital gains as the market turns up later on is outweighed—temporarily, at least—by a desire to avoid further losses while the decline continues. Investors will speculate in a bearish market and proceed to liquidate their investments.   The longer the maturities, the greater are the potential future losses, and hence the more eager will investors be to liquidate. Thus there develops the danger of a disorderly market, involving a decline in bond prices at an excessive speed.   A large volume of long-term debt adds to the danger that restrictive monetary policies will set into motion such a decline, and thus imposes a barrier to energetic use of such restrictions when needed.

Now it may be argued that there is nothing disorderly about a decline in bond prices.   An increase in interest rates and a decline in bond prices is the essence of an active policy of liquidity restriction.   The market forces that make for such a development are the vehicle of restrictive policy. Moreover, if maturities are long, less restrictive action may be needed to accomplish the desired result.   One of the advantages of a large and diverse public debt lies in its providing a medium by which changes in interest rates and credit conditions are transmitted promptly through the entire market, and this cannot occur without changes in security prices and yields.[1]   A speculative decline in bond prices will eventually hit bottom, and the market will turn up on its own accord.   These arguments have merit, and it is indeed difficult to define rigorously just what constitutes a disorderly market.   Yet, the contingency of a disorderly market cannot be neglected by responsible stabilization policy.   Public policy cannot permit a cumulative decline in bond prices at a rapid rate.   In the modern economy, public—and for that matter private—debt constitutes so important a component of the financial structure, and public credit so important an element of public policy, that such a situation must be avoided.   This, then, is the crux of the so-called conflict between debt and monetary policy.[2]

What matters here is that the contingency of a disorderly market is greater if the maturity of the outstanding debt is longer.   Because of this, a lengthening of maturities does not necessarily increase illiquidity per dollar of debt outstanding.   The positive relationship between maturity and stickiness may reverse itself after the debt advances beyond a certain

---

[1] See R. V. Roosa, "Interest Rates and the Central Bank," in *Money, Trade, and Economic Growth: In Honor of John Henry Williams*, The Macmillan Company, New York, 1951, pp. 270–295.

[2] The experience of the 1950s has shown that the fear of a disorderly market was exaggerated during the years immediately following the war, and especially that the "bonds must not fall below par" position was erroneous.   Yet the developments of these years also showed that the maintenance of an orderly market cannot be neglected.

maturity level.   Extreme long-term debt may assume the characteristics of very short-term debt if, in order to avoid a disorderly market, the central bank must step in and support the price of such debt.

All this suggests that lengthening the maturity structure beyond a certain point may become a matter of disutility rather than utility to the Treasury.   As noted before, the preferences of the Treasury as a borrower are not a mere mirror image of the preferences of private lenders.

Effects of Debt Structure on Level and Variability of Consumption

In our earlier discussion of the consumption effects of debt, we have argued that an increase in the supply of consols, while holding money constant, will tend to increase consumption via the Pigou effect, provided that the market value of total consols increases.[1]   The same holds for the addition of shorter debts.   Substitutions between short- and long-term debts that leave the total market value of debt unchanged may nevertheless change consumption, depending on resulting changes in the distribution of assets among consumers whose responses differ.

In addition, the maturity structure of the debt may effect the stability of consumption expenditures over the cycle.   To begin with, it is evident that the holding of liquid assets enables consumers to dissave.   Thus, the holding of claims may cushion the decline in consumption that results with a given decline in income.   At the same time, a liquidation of claims may accentuate a rise in consumption in a period of rising income.   On balance we arrive at a tendency toward built-in stability in the downward direction, combined with instability in the upward direction.   If short-term debt is more readily convertible into cash, these built-in effects will be more pronounced, the shorter the debt.   However, all government debt may be readily marketable, so that the consumer may liquidate long- as well as short-term debt.   Indeed, where interest rates decline in the downturn, long-term debt may be liquidated at a premium, which provides an additional inducement; and a corresponding check will be imposed by capital losses from liquidation in the upswing.

Suppose, now, that the consumer maintains his debt holdings.   If the rate of interest fluctuates with the cycle, the capital value of long-term debt, and hence the strength of the wealth effect, fluctuates in a counter-cyclical fashion.   As far as effects on consumption are concerned, the built-in stabilizing qualities of long-term debt appear superior.[2]

---

[1] See p. 537.

[2] We are not dealing here with nonmarketable debts such as savings bonds, which present a special problem.   Where the par value of the debt is fixed for the life of the bond, fluctuation in market price cannot occur.   The investor may be given an inducement to retain his bonds by relating yield to period held, but this is fixed in advance and not subject to cyclical variations.

Changes in Debt Structure and Their Timing

Thus far we have been concerned with the advantage of holding an existing debt in long or short terms.   Let us now consider the question of when the debt should be shortened or lengthened.

The Time Perspective.   It is usually argued that for a given total of debt, substitution of long- for short-term debt tends to reduce liquidity, just as the substitution of short-term debt for money reduces liquidity. It follows from this that substitution of long- for short-term debt is an appropriate means of restrictive action, called for usually under inflationary conditions.   These are conditions when the level of rates is high relative to the average of the cycle, thus raising expectations of lower rates in the future.   If the Treasury were to act as a private trader, this would suggest a shortening of its debts.   But the opposite seems called for when the Treasury acts as a compensatory agent.   This will hold even though the Treasury is left with a higher coupon bill during coming periods of lower rates.

As we have noted at the outset, there is nothing in the principle of least cost that rejects liquidity restriction because a cost is involved.   At the same time, the problem is one of accomplishing the desired restriction at least cost.   Hence there arises the question of the time period over which the cost is to be measured.   As noted before, this time perspective must be sufficiently long to cover the cost of the longest maturity offered.   The proper maturity mix might be thought of as that which corresponds to the needs of the average situation over the planning period.   The less flexibility there is in adjusting the debt structure by open-market operations in debts, the longer this planning period will have to be.   Debt management, by its inherent element of continuity, thus requires a longer planning period than do fiscal and purely monetary policies (changes in reserve requirements), which may be adjusted on an ad hoc basis.[1]

Nevertheless, at any one time, there is a choice among various approaches to restriction, including monetary, debt, and fiscal measures; and the proper weight, to be attributed to each, will depend upon the longer outlook as well as on the requirements of the immediate situation. Thus, it will be undesirable to meet a temporary need for restriction by lengthening maturities, if a sustained period of slack is expected to follow; or it may be desirable to lengthen maturities in a period short of full employment if a sustained period of inflation is expected thereafter. Both decisions bear upon the long-run picture, and must be matched in the short run by appropriate adjustments in monetary and/or fiscal measures.

[1] See p. 501.

The Appropriate Term Structure. To all this we must add again certain qualitative considerations, relating to the *kind* of expenditures that are curtailed in the private sector as liquidity is reduced. Substitution of long-term issues for short-term issues raises long rates relative to short rates. It reduces the availability of long-term funds to private borrowers and increases the availability of short-term funds; and vice versa if the public debt is shortened. The composition of the public debt thus affects the relative cost and availability of various types of private investment. Liquidity control, in other words, involves not only a problem of setting the proper level but also of obtaining the proper pattern of rates.

In the cyclical setting it has been argued that short rates in the boom should be high relative to long rates, though not necessarily above them. Short funds, if available to private borrowers, tend to flow into speculative activity of a destabilizing sort, while long-term funds are invested more soundly. Thus funds available to private borrowers should be diverted from short- to long-term use. There is no need for this in the depression, when recovery may be expected to start in short investment such as the restocking of inventories. Debt policy, by accentuating market-induced fluctuations in rate structure, may thus act to stabilize the direction of capital flow.

In the secular setting, an ample supply of long-term debt will prove advantageous to investors such as insurance companies and will compete with funds available for long-term investment in, say, private railroads or public utilities. Issuance of medium-term debt may be of interest to investors such as savings and loan associations and will compete with mortgage money; short-term debt will be of interest to commercial banks and compete with commercial credit, and so forth. On a more general basis, any increase in the supply of public debt raises the cost at which the private entrepreneur may obtain borrowed money relative to equity funds, thereby diverting private capital formation to industries financed by equity capital.

Restriction of any particular type of credit, or issuance of any particular type of debt, may give rise to compensating shifts on the private side of the capital and money market. However, these offsets will be of a partial sort only. The fact that the qualitative implications of debt policy cannot be determined easily should not be taken as an occasion to assume (as is done so frequently with regard to credit control) that they do not exist. Where one type of debt policy secures a result that is qualitatively preferable to another, it may be preferred even though the same degree of illiquidity (or reduction in private expenditures) is secured at a higher cost.[1]

[1] Considering the difficulties of choosing the proper maturity mix, one is tempted to

There is no avoiding the fact that debt policy has qualitative effects that must be taken into account. Given a perfect market, it may be argued that liquidity restriction at minimum cost will, in fact, provide a neutral solution; but as noted before, the market for claims is not perfect. In addition to the basic factor of uncertainty, further imperfections arise from statutory limitations on institutional lenders and other barriers to a perfect flow of funds between various sectors of the capital market. Much the same may be said for the monetary-policy approach to liquidity restriction. As evidenced by the recent discussion of credit rationing and the emphasis on the availability of funds,[1] there is little basis for the traditional belief that liquidity restriction is inherently neutral, whereas fiscal restriction is not.

D. THE INCIDENCE OF STABILIZATION POLICY

We must now move the problem of liquidity restriction back into the broader context of stabilization policy. Let us begin with a situation

---

take refuge in Simons's dictum that all public claims should be either in cash or consols, "*und sonst garnichts*" (to quote Marlene Dietrich). Thus with magic simplicity the problem of term structure is ruled out of court, and attention can be limited to the simpler problem of determining the proper supply of money and consols. (See Henry C. Simons, *Economic Policy for a Free Society*, University of Chicago Press, Chicago, 1948, chaps. 9 and 10.)

Aesthetics aside, there is little to be said for this plan. Reliance on consols only, and the not too different idea of open-market operation in bills only, places at best an unnecessary restraint on the use of liquidity policy; and at worst severely impairs its effectiveness. Moreover, the practice is bound to raise the cost of obtaining a given restriction.

There is no reason why the government should not accommodate the preferences of lenders to commit themselves at varying terms, thereby reducing the cost of purchasing illiquidity as well as improving the position of lenders. A policy of permitting consols only seems little different in nature from requiring that there be blue dresses or eight-cylinder cars only. Such prescriptions would simplify the economic process, but they would be inefficient in terms of economic welfare.

[1] The term *rationing* is used here to describe the allocation of a given supply of loanable funds among lenders at a cost below what the market will bear. This must be distinguished from changes in the lender's preference between different types of borrowers and a corresponding adjustment in his portfolio composition—an adjustment that occurs while the price for each type of loan continues to be cleared by the market. Allowance for this second type of adjustment, which underlies Keynes's concept of the "fringe of unsatisfied borrowers," is quite compatible with the traditional view of monetary restriction. It merely places emphasis on the lender's side of the market and on the heterogeneity of various debts. The allocation of funds on a nonmarket basis, involved in our concept of rationing, introduces a quite different concept, namely that of imperfection in the credit market. It is only the existence of this imperfection which can explain the proposition heard so frequently in recent years—that the effectiveness of restriction does not depend on the elasticity of the investment schedule.

where the prevailing pattern of stabilization policy—including proportional taxes or transfers by the Stabilization Branch, the level of bank reserves, and the structure of the debt—is such that aggregate demand is held at the appropriate level. Now suppose that certain changes occur, say an increase in the level of expenditures by the Allocation Branch or an upward shift in certain spending functions in the private sector. As a result, further restriction is called for. It can be accomplished in a number of ways.

Various tax rates may be increased, reserve requirements raised, open-market sales made, or the term structure of the debt lengthened. Depending on which approach or combination of approaches is chosen, the resulting course of the economy will differ. Various approaches to stabilization may result in different rates of growth as well as different states of distribution or incidence. The latter aspect returns us to what in an earlier connection was described as the differential incidence of alternative bundles of stabilization policy.

Fiscal versus Monetary Restriction

To be specific, let us assume that an upward shift in one or another spendings function has occurred in the private sector, and compare the distributional results that come about if this expansion is offset by (1) imposing a proportional income tax, which is the typical pattern followed by the fiscal sector of the Stabilization Branch, or by (2) monetary restriction imposed by way of raising reserve requirements.[1] It will be convenient, moreover, to assume that the desired restriction has already been accomplished by imposing the tax, and to examine what happens if the tax is withdrawn or reduced and a corresponding degree of monetary restriction is imposed instead. The result will measure the differential incidence between tax and monetary restriction.

Removal of Income Tax. The recipients of both wage income and capital income from old investment are benefited by the removal of the income tax. At the same time, and following our earlier reasoning, savers gain relative to consumers.[2] These results occur because the income tax discriminates against saving. Since saving rises as we move up the income scale, the net result tends to be regressive.

Monetary Restriction: New Contracts in Debt. As monetary restriction is imposed, interest rates rise. This is to the advantage of those who have uncommitted funds to lend, and to the disadvantage of those who wish to borrow.

Among the borrowers, the position of the government itself must be

---

[1] We are here referring to a truly proportional income tax, that is a flat rate tax without exemptions.

[2] See p. 263.

considered.   If the outstanding debt is of relatively long maturity, and if the period of restriction is short, the increase in interest rates may be reflected only slightly in the cost of borrowing to the government.   However, let us assume that the debt is sufficiently short and/or the period of restriction sufficiently long, so that the entire debt must be reborrowed at the higher level of rates.   This means that bond holders have gained at the cost of taxpayers.   The distributional result of this shift depends on who receives the interest and who pays the taxes needed to finance it.[1]

In order to estimate the distribution of net benefits that result from the tax-interest circuit, a number of problems must be faced.   First there is the question of just what tax is to be used.   Should we use the distribution of the average tax dollar under the prevailing tax structure or that of the marginal tax dollar; and if the latter approach is taken, how can we determine which is the marginal tax?   The answer depends on the type of debt to be refunded and who holds it.   It depends also on how we treat interest paid to such institutions as commercial banks.   Interest may be imputed either to holders of bank shares or to bank customers, the assumption being that service charges would be higher if commercial banks were not supported by interest received on public debt.   Thus the task of estimating the incidence of the tax-interest circuit is by no means simple.   Considering the postwar Federal debt in the United States and applying the distribution of the average tax dollar, it appears that the incidence of the tax-interest circuit is more or less neutral:[2] assuming finance by proportional income tax, it is clearly regressive.

Turning now to the market for private debt, those desiring to borrow new funds are placed at a disadvantage.   Where consumer or mortgage debt is concerned, the increased cost of borrowing is felt by the consumers directly.   While the ratio of such debt to income rises up to a point when moving up the income scale, it declines thereafter.   In the case of business debt, the situation is more difficult.   As business debt becomes subject to the higher rates, the increased cost may be added to price. In this case, it will be paid for by the consumer of the product or service in question.   The distributional result will thus be on the regressive side : The cost allocation is equivalent to financing interest on public debt by a sales tax on capital-intensive products; also, the holding of private debt is distributed less equally than that of public debt.   Alternatively, the increased cost of capital might be reflected in reduced wages, the result

[1] Depending on the propensities to spend of taxpayers and interest recipients, the required tax bill may exceed or fall short of the interest bill.

[2] See my "Monetary-debt Policy Revisited," in Carl J. Friedrich and Edward S. Mason (eds.), *Public Policy, 1940: a Yearbook*, Harvard University Press, Cambridge, Mass., 1941, p. 170.   For a more or less similar result, see Jacob Cohen, "Distributional Effects of the Federal Debt," *Journal of Finance*, vol. 6, no. 3, pp. 267–275, September, 1951.

being regressive in either case. Such, at least, will be the outcome in the short run. In the long run, effects on the level and efficiency of investment must be accounted for as well.

Monetary Restriction: Old Contracts in Debt. Before turning to this subject, let us consider the resulting decline in the market value of debt obligations that were outstanding prior to the increase in interest rates. In a sense this is to the disadvantage of old lenders and to the advantage of old borrowers. However, it is a qualified advantage or disadvantage only. The lender who holds such obligations does not suffer a loss in income stream, and he can look forward to the same payment at maturity as before. The drop in the market value of his investment merely reflects the fact that he cannot participate in the gain from higher yields until his obligations mature. For the borrower, this drop reflects the temporary gain derived by being able to postpone refunding at the higher rates until maturity. In a perfect credit market, this is all that need be said. At the same time, the lender may suffer an absolute loss if the credit market is imperfect, and credit standing is related to the market value rather than the maturity value of securities.[1] In this case, a corresponding advantage will accrue to the borrower. If lenders are identified with higher incomes and borrowers with lower incomes, the net change is to the advantage of the latter group.

Monetary Restriction: Growth. Viewing the problem in the long run, we may expect that the substitution of monetary restriction for restriction by proportional income tax will reduce capital formation relative to current consumption and hence result in a lower rate of growth. But this need not be the case with all types of monetary and fiscal restrictions. Substitution of restriction on installment credit for a tax on profits may well have the opposite result.[2] However, the assumption of a reduced rate of growth is reasonable for the comparison of general monetary and fiscal restriction.

If the substitution leads to a reduced rate of growth, this in turn may affect the division of factor shares between labor and capital, and hence the state of distribution. As shown in the preceding discussion, the effect of changes in the rate of growth upon factor shares is an exceedingly difficult problem, which defies simple prediction. There is no good reason to expect that the capital share in the national dividend should increase relative to the wage share, nor is there good reason to expect the opposite.[3] Either result may occur. Thus it is hardly possible to allow

---

[1] See p. 597.

[2] This is clearly the case if the restriction of installment credit goes to reduce consumer purchases on nondurables. If the production of durables is reduced, growth is curtailed because less future consumption is provided for.

[3] See p. 372.

for effects on growth in appraising the differential incidence of our two policies.

As the capital stock is reduced, or grows at a lesser rate, the marginal efficiency of investment rises or falls less rapidly.   The output per unit of capital is greater than it would have been otherwise, and a higher return can be paid on business debt without an increase in capital cost.   Thus, the implicit excise tax on the consumer, or income tax on the wage recipient—referred to previously when dealing with effects on new debt contracts—tends to be absorbed by the increased efficiency of capital. The final result will depend on the effects of a reduced rate of growth on factor shares.

One other aspect remains to be considered.   This is the fact that the increase in the rate of interest benefits savers relative to consumers.   It benefits higher incomes relative to lower incomes and strengthens the regressive effects noted in connection with the removal of the income tax. Barring a resulting increase in the wage share or the use of highly progressive taxes to finance interest on a large public debt, we are thus left with a presumption—though not a clear proof—that the differential incidence of our substitution of policies will be regressive.   This will be more apparent if the comparison is with fiscal restriction by a progressive income tax.

Similar comparisons can be drawn between the incidence of various types of liquidity restriction, such as general monetary restriction and lengthening of the debt structure; and these in turn may be compared with various approaches to fiscal restriction.   As we have noted before, the problem of incidence has no unique application to stabilization by taxation, but applies to other forms of stabilization policy as well. Differences in incidence must be taken into account when choosing between various approaches to stabilization, and they must be compensated for in the over-all budget plan by appropriate adjustments in the policy of the Distribution Branch.   Efficient policy requires that the stabilization function be discharged within the framework of the over-all budget plan and with proper regard for those other functions of budget policy performed by the Allocation and the Distribution Branches.

Name index

Ackley, G., 471, 504, 533, 550
Adams, H. C., 599
Adelman, M. A., 287
Alexander, S., 495
Allen, R. G. D., 474
Angell, J. W., 504
Arrow, K., 116, 118, 119, 129, 139

Bailey, M. J., 302
Barone, E., 302
Bastable, C. F., 230, 599
Bator, F. M., 374
Baumol, W. J., 139, 430, 474, 495
Bentham, J., 64, 65
Bergson, A., 140
Bernoulli, D., 99, 100, 104
Beveridge, W. H., 502
Birnbaum, E. A., 559
Bishop, R. L., 433
Black, D., 116, 128, 227, 232, 278
Blough, R., 331
Blum, W. J., 99
Bodin, J., 91
Boulding, K., 144, 150, 260, 280, 283, 544
Bowen, H. R., 76, 108, 116, 125, 137
Break, G. F., 141
Brown, E. C., ix, 169, 279, 313, 326, 337, 339, 342, 344, 346, 449, 484, 496, 506, 511

Brown, H. G., 379
Brownlee, O. H., 177
Buchanan, J. M., 117, 118, 128, 177, 182, 556
Bullock, C. J., 231
Burbank, H. H., ix
Butters, J. K., 169

Cannan, E., 227
Carver, T. N., 98
Chamberlin, E. H., 79, 282, 285, 299, 361
Clark, C., 52
Clark, J. M., 52, 503
Coates, W. H., 278, 287
Cohen, J., 582, 613
Cohen-Stuart, A. J., 95, 98, 101, 102
Cole, D., 239
Colm, G., 87, 175, 188, 328
Condorcet, M. J., 65
Cooper, G., 233, 237, 238, 243
Corlett, W. J., 142, 152, 251
Cournot, A. A., 79, 277, 287
Culbertson, J. M., 598

Dahl, R. A., 117
Dahlberg, A., 328
Dalton, H., 61, 113, 227, **292**
De La Riviere, 230

617

Subject index